THE ROLE OF THE FATHER IN CHILD DEVELOPMENT

Third Edition

Contributors

Henry Abramovitch, Ph.D.
Department of Behavioral Sciences
Sackler School of Medicine
Tel Aviv University

Henry B. Biller, Ph.D.
Department of Psychology
University of Rhode Island

Lisa A. Billings, Graduate Student
Section on Social and Emotional
  Development
National Institute of Child Health and
  Human Development

Raymond W. Chan, Graduate Student
Department of Psychology
University of Virginia

Mark Cohan, Graduate Student
Department of Sociology
University of Florida

E. Mark Cummings, Ph.D.
Department of Psychology
West Virginia University

Sandra H. Henderson, Ph.D.
Department of Psychology
University of Virginia

E. Mavis Hetherington, Ph.D.
Department of Psychology
University of Virginia

Cheryl A. Hosley, Graduate Student
Department of Psychology
Ohio State University

Jon L. Kimpton, Graduate Student
Department of Psychology
University of Rhode Island

Michael E. Lamb, Ph.D.
Section on Social and Emotional
  Development
National Institute of Child Health and
  Human Development

Charlie Lewis, Ph.D.
Department of Psychology
Lancaster University

William Marsiglio, Ph.D.
Department of Sociology
University of Florida

Raymond Montemayer, Ph.D.
Department of Psychology
Ohio State University

Anne Watson O'Reilly, Ph.D.
Department of Psychology
West Virginia University

Charlotte J. Patterson, Ph.D.
Department of Psychology
University of Virginia

Vicky Phares, Ph.D.
Department of Psychology
University of South Florida

Elizabeth H. Pleck, Ph.D.
Division of Human Development and
  Family Studies
University of Illinois

Joseph H. Pleck, Ph.D.
Division of Human Development and
  Family Studies
University of Illinois

Margaret M. Stanley-Hagan, Ph.D.
Department of Psychology
University of North Carolina at Charlotte

Kathleen J. Sternberg, Ph.D.
Section on Social and Emotional
  Development
National Institute of Child Health and
  Human Development

THE ROLE OF
THE FATHER IN
CHILD DEVELOPMENT

THIRD EDITION

EDITED BY MICHAEL E. LAMB

John Wiley & Sons, Inc.
New York • Chichester • Brisbane • Toronto • Singapore

Copyright © 1997 by John Wiley & Sons, Inc.
Published by John Wiley & Sons, Inc.

Library of Congress Cataloging-in-Publication Data:

The role of the father in child development / [edited by] Michael E.
    Lamb—3rd ed.
        p.   cm.
    Includes bibliographical references.
    ISBN 0-471-11771-4 (cloth : alk. paper)
    1. Fathers.   2. Father and child—United States.   3. Paternal
deprivation—United States.   4. Single-parent family—United States.
I. Lamb, Michael E., 1953–
HQQ756.R64   1996
308.874′2—dc20
                                                        96-4899
                                                        CIP

Printed in the United States of America
10 9 8 7 6 5 4 3

For
Frank
Jerry
Damon
Aya
Darryn
Jeanette
Philip

Who taught me so much about fatherhood

PREFACE

THIS EDITION OF *The Role of the Father in Child Development* marks the 20th anniversary of the first, published in 1976. The intervening decades have been marked by energetic and extensive research accompanied by thoughtful reconceptualization of fatherhood and father-child relationships. As a result, the third edition bears little resemblance to its ancestors. Instead, it contains a series of integrative summaries that represent the vibrant and productive scholarship that has done so much to illuminate our understanding of the father's many roles in child development.

Perhaps the biggest difference between the first and third editions of the collection is reflected in the consistent attempts by all contributors to view fathers in a broader social context. Whereas contributors to the first edition focused narrowly on fathers and father-child dyads, the contributors to this edition place fathers in the context of family systems and subsystems in which the relationships with and attitudes of mothers and siblings also play crucial roles. In addition, there is widespread recognition of the fact that fathers play a variety of roles in the family, with the relative salience of these roles varying across time and subcultural context.

All of the chapters were written especially for the volume, whose impressive size and scope attest to the amount we have learned about father-child relationships. Each of the contributors has made seminal contributions to our collective understanding of the specific topic about which he or she has written, and together they have painted a rich and highly nuanced account of fatherhood and paternal influences. One set of chapters survey father-child relationships at different stages of the children's lives. Others examine the effects of variations in paternal involvement in both intact and divorced families or focus on the special social and psychological circumstances that shape relationships, family climate, and child development. The unique situations faced by gay fathers, young fathers, stepfathers, and fathers whose children have special developmental needs are also examined closely. The resulting collection of chapters constitutes the first truly comprehensive and up-to-date summary of current scholarship concerning fathers, fatherhood, father-child relationships, and paternal influences.

The collection will be of special interest to clinical, developmental, and social psychologists and their students, as well as to psychiatrists, social workers, family lawyers, and other mental health professionals. In the face of an exploding scholarly literature, this collection provides a uniquely valuable integration of recent scholarship and research and will, I hope, shape conceptions of and research on fatherhood for years to come.

M. E. L.
Bethesda, MD

CONTENTS

THE ROLE OF THE FATHER IN CHILD DEVELOPMENT

Third Edition

CHAPTER 1

Fathers and Child Development: An Introductory Overview and Guide

Michael E. Lamb

National Institute of Child Health and Human Development

PREVIOUS EDITIONS of *The Role of the Father in Child Development* (Lamb, 1976, 1981c) contained encyclopedic introductory chapters in which I attempted to provide inclusive reviews of the primary and secondary literatures. Such endeavors are no longer possible, as the reference list for such a chapter would easily occupy more space than any of the chapters in this book! As a result, this edition of the collection instead includes an introductory chapter in which I attempt only to articulate major themes in our contemporary understanding of father-child relationships and paternal influences, while referring readers to the chapters that follow for more detailed reviews of the relevant literature.

Substantial progress has been made by scholars over the past 20 years. Hundreds of studies have enriched the empirical literature, while theorists have elaborated and refined the conceptual frameworks brought to bear on the understanding of paternal roles. When the first edition of this book was published in 1976, for example, social scientists in general, and developmental psychologists in particular, doubted that fathers had a significant role to play in shaping the experiences and development of their children, especially their daughters. As a result, contributors to the first edition all made concerted and often explicit efforts to demonstrate that fathers 1. indeed had a role to play in child development; 2. were often salient in their children's lives; and 3. affected the course of their children's development, for good as well as for ill. Though somewhat less defensive in tone, contributions to the second edition, published just five years later in 1981, not surprisingly emphasized the same conclusions. By contrast, the chapters in this volume all reflect widespread acceptance of the notion that fathers are often affectively and formatively salient, a conclusion that has encouraged a focus on more nuanced issues and concerns. Three merit special attention here: recognition that fathers play complex, multidimensional roles, that many patterns of influence are indirect, and that social constructions of fatherhood vary across historical epochs and subcultural contexts.

Fathers' Multifaceted Roles

Perhaps most important, researchers, theorists, and practitioners no longer cling to the simplistic belief that fathers fill a single unidimensional role in their families and in their children's eyes. Instead, they recognize that fathers play a number of significant roles—companions, care providers, spouses, protectors, models, moral guides, teachers, breadwinners—whose relative importance surely varies across historical epochs and subcultural groups. Only by considering the father's performance of these various roles, and by taking into account their relative importance in the socioecological context concerned, can we evaluate any father's impact on child development. Unfortunately, theorists and social commentators have tended in the past to emphasize only one paternal role at a time, with different functions attracting most attention during different historical epochs.

In earlier times, fathers were viewed as all-powerful patriarchs who wielded enormous power over their families (Knibiehler, 1995), and vestiges of these notions have survived until quite recently. According to Pleck and Pleck (Chapter 3 of this volume) and Lamb (1986), for example, during the colonial phase of American history fathers were primarily viewed as moral teachers, at least so far as the white colonists were concerned. By popular consensus, fathers were responsible for ensuring that their children grew up with an appropriate sense of values, acquired from the study of the Bible and other scriptural texts. With industrialization, however, primary focus shifted from moral leadership to breadwinning and economic support of the family. Then, perhaps as a result of the Great Depression, which revealed many men to be poor providers, social scientists came to portray fathers as sex-role models, with commentators expressing concern about the failure of many men to model masculine behavior for their sons. Throughout the twentieth century, fathers were urged to be involved with their children (Griswold, 1993), and following feminist and scholarly critiques of masculinity and femininity (Pleck, 1981), there emerged in the late 1970s a new concern with the "new nurturant father," who played an active role in his children's lives.

As these different conceptions have attracted public attention, of course, they have not completely supplanted other or earlier conceptions; most contemporary scholars would recognize all the images of fatherhood in the motivations and behavior of the men around them. In addition, each role is associated with one or more distinctive modes of influence on children. Clearly, breadwinning remains a key component of the father's role in most segments of society today (Barnett & Baruch, 1988; Baruch & Barnett, 1983; O'Hare, 1995; Pleck, 1983). Even in the vast majority of families with two wage earners, fathers are seen as the primary breadwinners, if only because of continuing disparities between the salaries of male and female workers. Economic support of the family constitutes an indirect but important way in which fathers contribute to the rearing and emotional health of their children. Furthermore, economic support (or the lack of it) is one of the ways in which noncustodial fathers influence their children's development (Hetherington & Stanley-Hagan, Chapter 11 of this volume).

A second important but indirect source of influence stems from the father's role as a source of emotional and concrete support to the other people, principally the mother, involved in the direct care of children (Parke, Power, & Gottman, 1979). The father's functioning as a source of emotional support tends to enhance the quality of mother-child relationships and thus facilitates positive adjustment by children; by contrast, when fathers are unsupportive and marital conflict is high, children may suffer (Belsky, 1990; Cummings & Davies, 1994; Cummings & O'Reilly, Chapter 4 of this volume). Fathers can also affect the quality of family dynamics by being involved in child-related housework, thus easing the mothers' workloads (Pleck, 1983, 1984). Paternal involvement in housework exemplifies another manner in which fathers influence children—by providing models of behavior that children can either emulate or eschew. Many of the behavior patterns acquired in childhood are the result of lessons derived from observing others and adjusting one's behavior accordingly.

Fathers also influence their children by interacting with them directly, and much of this book is concerned with the ways in which children are affected by caretaking, teaching, play, maltreatment, and neglect by their fathers. Most of the research on paternal influences is still concerned with such direct patterns of influence, even though fathers play multiple roles and affect their children's development in many ways other than via direct interaction.

Recognition of Indirect Patterns of Influence

Recognition that indirect patterns of influence are pervasive and perhaps more important than direct learning represents another of the major conceptual revolutions marking the 20 years of scholarship that have taken place between the first and third editions of *The Role of the Father in Child Development*. Whereas some contributors to the first edition provocatively proposed that some paternal influences might be mediated indirectly (the chapter by Lewis & Weinraub, 1976, was especially noteworthy in this regard), the extraordinary importance of indirect influences is now recognized universally. Indeed, almost every contributor to this volume underscores the extent to which fathers and children must be viewed as parts of complex social systems (notably, the family) in which each person affects every other reciprocally, directly, and indirectly. From this vantage point, of course, appraising the father's impact is much more difficult, both conceptually and statistically, but the newer perspectives promise much greater validity and, ultimately, generalizability.

Cultural Ecology

As in many areas of psychology, finally, researchers and theorists are slowly (and not consistently) recognizing the diverse array of family types and sociocultural expectations and demands that shape paternal roles, family processes, and child development. In practice, this means that fathers play differing roles in different subcultural contexts and that various groups hold contrasting views of what constitutes "the good father" (Hochschild, 1995). For example, breadwinning (and the indirect effects of financial security) may be of paramount importance in some contexts (as when the child was conceived outside of an enduring relationship) while moral guidance may be quite unimportant. For other families and communities, financial support may be unimportant, direct care and supervision crucial, and emotional support invaluable. Such variations in the relative salience of different aspects of fatherhood further complicate attempts to conceptualize and assess paternal roles and influences but, when appropriately recognized, promise to permit more valid and generalizable research on father-child relationships, even though the generalizability of many findings may be much narrower than researchers initially hoped.

Researchers have actually made limited progress to date in their efforts to discern and describe cross-cultural patterns and variations (Lamb, 1987), but they are at least more cognizant of limitations on the generalizability of their findings, and this augurs well for the future. Universal aspects of father-child relations and paternal roles may exist, but they must be demonstrated, not assumed as they were in the past. Careful attempts to describe father-child relationships in diverse cultural contexts would certainly help build the database needed for further progress in our understanding of father-child relationships; in the absence of such research, many of the contributors to this volume speak primarily to the models of paternity, fatherhood, and father-child relationships that dominate white North American middle-class society.

In the chapters that follow, two foci predominate: factors affecting the roles that fathers play or fail to play and the effects of variations in paternal behavior on child development. One set of concerns thus centers on fathers' motivations, histories, and psyches, while the other addresses the impact of these characteristics on their children. Logically, theory and research on "what makes fathers tick" should precede concern with their influence, although in practice, paternal influences have received much more attention from social scientists. In the next section, I first summarize evidence concerning the characteristics and determinants of paternal behavior and then review central conclusions regarding paternal influences on child development.

FATHERHOOD AND PATERNAL INFLUENCES

CHARACTERISTICS OF PATERNAL BEHAVIOR

Although scholars do not question the many other ways (direct and indirect) that fathers affect child development, the literature on paternal behavior is primarily concerned with interactions between fathers and children, and this limited focus is obvious in this section.

Partly in reaction to research designed to describe fathers' influences by studying what happens in their absence, a number of researchers initiated research in the mid-1970s designed to describe, often by detailed observation and sometimes also by detailed maternal and paternal reports, the nature and extent of paternal interactions with children (see chapters by Pleck, Lamb, Lewis, Biller & Kimpton, and Hosley & Montemayor in this volume). These studies have consistently shown that fathers spend much less time with their children than mothers do (see Pleck, Chapter 5 of this volume). In two-parent families in which the mother is not employed, fathers spend about 20%–25% as much time as mothers do in direct interaction or engagement with their children and about a third as much time being accessible to their children (Lamb, Pleck, Charnov, & Levine, 1987; Pleck, 1983; Pleck, Chapter 5 of this volume), although in general fathers assume essentially no responsibility (as defined by participation in key decisions, availability at short notice, involvement in the care of sick children, management and selection of alternative child care, etc.) for their children's care or rearing. Some fathers assume high degrees of responsibility, of course, but this small subgroup has not been studied extensively. In addition, average levels of paternal responsibility appear to be increasing, albeit slowly (Robinson, Andreyenkov, & Patrashev, 1988).

In two-parent families with employed mothers, the average levels of paternal engagement and accessibility both are substantially higher than in families with mothers who are not employed (Lamb et al., 1987; Pleck, 1983). In such families, paternal involvement in direct interaction and accessibility averages 33% and 65%, respectively, of the relevant figures for mothers. There is no evidence, however, that maternal employment has any effect on responsibility. Even when both mothers and fathers are employed 30 or more hours per week, the amount of responsibility assumed by fathers appears as negligible as when mothers are not employed. In addition, it is worth noting that fathers do not spend more time interacting with their children when mothers are not employed; rather the proportions just cited rise because mothers are doing less. Thus, fathers are *proportionally* more involved when mothers are employed, even though the extent of their involvement in absolute terms does not change to any meaningful extent. Over time, levels of paternal involvement have increased, but the changes are much smaller than popular accounts often suggest (Lamb et al., 1987; Pleck, Chapter 5 of this volume; van Dongen, 1995).

Both observational and survey data also suggest that mothers and fathers engage in different types of interaction with their children (Goldman & Goldman, 1983; Lamb, 1981a; Lamb, Chapter 5 of this volume; Lewis, Chapter 6 of this volume). These studies have consistently shown that fathers tend to "specialize" in play whereas mothers specialize in caretaking and nurturance, especially (but not only) in relation to infants. Although such findings have been repeated on multiple occasions and thus seem quite reliable, the results have often been misrepresented. Compared with mothers, fathers indeed spend a greater proportion of their time with children engaged in play, but they still spend a small proportion of their time in play. In absolute terms, most studies suggest that mothers play with their children more than fathers do, but because play is more prominent in father-child interaction (particularly boisterous, stimulating, emotionally arousing play), paternal playfulness and relative novelty may help make fathers especially salient to their children (Lamb, Frodi, Hwang, & Frodi, 1983). This enhanced salience may increase fathers' influence beyond what would be expected based on the amount of time they spend with their children.

These attempts to describe and quantify the nature and extent of paternal behavior have focused, of course, on children living in two-parent families. Ironically, while research has concentrated on parental behavior and parent-child relationships in such families, these families have become less common. More than half the children in the United States now spend part of their childhood in single-parent families, and similar trends are evident in other industrialized countries (Cherlin, 1992; Cherlin et al., 1991; Horn, 1995; Popenoe, 1989). Fatherlessness is particularly marked in impoverished African-American communities, and considerable concern has been expressed about its effects on the mothers and children in these families (Blankenhorn, 1995; Popenoe, 1996; Whitehead, 1993). To date, social scientists have been remarkably unsuccessful in their efforts to understand why so many men have removed themselves or allowed themselves to be excluded from their children's lives, although the adverse effects on child development have been well documented, as summarized below and by Hetherington and Stanley-Hagan (Chapter 11 of this volume).

DETERMINANTS OF PATERNAL BEHAVIOR

Although paternal behavior is multifaceted, embracing not only what fathers do but also how much of it they do, the existing literature on factors influencing paternal behavior focuses on variations in direct paternal involvement, ignoring much of what fathers do *for* their children by way of economic and emotional support within the family. This focus perhaps reflects the widespread assumptions that the extent of direct father-child interaction is of primary importance (for interventionists as well as for researchers) and that involvement and parent-child closeness are intimately associated, even though most studies of paternal involvement ignore the emotional quality of father-child relationships or find the quality and quantity of interaction to be unrelated (Grossman, Pollack, & Golding, 1988; Radin, 1994).

In this subsection I focus briefly on several factors that appear to affect paternal involvement. The discussion draws on an earlier suggestion (Lamb, 1986; Lamb et al., 1987) that one can conceive of motivation, skills and self-confidence, support, and institutional practices as a hierarchy of factors influencing paternal behavior. Favorable conditions must exist at each level if increased paternal involvement and broadened paternal behavior is to be possible and beneficial.

Motivation

Although researchers such as the Cowans (C. P. Cowan et al., 1985; P. A. Cowan, Cowan, & Kerig, 1993) and Grossman (Grossman et al., 1988) have made careful efforts to identify psychological or individual characteristics that influence the nature and extent of paternal behavior, most researchers have implicitly assumed that variations in the definition of fatherhood are determined more by subcultural and cultural factors than by individual characteristics (see also Jacobs, 1995). Many men set goals that depend on recollections of their own childhood, choosing either to compensate for their fathers' deficiencies or to emulate them. Many also express enjoyment of time spent with children—even adolescents (Larson & Richards, 1994). Indeed, survey data suggest that 40% of fathers would like to have more time to spend with their children than they currently have (Quinn & Staines, 1979). This implies that a substantial number of men are motivated to be more involved in relationships with their children. On the other hand, the same data suggest that more than half of the fathers in the country do not want to spend more time with their children than they currently do. Clearly, there is no unanimity about the desirability of increased paternal involvement. In addition, the identification of fatherhood with breadwinning serves to limit male involvement in child care, at least as much as do the constraints imposed by actual work time (Gerson, 1993). A powerful underlying assumption proposes that men are first and foremost workers and breadwinners whereas women are nurturers.

Changes in the level of paternal motivation have recently taken place, however, and can be attributed primarily to the women's movement and the questions it raises about traditional male and female roles. In addition, media hype about the "new father" has also affected motivation levels. The most impressive official program yet undertaken was initiated by the Swedish government in the early 1970s in an attempt to encourage men to become more involved in child care (Haas, 1992; Lamb & Levine, 1983) and overcome fears that active parenting and masculinity are incompatible. Continuing fears of this sort help explain why some motivational shifts have been so slow and particularly why the number of fathers who take a major role in child care has not increased much (nationally or internationally) despite tremendous changes in female employment patterns. Interestingly, however, researchers have not substantiated initial predictions that the levels and types of paternal involvement would be associated with measures of the men's masculinity or androgyny (see Pleck, Chapter 5 of this volume). In addition, institutional and cultural barriers, not only personality and motivational barriers, slow the pace of change and reduce average levels of paternal involvement. One indication of this can be found in the evidence of greater flexibility regarding the types of activities in which fathers engage, despite modest changes in the amount of time fathers spend with their children. Many fathers no longer avoid the messy child care activities they used to disparage, becoming (to the apparent chagrin of commentators like Blankenhorn, 1995) "co-parents" across a broad array of tasks.

Skills and Self-Confidence

Motivation alone cannot ensure increased involvement: Skills and self-confidence are also necessary. Ostensibly motivated men often complain that a lack of skills (exemplified by ignorance or clumsiness) prevents increased involvement and closeness. These complaints can be excuses, but they can also reflect a very real fear of incompetence and failure. The relevant skills can be obtained through participation in a growing number of formal skill-development programs (Levine & Pitt, 1995) or more informally through involvement in activities that children and fathers enjoy doing together. Such activities foster self-confidence and enjoyment, thereby promoting both further involvement and sensitivity. Sensitivity—being able to evaluate a child's signals or needs and respond appropriately—is also crucial to both involvement and closeness (Lamb, 1980). Both sensitivity and self-confidence are probably more important than specific skills where paternal behavior and influence are concerned. Many of the studies dealing with paternal influences show that the closeness of the father-child relationship—itself a consequence of sufficiently extensive and sensitive interactions—is a crucial determinant of the father's impact on child development and adjustment (see particularly the chapters by Lamb, Lewis, and Biller & Kimpton).

Support

The third factor influencing paternal behavior is support, especially support within the family from the mother. Like paternal attitudes, women's attitudes toward paternal involvement have changed slowly over the past two decades (Pleck, 1982; Polatnick, 1973–74). The same surveys that show a majority of men wanting to be more involved show that a majority of women do not want their husbands to be more involved than they currently are (Pleck, 1982; Quinn & Staines, 1979). This finding suggests that, although many mothers would like their partners to do more and are heavily overburdened by their responsibilities, a substantial majority are quite satisfied with the status quo, not only in the extent of paternal involvement but also in the range and type of activities in which fathers involve themselves (Hochschild, 1995). On the other hand, women overwhelmingly view breadwinning as a crucial role for husbands and fathers (O'Hare, 1995).

There may be many reasons for maternal hesitation about changing paternal roles. Some mothers may feel that their husbands are incompetent or fear that increased paternal involvement may threaten fundamental power dynamics within the family (Polatnick, 1973–74). Mother and manager of the household are the two roles in which women's authority has not been questioned; together they constitute the one area in which women have traditionally enjoyed real power and control. Increased paternal involvement may threaten this power and preeminence. The trade-off has dubious value because although many women have entered the workforce in the past three decades, many occupy low-paying, low-prestige positions with little prospect of advancement. Many women apparently prefer to maintain authority in the child care arena, even if that means physical and mental exhaustion. Their resistance is likely to persist until fundamental changes within society at large change the basic distribution of power. Economic conditions seem unlikely to reduce the need for both parents to obtain employment, and women continue to emphasize the need for husbands and fathers to be family breadwinners (O'Hare, 1995).

Within individual families, agreement between mothers and fathers regarding paternal roles may be of crucial importance. As mentioned earlier, family dynamics are formatively significant because fundamental conflicts between the parents have adverse effects on children's development. In this regard, it may be significant that two longitudinal studies of high father involvement (Radin, 1994; Radin & Goldsmith, 1985; Russell, 1983) found a remarkably high rate of family dissolution when the families were later relocated. Thus, despite initial harmony, substantial and fundamental problems concerning roles and responsibilities may arise later, particularly in times of ambivalence and confusion.

Institutional Practices

Institutional practices, particularly in the workplace, also affect paternal involvement, with the barriers imposed by the workplace ranked by fathers as among the most important reasons for low levels of paternal involvement (e.g., Haas, 1992; Yankelovich, 1974). Clearly, this is an important issue for many men, and it will be important as long as men take on and are expected to assume the primary breadwinning role. It is also true, however, that men do not trade work time for family time in a one-to-one fashion. Survey data show that women translate each extra hour of nonwork time into an extra 40–45 minutes of family work, whereas men translate each hour not spent in paid work into less than 20 minutes of family work (Pleck, 1983). Thus, while the pressures of work have a significant effect on parental involvement, the effects are different for men and women.

Paternity leave is the most frequently discussed means of enhancing paternal involvement, although flexible time scheduling would certainly be of greater value to employed fathers and mothers (Pleck, 1986). Two studies have shown that both mothers and fathers take advantage of flextime to spend more time with their children (Lee, 1983; Winett & Neale, 1980), but flextime remains an option open to relatively few workers.

Like the workplace, child care and educational institutions have traditionally made little effort to include fathers and have often acted in ways that exclude them or include them only in gender-typed ways (Klinman, 1986; Levine, Murphy, & Wilson, 1993).

Summary

Over the past two decades, fathers have expanded the definition of fathering, showing an increasing willingness to engage in a broad array of activities typically viewed as components of mothering. These changes have taken place alongside smaller changes in the extent to which fathers devote time to activities with and for their children and surprising resistance to the paternal assumption of parental responsibility. Both the changes and their slow pace appear attributable to secular changes, particularly in economic circumstances and maternal employment, as well as feminist critiques of traditional social structures. In addition, these slow but significant changes in the behavior of men who live with their children have occurred against a background of dramatic increases in the number of children who barely know or have almost no contact with their fathers. Attempts to understand paternal influences on child development must thus consider both the roles, functions, and impact of father-child relationships and the effects on child development of fatherless life-styles and the processes that lead to these circumstances.

PATERNAL INFLUENCES ON CHILD DEVELOPMENT

Over the past 40 years, more researchers have studied paternal influences on child development than have studied the determinants of paternal behavior, and the chapters in this volume only illustrate and underscore this fact. In order to summarize the voluminous literature on paternal influences, it is helpful to distinguish among three research traditions, each of which has contributed in important ways to our understanding of paternal roles.

Correlational Studies

Many of the earliest studies of paternal influences were designed to identify correlations between paternal and filial characteristics. The vast majority of these studies were conducted between 1940 and 1970, when the father's role as a sex-role model was considered most important, and as a result most studies focused on sex-role development, especially in sons (for reviews, see Biller, 1971, 1993; Lamb, 1981b). The design of these early studies was quite simple: Researchers assessed masculinity in fathers and in sons and then determined how strongly the two sets of scores were correlated. To the great surprise of most researchers, there was no consistent correlation between the two constructs, a puzzling finding because it seemed to violate a guiding assumption about the crucial function served by fathers. If fathers did not make their boys into men, what role did they really serve?

It took some time for psychologists to realize that they had failed to ask: Why should boys *want to be like* their fathers? Presumably they should only want to resemble fathers whom they liked and respected and with whom their relationships were warm and positive. In fact, the quality of the father-son relationship proved to be a crucial mediating variable: When the relationships between masculine fathers and their sons were good, the boys were indeed more masculine. Subsequent research even suggested that the quality of the father-child relationship was more important than the masculinity of the father (Mussen & Rutherford, 1963; Payne & Mussen, 1956; Sears, Maccoby, & Levin, 1957). Boys seemed to conform to the sex-role standards of their culture when their relationships with their fathers were warm, regardless of how "masculine" the fathers were, even though warmth and intimacy have traditionally been seen as feminine characteristics. A similar conclusion was suggested by research on other aspects of psychosocial adjustment and on achievement: Paternal warmth or closeness appeared beneficial, whereas paternal masculinity appeared irrelevant (Biller, 1971; Lamb, 1981b; Radin, 1981). The same characteristics are important with regard to maternal influences, suggesting that fathers and mothers influence children in similar ways by virtue of nurturant personal and social characteristics. Research summarized in this volume by Patterson and Chan (Chapter 14 of this volume) goes even further, indicating that the gender orientation of homosexual fathers does not increase the likelihood that their children will be homosexual, effeminate, or maladjusted.

As far as influences on children are concerned, in sum, very little about the gender of the parent seems to be distinctly important. The characteristics of the father as a parent rather than the characteristics of the father as a man appear to be most significant, although it is impossible to demonstrate that the father's masculine characteristics are of no significance. Biller (Biller, 1993; Biller & Kimpton, Chapter 8 of this volume) continues to underscore the crucial importance of distinctive maternal and paternal roles, and these themes are central to the claims of social commentators such as Blankenhorn (1995) and Popenoe (1996) as well.

Studies of Father Absence and Divorce

While the whole body of research that is here termed "correlational" was burgeoning in the 1950s, another body of literature, comprising investigations in which researchers tried to understand the father's role by studying families without fathers, was developing in parallel. The assumption was that by comparing the behavior and personalities of children raised with and without fathers, one could—essentially by a process of subtraction—estimate what sort of influence fathers typically had on children's development. The early father-absence and correlational studies were conducted in roughly the same era; not surprisingly, therefore, the outcomes studied were similar and the implications were similar and consistent with popular assumptions as well (for reviews, see Adams, Milner, & Schrepf, 1984; Biller, 1974, 1981, 1993; Blankenhorn, 1995; Herzog & Sudia, 1973; Whitehead, 1993). As indicated by Hetherington and Stanley-Hagan (Chapter 11 of this volume), boys growing up without fathers seemed to have "problems" in the areas of sex-role and gender-identity development, school performance, psychosocial adjustment, and perhaps in the control of aggression. The effects of fatherlessness on girls were less thoroughly studied, and they appeared to be less dramatic and less consistent.

Two related issues arising from the father-absence research must be addressed when evaluating these conclusions. First, even when researchers accept the conclusion that there are differences between children raised in families with the father present and those raised in families with the father absent, they must ask *why* those differences exist and *how* they should be interpreted. Second, it is important to remember that the existence of differences between groups of boys growing up with and without fathers does not mean that every boy growing up without a father has problems in the aspect of development concerned or that all boys whose fathers live at home develop normatively. One cannot reach conclusions about the status of individuals from data concerning groups, simply because there is great within-group heterogeneity. This again forces us to ask why such heterogeneity exists among children in father-absent families: Why do some boys appear to suffer deleterious consequences as a result of father absence while others do not? More broadly, the question is: What is it about father absence that makes for group differences between children in father-absent and father-present contexts, and what accounts for the impressive within-group variance?

Researchers and theorists first sought to explain the effects of father absence by noting the absence of male sex-role models in single-parent families. It was assumed that without a masculine parental model boys could not acquire strong masculine identities or sex roles and would not have models of achievement with which to identify (Biller, 1974, 1993). The validity of this interpretation is challenged by the fact that many boys without fathers seem to develop quite normally so far as sex-role development and achievement are concerned. Clearly, some other factors may be at least as (if not more) important than the availability of a male sex-role model in mediating the effects of father absence on child development. What might these factors be?

In a conceptual and empirical extension of research on the effects of father absence, many researchers initiated studies in the early 1980s designed to explore more carefully the ways in which divorce and the transition to fatherlessness might influence children's development. The results of these studies have underscored the many ways in which paternal absence influences children. First, divorce results in the absence of a co-parent—someone to help out with child care, perhaps to participate in tough decisions, and to take over when one parent needs a break from the incessant demands of child care (Maccoby, 1977). Following divorce, children consistently do better when they are able to maintain meaningful relationships with both parents, unless the levels of interparental conflict remain unusually high (e.g., Emery, 1982; Guidubaldi & Perry, 1985; Hess & Camara, 1979; Hetherington, Cox, & Cox, 1982, 1985; Kurdek, 1986; Wallerstein & Kelly, 1980). Second, economic stress frequently accompanies single motherhood (Pearson & Thoennes, 1990). The median and mean incomes of single women who head households are significantly lower than in any other group of families, and the disparity is even larger when one considers per capita income rather than household income (Glick & Norton, 1979; Horn, 1995; O'Hare, 1995). Third, the tremendous economic stress experienced by single mothers is accompanied by emotional stress occasioned by a degree of social isolation and continuing (though diminished) social disapproval of single or divorced mothers and their children (Hetherington et al., 1982). Fourth, children of divorce are often affected by the perceived, and often actual, abandonment by one of their parents (see Thompson, 1986, 1994, for reviews). Last, there are the "cancerous" effects of predivorce and postdivorce marital conflict. This may be an especially important issue because there can be little doubt that children suffer when there is hostility or conflict in the family (Amato, 1993; Amato & Keith, 1991; Cummings & O'Reilly, Chapter 4 of this volume). Since many single-parent families are produced by divorce and since divorce is often preceded and accompanied by periods of overt and covert spousal hostility, parental conflict may play a major role in explaining the problems of fatherless children.

In sum, the evidence suggests that father absence may be harmful, not necessarily because a sex-role model is absent, but because many aspects of the father's role—economic, social, emotional—go unfilled or inappropriately filled in these families. Once again, recognition of the father's multiple roles as breadwinner, parent, and emotional partner appears to be essential for understanding how fathers influence children's development.

Increased Paternal Involvement

Since 1980, several researchers have sought to identify the effects of increased paternal involvement on children. In most of these studies, researchers have compared the status of children in "traditional" families with that of children whose fathers either share in or take primary responsibility for child care (Lamb, Pleck, & Levine, 1985; Radin, 1994; Russell, 1983, 1986); other researchers have examined the correlates of varying paternal engagement (Koestner, Franz, & Weinberger, 1990; Mosely & Thomson, 1995). The effects of increased paternal involvement have been addressed in several major studies, and the results have been remarkably consistent. Children with highly involved fathers are characterized by increased cognitive competence, increased empathy, less sex-stereotyped beliefs, and a more internal locus of control (Pleck, Chapter 5 of this volume; Pruett, 1983, 1985; Radin, 1982, 1994). Again the question that has to be asked is: *Why* do these sorts of differences occur?

Three factors are probably important in this regard (Lamb et al., 1985). First, when parents assume less sex-stereotyped roles, their children have less sex-stereotyped attitudes themselves about male and female roles. Second, particularly in the area of cognitive competence, these children may benefit from having two highly involved parents rather than just one. This assures them the diversity of stimulation that comes from interacting with people who have different behavioral styles. Third, the family context in which these children are raised is important. In each of the studies cited above, a high degree of paternal involvement made it possible for both parents to do what was rewarding and fulfilling for them. It allowed fathers to satisfy their desires for closeness to their children while permitting mothers to have adequately close relationships with their children and to pursue career goals. In other words, increased paternal involvement may have made both parents feel much more fulfilled. As a result, the relationships were probably much warmer and richer than might otherwise have been the case. One can speculate that the benefits obtained by children with highly involved fathers are largely attributable to the fact that high levels of paternal involvement created family contexts in which the parents felt good about their marriages and the child care arrangements they had been able to work out.

In all of these studies, fathers were highly involved in child care because both they and their partners desired this. The effects on children appear quite different when fathers are forced to become involved, perhaps by being laid off from work while their partners are able to obtain or maintain their employment (Johnson & Abramovitch, 1985). In such circumstances, wives might resent their husbands' inability to support their families while husbands resent having to do "women's work" with the children when they really want to be out earning a living and supporting their families (see Johnson & Abramovitch, 1988; Russell, 1983). Not surprisingly, this constellation of factors appears to have adverse effects on children, just as the same degree of involvement has positive effects when the circumstances are more benign. The key point is that the extent of paternal involvement may be much less significant (so far as the effects on children are concerned) than the reasons for high involvement and the parents' evaluation thereof.

In sum, the effects of increased involvement may have more to do with the context than with father involvement per se. It seems to matter less who is at home than how that person feels about being at home, for the person's feelings will color the way he or she behaves with the children. Parental behavior is also influenced by the partner's feelings about the arrangement: Both parents' emotional states affect the family dynamics.

Summary

Viewed together, the results summarized here offer important insights to our understanding of paternal influences. First, fathers and mothers seem to influence their children in similar rather than dissimilar ways. Contrary to the expectations of many psychologists, including myself, who have studied paternal influences on children, the differences between mothers and fathers appear much less important than the similarities. Not only does the description of mothering resemble the description of fathering (particularly the version of involved fathering that has become prominent in the late 20th century) but the mechanisms and means by which fathers influence their children appear similar to those that mediate maternal influences on children. Stated differently, students of socialization have consistently found that parental warmth, nurturance, and closeness are associated with positive child outcomes whether the parent or adult involved is a mother or a father. The important dimensions of parental influence are those that have to do with parental characteristics rather than gender-related characteristics.

Second, as research has unfolded, psychologists have been forced to conclude that the characteristics of individual fathers—such as their masculinity, intellect, and even their warmth—are much less important, formatively speaking, than are the characteristics of the relationships that they have established with their children. Children who have secure, supportive, reciprocal, and sensitive relationships with their parents are much more likely to be well-adjusted psychologically than individuals whose relationships with their parents—mothers or fathers—are less satisfying. Likewise, the amount of time that fathers and children spend together is probably less important than what they do with that time and how fathers, mothers, children, and other important people in their lives perceive and evaluate the father-child relationship.

Third, individual relationships are now often seen as less influential than the family context. Fathers must thus be viewed in the broader familial context; positive paternal influences are more likely to occur not only when there is a supportive father-child relationship but when the father's relationship with his partner, and presumably other children, establishes a positive familial context. The absence of familial hostility is the most consistent correlate of child adjustment, whereas marital conflict is the most consistent and reliable correlate of child maladjustment.

Fourth, these factors all underscore the fact that fathers play multiple roles in the family and that their success in all these diverse roles influences the ways in which they affect their children's development and adjustment. Fathers have beneficial effects on their children when they have supportive and nurturant relationships with them as well as with their siblings, when they are competent and feel fulfilled as breadwinners, when they are successful and supportive partners, and so on.

Fifth, the nature of paternal influences may vary substantially depending on individual and cultural values. A classic example of this can be found in the literature on sex-role development. As a result of cultural changes, the assumed sex-role goals for boys and girls have changed, and this has produced changes in the effects of father involvement on children. In the 1950s, gender-appropriate masculinity or femininity was the desired goal; today androgyny or sex-role flexibility is desired. And whereas father involvement in the 1950s seemed to be associated with greater masculinity in boys, it is associated today with less sex-stereotyped sex-role standards in both boys and girls. Influence patterns also vary substantially depending on social factors that define the meaning of father involvement for children in particular families in particular social milieus. More generally, this underscores the variation in the relative importance of different paternal functions or roles across familial, subcultural, cultural, and historical contexts. There is no single "father's role" to which all fathers should aspire. Rather, a successful father, as defined in terms of his children's development, is one whose role performance matches the demands and prescriptions of his sociocultural and familial context. This means that high paternal involvement may have positive effects in some circumstances and negative effects in others. The same is true of low paternal involvement.

OUTLINE OF THE BOOK

The next four chapters attempt to place fatherhood, fathers' roles, and paternal influences into context and perspective. In the first of these chapters, Abramovitch (Chapter 2) focuses on key images of fatherhood that are represented in the Scriptures (especially in the Old Testament) and attempts to articulate the implications of these images for contemporary fathers and their behavior. As in literature, religious imagery can provide insights into popular fears and beliefs, and many of these have maintained their relevance over time.

Like Abramovitch, Elizabeth and Joseph Pleck (Chapter 3) attempt to review the status and role of fathers historically. Their focus is limited to four centuries of American history, however, as they articulate the changes over this period in the dominant portrayals of fatherhood. Originally viewed as a stern patriarch by white colonial settlers, "the father" is shown to have evolved through several stages into the more democratic, warm, and involved figure of much contemporary discourse. Of course, as the Plecks point out, this picture is more representative of changes that have taken place in the dominant white culture than it is of fathers' roles in other prominent subcultures, including black and Native American cultures.

In Chapter 4, Cummings and O'Reilly place fathers not in historical but in family context. They review a wealth of evidence that paternal influences are mediated in many important ways by the quality of the relationships that fathers establish with their partners, because this has a powerful impact on family climate, which in turn shapes children's experiences and development. Family conflict has harmful effects on children in part because it adversely affects the behavior and involvement of both parents and in part because of the undesirable behavior modeled for young children in such circumstances. As indicated earlier, researchers have become increasingly aware of the important role played in children's development by marital quality and conflict.

One of the factors that influences marital quality is paternal involvement, and there has been considerable debate, particularly over the past decade, about the appropriate levels of involvement that fathers should adopt (Pleck, Chapter 5). As indicated above, researchers have argued that the effects of father involvement on children depend greatly on whether both parents want increased paternal involvement, as this affects the affective family climate. Other evidence suggests further that variations in father involvement may directly affect children's development by producing changes in the level, extent, and type of contact that children have with both of their parents.

In Chapters 6 through 9, the focus shifts to the character and influence of father-child relationships in the four major phases of childhood. Lamb (Chapter 6) begins the section by discussing the development of father-infant relationships. As he notes, relationships between fathers and infants have been studied widely and thoroughly over the past two decades. Researchers have gathered substantial evidence that infants form attachments to both mothers and fathers at about the same point during the first year of life, although most infants develop a preference for their primary care providers. Observational studies have also shown that fathers are often associated with playful and vigorously stimulating social interaction, which may affect their salience and impact, although these playful tendencies apparently do not diminish the potential of both mothers and fathers to behave sensitively and responsively.

Fathers continue to interact playfully with their preschool-aged children (as discussed by Lewis in Chapter 7). Unfortunately, very few of the many studies of father-child interaction have been longitudinal in nature. As a result, relatively little is known about patterns of development, influence, and change. Lewis does adduce interesting evidence that fathers may be more affected than mothers are by being observed in public settings, however. This finding may be important not only to those trying to understand paternal influences but also to those striving to design empirical studies.

Where school-aged children are concerned, argue Biller and Kimpton in Chapter 8, there is substantial evidence that both mothers and fathers make unique contributions. Children who benefit from "the two-parent advantage" are thus exposed to a wider range of interests, activities, and experiences than those who have only one parent. Biller and Kimpton review a substantial body of evidence that children who have active, committed, and involved fathers generally perform better cognitively, academically, athletically, and socially than do children who do not benefit from such involvement.

Whereas researchers have made considerable advances in their attempts to study the relationships between fathers and infants, preschoolers, and school-aged children, they have made considerably less progress in their attempts to understand father-adolescent relationships. The evidence reviewed by Hosley and Montemayor in Chapter 9 suggests that there are several important differences between adolescents' relationships with mothers and with fathers. Father-adolescent relationships appear more distant, less intimate, and less intensive, whereas adolescent-mother relationships involve more closeness, self-disclosure, and affection. The possible effects of these differences on children's development have yet to be explored, particularly in the absence of evidence about fathers' expectations and goals for relationships with their adolescent offspring.

Although the authors of Chapters 5 through 9 disagree somewhat about the formative importance of individual paternal characteristics relative to characteristics of the families and their sociocultural context, all these authors discuss the important ways in which family climate mediates paternal influences on child development regardless of the children's ages. This issue is placed in especially stark relief when research on families whose children have special needs is reviewed (Lamb & Billings, Chapter 10).

Parents in such families face more stress, and the ability to cope with these increased demands is often determined by the willingness of fathers not only to support their wives emotionally and financially but also to assume for themselves some of the additional burdens that pertain to the care and rearing of handicapped children. In these families, therefore, the children's special needs not only impose additional strains on the family system but by so doing underscore the importance of family dynamics rather than individual paternal characteristics in shaping children's development.

Unfortunately, an increasing number of children in the United States experience their parents' divorce before the end of their adolescence. Indeed, approximately 50% of the young children in this country spend some portion of their life in single-parent families, and not surprisingly, many theorists and researchers have studied the effects of divorce on fathers and their children. Hetherington and Stanley-Hagan (Chapter 11) review this literature, showing that divorce typically has painful adverse effects on mothers, fathers, and their children. Longitudinal as well as cross-sectional studies of children raised in single- and two-parent families consistently show that children who experience their parents' divorce are more likely to suffer developmental difficulties and maladjustment during their childhood and adolescence. The nature and extent of these effects depends on a number of factors, including the socioeconomic circumstances of mother-headed families, the extent to which the physically absent fathers remain financially responsible for their children, and the extent to which fathers maintain salient and significant relationships with their children following divorce.

Another aspect of fatherhood in divorced families is explored by Hetherington and Henderson (Chapter 12) in a chapter concerned with stepfathers. Hetherington and Henderson review evidence that the entry of stepfathers does not, as commonly assumed, obviate all the adverse effects of father absence on child development, even though stepfathers often provide financial resources and reduce some of the social and emotional difficulties faced by single mothers. On the other hand, stepfathers frequently find themselves in uncertain situations, with neither the status nor the responsibilities of biological fathers and with considerable amounts of conflict with both their stepchildren and their partners' former spouses. Some of the difficulties involved in navigating these stresses are discussed by Hetherington and Henderson, who describe adaptation within stepfamilies as a continuous process, rather than a static resolution, whose nature depends on the circumstances and the individuals involved.

Chapters 13 and 14 deal with smaller groups of fathers whose characteristics make them unusual. In the first, Marsiglio and Cohan (Chapter 13) review the literature on young fathers and their impact on child development. Although much has been written about the effects of adolescent pregnancy and parenthood on young children, it has only recently been recognized that the majority of men involved in adolescent pregnancies are not themselves adolescents (Elster & Lamb, 1986). Many are still younger than average at the time of their children's birth, however, and they tend to have characteristics that make them somewhat immature psychologically and socially (Lamb, Elster, Peters, Kahn, & Tavaré, 1986). These characteristics, along with the fact that many young fathers are not married to their children's mothers and are often unwilling or unable to provide financially for their children, add to the developmental difficulties faced by these children.

By contrast, the gay fathers discussed by Patterson and Chan (Chapter 14) tend to be financially secure. Many gay fathers have children in the context of heterosexual relationships before "coming out," and the difficulties faced by their children involve coming to terms with the gender orientation of their fathers. Other gay fathers become parents through artificial insemination, adoption, or foster parenthood, but in each case the stresses occasioned by societal hostility toward homosexuals rather than the economic stresses faced by fathers impose the greatest burden on these fathers and their children. Although the literature is scanty, the bulk of the evidence suggests that children in the care of gay fathers develop normally, without significant increases in the rates of psychosocial maladjustment. The possibility that developmental trajectories depend on the social and structural circumstances of relationships involving gay fathers has yet to be explored, however.

Psychological maladjustment among fathers and their offspring is the focus of Chapter 15. Phares attempts to provide a comprehensive review of the research literature documenting the extent to which paternal maladjustment has adverse consequences for children's development as well as the extent to which filial maladjustment is associated with various aspects of the father-child relationship. Much of the emergent literature reviewed by Phares is designed to address an earlier overemphasis on either paternal absence or the roles of maternal deficiency, deviance, and deprivation in filial maladjustment. Chapter 15 includes summaries of recent research on the etiology of conduct disorders, antisocial personality disorder, alcohol abuse, depression, anxiety disorders, schizophrenia, autism, attention deficit/hyperactivity, and eating disorders, with a special focus on associations with paternal characteristics.

Finally, Sternberg (Chapter 16) discusses fathers in violent families. After reviewing the limited available evidence on the effects of various types of family violence (paternal abuse of mothers and children, as well as maternal abuse of fathers) on the growth, development, and adjustment of children raised in violent families, Sternberg speculates about the mechanisms whereby violence alters and distorts paternal influences on child development. She reminds us once again how fathers' influences can be both positive and negative.

CONCLUSION

As we approach the twenty-first century, our conception and understanding of fatherhood and paternal influence patterns is considerably greater than it was as little as two decades ago, when *The Role of the Father in Child Development* (Lamb, 1976) first appeared. The chapters that follow illustrate the intensity of research on these topics and paint an increasingly detailed and complex picture of both the factors that influence paternal behavior and how fathers influence their children's development by the way they treat them, by the way they treat the children's mothers, and by their psychological and physical neglect. While much remains to be learned, the progress to date is noteworthy.

As argued in this chapter, recent study has been characterized by increasing awareness of the cultural and historical boundedness of much research. There is no single role that fathers play in families or in their children's development, and the relative importance of the father's many roles varies across subcultures and historical epochs. Limiting the generalization of research findings and exploring the major cultural variations in paternal behavior will continue to dominate future research on fatherhood and its relation to child development. There is now little doubt that fathers influence child development profoundly, and often negatively; the challenge for the future is to better understand the many, direct, indirect, and complex patterns and processes of influence. The chapters in this book summarize what we have already learned and identify fertile areas for future research.

CHAPTER 2

Images of the "Father" in Psychology and Religion

Henry Abramovitch

Sackler School of Medicine, Tel Aviv University

I N THIS CHAPTER I review some of the dominant themes concerning the images of the father in psychology and religion. I make no attempt to be comprehensive but focus on key images using mythological, biblical, and contemporary sources. After reviewing historical changes in the image of masculinity and the father, I proceed to examine and illustrate the impact each image of the father has on his children.[1]

HISTORICAL CHANGES IN THE IMAGE OF THE FATHER

At the outset of this century, the father played a central role in both psychology and religion. "God the Father" was the dominant metaphor in Western religion, and in the new depth psychology, the castrating, or Oedipal, father was seen as the major force in the development of personality. Moreover, it was argued that an individual's emotional attitude toward religion was a reflection of and consolation for one's relationship with the personal father. The father reigned supreme, at least in theory. There was no need for a "Father's Day" to correspond to "Mother's Day" since, as one Japanese friend noted is still true in the Pacific Rim, "Every day was father's day!"

More recently, the role and image of the father has continued to decline in potency, authority, and importance. Contrast the popular American TV show of the fifties, "Father Knows Best" with the best-known contemporary image of the father in popular culture, Homer Simpson. The former father was a wise, mature, guiding force in the lives of his children, while the latter is a foolish, self-centered slob, whose children far exceed him in the once fatherly virtues of wisdom, maturity, and discipline.

The decline of the father is related to a radical alteration that occurred in the image

---

1. Certain parts are adapted from Abramovitch (1994a, 1994b, 1995).

of men and the corresponding concept of masculinity. This attitude is well expressed in Peter Tatham's *The Making of Maleness* which begins as follows:

> Until about thirty years ago, the nature of a man and his masculinity was little questioned. Generally speaking, it was assumed that a man would inevitably wish to be strong, powerful, and decisive, and that he would concern himself more with what went on outside the home than with domestic details. Since this ideal was assumed to arise in some way from his actual biological nature, it was therefore inescapable. Any individual who found it hard to reach this goal could be tolerated, patronized, or even pitied, provided he was seen to agree that he was failing as a man. By acknowledging his failure, he implicitly endorsed the correctness of the model. Individuals or groups, on the other hand, who appeared deliberately to flout this view of being a man were deeply disturbing. They might have included aesthetes, homosexuals, pacifists, foreigners; and their fate was scorned as deviant, to be criminalized, conquered, or otherwise controlled. Women were also expected to go along with this view of manliness, which inevitably made inferior persons of them also. (Tatham, 1992, pp. xv–xvi)

From this secure position of a divinely ordained sense of masculinity, males have become increasingly confused about their own nature. Castigated as brutal, patriarchal, and sexually abusing, images about men have tended to split into "savage men" who indeed abuse and abandon their loved ones and what Robert Bly in his book *Iron John: A Book about Men* (1990) has called "soft men." These soft men are "lovely, valuable people" with a gentle attitude to life. "But many of these men are not happy," Bly observes. "You quickly notice the lack of energy in them. They are life-preserving but not exactly life-giving. Ironically, you often see these men with strong women who positively radiate energy" (Bly, 1990, p. 3). Underneath this lack of energy, Bly finds tremendous grief and anguish about the remoteness of their fathers. In the turmoil of his current relationships, the soft man cared for his partner, felt her pain, and even provided comfort. He was empathetic and nurturing, but what he lacked was *resolve:* He could not say what he really wanted and stick to it. If a person does not feel himself to be an initiated male, he will have difficulty becoming an adequate father. Such men seem to be saying, "If I am not a real man, how can I be a real father?"

In the past few years, there seems to have been a reversal of fortunes in the attempt to rediscover or re-create a postfeminist image of a strong yet gentle man. Such men exude the pathos and resolve of the "wild man." They are initiated into men's mysteries, in touch with their own inner and outer nature while preserving a healthy sense of their own "wildness." The change is also reflected in new social movements such as the heterogeneous but growing international "men's movement" inspired in part by Robert Bly's book.

With an exploration of a new masculinity came a renewed interest in the father. The dominant themes of the recent explosion of writings stress one above all others: the absence of the father and the yearning for reunion. A review of some of the recent titles in the psychology of the father clearly reflects the central importance of the image of the absent father: Alix Pirani, *The Absent Father;* Samuel Osherson, *Finding Our Fathers;* Guy Corneau, *Absent Fathers, Lost Sons* (translated from the French *Pere Manquant. Fils Manquée*); Alfred Collins, *Fatherson: A Self Psychology of the Archetypal Masculine;* and Gregory Max Vogt, *Return to the Father: Archetypal Di-*

mensions of the Patriarch. In sharp contrast, other influential texts on the adult development of men, such as Levinson's *The Seasons of a Man's Life* (1978) and Moore and Gillette's *King, Warrior, Magician, Lover: Rediscovering Masculine Potential* (1990), do not even mention the word "father" in their indexes.

The key element in all these empirical, mythological, comparative studies is the suffering of the abandoned son, yearning for a father who is loving and emotionally available and who is able to initiate his son into the world of the mature masculine, the realm of "true men." As Osherson puts it, "the psychological and physical absence of fathers from their families is one of the greatest underestimated tragedies of our times" (Osherson, 1986, p. 6).

Osherson cites research in the contemporary United States that clearly reflects the feelings of emotional neglect and physical abandonment. In one survey of over 7,000 men, none said they had been or were close to their fathers! Another study revealed that barely 1% described good relations with their fathers, and in a detailed clinical research study barely 15% revealed evidence of a history of "nurturance and trust-worthy warmth and connection" (Osherson, 1986, p. 5). The remoteness of such fathers exposes sons and daughters not to the man himself but only to his moods. As Bly puts it, there is "temperament without teaching" (Bly, 1990, pp. 96–98).

Mitscherlich (1969), the German psychoanalyst, suggests that the inability of fathers to share with their children the nature of their worklife day by day, and season by season, as was possible in many traditional societies, creates black holes in the child's psyche. In the place of a caring, strong inner father, demons appear. These demons undermine the image of the father and tell the child that the father's work is bad and that the father himself is evil. The result is widespread "paternal deprivation" resulting in what has been called "father hunger," the yearning for a good or good enough father, or an "internal father who does not care," a child's misinterpretation of fatherly distance (Cath, Gurwitz, & Ross, 1982; Shapiro, 1984, p. 69). Such father hunger has been linked to a wide variety of dysfunctions: the etiology of narcissistic disorders (Carvalho, 1982), drug abuse, antisocial personality disorder, and conduct disorders (Kaplan & Sadock, 1994), all of which lay down a basis for an intergenerational cycle of continuing paternal deprivation.

A second consequence of such life without father is that children, but especially sons growing up without direct access, tend to view the father through their mother's eyes. As a result they will tend to see men and their own masculinity from a woman's viewpoint. This tendency alienates them from their own sense of themselves as males. When such a son becomes a father, he never feels at home with himself, since his connection with himself is mediated via an Other.

THE ARCHETYPAL IMAGE OF THE ABSENT FATHER

Many authors discuss "the absent father" as if it were a new and recent phenomenon, and they may be correct. Certainly many cultures including the Biblical put enormous importance on becoming a father. On the other hand, the yearning of a lost son for an absent father seems to be a widespread if not universal theme among the world's religions and literature, and therefore it likely has archetypal significance.

The dominant image of the absent father in both psychology and religion is perhaps best reflected in the central image of Christianity, Jesus on the cross. Just before his death, the Son cries out in a loud voice, "Eli Eli lama sabachthani?"—that is, "My God, my God, why have you deserted me?" (see Matthew 27:46–47, quoting Psalm 22:1). Jesus, the son who never became a father, dies in the heartbreak of feeling abandoned by the most important of fathers. The image of a son suffering the torments of an absent father has lost none of its potency. It still dominates the discussion by sons of their personal and heavenly fathers.

Many classics of Western literature also hinge on the father-son relationship. Shakespeare's *Hamlet,* Homer's *Odyssey,* and the story of Joseph in the Bible all revolve around the fate of the son separated from his father. Hamlet returning home from his university studies finds his father dead, his mother remarried, and himself displaced from the crown. In Hamlet's dramatic meeting with his father's ghost, his father demands, "If thou didst ever thy father love . . . Revenge his foul and most unnatural murder" (act 1, scene 5, 23–25). But Hamlet, like today's soft man, lacks resolve. He is unable to identify fully with his dead father's wishes as a "father's son" and act; nor is he able to mourn his dead father and accept the new reality. The result of his inability to resolve this conflict of fatherly loyalty leads to uncontrolled aggression with tragic consequences for all.

The *Odyssey* likewise begins with the problem of the absent father. Telemachus, Odysseus's son, says to an unknown guest,

> My mother says I am his son, but I don't know myself; I never heard of anyone who did know whose son he was. . . . If he were dead, it would not hurt me so much; if he had fallen before Troy among his comrades, or if he had died in the arms of his friends, after he had wound up the war. Then the whole nation would have built him a barrow, and he would have won a great name for his son as well in days to come. But now, there is not a word of him. The birds of prey have made him their prey; he is gone from sight, gone from hearing, and left anguish and lamentation for me. (*Odyssey,* Book 1; trans. Rouse, 1937, p. 16)

Telemachus appears as a lost son, unable to idealize or mourn his long-absent father; nor is he able to defend his father's house and patrimony. The stranger is of course Athena in disguise, come to Ithaca to put heart into Odysseus's son. Athena's advice is

> Get the best ship you can find, put twenty oarsmen aboard, go and find out about your father and why he is so long away. Perhaps some one may tell you, or you may hear some rumour that God will send, which is often the best way for people to get news. . . . Then, if you hear that your father is alive, and on his way back, for all your wearing and tearing you can bear up for another year. But if you hear that he is dead and no longer in this world, come back here yourself to your own home, and build him a barrow, and do the funeral honours in handsome style, as you ought, and give away your mother to some husband. . . . Indeed, you ought not to play about in the nursery any longer; your childhood's days are done. (Book 1, Rouse, 1937, pp. 17–18)

Athena's advice seems a model of psychotherapy for a lost son. Telemachus even says to the disguised stranger, "You might be a father speaking to his own son."

Telemachus does spend the next three books of the epic searching for his father. In the end, when they find each other, Odysseus says what many contemporary males yearn to hear, "I am your father, for whom you have mourned so long and put up with the wrongs and violence of men" (Book 16, Rouse, 1937, p. 184). As if to reinforce the theme of father-son reunion, the epic ends with reconciliation between Odysseus, his son, and his own father, who can cry, "What a day is this, kind gods! I am a happy man. My son and my son's son are rivals in courage" (Book 24, Rouse, 1937, p. 271).

Nor does the yearning for one's father apparently resolve itself in youth. In the poignant memoir *I Had a Father,* Clark Blaise (1993, p. 6) writes, "I don't know any man my age who wouldn't want his father back, no matter how deformed their relationship had been. I don't know of any man my age, with the possible exception of Philip Roth, who achieved a proper parting with his father, who didn't feel cheated of one last sailing, one last drink, one last drive to the sunset." Christianity, with a bleaker view of life, leaves to parable (the parable of the "prodigal son") or a "better world," the wish of an ultimate reconciliation between father and son.

THE IMAGE OF THE MURDEROUS FATHER

If the shadow of the absent father is long, it is perhaps still not as dark as the malevolent image of the murderous father. Ross (1982, 1986, 1992) and others drew renewed attention to the legend of Oedipus. In that story, Laius, Oedipus's father orders his infant son killed, and he is left to die on a Theban hillside. The infant, however, is found by a shepherd who raises the child. Later, as a young man, making his way in the world, he comes to a narrow bridge, wide enough for only a single man to pass. He sees an old man coming in the other direction and brashly asks the old man to stand aside for the young. When the old man stubbornly refuses, they fight and Oedipus unknowingly kills his old father, now wandering away from his kingdom. Oedipus goes on to save the city from a plague by answering the riddle of the Sphinx and unknowingly to marry his mother, the queen. Only much later in life, when he is a grandfather and another plague devastates the city, does the truth gradually emerge.

Freud in his famous analysis of the tale claimed that it revealed the unconscious desire of sons to murder their fathers and marry their mothers. Ross demonstrated convincingly that Freud "misread" the myth, enacting the story of his own childhood as he saw it from the perspective of an adult "wounded healer." Freud systematically ignored the beginning of the story as a tale of child abuse. Laius, the father, in collusion with his wife, Jocasta, sought to kill their new-born child. He also failed to see the meeting at the narrow bridge as the inevitable clash between generations, in which the old must give way to a successor generation.

The story of Oedipus becomes not a story of unconscious desires on the part of the son but the inevitable consequences of the "darker side of fatherhood." Closer inspection of the original tale reveals a darker side of Laius the father. Laius, like Hamlet, was a son displaced by his uncle. Taking refuge with neighboring King Pelops, he returned the favor by sexually abusing the king's very young son. In turn, the king cursed his guest saying that Laius would be slain by his own son. Laius, subsequently king of Thebes, refused to have sex with his wife, but she got him drunk and thereby conceived the son (cf. Genesis 19 for the similar story of Lot's daughters).

Laius, the unwilling father, commands his wife to kill the child by exposure, and it is she who turns the infant over to his would-be death.

Such behavior constitutes what Ross popularized as the "Laius complex" (Ross, 1992, p. 333): the urge to sodomize and murder one's own children. The actions of Laius are echoed by other Great Father figures like Chronos, Pharoh, and Herod who are envious of the young. "Infanticidal envy continues to afflict fathers. Many fathers are unable to overcome the envy they harbour for the son in the womb or for the son sucking at the breast" (Shapiro, 1984, p. 72). Shapiro goes on to say that the child's first task is often to survive their father's envy.

THE FIRST FATHER

Laius does appear as the archetypal all-bad father, an unwilling, sexually abusing, absent father, who experiences his children as murderous competitors. More interesting is his Biblical counterpart Abraham, who combines loving and murderous aspects. Abraham, in Jewish and Christian tradition (though not apparently in Islam), is often considered the archetypal patriarch, The First Father. His name illustrates this identity and is said to mean "the father of many nations." It is through him that God binds his descendants in an everlasting covenant; Abraham is the first father to lay the sign of circumcision covenant on his son's penis, and he is the one who will teach his sons to "do what is right and just" so that God may bring about all that has been promised. Abraham is a father intimately concerned with his sons' lives and their spiritual progress. Not surprisingly, then, he is known to Jewish tradition as "Our Father Abraham" and to Christians as "Father Abraham," declared to be the ideal exemplar of fatherhood.

This fatherly facade, however, breaks down under closer inspection. Abraham's relationship with his own sons Ishmael and Isaac has a darker side. In both cases, he neglects them "in utero": allowing Sarah to torture the pregnant Hagar, who flees into the desert, or allowing the possibly pregnant, or about to become pregnant, Sarah to spend the night in a king's harem. In both cases, Abraham's sons are rescued only by divine intervention. The case against Abraham approaches charges of attempted child abuse in his treatment of his sons as young men. Ishmael is disinherited and banished to die of thirst in the desert (a fate narrowly averted). Isaac is almost murdered in a ritual sacrifice on Mount Moriah. Again, in both cases it is by divine, and not paternal, intervention that the son does not die. Far from being the ideal father, in these cases Abraham appears to suffer from a severe Laius complex. His neglect and abuse are all the more surprising given his enormous desire for sons and for continuity.

The traditional interpretations of the strange episode recounted in Genesis 22, known in Hebrew tradition as the *akeda*, "the binding of Isaac," stress the issue of obedience and authority. God the Father commands Abraham the father to offer up his son as a holocaust sacrifice on the place He will show to him. It is at this moment that Abraham the father must choose. Does his supreme loyalty lie with his son or his God? Abraham is typically praised for remaining a spiritual son rather than a protective father and agreeing to "the grossest violation of the human order" (Abramovitch, 1994a). Abraham, however, was no ordinary father, for he *did* solve the riddle of fatherhood in a way analogous to Oedipus's solving the riddle of the sphinx and so deserves the title The First Father.

To better understand Abraham's role, we need to explore the overall relations between sons and fathers in biblical narrative. Within biblical narrative, the most common and concise biography presents a person in his main social role, as that of a paternal ancestor, part of an unfolding chain of sons becoming fathers. In these genealogical lists, the birth of a son is the marker event separating everything that came before from all that is to follow. These lists, therefore, describe an unbroken chain of ancestral descent from father to son. Not to have a son (and therefore never to attain the status of father) means in biblical context to be "cut off," separated from the main line of biospiritual evolution. It means to die alone, cut off. In contrast to much of psychoanalytic thought, which is given from the son's point of view, biblical psychology might be said to be "father centered."

One of the key functions that fathers play is to pass onto their children their status and social roles (Hewlett, 1992). Anthropologists have suggested that such succession normally proceeds along one of two patterns: the *genealogical* pattern, or inheritance by birthright, or the *charismatic* pattern, or inheritance by selection. The benefits of genealogical succession are assured succession. Everyone will know in advance who will be the next healer, king, or high priest. The drawbacks of such succession are equally clear: The new man may be unfit for the job. The two books of Kings in the Bible contain examples of such bad hereditary rulers. In contrast, the charismatic pattern involves complementary benefits and dangers. One receives someone right for the office, but the transition may involve a disruptive period of uncertainty and civil war, as recounted in Judges and Samuel, until succession is assured. Normally, genealogical and charismatic succession are mutually exclusive. Moses was a charismatic leader par excellence. But he created a split system of succession: priesthood was inherited from father to son; political leadership remained charismatic. Significantly, Moses passed over his own sons to appoint Joshua as his chosen political successor (cf. Deuteronomy 34:9, "Joshua son of Nun was filled with the spirit of wisdom, for Moses had laid his hands on him") and his brother Aaron to found a hereditary priest caste (cf. Exodus 29:4–9; Numbers 20:23–28).

The Hebrew tradition starting with Abraham, however, yearned to combine genealogical and charismatic succession. Abraham, like many fathers after him, wished that *his* son would inherit *his* God, so that his son could say "my God" is "God of my fathers." In this way, a biological son would become the spiritual successor, son-and-disciple.

The tension between hereditary and charismatic succession appears dramatically when one reviews the relations between fathers and sons in the main narrative text of Scripture. There are few good fathers and few, if any, instances of uncomplicated succession (for a more complete analysis, see Abramovitch, 1994a). Neither Adam, Noah, Isaac, Jacob, Reuben, Judah, nor even Joseph can be described as a successful father. In later generations, Moses, Aaron, Gideon, Avimelech, Eli, Samuel, Saul, David, and even Solomon are failures in some important aspect of their fathering.

Most biblical fathers undergo traumatic loss in relation to their sons. Adam, like David after him, loses two sons in one blow, through the double curse of fratricide and exile; Noah and Saul curse their own sons; Jacob, Moses, and Saul, inadvertently, one might say even unconsciously, send their sons on missions that (almost) lead to their death. Terah, Jacob, Judah, Eli, and David all experience the death of at least one son. Indeed, there is hardly a clear-cut case where a father successfully initiates his first-born son as his chosen spiritual successor.

The case of Samuel is instructive on this point. The text of 1 Samuel 8:1–7 depicts a crisis of continuity, when Samuel, a charismatic spiritual leader, tries to make his biological sons his spiritual heirs:

> When Samuel grew old, he appointed his two sons as judges over Israel. The name of the first born was Joel, that of the younger Abijah; there were judges in Beersheva. But his sons did not follow his ways; they wanted money, taking bribes and perverting justice. Then all the elders of Israel gathered together and came to Samuel at Ramah. "Look," they said to him, "you are old and your sons do not follow your ways. So give us a king to rule over us, like the other nations." It displeased Samuel that they should say, "Let us have a king to rule us." (trans. *The Jerusalem Bible,* 1968)

Here we can see most clearly the clash between the two systems of inheritance: the elders demanding a system of assured succession and Samuel's paternal injury when the people rightly reject his children as unworthy. The question remains for Samuel, as for Eli his mentor (or even for Moses, David, and Solomon), why he was not a more effective moral influence on the characters of his sons.

In sharp contrast is the relationship between Isaac and his son Esau. Here, on Isaac's deathbed, was a clear occasion when a father wished to pass on his hereditary and spiritual inheritance to his first, beloved son. In one of the most tender moments between a father and son in all Scripture, they learn to their horror that this unique opportunity has been lost:

> No sooner had Jacob left the presence of his father Isaac—after Isaac had finished blessing Jacob—than his brother Esau came back from the hunt. He too prepared a tasty dish and brought it to his father. And he said to his father, "Let my father sit up and eat of his son's game, so that you may give me your innermost blessing." His father Isaac said to him, "Who are you?" And he said, "I am your son, Esau, your first born!" Isaac was seized with very violent trembling. "Who was it then," he demanded, "that hunted game and brought it to me? Moreover, I ate of it before you came, and I blessed him; now he must remain blessed!" When Esau heard his father's words, he burst into wild and bitter sobbing and said to his father . . . "Have you but one blessing, Father? Bless me too, Father!" And Esau wept aloud. (Genesis 27:30–38, trans. Jewish Publication Society, 1978)

In theological terms one may see how universal issues of power, rivalry, and envy with one's personal father are contrasted with the possibility of a personal destiny under the guidance of a spiritual father.

Now we can return to Abraham and the riddle of fatherhood and suggest a new interpretation of the *akeda.* Abraham in most Hebrew interpretations is pictured as willingly going off to kill his son, at God's command. In Jewish legend Satan, the Adversary, sensibly tries to stop him by appealing to his humanity: How can he kill an innocent victim, in whom all the promises are imminent?

I suggest that the *akeda* is a symbolic enactment of the filicidal urge of the Laius complex. It touches the universal moment when fathers wish to kill their sons, whether out of a power urge, in a momentary rage, or whatever. But Abraham is Laius with a difference! Having been ready to kill, he is stopped, looks up, and conceives new possibilities and displacements for this bloody urge. This resolution is part of the horrible fascination bound up in the story: the reader must face his own hidden feelings. Would I too be willing to kill my son, even for some ultimate value? Would I too let myself be sacrificed by my father for some unseen vision? The story provides its own suspense and catharsis, allowing fathers to experience and dissipate the tensions between the generations.

The *akeda* has another dimension, namely, to resolve the tension between the two types of succession. If we examine the *akeda,* not from the father's point of view but from the son's, we may argue that this trauma is also a ritual initiation of Abraham's son to Abraham's God. Abraham has no other son. If Isaac is unworthy, as presumably Ishmael was, then Abraham is lost, cut off. In order to assure himself and Isaac of his worthiness, Abraham binds Isaac to God, as surely as he bound the boy to the altar. Once Isaac is an acceptable sacrifice, he is "sanctified" to God, no less than Samuel. Isaac, too, may hear the blessings and promises Abraham has heard so many times, and in this way Isaac is accepted as Abraham's spiritual heir. It is striking that the *akeda* illustrates the exclusivity between the two types of inheritance. In order for Isaac to become a prophet, Abraham must be willing to lose him as his own beloved son. No other father in the Bible successfully resolves the paradox of continuity by birthright versus continuity by being chosen. No other father makes such a good match for his son, lives to see grandchildren, and becomes, "dying at a ripe old age, an old man who had lived his full span of years" (Genesis 25:8), buried by both his sons. By enacting and rejecting the filicidal urge and by fusing the genealogical and charismatic, Abraham did solve the riddle of fatherhood and remains Our Father Abraham, truly The First Father.

Implicit in the *akeda* story is the complementary image of the abandoned father. This image is best exemplified by the experience of the aging father, Jacob or David, each of whom loses a son in a murderous game of sibling rivalry. Jacob, Scripture says, "mourned his son for a long time. All his sons and daughters came to comfort him, but he refused to be comforted. 'No,' he said, 'I will go down in mourning to Sheol beside my son.' And his father wept for him" (Genesis 37:35, trans. *The Jerusalem Bible,* 1968). Such interminable mourning for a lost, favorite son is surely as potent as the yearning of a son for an absent father, however painful it must be for surviving children.

David's case is all the more pathetic. When his rebellious son Absalom (in Hebrew, *ab* "father" and *shalom* "peace"; hence, ironically, "Peace upon father") is killed, the old king cries out, "My son Absalom! Would I have died in your place! Absalom, my son, my son!" (2 Samuel 19:1). If one image of the father is as murderous father, then the complement is the father who is blind to the evil in his sons, blind even to the attempts of sons to slay their fathers. If there is an underlying connection between these complementary images—murderous father/murderous son, absent father/absent son—it may lie in the fact that father and son often use each other as mirroring selfobjects, using each other to feel good or bad about one's self (Collins, 1994). The success of the son reflects back on the father; the success of the father reflects outward toward the son. But the reverse is likewise true. The failure of the son attacks the father's sense of himself. Two common strategies fathers (and sons) may adopt to deal with this tension are to destroy the bad self-object, the strategy of the murderous father, or to abandon the son as a self-object, the strategy of the absent father. Only when such a symbiotic use of each other as self-objects resolves into an individuated relation can father and son come to know each other as genuine persons.

The paternal tendency to select a "chosen son," so much in evidence in the Bible, is not without its own darker side. Each chosen son (or daughter), necessarily, implies a rejected child. Each rejection is itself a source of abandonment, resentment, frustration, and possibly aggression. One author, writing in *Fatherhood* (French, 1992), a collection of essays by sons of famous fathers, puts it most vehemently: "Any parent who even thinks of having a 'favourite child' is guilty of spiritual infanticide" (Edwards, 1992, p. 69).

THE GOD OF LOVE AS "SKY FATHER"

In contrast to the terrors of a murderous or abandoning father is the tender security of a loving father, characterized by the God of the New Testament. This God is the God of the Ten Commandments shorn of his jealous, vengeful aspect. But whereas the God of the Old Testament is the source of both good and evil, the New Testament has an extraneous source of evil in the form of the fallen angel Lucifer or the Devil. Psychodynamically, one can maintain a idealized loving relationship with the father, but only by the defense mechanism of splitting, in which God, Father, and Son are all good, while the devil and the sinner are all bad.

The God of the New Testament is often spoken of as "The Father." However, as the Lord's Prayer makes clear, ("Our Father in heaven . . . your will be done on earth as in heaven"; Matthew 6:9–10, trans. *The Jerusalem Bible*), this father is a "sky father." The sky father as a psychological type is a remote, all-seeing, spirit, who lays down divine law (Coleman & Coleman, 1981). The first quality of such sky fathers is remoteness. Like African high gods, such sky gods must be approached via an intermediary and cannot be approached directly. In Christianity, Jesus the Son is such a link to the Father: "No one can come to the Father except through me. If you know me, you know my Father too" (John 14:6–7, trans. *The Jerusalem Bible*). A second characteristic of a sky god is pervasiveness. From his vantage point in the heavens, the sky god sees all. In this role, he may act as judge and absolute authority, whose word is final ("The Lord can rescue the good from the ordeal, and hold the wicked for their punishment until the day of Judgement"; 2 Peter 2:9, trans. *The Jerusalem Bible*). Indeed the word *logos* is a central aspect of the father. *Logos* refers to "the Word" (as in the Gospel of John, which begins "In the beginning was the Logos . . ."), but more specifically rationality, logic, intellect, language, law. Third, the sky god exemplifies spirit, the creative wind of creation, in contrast to the matter of the "earth mother" ("Now the earth was a formless void, there was darkness over the deep, and God's spirit hovered over the water"; Genesis 1:1, trans. *The Jerusalem Bible*). The sky father of Christianity is a nurturing-forgiving authority ("Give us today our daily bread and forgive us . . ."), and it is this aspect of "loving kindness" that differentiates the Christian image of God the Father from that of Zeus, the sky god of Greek mythology.

Bolen (1989) has analyzed Zeus as a sky father. Zeus is remote, obsessed with power. His symbols of thunderbolt and eagle exemplify his tendency to decisive action and swift retribution. He is amoral but authoritarian, one who must have the last word and who sees children as subordinates whose obligation is "to be obedient and carry out his will. . . . He expects loyalty in return, and feels betrayed when a subordinate or child 'grows up' and then differs from him" (Bolen, 1989, p. 54). With a Zeus-like sky god, there is no possibility of reconciliation, except on his terms. Zeus is thus "the archetype of a dynastic father. He wants many children and grandchildren to carry on after him, and to this end he tries to impose his will on what his children do in the world, not only in his lifetime but also beyond the grave." Zeus, who himself survived a Laius-like attack by his father, Cronos, tends to see his own sons and supporters as potential rivals. His brother Poseidon, ruler of the sea, in contrast exemplifies the father who is passionate in his fidelity toward his sons but impulsively destructive when enraged. As such, Poseidon, given the epithet "Earthshaker," the sender of earthquakes and tidal waves, is the mythological model of the abusing father.

Although one's biological father is the first candidate to play a godlike role of authoritative sky father, any father figure can assume the role. Consider Ernest Jones's son, who describes how his father's mentor, Sigmund Freud, assumed the mantle of sky father for both of them:

> I admired my father enormously. . . . Then, being the son of a dedicated Freudian was bound to confront me with a particular difficulty. I learned (not from my father, who was averse to talking about professional matters and certainly never sought to indoctrinate me, but from my general reading) of the existence of the Oedipus complex. I don't recall my exact age at the time, but I know I was seized with panic. Did I really want to kill my father? Did I want to make love with my mother? (The idea held no attractions whatever for me.) I asked my father, attempting to put on an air of detached intellectual curiosity, whether this complex is indeed universal in humankind or whether it admitted of exceptions. He assured me it was an integral part of the human condition, whether in the primeval forest or in the most sophisticated and cultivated environment. To have discovered its universality, he explained, was the mark of Freud's genius. I felt—as the son of a Calvinist preacher might have felt on making acquaintance with the doctrine of original sin—the weight of an inescapable doom. I did not want to hate my father; yet by failing to hate him, I should be repudiating his creed. . . .
>
> In his world, however, he was not the supreme authority, that position being reserved for Sigmund Freud. It was painful for me to realise that there was someone who could correct or rebuke my father, just as the headmaster of my school could correct or rebuke me. Many years later, I read my father's letters home to my mother from San Cristoforo—the place where, in 1923, the mandarins of psychoanalysis, led by the egregious Otto Rank, convinced Freud that Jones was an unworthy disciple and imposed a humiliating censure on him. When I read these letters, my father was long dead (so was Rank) and I was almost sixty years old. But I felt the same mingling of grief and outraged

anger—"how dare they do this to my father?"—that I might have felt had I been still a boy. (Jones, 1992, pp. 25–27)

Jones the son seems caught between his own idealization of his personal father, and his father's own idealization of Freud as the Great Father. The accompanying identification makes his father's humiliation his own. It is remarkable that Jones, like many psychoanalysts, psychiatrists, and other psychotherapists (Maeder, 1989), was insensitive to his son's needs and the dilemma of being the son of a famous father. The tragic double standard in which fathers give time and sensitivity to other people's children but not to their own is summed up in the well-known joke: Question (to the child of a doctor or therapist): What do you want to be when you grow up? Answer: A patient!

LOYALTY AND DISLOYALTY: A RESOLUTION

It is striking to recall that the Fifth Commandment is the only one of the commandments to carry the explicit promise of a reward: "Honor your father and your mother so that you may have a long life" (Exodus 20:12, trans. *The Jerusalem Bible*). The literalist interpretation of this reward refers to the absolute right of life and death that parents in the Bible had over their children. According to Deuteronomy 21:18–21, parents were able to put to death a "stubborn and rebellious son who will not listen to the voice of his father or the voice of his mother." But a more generous approach suggests that in honoring their progenitors, children were "choosing life." The appropriate reward would be long life, in which children honoring parents are, in turn, honored by their own children. In this way, honoring parents creates life-affirming *karma* that perpetuates life. The opposite act, dishonoring parents, ruptures the flow of intergenerational vitality and thereby breaks the cycle of life. More cynically, the need for a reward suggests what Freud originally argued. Given the unconscious emotional ambivalence between children and fathers, one needs positive reinforcement of the most concrete kind to counter the natural tendency toward disrespect and rebellion.

A more sensitive resolution of how the sins of the father will not be visited upon the son comes from the story recorded in the Hebrew Mishna, a second-century compilation of Jewish law (Eduyot 5:7). It deals with a subject familiar to contemporary academics, a vicious disagreement among scholars. One rabbi, Akavia, son of Mehalalel, resisted the majority opinion on some four points of law. The majority begged him to relent and offered him the presidency of the *sanhedrin,* the central rabbinical court, as an incentive to compromise, but he remained steadfast in his refusal and suffered social isolation as a result. When he was old and about to die, he called his son to him and instructed him as follows:

You must follow the majority on these four points of law. I could not go along with the majority on this issue, since I learned this particular *teaching* from two of my teachers. The other Rabbis had learned their version from their two teachers, so each was right to remain adamant in his position. But you, my son have heard this opinion only from me, a single source and therefore I insist that in this matter you are required to accept the majority opinion.

Rabbi Akavia seems acutely aware of his son's dilemma of how to be loyal to his father and yet not suffer his father's fate of being cut off from the community. This father works out a brilliant solution. By his father's command, the son must abide by the majority decision of the community. In this way, the son is indeed a loyal son but does not carry the dispute into the next generation. Many disputes within families, in professional associations, and between nations have their roots in past quarrels. These feuds are then passed onto the next generation so that the "sins of the fathers" become the bitter fruit of the sons, who must choose between the community and their fathers. Generative fathers are able to devise creative ways to nurture their sons' loyalty in a way that breaks the intergenerational cycle of discord.

The generative Rabbi Akavia is better known for a series of questions and answers recorded in another section of the Mishna (The Saying of the Fathers 6:3) which begins "Know . . . from where you have come?" To which is answered: "A stinking drop (of semen)." Akavia's answer seems to suggest a necessary de-idealization of father as progenitor. The other questions (Where you are going? and Before Whom must you stand in judgment?) stress the primacy of the Great Father, who takes precedence over father of bodily form.

THE GOOD ENOUGH FATHER

What then is the image of the good enough father? The English Jungian analyst Andrew Samuels (1985, 1989, 1993) has provided the most compelling image of what good enough fathering might entail.[2] Drawing on clinical material, he suggests that the pathologies of the father lie in the physical and psychic distance between a father and his children on two key dimensions, the erotic and the aggressive. A father who is too close or too remote will not be good enough. A father too close erotically will be perceived as "incestuous," if not actually abusive, leading to a distorted relation to sexuality and relationships. An erotically distanced father will leave his child disconfirmed in relation to his or her own body and basic self-worth. When a father is too close aggressively, the child will be overwhelmed and symbolically castrated, unable to stand up to authority or for himself. An emotionally absent father leaves the child unprepared for the world and prone to self-doubt, if not actual violence.

In contrast, the good enough father is able to successfully maintain the golden mean. Such a father is close but not too close, strong but not overwhelming, loving but not seductive, supportive but able to discipline, caring but encouraging autonomy. The image of such a good father implies a fusion of a sky father with the intimate fathers, reported among the Aka pygmies (Hewlett, 1992): a wise all-seeing father who is also able to hold his child tenderly in his arms; a father who is able to support his children physically, emotionally, spiritually, and so provide them with enough backbone to become autonomous caring individuals in their own right; a father who is both lord and "Daddy." The difficulty for fathers is how to combine the contrasting imagery of authority and intimacy into a coherent whole.

---

2. Other authors writing from a Jungian perspective who have also made important contributions to the subject of fathers include Beebe (1985), Berry (1993), Bolen (1989), Collins (1994), Gurian (1992), Henderson (1967), Hopcke (1991), Leonard (1983), Madi (1987), Monick (1987), Pedersen (1991), Tatham (1992), and Vogt (1992).

How the imagery of the father may suddenly shift and reemerge in such a new way is recounted in *What Men Really Think* by Mark Baker (1992). At the end of the chapter on "dads," he tells how he received "two gifts" from his father when he interviewed him for the book: "First of all, he told me the story of his life in a plain, man-to-man way that I hadn't heard before" (Baker 1992, pp. 273–74). Specifically, he learns how his father's joining the Marines at 17 during World War II was not a great adventure but "a desperate attempt to escape from a broken home where he had borne too much of the burden for supporting and holding together the family since at least the age of 12." He had volunteered as a suicidal gesture "never intending to come home again except in a box." But just before going into action, he received a letter from his mother saying she had now remarried and "everything would be just fine." It was this last-minute news that allowed him to be one of the few survivors of the murderous onslaught that followed. Baker continues,

> The second gift came after the interview was over and the tape recorder was turned off. We were just sort of winding down with a little small talk about my two sons, when my dad turned to me and said, "I don't know what you're doing or how you're doing it, but keep it up. It's working." That quiet confirmation from my father of me and my life, my manhood, meant the world to me. That's the handful of words so many men wait for all their lives but never hear. (Baker 1992, p. 274)

These themes of death-continuity, separation-reconciliation, and rejection-confirmation within the father-son relationship are poignantly expressed in the story of Jacob and Joseph. Jacob, the father, believes his son is lost forever and lapses into interminable mourning. Joseph, the son, succeeds in a foreign land, but is cut off from the father. When father and son finally meet, they embrace, with the son weeping "for a good while" and his father saying, "Now I can die, having seen for myself that you are alive" (Genesis 46:30, trans. Jewish Publication Society, 1978). These stories show how the reconciliation between father and child is one of the fundamental projects in a person's life.

CHAPTER 3

Fatherhood Ideals in the United States: Historical Dimensions

Elizabeth H. Pleck and Joseph H. Pleck
University of Illinois at Urbana-Champaign

I N THE CONVENTIONAL WISDOM, over four centuries of American history the stern patriarch of the colonial settlers changed into the involved father of today, as the hierarchical model of domestic government gave way to the modern democratic ideal (Griswold, 1993). Gone was the moral guide, distant and cold, rod in one hand and Bible in the other. In his place stood the playmate, pal, coach, child development specialist, diaper changer, chauffeur, and childbirth attendant of modern film and advertisements.

It is easy to find flaws in this generalization about the changing American father. Some of today's dads are distant and gruff, remote and icy, violent, or irresponsible, not genial or kind. Many do not see their children on a regular basis and are not a significant presence in their children's lives. Moreover, the stern image of the colonial patriarch ignores the diversity of colonial fathering. In *The Protestant Temperament* Philip Greven, Jr. (1977) described three styles of parenting common among white Protestants from the colonial period to the early nineteenth century. The evangelicals conform most closely to our image of the stern patriarch. They believed in breaking the child's will, and in corporal punishment liberally administered. The moderates wanted to bend the will of the child, not break it. Famous fathers who belonged in this second group, such as Thomas Jefferson, Benjamin Franklin, and John Adams, sought to compel their children out of love and duty, not fear. A third type of parent, the genteel, were more permissive. Many Southern planters often left corporal punishment to tutors and servants. They did not try to inspire fear in children, but instead tended to indulge them.

The more serious problem with the stern to involved trajectory is that it fails to capture the ethnic and racial diversity of American society. The first American fathers were Indian men, who were not concerned about maintaining authority or commanding obedience of children. Many were not patriarchs at all, since they belonged to tribes that traced lineage through the female line. Families in such tribes might dwell in longhouses or hogans that contained related kin members on the mother's side. Fathers did not live with their children. The mother's brother, rather than her husband, often took the father's role in childrearing. Even Indian men in patrilineal tribes did not expect children to be obedient out of fear. Indian mothers and fathers rarely used corporal punishment in disciplining their children. They believed that the community, rather than an individual parent, was responsible for the proper behavior of children (Mintz & Kellogg, 1988).

Moreover, the augmentation of hoe agriculture, performed by women, with men's hunting, trapping, and fishing required paternal absence. In many Indian villages, men and older boys left the village for months at a time to hunt, fish, trade, make war, and engage in diplomacy. Women educated the young and carried on village life. Whites, who saw Indian men resting in villages after having returned from hunting, described overburdened women and lazy men. As would be typical in the encounter between cultures with different concepts of proper gender roles, the Indian way of fathering was considered inferior. Most of the efforts by whites to assimilate Indians were designed to make Indian men into breadwinners, that is, farmers who used the plow in tending fields, and Indian mothers into housewives (Jensen, 1977; Perdue, 1985).

That our story usually begins with stern colonial white men rather than gentle Indian fathers may tell us something about racial bias in American history writing. The reality was that colonial fathers were red, black, brown, as well as white. Although, after the European colonizers arrived, the largest group of fathers were white, propertied, and Protestant, diverse styles of fathering and diverse ideals of fatherhood have always coexisted in American history.

At the same time, there was a single culturally dominant ideal of fatherhood. The purpose of this review is to provide a cultural history of those ideals, the standards of respectability, rectitude, proper thought, and deed, expected of men. The ideal of fatherhood was essentially a set of implicit rules about what constituted a good father. It could be written down, however, by ministers, or later by childrearing experts. Although all colonial rulemakers were men, women began to furnish advice to men about fathering beginning in the nineteenth century. Since that time female as well as male experts have shaped the ideology of fatherhood.

There is another story to be told as well that concerns the actual conduct of fathers, good and bad, the quality of their relationships with their children, the quantity of the contact, the tasks and responsibilities fathers undertook. We know a little about this second topic, but less than about the first, despite the excellent book *Fatherhood in America* by Robert Griswold (1993). Scholars and researchers, who began the study of gender by examining women's experience, have in the last decade added new work on the history of men (Bederman, 1995; Carnes, 1989; Carnes & Griffen, 1990; Chauncey, 1995; Clawson, 1989; Griswold, 1993; Rotundo, 1985). Still, most of this research concerns masculinity, boyhood, or gay life, rather than fatherhood. There is still not enough information to write a history of the father-son talk, the dynamics of the relationship between black middle-class fathers and their children, or the story of the modern Hispanic father.

Why learn about the ideals of fatherhood at all, when so many may not live up to them? In our own times, the "new father" who changes diapers, schedules medical appointments, and knows the name of his child's teacher is the ideal. But national time use surveys suggest that he is not the norm (J. Pleck, 1985; J. Pleck, Chapter 5 of this volume). Moreover, people often behave at variance with their own ideals. Upper-middle-class fathers today often uphold the ideal of equality in discourse, but not in practice, whereas working-class husbands often adhere to traditional gender norms but engage in considerable sharing of housework and child care out of necessity (Hood, 1983). However, it is still important to know what paternal ideals are, even if fathers do not always practice them, since they still use them as a guide for behavior and as a basis for judging others. Similarly, knowing the ideal of fatherhood reveals by inference what its opposite, bad fathering, was.

English common law, which the American colonists inherited, gave fathers a great deal of power over their children. It gave the father an absolute right to custody, in the event of separation or a divorce. A man's children were not only his property, but his responsibility to provide for and educate properly. In the nineteenth century, appellate court judges began to modify these rules. Many judges respected the father's presumptive right to custody, but argued that such rights could be superseded if maternal custody best served the child's welfare. Some judges insisted that the custody decision had to be made according to a standard that determined the best interests of the child. Others held that the mother was the preferable parent. The "tender years" doctrine favored the mother as a caretaker for infants and prepubescent and disabled children. Daughters of all ages, judges often held, were best left with their mother. Courts generally preferred the mother as a custodial parent for all children by the end of the nineteenth century, except if she was unfit (Grossberg, 1983; Mason, 1994; Zinaldin, 1979). Most divorced mothers, even today, have physical custody of their children. What is new since the 1970s is that the tender years doctrine has disappeared. The new rules have their own biases, but judges no longer automatically assume that custody should be given to the mother.

STERN PATRIARCHS AND OTHERS

The history of child custody provides one indication of changes in the paternal role; the evolution of dominant ideals furnishes another.[1] The ideal father of the colonial period was the stern patriarch. In the period from 1830 to 1900 he was the distant breadwinner. The ideal was the genial dad and sex-role model between 1900 and 1970, and since then, dad is supposed to be a co-parent, who shares equally with his wife in the care of children. In examining four chronological periods we can discern the nature and origins of the culturally dominant ideals of fatherhood and the degree to which fathers may have accepted, adopted, and put into practice these ideals.

The dominant ideal of stern fatherhood in colonial America was the one held by the Protestant, farming majority in the North, but not the white Southern colonies, according to Greven (1977). Two of his types, the evangelicals and the moderates,

---

1. J. Pleck (1987) proposes a four-stage model for the history of fatherhood ideals, which differs in some respects from the one presented here. Rotundo (1985) divides the history of American fatherhood into three stages and does not emphasize the father's role as a sex-role model. Griswold (1993) traces in much greater detail developments similar to the ones recounted here. For other general reviews of the history of fatherhood, see Stearns (1991), LaRossa, Gordon, Wilson, Bairan, & Jaret (1991), Bloom-Feshbach (1981), and Demos (1986). Bernard (1981) examines one of the four dominant cultural ideals, that of the male breadwinner.

both conformed to the ideal of the stern patriarch, but the evangelicals fit the mold more closely than moderate fathers. Among both groups, Protestant fathers wanted to make their home a small religious temple and install the male head of household as the domestic spiritual leader (Morgan, 1966; Stone, 1977). Fathers thus ruled the family government, presided over daily prayers, and taught their children how to read and interpret the Bible. (It was believed that women could not be trusted to provide a proper religious education.) They were also the protectors of their families from marauding Indians, or the ravages of wind and storm. Although a farm mistress, defending her home, might brandish an ax or fire a shotgun, the husband and father was usually expected to protect his wife and children from danger (Demos, 1970; Ulrich, 1983).

Until they were about three years old, both boys and girls were primarily their mother's responsibility. So much were infants under the mother's care that they were often described as "her babies." At about age three, a boy became more his father's charge, although his mother still provided for his physical care (Rotundo, 1985). A girl received most of her guidance and training from her mother. The language of the colonists mirrored the distinct gender assignment of children to the same-sex parent. A father might speak of "his sons" and a mother of "his boys," whereas a mother might write of "her daughter" and a father of "your daughters" (Norton, 1980).

Spanish and Hispanic fathers in the Southwest and California also believed that fathers should be stern patriarchs, who deserved unquestioning obedience from their children. A son appearing before his father had to ask permission before smoking, sitting, or wearing a hat. The major difference with the New England colonists was that responsibility of Hispanic fathers to sons and daughters was wrapped in a code of honor. A father had to teach his sons to be manly and adhere to this code. He also had to pay special attention to protecting the virginity and reputation of unmarried daughters. Any stain on a daughter's reputation permanently damaged her marriage prospects and her family's sense of honor (Gutierrez, 1991).

In all these respects, Southern white fathers of the planter class resembled Spanish and Hispanic fathers. They, too, adhered to a code of honor and sought both to teach their sons to be manly and to keep their unmarried daughters virginal. However, a Southern father allowed his son to be rude, talk back, and disobey at times, and did not demand the many deferential customs Hispanic fathers expected (Greven, 1977; Stowe, 1987; Wyatt-Brown, 1982).

Virtually all colonists in every region believed that fathers, not mothers, provided the best examples of proper moral character for girls as well as boys. Women, it was held, were excessively fond of their children and governed by their passions, rather than by reason (Ulrich, 1983). Maternal love was not regarded as an essential ingredient in childrearing. In the colonial period, ministers and others writing on the subject of childrearing addressed themselves either to fathers or both parents, rarely singling out mothers. Some writers gave men and women equal responsibility for child discipline, whereas others set a lower value on mothers' contribution than on fathers'. The qualities considered essential to good childrearing—rationality, self-control, and theological understanding—were believed to reside in men, rather than women.

It is important to point out that our colonial forebears respected the stern father, but castigated the cruel one. It has been charged that fathers in colonial America and even farther back in time were often brutal and indifferent to their many offspring

(DeMause, 1974; Shorter, 1975; Stone, 1977). Accustomed to the frequent death of infants, they saw no reason to lavish much attention on any child. As the primary disciplinarians, they resorted to the rod and the whip when necessary. Children were necessary labor on the farm, but little else. Historians have gone to great lengths to refute this view of parental indifference (Pollack, 1983). John Demos, in searching the court records of colonial Massachusetts, could not find a single child burned or scalded by an errant father (or mother). There were indeed few complaints of child abuse in colonial times. There is no sure way of knowing whether the lack of complaints proves a low incidence of abuse or an unwillingness to report it to authorities. There were more reports of abused servants than children. Servants complained if permanently injured or maimed. Presumably punishment and even abuse that fell short of that standard was not reported (Gutierrez, 1991; E. Pleck, 1987). Still, colonials did have a definition of excessive punishment, and a father was expected not to punish in anger (Demos, 1986).

As property owners in a society where land, rather than cash, was the main form of wealth, landowning fathers controlled a valuable resource that affected the future of their sons and daughters. They could decide when to give a son a plot of land and thus grant him economic independence. If a father could bestow such favors, he could also withhold them. Many sons, farming on their own as young adults, did not receive clear title to the land until a father's death. So long as the father had arable land to distribute, he could put his adult sons on a short leash. As coastal areas became settled, and soil depleted, sons went went to start their own farms, or moved to the cities. As a result, the bonds of parental control grew looser (Greven, 1972).

Southern planters and landowning Hispanic fathers arranged marriages for their children (Gutierrez, 1991; Stowe, 1987). Most other fathers in the American colonies did not. By disapproving of a match, however, fathers of means could withdraw the financial resources necessary for the couple's well-being. Fathers seemed to have been more concerned about the finances, rather than the true affections, of a prospective suitor. A father might investigate the economic worthiness of a prospective bridegroom or the financial standing of a daughter-in-law's family. Mothers, by contrast, were more concerned that a girl might marry too soon (Rothman, 1984).

The patriarchal father of colonial times was supposed to be and often was an active, involved parent. His farm was his place of work, and that of his wife, children, and servants, or slaves, if he had them. A son worked at his father's side in doing farm labor and thereby learned his future calling. Urban artisans taught sons a trade or apprenticed them to another artisan to learn a skill. The one exception to the daily involvement of fathers in the life of their children was childbirth. A husband visited a woman in labor but left when the pains increased or birth seemed imminent. In all cultures of colonial America, fathers were expected not to be present at the birth of their child (Leavitt, 1988). However, they were there if women friends and relatives were unavailable.

Until the pioneering research of Herbert Gutman, it was thought that the frequency of sale meant that the slave father was essentially an absent and uninvolved father. Gutman (1976) discovered that the slave father resembled in many respects the father among poor white farmers. In the majority of cases, the slave father lived with his wife and children in a log cabin. Some fathers, who lived on a neighboring plantation, received permission from the master to visit wife and children once a week or on holidays. When such permission was denied, they often became runaways so that they could see their families.

However much he might have wanted to, the slave father could not play the role of physical protector of his wife and children. He was a strict disciplinarian, who expected obedience and punished with the whip. He sometimes provided religious instruction, told stories and sang songs, and was especially involved in teaching his sons to hunt and fish (Genovese, 1974; Jones, 1985). He spent his evenings and free time in trying to provide additional food, or even income, for his family. In several respects his role was unique. Slaves were especially likely to name their sons after a father to preserve his memory, in the event he was sold. It was far less common for daughters to be named for their mothers (Cody, 1982; Gutman, 1976). The slave father and his wife had to teach their children how to survive the physical and psychological assaults of slavery. A child had to learn when to fight and when to acquiesce. Fathers and mothers often had to offer lessons in accommodation, or outward deference to white overseers and masters. Masters, who could sell a man's children, or sell a father away from his children, taught the cruelest lesson of all. Most sales were individual ones, which separated one family member from the rest of his or her kin. After slaves were emancipated, many a father set about searching for his lost children (Litwack, 1979). But as long as the system endured, the slave father lacked the legal rights of a free man and had only limited authority over his children.

DISTANT BREADWINNERS AND OTHERS

A new ideal of fatherhood emerged among the middle classes between the American Revolution and the 1830s. The mother, not the father, was assumed to be the primary parent; the father's role became passive rather than active. Accordingly, when children went astray it was mothers who were to blame. The Victorians liked to say that behind every great man was a dutiful, pious mother. Public and Sunday schoolteachers, mainly women, replaced fathers in providing children with secular and religious instruction (Vinovskis, 1988). Still, the father set the moral standard for the family and served as the last resort in administering serious punishment (Demos, 1986; Rotundo, 1985). The distant breadwinner was still assumed to be the physical protector of his wife and children, but his responsibility in this area was not emphasized, perhaps because his family was not assumed to be in imminent danger. Fathers no longer exercised veto power over a child's choice of a future mate. But a son did ask his father's permission to enlist in the Civil War, even though he may have been ready to sign up without it (Frank, 1992).

The single largest reason for the change in father's role was economic. The ideal father was now a clerk or a businessman, not a farmer (Ryan, 1981). He might leave home each day to commute to a counting house, or take frequent trips on business. Even if he came home for the noon meal and dinner, his head might be buried in a newspaper. Fathers might find the home a refuge from the cutthroat competition of the business world, but they often spent their evenings at the lodge, a club, the saloon, or playing cards at a friend's home (Carnes, 1989). As had been true before, daughters received training in their future life's work from their mothers. But the new respect accorded mothering, and the deep belief in the purity and saving power of maternal love, encouraged daughters to form strong emotional attachments with their mothers, not fathers (Smith-Rosenberg, 1975). Middle-class sons, however, still sought a father's counsel regarding education, finance, occupational choice, and political affairs (Rotundo, 1985).

As a result of the economic changes brought by the Industrial Revolution as well as the greater respect accorded maternal love, by the 1830s, the mother, rather than the father, was seen as the more powerful agent in developing a child's character (Cott, 1977; Ryan, 1981). Reason was debased as the currency for proper parenting. Women were considered to be fitted by nature—by their mother's heart—for raising children. Male aloofness and distance was now seen in a less favorable light. Rotundo (1985) has suggested that fathers could express more affection with their daughters than with their sons because a man did not expect his daughter to achieve worldly success. While many men may have withdrawn emotionally as well as physically from the kind of home Currier and Ives depicted, a father's feelings for his son might break through—for example, if his son was wounded in battle. Although it was not routine, fathers, rather than mothers, traveled to Civil War army camps to nurse wounded sons (Frank, 1992).

If industrialization separated home and work among the middle class, it may also have enlarged the class of bad fathers. The bad father is always the mirror image of the good one. In colonial times the bad father did not marry a girl if he got her pregnant, and the even worse one failed to provide support for the child. The bad father also did not provide proper moral and religious instruction for his children. The bad Victorian father, by contrast, was often seen as lower class, irreligious, a foreigner, or a man of color.

Because breadwinning became so central to fatherhood in the nineteenth century, the failure to support a family, always a grievous sin, took center stage in Victorian melodrama and temperance tracts. As one of the largest social movements in the nineteenth century, the temperance crusade depicted for its audience the alcoholic father who squandered his wages, thus depriving his family of food and comforts. Although these depictions frequently included physical abuse of wife and children, even incest, abandonment of the breadwinning responsibility was in many ways the most central flaw (Epstein, 1981; E. Pleck, 1987). At his worst, the bad father deserted his wife and children, forcing them to beg or depend on charity. Such a man was often portrayed as lower class, often Irish Catholic, both because there was a kernel of truth in the stereotype and more importantly, because the native-born Protestant middle class prided itself on its cultural and religious superiority to the poor and the immigrant (Diner, 1983; Stansell, 1986).

Indeed, the immigrant father, who lost something of the mantle of the patriarch when he immigrated to America, was forced by American circumstance to become a shadowy figure in the lives of his children (Rubel, 1966; Thomas & Znaniecki, 1918). By inclination, he wanted to be much like the ideal colonial father, a man honored, revered, respected, feared, and unquestioningly obeyed by his children. As the family leader, he decided which children to send to work, or whether to move to America. He believed a large family was an economic resource and proof of his virility. He sought to be able to veto his children's choice of a mate and guard the virginity of his unmarried daughters (Ewen, 1985; Sanchez, 1993; Yans-McLauglin, 1981).

The difficulty for the immigrant father and his children was that America did not permit him to be the kind of father he wanted to be. He had not been the sole bread-winner in the Old Country, and did not expect to be so here (Glenn, 1990). But the American landscape was different in other respects. The father's children became his guides to America, since he often spoke no English, or theirs was better than his. A man who left home before his children were awake and returned after they were asleep had little time to spend with his children. Morris Rosenfeld expressed his regret for his absence in "My Little Boy," published in 1914 (Karp, 1976):

> Ere dawn my labor drives me forth
> I have a little boy at home
> That seldom do I see
> Ere dawn my labor drives me forth
> 'Tis night when I am free
> A stranger am I to my child
> And strange my child to me.

The immigrant father could be absent for months, even years, taking seasonal jobs in unskilled labor to support the family, if he had come to America and left his family behind. He vacillated between wanting his son to follow in his footsteps and want-ing him to lead a better life (Covello, 1967; Handlin, 1951; Howe, 1989). When a father commanded his children to come home at a certain hour, marry the suitor he chose, speak the native tongue, or turn over an entire paycheck, they often responded with derision, embarrassment, blows, laughter, or subterfuge. Immigrant mothers of-ten tried to mediate these conflicts (Griswold, 1993; E. Pleck, 1983).

Whether immigrant or native born, rural fathers of the nineteenth and early twenti-eth centuries faced similar conflicts. If the weather was good, and the land sufficient, the farming father could fulfill his goal of leading the family economic enterprise and providing for his family. But young sons and daughters were attracted to the excite-ment and freedom of city life. Rural sociologists in the 1920s interviewed farmers' adult sons and daughters to learn why so many of them were flocking to the city. They learned that the children resented their father's discipline, even his hovering presence, and the hard labor he demanded of them. In comparison with urban chil-dren, rural sons and daughters were more critical of their fathers, and less likely to confide in them or show them affection (Griswold, 1993).

"DADS" AND OTHERS

We use the term "dad" to refer to the new ideal of fatherhood emerging in the twenti-eth century, the father who was a close rather than distant paternal figure, who took on mainly fun activities with children.[2] Previous authors have offered various dates for the origins of this model of fatherhood. Some attribute the rise of the dad to the 1950s (J. Pleck, 1987), and others trace it to the 1920s (Griswold, 1993; LaRossa & Reitzes, 1993). Magazine writers proclaimed the ideal around the turn of the century (Marsh, 1990), although it was amplified and publicized in the 1920s as part of the

2. The term "dad" was used as early as the 1860s, but had not yet acquired its modern meaning of male parent who is a playmate and chum of the child (Frank, 1992).

new concept of companionate marriage (Mintz & Kellogg, 1988). The dad was expected to be involved in childrearing for the sake of the child. But he did not share equally in the tasks and responsibilities of childrearing. The dad was also a symbol of the bourgeoisie and, thus, a marker dividing the middle from the working class. Because this was so, fathers not of the middle class were likely to be thought of in terms of class stereotypes, that is, they were seen as excessively masculine, violence prone, authoritarian, and impulsive. A more detailed investigation of the decades between 1900 and 1970 might reveal important shifts within the ideal and its various rationales during this period. However, the essence of this ideal persisted and managed to weather relatively intact two world wars, the Great Depression, and the suburban barbecue of the 1950s.

The dad was expected to take daily (although not equal) responsibility for bringing up children and the details of running a household. He was expected to play with sons and daughters, instruct them, see that they did their homework, and take them on outings and camping trips. He could offer them hugs and expressions of affection; he was expected to be a chum especially with his sons, and teach them how to play football or baseball. There was less emphasis on the father's role as a disciplinarian. Most fathers no longer played a role in a child's choice of a marriage partner. At best, they might try to negotiate the time when a son or daughter would return from a date. Since courting no longer occurred in the family parlor, fathers could not exercise much supervision, even if they had been so inclined (Bailey, 1988). In the realm of childbirth, a father was not expected to be present at the birth of a child (Leavitt, 1988).

The prosperity and security of the middle class and the growth of the suburbs made possible this new ideal of fatherhood. Even so, this father could be a manager, but not a storeowner, who worked evenings and weekends at his establishment, or a traveling salesman, so busy covering his territory that he spent little time at home. The ideal dad had to have enough leisure time to be able to devote to his family. Men were expected to spend more time at home, and less at their clubs or lodges. Indeed, the heyday of the lodge seems to have passed by about 1890 (Carnes, 1989). A larger house in the suburbs also created the appropriate setting for backyard play (Marsh, 1990). The creators of this ideal were Ennis Richmond, Carl Werner, Bernard Mac-Fadden, and other authors of advice books on how to raise boys, and the home economists, such as Martha and Robert Bruere. The main justification these authors gave for paternal involvement was that fathers could prevent sons from falling into "evil ways." But distrust of mothers, created by the fear that men were not manly enough, also spurred interest in fatherhood. The regard in which fathers were held seemed to rise, just as the luster on motherhood began to tarnish. Mothers no longer enjoyed the unqualified esteem in which they were held in the nineteenth century. Too much mother-dominated childrearing, it was believed, produced unmanly boys (Marsh, 1990; J. Pleck, 1983).

Although magazine writers and home economists at the turn of the century invented the ideal dad, it was a much larger group of psychologists, sociologists, social workers, home economists, and family service counselors who propagated the idea in the 1920s (Griswold, 1993). Elaborating fears of the effeminate boy and the much older fear of excessive maternal love, advisors stated repeatedly that too much mothering was bad for the child. It caused in children maternal fixation, dependence on mothers, and personal immaturity. They argued explicitly that fatherly involvement was good for the personal growth and development of the child. Good mothering alone was not enough, they argued, and fathers made a different and unique contribution. They could provide a model of true manhood. A son who had played baseball with his father and gone camping with him would grow up to be independent and self-reliant. Moreover, the daughter who enjoyed her father's love and attention could choose the right man to marry.

Interestingly, cartoons depicting father-as-bumbler began appearing in *The Saturday Evening Post* and elsewhere in the 1920s, at precisely the same time that experts were first calling for greater paternal involvement in childrearing. Cartoons in the 1930s and 1940s were kinder, perhaps out of sympathy for men's plight during the depression and later out of respect for their wartime service (LaRossa et al., 1991). The bumbling father of the 1920s did not know how to control or discipline his children. He could not cook a meal or put his children to bed without tripping over his shoelaces. One explanation of the comic image is that the portrayal of the foolish dad was designed to enforce conformity to the new standard of fatherhood (Day & Mackey, 1986). Or were cartoonists in the 1920s actually protesting against the advice of the experts?

In the 1930s, Lewis Terman and Catherine Miles in *Sex and Personality* (1936) developed the concept of psychological "masculinity-femininity." They contended that central to normal, mature personality was possessing sex-appropriate psychological traits. Conversely, they argued that a certain number of adults became deviants, that is, effeminate men or masculine women. One step beyond this level of deviance were genuine "inverts," that is, homosexuals, incapable of feeling heterosexual attraction. At one level, Terman and Miles were simply adding a theoretical basis and a method of testing (masculinity-femininity scales) to the general arguments about gender development of the 1920s (J. Pleck, 1981). At another level, their work can be seen as psychologists' response to the devastating impact of the Great Depression on the cultural definition of manhood: an attempt to demonstrate that manhood should be defined not by holding a job, but by acquiring psychological masculinity as a boy. Childrearing literature and newspaper columns reveal that middle-class fathers were attuned to popularized versions of the ideas of Terman and Miles. Angelo Patri, a New York City junior high school principal, published a nationally syndicated advice column in the 1930s. Fathers in their letters to Patri worried about teaching children about sex, about sons who were insufficiently masculine, and about poor school performance (Griswold, 1993; LaRossa & Reitzes, 1993).

During the Great Depression unemployed and underemployed men had plenty of time to spend with their families, to be the pals to their children they had always wanted to be. While employed men had much less time to devote to their children, they seem to have felt better about the hours they spent, since they were also fulfilling their breadwinning responsibility. Men who failed to provide grew irritable, despondent, abusive, or withdrawn (Komarovsky, 1940; LaRossa & Reitzes, 1993). Many deserted their families entirely. Children, who had all along told interviewers how much they longed for fathers to spend more time with them, actually preferred fathers who brought home money to the family (Lynd & Lynd, 1929). When fathers failed to do so, children, especially teenagers forced to become family breadwinners, blamed their fathers and rebelled (Cole, 1963). For every adolescent who was angry or rebellious with his or her unemployed father was another who felt only pity. But the central lesson of the depression was that paternal involvement was never the main goal of fathers or their children: money was (Griswold, 1993).

The full employment that World War II made possible seemed to bring a temporary end to the problem of paternal unemployment. The father employed in war production was earning a good living. After considerable debate, Congress decided to include fathers in the draft to serve in the armed forces. The proponents had a simple reason: they needed the men. The opponents of drafting wartime fathers gave as their arguments the need of fathers to maintain small businesses and the father's role in preventing juvenile delinquency (Griswold, 1993).

Wartime mobilization also interacted with the cultural definition of fatherhood in another way. The failure of many young men, fathers or otherwise, to pass army physicals led to charges that overly solicitous mothers and absent fathers had made sons soft, too weak or cowardly to fight (Griswold, 1993). Phillip Wylie in *Generation of Vipers* (1942) argued that mothers had protected too many boys from the inevitable struggle with their father, the elemental struggle that would bring a boy into manhood and independence. Mothers were overprotective, but at the same time fathers were also too passive. Such passive fathers failed to punish children, make decisions, were excessively concerned with being liked by children, acted childlike, and neglected to tell sons "the facts of life."

Excessively powerful mothers and passive, uninvolved fathers, it was also argued beginning in the 1940s, produced homosexual sons. There was no comparable attention to the mix of maternal and paternal qualities that led daughters to become lesbians because homosexuality was more stigmatized and more feared for males than females (Chauncey, 1995). It was believed that homosexual sons favored their mothers over their fathers because their fathers had shown them little affection.

In the 1950s dad was supposed to be in the basement, working on a do-it-yourself project, in the driveway, teaching his son about cars, or in the backyard, putting steaks on the grill. Articles in popular magazines, such as "A Build-up for Dad" and "Fathers are parents, too" published in the 1950s, could have been written in the 1920s (May, 1988). But the 1950s saw a new rationale for involved fathering: men themselves would find it creative and enjoyable. In fact, fathering was touted as the best of men's hobbies, a more meaningful activity than a career or occupation (May, 1988). The opening credits of "Father Knows Best" showed Jim, dressed in a business suit and carrying his hat, leaving for his office at the insurance agency. In the next sequence he was shown returning from work, as his wife and children gathered to greet him. While the domestic imagery originated in the era of the distant breadwinner, the activity in the home—managing and settling disputes, and comforting the distressed— conveyed the ideal of the Genial Dad (Haralovich, 1992). Both white working-class fathers in sitcoms, such as Stuart Erwin in "The Trouble with Father," and their middle-class counterparts, Jim Anderson, Ward Cleaver, and Ozzie Nelson, were portrayed as bumblers. These men were often manipulated by their wives, who had an intuitive and empathic understanding of the best course. There were no black, Asian, or gay fathers on television in the 1950s.

Like the 1940s, the fifties dad had to make sure that his son did not become a sissy or a homosexual. Good fathering was also viewed as the best prevention for the authoritarian tendencies reflected in communism and fascism. The nurturing, affectionate dad, social researchers claimed, would produce tolerant, democratically inclined children (Griswold, 1993). But the most noteworthy new outcome to be connected to inadequate or absent fathering was juvenile delinquency. To Terman and Miles, the problem for boys was that they might not be masculine enough. In the 1950s hypermasculinity, that is, exaggerated masculine behavior, interpreted as a defense against unconscious feminine identification, began to be seen as a problem as well, and delinquency was its principal manifestation.

Researchers gave special attention to juvenile delinquency and father absence among black youth (Gilbert, 1986). Because of father absence among blacks, the psychologist Thomas Pettigrew argued in 1964 that "the sex role identity problems created by the fatherless home are perpetuated in adulthood" (Pettigrew, 1964). The next year Daniel Patrick Moynihan (U.S. Department of Labor, 1965) borrowed from Pettigrew's analysis, and from E. Franklin Frazier's studies of the black family (Frazier, 1939). He argued that the internal dynamics of the black family lay at the heart of the problem of black poverty. The problem, according to Moynihan, was the matriarchal family structure common among blacks. In this family structure, fathers were absent. Black sons grew up with a frustrated sense of masculinity, which they overcompensated for in violence, or crime. One solution was for black sons to receive appropriate manly roles by going into the military. Moynihan wrote, "Given the strains of the disorganized and matrifocal family life in which so many negro youth come of age, the Armed Forces are a dramatic and desperately needed change: a world away from women, a world run by strong men of unquestioned authority" (U.S. Department of Labor, 1965). Another was for the government to provide job training for black men, as a means of encouraging marriage and family stability.

With the notable exception of Cliff Huxtable, the physician father in "The Cosby Show," a popular television program of the 1980s, the black father has usually been portrayed as the opposite of the good father, irresponsible or absent, and sometimes physically brutal (Berry, 1992). He has thus been viewed as aberrant, a man who did not live up to the ideal. The realities of black fatherhood are diverse, and vary greatly, according to the father's social class. Still, one cannot escape major transformations in black family structure that have occurred since the Moynihan Report appeared. The female-headed household today is the dominant family form among African Americans. Only a minority of African American children today live with their biological fathers throughout their childhoods (Bumpass & Sweet, 1989).

The disagreement is not about these statistics, but about their meaning. On the one hand, some argue that lower down the social scale one moves, the more one finds an alternative system of fatherhood and family. Like Indian matrilineal families, brothers of the mother and other male kin play a paternal role in the family. Moreover, some argue that many mothers view the father of the family as a family friend, who can help from time to time, rather than as a failed provider (Stack, 1974). On the other hand, others insist that most blacks hold the dominant culture's conception of the father as a breadwinner and involved dad, but understand that many men fail to live up to this ideal (Furstenberg, 1995; Liebow, 1967). Black children, too, want a father who is a breadwinner and regard jobless fathers and men who fail to provide child support as disappointments. Since the Moynihan Report a sexual revolution among teens and the declining availability of jobs for unskilled and uneducated workers in large cities has compounded the problem. The sociologist William J. Wilson (1987) argued that in addition to the economic difficulties, "the lack of community norms to reinforce work increases the likelihood that individuals will turn to either underground illegal activity or idleness or both."

THE CO-PARENT AND OTHERS

There were many shifts and subthemes in the cultural perceptions of the modern, involved dad between 1900 and 1970. But a new element, starting in the 1970s, signaled the emergence of a model that was fundamentally new. This new element was that fathers should be highly involved as part of an egalitarian relationship between husbands and wives called for by feminism (Fein, 1978; Furstenberg, 1988; LaRossa, 1988; Parke & Tinsley, 1984). The term we choose for this new model—the co-parent father—makes central the father's coequal responsibility for parenting. The co-parent father of the 1970s was expected to be not only involved but an equal participant with his wife in the physical care of the child, even a labor coach and attendant at childbirth (Rotundo, 1985). The latest version of Dr. Benjamin Spock's *Baby and Child Care* stated the new norm: "The father—any father—should be sharing with the mother the day-to-day care of their children from birth onward. This is the natural way for the father to start the relationship, just as it is for the mother" (Spock & Rothenberg, 1992, p. 28). The rationale for the dad was to serve the needs of the child's development; the main rationale for the co-parent was to share equally in the burden of child care. He was expected to carry his share of the load because it was the fair thing to do; as an afterthought, advocates argued that fathering was fun and enhancing for the father.

In providing both care and attention to his children, the co-parent was expected to give equal attention to his daughters as to his sons. There was little emphasis on the father's distinctive role as a disciplinarian. Rather, childrearing books usually offered their advice about effective punishment to parents in gender-neutral language. If the ideal father and his wife were divorced, he was expected to share the custody of his children and take an active and equal role in their care.

Fathers were no longer asked to play a part in raising a son in order to prevent him from becoming a sissy. Instead, their participation would help make boys less gender-stereotyped and more nurturant. In one strand of feminist writing in the 1970s, women's abilities to empathize, disclose, and connect with others were seen as personality strengths men had been deprived of (Chodorow, 1978; Dinnerstein, 1976; Gilligan, 1982). Feminist theorists claimed that men were socially unskilled at childrearing, though not innately so. One after another endorsed the idea of egalitarian parenting (Chodorow, 1978; Dinnerstein, 1976; Hochschild, 1989; Okin, 1989; Ruddick, 1989). A father might produce an androgynous son not by acting manly or serving as a male role model, but by performing routine care of the child. Indeed, the prevalence of the term co-parent, beginning in the 1970s, indicated that to many the roles of mother and father were regarded as equal and interchangeable.

The idea of the co-parent father was a response to feminism, the growth in maternal employment, and the concomitant demand from employed women that husbands share in housework and child care. In 1950, 25% of married women living with their husbands held paying jobs; by 1990, the figure was nearly 60%. The growth in paid work among mothers with even preschool children was especially dramatic. The man of the house was no longer the sole breadwinner. In 1960, 42% of households were supported by a sole male breadwinner; in 1988 the figure was 15% (Wilkie, 1993). This latter trend also came about because of the growth of women's employment, along with the rise of divorce, and single-parent households, mainly headed by women. Only a small percentage of wives and mothers earned more than their husbands, or as much, but an increasing number were contributing one-third or more of family income. The surge in job holding among women, in female college graduates and the dissatisfactions of these women, along with the heightened concern about equality and rights from the social movements of the 1960s, fueled the demands for a new women's movement (Cohen, 1988; Evans, 1979). To Betty Friedan in *The Feminine Mystique* (1963) a clean home or well-behaved children were no longer considered the most important accomplishments of a woman's life. She attacked the idea that women, not men, should sacrifice their wants and needs on behalf of the family.

Skeptics about this change in the father role argue that the "new father" is largely a cultural myth, propagated in movies and television commercials, that masks the reality that most housework and child care is still done by women (LaRossa, 1988). Others argue that the ideal of the "new father" is mainly one of the upper middle class, who now see men not of their class as culturally inferior because they have failed to adopt this new ideal (Griswold, 1993; Hondagneu-Sotelo & Messner, 1994). First of all, it is clear that the role of father as breadwinner has not disappeared, although it is not as strongly held as it once was (Gerson, 1993). In 1989, 47% of a representative sample of American men believed it was best for men to be the sole breadwinner in a family, compared with 69% in 1972 (Wilkie, 1993). National surveys confirm that belief in the co-parent dad is greatest in the upper middle class. Representative samples of men in the American population, from 1972 to 1989, were asked whether they agreed with the statement that "it is much better for everyone involved if the man is the achiever outside the home and the woman takes care of home and family" (Thornton, 1989, p. 877; Wilkie, 1993). The strongest disagreement with the statement came from well-educated men. Disagreement was also more common among political liberals, those under 55, and men whose wives were employed full time. Although related to education and other variables, pollsters found disagreement with the traditional gender ideology implicit in the question had increased dramatically in the population as a whole from 1972 to 1989, suggesting that an ideal held by well-educated liberal men had spread throughout the general population of younger men (Wilkie, 1993). The middle-class nature of the new ideal should come as no surprise, because all of the previous major new ideals have emerged from this class. At the same time, the new ideal of fatherhood in fact reflects the reality that resident fathers today, thought not sharing truly equally, are still more involved in childrearing than their fathers and grandfathers (see Caplow, Bahr, Chadwick, Hill, & Williamson, 1982; J. Pleck, Chapter 5 of this volume).

The juggling of child care and commuting to two different jobs required adjustments in men's and women's schedules and sets of responsibilities. A mother made the dentist appointments, attended the PTA meetings, kept a list of babysitters, and stayed home when the children were sick. The father functioned as the mother's deputy, performing while his wife retained responsibility to make sure that the tasks were done (Lamb, Pleck, Charnov, & Levine, 1985). Most often she had to ask for help, rather than expect 50-50 sharing as a matter of course. Psychologists, writers, and firsthand testimonials by men, urging greater paternal involvement, appeared in a steady stream, beginning in the 1970s. The popular film *Kramer vs. Kramer* (1980) portrayed sympathetically the involved father whose exwife relinquished control to him of their son, even though she was victorious in a bitter custody battle. He, too, was portrayed as a bumbler, an incompetent who could not make his son French toast for breakfast without causing a fire in the kitchen. But before the movie ends, he is able to cook breakfast quickly and with aplomb. In the 1980s more fathers than mothers populated television commercials, and they were often shown cuddling an infant or pushing a stroller (Coltrane & Allan, 1994).

The emergence of the "co-parent father" in the brief period of time since the 1970s is a significant development, on a par with the emergence of the ideal of the dad in the period immediately preceding it. However, there are two other important but not as culturally dominant trends in the social representation of fatherhood that appeared in this same period. The first was the cultural discourse about the "deadbeat dad," the very opposite of the co-parent (Furstenberg, 1988, 1990). He was nonresident, noninvolved, and nonsupporting. The deadbeat dad did not appear in television commercials, but instead emerged in public debate about father's rights, welfare reform, child support enforcement, and prevention of teen pregnancy. According to Furstenberg, rising rates of deadbeat dads arose from the same sources as increased involvement among the fathers who remain present, namely, the decline in the male provider role, and what he terms the "decline in the gender division of labor" (which apparently refers to a greater provider role for women). Furstenberg argues, however, that the new phenomenon is that deadbeat dads, once primarily a lower-class problem, were increasing among the middle class (Furstenberg, 1988). Such a view conforms to the idea of Barbara Ehrenreich, who argued that, beginning with the *Playboy* philosophy of the 1950s, men had begun to loosen their commitment to the family and regard marriage, fatherhood, and supporting a family as burdens they no longer wanted to carry (Ehrenreich, 1983).

The other trend in the decades since 1970 was the backlash against the women's movement that began with opposition to abortion rights and the Equal Rights Amendment in the 1970s and led to a general indictment of feminism and a call to return to "family values." This political slogan, first of the Republicans, then also picked up by the Democrats, concerned not only family structure (two-parent, wife probably not employed) as well as beliefs about sexuality, religion, hard work, and morality (Coontz, 1992; Faludi, 1992; Skolnick, 1991). This backlash fueled men's demand for greater custody rights after divorce, opposition to married women's employment, and divorce. Some writers and politicians, responding to the more conservative climate of the times and the renewed influence of the religious right in American culture and politics, favored a reassertion of a distinctive paternal authority, a return to stern patriarchy. They argued that fathers make a unique contribution to childrearing in asserting control, which promotes the development of responsible adults (Blankenhorn, 1995).

CONCLUSION

The leaven of history and culture creates our ideas of fatherhood (Demos, 1986). Slowly culture changes, and so do our beliefs about what fathers should be. The role of the father as breadwinner has often been assumed to be the overwhelming dominant image of the American father, yet in fact it was not the strongest one at the beginnings of American history, and it is under challenge today. Earlier ideals remain as subterranean layers underneath the prevailing one and as dominant ideals in some subcultures. Nonetheless, the ideal of the father as breadwinner still remains today a powerful force.

In every period of American history, new economic imperatives as well as changes in the nature of the family, domestic ideals, and mothers' roles have been among the forces promoting new ideals. The central economic imperative has been the new economic relations between work and family, either changes in fathers' work, mothers', or both. Women have often encouraged a change in fathering, but men have been promoters of new ideals of fatherhood as well. While ideals have promoted change in gender roles, they have also helped to buttress class distinctions, serving as a sign of the more privileged class's conception of its enlightened attitude toward fathering (Griswold, 1993; LaRossa, 1988).

The ideal father of colonial America, the twentieth-century dad, and the co-parent of today share one similarity. All three types of fathers were expected to be active and involved. But the colonial father spent most of his day with his family; the modern father and co-parent does not. The parental role may have been more satisfying for fathers when it was integrated into a religious and rural way of life, but it may not have been that way for adolescent sons and daughters. Despite these similarities with previous ideals, the ideal of the co-parent also represents an important departure from the past. All previous ideals have assumed and reinforced a gender division of labor in domestic and breadwinning responsibilities. The ideal of the co-parent, on the other hand, assumes that fathers and mothers must share the tasks and responsibilities of childrearing equally and that their roles are interchangeable.

There is nothing new in our public discourse about the good dad versus the bad one. The bad dad has always been the man who failed to live up to his parental responsibilities. Those responsibilities have always been defined in part as acknowledgment of paternity and responsibility for child support. Even though the good dad has possessed a variety of qualities, failure as a breadwinner has always been a significant feature of the bad dad. Our culture has always thought that bad dads are mainly found at the lower end of the social scale. Ultimately, discourse about the good dad and the bad dad has never been simply about fatherhood, but also about the lines we draw between the respectable classes and the disreputable ones. It invariably reflects the fear that children of abandoning fathers will become dependent on the state for support.

Ever since the 1900s, men, and some women, have called for men to become more involved and active as parents. The rationales for why they should do so have undergone a dizzying number of turns. The ideal that emerged in the 1970s is still comparatively new. If history is any guide, it should last for some time to come. But the history of fatherhood also cautions us to expect more and newer ideals of fatherhood, as the economy, the culture, and the family all continue to undergo substantial alteration. We can also expect the experience of fathering to continue to change, albeit slowly, and for the behavior of fathers to lag much behind changes in the ideals.

CHAPTER 4

Fathers in Family Context: Effects of Marital Quality on Child Adjustment

E. Mark Cummings and Anne Watson O'Reilly
West Virginia University

FATHERS ARE increasingly recognized as playing an important role in children's adjustment, although the topic remains understudied 20 years after attention was called to this gap in the literature (Lamb, 1976). Fathers are significant contributors to many aspects of family functioning pertinent to children's well-being and development (Belsky, 1981; Lamb, 1976). The effects on children of growing up in fatherless homes is a national concern, reflecting awareness of the negative impact of such homes on many children (Broder, 1993; McLanahan & Sandefur, 1994). Children of divorce undergo significant declines in the quality of parenting, economic circumstances, and outside sources of psychosocial support and are faced with fears of abandonment by one or both parents (NICHD Consensus Statement on the Effects of Divorce and Custody Arrangements, in press).

One obstacle to understanding the role of fathers in families is that relatively sophisticated and complex models of family functioning are required. Despite frequent proscriptions to do otherwise (e.g., Bell, 1979), the implicit assumption of much family research remains that parents influence their children only through parent-child interaction.

The father's influence on children cannot be adequately conceptualized only in terms of father-child interactions but must be understood in terms of a broader family context. Fathers affect multiple dimensions of family functioning and are, in turn, themselves influenced by multiple factors outside of their relationships with their children (Lamb, 1976). Adequate conceptualization of the effects of fathers requires recognition of this interplay of multiple family systems (Minuchin, 1985).

In particular, marital quality at the same time is a product of the father's influence and affects the father's functioning in the family (Belsky, 1981, 1984). Links between marital quality and children's adjustment have long been reported (e.g., Baruch & Wilcox, 1944; Hubbard & Adams, 1936; Rutter, 1970; Watson, 1925; see Emery, 1982; Grych & Fincham, 1990, for reviews). Interparental conflict has been related to the effects on children of family dysfunction, including divorce and custody arrangements (Amato & Keith, 1991; Block, Block, & Gjerde, 1986; Thompson, 1994), parental depression (Downey & Coyne, 1990), parental alcoholism (West & Prinz, 1987), and physical abuse (Jouriles, Barling, & O'Leary, 1987; Wolfe, Jaffe, Wilson, & Zak, 1985). On the other hand, constructive marital relations may be positive influences, teaching children valuable lessons about conflict expression and negotiation (Cummings & Davies, 1994a). Thus, in their leading textbook, Hetherington and Parke (1993, p. 423) state that "a satisfying marital relationship is . . . the cornerstone of good family functioning which directly or indirectly facilitates effective parenting, positive sibling relationships, and the development of competent, adaptive children."

This chapter focuses on the father's influence on children's development in the context of marital quality. One direction is simply to examine the effects of marital quality on multiple family systems and the functioning of children. Since fathers are cocontributors to marital quality, these influences can be attributed, in part, to fathers.

A second, related direction is to begin to articulate those effects that are *specifically* due to fathers. Fathers have only recently been considered in research as distinct members of the marital dyad, and theoretical models of marital functioning have neglected the father. Thus, effects are typically cast in terms of marital quality from the mother's perspective, the influence of marital quality on mother-child relations, or interrelations between marital quality and the mother's adjustment. There is simply a need for the greater inclusion of fathers in research, and more study of the father's perspective and particular contributions.

Further, a process-oriented understanding of family functioning requires more specificity, differentiation, and precision in the study of cause-and-effect relationships (Cummings, 1995b). The disaggregation of mother and father effects is another step toward a more sophisticated model of family functioning. Accordingly, the available evidence will be reviewed, and exploratory questions raised, toward stimulating further study of the specific effects and outcomes due to fathers in the context of marital relations.

We close by examining a theoretical model centering on emotional security as an account for some important effects of marital quality and fathering on children's adjustment. A gap in research on marital quality as a context for child development is that theory has not kept pace with research. Relatively little elaboration of conceptual models has occurred in response to a multitude of recent findings, and there remains little theoretical foundation for understanding father effects in relation to other family influences and general processes of child development. An emotional security hypothesis is described toward the goal of contributing to a theoretical level of analysis of relations between these variables, including the positive effects of marital quality, and the less desirable outcomes associated with discordant marital relations.

FATHERS IN THE CONTEXT OF MARITAL QUALITY: A FRAMEWORK

Figure 4.1 illustrates pathways through which fathers and marital relations affect family functioning and, in turn, are influenced by various family systems. Specifically, in this framework, the father's behavior in the marital context affects parenting, parental

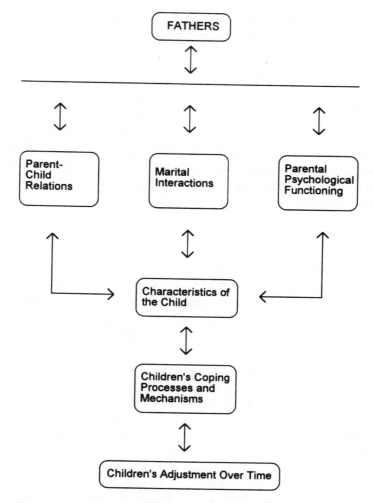

Figure 4.1   Fathers in the context of marital quality: A framework

psychological well-being, and children's functioning. In turn, these various systems influence the father's functioning. Thus, for example, marital quality may influence the father's (or mother's) psychological well-being, which, consequently, affects the quality of parenting and subsequent marital functioning.

These factors are represented in terms of several interrelated pathways: 1. *parent-child relations*—relations between marital quality and parent-child relationships, including effects on fathering; 2. *marital interactions*—the influence of exposure to marital interactions and conflict on children, including consideration of the father's particular interpersonal style in interaction with the mother; and 3. *parental psychological functioning*—effects on children of the father's psychological profile that relate to marital functioning (e.g., the father's physical abuse of the mother; Jaffe, Wolfe, & Wilson, 1990), or the mother's psychological profile attributable to the father's through marital functioning.

Children, in turn, may affect marital quality and parenting, including the father's behavior. Thus, certain characteristics of children may be relatively stable regardless of family circumstances (e.g., temperament; Pedlow, Sanson, Prior, & Okerlaid, 1993) and may influence parental resources, caregiving abilities, and the marital relationship (Bugental, Mantyla, & Lewis, 1989; Lee & Bates, 1985; van den Boom & Hoeksma, 1994).

The outcomes of these transactions between the child and family environment are represented as children's coping processes and mechanisms in Figure 4.1. Briefly, our assumption is that marital functioning does not lead directly to significant outcomes in children but affects children through a series of microsocial processes occurring interactively over a period of time, that is, gradual adaptations by children to family circumstances. We hold that the identification of these specific coping patterns-in-social-context should be the long-term goal for research since it is these processes that ultimately mediate relations between family experiences, on the one hand, and child development outcomes, on the other. Thus, children's adjustment over time (see Figure 4.1) is understood in terms of specific adaptive or maladaptive emotional, social, or cognitive response patterns and dispositions.

The review that follows is guided by this outline, following two themes: the effects of marital quality assessed at a dyadic level of analysis, that is, without the specific identification of father effects, and evidence or at least speculation about father effects in the context of marital relations. To illustrate this latter theme, the father is presented as a distinct element in Figure 4.1, with reciprocal pathways between the father and the multiplicity of family systems.

Finally, this framework is a heuristic and does not exhaustively represent influences within the family that may be attributed to fathers. For example, marital quality and fathering influences sibling relationships. Briefly, several studies indicate that sibling relationships are more negative in association with high marital conflict (e.g., Brody, Stoneman, McCoy, & Forehand, 1992), but one study suggests that siblings may also emotionally buffer or help each other when faced with parental conflicts (Cummings & Smith, 1993). Father effects per se have not been isolated, but questions about gender and cross-gender effects may be of particular interest (e.g., Kerig, Cowan, & Cowan, 1993): Are male and female siblings differentially affected in their relationships with the father across varying degrees of marital quality, and what are the outcomes for boy-boy, girl-girl, and opposite-sex sibling dyads?

MARITAL QUALITY AND PARENT-CHILD RELATIONS

GENERAL EFFECTS OF MARITAL QUALITY

Consistent with the framework outlined in Figure 4.1, a significant body of evidence has accumulated indicating that marital quality affects the quality of parent-child relationships. In particular, marital conflict has been associated with the quality of parenting practices and parent-child attachment (see recent reviews in Cummings & Davies, 1994a, 1995; Davies & Cummings, 1994). Given the recency of the reviews on this topic, limited space will be devoted to this work here.

High marital quality supports high-quality parenting and is linked with greater similarity between mother-child and father-child relations. In harmonious marriages, mother-child and father-child relations are both more positive, and mothers and fathers are more likely to have similar, shared, and reciprocal roles within the family. Thus, in harmonious marriages both parents give more favorable ratings of their children and the parental role (Goldberg, 1990); they speak to their children with more complex sentence structures (Pratt, Kerig, Cowan, & Cowan, 1992); child care is more often shared (Goldberg, 1990); there is more agreement between the parents on problem child behaviors and parenting issues (Gjerde, 1988; Goldberg, 1990); there is greater child attachment security and child sociability (Goldberg & Easterbrooks, 1984; Howes & Markman, 1989); and parents evidence more positive teaching styles and greater responsivity and sensitivity (Brody, Pellegrini, & Sigel, 1986). Further, when marital quality is high, if children are close to one parent they are likely to be close to the other (Booth & Amato, 1994). Also, high marital quality can buffer the effects of negative childhood experiences so that individuals are better parents (Cohn, Cowan, Cowan, & Pearson, 1992).

Unfortunately, low marital quality undermines parenting. Several examples serve to illustrate this point. Holden and Ritchie (1991) found that the presence of marital aggression predicted maternal reports of high parenting stress, a lack of parental warmth, and inconsistency in childrearing and observations of parent-child conflict and low parental involvement. Hetherington and Clingempeel (1992) reported that marital conflict was positively related to parental negativity and negatively related to parental warmth. With regard to parent-child attachment, M. J. Cox and Owen (1993) found that marital conflict during prenatal and early infancy periods was associated with insecure parent-child attachment at age one. Similarly, Howes and Markman (1989) reported that high marital conflict predicted the later development of insecure parent-child attachment. Finally, sequential analyses described in Christensen and Margolin (1988) revealed that the probability of parent-child conflict increased significantly after the occurrence of marital conflict.

These findings are consistent with the view that marital relations can be a source of support for, or can undermine, the parenting role (Belsky, 1984). However, many questions remain as to why this is the case. On the one hand, do positive marital relations support or increase the parents' capacities for emotion regulation in the context of the family, for example, by increasing their sense of emotional security, with positive implications for their pattern of interactions with family members, including the children? On the other hand, does marital conflict distract or otherwise preoccupy the parents so that less time is available for childrearing duties, the parent's capacities for emotional or behavioral regulation are reduced, and parental stress in interaction with children is increased?

A limitation of this literature is the overreliance on questionnaire and correlational methods, so that conclusions about causality cannot (or at least should not) be made with confidence. Some data collection methods do support a logic of causality (e.g., longitudinal research or sequential analyses). However, Fincham (1994) has correctly observed that "the logic that supports causality should not be confused with the controlled, experimental study so familiar to psychologists" (p. 125).

Another limitation is that family contexts are often not precisely defined and differentiated. For example, marital conflict has very different effects on children depending on how the parents express or resolve their differences (Davies & Cummings, 1994). Constructive discussions of marital differences may have positive effects on children (B. Beach, 1995). Analogue or experimental research would permit more precise tests of hypotheses about causality and the impact of specific marital contexts (Cummings, 1995b; see also Jouriles & Farris, 1992, described below).

SPECIFICATION OF FATHER EFFECTS IN MARITAL CONTEXT

Another theme for the study of the impact of marital quality on parenting is to differentiate effects on mothering and fathering. The quality of marital functioning has different implications for men and women, including their behavior as parents (e.g., Lamb & Elster, 1985; Markman & Kraft, 1989). The father influences, and is influenced, in these relationships (see Figure 4.1).

While mother-child and father-child relationships are likely to be positive and relatively similar when marriages are harmonious, differences between the quality and nature of these relationships increase as marital quality declines. A body of research that has accumulated relatively recently indicates that father-child relationships are more vulnerable to low marital satisfaction than are mother-child relationships. Thus, poorer marital quality has a more negative impact on father-child relationships than on mother-child relationships (Amato & Keith, 1991; Belsky, Rovine, & Fish, 1989; Belsky, Youngblade, Rovine, & Volling, 1991; Booth & Amato, 1994; Easterbrooks & Emde, 1988; Goldberg & Easterbrooks, 1984; Goth-Owens, Stollak, Messe, Peshkess, & Watts, 1982; Parke & Tinsley, 1987).

For example, Rossi and Rossi (1990) reported that current marital unhappiness reduced ratings of parent-child affection for fathers but not for mothers. Lamb and Elster (1985) found that social support and mother-father engagement predicted the degree of involvement and engagement for fathers but not for mothers. In fact, the findings of some studies have suggested that mothers compensate for low marital quality by being more supportive of the children (Belsky et al., 1991).

More negative outcomes for father-child relationships than for mother-child relationships have been reported with particular consistency when there is high marital conflict or divorce (Amato, 1986; Amato & Booth, 1991; Peterson & Zill, 1986; White, Brinkerhoff, & Booth, 1985). Thus, while divorce is linked with poorer relationships with both parents, effect sizes are typically greater for fathers than for mothers (Amato & Keith, 1991). Decreased contact, eroded affective ties, and fewer exchanges of assistance are more likely to occur for fathers than for mothers (Amato, Rezac, & Booth, in press; Booth & Amato, 1994; Cooney, 1994; Rossi & Rossi, 1990). On the other hand, there is a suggestion in some research that getting along with the father may have more impact on the development of adjustment problems in children than getting along with the mother (Prucho, Burant, & Peters, 1994).

The bases for the greater effects of marital quality on fathering than on mothering are not well understood. Several hypotheses have been advanced. For example, women may be better at compartmentalizing the spouse and parent roles, resulting in less carryover from marital relations to parenting for mothers (Belsky et al., 1991). Mothers' attitudes about gender roles may serve a "gatekeeper" function with regard to fathers' participation in childrearing as marital relations worsen (Katzev, Warner, & Adcock, 1994). Another hypothesis is that motherhood is a more fundamental role for women than is fatherhood for men (E. Thompson & Walker, 1989). For fathers, parental and husband roles are more fused (Belsky, Gilstrap, & Rovine, 1984).

Fathers display less negative and more sensitive behaviors when interacting with their children when they report higher marital satisfaction (Belsky et al., 1991).

Further, the direction of effects and the pattern of causal relations between variables are unclear. Fathers who are less sensitive overall may be more prone to both dysfunctional marriages and poor fathering. Men are more likely than women to withdraw both from marriages (Christensen & Heavey, 1990; Christensen & Shenk, 1991) and from their children (Howes & Markman, 1989) as marital relations worsen. Dickstein and Parke (1988) reported that paternal marital satisfaction was a significant predictor of the social referencing of fathers by infants but maternal marital satisfaction was not a significant predictor of referencing to mothers. Thus, suggestive of the emotional withdrawal of fathers from their children when marital quality is low, dissatisfied fathers may not be a good source of information for children when they look to the father for cues to emotional responding in ambiguous or stressful social contexts. Another possibility is that the father's negative parenting has more negative impact. Thus, Katz and Gottman (1995b), based on structural equation modeling, reported that rejecting parenting by fathers is associated with higher heart rates in children and more negative behavior toward parents in parent-child interaction.

Given the complexity of the interrelationships reported in correlational research, and the corresponding uncertainty about the directions of effects, experimental studies testing specific hypotheses can make a valuable contribution. In an ingenious study, Jouriles and Farris (1992) manipulated the interactions of parents and then examined the effects of such manipulations on family interactions. Families were assigned to either conflictual or nonconflictual marital interaction conditions, and then interactions between either the mother or father with the son were examined. Relative to the nonconflictual conditions, the conflictual conditions resulted in more confusing and threatening commands by fathers to sons, and less compliance of sons with fathers' commands. Thus, experimental studies support field research in indicating that marital conflict more negatively affects father-child than mother-child interactions.

Cross-sex relations may be particularly influenced by marital quality. Gender-role differentiation between the spouses typifies distressed marriages (Gottman & Levenson, 1988; Markman & Kraft, 1989), and gender differentiation in parent-child relations may also increase as marital relations worsen. There is some evidence that the mother-son relationship is more sensitive to marital quality than is the mother-daughter relationship. For example, mothers make greater maturity demands of their sons and show more negativism toward them as marital quality declines (Goldberg, 1990; Olweus, 1980). However, there is greater research support for the notion that the father-daughter relationship is particularly influenced by marital quality (Belsky et al., 1989; Booth & Amato, 1994). For example, Kerig et al. (1993) reported that fathers with higher marital satisfaction were more positive and assertive with first-born daughters, compared to first-born sons, and their daughters were more compliant to their commands. Goldberg and Easterbrooks (1984) found that marital satisfaction was linked with secure father-daughter attachments, whereas the security of mother-child attachments was unrelated to marital adjustment. By contrast, father-son relationships have been reported not to undergo long-term decline, even under certain circumstances of divorce (Booth & Amato, 1994).

THE DIRECT EFFECTS OF EXPOSURE TO MARITAL INTERACTION

GENERAL EFFECTS OF EXPOSURE TO MARITAL INTERACTION

As shown in Figure 4.1, marital quality can have direct effects on children's functioning due to exposure to marital interactions, independent of any effects due to parenting. Among the various forms of interparental interactions, interparental conflict is most consistently linked with children's adjustment problems (Cummings, 1994; Grych & Fincham, 1990). For example, overt hostility between the parents forecasts child behavior problems better than marital apathy and covert tension (e.g., Jenkins & Smith, 1991). Marital conflict is a better predictor of children's adjustment problems than is general marital distress (e.g., Emery & O'Leary, 1984).

Further, there is considerable evidence, including experimental demonstrations that cogently pinpoint the direction of effects and causal relations, that adults' conflicts have direct "exposure effects" on children's emotionality, physiological functioning, and social behavior, including their aggressiveness toward peers and their disposition to become enmeshed in parental conflicts (Cummings & Davies, 1994a). While experimental manipulation of actual marital conflict is not ethically feasible, various innovative analogue, experimental studies have been devised to test key process relations. Confidence in the findings is increased by the fact that field and laboratory studies have, in general, converged in demonstrating the central conclusions (Cummings, 1995b). Again, because of the recency of reviews (Cummings, 1994; Cummings & Davies, 1994a; Davies & Cummings, 1994), the treatment here focuses briefly only on some the main messages of research as examples.

Children's Aggression Increases

Consistent with clinical field studies reporting links between marital conflict and children's aggression (Emery, 1982; Grych & Fincham, 1990), a series of laboratory studies shows that children's aggression increases following exposure to unresolved conflicts between adults. Thus, one study examined the responses of two-year-old friends (Cummings, Iannotti, & Zahn-Waxler, 1985). The children played freely while two female actors came and went. First, the actors were friendly. Later, they returned and became angry at each other. Finally, they came back and resolved their dispute. Interchild aggression increased following the two-year-olds' exposure to the fight and declined again after the resolution. A control group of children exposed to a series of emotionally neutral interactions showed no change in aggression over time. Other studies have replicated these relations (e.g., Cummings, 1987; Klaczynski & Cummings, 1989).

Conflict Expression

Contextual variations in how conflicts are expressed also influence how conflict affects children. Children are partricularly disturbed by physically aggressive interactions between the parents (e.g., Cummings, Vogel, Cummings, & El-Sheikh, 1989), which are linked with their development of adjustment problems (Grych & Fincham, 1990). Grych and Fincham (1993) reported that intense conflicts and conflict about child-related themes were particularly distressing to children.

Sensitization

Children's regulatory problems increase as a function of increased exposure to unresolved conflicts. Repeated exposure in the laboratory has been shown to result in increased distress and aggressiveness toward peers. A history of exposure to marital hostility in the home is associated with increased distress responding and taking responsibility for the parent during experimental presentations of parental conflicts (J. S. Cummings, Notarius, Pellegrini, & Cummings, 1989). Greater history of marital conflict also is linked with greater distress responding and taking responsibility for the parent in marital conflicts occurring in the home as described in parental diaries (Cummings, Zahn-Waxler, & Radke-Yarrow, 1981). Further, experiments have shown that mild inductions of sensitization can be produced in the laboratory in response to artificially created "marital conflict histories" (e.g., El-Sheikh & Cummings, 1995). The strength of support for sensitization processes make it a requirement that any theoretical model account for it.

Positive Dimensions of Marital Quality: The Impact of Conflict Resolution

On the other hand, the resolution of conflict substantially alters the meaning and interpretation of conflict from the child's perspective. Thus, children's reactions to the same conflict expression are dramatically changed if the conflict is resolved (e.g., Cummings et al., 1989). Children often report nonnegative, or even positive, emotions in reaction to resolved conflicts. Further, children benefit from any progress toward resolution; that is, resolution does not have to be complete for benefits to accrue. Children may also detect resolution behind closed doors and respond positively to explanations of resolutions that they do not observe themselves (Cummings, Simpson, & Wilson, 1993). Furthermore, the emotionality as well as the content of conflict endings (e.g., angry vs. emotionally pleasant apologies) affects appraisal and responding, even among young children (Simpson & Cummings, 1996), with positive emotional and content elements each associated with more positive reactions. Thus, the data suggest that children's reactions to adults' conflict are not a process of emotional contagion, but are highly sensitive to what the conflict finally communicates about the status of the interpersonal relationships, with positive conflict endings linked with less negative, and more positive, reactions by children.

Exposure to Other Dimensions of Positive Marital Relations

Marital disputes that are constructive and emotionally positive are associated with positive affective responses by the children (Easterbrooks, Cummings, & Emde, 1994). Further, exposure to interparental disagreements may also hold benefits, depending upon how they are enacted. For example, positive problem-solving strategies and behaviors exhibited by the parents have been linked to more effective strategies in conflict situations by the children (Beach, 1995), although this question has received scant study.

In addition, children are also exposed to many types of marital interactions that do not induce stress (e.g., playful interactions and routine activities) but, on the contrary, may bring them pleasure. For example, while tinges of jealousy may be evident, children seem to enjoy observing affectionate exchanges between their parents. Children often smile or laugh when exposed to interparental affection (Cummings et al., 1981; Cummings, Zahn-Waxler, & Radke-Yarrow, 1984).

SPECIFICATION OF FATHER EFFECTS PERTAINING TO EXPOSURE TO MARITAL INTERACTION

Figure 4.1 also calls attention to the need to isolate the impact of the father's versus the mother's behaviors in marital interaction from the perspective of the child. What is the father's particular role in marital relations from the children's perspective? Does the father's playfulness toward the mother bring children particular pleasure and a sense of security? Does their conflict behavior in front of children involve different expressions of emotionality or different themes in terms of content? Are fathers more or less prone to initiate, or agree to, resolution? Are the father's styles of conflict negotiation and resolution in a family context different? Do patterns of conflict expressions and resolution by fathers during marital interactions have different effects on children than do conflict expressions by mothers?

Pertinent to this issue, Crockenberg and Forgays (1996) videotaped marital couples working toward the resolution of conflicts and showed parts of the tapes to their children. Girls judged their fathers to be more angry than did boys, despite the absence of differences between the father of boys and girls according to independent observers. Girls also evidenced a trend ($p = 0.06$) toward reporting more negative emotional responses to fathers than did boys. These findings are consistent with other evidence of the vulnerability of the father-daughter relationship to marital conflict (e.g., see Kerig et al., 1993).

There are also some leads for future research on these questions. For example, marital interaction research indicates differences between the behavior of men and women in marital conflict (see review in Cummings & Davies, 1994a). Thus, while men and women are equally likely to physically aggress, males may engage in more extreme acts of aggression and are more often identified as spouse abusers (Jaffe, Wolfe, & Wilson, 1990). Further, interspousal aggression is associated with physical aggression toward the children (Hughes, 1988; Jouriles et al., 1987). Interspousal aggression and the physical abuse of children each predict children's sensitization to conflict in the form of heightened emotional reactivity, aggressiveness, and caretaking behavior toward the parents (e.g., Cummings, Hennessy, Rabideau, & Cicchetti, 1994; J. S. Cummings et al., 1989). Futher, witnessing and being victims of physical abuse may be linked with similar problems in adjustment (Jaffe, Wolfe, Wilson, & Zak, 1986). Recent work indicates that children who are both witnesses and victims experience greater adjustment problems than children who experience only one of these forms of familial violence (Sternberg et al., 1993). An interesting, but unanswered, question is whether the same act of hostility is more disturbing for children when enacted by fathers than by mothers.

As marital distress increases, a demand-withdraw pattern sometimes develops in which the demonstrative spouse presents increasing grievances and criticisms, and the partner, in turn, becomes more and more passive and defensive (Christensen & Heavy, 1990). Women are more likely to become pressuring and blaming as conflict becomes more frequent and intense, whereas men more frequently withdraw (Markman & Kraft, 1989; Notarius & Markman, 1993). Thus, in some distressed marriages, the father's expressions of anger may be more passive, that is, the "silent treatment," which may be as emotionally disturbing to children as verbalized anger (Cummings et al., 1989). Katz and Gottman (1993) recently reported that marital interaction patterns classified as Mutually Hostile predicted children's externalizing behavior problems three years later, whereas a Husband Angry and Withdrawn pattern was related to children's internalizing problems.

Finally, observations of family conflicts around the dinner table were reported by Vuchinich, Emery, and Cassidy (1988). Fathers made more authority moves than did others during family conflicts, mothers mediated more often, and children tended to use distraction strategies. Daughters intervened more frequently than sons in disputes, except marital conflicts. More recently, Vuchinich, Wood, and Vuchinich (1994) reported that parental warmth and better family problem solving were highly correlated.

PARENTAL PSYCHOLOGICAL FUNCTIONING AND MARITAL QUALITY

Relationships between marital quality, parental psychological functioning, and children's adjustment are also indicated (see Figure 4.1). The marital relationship is a first-order support system for parents with influence on positive and negative functioning by parents (Belsky, 1984; Belsky et al., 1989; Cohn et al., 1992; Rutter, 1980). Positive marital relations foster emotional well-being in the parents. On the other hand, marital distress "is the most common reason why people seek psychological help" (Bradbury & Fincham, 1990, p. 3) and predicts emotional distress, depression, negativity, and violence in the parents (S. R. H. Beach & Nelson, 1990; Hershorn & Rosenbaum, 1985).

The parents' psychological functioning influences children's adjustment (Cummings & Davies, 1994b). Further, marital conflict has been identified as a factor in children's adjustment when parents have psychological problems (Downey & Coyne, 1990; West & Prinz, 1987). Marital quality and parental psychological adjustment may each add to the prediction of parenting quality (M. J. Cox, Owen, Lewis, & Henderson, 1989).

GENERAL EFFECTS OF MARITAL QUALITY

Research has typically focused on interrelations among marital quality, maternal psychopathology, and child adjustment. Maternal depression illustrates this pathway of influence within the family system. A sizable literature indicates that marital quality and maternal depression are related and, further, that maternal depression factors in children's risk for adjustment problems (Downey & Coyne, 1990).

Maternal depression covaries with marital conflict (e.g., Coyne, Burchill, & Stiles, 1991; Gotlib & Wiffen, 1989). A direction of causality from marital conflict to maternal depression is indicated by some studies (see review in Beach & Nelson, 1990). Further, marital discord may mediate the effects of maternal depression on children and be a more prominent predictor of certain child outcomes than maternal depression per se. For example, A. D. Cox, Puckering, Pound, and Mills (1987) reported that interrelations between maternal depression and marital discord were reciprocal rather than unidirectional and that marital discord was more closely related to problems in mother-child interaction.

On the other hand, relatively little is known about the undoubtedly positive and supportive role of marital relations in many families with parental depression. With regard to marital discord important questions also remain: Do marital conflicts in families with parental depression differ in important ways from conflicts in families without parental depression, and what are the implications of specific forms of conflict expression in the broader context of family emotionality for children's adjustment? What psychological dimensions in children are affected by parental depression, and are there common links between the psychological processes activated by various forms of negative emotionality in the family?

SPECIFIC FATHER EFFECTS IN MARITAL CONTEXT

In the sense that fathers influence mothers' psychological adjustment as a function of the marital relationship, there is evidence for father effects as outlined in Figure 4.1. Specific negative elements of husband-wife relations have been identified as elevating the risk for depression in mothers (e.g., lack of support and the stressful effects of marital conflict; see review in Beach & Nelson, 1990). On the other hand, a supportive relationship with the husband is associated with reduced depressive symptomatology in mothers (S. R. H. Beach, Arias, & O'Leary, 1987).

There has been less study of relations between marital conflict, the father's psychopathology, and child adjustment. For which particular forms of psychopathology are fathers most at risk as a function of marital conflict, and what are the effects on children's adjustment? How do positive versus discordant relations with mothers affect fathers' psychological adjustment, and what are the sequelae for children of forms of psychological problems induced in fathers by marital conflict?

CHARACTERISTICS OF THE CHILD

As shown in Figure 4.1, the characteristics of the child also undoubtedly factor in responding. This is yet another gap in this literature, particularly with regard to process variables, such as temperament or biological factors, as opposed to marker variables, such as age or gender (Cummings & Davies, 1994a). There are promising directions emerging with regard to the assessment of temperament (Kagan, 1994) and biological factors (e.g., Dawson et al., 1994; Fox, Calkins, & Bell, 1994; Rothbart, Posner, & Rosicky, 1994). Thus, vagal tone has been identified as related to individual differences in children's capacity to regulate emotion and buffering from the negative effects of marital conflict (Katz & Gottman, 1995a). However, on a cautionary note, identifying the operation of biological systems in children's responding to social contexts does not resolve questions of cause and effect, and the relative primacy of internal (biological) versus external (social) systems. Further, the operation of biological systems underlying regulatory processes still must ultimately be understood in relation to specific contexts of individual children's experience, both immediate and historical.

CHILDREN'S COPING PROCESSES AND MECHANISMS

The "stress and coping" tradition of research and theory offers a useful heuristic for conceptualizing complex social processes at a microsocial level, as reflected in Figure

4.1. These notions are relevant for a process-oriented model for interrelations between fathers, marital quality, and child adjustment.

Lazarus and Folkman define stress as "a particular relationship between the person and the environment that is appraised by the person as taxing or exceeding his or her resources and endangering his or her well-being" (1984, p. 19). Coping is conceptualized as a dynamic process, that is, "the changing thoughts and acts that the individual uses to manage the external and/or internal demands of a specific person-environment transaction that is appraised as stressful" (Folkman, 1991, p. 5). When coping is viewed from a contextual perspective, emphasis is placed on the specific thoughts and acts that the individual uses to cope with specific contexts, as guided by personal appraisals of situations, especially perceived ability to cope, that is, coping efficacy. Individual differences also figure prominently, including personal dispositions, family history, age, and sex. Interactions between the individual and specific environmental contexts find expression in multidimensional coping processes and strategies that develop into stable patterns leading over time to either adjustment or maladjustment in functioning (see also Sroufe & Rutter, 1984).

RESPONSE PROCESSES ASSOCIATED WITH MARITAL QUALITY

High marital quality may greatly support and foster positive emotional experience and social competencies in both parents and children. However, historical experiences with frequent, destructive marital conflicts appears to leave a "residue"; that is, children are more sensitive and reactive to adults' conflicts (Cummings, 1994), and perhaps family stresses more generally (Ballard, Cummings, & Larkin, 1993; Cummings & el-Sheikh, 1991). These effects may reflect emotional insecurity (Davies & Cummings, 1994), rejection sensitivity (Feldman & Downey, 1994), or other processes related to problems in emotionality and emotion regulation (R. A. Thompson, 1991, 1994; Wilson & Gottman, 1995).

In addition, negative emotionality between the parents also disrupts parental functioning. Problems of emotional expression and regulation are highly significant to the experienced quality of marital relations and parental psychological functioning (Gottman, 1994; Notarius & Markman, 1993). Spouses do not "get used to" marital discord. Instead, as marital distress increases, marital partners become sensitized to conflict. Marital interactions are characterized by escalating and reciprocal negativity, more prolonged conflict episodes, and greater enmeshment by the parents in coercive conflict processes (Bradbury & Fincham, 1987; Levensen & Gottman, 1983; Margolin & Wampold, 1981). Thus, negative emotionality and behaviors between the father and mother may be a primary influence in the chain of events in distressed marriages for both parents and children.

RESPONSE PROCESSES ASSOCIATED WITH THE FATHER IN MARITAL CONTEXT

Given the above discussion, it is perhaps not surprising that there has been little identification of response processes associated specifically with the father, although some leads are evident in various places in this review. Toward stimulating future research, we would like to call attention once again to gender differences and cross-gender effects as directions for future work. Do fathers feel more protective of their sons, and mothers more protective of their daughters, during marital conflict? Do boys and girls more often take sides with the same-sex parent than the opposite-sex parent? A more complex scenario is that boys and girls are equally likely to help either parent in satisfied marriages (i.e., relatively unlikely to become involved at all; see Cummings & Davies, 1994a), but boys take sides with the father, and girls take sides with the mother, in distressed marriages (e.g., Booth & Amato, 1994; Kerig, Cowan, & Cowan, 1993).

Finally, it is intriguing that few gender differences in children's immediate reactions to marital conflict are found (Cummings & Davies, 1994a), but differences between boys and girls are frequently reported in their coping processes and adjustment problems (Cummings, Davies, & Simpson, 1994; Grych & Fincham, 1993). What accounts for these results? Possible gender differences between the parents in conflict expression and their behavior within the family toward same-sex versus opposite-sex children are an intriguing avenue for future research.

CHILDREN'S ADJUSTMENT AND MARITAL QUALITY

Finally, completing the journey through the elements outlined in Figure 4.1, children's adjustment has been shown to be a function of marital quality. For example, correlations between child problems and marital conflict are typically low to moderate in magnitude (Grych & Fincham, 1990). However, marital conflict is more closely associated with negative child outcomes in distressed families (Wolfe et al., 1985). The extremity and form of expression of conflict are likely to be factors in the strength of association between marital conflict and problems in children's adjustment.

Children from high-conflict homes are especially vulnerable to externalizing disorders, including excessive aggression, noncompliance, and delinquency. Relationships between marital conflict and children's internalizing problems are less robust, but there are unanswered questions about whether the relatively subtle behaviors that reflect internalizing problems are underreported, which would attenuate the findings (Cummings & Davies, 1994a).

Thus, research has documented significant associations between marital quality and children's adjustment, as we noted at the outset. However, at this stage in the field's development, simply demonstrating that family variables are correlated is reaching a point of diminishing returns. Research is now needed to explain the bases for these associations, the direction of effects, and the causal relations so that viable theories about the effect of family, including fathers in a family context, can be supported (Cummings, 1995b).

FATHERS IN A FAMILY CONTEXT: AN EMOTIONAL
SECURITY HYPOTHESIS

The chapter closes with a discussion of a theoretical model. Specifically, an emotional security perspective is described based on work on marital conflict and children (Davies & Cummings, 1994), which is extended to include consideration of fathers in families. Research supports a broad family-wide pattern of influences on children's sense of emotional security, with implications for their psychological adjustment

(Cummings & Davies, 1995). Notably, the ability to successfully regulate emotion and arousal pertinent to an individual's sense of emotional security have emerged as salient processes in both the marital relations and child development literatures. Emotional security functions have been identified as an important process in adult love relationships (Brennan & Shaver, 1995; Hazen & Shaver, 1987) and may be stable and transmitted across generations within the family (Benoit & Parker, 1994). This theoretical model shows promise for organizing the results of studies pertaining to fathering and for suggesting future directions for research.

THE GENERAL MODEL OF EMOTIONAL SECURITY

Davies and Cummings (1994; see also Cummings & Davies, 1995) have proposed that children's sense of emotional security derives from the quality of the marital relationship as well as from the quality of parent-child relationships. Recently, they have described a specific definition for emotional security (Cummings & Davies, 1996): "Emotional security is a latent construct that can be inferred from the overall organization of children's emotions, behaviors, thoughts, and physiological response, and serves a set goal by which children regulate their own functioning in social contexts, thereby directing social, emotional, cognitive, and physiological reactions."

Notably, children have sound bases for concern about the quality of marital relations. Marital quality may have implications for the future intactness of the family. Family dissolution as an end result of destructive marital conflict drastically reduces the psychological availability of the noncustodial parent, while also causing economic hardship and many difficult life changes.

A family-wide perspective on the origins of children's sense of emotional security is supported by recent research. Intercorrelations have been reported between attachment security, marital quality and conflict, parental psychological functioning, parenting practices, and children's psychological adjustment (e.g., see reviews in Cummings & Davies, 1994a; Davies & Cummings, 1994). For example, children are more likely to form insecure attachments to mothers with depression, with marital quality and parenting practices each implicated in the adjustment of children of depressed parents (Cummings, 1995a; Cummings & Davies, 1994b).

Further, consistent with the framework outlined in Figure 4.1, children's impact upon their parents merits consideration. Specifically, a negative affective cycle may occur within families, with parental dysfunction leading to child emotional disregulation, and children's behavioral and emotional dysfunction undermining the emotional quality of parent-child and marital relationships. Thus, diminished capacities by children to regulate their own emotionality and social behavior (e.g., aggressiveness and conduct problems) due to marital disturbance erode parent-child relationships and place further stress on marriages (Bugental et al., 1989; Mangelsdorf, Gunnar, Kestenbaum, Lang, & Andreas, 1990).

Specific coping processes and mechanisms have been linked with emotional security, including children's 1. capacity to regulate their own emotional arousal, 2. decreased responsibility-taking, guilt, and shame about the parents' conflicts, and 3. more positive internalized representations or working models of self and family (e.g., less perceived threat, increased confidence in the predictability of parents' behavior, and higher self-esteem and worth). These interrelated processes may each factor in children's decreased risk for the development of adjustment problems over time in nondistressed families.

EMOTIONAL SECURITY AND CHILDREN'S GENERAL WELL-BEING

The construct of emotional security also calls attention to the importance of children's emotionality at a more inclusive level of analysis than simply diagnoses of psychopathology. Research has focused on clinical levels of disorders in children, but the quality of children's emotional lives is much more than that. Further, children from discordant families may be more prone to the experience of psychological pain and a relative absence of psychological pleasure. These affective experiences are significant from a mental health perspective for children, whether or not formal diagnoses of psychopathology are merited.

Emotional relationships between fathers, mothers, and children are more full-bodied than simply emotional security versus insecurity, including a richer experience of the intense affects that are central to children's and adult's enjoyment of, or lack of pleasure in, their lives (J. S. Wallerstein, 1995, personal communication). In particular, Emery (1994) has suggested that psychological pain is a sequelae of the loss of contact with noncustodial fathers. Children love both their father and mothers, strongly want contact with both, and have worry and compassion for both. A limitation of research is the overpathologizing of family functioning, and a lack of assessment of subclinical aspects of children's emotional well-being (e.g., pleasure, enjoyment, minimal worry and other psychological pain). Further, children's emotional well-being in the broader sense of the term may have long-term mental health implications (e.g., in terms of proneness for later adult depression and dysfunctional adult relationships) that are not immediately apparent at the time of family dysfunction.

EMOTIONAL SECURITY AND FATHER EFFECTS

Research is only beginning to map relations between fathers, children, and emotional security in a family context, however. The importance of attachment security for children's adjustment has been the subject of much study but is typically limited to mother-child attachments (Bretherton, 1985).

Broader conceptualizations of the family-wide origins of emotional security are likely to account for substantially more about the course of children's development. Specifically, conceptions of emotional security can usefully be extended to include the functioning of the marital relationship from the children's perspective and the significance of fathers and other family relationships (e.g., siblings, grandparents, or other familial and extrafamilial relationships). Further, interparental relationships can also be thought of in these terms, including patterns of marital emotionality and emotional expressiveness, and interparental attachments and the parents' childhood attachments.

Links have been reported between marital harmony and more secure father-daughter attachments (Goldbert & Easterbooks, 1984) and marital conflict and less secure infant-father attachment (Volling & Belsky, 1992). Cohn, Silver, Cowan, Cowan, and Pearson (1992) reported that men with secure internal working models of attachment had better-functioning marriages than men with insecure childhood attachments. Further, women with insecure childhood attachments had less conflictual and more harmonious marriages when married to men with secure childhood attachments than when married to men with insecure childhood attachments. Cohn et al. (1992) found that children of fathers with secure childhood attachments, in comparison to children of fathers with insecure childhood attachments, were more task-oriented and displayed more warmth and less negative affect. In addition, in comparison to marriage to men with insecure childhood attachment, marriage to men with secure childhood attachments fostered better parenting styles by mothers with insecure childhood attachments and more warmth between the mothers and their children.

NEW DIRECTIONS

The integration into child development research of conceptualizations of adult attachments and marital functioning logically indicates the value of inclusion of information about the security of the father's current and past attachments. As noted above, even the scant research thus far accomplished supports that such notions may help explain the functioning of both fathers and mothers in a family context. Further, the interface of 1. marital relations and parenting and 2. the emotionality of parental and child behaviors are questions that need to be addressed for more advanced understanding of children's functioning in family contexts.

Thus, parent-child relationships are embedded in a social context that includes the marital relationship, social networks, and occupational experience of parents (Belsky, 1990). Fathers are likely to figure importantly in each of these emerging extensions of the construct of emotional security from a family-wide perspective.

Issues of emotional security are pertinent to children's behavior in intact families and also to how children cope during and following marital dissolution (Hill, 1988). Emotional security conceptualizations might be productively extended to the study of children's functioning when marital dissolution occurs, or in single-parent families. Fathers, or men who are the closest equivalent to fathers in these family contexts, may play an important role in such childrearing environments.

Such work, which is likely to be more sensitive to the quality of children's emotional lives, will better reflect the full range of child development outcomes than simply global, questionnaire-based assessments of psychopathology (Simons, Whitbeck, Beamon, & Conger, 1994). The bottom line is that more process-oriented assessments and conceptualizations that include all important family members, including fathers, in their purview are needed to avoid oversimplification of the impact of family phenomena and foster better understanding of child development prospects (Clark & Barber, 1994). To find answers to complex questions regarding directions of effects and causal relations, work must move beyond correlational, field research to the process-oriented study of multiple family systems and multiple response processes and must utilize multiple methods, including experimental methods (Cummings, 1995b).

CHAPTER 5

Paternal Involvement: Levels, Sources, and Consequences

Joseph H. Pleck

University of Illinois at Urbana-Champaign

THIS CHAPTER REVIEWS recent research concerning the levels, origins, and consequences of paternal involvement. Its focus is restricted to adult fathers in heterosexual two-parent families, as other chapters in this volume consider other important paternal groups. Investigations conducted in the United States provide most of the data discussed here, but some research from other industrial countries is included.

Several themes guide the chapter. Data on fathers' average level of involvement are of great interest to many people, but these assessments vary considerably according to many factors, not least the measures used. Descriptive results on fathers' average levels of involvement are actually far more variable than is generally realized. Nonetheless there is a tendency to think that the question "How involved are U.S. fathers?" should have a simple answer.

Further conceptualization is needed of the origins and sources of paternal involvement. Lamb, Pleck, Charnor, and Levine (1985; Pleck, Lamb, & Levine 1986) proposed a four-factor model for its sources: motivation, skills and self-confidence, social supports, and institutional practices. This framework needs to be integrated with other available models for the determinants of fathering, and with more general theoretical perspectives on parental functioning.

Because the construct of paternal involvement called attention to an important dimension of fathers' behavior neglected in prior research and theory, it was an important advance. However, the utility of the construct in its original, content-free sense now needs to be reconsidered. The critical question is: How good is the evidence that fathers' *amount* of involvement, without taking into account its content and quality, is consequential for children, mothers, or fathers themselves? The associations

I wish to thank Catherine Huddleston, Talley Arnold, Lynne Borden, Thomas Rane, and Michael Lamb for their assistance in the preparation of this chapter.

with desirable outcomes found in much research are actually with positive forms of paternal involvement, not involvement per se. Involvement needs to be combined with qualitative dimensions of paternal behavior through the concept of "positive paternal involvement" developed here.

CONCEPTUAL AND METHODOLOGICAL ISSUES

At the outset, it is valuable to consider how the involvement construct emerged, its operationalization, and related methodological and conceptual issues. Lamb, Pleck, Charnov, and Levine (1985, 1987) proposed the construct of paternal involvement as including three components: 1. paternal engagement (direct interaction with the child, in the form of caretaking, or play or leisure); 2. accessibility or availability to the child; and 3. responsibility for the care of the child, as distinct from the performance of care. Before the formulation of this construct, the paternal behaviors and characteristics studied in father-present families included only qualitative ones such as masculinity, power, control, warmth, responsiveness, independence training, playfulness, and the like. By comparison, involvement is a content-free construct, concerning only the quantity of fathers' behavior, time, or responsibility with their children.

Sources of the Involvement Construct

The construct of paternal involvement reflected both social and methodological developments during the preceding decade. On the social side, the apprehensions about fathering emerging in the 1980s focused primarily on whether children were getting enough fathering, and whether fathers were doing enough to reduce the childrearing burden of employed mothers. The one exception, albeit an important one, was the increasing awareness of physical and sexual abuse by fathers. But most attention nonetheless went to the amount, not the kind, of fathering children received. This worry was also expressed in the growing concern about father absence, whose rates had risen markedly. Of course, the empirical correlates of father presence versus absence are not necessarily the same as the correlates of fathers' degree of involvement in father-present families (Lamb, Pleck, & Levine, 1985; Pederson, 1976). But underlying the interest in both topics is concern about the effects of the amount of paternal involvement.

Methodologically, the development of the involvement construct was also fostered by the availability of a new kind of data: time "diaries" from national representative samples or other large-scale probability samples, from which data about fathers' time with children could be coded. This methodology fell into disuse after its introduction by home economists in the 1920s, but was taken up again in earnest by economists and sociologists in the late 1960s. Other researchers began collecting time use data by simply asking respondents to estimate their time in child care and other activities. Results from time use research began appearing in the family studies literature in the late 1970s (Pleck, 1977, 1983, 1985). Through the concept of paternal involvement, these data became meaningful to human development. Compared to most developmental and family studies research, these data had the advantage of being based on large probability samples of known generalizability. Since several major time diary studies were replicated across time, they also made it possible to track secular trends in father involvement.

OPERATIONALIZATIONS: INVOLVEMENT VERSUS POSITIVE INVOLVEMENT

In addition to time diary or other time estimates, other measures have been explicitly developed for the assessment of paternal involvement. In a particularly thorough operationalization, McBride's (1990; McBride & Mills, 1993) Interaction/Accessibility Time Chart discriminates four subcategories of engagement (defined as using play, functional, parallel, and transitional), accessibility, and responsibility, and also distinguishes workday versus nonworkday levels of engagement and responsibility. Radin (1994) notes that many investigators have supplemented or elaborated the involvement concept to include other elements such as fathers' proportion of involvement and specific activities such as play. Her own widely used Paternal Index of Child Care Involvement (PICCI) assesses five components, labeled statement of involvement, child-care responsibility, socialization responsibility, influence in childrearing decisions, and accessibility. Paternal involvement is reported in absolute terms for some components, and in proportional terms for others.

The most important shift represented by Radin's and many other operationalizations of involvement, however, has not been made explicit. The PICCI socialization and child-care subscales ascertain level of involvement through assessing activities that are not just indicators of overall time spent with the child, but are specific activities likely to promote development. For example, the socialization subscale includes "helping children with personal problems" and "helping children to learn," and the childrearing decision subscale includes deciding "when children are old enough to learn new things." Thus, the summary score reflects a composition of positive paternal involvement rather than involvement in the original, content-free sense. The same is true in many other measures. Volling and Belsky's (1991) summary measure of "observed father-infant interaction" includes frequency of responding, stimulating or arousing, caregiving, and expressing positive affection. This measure seems to correspond to Belsky's (1984) conceptualization of "growth-facilitating parenting" and "parenting that is *sensitively* attuned to children's capabilities and to the developmental tasks they face" (p. 85). Snarey (1993) assesses fathers' engagement in their children's intellectual development, social development, and physical development during childhood and during adolescence. In the 1987–88 National Survey of Families and Households (NSFH), fathers with preschool children only (ages 0–4) were asked about the frequency of three activities with their child or children: "outings away from home (e.g., parks, zoos, museums)," playing at home, and reading. Men with school-aged (5–18) children responded about the frequency of "leisure activities," working on projects or playing at home, having private talks, and helping with reading and doing homework (Marsiglio, 1991b). Amato's (1987) summary variable of "paternal support" incorporates positive paternal activities along with reports of the father's being a favorite person to have talks with and the person in the family the child tells if he or she is really worried. Because of the particular behaviors and relationship characteristics at issue, all these measures assess positive paternal involvement.

The more general point is that in addition to quantitative level of involvement, the content or quality of paternal involvement can also be assessed. Realizing that these are distinct dimensions has several implications. For one thing, their interrelationship can be investigated empirically. Intercorrelations among PICCI subscales appear to vary considerably in different samples (Ahmeduzzaman & Roopnarine, 1992; Harold-Goldsmith, Radin, & Eccles, 1988; Radin, 1994; Roopnarine & Ahmeduzzaman, 1993; Sagi, 1982; Tulananda, Young, & Roopnarine, 1994). The associations of PICCI scales and assessments of quantitative involvement with qualitative involvement measures is generally low (Bailey, 1994; Grossman, Pollack, & Golding, 1988; Radin, 1994),[1] although a few studies report stronger correlations (Amato, 1987; Sagi, 1982). In addition, the hypothetical influence of involvement on child outcomes can be formulated in two related ways. Good child outcomes should be predicted better by the combination of high quantitative involvement and high quality than by either dimension alone.[2] To date, no research has directly tested this obvious hypothesis. An alternative formulation is that good outcomes are a function of positive paternal involvement rather than paternal involvement per se. As will be seen later, most investigations of child outcomes have actually examined associations with positive paternal involvement.

OTHER METHODOLOGICAL AND CONCEPTUAL ISSUES

Several remaining issues merit discussion. First, there has been long-standing concern with the validity of assessments of paternal involvement, particularly when reported by fathers themselves. Several studies using father-mother pairs, however, have found high agreement between fathers' reports of their involvement and wives' assessments (Ahmeduzzaman & Roopnarine, 1992; Levant, Slattery, & Loiselle, 1987; Roopnarine & Ahmeduzzaman, 1993; Smith & Morgan, 1994; Tulananda et al., 1994). However, in a nonpaired sample, Peterson and Gerson (1992) observed dramatic discrepancies between the average extent of fathers' participation in selecting their child's current nonparental child-care arrangement reported by fathers and by mothers, although McBride and Mills (1993) did not. Research needs to investigate the reliability of assessments of parental involvement further.

For one commonly used form of assessment, fathers' estimates of the amount of time they spend with their children, validity may be low. Time use is often assessed with respondents' estimates rather than full-scale time diaries because the latter are so laborious for respondents to complete, tending to crowd out the other measures needed for theoretically driven analyses of origins and consequences of paternal involvement. Although research using respondents' more global estimates of their time spent with children has made a contribution (Pleck, 1985), recent work on the cognitive evaluation of survey questions suggests that the error variance in such measures is considerable (Forsyth, Lessler, & Hubbard, 1992). The difficulty is that making such estimates is a reconstructive process, and subjects vary in the cognitive techniques they use to do it. Unless subjects are given guidelines about how to make an estimate,[3] variance in their responses is likely to reflect differences in their recon-

---

1. For the research by Radin, by Russell, by Sagi, and by Lamb, Hwang, Frodi, and colleagues, citations are generally given to more recent summary publications. For more complete citations of publications from these studies, see the reference lists of the publications cited here.

2. Besides Lamb, Pleck, and Levine's (1985) early expression of this hypothesis, it has been explicitly formulated elsewhere only in a footnote in Ihinger-Tallman, Pasley, and Buehler (1993).

3. Levant et al. (1987) and McBride and Mills (1993) provide examples of instructions and response formats for respondents that reduce error due to respondents using different estimation methods and increase the validity of respondents' estimates. However, these approaches require individual administration.

structive techniques as much or more than their actual time use patterns. The error introduced considerably weakens analyses of the correlates of involvement.

Second, assessment of paternal involvement with a specific child should be distinguished from involvement summed or averaged across all children (for fathers who have more than one child). Drawing on the distinction between shared and nonshared environmental influences in behavioral genetics (Plomin, 1989), different children of the same father receive both a shared component of paternal influence and a nonshared or unique component. One analysis estimated that 31% of the total variation in paternal behavior toward children, and 26% of the total variation in paternal affect, actually occurs between siblings (i.e., within families) rather than between families (Harris & Morgan, 1991). Future research should explore the extent to which generic versus child-specific components of paternal involvement and other paternal behaviors can be empirically distinguished and should investigate how their predictors or consequences vary.

Finally, most fathers may perceive provision of economic support as their main contribution to their children's well-being. Since the involvement construct includes forms of involvement traditionally shown by mothers but excludes breadwinning, a possible critique is that involved fatherhood is therefore "mother-defined fatherhood" (Blankenhorn, 1995). Three questions need to be distinguished. Should the concept of involvement include breadwinning? Is involvement the only important component of fathering, and specifically, does breadwinning promote development? And, should breadwinning be viewed as a component only of fatherhood, or of motherhood as well?

Lamb et al.'s definition does reflect what "involved father" means in everyday discourse. Calling a father highly involved who is a good economic provider but who is low in engagement, accessibility, and responsibility would seem inaccurate to most people. But the concept of involvement was never intended to encompass all important paternal behavior. Lamb et al. (1987; Lamb, Pleck, & Levine, 1985) explicitly argued that involvement is only one of several modes of paternal influence on child development. As evidenced for example by the negative association between family income and adolescent risk behaviors (J. D. Hawkins, Catalano, & Miller, 1992), parental breadwinning promotes positive development as well. Whether breadwinning is a uniquely paternal behavior is ultimately a value question. Some theoretical analyses view resource provision as one of several essential parental functions, without linking these functions to gender (Small & Eastman, 1991). In the example just given, it is possible that fathers' contribution to family income has a stronger or unique protective effect on adolescent risk behaviors compared to mothers' contribution, though it seems unlikely. But whether parenthood should be viewed as inherently gender-differentiated cannot be answered definitively on empirical grounds. Whatever the answer, it is appropriate to exclude breadwinning from the concept of father involvement so long as it is recognized that involvement is not the only important paternal behavior.

The chapter next considers recent data on levels of paternal involvement. This section emphasizes time use data assessing involvement in the original content-free sense, partly because of the considerable interest in paternal time per se and partly because these data describe paternal involvement in an easily interpretable metric. Subsequent sections examine the sources and consequences of involvement, utilizing a broader range of data, distinguishing where possible paternal involvement per se from positive paternal involvement. The three components of involvement are also distinguished to the extent the data permit.

LEVELS OF PATERNAL INVOLVEMENT

ENGAGEMENT AND AVAILABILITY

Table 5.1 summarizes recent data concerning fathers' engagement and accessibility. These data are presented in two ways: paternal involvement relative to maternal involvement and paternal involvement in absolute terms. In reviewing earlier research, Lamb, Pleck, Charnov, and Levine (1985) and Lamb et al. (1987) noted that estimates of the time fathers spend with their children vary widely because studies assess engagement or accessibility and because each of these components can be operationalized narrowly or broadly. However, results across studies are more comparable if fathers' time is expressed as a proportion of mothers' time.

Averaging across studies from the 1980s and 1990s, fathers' proportional engagement is somewhat over two-fifths of mothers' (43.5%), and their accessibility is nearly two-thirds of mothers' (65.6%). These figures are somewhat higher than the corresponding averages in the 1970s and early 1980s studies—about a third for engagement and about a half for accessibility (Lamb, Pleck, Charnov, & Levine, 1985a).

Fathers' absolute levels of engagement and accessibility are higher with young children than with adolescents. For young children, in studies distinguishing weekdays from weekend days, the best available estimate for paternal engagement time is 1.9 hours for weekdays, and 6.5 hours for Sundays. In addition to distinguishing workdays from nonworkdays, the study yielding this estimate (McBride & Mills, 1983) has the strength of using a guided interview procedure to assess engagement and accessibility time. Engagement estimates for younger children, not distinguishing type of day, range from 2.0 to 2.8 hours/day. For adolescents, current estimates of paternal engagement from U.S. studies range from 0.5 to 1.0 hours for weekdays, and 1.4 to 2.0 hours for Sundays, with more time reported with sons than with daughters.[4] Accessibility estimates are higher, ranging from 2.8 to 4.9 hours/day for younger children (9.8 hours/day for Sundays), and 2.8 hours/day for adolescents.

These estimates contrast markedly with the figures disseminated in the media. A statistic frequently cited recently is 12 minutes/day (Skow, 1989) because it is the only specific estimate of fathers' average time in child care given in Hochschild and Machung's (1989) influential *Second Shift*. However, this number was derived from a study nearly 25 years old at the time of Hochschild and Machung's publication and concerned fathers' child-care time only on workdays (Pleck, 1992a, 1992b).[5]

---

4. Using 1981 follow-up data from respondents included in the 1975–76 Study of Time Use, Nock and Kingston (1988) also provide detailed tabulations for time in specific engagement activities and all accessibility activities for single- and dual-earner fathers and mothers, with and without preschool children.

5. In an earlier period, the estimate of father's average daily time with children cited most frequently was Rebelsky and Hanks's (1971) figure of 37 seconds/day, actually a mathematical impossibility since one of the 10 fathers in the sample studied was reported as spending 22 minutes/day.

Table 5.1   Levels of Paternal Involvement: Engagement and Accessibility

Type of Paternal Involvement	Finding	Sample and Comments	Study
		Relative Level[a]	
Engagement	30%	1985, U.S.; adults ages 18–65	Robinson et al., 1988
	40%	1986, small Midwestern city; adults ages 18–65	Robinson et al., 1988
	37%	1987–88 NSFH; fathers with target child ages 0–4	Blair & Hardesty, 1994
	45%	Dual- and single-earner[b] fathers with school-aged daughters	Levant et al., 1987
	83%	Dual-earner fathers with children ages 3–5	McBride & Mills, 1993
	41% (fathers' reports); 37% (mothers' reports)	Black married fathers with children ages 3–5	Ahmeduzzaman & Roopnarine, 1992
	37% (fathers' reports); 40% (mothers' reports)	Puerto Rican fathers with children ages 3–5 in a Northeastern U.S. city	Roopnarine & Ahmeduzzaman, 1993
	35% (fathers' reports); 38% (mothers' reports)	Fathers with children ages 3–5	Tulananda et al., 1994
Accessibility	72%[c]	1981–83 National Longitudinal Surveys (NLS)	Goldscheider & Waite, 1991
	82%	Dual- and single-earner fathers with children ages 3–5	McBride & Mills, 1993
	43%	Dual- and single-earner fathers with school-aged daughters	Levant et al., 1987
	50%	Dual-earner fathers	Leslie et al., 1991
	73%	Dual-earner fathers with children ages 0–10	Haas, 1988
	64%	Dual-earner fathers with children ages 0–5	Jump & Haas, 1987
	75%	Fathers with adolescents; uses Experience Sampling Method (ESM)	Larson, 1993
		Absolute Level	
Engagement	2.4 hrs/day in physical care	NSFH; fathers of children ages 0–4	Blair & Hardesty, 1994
	2.8 hrs/day	Black married fathers with children ages 3–5	Ahmeduzzaman & Roopnarine, 1992
	2.7 hrs/day (fathers' reports); 2.5 hrs/day (mothers' reports)	Puerto Rican fathers with children ages 3–5 in a Northeastern U.S. city	Roopnarine & Ahmeduzzaman, 1993

Table 5.1 (*Continued*)

Type of Paternal Involvement	Finding	Sample and Comments	Study
	1.9 hrs weekdays; 6.5 hrs Sundays	Dual- and single-earner fathers with children ages 3–5	McBride & Mills, 1993
	2.0 hrs a day alone or with mother, 0.5 hrs a day alone	Dual- and single-earner fathers with school-aged daughters	Levant et al., 1987
		1986 Father and Child Survey, U.S.; fathers with children ages 10–15:	Ishii-Kuntz, 1994
	1.0 hr weekdays; 2.0 hrs Sundays	Sons	
	0.5 hrs weekdays; 1.4 hrs Sundays	Daughters	
		1986 Father and Child Survey, Japan; children ages 10–15:	Ishii-Kuntz, 1994
	0.3 hrs weekdays; 1.3 hrs Sundays	Sons	
	0.4 hrs weekdays; 1.4 hrs Sundays	Daughters	
Accessibility	4.9 hrs weekday; 9.8 hrs Sundays	Dual- and single-earner fathers with children ages 3–5	McBride & Mills, 1993
	3.9 hrs a day	Dual-earner fathers with children ages 0–5	Jump & Haas, 1987
	2.8 hrs a day	Dual-earner fathers with children ages 0–10	Haas, 1988
	2.8 hrs a day	Fathers with adolescents	Almeida & Galambos, 1991
	Child present 27% of fathers' time	Fathers with adolescents; uses ESM	Larson, 1993
	Child present 50% of fathers' time	Above study, excluding time working or commuting	Larson, 1993

Note. In this and later tables all samples are from the United States unless otherwise indicated. Year of data collection reported for some but not all studies.

[a]Fathers' time expressed as a proportion of mothers' time; see discussion in text.

[b]Earner status is reported here when emphasized in the study's sample description.

[c]Calculated from data indicating fathers performed 42% of the total child care.

RESPONSIBILITY

Fathers' average share of responsibility is substantially lower than mothers' (Leslie, Anderson, & Branson, 1991; McBride & Mills, 1993; Peterson & Gerson, 1992), and lower than fathers' share of engagement or accessibility (McBride & Mills, 1993). Recent studies have focused particularly on responsibility for selecting nonparental child-care arrangements (Leslie et al., 1991; Peterson & Gerson, 1992). Research has yet to identify any child-care task for which fathers have primary responsibility.

Federal surveys of the child-care arrangements of families with employed mothers provide data relevant to paternal responsibility. In the 1991 survey, 23% of employed married mothers with a child under five years reported that the father was the primary child-care arrangement during the mother's working hours (O'Connell, 1993).[6] In addition, 7% of single working mothers reported the father as the primary arrangement. In two-parent families, fathers are the primary arrangement as often as child-care centers and preschools combined (24%), and as often as family day-care homes (23%). Fathers are also more likely to be the primary arrangement than are grandparents (16%). The relatively high rate of primary paternal care in dual-earner families suggests that for a significant period of the workweek, a substantial minority of fathers have a high level of responsibility.

HAS PATERNAL INVOLVEMENT INCREASED IN RECENT DECADES?

Lamb, Pleck, Charnov, and Levine (1985; Pleck, 1985) recounted data from one study indicating that fathers' engagement time increased between 1924 and 1977, and from three studies suggesting it rose between the mid-1960s and early 1980s. Lamb (1987) and Pleck (1985) also cited Juster's comparison between 1975 and 1981 as further evidence of increasing paternal involvement. Two more recent comparisons corroborate the increase in paternal engagement between the 1960s and 1980s, and a third study suggests an increase in paternal responsibility since the late 1970s.

Robinson, Andreyenkov, and Patrushev (1988) conducted surveys in Jackson, Michigan, in 1986 and 1966, and in representative U.S. national samples in 1985 and 1965. Data on time with children are reported by gender, but not by parental status.[7] However, if the figures are adjusted for the proportions who have children in each year, fathers' total time with children increased over these two decades by 25% in the Jackson sample and by 33% in the United States as a whole. Since, in families with children, the average number of children present was lower in the mid-1980s than in the mid-1960s, the increase in paternal engagement time is even greater on a per child basis.

Federal surveys of working mothers' child-care arrangements for preschoolers suggest that paternal responsibility has increased in the last two decades. Compared to the 23% of married employed mothers who reported fathers as their primary child-care arrangement in 1991, 17% did so in 1977 (O'Connell, 1993). Presser (1989) cites other evidence that father care for children during mothers' working hours increased between 1965 and 1985.

In a critique of the earlier comparisons that Lamb (1987) and Pleck (1985) offered as evidence of change, LaRossa (1988) holds that since the turn of the century "fatherhood has not changed (at least significantly), if one looks at the conduct of fatherhood—how fathers behave vis-à-vis their children" (p. 451). The first criticism is that in Juster's (1985) longitudinal comparison of a sample of fathers interviewed in 1975 and 1981, and for Caplow, Bahr, Chadwick, Hill, and Williamson's (1982) contrast between 1924 and 1977, the measure used assesses only one aspect of involvement

---

6. Although paternal caretaking does occur more often when the father is unemployed, the more usual situation is that one or both parents works a nonday shift, which they sometimes select as a strategy to reduce child-care costs.

7. For this reason, Robinson et al.'s 1985 and 1986 data were used in Table 5.1 only to estimate fathers' proportional engagement, not to report fathers' absolute level of engagement.

and does not distinguish between one-on-one and less intense interaction. While this is true, increases are evident for the measures that are available. LaRossa further criticizes the paternal increase shown in Juster's comparison on the grounds that mothers' time with children increased by the same absolute amount. However, mothers' engagement has not increased in other trend analyses of time diary data (Robinson, 1977a; Robinson et al., 1988). But even if it did, the fathers' increase would not necessarily be less meaningful, especially since the fathers' proportional increase is far greater. In summary, the increase in paternal involvement observed in these studies is not large in absolute terms, and fathers remain a long way from parity with mothers. Nonetheless, evidence from five comparisons reviewed earlier (Lamb, 1987; Lamb, Pleck, Charnov, & Levine, 1985; Pleck, 1985) and three additional comparisons discussed here are consistent in documenting clear increases in paternal engagement and responsibility, especially over the past three decades.

SOURCES OF PATERNAL INVOLVEMENT

Lamb et al. (1987; Pleck et al., 1986) proposed that four factors influence the level of paternal involvement: motivation, skills and self-confidence, social supports, and institutional factors or practices. The constructs emphasized in other available theoretical frameworks for the determinants of parenting and fathering have clear relationships to Lamb et al.'s (1987) four factors. For example, the cognitions and beliefs about parenting highlighted by Abidin (1992) contribute to motivation, and this theorist explicitly calls for greater attention to the role of parental "motivational systems." Motivation is also related to Ihinger-Tallman et al.'s (1993) concept of "father parenting role identity" (for a related discussion, see A. J. Hawkins, Christiansen, Sargent, & Hill, 1993; Krampe & Fairweather, 1993; Marsiglio, 1991a). Motivation for involvement can be interpreted as a central dimension of fathers' personality and developmental history, key factors in Belsky's (1984; Vondra & Belsky, 1993) process model of parenting. Skills are grounded in developmental history as well. Marriage and the workplace in Belsky's model are components of Lamb et al.'s social supports and institutional factors, respectively.

After briefly reviewing the sociodemographic correlates of paternal involvement, this section uses Lamb et al.'s four-factor framework as the basis for organizing the considerable body of data now available. The potential role of biogenetic factors in paternal behavior is not discussed here (Lamb, Pleck, Charnov, & Levine, 1985; Lamb et al., 1987). For certain categories of potential influences, available results are summarized in tables.

CHILD CHARACTERISTICS AND PATERNAL SOCIODEMOGRAPHIC CHARACTERISTICS

Child's Gender
Recent studies generally support the conclusion of earlier reviews that fathers are more involved with sons than with daughters (Amato, 1987; Barnett & Baruch, 1987; Blair, Wenk, & Hardesty, 1994; Goldscheider & Waite, 1991; Harris & Morgan, 1991; Ishii-Kuntz, 1994; Marsiglio, 1991b). Radin (1994) also noted that there is greater stability over time in fathers' degree of involvement with sons, perhaps indicating

that paternal involvement with sons is in some way more deeply grounded in fathers' paternal identities.

The generalization of fathers' great involvement with sons requires some further specification, however. The gender differential appears to be greater with older children, and several studies find no gender difference in parental involvement with younger children (Marsiglio, 1991b; Palkovitz, 1984; Roopnarine & Ahmeduzzaman, 1993; Tulananda et al., 1994). The gender differential is also greater for paternal play than for caretaking (Levy-Shiff & Israelashvili, 1988). In a study of sibling pairs in the National Survey of Children, Harris and Morgan (1991) also observed that daughters with brothers are advantaged in terms of paternal attention relative to other daughters, and that sons are also advantaged by being the only boy. Japanese fathers actually spend less time with school-aged sons than with daughters (Ishii-Kuntz, 1994).

Child Age

As shown in Table 5.2, fathers are less involved with older children, except in reading (Marsiglio, 1991b).[8] Since mothers also report spending less time with older children (Pleck, 1985), the question of greater interest is how the decline of parental involvement with age of child differs by parental gender. Three of the four available studies indicate that with older children, fathers' involvement relative to mothers' is higher. Thus, fathers' involvement declines proportionally less than mothers' as children get older, no doubt because fathers' initial baseline is lower.

Family Size

In families with more children, fathers tend to contribute a higher proportion of the total parental interaction, although some studies find no association. In some investigations, fathers' absolute amount of engagement with young children is higher when there are fewer children, and maintaining high initial involvement is more likely. But others find no relationship between family size and involvement, and one analysis among older children finds a negative relationship (Marsiglio, 1991b), perhaps because when families are large, the younger children present may require a disproportionate share of the fathers' time or the father may feel greater breadwinner pressure.

Other Child Characteristics

Fathers are more involved with first-born than later-born children, and with infants born prematurely. Both relationships may hold for mothers as well. In single-earner families, fathers are more involved with infants who have difficult temperaments, perhaps because fathers may feel a particular need to give the mother relief from a difficult infant if she is home full time with him or her. Other child characteristics potentially influencing paternal involvement have received little attention.

Fathers' Socioeconomic Characteristics

As indicated in Table 5.3, the association of paternal involvement with education, occupation, income, and composite measures of socioeconomic status is not consis-

---

8. Older studies were excluded in Table 5.1 concerning levels of paternal involvement but are included in this and later tables.

Table 5.2   Associations between Paternal Involvement and Childrens' Characteristics and Family Size

Childrens' Characteristics	Finding	Sample and Comments	Study
Age	Older children: less accessibility	1977 Quality of Employment Survey	Pleck, 1985
	Older children: less engagement	1975–76 Study of Time Use	Pleck, 1985
	Older children: less absolute and relative accessibility, no relationship to other components	Fathers with kindergartners and fourth-graders	Barnett & Baruch, 1987
	Older children: less positive engagement	Australian fathers	Amato, 1987
	Within both age groups: less positive engagement, but reading higher with age among ages 0–4	NSFH; fathers with target child ages 0–4, 5–18	Marsiglio, 1991b
Family size	Larger families: no relationship to absolute engagement	Fathers with children ages 48–60 months	Baruch & Barnett, 1981
	Larger families: higher relative accessibility, no relationship to other components	Fathers with kindergartners and fourth-graders	Barnett & Baruch, 1987
	Larger families: higher relative accessibility	NSFH; fathers with target child ages 0–4	Ishii-Kuntz & Coltrane, 1992
	Larger families: no association with relative accessibility	1981–83 NLS	Goldscheider & Waite, 1991
	Larger families: lower positive engagement among older children; no association among younger children	NSFH; fathers with target child ages 0–4, 5–18	Marsiglio, 1991b
	Smaller families: higher involvement	Fathers with children ages 0–10	Russell, 1983, 1986
	Smaller families: maintenance of high initial involvement	Fathers with children ages 3–6	Radin, 1994
Other child characteristics	Birth order: higher positive engagement with first-born than with later children	Fathers with children ages 0–2	Rustia & Abbott, 1993
	Premature infants: more positive engagement	Fathers with infants	Yogman, 1987
	Infants with difficult temperaments: more positive engagement among single-earner fathers	Dual- and single-earner fathers with infants	Volling & Belsky, 1991

Note. In this and later tables, involvement components are assessed in absolute terms unless noted. The type of paternal involvement is distinguished when possible. The generic term "involvement" is used for the Paternal Index of Child Care Involvement (PICCI; Radin, 1994) summary score and for other measures for which form of involvement cannot be distinguished.

Table 5.3 Associations between Paternal Involvement and Fathers' Socioeconomic Characteristics

Fathers' Socioeconomic Characteristics	Finding	Sample and Comments	Study
Education	No consistent relationship	Review of nine studies prior to 1980	Pleck, 1983
	Higher education: higher positive engagement	NSFH; fathers with children ages 5–18	Blair et al., 1994
	Higher education: higher relative accessibility	1981–83 NLS	Goldscheider & Waite, 1991
	Higher education: less physical caregiving; no relationship with other components	Dual-earner fathers with children ages 0–10	Haas, 1988
	Higher education: more involved	Fathers with children ages 0–10	Russell, 1983, 1986
	No relationship	Fathers with kindergartners and fourth-graders	Barnett & Baruch, 1987
	No relationship	Dual- and single-earner fathers with infants	Volling & Belsky, 1991
	No relationship	NSFH; fathers with children ages 0–4	Cooney et al., 1993
	Higher education: more positive engagement	Black married fathers with children ages 3–5	Ahmeduzzaman & Roopnarine, 1992
	No relationship	NSFH; fathers with target child ages 0–4	Ishii-Kuntz & Coltrane, 1992
Occupational prestige	Higher prestige: less involved	Dual- and single-earner fathers	Dubnoff, 1978
	Involvement highest in lower-white collar and professional fathers; involvement lowest in blue-collar, middle, or high management positions and self-employed fathers	Men ages 25–45	Gerson, 1993
	High occupational status: more play	Fathers with newborns, followed to age 5	Grossman et al., 1988
Income	No relationship	Review of three studies prior to 1980	Pleck, 1983
	Higher income: more positive engagement	NSFH; fathers with target child ages 5–18	Blair et al., 1994

Table 5.3 (*Continued*)

Fathers' Socioeconomic Characteristics	Finding	Sample and Comments	Study
Income	No relationship to relative accessibility	1981–83 NLS	Goldscheider & Waite, 1991
	Higher income: less physical care, no relationship to relative accessibility	Dual-earner fathers with children ages 0–10	Haas, 1988
	Higher income: more positive engagement	Black married fathers with children ages 3–5	Ahmeduzzaman & Roopnarine, 1992
	No relationship	Puerto Rican fathers with children ages 3–5 in a Northeastern U.S. city	Roopnarine & Ahmeduzzaman, 1993
Composite social class	No relationship	Men ages 25–45	Gerson, 1993
	Higher composite social class: more play, no relationship to other components	Fathers with newborns, followed to age 5	Grossman et al., 1988
Race/ethnicity	No consistent relationship	Review of five studies prior to 1980	Pleck, 1983
	Black fathers more involved than white fathers	Black and white fathers with preschoolers	McAdoo, 1988
	Black fathers more involved than white fathers	Middle-class black fathers	Allen, 1981
	Black fathers talk more and report more positive engagement with older children, not with younger children	NSFH; fathers with target child ages 0–4, 5–18	Marsiglio, 1991b
	Black fathers show lower relative accessibility	1981–83 NLS	Goldscheider & Waite, 1991
	No differences among Puerto Rican, African American, and Euro-American fathers	Fathers with children ages 3–5; uses PICCI	Roopnarine & Ahmeduzzaman, 1993

tent. However, involvement may vary by occupational category in a more complex fashion, illustrated by Gerson's (1993) report that daily participation in child care is highest among fathers in lower white-collar jobs and professional jobs, and lowest among fathers in blue-collar and middle or high management positions and self-employed fathers. With education controlled, fathers' income per se is positively associated with engagement with older children, but not with their proportional share of child care. (Associations with fathers' employment status, fathers' work hours, family income, and parents' relative income are discussed later.)

Race and Ethnicity

The association of parental involvement with race is also not consistent. However, there is some indication in recent large-scale surveys that, with older children, black fathers show higher engagement than white fathers. However, fathers' relative accessibility is lower among blacks in the National Longitudinal Survey (NLS). In the one available study, Puerto Rican fathers' involvement does not differ from Euro-American fathers'.

Theoretical Implications

Although the associations between paternal involvement and the characteristics considered here are usually not put in a theoretical context, they should be. Any observed differentials in paternal involvement by children's age or gender presumably occur because fathers' motivation or skills for involvement vary according to these characteristics. Socioeconomic status and race may function as proxies for differences in beliefs and background experiences which contribute to motivation and skills for involvement, as well as differences in social supports and in the characteristics of fathers' jobs. Available research has not as yet investigated the extent to which differential paternal involvement by child characteristics and paternal demographic characteristics is mediated by these or other theoretically relevant constructs.

I. MOTIVATION

Motivation is influenced by the individual's developmental history, personality characteristics, and beliefs.

Developmental History: Own Father's Involvement

The aspect of developmental history receiving most attention is the fathering the individual received from his own father. The two opposing hypotheses are that fathers *model* their own fathers' involvement (whether low or high) or *compensate* for their fathers' lack of involvement (however, compensation occurs only if own-fathers' involvement was low). The modeling hypothesis is directly supported by some studies (Haas, 1988; Manion, 1977; Reuter & Biller, 1973; Sagi, 1982), and also by associations between own-fathers' involvement and stability of high paternal involvement over time (Radin, 1994), and fathers' comfort in an active parenting role (Jump & Haas, 1987). The compensation hypothesis is supported by other research (DeFrain, 1979; Eiduson & Alexander, 1978). Compensation is also supported by associations between low own-fathers' involvement and fathers' planning prior to birth to be the primary caretaker (Pruett, 1987), and between high involvement and perceiving low quality in the fathering one received (Barnett & Baruch, 1987). In qualitative studies, most men do not view their own fathers as positive models (though a minority do) and want to be better role models for their own children than their fathers were to them (Daly, 1993; Ehrensaft, 1987). In a few studies, paternal involvement and own-fathers' involvement are unrelated (Gerson, 1993; Radin, 1994), perhaps indicating that both modeling and compensation are occurring in subgroups roughly equal in size.

Future research in this area needs greater theoretical grounding. For example, the results of the considerable research on factors promoting or inhibiting modeling have not been utilized. The son's affective evaluation of his father's involvement is likely to be a key moderator: The son models his father's level of involvement when the son's affective response to it is positive but compensates for it when his response is negative. In addition, own-fathers' level of involvement should be assessed by means other than subjects' retrospective reports, a serious flaw in all existing studies because of the potential for confounding biases. Longitudinal data will hopefully become available in the future that permit even better comparisons. Researchers should also heed Daly's (1993) perceptive observation that fathers, rather than modeling after a single individual, instead have "fragmented models" and select behaviors to incorporate from a variety of others, especially peers.

Developmental History: Fathers' Age, Marital History, and Other Characteristics
The context in which fathers function varies according to their age, marital history, and other developmental history. A few studies, some with age of children controlled, find that older fathers are more engaged with their children (Coltrane, 1990; Haas, 1988), but most find no association (Ahmeduzzaman & Roopnarine, 1992; Cooney, Pederson, Indelicato, & Palkovitz, 1993; Gerson, 1993; Grossman et al., 1988; Marsiglio, 1991b; Robinson, 1977b; Russell, 1983, 1986; Volling & Belsky, 1991), and one study finds paternal age negatively associated with accessibility and responsibility among African American fathers (Ahmeduzzaman & Roopnarine, 1992).

Using a typology combining paternal involvement and affective evaluation of one's paternal role, Cooney et al.'s (1993) analysis of NSFH data observed intriguing differences among men who became fathers "early" (the youngest quartile, at age 23 or younger), "on time" (age 24–29), and "late" (the oldest quartile, age 30 or older). Among early fathers the modal pattern was uninvolved fathering/positive affect. For on-time fathers, the uninvolved/negative pattern was most common. Late fathers showed two modal patterns: involved/positive and involved/negative, with marital satisfaction and work hours most influencing whether fathers' affect was positive or negative. Cooney et al. interpreted these patterns in terms of the extent to which fathers had competing roles and had accumulated psychological resources. These findings suggest fatherhood that is "on time" may actually not be optimal.

Stepfathers show lower levels of engagement than biological fathers (Blair et al., 1994; Marsiglio, 1991b). Fathers say they feel more like a father to their stepchildren if one or more of their biological children also lives with them (Marsiglio, 1992). Growing up in a stepfamily or single-parent family is unrelated to paternal involvement (Goldscheider & Waite, 1991). Interestingly, Goldscheider and Waite report that the strongest predictor of low proportional involvement is living away from one's parents before marriage. If a male lives with other males prior to marriage, this may establish a low baseline for his level of domestic work, and living with a female prior to marriage may do the same.[9] Finally, with hours of work controlled, fathers with disabilities are proportionally more involved with their children (Goldscheider & Waite, 1991).

Developmental History: Early Socialization, Proximal Socialization, and Other Factors

Early and proximal socialization experiences deserve more investigation as determinants of paternal involvement than they have received. Such factors as experience in babysitting or working in youth recreation, caring for younger siblings, and even simply having younger siblings should be investigated. Currently, Gerson's (1993) study provides the only direct evidence that fulfilling experiences in caretaking earlier in life (albeit retrospectively reported) contribute to paternal involvement later. This study also classified men according to whether, as adolescents, they had a breadwinner orientation or a non-breadwinner orientation when they imagined their future lives. Middle-class men were equally likely to be classified as involved fathers later in life whether they initially had a breadwinner orientation (among whom 35% were involved fathers) or a non-breadwinner orientation (36%). But among men from working-class backgrounds, those initially oriented to breadwinning were much less likely to be involved fathers (21%) than were those not oriented to breadwinning (38%). Early socialization may thus be more determinative of later paternal involvement in working-class than in middle-class men.

Paternal involvement and engagement are associated with more proximal socialization experiences such as reading books on child care before and during pregnancy (Russell, 1983, 1986), attending the birth (Russell, 1983, 1986; but see Palkovitz, 1985), "rehearsing" for parenthood (e.g., amount of daydreaming involving being a parent, parental feelings, and reaction to quickening; (Feldman, Nash, & Aschenbrenner, 1983), and taking days off from work immediately after birth (Pleck, 1993). However, these associations may result from selection factors; that is, these experiences and higher involvement later may both result from common predisposing factors.

Evidence that early socialization experiences may have a causal influence is provided by the Six Cultures study (Whiting & Edwards, 1973). In several of the East African societies investigated, although girls are preferred, it is acceptable to assign preadolescent boys responsibility for infant care if there are no female siblings available because they are assisting in farming or are in school. In some of these societies, half or more of the boys age five and over regularly took care of infants. In these societies, gender differences in preadolescent children's behavior are far smaller than in others, suggesting that task assignment is a principal mechanism of gender socialization. A further analysis revealed an even more direct link between boys' providing early infant care and their behavior toward children. Among the Oyugis (western Kenya), by a fluke of sex ratio many households had no girl of appropriate age, so a large number of boys cared for infant siblings. Ember's (1973) analyses within this sample showed that providing infant care, distinct from other domestic chores, was uniquely associated with boys' showing more responsible and prosocial behavior toward other children.

---

9. Although Goldscheider and Waite interpret a parallel finding for women, they do not comment on this finding for males.

Personality Characteristics: Gender-Role Orientation

Many studies concern gender-role orientation, that is, the extent to which individuals report themselves as having masculine (M) and feminine (F) traits, assessed by the Bem Sex Role Inventory (BSRI) and by the Personal Attributes Questionnaire (PAQ; for a review, see Lenney, 1991). Most of this research conceptualizes gender-role orientation as a determinant of involvement, although it expresses cautions about causal inference (Lamb et al., 1987; Lamb, Pleck, & Levine, 1985). Several cross-sectional comparisons find that involved fathers are more likely to be androgynous, that is, high in both M and F (Palkovitz, 1984; Rosenwasser & Patterson, 1984–85), or are higher in F (Russell, 1983, 1986). However, other cross-sectional studies find no associations (DeFrain, 1979; Lamb, Frodi, Hwang, & Frodi, 1982; Levant et al., 1987; Radin, 1994). A small-sample longitudinal analysis, relating fathers' BSRI scores during pregnancy to involvement with the child five years later, also found no relationships (Grossman et al., 1988). One study found that although BSRI dimensions were unrelated to overall involvement, M predicted low physical care and high decision making (Radin, 1994).

Future research should employ longitudinal designs that permit assessment of causal direction. Research should also formulate and test further hypotheses about the types of involvement that are theoretically related to M and the types related to F, as suggested by Radin's (1994) findings. Future studies should also make use of conceptual developments in the construct of gender-role orientation. Some research distinguishes positive and negative forms of both M (i.e., M+, M−) and F (F+, F−), finding they have different correlates (Spence, Helmreich, & Holanan, 1979). For example, adolescent risk behaviors appear associated with the negative but not the positive components of M and F (reviewed in Pleck, Sonenstein, & Ku, 1994b). An obvious hypothesis is that father involvement is a function of positive F, and perhaps of positive M as well. This distinction might also figure in fathers' modeling as opposed to compensating for the involvement of their own fathers. Modeling may occur when the male perceives his own father as high in positive M or F, and compensation if he perceives own father as having negative M or F.

Other Personality Characteristics

Positive paternal engagement is generally associated with self-esteem (Blair et al., 1994; Coysh, 1983; Volling & Belsky, 1991 [at three months in pooled sample, but not other comparisons]; cf. A. J. Hawkins & Belsky, 1989); with overall life adaptation (successful coping with tasks of adulthood concerning work, marriage, freedom from symptoms, and relationship with own parents) during pregnancy (Grossman et al., 1988); with low depression (Blair & Hardesty, 1994); and with parental awareness, a cognitive-developmental construct concerning the maturity of parents' understanding of children and the parent-child relationship (Levant et al., 1987). Findings are inconsisent concerning relationships with empathy (Palkovitz, 1984; Volling & Belsky, 1991). Involvement is unrelated to social desirability response set (Palkovitz, 1984).

Beliefs

In many studies, paternal involvement is higher among men with more egalitarian beliefs about women or about gender roles (Bailey, 1991; Baruch & Barnett, 1981; Blair et al., 1994; Goldscheider & Waite, 1991; Ishii-Kuntz & Coltrane, 1992; Levant et al., 1987). But nearly as many studies fail to confirm the relationship (Crouter, Perry-Jenkins, Huston, & McHale, 1987; Marsiglio, 1991b; McHale & Huston, 1984; Pleck, 1985). The one available study using a measure specifically assessing traditional attitudes toward masculinity finds no association (Barnett & Baruch, 1987; for discussion of the linkages among attitudes toward women, toward gender roles, and toward masculinity, see Pleck, Sonenstein, & Ku, 1994a). Belief that the fathers' role is important in child development is associated with higher paternal involvement (Palkovitz, 1984; but see McBride & Mills, 1993). Lamb et al. (1982) reported that valuing parenting over work was associated with Swedish fathers' prebirth plans to take parental leave, but not with their actual leave-taking behavior.

Paternal "Identity"

Ihinger-Tallman et al. (1993) and others (A. J. Hawkins et al., 1993; Marsiglio, 1991a; Snarey, 1993) have argued that paternal behavior needs to be understood as an expression of paternal identity. Ihinger-Tallman et al. define fathers' "parent-role identity" as the "self-meanings attached to the status and associated roles of parenthood." Hawkins et al. discuss the development and importance of the "fathering self" and the place of fatherhood in adult men's life structure. Also related to paternal identity are "generative fathering" (A. J. Hawkins et al., 1993; Snarey, 1993), and Abidin's (1992) concept of "commitment to the parental role," that is, the beliefs and self-expectations constituting the individual's working model of the "self-as-parent." Recent psychoanalytic literature has also given considerable attention to the concept of paternal identity and factors influencing its development (Cath, Gurwitt, & Ross, 1988).

The construct of paternal identity can be viewed as an integration of the individual's developmental history, personality characteristics, and beliefs related to fathering. Although not using the term identity, Levy-Shiff and Israelashvili's (1988) description of the personality characteristics associated with high paternal involvement in caretaking—being high on sensitivity, perception, and openness to experience, accepting obligations and commitments, and viewing fatherhood as "a self-enriching experience that gratifies psychological and social needs"—seems a summation of generative paternal identity. Baruch and Barnett's (1986a) finding that behaviorally involved fathers rate themselves as highly psychologically involved with their children is also consistent with the identity perspective. Ihinger-Tallman et al. (1993) report significant positive associations between paternal involvement and paternal identity, the latter assessed by a measure encompassing parental role satisfaction, perceived competence, investment, and role salience.

II. SKILLS AND SELF-CONFIDENCE

Fathers' self-perceived competence in interacting with children is associated with their involvement (Baruch & Barnett, 1986a; McHale & Huston, 1984), although Crouter et al. (1987) observed this relationship only among sole-breadwinner fathers. Involvement is also predicted by fathers' holding positive beliefs about men's competence with children (Russell, 1983, 1986) and men's ability to be close to children (Haas, 1988). Fathers' knowledge of development is associated with positive engagement, though not time in routine care (Bailey, 1993). Several interventions to promote parenting skills among fathers have increased involvement (Cowan, 1988; Klinman, 1986; Levant & Doyle, 1983; McBride, 1990).

III. SOCIAL SUPPORTS AND STRESSES

This section focuses on the role of wives and the marital relationship as determinants of paternal involvement; the consequences of paternal involvement for marriage are considered later. Before reviewing marital dynamics per se, the relation of paternal involvement to mothers' employment and other maternal characteristics should be considered.

Maternal Employment Characteristics

As shown in Table 5.4, father's proportional share of total parental involvement is consistently greater when mothers are employed. The more controversial question is whether fathers' absolute level of involvement is also higher. As suggested by the inconsistency in results in Table 5.4, if maternal employment does lead to an increase in fathers' absolute involvement, it is not large, robust, or generalized.

Paternal involvement has no consistent association with the mother's earnings or share of family income, or how she or her husband perceives her job. There is some indication that fathers are more involved if they perceive their wives as having better career prospects than themselves, or if fathers wanted a career-oriented partner. However, involvement is also greater when mothers' occupational status is lower in the one available study. When wives work more hours, fathers' proportional involvement is greater. Results are inconsistent on whether wives' number of hours worked predicts a higher absolute level of paternal involvement in samples restricted to dual-earner families. Whether wives work nonday shifts, have frequent overtime, or have control over their work schedule is generally unrelated to paternal involvement.

Other Maternal Characteristics

As reported in Table 5.5, fathers with older wives are more involved. In half the available studies, fathers are more involved when mothers have more education. Fathers are not more involved when mothers have disabilities, although fathers' own disabilities are associated with greater involvement (Goldscheider & Waite, 1991).

Fathers are more involved when wives currently have positive relationships with their own fathers. There is some evidence that paternal involvement is higher when the mother's father was less involved with her and her mother was employed during the mother's childhood, but it is not consistent. Paternal involvement is higher when mothers hold liberal attitudes toward gender but is unrelated to maternal gender-role orientation. Finally, in a personality-focused longitudinal study (Grossman et al., 1988), the strongest single predictor of low paternal involvement with children at age five was the mother's, during pregnancy, being rated high in autonomy (defined as viewing and valuing the self as distinct from others, based on a clinical interview). Methodologically, however, this association is confounded by the fact that part of the definitional criteria for autonomy was "participating in and enjoying activities carried out alone." If mothers generally prefer doing things alone, low paternal involvement is not surprising.

It has been argued that following divorce, mothers act as "gatekeepers" of fathers' involvement (Ihinger-Tallman et al., 1993). The evidence to date for maternal gate-

Table 5.4   Associations between Paternal Involvement and Mothers'
Employment Characteristics

Mothers' Employment Characteristics	Finding	Sample and Comments	Study
Employment status	Fathers' relative and absolute involvement higher when mother is employed	1977 Quality of Employment Survey	Pleck, 1985
	Fathers' relative involvement higher when mother is employed, absolute involvement not higher	1975–76 Study of Time Use	Pleck, 1985
	No relationship to positive engagement	Fathers with children ages 3–4	Bailey, 1991
	No relationship to positive engagement	NSFH; fathers with target child ages 5–18	Blair et al., 1994
	No relationship to positive engagement	Fathers with children age 1, followed to age 6	Gottfried et al., 1988
	No relationship to positive engagement	Fathers with children age 1, followed to age 12	Gottfried et al., 1994
	Fathers' engagement higher on workdays when mother is employed, no relationship to other components	Dual- and single-earner fathers with children ages 3–5	McBride & Mills, 1993
Absolute earnings, or share of marital earnings	No relationship	1981–83 NLS	Goldscheider & Waite, 1991
	No relationship	Dual-earner fathers with children ages 0–10	Haas, 1988
	No relationship	NSFH; fathers with target child ages 0–4	Ishii-Kuntz & Coltrane, 1992
	No relationship	Dual-earner fathers	Leslie et al., 1991
Occupational prestige	Higher prestige: more play, no relationship to other components	Fathers with newborns, followed to age 5	Grossman et al., 1988
Father perceives mother as having better career prospects than his	Lower involvement	Men ages 25–45	Gerson, 1993
Father wanted career-oriented partner	Higher involvement	Men ages 25–45	Gerson, 1993

Table 5.4 *(Continued)*

Mothers' Employment Characteristics	Finding	Sample and Comments	Study
Father's commitment to mother's career	No relationship	Dual-earner fathers with children ages 0–5	Jump & Haas, 1987
Perceives her employment as "career," "job," or "something in between"	No relationship to responsibility for selecting child-care arrangements	Dual-earner fathers	Leslie et al., 1991
Work hours	More hours: more relative accessibility	1981–83 NLS	Goldscheider & Waite, 1991
	More hours: more relative engagement	NSFH; fathers with target child ages 0–4	Ishii-Kuntz & Coltrane, 1992
	More hours: more relative accessibility in dual-earner fathers, no other relationships	Fathers with kindergartners and fourth-graders	Barnett & Baruch, 1987
	No relationship to responsibility for selecting child-care arrangements	Dual-earner fathers	Leslie et al., 1991
	No relationship to accessibility	1977 Quality of Employment Survey: dual-earner fathers	Pleck & Staines, 1985
	More hours: higher relative accessibility, no relationship to other components	Dual-earner fathers with children ages 0–10	Haas, 1988
	More hours: more responsibility, but not more engagement or accessibility; when mothers' hours increased over time, fathers' accessibility and responsibility increased, but not engagement	Fathers with adolescents	Almeida et al., 1993
Overtime frequency	More overtime: higher proportion of child care	Dual-earner fathers with children ages 0–10	Haas, 1988
Workshift	No relationship	1977 Quality of Employment Survey: dual-earner fathers	Pleck & Staines, 1985
Schedule flexibility	More flexibility: higher relative accessibility, no relationship to other components	Dual-earner fathers with children ages 0–10	Haas, 1988
	No relationship	Dual-earner fathers	Leslie et al., 1991

Table 5.5　Associations between Paternal Involvement and Mothers' Other Characteristics

Mothers' Other Characteristics	Finding	Sample and Comments	Study
Age	Older mother: more relative accessibility	1981–83 NLS	Goldscheider & Waite, 1991
	Older mother: more physical caregiving, less emotional caregiving	Dual-earner fathers with children ages 0–10	Haas, 1988
	Older mother: less positive engagement	Fathers with first-born infants	Feldman et al., 1983
	Older mother: less accessibility and play	Fathers with newborns, followed to age 5	Grossman et al., 1988
Education	No relationship	NSFH; fathers with target child ages 0–4	Ishii-Kuntz & Coltrane, 1992
	No relationship	NSFH; fathers with target child ages 0–4, 5–18	Marsiglio, 1991b
	No relationship	Fathers with kindergartners and fourth-graders	Barnett & Baruch, 1987
	No relationship	Dual-earner fathers with children ages 0–10	Haas, 1988
Disability	No relationship to relative accessibility	1981–83 NLS	Goldscheider & Waite, 1991
Positive relationship with her own father	Positive engagement	Fathers with first-born infants	Feldman et al., 1983
Own father was uninvolved	Less involved in physical care, no relationship to other components	Dual-earner fathers with children ages 0–10	Haas, 1988
	More involved at time 1, more involved at time 2 with daughters only	Fathers with children ages 3–6, followed up 4 yrs and 11 yrs	Radin, 1994
Own mother was employed	More involved	Fathers with children ages 3–6, followed up 4 yrs and 11 yrs	Radin, 1994
	No relationship	Dual-earner fathers with children ages 0–10	Haas, 1988
Believes fathers can do more child care	Positive engagement and accessibility	Dual-earner fathers with children ages 0–10	Haas, 1988
Attitudes toward gender	Liberal attitudes toward women: positive engagement	Fathers with children ages 48–60 months	Baruch & Barnett, 1981
	Liberal attitudes toward women: no relationship	NSFH; fathers with target child ages 0–4	Ishii-Kuntz & Coltrane, 1992

Table 5.5 *(Continued)*

Mothers' Other Characteristics	Finding	Sample and Comments	Study
Attitudes toward gender	Liberal attitudes toward women: no relationship	NSFH; fathers with target child ages 0–4, 5–18	Marsiglio, 1991b
	Liberal views toward masculinity: accessibility	Fathers with kindergartners and fourth-graders	Barnett & Baruch, 1987
	Belief that maternal employment has positive consequences for children: no relationship	Dual-earner fathers with children ages 0–10	Haas, 1988
Believes children benefit from paternal involvement	Fathers have more engagement	Fathers with first-born infants	Palkovitz, 1984
Other personality dispositions	Rated high in autonomy: fathers less involved	Fathers with newborns, followed to age 5	Grossman et al., 1988

keeping in two-parent families is relatively weak and indirect. Paternal involvement is often but not always related to maternal employment characteristics that might lead wives to want greater paternal involvement. Paternal involvement is associated with wives' nontraditional attitudes about gender and wives' positive beliefs about fatherhood. However, this association may result from selection factors.

Marital Dynamics

There is some indication that absolute level of paternal involvement is lower in marriages of longer duration (Blair et al. 1994). However, this factor is positively correlated with the parents' ages, and negatively correlated with the age of the youngest child, variables not controlled in this particular analysis. Higher paternal involvement is predicted by higher husband share of the couples' prenatal division of labor (Coysh, 1983; Volling & Belsky, 1991). The most direct evidence available documenting the facilitating role of wives' support is that fathers' work-family role strain is lower when they perceive greater support from their wives (O'Neil & Greenberger, 1994).

Marital adjustment or satisfaction has sometimes been interpreted as a consequence of level of paternal involvement (e.g., Crouter et al., 1987; Jump & Haas, 1987; Russell, 1983, 1986), but it has more often been considered a source. In cross-sectional studies, high paternal involvement is found to be associated with good marital adjustment (Blair et al., 1994; Jump & Haas, 1987; McBride & Mills, 1993) about as often as with poor marital adjustment (Crouter et al., 1987; Gerson, 1993; Russell, 1983, 1986). Negative associations are found more often when the marital measures used concern frequency of conflict or disagreement rather than global measures of marital adjustment. Crouter et al.'s study suggests the negative association may be restricted to or at least stronger in dual-earner families.

However, in longitudinal studies investigating marital adjustment as a source of paternal involvement, the association is more consistently positive. These studies include research relating prenatal level of marital adjustment to paternal involvement in the first year (Coysh, 1983; Feldman et al., 1983; Levy-Shiff & Israelashvili, 1988; but see Grossman et al., 1988) as well as studies explicitly relating the degree and direction of change over time in marital adjustment to change in involvement (Volling & Belsky, 1991). When marriages deteriorate in quality, paternal interaction also becomes more negative and intrusive (Belsky, Youngblood, Rovine, & Volling, 1991; Brody, Pillegrini, & Sigel, 1986). There is some evidence that mothers, by contrast, become more involved with children when marriage deteriorates, in a more compensatory process (Belsky et al., 1991).

Overall, greater father involvement may indeed be associated with more frequent disagreements and conflicts. If both parents are actively involved, differences in child-rearing styles may be more of an issue and mishaps in communication and arrangements may occur more frequently. Nonetheless, high paternal involvement appears far more often grounded in good marital relationships than in poor ones. (See Cummings & O'Reilly, Chapter 4 of this volume, for a review of the impact of marital quality on child adjustment.)

Other Social Supports and Stresses

Social supports for involved fatherhood from outside the marital relationship appear to be weak. In contrast to women's social networks, men's networks provide them with less encouragement and fewer resources relevant to child care (Lein, 1979). Involved fathers may encounter hostility from acquaintances, relatives, and workmates (Hwang, Elden, & Frannson, 1984; Russell, 1983, 1986). Social-psychological studies also provide some evidence of negative attitudes toward men who are involved with children in other than stereotyped ways (Raine & Draper, 1994).

In investigations of the association between paternal involvement and social supports, Roopnarine and associates (Ahmeduzzaman & Roopnarine, 1992; Roopnarine & Ahmeduzzaman, 1993; Tulananda et al., 1994) examine frequency of communication around child issues with kin, extrafamilial individuals, and institutions among African American, Puerto Rican, Euro-American, and Thai fathers. In the African American sample, extrafamilial communication was positively correlated with positive engagement and negatively correlated with accessibility. This pattern may indicate that engaged fathers seek out supportive communication with nonkin individuals, which in turn reinforces their engagement. But in addition, nonkin individuals may provide care, which substitutes for fathers' accessibility.

Family economic distress may be associated with increased quantity, though not quality, of paternal involvement (Harold-Goldsmith et al., 1988; McLoyd, 1989). Low family income per se appears unrelated (Haas, 1988; Ishii-Kuntz & Coltrane, 1992; Volling & Belsky, 1991). General level of parental stress is also unrelated to paternal involvement (McBride & Mills, 1993). Stress may be less important as a predictor of paternal involvement than as a moderator of its effects, as suggested by Almeida and Galambos's (1991) finding that increasing involvement with adolescents is associated with more frequent father-adolescent conflicts among stressed fathers, but with less frequent conflicts among nonstressed fathers.

IV. INSTITUTIONAL FACTORS AND PRACTICES

The institution impacting on fathers' involvement to receive most attention is the workplace. Relevant here is research on characteristics of fathers' employment, fathers' levels of work-family conflict, desire for supportive workplace policies, and their actual use of workplace policies.

Fathers' Employment Characteristics

As indicated in Table 5.6, unemployed fathers have been overrepresented in studies of primary caretaking fathers and spend more time with their children. However, while higher in quantity, it is not necessarily higher in quality. Fathers' number of hours worked is, perhaps surprisingly, not significantly related to their involvement, in the majority of studies. Negative associations are found only for accessibility and for more discretionary forms of engagement such as reading and leisure activities. Fathers who work on weekend days report lower accessibility, but involvement is generally unrelated to other specific schedule characteristics. Fathers' degree of control over their schedule is not consistently associated with greater involvement in cross-sectional analyses, but it is in experimental studies comparing fathers before and after the introduction of flextime (see below). Fathers are more involved if they have "fluid employment trajectories" (Gerson, 1993) and if they view the breadwinner obligation as being shared with their wives (Haas, 1988). Associations of involvement to job satisfaction and job commitment are inconsistent.

Fathers' Work-Family Conflicts and Desire for Family-Supportive Policies

The extent to which fathers experience work-family conflict and want more family-supportive policies from their own employers are other indicators of the degree to which workplace factors limit paternal involvement. Table 5.7 indicates that substantial proportions of working fathers report stress in combining work and family roles, or say they are interested in using specific policies to reduce this stress, and in some surveys, men's levels equal or exceed women's. Men's interest in using specific policies to reduce work-family stress is also increasing.

Effects of Workplace Policies and Practices

The most direct evidence on the extent to which workplace policies and practices limit paternal involvement concerns the empirical links between involvement and these policies and practices. Work-family supports, assessed by items concerning the degree to which the workplace and coworkers provide a supportive environment for parenting and family responsibilities, are associated with higher engagement (Volling & Belsky, 1991). About the same proportion of fathers as mothers change their schedules when flextime is introduced (Winett & Neale, 1980), and those who change their schedules spend more time with their children (Lee, 1983; Winett & Neale, 1980). Another alternative work schedule, the four-day (compressed) work week, also fosters greater paternal involvement (Maklan, 1977).

Few U.S. fathers take advantage of formal parental leave policies, although utilization is increasing. Enough fathers have wanted formal paternity leave that a substantial body of case and administrative law has established fathers' entitlement to child-

Table 5.6   Associations between Paternal Involvement and Fathers'
Employment Characteristics

Fathers' Employment Characteristics	Finding	Sample and Comments	Study
Employment status	Unemployed: increased involvement	Dual- and single-earner fathers with infants	Pruett, 1987
	Unemployed: increased involvement	Fathers with children ages 0–10	Russell, 1983, 1986
	Unemployment: increased quantity of caretaking, but not necessarily increase in quality	Fathers with preschool and kindergarten children	Harold-Goldsmith et al., 1988
	No relationship	NSFH; fathers with target child ages 0–4	Blair et al., 1994
	No relationship	NSFH; fathers with target child ages 0–4, 5–18	Marsiglio, 1991b
Work hours	More hours: less reading and leisure activities, no relationship to other activities	NSFH	Marsiglio, 1991b
	No relationship	1981–83 NLS	Goldscheider & Waite, 1991
	More hours: less relative accessibility	NSFH; fathers with target child ages 0–4	Ishii-Kuntz & Coltrane, 1992
	No relationship	Dual-earner fathers with children ages 0–10	Haas, 1988
	More hours: less accessibility	1977 Quality of Employment Survey: employed fathers	Pleck, 1985
	No relationship	1977 Quality of Employment Survey: dual-earner fathers	Pleck & Staines, 1985
	No relationship	1975–76 Study of Time Use	Pleck, 1985
	More hours: less time spent in leisure activities only	Dual- and single-earners with children ages 1–1.5	Crouter et al., 1987
	No relationship with responsibility for choosing child-care arrangements	Dual-earner fathers	Leslie et al., 1991
"Fluid employment trajectories"	Increased involvement	Men ages 25–45	Gerson, 1993
View breadwinner obligation as shared with mother	More involvement	Dual-earner fathers with children ages 0–10	Haas, 1988

Table 5.6   (*Continued*)

Fathers' Employment Characteristics	Finding	Sample and Comments	Study
Work weekend days regularly	No relationship	1977 Quality of Employment Survey: dual-earner fathers	Pleck & Staines, 1985
Work nonstandard shift or second job	No relationship	1977 Quality of Employment Survey: dual-earner fathers	Pleck & Staines, 1985
Work afternoon shift and have control over shift	More accessibility	1977 Quality of Employment Survey: dual-earner fathers	Staines & Pleck, 1986
Degree of control over work schedule	No relationship	Dual-earner fathers with children ages 0–10	Haas, 1988
	No relationship	1977 Quality of Employment Survey: dual-earner fathers	Staines & Pleck, 1983
	More control: more involvement	Fathers ages 25–45	Gerson, 1993
	No relationship	Fathers in federal agencies with or without flextime (cross-sectional comparison)	Bohen & Viveros-Long, 1981
	More control: more involvement	British fathers, before and after introduction of flextime	Lee, 1983
	More control: more accessibility	Fathers, before and after introduction of flextime	Winett & Neale, 1980
Job satisfaction	Higher job satisfaction: lower accessibility	Fathers with newborns, followed to age 5	Grossman et al., 1988
	No relationship	Dual-earner fathers with children ages 0–10	Haas, 1988
Psychological investment in job	High involvement: less play, less weekday accessibility	Fathers with first-born infants	Feldman et al., 1983
	No relationship	Fathers with newborns, followed to age 5	Grossman et al., 1988

care leave when employers provide it to mothers (Pleck, 1993).[10] Other data indicate that most fathers take short, "informal" parental leaves using vacation, sick days, and other discretionary time off (Pleck, 1993). Estimates of the proportions taking informal leave range from 75% to 91%, and the length averages five days (Bond, Galinsky, Lord, Staines, & Brown, 1991; Essex & Klein, 1991; Hyde, Essex, & Horton, 1993;

10. For recent reviews of fathers' usage of parental leave in Sweden, see Haas (1992, 1993) and Pleck (1993).

Table 5.7 Fathers' Work-Family Conflicts and Desire for Family Support Policies

Variable	Finding	Sample and Comment	Study
Stress in combining work and family roles	36% fathers reported "a lot of stress" in balancing work and family; 37% mothers	1,600 employees in a public utility and high-tech company in the Northeast	Trost, 1988
	72% fathers reported difficulties with child care; 65% mothers	1,200 employees in a Minneapolis company	Trost, 1988
	70% fathers reported general "dual-career problem;" 63% mothers	1,200 employees in a Minneapolis company	Trost, 1988
	34.4% dual-earner fathers report "some" or "a lot" of work-family conflict; 40.5% single-earner fathers report "some" or "a lot" of work-family conflict; 44.1% dual-earner mothers report "some" or "a lot" of work-family conflict	1978 Quality of Employment Survey	Pleck et al., 1988
	Fathers' reports of stress are substantial but less frequent than mothers	3,566 employees in 33 companies in Portland	Regional Research Institute for Human Services, 1987
Lateness and missing work	Fathers miss work or are late more often than nonfathers	32,000 employees in 103 companies in 5 cities	Emlen, 1987
Hostility from supervisors and coworkers	Involved fathers may encounter hostility	Swedish fathers	Hwang et al., 1984
	Involved fathers may encounter hostility	Fathers with children ages 0–10	Russell, 1983, 1986
	Greater for fathers than mothers	Dual- and single-earner husbands	Bolger et al., 1989
Miss work if child-care arrangements break down	Fathers less likely than mothers	495 fathers and mothers in 8 organizations	Shinn et al., 1987
Negative consequences of work-family conflicts	Missing work when child-care arrangements break down is more strongly associated with stress, poor health, and diminished well-being in fathers than in mothers	495 fathers and mothers in 8 organizations	Shinn et al., 1987
Interest in policies to reduce work-family stress	1985: 18% fathers wanted option of part-time work to be with their children; 1988: 33% wanted this option	Large sample of Dupont employees	Thomas, 1988

Table 5.7   (*Continued*)

Variable	Finding	Sample and Comment	Study
Interest in policies to reduce work-family stress	1986: 15% of fathers interested in parental leave plan for newborns; 1991: 35% wanted this option	Large sample of Dupont employees	"Labor Letter," 1991
	1986: 40% of fathers interested in parental leave plan for sick children; 1991: 64% wanted this option	Large sample of Dupont employees	"Labor Letter," 1991

Pleck, 1993). The liberality of the employer's leave policy is a significant predictor of how many days fathers take off (Hyde et al., 1993). The more days taken off from work, the more involved they are with their child later on (Hwang, 1987; Lamb et al., 1988; Pleck, 1993). These associations do not necessarily show that taking time off from work at birth causes higher levels of later paternal involvement, since both might result from common selection factors in the father or family situation. However, these associations do suggest that the availability of parental leave, formal or informal, supports paternal involvement.

OVERVIEW

As Lamb, Pleck, Charnov, and Levine's (1985) four-factor model indicates, paternal involvement is multiply determined. No single predictor exerts a predominant influence. Further, hardly any predictor is significantly associated with paternal involvement in all available studies, suggesting that associations with involvement of even the most consistent variables may vary in different contexts. Variables associated with paternal involvement may act together additively, paralleling the concept of cumulative risk in the study of risk outcomes. That is, the presence or absence of a particular factor may be less important than the cumulative number of predisposing characteristics.

Factors promoting father involvement may also operate interactively. Indeed, part of Lamb et al.'s original formulation was the notion that the four factors exert influence in a specific sequence. For skills, self-confidence, and social supports to predict involvement, motivation has to be present. Likewise, for institutional practices to be a limiting factor, the three prior factors need to be in place. This part of Lamb et al.'s conceptualization provides a way of understanding why most fathers do not seek out fatherhood education programs (motivation for greater involvement is low) but fathers who enroll appear to increase their involvement (among the motivated, skills may be a limiting factor). Most fathers of newborns do not take formal paternity leaves (suggesting that for most, at least the job expectation of continuing work after birth is not a limiting factor). At the same time, a small minority have struggled to obtain formal leave at considerable personal cost (among the subgroup with motivation, skills, and other supports, workplace demands are indeed a barrier).

In a related vein, Ihinger-Tallman et al. (1993) postulate eight factors moderating the relationship between paternal identity and actual involvement, such as mother's preferences and beliefs, father's economic well-being and employment stability, and so forth. If paternal identity is interpreted as a motivational factor, then Ihinger-Tallman et al.'s predictions overlap Lamb et al.'s. In a partial test of Lamb et al.'s notion, Haas (1988) hypothesized that workplace factors have stronger associations with paternal involvement among fathers with positive attitudes toward involvement than among those with negative attitudes. Haas's analysis did not support the hypothesis, however.

Mothers' employment status has received particular attention as a potential moderator of factors influencing paternal involvement. Several studies find support for the notion that single-earner and dual-earner families are different ecological contexts for paternal involvement, with father involvement more a function of his personality in the former, but more a function of structural factors in the latter (Barnett & Baruch, 1987; Crouter et al., 1987; Volling & Belsky, 1991). However, their results regarding the specific personality or structural factors related to involvement in the two kinds of families are not consistent. This may indicate that there may also be further ecological differences within samples of single-earner families, and of dual-earner families. Future research should explore further how factors associated with paternal involvement may act as cumulative predisposing factors, how they may interact with each other, and how their influence varies in different ecological contexts.

CONSEQUENCES OF PATERNAL INVOLVEMENT

CONSEQUENCES FOR CHILDREN

At the outset, the consequences of paternal involvement need to be distinguished from the effects of other paternal characteristics (Lamb, Pleck, & Levine, 1985). Earlier reviews have focused on child outcomes associated with paternal warmth, masculinity, socialization practices, and relationship characteristics (Biller, 1981; Hoffman, 1981; Radin, 1981), topics not covered here. The effects demonstrated suggest that even when fathers are relatively uninvolved, their characteristics have an impact on their children.

Most research on the consequences of paternal involvement focuses on direct effects (i.e., father to child). However, because paternal and maternal behavior can influence each other (Belsky, 1981; Belsky & Volling, 1987; Dickie, 1987; Parke & Anderson, 1987), paternal involvement can also influence the child indirectly by virtue of its effects on mothers. Paternal involvement can also have indirect effects through its impact on sibling relationships, as in Volling and Belsky's (1992) finding that facilitative and affectionate fathering is associated with prosocial sibling interaction. Father involvement also influences children's peer relationships, thus affecting developmental outcomes through yet another pathway (MacDonald & Parke, 1984).

Earlier reviews suggested that direct effects of quantity of paternal involvement on infant attachment are minimal because fathers' style of interaction is more influential for this outcome (Lamb, 1987; Lamb, Chapter 6 of this volume; Lamb, Pleck, Charnov, & Levine, 1985). For other early childhood outcomes, preschool children of substantially engaged and accessible fathers (i.e., performing 40% or more of the within-family child care) show more cognitive competence, more internal locus of control, more empathy, and less gender-role stereotyping (Lamb, 1987; Radin, 1994). Other studies confirm positive associations between these outcomes and involvement, especially positive engagement.

For example, degree of positive paternal engagement in the month following birth has an independent association with infants' cognitive functioning at one year (Nugent, 1991). A factor probably contributing to this effect is that fathers who are more engaged perceive their infants as more cognitively competent (Ninio & Rinott, 1988). Gottfried, Gottfried, and Bathurst (1988) report significant relationships between positive father engagement and WISC IQ, academic achievement, and social maturity at ages six and seven, including some associations between engagement at age six and these outcomes assessed a year later. Positive paternal engagement is significantly related to a cluster of outcomes including self-control, self-esteem, life skills, and social competence in both elementary-age children and adolescents (Amato, 1987). Positive paternal involvement or engagement is also associated with less gender stereotyping in children (Carlson, 1984; but cf. Baruch & Barnett, 1986b). Adolescents with positively involved fathers at ages 3–5 and ages 7–9 hold less traditional views as adolescents about dual-earner couples and about parents sharing child care (Williams, Radin, & Allegro, 1992).

An important recent analysis uses data from the NSFH to assess the association between positive paternal engagement and outcomes in children aged 5–18 in two-parent families, with positive maternal engagement, parental control, and race and sociodemographic background controlled (Mosley & Thomson, 1995). For both boys and girls, high positive paternal engagement is significantly associated with lower frequency of externalizing and internalizing symptoms, and higher sociability (getting along with others, carrying out responsibilities, and doing what parents ask). In addition, high positive engagement predicted in boys fewer school behavior problems, and in girls more self-direction (is willing to try new things, keeps self busy, is cheerful and happy). The inclusion of level of positive maternal engagement as a control variable is especially valuable since the results therefore establish that father engagement is associated with children's well-being net of any effect for mothers' engagement, which cannot be said for most studies showing positive correlates for positively engaged fathering. However, the effects of positive paternal engagement are smaller in magnitude than those of race and poverty.

Another finding is particularly relevant to recent arguments that the kind of increased paternal involvement needed today is only its more traditional forms, emphasizing authority and limit setting (Blankenhorn, 1995). For boys, high parental control was associated with more problems (school behavior, externalizing, and internalizing) and lower sociability and initiative. The effect on school problems was significantly greater among boys from poor familes[11] (see also Amato, 1987). Parental control could be a response rather than a cause of the school behavior and externalizing problems. But this interpretation seems less plausible since high parental control is also associated with child outcomes that do not ordinarily elicit parental control efforts (internalizing problems, less sociability, and less self-direction).

Two other recent analyses from long-term longitudinal studies further confirm the

---

11. Unlike the engagement variable, the measure of control was available only for the parents combined.

positive consequences of paternal involvement. Koestner, Franz, and Weinberger (1990) investigated determinants of empathic concern for others, based on adjective self-ratings, at age 31, using a sample first studied by Sears, Maccoby, and Levin (1957). Among eight dimensions of maternal behavior and three dimensions of paternal behavior at age five, and with gender controlled, the strongest predictor of empathic concern in both men and women was high level of paternal child care, accounting for more variance (13%) than the three strongest maternal predictors combined. Snarey (1993), studying fathers drawn from a sample initiated in the 1940s (Glueck & Glueck, 1950), coded degree of active engagement in their children's intellectual development, social development, and physical development during childhood and during adolescence, in the 1950s and 1960s. With other factors controlled, positive paternal engagement explained 11%–16% of the variance in daughters' and sons' educational mobility relative to their parents, and 6%–13% of their occupational mobility, assessed when the children were in their 20s.

Finally, in addition to child and adolescent outcomes, paternal involvement also influences the quality of father-child relationships. In a short-term longitudinal study focusing on the father-adolescent relationship, more accessible fathers are more accepting of their adolescents, and involvement predicts increasing acceptance over time as reported both by the father and the adolescent (Almeida & Galambos, 1991).[12] As noted earlier, the effects of paternal involvement also varied according to fathers' level of stress: Among stressed fathers, increasing level of involvement with adolescents is associated with more frequent father-adolescent conflicts, but among non-stressed fathers, with less frequent conflicts.

CONSEQUENCES FOR MOTHERS AND FOR MARRIAGE

There is great interest in the long-term effects of greater paternal involvement on women's labor force success, but solid evidence is currently unavailable. Such analyses will become possible, however, as national data sets such as the NSFH that include assessments of paternal involvement collect later waves of data. Baruch and Barnett (1986a) concluded from a cross-sectional association that greater father involvement leads to lower overall life satisfaction in mothers. However, the alternative interpretation is that fathers' greater involvement is a response to mothers' low life satisfaction, which, like depression, impedes effective parenting. Little other evidence is available concerning effects of paternal involvement on mothers' well-being.

Marital satisfaction or adjustment has been viewed as both a source and consequence of paternal involvement, as noted previously. In the cross-sectional research reviewed earlier, the association between fathers' involvement and measures of marital adjustment is positive about a often as it is negative, with negative associations more common when the marital measures concern frequency of conflict rather than global evaluation of quality of marriage. Several analyses provide detail about the perceptions on fathers' and mothers' parts that may be grounds for conflict.

Regarding fathers' perceptions of mothers, fathers in one cross-sectional study who were more involved expressed more dissatisfaction with their wives' amount of time

---

12. Although more frequent and intense father-adolescent conflicts as reported by the father were also associated with great paternal involvement, this association was not corroborated in the adolescent data.

with the child, work schedule, and overall time allocation. Wives of more involved husbands were aware that their husbands had higher dissatisfaction but were not more dissatisfied with themselves in these regards (Baruch & Barnett, 1986a). In Haas's (1988) study in dual-earner couples, fathers may also be more involved because they are concerned that mothers' employment could have negative effects on the children. Since the wives of involved fathers in the same study more often thought that maternal employment benefited children, conflicts would not be surprising. However, these conflicts should be interpreted as a result of differing perceptions of the wives' employment, not of paternal involvement. Baruch and Barnett (1986a) concluded that greater father involvement leads fathers to view their wives as less competent parents. However, the association could reflect causality in the opposite direction: Fathers are more involved because their wives are less competent. Nonetheless, even if paternal involvement is a cause rather than a result of perceiving low maternal competence, it is not surprising that father involvement in this context could be associated with marital conflict.

Concerning mothers' perceptions of fathers, in one study wives reported being more satisfied with fathers' amount of time with the children when fathers were more involved, but the fathers themselves perceived their wives as being more dissatisfied with them (Baruch & Barnett, 1986a). Another study found that wives of more involved fathers were actually more likely to think their husbands should do more (Haas, 1988). These discrepancies may indicate that fathers have difficulty perceiving accurately their wives' view of them or that wives may have difficulty communicating it. Alternatively, more involved fathers may face, or at least think they face, a "revolution of rising expectations" from their spouses.

Some longitudinal research suggests that fathers' self-perceived competence and satisfaction in their paternal role has positive consequences for marriage (see review in Snarey, 1993). The evidence concerning consequences of positive paternal involvement, though limited, is positive. In Snarey's (1993) study, offering positive paternal engagement during childhood accounted for 12% of the variance in fathers' marital success at midlife (coded as divorced, still married with unclear enjoyment, or still married with clear enjoyment) with the first wife, who was the mother of the children with whom the father's involvement was assessed. Paternal engagement during adolescence contributed an additional 9%, with sociodemographic factors controlled.

In the short run, Russell's conclusion (1983, 1986) that increased paternal involvement entails both costs as well as benefits for marriage seems judicious. Snarey's evidence suggests optimism concerning longer-run effects on marriage, and therefore for mothers and fathers. Of course, this optimism must be cautious since finding about the consequences of paternal involvement in the 1950s and 1960s on marital outcomes in the 1970s are not necessarily generalizable to the present.

CONSEQUENCES FOR FATHERS

As with impact on marriage, other dimensions of fathering beside involvement potentially influence fathers' well-being. For example, in fathers of preschoolers, work-family role strain is lowest when their pattern of role commitments entails low work commitment and high parental commitment (Greenberger & O'Neil, 1990). With job role quality and marital role quality controlled, fathers' parental-role quality is a significant predictor of psychological distress (Barnett, Marshall, & Pleck, 1992). In longitudinal analyses, paternal competence and satisfaction is associated with positive effects on fathers' development and community participation (Heath, 1978, 1991).

Available evidence about the cross-sectional associations of involvement with paternal personality, attitudes, and several dimensions of self-perceptions was summarized in a previous section. Most of the relationships found could be interpreted alternatively as effects of paternal involvement on fathers. Indeed, one study of paternal engagement and depression argued that low engagement leads to depression (Blair & Hardesty, 1994). While it seems more parsimonious that depression leads to low paternal engagement, bidirectional influence is possible in this relationship as well as in relationships with gender-role orientation, self-esteem, empathy, gender-role attitudes, attitudes toward fathering, paternal identity, parenting skills, and self-perceived parental competence. When associations are found with self-esteem, empathy, parenting skills, and competence, they are positive, suggesting that high involvement is associated with desirable outcomes. However, these relationships are not found consistently, indicating that linkages to positive outcomes do not occur in all contexts.

Other cross-sectional analyses focus on role conflict and satisfaction. More involved fathers feel they lack time for their careers and that their family responsibilities interfere with their work, but they also feel less strain in their family role performance (Baruch & Barnett, 1986a). In dual-earner families, more involved fathers experience more work-family stress, although in single-earner families they report less stress (Volling & Belsky, 1991). Also in dual-earner families, more accessible fathers are more likely to feel bothered about their having a nontraditional role (Jump & Haas, 1987). The negative perceptions associated with high involvement seem more likely to be results rather than causes. For the finding involving single-earner fathers, however, causality may be reversed: In this group low work-family stress may facilitate high involvement. In spite of these perceived stresses and conflicts, however, more accessible fathers do not report being less satisfied with their parental role overall (Jump & Haas, 1987). One interpretation is that although high involvement entails the costs just noted, fathers experience compensating benefits.

Two longitudinal studies provide evidence about short-term and long-term consequences on men's well-being. Of the voluminous research literature on the transition to parenthood, only A. J. Hawkins and Belsky (1989) examine postnatal outcomes as a function of fathers' degree of participation in infant care. In this study, fathers of boys generally declined in self-esteem over the transition while fathers of girls increased in self-esteem. Fathers showed the opposite pattern on a measure of empathy. Additionally, the more involved fathers were with children of either gender, the more they declined in self-esteem. One possible interpretation of the decline in self-esteem among fathers of boys is that boys are more difficult to care for, and fathers of boys are more involved with them. Although achieving the status of fatherhood has an overall positive effect, the difficulties fathers experience caring for boys lower self-esteem to a great degree. Another interpretation was that since the self-esteem measure was highly correlated with traditional masculine traits, fathers of sons are demonstrating "nontraditional development for men [i.e., decrease in masculinity, increase in femininity] and the influence of gender-linked father involvement on this development," which Hawkins and Belsky view as beneficial (p. 381).

In addition to the marital and child outcomes discussed earlier, Snarey's (1993) analysis examined the long-term effects of positive paternal engagement on fathers' occupational mobility and their "societal generativity" assessed at midlife. Positive engagement during childhood and during adolescence was positively related to fathers' occupational mobility, accounting for 6% of the variance with other factors controlled. Thus, rather than impeding men's career progress, greater involvement actually fostered it. Societal generativity, coded from intensive interview data, assessed the extent to which subjects "demonstrated a clear capacity for establishing, guiding, or caring for the next generation through sustained reponsibility for the growth, well-being, or leadership of younger adults or of the larger society," but explicitly excluding his own children (p. 98). With level of psychosocial development prior to parenthood and other factors controlled, positive paternal engagement, particularly supporting the child's socioemotional development, explained 14% of the variance in men's midlife generativity. Another study also finds that generativity is linked specifically to fathers' positive social engagement, not to their routine care (Bailey, 1992).

Overall, higher paternal involvement exacts some costs for fathers in the short run in terms of increased levels of work-family conflict (in dual-earner couples) and decreased self-esteem as traditionally assessed. These costs do not appear to reduce overall satisfaction with parenthood, however. Limited longitudinal evidence suggests that in the long term, high involvement has a modest positive impact on career success and a greater positive effect on at least one personality outcome, fathers' societal generativity. These data are consistent with A. J. Hawkins et al.'s (1993) and Snarey's (1993) argument that although fathers who become highly involved may experience significant disequilibrium and stress in the short run, these experiences stimulate them ultimately to achieve higher levels of functioning.

CONCLUSIONS

Several conclusions appear warranted from the research conducted since Lamb, Pleck, Charnov, and Levine (1985) proposed the construct of paternal involvement. Further evidence has accumulated that paternal involvement has increased over the last three decades, both in proportional and absolute terms. Fathers' level of engagement in recent studies averages somewhat over two-fifths of mothers compared to one-third in the research reviewed a decade ago by Lamb et al., and accessiblity averages about two-thirds compared to one-half in the earlier review. In absolute terms, the best available current estimate for paternal engagement time with young children is 1.9 hours for weekdays, and 6.5 hours for Sundays. Accessiblity estimates for fathers of young children range from 2.8 to 4.9 hours/day (9.8 hours/day for Sundays).

Progress has been made in exploring the courses of paternal involvement. Nonetheless, several important categories of potential influences have received remarkably little attention. Research on skills and self-confidence as facilitating factors is especially thin. Childhood and adolescent experiences as well as experiences more proximal to parenthood promoting paternal motivation, skills, and self-confidence need far more study than they have received. Most studies exploring attitudinal influences employ general-purpose measures of attitudes about gender, rather than attitudes focusing more specifically on masculinity and fatherhood. Indeed, the salient dimensions of fathering-related attitudes and how attitudes toward fathering and masculinity intersect are not well understood. While there has been significant progress in the last decade in understanding how fathers' marriage and fathers' workplaces act as contexts for paternal involvement, research now needs to move to the next level of conceptualization of the role these two environments play in fathering. Paternal identity as an overarching construct needs further development. How paternal involvement is embedded in fathers' own adult and life course development is still largely unexplored terrain.

Lamb et al.'s model specifying motivation, skills and self-confidence, social supports, and institutional practices as the key facilitating factors for paternal involvement continues to be useful. At the same time, research on fatherhood should also make use of the more general models of parenthood and parental behavior that have emerged, as well as more developmental frameworks for fathering. Studies should move beyond examining only the associations of individual predictors with involvement, giving more attention to ways in which predisposing factors may have a cumulative or interactive influence. In such investigations, it is unlikely that one overall model will be consistently validated. Rather, the specific factors that act cumulatively or interactively to influence paternal involvement probably vary, perhaps substantially, in different ecological contexts.

The development most affecting the study of both sources and consequences is the tacit shift in measurement noted throughout this chapter from paternal involvement per se to positive paternal involvement. The research Lamb et al. cited in formulating the construct assessed involvement in purely quantitative way, in particular via time diary and other time use measures. As research has evolved, however, the content and quality of the involvement have gradually become incorporated in the measures. Since most measures used currently incorporate a substantial component of positive content, they actually assess positive paternal involvement. These measures tap the dimension of paternal behavior that actually should be of primary interest. Positive paternal involvement means high engagement, accessibility, and responsibility with positive engagement behaviors and stylistic characteristics. In essence, positive involvement means not just "going through the motions" of fatherhood. Positive paternal involvement may be the essence of what A. J. Hawkins et al. (1993) conceptualize as "generative fathering."

Evidence has continued to accumulate, including some from longitudinal research, that positive paternal engagement is associated with desirable outcomes in children, adolescents, and young adults. Several important new studies report evidence that positive paternal engagement promotes psychosocial development in fathers themselves. Research on consequences is weakest concerning effects on marriage and on mothers. Some headway has been made in understanding how paternal involvement is embedded in marital relationships, with marital quality being a source and consequence of involvement in a simultaneous and complex fashion, but much remains unknown.

Finally, considering the research conducted on consequences as a whole, there is an implied hypothesis that the different components of paternal involvement benefit different parties. The research available seems to test the notion that positive engagement has benefits for children and fathers, while paternal accessibility and respon-sibility offers potential benefits to mothers, perhaps primarily employed mothers. Of course, direct positive effects on some parties may lead to indirect benefits for others. This general hypothesis needs to be tested more explicitly. Currently, the PICCI and the measures used in many other studies assess multiple dimensions of involvement but do not permit researchers to explore differential correlates.

CHAPTER 6

The Development of Father-Infant Relationships

Michael E. Lamb

National Institute of Child Health and Human Development

S INCE 1970 there has been considerable research on the development of father-infant relationships. It is widely recognized today that most infants develop within complex social systems, even though researchers have continuing difficulty studying and conceptualizing the multidirectional influences involved. In addition, most of the research has been concerned with the behavior and impact of fathers in traditional families, wherein mothers stay home with their infants while fathers are the families' sole economic providers. Such families are increasingly unrepresentative, however, and this restricts the generalizability of the research, as does the common focus on affluent Euro-American families in the United States.

When research on human father-infant relationships first began, researchers sought to determine whether (and when) most infants formed relationships with their fathers. Having shown that most infants indeed became attached to their fathers, investigators then attempted to define the similarities and differences between mother- and father-infant relationships, both directly, and via the impact of these relationships on maternal behavior. At about the same time, two other issues became popular: describing paternal behavior and assessing the formative significance of father-infant relationships. Clearly, the concerns of researchers have become broader and more inclusive over the years, and each of these issues is addressed in this chapter, although not in the order in which each achieved prominence. Instead, I start with the research on paternal responsiveness or sensitivity, particularly to very young infants. I then consider the development of father-infant attachments, evaluating the proposition that there is a preference hierarchy among attachment figures in which mothers typically are preferred over fathers. In the third section, I describe research on the differences and similarities between maternal and paternal behavior. Paternal influences on devel-

I am grateful to Kimberly Monroe and Katie Britten for assistance in the preparation of this chapter.

opment are considered in the fourth and patterns of indirect effects in the final substantive section.

PATERNAL SENSITIVITY

Sensitivity or responsiveness to infant signals is a topic that has been of interest to developmental psychologists for many decades, although the concept has been operationalized in many different ways. Perhaps the most useful formulation is that of the ethological attachment theorists (Ainsworth, 1973; Bowlby, 1969; Lamb & Easterbrooks, 1981; Lamb & Gilbride, 1985; Lamb, Thompson, Gardner, & Charnov, 1985) who propose that infants are biologically predisposed to emit signals (e.g., cries and smiles) to which adults are biologically predisposed to respond. When adults consistently respond promptly and appropriately to infant signals, infants come to perceive them as predictable and reliable. This perception fosters the formation of secure infant-parent attachments (Ainsworth, Blehar, Waters, & Wall, 1978; Lamb, 1981; Lamb et al., 1985), whereas insecure attachments may result when adults do not respond sensitively. When they respond rarely, no attachments may develop at all. Determining whether fathers are appropriately responsive to their infants is thus of crucial importance.

After observing parents in a waiting room containing an infant and its mother, Feldman and Nash (1977, 1978; Feldman, Nash, & Cutrona, 1977; Nash & Feldman, 1981) concluded that sex differences in "baby responsiveness" waxed and waned depending on the subject's age and social status and were not determined by innate gender differences. Females were more responsive than males in early adolescence and in early parenthood, whereas there were no sex differences among eight-year-olds, childless couples, and unmarried college students. By contrast, no sex differences in responsiveness to infants were evident when Frodi and her colleagues (Frodi, Lamb, Leavitt, & Donovan, 1978; Frodi, Lamb, Leavitt, Donovan, Neff, & Sherry, 1978) studied the psychophysiological responses of mothers and fathers watching quiescent, smiling, or crying infants on a television monitor. Later Frodi and Lamb (1978) found no sex differences in physiological responses among either 8- or 14-year-olds, although 14-year-old girls were more behaviorally responsive than males in a waiting room situation similar to Feldman's. Ten-year-old girls were more behaviorally responsive than 15-year-olds, underscoring the importance of developmental changes in social roles (Frodi, Murray, Lamb, & Steinberg, 1984). Like Feldman and Nash, we concluded that there were no biologically based sex differences in responsiveness to infants and that behavioral dimorphisms emerged in response to societal pressures and expectations.

Most fathers report being elated when their infants are born (Greenberg & Morris, 1974), frequently visit hospitalized newborns (Levy-Shiff, Sharir, & Mogilner, 1989; Marton & Minde, 1980), and continue to feel emotionally connected to their infants, such that fathers and mothers are equivalently anxious about leaving their babies in someone else's care (Deater-Deckard, Scarr, McCartney, & Eisenberg, 1994). New fathers (and, indeed, unrelated male medical students) behave just as mothers do when introduced to their newborn infants (Klaus, Kennell, Plumb, & Zuehlke, 1970;

Rödholm & Larsson, 1979, 1982). When blindfolded and denied access to olfactory cues, Israeli fathers were able to recognize their infants by touching their hands, just as mothers were (Kaitz, Lapidot, Bronner, & Eidelman, 1992; Kaitz, Shiri, Danziger, Hershko, & Eidelman, 1994). Fathers could not recognize their infants by touching their faces, however, whereas mothers could do so (Kaitz, Meirov, Landman, & Eidelman, 1993; Kaitz et al., 1994), perhaps because the mothers had spent more time with their infants prior to testing (6.8 hours vs. 12.6 hours on average). Interestingly, both mothers and fathers were better at identifying their own newborns by touching their hands than by touching their faces.

Unstructured observations of mother-father-newborn interaction in a maternity ward reveal that fathers are neither inept nor uninterested in interaction with their newborns. Indeed, all but a couple of measures employed by Parke and his colleagues showed that fathers and mothers were equivalently involved in interaction (Parke & O'Leary, 1976; Parke, O'Leary, & West, 1972). When observed feeding their infants, both fathers and mothers responded appropriately to infant cues (Parke & Sawin, 1977), although fathers tended to yield responsibility for childtending chores to their wives when not asked to demonstrate their competence for investigators. Power and Parke (1983) subsequently reported that, when observed playing with their eight-month-olds, fathers were less sensitive to cues regarding the infants' interests and activities than mothers were. In addition, fathers were somewhat less likely to retrieve their crying infants than mothers were (Donate-Bartfield & Passman, 1985). On the other hand, fathers and mothers both adjust their speech patterns when interacting with infants—speaking more slowly, using shorter phrases, and repeating themselves more often when talking to infants than with other adults (Blount & Padgug, 1976; Dalton-Hummel, 1982; Gleason, 1975; Golinkoff & Ames, 1979; Kauffman, 1977; Phillips & Parke, 1979; Rondal, 1980). Indeed, Warren-Leubecker and Bohannon (1984) reported that fathers increased their pitch and frequency range even more than mothers did when speaking to two-year-olds. Interestingly, infants learn to use labels ("papa," "dada," etc.) for their fathers earlier than for their mothers (Brooks-Gunn & Lewis, 1979), perhaps because frequent paternal absences make it necessary to refer to them more often.

Both parents are sufficiently sensitive to developmental changes in their children's abilities and preferences that they adjust their play and stimulation patterns accordingly (Crawley & Sherrod, 1984). When asked to instruct their eight-month-olds, mothers and fathers behaved quite similarly, although the fathers prohibited their infants' activities and talked more than the mothers did (Brachfeld-Child, 1986). These differences may have reflected differences in sensitivity, although several other interpretations are possible. Mothers' and fathers' perceptions of their infants' temperament are correlated, though not highly, suggesting that they may be sensitive to different infant tendencies and characteristics, that they have different types of experiences with their infants, or that their personalities affect their perceptions (Lamb, Frodi, Hwang, & Frodi, 1983b; Mebert, 1989).

Although fathers can be as responsive to infants as mothers are, their behavior is often less sensitive. In a large study of mother- and father-infant interaction, for example, Heermann, Jones, and Wikoff (1994) reported similar factor structures in ratings of mother- and father-infant interaction, although fathers were rated lower than mothers on all scales and at every age. Fathers were either less sensitive than mothers in absolute terms, or the ratings were biased in favor of maternal styles. In addition, Belsky, Gilstrap, and Rovine (1984) reported that, although fathers were less actively engaged in interaction with their one-, three-, and nine-month-old infants than mothers were, the differences narrowed over time. Individual differences in paternal engagement were quite stable over time, especially between three and nine months, although other studies have shown that paternal sensitivity varies depending on the fathers' circumstances, marital relationships, and personalities. Thus, fathers were consistently more involved in interaction with their infants when they were highly engaged in interaction with their partners (Belsky et al., 1984), whereas fathers who were more involved in the treatment of their medically compromised infants appeared to interact more positively than did those who were more distressed by their infants' ill-health (Darke & Goldberg, 1994). Levy-Shiff and Israelashvili (1988) found that Israeli fathers who were rated prenatally as warm and interested played more with their nine-month-olds, whereas prenatal perceptiveness, sensitivity, and a tolerance for external intrusions were correlated with greater involvement in caretaking. In addition, paternal responsiveness probably varies depending on the degree to which the fathers assume responsibility for infant care: caretaking experience appears to facilitate parental responsiveness (Donate-Bartfield & Passman, 1985; Zelazo, Kotelchuck, Barber, & David, 1977). Because fathers interact with their infants less and assume less responsibility for child care than mothers do, it seems likely that paternal sensitivity should decline over time relative to that of mothers. These variations and developmental changes notwithstanding, most fathers are sufficiently responsive to their infants that attachments should form provided that a sufficient amount of father-infant interaction takes place.

THE EXTENT OF FATHER-INFANT INTERACTION

This raises an obvious question: How much time does the "average" father spend with his infant? As one might expect, estimates vary widely even when one considers only traditional family structures in which fathers have primary responsibility for breadwinning. In one early study, mothers reported that the fathers of 8- to 9 ½-month-old infants were home between 5 and 47 hours per week at times when the infants were awake (Pedersen & Robson, 1969). The average was 26 hours, and the fathers reportedly spent between 45 minutes and 26 hours each week actually interacting with their babies. From interviews with the parents of 6- to 21-month-olds, meanwhile, Kotelchuck (1975) determined that mothers spent an average of nine waking hours per day with their children, whereas fathers spent 3.2 hours. The parents interviewed by Golinkoff and Ames (1979) reported figures of 8.33 and 3.16 hours, respectively, while interviews with the Israeli parents of nine-month-old infants suggested that the average father spent 2.75 hours available to his infant each day, with 45 to 50 minutes spent in actual interaction (Ninio & Rinott, 1988). These Israeli fathers averaged one caretaking task per day, but seldom (once every 10 days) took sole responsibility for their infants. English fathers interviewed by Lewis (1984) reported engaging in one activity with their children each day—strikingly more than their own fathers, although less than the Irish fathers studied by Nugent (1987). German and Italian fathers, by contrast, appear much less involved (New & Benigni,

1987; Nickel & Köcher, 1987). Swedish fathers are probably the most active (Hwang, 1987); they spend an average of 10.5 hours per nonworkday with their children—almost as much as mothers do—and 37 hours per week in dual-earner families, again almost as much as mothers do (Haas, 1992, 1993). In contrast, the American fathers interviewed by Lewis and Weinraub (1974) reported much less interaction than this: the average was 15 to 20 minutes per day. The variability among these estimates presumably is attributable to socioeconomic, subcultural, and demographic differences among the populations studied (e.g., Bronstein & Cowan, 1988). Like Gottfried, Gottfried, and Bathurst (1988), Crouter, Perry-Jenkins, Huston, and McHale (1987) reported that fathers in dual-earner families were more involved in child care than were fathers in single-earner families, although the mothers' employment status did not affect paternal involvement in leisure activities, and fathers' sex-role attitudes did not predict the types of paternal involvement (McHale & Huston, 1984). The extent of paternal involvement may also differ depending on the amount of encouragement and support fathers receive: Lind (1974), for example, found that Swedish fathers who were taught how to care for their newborns and were encouraged to do so were more involved with their infants three months later, while Parke and Tinsley (1985) and Parke and Beitch (1986) reported that the greater burdens imposed on families by the birth of preterm babies facilitated paternal involvement. McHale and Huston (1984) also reported that fathers who perceived themselves as more skillful were more involved later. Short-term interventions for new fathers do not appear to influence paternal behavior or involvement (Belsky, 1985; Pannabecker, Emde, & Austin, 1982; Parke & Beitch, 1986), although Myers (1982) reported that fathers became more knowledgeable and more involved when they were shown how to conduct Brazelton (BNAS; Brazelton, 1973) assessments of their newborns. Consistent with this, Ninio and Rinott (1988) reported that the Israeli fathers who were more involved with their nine-month-olds also attributed the greatest levels of competence to them. Apparently perceptions of infant competence and paternal involvement reinforce one another. Grossman and Volkmer (1984) reported that the predelivery desire of German fathers to be present during delivery had a greater impact on their reported involvement than did actual presence during childbirth. This outcome was not surprising in light of Palkovitz's (1985) conclusion that birth attendance, in and of itself, does not appear to have consistent, clear, or robust efforts on paternal involvement or behavior. On the other hand, birth attendance followed by extensive postpartum father-infant interaction in the hospital may stimulate greater paternal involvement and engagement (Keller, Hildebrandt, & Richards, 1985). And whatever the factors that influence fathers' tendencies to be more or less involved in interactions with their children, there appears to be substantial stability, at least during the period from birth through the first 30 months (Lamb et al., 1988). Not surprisingly, work demands played an important role in determining how involved the Swedish fathers in this study were, just as they did in a later study conducted in the United States (Hyde, Essex, & Horton, 1993). Pruett (1985; Pruett & Litzenburger, 1992) also reported substantial stability over time in relative paternal involvement, although his sample was very small. Over a one-year period Nugent (1987) reported considerable stability in the involvement of Irish fathers.

Evidently, the extent of paternal involvement varies greatly depending on the parents' ideology, personality, and work roles (Marsiglio, 1993, 1994; Radin, 1994). Unfortunately, although most theorists believe that regular interaction is necessary for attachments to form, it has not been possible to specify how much interaction is necessary, perhaps because the quality of interaction is even more important than its quantity (Schaffer & Emerson, 1964). Furthermore, Schaffer's (1963) research on hospitalized infants suggested that the amount and quality of social interaction facilitated the formation of bonds to people other than the sources of stimulation. The quality of mother-infant interaction may thus facilitate the formation of father-infant attachments and affect the amount of interaction necessary for father-infant attachments to form. Evidence reviewed in the next section suggests that most infants must have enough "quality" interaction with their fathers because most infants do become attached to their fathers.

THE DEVELOPMENT OF FATHER-INFANT ATTACHMENTS

As early as 1964 Schaffer and Emerson asked whether and when infants formed attachments to their fathers. Mothers reported that their infants began to protest separations from both parents at seven to nine months of age, and that by 18 months of age 71% protested separation from both parents. Babies formed attachments to those with whom they interacted regularly; involvement in caretaking seem insignificant.

Pedersen and Robson (1969) also relied on maternal reports, although their focus was on responses to reunion rather than on separation protest. Seventy-five percent of the mothers reported that their infants responded positively and enthusiastically when their fathers returned from work, and this led Pedersen and Robson to conclude that these infants were attached to their fathers. Among the boys, intensity of greeting was correlated with the frequency of paternal caretaking, paternal patience with infant fussing, and the intensity of father-infant play. Among daughters, however, intensity of greeting was correlated only with reported paternal "apprehension" about the girls' well-being.

Separation protest was the primary focus when observational studies of father-infant attachment began in the 1970s. Kotelchuck (1972) reported that 12-, 15-, 18-, and 21-month-old infants predictably protested when left alone by either parent, explored little while the parents were absent, and greeted them positively when they returned. Few infants protested separation from either parent when the other parent remained with them. A majority (55%) of the infants were more concerned about separation from, and thus seemed to prefer, their mothers, but 25% preferred their fathers and 20% showed no preference for either parent. Similar results were obtained in several studies using the same experimental procedure (Lester, Kotelchuck, Spelke, Sellers, & Klein, 1974; Ross, Kagan, Zelazo, & Kotelchuck, 1975; Spelke, Zelazo, Kagan, & Kotelchuck, 1973; Zelazo et al., 1977). Later research confirmed, not surprisingly, that infants and toddlers also protested being left by either their mothers or fathers in nursery school settings (Field et al., 1984). Somewhat unexpectedly, however, Spelke et al. (1973) found that infants protested least when they had highly involved fathers, and that heightened paternal involvement also delayed the onset of separation protest. American infants with highly interactive fathers strongly protested separation from both parents at 15 and 18 months of age (Kotelchuck, 1972), whereas those with less interactive fathers protested at 12 months of age (Spelke et al., 1973).

Guatemalan infants, who rarely interacted with their fathers, protested separation at nine months (Lester et al., 1974). In general, the data indicated that babies who experienced a great deal of interaction with their fathers started to protest separation later than those whose fathers were uninvolved, and the phase during which protest occurred was briefer when involvement was greater. The consistently counterintuitive nature of these correlations suggests that the intensity of separation protest may not index the intensity of attachment.

The other dependent measures recorded in Kotelchuck's studies yielded more interpretable findings, however. Low paternal involvement in caretaking was associated with reduced interaction and proximity seeking in the laboratory (Kotelchuck, 1972; Spelke et al., 1973), and an intervention study (Zelazo et al., 1977) showed that when paternal involvement at home increased, there was a concomitant increase in the amount of father-infant interaction in the laboratory. Measures of separation protest were unaffected.

Cohen & Campos (1974) also observed infants' responses to brief separations from each of their parents as well as their propensity to seek comfort from the adult remaining with them. Distress did not discriminate between mothers and fathers, but on measures such as frequency of approach, speed of approach, time in proximity, and use of the parent as a "secure base" from which to interact with a stranger, 10-, 13-, and 16-month-old infants showed preferences for their mothers over their fathers, as well as clear preferences for fathers over strangers. Likewise, Lewis and his colleagues reported that one-year-olds touched, stayed near, and vocalized to mothers more than to their fathers in 15-minute free-play sessions, whereas no comparable preferences were evident among two-year-olds (Ban & Lewis, 1974; Lewis & Ban, 1971; Lewis, Weinraub, & Ban, 1972). By contrast, Feldman and Ingham (1975), Lamb (1976c), and Willemsen, Flaherty, Heaton, and Ritchey (1974) reported no preferences for either parent over the other in different laboratory procedures focused on responses to separation and reunion.

By the mid-1970s, therefore, there was substantial evidence that children developed attachments to their fathers in infancy. It was unclear how early in their lives infants formed these attachments, however, since there were no data available concerning the period between six and nine months of age during which infants form attachments to their mothers (Bowlby, 1969). There was also controversy concerning the existence of preferences for mothers over fathers, and there were no data available concerning father-infant interaction in the unstructured environment rather than in the laboratory.

It was in this context that I initiated a naturalistic longitudinal study of mother- and father-infant attachment in 1974. Lengthy home observations revealed that 7, 8-, 12-, and 13-month-old infants in traditional Euro-American families showed no preference for either parent over the other on attachment behavior measures, although all showed preferences for the parents over relatively unfamiliar adult visitors (Lamb, 1976b, 1977c). Similar patterns were evident in a later study of 8- and 16-month-old infants on Israeli kibbutzim (Sagi, Lamb, Shoham, Dvir, & Lewkowicz, 1985). Measures of separation protest and greeting also showed no preferences for either parent in the North America study (Lamb, 1976b), but the situation changed during the second year of life. Boys began to show significant preferences for their fathers on the attachment behavior measures, whereas girls showed no significant or consistent preference for either parent (Lamb, 1977a). By the end of the second year, all but one of the nine boys studied showed consistent preferences for their fathers on at least four of the five attachment behavior measures (Lamb, 1977b). These findings appear to be at odds with Bowlby's (1969) claim that there is a hierarchy among attachment figures, with the primary caretaker usually becoming the preferred attachment figure. The data were not really appropriate for testing this hypothesis, however. According to attachment theory, preferences among attachment figures may not be evident in stress-free situations in which infants do not need comfort from or protection by attachment figures. Under stress, however, infants should focus their attachment behavior more narrowly on primary attachment figures. In fact, when these infants were distressed, the display of attachment behaviors increased, and the infants organized their behavior similarly around whichever parent was present. When both parents were present, however, distressed 12- and 18-month-olds turned to their mothers preferentially (Lamb, 1976a, 1976e), whereas 8- and 21-month-olds showed no comparable preferences (Lamb, 1976c, 1976d). Evidently the hierarchy among attachment figures is marked only during a relatively brief period. Notice also that mothers were deemed more reliable sources of comfort and security, even though fathers become more desirable partners for playful interaction, especially with boys (Clarke-Stewart, 1978; Lamb, 1977a, 1977c). In addition, affiliative behavior measures showed preferences for fathers throughout the first two years of life (Clarke-Stewart, 1978; Lamb, 1977a, 1977c).

In a longitudinal study of traditional and highly involved Swedish fathers and their partners, Lamb, Frodi, Hwang, and Frodi (1983a) found that 8- and 16-month-olds showed clear preferences for their mothers on measures of both attachment and affiliative behavior, regardless of the fathers' relative involvement in child care. One reason for this unexpected result may have been that these Swedish fathers were not especially active as playmates; Lamb et al. speculated that playfulness may serve to enhance the salience of fathers, and that in the absence of such cues infants develop clear-cut preferences for their primary caretakers. (Even today, many Swedish fathers do not take advantage of social policies that would allow them to share in or assume primary responsibility for their infants' care: Haas, 1992, 1993; Lamb & Levine, 1983). Frascarolo-Moutinot (1994) reported that Swiss fathers and mothers were both used as secure bases and sources of security only when the fathers were quite highly involved in a variety of everyday activities with their infants ("the new fathers"). By contrast, Swiss infants with traditional fathers clearly obtained more comfort and security, even at home, from their mothers than from their fathers. Increased paternal involvement thus does seem to strengthen infant-father attachment although as long as mothers assume primary responsibility for child care, they appear to be preferred attachment figures. Most infants, however, clearly form attachments to their fathers.

CHARACTERISTICS OF MOTHER- AND FATHER-INFANT INTERACTION

Even in the first trimester, fathers and mothers appear to engage in different types of interactions with their infants. When videotaped in face-to-face interaction with their 2- to 25-week-old infants, for example, fathers tended to provide staccato bursts of both physical and social stimulation, whereas mothers tended to be more rhythmic and containing (Yogman, 1981; Yogman et al., 1977). Mothers addressed their babies with soft, repetitive, imitative sounds, whereas fathers touched their infants with rhythmic pats. During visits to hospitalized premature infants, mothers were responsive to social cues and fathers to gross motor cues (Marton & Minde, 1980), and although Israeli mothers visited and interacted with hospitalized preterm infants more than fathers did (Levy-Shiff, Sharir, & Mogilner, 1989), fathers were consistently more likely to stimulate and play with their infants and less likely to engage in caretaking. These findings contradict Marton, Minde, and Perrotta's (1981) suggestion that the preterm nursery has a homogenizing effect on parental behavior.

When observed at home with infants over six months of age, fathers tend to engage in more physically stimulating and unpredictable play than mothers do (Clarke-Stewart, 1978; Crawley & Sherrod, 1984; Frascarolo-Moutinot, 1994; Lamb, 1976b, 1977c; Power & Parke, 1979; Teti, Bond, & Gibbs, 1988), although rough physical play becomes less prominent as children grow older (Crawley & Sherrod, 1984). Since these types of play elicited more positive responses from infants, young children prefer to play with their fathers when they have the choice (Clarke-Stewart, 1978, 1980; Lamb, 1976b, 1977c). Mothers are more likely to hold their 7- to 13-month-old infants in the course of caretaking, whereas fathers are more likely to do so during play or in response to the infants' requests to be held (Belsky, 1979; Lamb, 1976c, 1977c). It is thus not surprising that infants respond more positively to being held by their fathers than by their mothers (Lamb, 1976a, 1977c). On the other hand, Frascarolo-Moutinot (1994) reported that fathers were also more intrusive than mothers were, and all researchers agree that most of the differences between mothers and fathers are not large. Both parents encourage visual exploration, object manipulation, and attention to relations and effects (Teti et al., 1988; Power, 1985).

Fathers and mothers do not simply play differently; play is an especially salient component of father-infant relationships. According to Kotelchuck's (1975) informants, mothers spent an average of 85 minutes per day feeding their 6- to 21-month-olds, 55 minutes per day cleaning them, and 140 minutes playing with them. The comparable figures for fathers were 15, 9, and 72 minutes. According to parental diaries (Yarrow et al., 1984), the average father spent 6 and 7.3 hours per week playing with his 6- and 12-month-old, respectively (43% and 44% of the time spent alone with the infant) compared with 17.5 and 16.4 hours by the mother (16% and 19%, respectively, of the time she spent alone with the infant). Clarke-Stewart (1978) also suggested that fathers were consistently notable for their involvement in play, although their relative involvement in caretaking increased over time. Rendina and Dickerscheid (1976) did not record maternal behavior, making a comparison of maternal and paternal behavior impossible, but the fathers they studied also spent most of their time in playful interaction; on average, only 3.8% of the time was spent in caretaking.

It is not only affluent Euro-American fathers who specialize in play; Hossain and Roopnarine (1994) reported that middle-income African American fathers were also more likely to play with their infants than to feed or clean them despite claiming (like many Euro-American fathers) that parents should share child-care responsibilities (Hyde & Texidor, 1988). English fathers are also more likely than mothers to play with rather than care for both normal and handicapped infants and toddlers (Lewis,

1986; McConachie, 1989; Richards, Dunn, & Antonis, 1975). By contrast, fathers on Israeli kibbutzim did not play with their 8- and 16-month-olds more than mothers did, although the mothers were much more actively involved in caretaking and other forms of interaction than the fathers were (Sagi et al., 1985). Swedish fathers are not notably more playful than mothers (Frodi, Lamb, Hwang, & Frodi, 1983; Lamb, Frodi, Hwang, & Frodi, 1982; Lamb et al., 1983a), nor are Aka pygmy fathers whose behavior is similar to that of mothers (Hewlett, 1987, 1990).

Patterns of parental behavior may differ when both parents work full time during the day (Pedersen, Cain, Zaslow, & Anderson, 1982). Working mothers stimulated their infants more than nonworking mothers did, and they were far more active than their husbands were. As expected, fathers with nonworking wives played with their infants more than mothers did, but this pattern was reversed in the families with working mothers. Likewise, Field, Vega-Lahr, Goldstein, and Scafidi (1987) reported that employed mothers were much more interactive in face-to-face interactions with their infants than employed fathers were. Perhaps this explains why mothers' return to paid employment is sometimes associated with changes in the security of infant-father but not infant-mother attachment (Owen, Easterbrooks, Chase-Lansdale, & Goldberg, 1984).

There is no solid evidence yet available concerning the origins of paternal and maternal interactive styles. Brazelton and his colleagues (1979) have argued that they reflect biologically determined differences that very young infants innately "expect" and thus elicit from parents who behave inappropriately. Because this notion attributes greater cognitive and perceptual skills to young infants than they are known to possess (Lamb & Sherrod, 1981), it seems more likely that the different parental styles reflect the social roles assumed by men and women. Several researchers have thus studied families marked by nontraditional parental roles. Field (1978) reported that primary caretaking fathers behaved more like mothers than secondary caretaking fathers did, although fathers engaged in more playful and noncontaining interactions than mothers did regardless of their involvement in child care. Field et al. (1987) later reported that employed mothers were more actively involved in face-to-face interaction than employed fathers were, but unfortunately this study included no unemployed parents. Pruett (1985; Pruett & Litzenburger, 1992) studied no fathers who were not highly involved in infant care but repeatedly remarked on the distinctive playfulness of these fathers. Frascarolo-Moutinot (1994) reported no differences in playfulness between "new fathers" and "traditional" fathers, although the wives of the new fathers were less intrusive and controlling than the wives of traditional fathers. Lamb and his colleagues (Lamb, Frodi, Frodi, & Hwang, 1982; Lamb, Frodi, Hwang, Frodi, & Steinberg, 1982a, 1982b) reported that mothers were more likely than fathers to vocalize, display affection to, touch, tend to, and hold their infants whether or not their partners took a month or more of paternity leave. These findings were replicated in another study of Swedish parents by Hwang (1986); again, mothers were much more active during the observation than their partners were, regardless of the mens' relative involvement in child care. On traditional Israeli kibbutzim, meanwhile, child care is primarily the responsibility of professional caretakers (*metaplot*) rather than either parent. Yet despite this, and the fact that the two parents spent equivalent amounts of time with their children during the late afternoon "love hours," sex-of-parent differences were still prominent. Mothers engaged in more caretaking and were generally more interactive than fathers were; fathers were not distinguished by their involvement in play, however (Sagi et al., 1985).

Overall, these findings suggest that the distinctive maternal and paternal styles are quite reliably evident when North American, British, and Irish families are studied, but are not typical in all cultures. When these differences exist, however, they appear quite resistent to change.

PATERNAL INFLUENCES ON INFANT DEVELOPMENT

Many reviewers have speculated that fathers affect the development of sex-role and gender identity, especially in boys (e.g., Bronstein, 1988; Lamb & Stevenson, 1978; Parke, 1979), and this speculation was strengthened by evidence that fathers interact preferentially with sons from shortly after delivery. Parke and O'Leary (1976) found that American fathers vocalized to, touched, and responded to their first-born sons more frequently than their first-born daughters, and similar tendencies were evident among British fathers (Woollett, White, & Lyon, 1982). In a later study of three-week-olds and three-month-olds, Parke and Sawin (1975) found that fathers looked at sons more than at daughters and provided them with more visual and tactile stimulation than they did daughters. Mothers, in contrast, stimulated girls more than boys. Fathers were also more likely to diaper and feed three-month-old sons than three-month-old daughters (Parke & Sawin, 1980). Fathers were warmer and more sensitive with three-month-old sons than with daughters (Cox, Owen, Lewis, & Henderson, 1989), as well as more attentive to older infants (Rendina & Dickerscheid, 1976; Weinraub & Frankel, 1977). In Israeli kibbutzim, fathers spent more time visiting their four-month-old sons than their four-month-old daughters (Gewirtz & Gewirtz, 1968). Even among the nomadic !Kung Bushmen, fathers spent more time with sons than with daughters (West & Konner, 1976).

Some studies suggest that sex-differentiated treatment intensifies during the second year of life when fathers sometimes make themselves especially salient to sons (e.g., Lamb, 1977b). Thus, fathers verbalized to their sons more than to their daughters during the second year (Lamb, 1977a, 1977b), and they reported spending more time (about 30 minutes more per day) playing with first-born sons than with first-born daughters (Kotelchuck, 1976). At least some parents of boys believe that fathers play a special role (as play partners and role models), whereas those with daughters do not think that mothers and fathers play different roles (Fagot, 1974).

Although they did not study mothers, Snow, Jacklin, and Maccoby (1983) reported clear difference between father-son and father-daughter interaction involving one-year-olds; fathers prohibited boys more than girls, gave more toys to girls than to boys, and vocalized more to girls, who remained physically closer to their fathers. English fathers are much more concerned about gender-inappropriate behavior than mothers are (Jackson, 1987; Lewis, 1986) and respond to their children accordingly (McGuire, 1982).

Larger-scale studies have revealed few consistent differences between maternal and paternal responses to the behavior of 12-, 18-, and 60-month-olds, however (e.g., Fagot & Hagan, 1991). Fathers were not especially concerned about the need to socialize their sons preferentially, and they were not especially involved in the promotion of stereotypically sex-appropriate behavior—findings that were confirmed in a meta-analysis by Lytton and Romney (1991) and a narrative review by Siegel (1987). Caldera, Huston, and O'Brien (1989) likewise reported that fathers were not especially involved in efforts to shape the sex-stereotyped behavior of their toddlers, although different types of toys "pulled" for different types of play and different types of parent-child interaction. Power and Parke (1986) reported that the frequency of socialization demands increased with age between 11 and 17 months of age, although there were few differences between mothers and fathers. Both parents were more likely to discourage aggression and encourage prosocial behavior in girls than in boys, and to encourage household responsibilities and turn-taking in boys. The results of recent studies have thus failed to support claims regarding the special responsibility of fathers for sex-role socialization in infancy. Research reviewed in the previous section clearly shows that fathers present sex-stereotyped models from which their infants may learn.

Other researchers have explored paternal influences on cognitive and motivational development. This focus was attributable partly to evidence concerning the impact of mother-infant interaction on cognitive development (see Stevenson & Lamb, 1981, for a review) and partly to evidence that male (though not female) infants raised without fathers were less cognitively competent than infants raised in two-parent families even though mothers in single- and two-parent families behaved similarly (Pedersen, Rubenstein, & Yarrow, 1979). Other adults did not seem able to fill the void left by the infants' fathers. In a later study of infants whose fathers were present, Yarrow et al. (1984) reported that paternal stimulation had an especially important role to play in the development of boys' (but not girls') mastery motivation in the first year of life. Wachs, Uzgiris, and Hunt (1971) likewise reported that increased paternal involvement associated with better performance on the Uzgiris-Hunt scales.

In her observational study of 15- to 30-month-olds, Clarke-Stewart (1978) found that intellectual competence was correlated with measures of maternal stimulation (both material and verbal), intellectual acceleration, and expressiveness, as well as with measures of the fathers' engagement in play, their positive ratings of the children, the amount they interacted, and the fathers' aspirations for the infants' independence. However, examination of the correlational patterns over time indicated that the mothers affected the children's development and that this, in turn, influenced the fathers' behavior. In other words, paternal behavior appeared to be a consequence of, not a determinant of, individual differences in child behavior. Similarly, Hunter, McCarthy, MacTurk, and Vietze (1987) reported that, although the qualities of both mother- and father-infant interaction in play sessions were individually stable over time, the paternal variables were not associated with differences in the infants' cognitive competence, whereas the indices of maternal behavior were predictively valuable. These findings illustrate a notion we pursue in the next section—that children develop within family systems in which all parties affect and are affected by one another. Influences do not always run directly from parents to children.

Although mothers and fathers both adjust their speech characteristics when speaking to infants, some differences between maternal and paternal communicative patterns remain. Gleason (1975) and Rondal (1980) have suggested that because fathers use more imperatives, attention-getting utterances, and state sentences than mothers do, they contribute in unique, though still poorly understood, ways to linguistic development. Infants clearly view both parents as potential sources of information: in ambiguous settings, they look to either parent for clarification, and they are equally responsive to information from mothers and fathers (Hirshberg & Svejda, 1990; Dickstein & Parke, 1988).

Attachment theorists believe that maternal sensitivity determines the security of infant-mother attachment and thus of subsequent psychological adjustment (Ainsworth et al., 1978; Lamb, 1987; Lamb et al., 1985), and it seems reasonable to assume that individual differences in paternal sensitivity influence the security of infant-father attachment. In a meta-analysis combining data from 11 studies in which infants had been assessed in the Strange Situation with both their parents, Fox, Kimmerly, and Schafer (1991) reported that infants tended to have attachments of similar type with both parents, although convergence was quite weak. These findings might reveal concordant parenting styles or—more likely—the fact that inherent differences in infant temperament also influence the quality of infant-parent attachment in the Strange Situation. Bridges, Connell, and Belsky (1988) also showed that the structure of infant behavior in the Strange Situation differed depending on whether infants were with their mothers or fathers, again suggesting that infant-mother and infant-father attachments are individually unique, distinctively influenced by the adults' characteristics. It is thus especially important to assess infant-mother and infant-father attachment as well as infant temperament when attempting to assess the relative importance of these different factors on child development.

Other researchers have confirmed that variations in paternal behavior influence the security of infant-father attachment. Cox, Owen, Henderson, and Margand (1992) reported that fathers who were more affectionate, spent more time with their three-month-olds, and had more positive attitudes were more likely to have securely attached infants nine months later. Father-infant attachments are more likely to be insecure when fathers report high levels of stress (Jarvis & Creasey, 1991).

The effects of infant-father attachment on subsequent behavior have also been studied. In a study of infants on Israeli kibbutzim, Sagi, Lamb, and Gardner (1986) reported that the security of both mother- and father-infant attachment were associated with indices of the infants' sociability with strangers: Securely attached infants were more sociable than insecure-resistant infants. Earlier, Lamb, Hwang, Frodi, & Frodi (1982) reported that Swedish infants who were securely attached to their fathers were more sociable with strangers, although there was no association between the security of infant-mother attachment and sociability in their sample. Main and Weston (1981) found that the security of both mother-infant and father-infant attachments affected infants' responses to an unfamiliar person (dressed as a clown). Unfortunately, it was not possible to determine which relationship had the greater impact since the clown session took place at the same time as the assessment of the mother-infant attachment—six months before assessment of the father-infant attachment. It seems plausible, however, that the relationship with the primary caretaker would be more influential, although it would behoove researchers to assess relationships with both parents when attempting to assess parental influences on child development.

Fagot and Kavanagh (1993) underscored the importance of considering the quality of attachment to both parents. Both parents found interaction with insecurely attached infants less pleasant, and both tended to become less involved in interactions with insecurely attached boys, a factor that may explain the greater likelihood of behavior problems among boys. Interestingly, fathers had unusually high levels of interaction with insecure-avoidant girls, who received the fewest instructions from their mothers. In a study of 20-month-olds, Easterbrooks and Goldberg (1984) found that the children's adaptation was promoted by both the amount of paternal involvement and the quality or sensitivity of their fathers' behavior. Interestingly, the quality of interaction appeared to be more influential than the extent of paternal involvement. Neither the security of infant-mother nor infant-father attachment influenced the adjustment at age five of infants raised on traditional kibbutzim (those with central dormitories for children), although the security of the infant-caretaker relationship was influential (Oppenheim, Sagi, & Lamb, 1988). Recent research also suggests that fathers and mothers may have distinct influences on the development of peer relationships. MacDonald and Parke (1984), for example, found that physically playful, affectionate, and socially engaging father-son interaction was correlated with the boys' later popularity, whereas mothers' verbal stimulation was associated with popularity. In addition, rejected-aggressive boys reported receiving less affection from their fathers (but not from their mothers) than did rejected-nonaggressive and neglected boys. And although the security of infant-father attachment did not predict the quality of later sibling interaction, there was a nonsignificant tendency for sibling interaction to be more positive if fathers had positive relationships with the older children when they were three years old.

Some of the speculations concerning paternal influences focus less on the specific differences between maternal and paternal styles than on the fact that they differ in many ways. In the early months, for example, it may be easier for infants to learn to recognize the characteristic features of one parent when they are exposed relatively frequently to a distinctly different person. Furthermore, because mothers and fathers represent different types of interaction, infants are likely to develop different expectations of them, which should in turn increase their awareness of different social styles and perhaps facilitate a perceptual sensitivity to such subtle differences (Lamb, 1981). This would contribute to the development of social competence. Pedersen et al. (1979) found that the degree of paternal involvement (as reported by mothers) was positively correlated with the social responsiveness of five-month-olds. Overall, the evidence suggests that the security of infant-father attachments, like the security of infant-mother attachment, is influenced both by the parents' behavior and by the child's temperaments. The security of infant-father attachment appears to have a unique and independent influence on the child's development, although in traditional families, the impact may be less than the security of the infant-mother attachment.

DIRECT AND INDIRECT EFFECTS

Fathers not only influence children directly; they also affect maternal behavior, just as mothers influence paternal behavior and involvement (Belsky, 1981; Lamb, 1986; Lewis, Feiring, & Weinraub, 1981). Indeed, although pre- and postpartum measures of the father's personality clearly influence the type, quality, and extent of involvement in postpartum relationships with infants (Belsky, 1985; Cox & Owen, 1991; Cox et al., 1989; Feldman & Nash 1985; Feldman, Nash, & Aschenbrenner, 1983; Heinicke,

1984; Levy-Shiff, Goldschmidt, & Har-Even, 1991; Levy-Shiff & Israelashvilli, 1988; Palkovitz, 1984), there is substantial evidence that the quality of the marital relationship is crucial as well. Pedersen, Anderson, and Cain (1977), for example, showed that the affective quality of parent-infant interaction could be predicted from observational measures of mutual criticism in the spousal relationship. Price (1977) reported that the ability of mothers to enjoy and be affectionate with their infants was associated with the quality of the marital relationship, and Minde, Marton, Manning, and Hines (1980) reported that the quality of the marital relationship predicted the frequency of maternal visits to hospitalized premature infants. Henneborn and Cogan (1975) and Anderson and Standley (1976) reported that women whose husbands were supportive during labor were themselves less distressed, and Feiring (1976) found that women who reported supportive relationships with "secondary parents" (spouses, lovers, or grandparents) were more sensitively responsive to their infants. Paternal and familial support may be an especially significant determinant of maternal sensitivity today, when many young mothers feel the conflicting attractions of parenthood and career aspirations (Lamb, Chase-Lansdale, & Owen, 1979; Lamb, Owen, & Chase-Lansdale, 1980). Durrett, Otaki, and Richards (1984) found that the Japanese mothers of securely attached infants reported greater levels of spousal support than did the mothers of insecurely attached infants. Mothers whose husbands evaluated their maternal skills positively were more effective in feeding four-month-old infants (Pedersen, 1975), whereas the frequency of the parents' comments about the baby is correlated with the amount of father-infant interaction as are the frequency of comments not about the baby and the frequency of ignoring (Belsky, 1980). After controlling for individual differences in the fathers' psychological adjustment, Cox et al. (1989) reported that fathers in close confiding marriages have more positive attitudes toward their three-month-old infants and toward their roles as parents than did fathers in less successful marriages, whereas mothers in close confiding marriages were warmer and more sensitive. Similar results were reported by Levy-Shiff and Israelashvilli (1989), although Crouter and her colleagues (1987) reported that, at least in dual-earner families, increased paternal involvement in child care was often at the expense of marital happiness. Goldberg and Easterbrooks (1984) reported that good marital quality was associated with both more sensitive maternal and paternal behavior as well as higher levels of functioning on the part of the toddlers studied. Easterbrooks and Emde (1988) speculated that the quality of the marital relationships may be especially influential soon after birth, although Gable, Crnic, and Belsky (1994) reported powerful associations among marital quality, the quality of parent-child relationships, and child outcomes in a study of two-year-olds. Infants characterized by negative emotionality early in the first year tended to become more positive when they had active, sensitive, and happily married mothers, whereas some infants became more negative when their fathers were dissatisfied with their marriages, insensitive, and uninvolved in their children's lives (Belsky, Fish, & Isabella, 1991). Meanwhile, Heinicke and Guthrie (1992) reported that couples who were well adapted to one another, or whose adaptation increased over time, provided better care than parents whose spousal adaptation was poor or declining, a set of findings consistent with earlier reports of adaptation over shorter periods of time (Durrett, Richards, Otaki, Pennebaker, & Nyguist, 1986; Engfer, 1988; Heinicke, Diskin, Ramsey-Klee, & Oates, 1986; Heinicke & Lampl, 1988; Jouriles, Pfiffner, & O'Leary, 1988; Meyer, 1988). Consistent with this, Goldberg and Easterbrooks (1984) reported that high levels of marital adjustment were associated with more positive parental attitudes and behavior, as well as secure infant-parent attachments. Belsky et al. (1984), Lamb and Elster (1985), and Dickie and Matheson (1984) all reported that fathers' interactions with their infants were influenced by the ongoing quality of interaction with their partners much more profoundly than mothers' behavior was. This may be because paternal behavior and engagement are somewhat discretionary, whereas maternal behavior is driven by clearer conventions and role definitions. In any event, both maternal and paternal attitudes influence paternal behavior (Palkovitz, 1984), and marital conflict appears to have a more harmful impact on socioemotional development than does parent-child separation or father absence (see Cummings & O'Reilly, Chapter 4 of this volume).

In addition to correlational studies exploring the impact of marital quality on maternal and paternal behavior, researchers have shown that the mere presence of either parent influences the interaction between the other parent and the infant. In general, the presence of the other parent leads to a reduction in interaction between parent and child—whether the interaction takes place at home (Belsky, 1979; Clarke-Stewart, 1978; Pedersen, Anderson, & Cain, 1980) or in structured laboratory settings (Lamb, 1976a, 1976e, 1977a, 1978, 1979). A similar effect has been noted in naturalistic studies at home and in public places (Cleaves & Rosenblatt, 1977; Hwang, 1986; Liddell, Henzi, & Drew, 1987; Rosenblatt, 1974) as well as in studies of maternal and paternal speech (Golinkoff & Ames, 1979; Stoneman & Brody, 1981). Interestingly, Stoneman and Brody found that children did not accommodate to the social setting as much as their parents did, and Hwang (1986) reported that traditional Swedish fathers were much more affected by their partners' presence than shared-caretaking fathers were. Traditional fathers engaged in more interaction where alone than with their partners, whereas highly involved fathers behaved similarly in the two contexts. Lewis and Kreitzberg (1979) reported that the fathers and mothers of first-borns vocalized to their infants more than the parents of later-borns did—perhaps because, as the authors report, other siblings were often present during the observations. Lytton (1979) found that paternal presence increased the likelihood that mothers would respond positively to toddlers' compliance, reduced the number of maternal efforts to exert control, and increased the mothers' effectiveness as disciplinarians.

CONCLUSION

Clearly fathers can no longer be deemed "forgotten contributors to child development" (Lamb, 1975) because the relationships between fathers and infants are now being studied widely and thoroughly. Of course, many important questions remain unanswered, but at least some issues have been resolved. First, there is substantial evidence that infants form attachments to both mothers and fathers at about the same point during the first year of life. Second, a hierarchy appears to exist among attachment figures such that most infants prefer their mothers over their fathers. These preferences probably develop because the mothers are primary caretakers; they might well disappear or be reversed if fathers were to share caretaking responsibilities or become primary caretakers, which few have done.

Third, the traditional parental roles affect styles of interaction as well as infant preferences. Several observational studies have now shown that fathers are associated with playful—often vigorously stimulating—social interaction, whereas mothers are associated with caretaking. These social styles obviously reflect traditionally sex-stereotyped roles, and it has been suggested that they play an important role in the early development of gender role and gender identity. We do not yet know whether the maternal and paternal styles are purely products of social influences or whether innate tendencies play a role as well. We do know, however, that both mothers and fathers are capable of behaving sensitively and responsively in interaction with their infants. With the exception of lactation, there is no evidence that women are biologically predisposed to be better parents than men are. Social conventions, not biological imperatives, underlie the traditional division of parental responsibilities.

In the immediate future, the most conceptually important advances will involve attempts to determine how patterns of interaction within the family system affect the course of infant development. It is clear that the way either parent interacts with the infant is determined jointly by his or her personality, relationship with the spouse, and the infant's unique characteristics, but we do not know just how these diverse influences complement and supplement one another.

CHAPTER 7

Fathers and Preschoolers

Charlie Lewis
Lancaster University

TWENTY YEARS ago fatherhood fell under the gaze of developmental psychologists. *The Role of the Father in Child Development* (Lamb, 1976, 1981a) provided the major summary of this wave of theory and reflected the sheer volume of research and discussion that was produced. A 15-year gap between the second and third editions allows us sufficient distance for reflection on just what was achieved in this outpouring of research. Frank Pedersen (1980) likened this wave of fatherhood investigations to a "break" in a cycle race, in which a small group of pioneers set a quicker pace and new directions for the pack of researchers to follow. I will reflect upon the research on preschoolers to see where the break led us and will focus largely on studies published after the 1981 edition, since most of the research before that date is extensively summarized in that volume.

There are three main sections in this chapter. The first examines the nature of paternal interaction with preschoolers. The aim is to show that paternal styles are not driven by simple imperatives, so we cannot talk of distinctive patterns of father-child interaction. The second section reconsiders men's family roles by examining the public observation of fathers. This serves two purposes. First, it shows that research on parent-child interaction should be understood as a public display rather than a demonstration of the "essence" of the relationship. The available data suggest that men may be more influenced by being observed than women. However, the second reason for focusing upon father-child interaction as a public activity stems paradoxically from the fact that much of that interaction takes place in public and appears to be more distinctive than that witnessed in the home. It will be argued that the representational significance of such public displays is important. In the third section the issue of whether we have sufficient evidence to conclude that fathers influence preschoolers' development will be considered. As is the case with father-child interaction there is little to suggest that paternal styles have unique influences on children. Only in subtle ways can we discern "paternal effects." In order to understand just why this is the case it is necessary to set the scene with some reflection upon what has been said about fathers and the constraints upon their involvement in family life.

FATHERS' ROLES IN EARLY CHILD DEVELOPMENT

> There is no doubt that fathers are important contributors to child development. In particular, fathers significantly affect the development of sex roles, cognitive abilities and achievement motivation. (Weinraub, 1978, p. 127)

Two clear and yet contradictory themes are apparent in the 1970s wave of fatherhood research. As Weinraub's statement suggests, there was a strong conviction that men must have an influence on their children's development. Both the major theories of the day, psychoanalysis and social learning theory, held that identification with same-sex parents is critical in the areas highlighted by Weinraub. Yet a parallel theme in the fatherhood literature played down the role performed by men in influencing their children's development: "Although most research on the father-child relationship has been focused upon the presumed effects, the literature in this area is remarkably inconclusive" (Lamb, 1981b, p. 24). More often than not authors expressed two opinions simultaneously—that fathers provide an essential ingredient to the child's psychological development, but to understand fathers we need to grasp that other factors are involved.

Weinraub's assertion is singled out because it was her contributions to the first two editions of this book which expressed so clearly just what the "break" from research tradition did in theoretical terms (Lewis, Feiring, & Weinraub, 1981; Lewis & Weinraub, 1976). Far from making bland statements about the "effects" of paternal involvement, these two chapters attempted to explore ways of moving beyond simple cause-effect relationships in parent-child influence (see also Clarke-Stewart, 1977). Rather, they attempted to place fatherhood into a social network of relationships involving extended kin members and "indirect" as well as direct (i.e., interactional) influences upon the child. Such indirect influences included factors like paternal emotional support for mothers, "representational" influences, like the place of the father in the child's symbolic understanding of parenthood, and "transitive" influences, like the effects of a close spousal relationship on the child.

Taken together, these chapters by Lewis and Weinraub offered some solutions to the call made by Lamb (1975) for more longitudinal data and a process model of paternal involvement. Such a perceived need was not new. As Layman (1961, p. 107) suggested, "We can delineate the ideal role of the father in relation to effective functioning of the child only if we consider many variables. These include the role assumed by the mother, the mother-father relationship, the specific subculture of which the family is part and the social class to which the family belongs." More recent analyses have continued to reflect this theme:

> To understand dimensions of parenting and to adequately conceptualise the predictors of fathering one needs to integrate variables in each of the following domains: psychological, marital, sociocultural and parental. In addition it is our contention that the study of fathering should occur within the context of a complex, interactive systems approach, one in which both direct effects (predic-

tions from fathers' own characteristics) and indirect effects (predictions from wives' characteristics) can be examined over time. (Grossman, Pollack, & Golding, 1988, p. 82)

Systemic models of family development like Belsky's (1981) have continued this theme and attempted to integrate such potential influences upon family development. His model states that the determinants of parenting derive from the child, the parent, and the parents' relationship. It has been very illuminating in the analysis of the various factors that conspire together to produce a parent-child relationship and has crystallized many of the ideas outlined in the earlier editions of this book and by authors like Layman. It has also made us focus upon fatherhood as a sociological construct, since father-child relationships seem qualitatively different from mother-child relationships. As Belsky (1990, p. 887) summarizes,

Investigators have repeatedly found that spousal support of both the emotional (e.g., love, intimacy) and instrumental (e.g., child care tasks) variety is associated with enhanced parental performance—of mothers and fathers alike. . . . There is some indication that patterns of fathering are more systematically related to patterns of marital interaction or measures of marital adjustment/satisfaction than are patterns of mothering . . . perhaps because men's parental roles are less scripted by social convention.

It is the difference between mother-child and father-child relationships that has dominated theorization within sociological reflections on family development (e.g., Backett, 1982; Berger & Kellner, 1964; La Rossa, 1977), but only touched upon in psychological research (Lewis, 1986). These analyses have highlighted the complexities of the relationships between parents in determining the part played by fathers in families. In many respects the break within psychological studies has been a move, albeit implicit, into a sociological domain. This domain is not one where maternal and parental roles are functionally determined by male "instrumentality" and the female "expressiveness" (Parsons & Bales, 1955). Fatherhood is "less scripted by social convention" not because men are "forgotten contributors to child development," but because they continue to be written (and to write themselves) into a role away from the center stage of family interactions. The demands of work, men's relative lack of reward for their commitment to family life, the subtle negotiations between partners in determining the part played by the men in families—all contribute to our understanding of fatherhood, as theoreticians and participants. In order to demonstrate that mothers' and fathers' access to the domain of parenting is unequal, this analysis of the father's role begins with an examination of the "problem" of fatherhood. Most of the analysis will focus upon resident fathers, even though some studies suggest that 31%–40% of preschoolers live at one time or another without their fathers (Mott, 1990).

How Practically Involved Are Fathers of Preschoolers?

If we leave aside the fact that many fathers absent themselves from the home during the child's preschool years and the much discussed problems of selecting criteria of involvement (McKee, 1982), how much do men contribute to the care of their young offspring? Two themes appear to link research over the past 50 years. The first is that in industrial cultures most men take on a secondary role, filling in only when they are "needed" and rarely taking responsibility for the child's daily routine. The second is that despite their rather limited range of roles, there is variation between men in most cultural settings.

Fathering as a Secondary Activity

The 1980s and 1990s have witnessed a dramatic increase in discussion about changing paternal roles (see Lewis & O'Brien, 1987, for a critique). Yet the reality of social change has been far less in evidence. For example, in Australia it has been estimated that in fewer than 2% of families do fathers share child-care tasks equally with mothers, and the proportion of "highly involved" men is less than 10% (Russell & Radojevic, 1992). Meanwhile 60% of "traditional" fathers have never looked after their children alone (Russell, 1983). The patterns in other industrial cultures are similar (see, e.g., Lamb, 1987), particularly when it comes to the 90% who are not highly involved.

Large-scale surveys reveal just how little men do with their children. Osborn and Morris (1982) examined paternal involvement in over 13,000 five-year-olds in a British national cohort study. Four aspects of care were selected for scrutiny: looking after the child without the mother, putting him or her to bed, depositing or collecting the child from nursery school or preschool, and reading to him or her. One-quarter of all fathers were reported not to have carried out any of these tasks over the past week, while only 4% had performed all four. The task of putting the child to bed offers wide opportunities for expression of parental affection, teaching through recapping on the day's activities, storytelling, and generally maintaining their relationship. While 49% of the fathers were reported to have participated in the past week, a similar proportion (43%) were recorded to be at work sometimes or usually until after the child's bedtime. The latter group contained more blue-collar workers, often because they worked shifts. Other studies show that families often take pains to compensate for this enforced separation between men and their children. For example, Newson and Newson (1968) found that in 16% of families the four-year-old was often allowed to get out of bed when daddy came home.

While in most families mothering is more conspicuous than fathering, the latter can be important or at least visible. Studies over the past 30 years have shown that men fitted their parenting commitments around their wives' routines (Lewis, 1986; Newson & Newson, 1968), when the need or opportunity arises (Osborn & Morris, 1982). So in industrial cultures over the past generation 30% of fathers have regularly put the preschooler to bed (Newson & Newson, 1968), particularly when the mother works a fixed, nonday shift (Presser, 1988). Likewise paternal involvement may increase if circumstances demand. Knafl and Dixon (1984) studied fathers' care for young children hospitalized for a nonemergency, minor procedure. Sixty-eight percent altered their work schedules to spend time with their child, often unofficially. Most of those who took annual leave visited daily and usually for 8 to 12 hours. All but three of the rest of the fathers fitted visiting around their work.

Variations between Fathers

The Osborn and Morris data, cited above, reveal also that fathers' contributions to child care are characterized by wide individual differences. When parents keep a daily record of paternal involvement with their preschoolers, variations in their availability are great. For example, Underwood (1949) found in a small sample that the weekly involvement of men was between one hour, thirty minutes and 19 hours, 37 minutes. Similar differences between highly involved men and those on the margins of family routines have been reported with reference to a variety of child-care tasks (e.g., Lewis, 1987). While there may be a few cultural exceptions (Hewlett, 1987), such variations testify to the expendability of fathers in many families and cultural settings.

What determines paternal involvement in any particular setting? In the late 1970s studies suggested an association between male nurturance or androgyny and greater paternal involvement in child care (De Frain, 1979; Russell, 1978). However, this research did not ascertain whether this connection was a causal one and if so in which direction. More recent investigations have suggested that the picture is more complex. While longitudinal research confirms the earlier findings, it suggests that concepts like "nurturance" need to be unpacked. First, personality attributes of the father seem to be important. Second, characteristics of the mother also seem to be related to the amount of care giving the father does. Grossman et al. (1988) reported that mothers who had greater feelings of autonomy and those in certain occupations had more involved husbands. Third, and perhaps more important, the couple's employment patterns play a key role. Not only are some unemployed men far more involved than their employed peers (e.g., Radin & Goldsmith, 1989), but hours of parental paid work have been found to be the most accurate predictor of paternal involvement in child care (Lewis, 1986).

PATERNAL INTERACTION WITH PRESCHOOLERS

Given that even in two-parent (i.e., father-resident) families fathers spend much less time with their children than do mothers, what effect does this have on the children's socialization? Do parents adopt different styles with their preschoolers, and if so do these behavioral styles have any obvious influences on the child's psychological development? In many respects we might expect fathers to adopt different parental styles in interaction, either because they identify more with "masculine values" or simply as a result of their relative distance from the nurturant side of parental life. Certainly such assumptions are apparent in both social learning and psychoanalytic theory.

Over many decades commentators have been divided over the possible contribution by each parent to interactions. The bulk of research has failed to identify stylistic differences, using a variety of measures. For example, the spate of studies following parent-infant interaction into the early preschool period (Pedersen, 1980) revealed many more similarities between parents than differences (see Lewis, 1982, for a discussion). Clarke-Stewart (1980), for example, examined children at 30 months of age at home with their parents. By and large the quality of father-child interaction was equivalent to that of mothers and children as measured by paternal responsiveness, stimulation, affection, and teaching. Laboratory studies in the same wave of research produced similar results. For example, Pakizegi's (1978) observations of three-year-olds with their parents identified a typical pattern. Adults' play with preschoolers tends to support the latter's activities, in exploring toys or developing lines of play. Similarly the child's approaches to each parent consist of a large proportion of requests for information or action (38% of all child actions) and a fair amount (8%) of "bossing" the parent, confirming that fathers as well as mothers can be the unacknowledged "victims" of their children's activities (Patterson, 1980). Research since the major wave of psychological studies has tended to confirm the similarity between parents in the nurturance they report (Bentley & Fox, 1991), their disciplinary regimes (e.g., Hart, de Wolfe, Wozniak, & Burts, 1992), and their teaching styles in various observational settings (Worden, Kee, & Ingle, 1987).

However, the tide of opinion has been hard to stem. Many parents and researchers assume that parental roles have different impacts on the child. Two issues recur: The first is that fathers may use particular play styles that are distinctive. It is their physical strength that is cited as particularly salient to the child's understanding of masculinity. One large-scale survey reported that fathers are more likely than mothers to engage in physical play bouts with their children and that this peaks in the preschool period of development (MacDonald & Parke, 1986). Second, and as a result of such reported differences, many continue to assume that paternal activities exert a clear influence on early sex-role development: "Parents treat boys and girls differently . . . and this differential shaping is particularly strong in the toddler and preschool years. Furthermore, fathers are more likely to enforce differential treatment than are mothers" (Williams, Radin, & Allegro, 1992, p. 458). As sex-role development is considered to be the most likely area of paternal influence we will compare it as a paradigm case in the first part of this section. The second part will compare maternal and paternal linguistic input on the child's development.

DO FATHERS ENCOURAGE SEX-ROLE DEVELOPMENT?

The link between paternal style and the child's sex role development has been a focus of attention for many decades, and the early literature is well summarized by Biller (1981). The topic is particularly relevant to this review because the preschool period has attracted so much attention. It has been estimated that almost 80% of published papers on parental influences on sex-role development focus upon children under the age of six (Lytton & Romney, 1991). The debate has been dominated by two theoretical perspectives. The first perspective was voiced by Maccoby and Jacklin (1974) in response to the argument that both parents treat their sons and daughters differently. They reviewed the existing literature (many hundreds of studies) and claimed that the evidence for differential socialization as the cause of sex differences in children's behavior was hardly conclusive. In response to Maccoby and Jacklin, Block (1976) argued that the null results from their survey resulted from the failure of researchers to focus upon mothers and fathers as different agents of socialization. She argued that fathers interact with their sons and daughters in different ways. Block's claims were reminiscent of Reciprocal Role Theory (Johnson, 1982) and were taken up by proponents of the view that fathers have a central role, particularly in early childhood (e.g., Power, 1981).

The debate has continued despite attempts to quash it once and for all. Two reviews have attempted to demonstrate that the evidence to support a "paternal socialization" hypothesis is insufficient. In 1987 Siegal reviewed 39 published studies and found only two common themes. In these studies fathers were found consistently to engage in physical play more with sons than with daughters and to encourage their children to play with sex-typed toys. Yet in all other respects they were indistinguishable from mothers. More recently, Lytton and Romney (1991) carried out an even more extensive meta-analysis of 172 studies, involving almost 28,000 participants and a variety of interview, observation, and questionnaire measures. Their analysis reveals a great variety of patterns of mother-child and father-child interaction. Some factors apparent in a few studies were nonsignificant in others. For example, in two American reports fathers encouraged sons more than daughters to achieve. However, in 20 further studies they did not, nor did they when all the difference scores were analyzed using a pooled standard deviation. In keeping with Siegal's (1987) results they found the only consistent factor to emerge from Lytton and Romney's analysis was their encouragement of sex-typed activities, but their influence was only small: 0.3–0.5 of one standard deviation. Any trends toward a parental sex difference in interaction styles diminished with age. They therefore conclude, "The present meta-analysis has demonstrated a virtual absence of sex-distinctive parental pressures, except in one area" (Lytton & Romney, 1991, p. 288).

Lytton and Romney's (1991) analysis appears to undermine Block's (1976) contention that there are clear parental differences in the treatment of boys and girls. It is supported by more recent work that suggests that even the encouragement of sex-typed activities disappears once father and child are actively at play (Idle, Wood, & Desmaris, 1993). Yet there are some grounds for not dismissing the parental socialization hypothesis completely. Lytton and Romney admit that despite the lack of significant results many of the nonsignificant trends concerning parental differentiation were in the expected direction. The failure of the meta-analysis to obtain significant results could be the result of a poverty of incisive measures to tease apart the various layers of interactional complexity. So, terms like parental "restrictiveness" or "encouragement of dependence" might not be subtle enough to reveal the true extent of the differences between parents in their differentiation of boys and girls. As Lytton and Romney admit, their analysis was very much at the behavioral level. This might obscure relationship factors or mutual influences between parent and child. Meta-analysis has obvious benefits, but might miss the crucial level of analysis.

Lytton and Romney's data stand in contrast to many strands of research evidence that seem to show that parents play a part in sex-role socialization, but that do not appear obviously to tie together into a coherent thread of an argument. Researchers have turned to consider why there are such inconsistencies in the literature. Large-scale reviews and meta-analyses lump together children of different ages and categories that become approximations. It may be that parental influences on the child are time specific or change in subtle ways as the child's interests and capabilities develop. Beverly Fagot has long argued that the transition between infancy and early childhood (18–30 months) is a critical period in sex-role development at which time parents make their mark on males and females. She claims that overarching analyses assume a homogeneity of parental effects as if they are, or should be, consistent over the child's development. In one recent study, for example, she examined parent-child interaction for four one-hour sessions in the home at 12 months, 18 months, and again at around the child's fifth birthday (Fagot & Hagan, 1991). Parental reactions to the child at 18 months were different from those earlier and later. They reacted more negatively, particularly when their sons attempted to communicate, and were more encouraging of their sons' stereotypical masculine play. At the same time, late infancy marked a time when parents were more rewarding of their daughters' attempts to communicate and of their sons' negative actions. If either parent was more positive about stereotypical activities it was fathers, who encouraged more gross motor activities than mothers.

Fagot and Hagan's study suggests that we should be cautious about completely ruling out parental influences. In keeping with their previous work (Fagot, 1985), it shows that the time when children are acquiring language at a most rapid rate may be marked by more clear "messages" about sex-appropriate behavior. Further research will have to examine, first, whether or not there are clear sex-of-parent influences, or more subtle sex-of-child × sex-of-parent interactions, and, second, the nature of any critical periods of influence. There is some evidence to support the view that each of these layers of influence may operate a little later in the preschool period, at ages three to four. In other studies fathers appear to demonstrate an interest in manipulating objects during free play, while mothers seem to be more intent on instructional activities (e.g., Stevenson, Leavitt, Thompson, & Roach, 1988). There is further evidence to suggest that fathers exert more control on their interactions with four-year-olds, particularly their sons to whom they appear to demonstrate more instrumentality and less warmth (Bright & Stockdale, 1984; Frankel & Rollins, 1983). If given a specific task to do one-to-one with their children, fathers may impose more demanding strategies on their daughters (McGuillicuddy-deLisi, 1988). Such differences might indicate that in free play fathers attempt to act like "one of the boys" with their sons, while in more pedagogical settings they may want their daughters to demonstrate their cognitive-linguistic skills. It is to the meaning of such observed differences that we examine in the next major section.

FATHER-CHILD LANGUAGE

If research examining the minute details of behavioral interaction has been the hallmark of research on fathers and their infants (e.g., Berman & Pedersen, 1987; Pedersen, 1980), then studies of parent-child language have been typical of investigations into the preschool period. This wave of research was prompted by a small study by Gleason (1975) who analyzed the speech addressed to preschoolers of a range of ages to see if fathers modify their language, as mothers do, to suit the linguistic capabilities of the child. Gleason found that while fathers do use "child-directed speech" they also occasionally breach such modification by using words like "aggravating," "dingaling," and "brontosaurus" which are beyond the two- to three-year old child's capabilities. She provocatively suggested that fathers act as a "bridge" to the outside world. As a result of their relative incompetence men may inadvertently stretch their children's linguistic skills. The task of much research since has to evaluate the "bridge" hypothesis further (Mannle & Tomasello, 1987).

In many respects the data on parent-child language echoes those on sex-role development, in that some measures suggest differences between parents whereas others do not. Analyses of the amount (Masur, 1982) and structure (Fash & Madison, 1981) of parental language both in free play and in specific play tasks confirm Gleason's suggestion that "fatherese" does make the same concessions to the child as "motherese" does. Mothers' and fathers' language is particularly similar when the linguistic corpus is collected from triadic (mother-father-child) interaction (Hladik & Edwards, 1984; Pellegrini, Brody, & Stoneman, 1987). By age five, the conversational rhythm of turn taking and mutual influence between parent and child appear to be similar for mothers and fathers (Welkowitz, Bond, Feldman, & Tota, 1990).

However, there are some differences between parents in most published studies. Some support the "bridge" hypothesis in that it seems as if paternal language is often not as fine-tuned as that of mothers. For example, Pratt, Kerig, Cowan, and Cowan (1992) compared the most commonly used measure of linguistic structure, the Mean Length of Utterance (MLU), in both parents and their three-year-olds. Maternal MLU was significantly more positively correlated with the child's MLU than was paternal MLU, suggesting that mothers are more adept at fine-tuning their speech. Furthermore, the child's MLU was related to functional aspects of maternal speech like the mother's responsiveness. Pratt et al.'s data are complemented by research that shows that fathers' language questions preschoolers' conversational violations more (Pellegrini et al., 1987), it is less helpful to the child's bid to communicate (Austin & Braeger, 1990), it can be more highly redundant than the child will appreciate (Fash & Madison, 1981), and it can be highly controlling (McLoughlin, Schutz, & White, 1980).

The above patterns of findings appear to be consistent despite their relative complexity. They seem to indicate support for the bridge hypothesis in that fathers modify their language to communicate with their preschoolers, but they fail to demonstrate such sensitivity at all times. Just why men might do this is unclear. It is usually assumed that fathers are simply incompetent. They may consciously attempt to extend their child's skills, although the existing data (to be examined later) do not clearly suggest that this "strategy" is effective. In the next section we shall see that the picture is more complicated, so we cannot restrict our analysis to the bridge hypothesis. Research on parental language also suggests interesting influences of the child's sex on their output. Some studies report that parents appear to discriminate between children of the same or the opposite sex. For example, when playing a structured game with their five-year-olds, mothers and fathers use more complex language with opposite-sex children (McLoughlin et al. 1980), while they discuss future plans with the same-sex child (Masur, 1982). More easily interpretable findings are main effects of the child's sex. Reese and Fivush (1993) examined the conversational styles of parents with their three-year-olds when sharing reminiscences about the child's past. Fathers and mothers talk longer and use more elaborate language with daughters even though their sons are equally proficient language users. Reese and Fivush argue that in domains of experience linked with girls', rather than boys', interests, parental language is highly sex typed.

So, rather than addressing their children in ways that simply reflect their general sensitivity to the child's level of skill, parents have been found to alter their language dependent upon the context. Further research seems to support the findings of Reese and Fivush in that parents and preschoolers appear to modify their language as a result of the structure of the setting in which their language is recorded (Lewis & Gregory, 1987; Welkowitz et al., 1990). There is therefore an element of doubt in interpreting data on early language interchanges between parents and preschoolers. Such doubt matches the findings on sex differences concerning just what such data demonstrate. If parents change their behavior dependent upon minor factors like the toys that are available to them, then this suggests that we have to situate theoretical claims about what is recorded in terms of parents' interpretations of the research experience as a public activity.

FATHERING OBSERVED: PUBLIC INFLUENCES

Many reasons have been put forward as to why patterns of paternal engagement with preschoolers appear to show sex of parent or child influences in some circumstances but not in others. The usual argument is that any significant effects may simply be Type 1 errors or effects that do not have much significance in terms of predicting variance in the child's "outcome" measures (e.g., Lytton & Romney, 1991). Alternatively, it is suggested that fathers may interact with their preschoolers in unique ways, but these are somehow not captured by existing methods. An analysis of the social psychology of the observation process itself in this section reveals that research on fathers may be particularly problematic in terms of how we interpret maternal versus paternal data. If we admit that observation is a public enterprise and that fathers ordinarily engage in publicly observed interactions, then we may learn a great deal about their relationships with preschoolers and perhaps even about how patterns of influence might be transmitted.

ANALYZING FATHER-CHILD INTERACTIONS

In much research on paternal interactions fathering continues to be treated as a set of behaviors that are prompted in men when they come into contact with their children. The child may have an influence upon the interaction (cf. Bell, 1968), but by and large the father's actions are treated as unreflexive. Yet there are strong grounds for assuming that parents react in different ways to being observed—that observation is essentially a means of displaying skills within particular contexts. For a start there is clear evidence that fathers' interaction styles are influenced by their socioeconomic circumstances (Radin & Epstein, 1975; Roberts, 1987). Such patterns raise the issues of what influences fathers' styles in the first place and why.

What are the particular elements of paternal style? As mentioned earlier most theoreticians assume that biological or socialization differences are revealed by significant sex-of-parent effects. However, research has demonstrated that the picture is more complex. If mothers and fathers are given a range of tasks to do, then the major influence on their way of interacting with their preschooler is the activity, not the sex of the parent (Lewis & Gregory, 1987; Ross & Taylor, 1989; Worden et al., 1987). For example, Ross and Taylor set up a study that examined dyadic parent-son interaction bouts in two playrooms, one with stereotypical "maternal" objects like books and puzzles, the other with "paternal" objects like trucks and balls. Boys were chosen on the grounds that sex-of-parent differences are stronger for boys than girls. The order of each parent-child play session (one for each parent in each playroom) was balanced, and there were four weeks between each session. There were some sex-of-parent effects, but there were clear playroom influences on both parents' activities. In the "maternal" playroom mothers and fathers engaged in more reading, constructive play, and instructional play, while in the "paternal" playroom parents and children played more, particularly in physical games and pretense. The children appeared to display greater positive affect when with their parent adopted a "paternal" style of play. Thus Ross and Taylor (1989, pp. 30–31) conclude,

> Parents adapt their style of play to differences in context and to the differences in the play of their children. Thus the play style differences between parents are far from obligatory and should be evaluated in the context of parental flexibility. . . . It seems that the children were the leaders in this environment, and the sex differences in parental play styles reflected the fathers' greater willingness to join actively in the play of their sons.

Some cautions must be made about Ross and Taylor's conclusion, as summarized in this quotation. First, their analysis does not, as they suggest, allow us to infer that the order of "influence" was from child to adult. Second, they did not provide evidence to show that fathers enter into stereotypical, or active, play patterns willingly. These readings of their data seem compelling but need to be substantiated by further evidence, utilizing sequential analysis that allows for causality to be inferred rather than assumed. Yet the differences between playrooms suggest that contextual factors might account for any sex-of-parent effects that are found in studies of parent-child interactions. Two reasons why this might be the case are apparent. The first, which I will discuss in the next section, is that father-child relationships are often punctuated by brief encounters between events in the child's routine, like between bathtime and bedtime. Such "situational" constraints might in some way stage manage the father's relationship with his child.

The second possible issue concerns "experimenter" (Rosenthal, 1966) or "reactivity" (Haynes & Horn, 1982) effects, which refer to the ways in which individual activities may be a result of being observed. It is very hard to pinpoint such factors, and very few studies have attempted to address their significance (Lewis, 1985; Russell, Russell, & Midwinter, 1992). The more comprehensive study by Russell et al. attempted to come to grips with the possible differential effects of observation on mothers and fathers, as suggested by Lewis (1985). Technical analyses of the research process have long suggested that individuals might change their interactions when being observed either to "look good" or from anxiety (e.g., Blurton Jones, 1972). The grounds for assuming that mothers and fathers may react in different ways during a "natural" observation session stem from the different types of relationship that they have with their children. Russell et al. observed families with a preschooler, a school-aged child, and both parents in the early evening around the time of a family meal. Like other research of this type, the observation started half an hour before "dad" arrived home and continued for one hour. Afterwards the parents were interviewed alone about specific events in the family interaction and whether each was "typical." Eighty percent of parents reported some degree of influence of the act of observation. More than their wives, those fathers who reported a greater inhibition were found to initiate less play and to demonstrate less affection to their primary-school-aged child. In summarizing this study Russell and Radojevic (1992, p. 301) comment, "The evidence suggests that fathers are more influenced by the observer's presence when observed at home than mothers are, and perhaps the observational method is less valid for the study of fathers than for mothers."

COMING OUT: FATHERS IN THE PUBLIC EYE

Russell and Radojevic's conclusion may well be correct and calls for further research. Yet it overlooks the fact that many fathers will mainly engage in interactions with their preschoolers which are triadic or polyadic. At home the short bursts of paternal play are usually within sight or earshot of the mother (Lewis, 1986). In addition much father-preschooler interaction takes place outside the home and is open to public scrutiny. Young children accompany their fathers to the park or on shopping expeditions (Lewis, 1986), while the later preschool years are often characterized by fathers and their children developing a shared interest, like fishing (Newson & Newson, 1976), which involves exposure to the public gaze. Over the past 15 years a small group of studies has examined the involvement of male caregivers in a variety of public settings. These give rare insights into the division of domestic labor and the complexities of paternal experience. What men do in public is "relatively uncontaminated by the observer's presence" (Amato, 1989, p. 982). However, it is still a public demonstration of their commitment witnessed not only by their family and friends but also by the world at large.

The preschool period appears to be the time when in many settings fathers appear to make themselves salient to their children in public places. Indeed, a trip to the park or the store may be an integral feature of paternal involvement. One massive study of the structure of social groups involving children in 18 cultures found a peak of male involvement with young preschoolers compared with infants or school-aged children (Mackey, 1985). While home-based studies appear to suggest no overall rise in paternal involvement (Lamb, 1987), or even a decline after infancy (Coverman & Sheley, 1986), research on fathering in public supports Mackey's observations. Such observations provide a window into the nature of fatherhood, particularly expectations about sex roles and the transmission of cultural norms.

If parent-child groups are examined in public settings like amusement parks, fast-food outlets, and shopping centers in the early evening or on weekends, large amounts of father-child interaction are in evidence. Amato (1989) observed 2,500 preschoolers in a variety of such settings for as long as it took an adult to demonstrate a gesture of care, like holding the child's hand. Most observations lasted less than a minute before such an action was recorded. He noted the size of the group, its ethnicity, the sex of the child, and the sex of the adult who provided care for the child, even if that gesture was momentary. He found that males were recorded to have cared for their charges in 42% of observations where it was possible to distinguish one caregiver. While the time of day selected for observation to optimize paternal involvement, the proportion of male caregivers is much higher than would be expected from stereotypes about males as figures who are psychologically absent from family life.

In many respects the public domain reflects the private world of the home. Men were much more likely to display care-giving gestures in parks than in shopping centers and restaurants. As a specialist in fun and play the father is less likely to take responsibility for the preschooler in a setting which is stereotypically female—the kitchen in the home or the public dining area. Sex-role norms toward children are also reproduced in the public domain. Amato (1989) observed that more boys (48%)

than girls (38%) were cared for by male adults. Male involvement was greater in recreational settings like parks than in restaurants or shopping malls. Perhaps the most revealing data concern the interaction between the sex of the adults and the age of the child. Very few infants (5%) were cared for by men in same-sex groups. Male care for preschoolers was still much greater in mixed-sex groups (56%) than in single-sex male groups (32%).

From Amato's study it seems that men display their commitment to parenting more to preschoolers than to infants and more to boys. Either these patterns represent "typical" levels of involvement or they may reveal the importance of public interaction for communicating to the child just what is culturally appropriate despite any equal treatment boys and girls might receive inside the home (cf. Lytton & Romney, 1991). The "public display" argument seems more likely. It must be borne in mind that large numbers of younger preschoolers and girls received attention from their fathers in Amato's and other similar studies. But the emphasis on father-son relationships might have particular salience to the child, particularly in light of differential parental behavior. Burns, Mitchell, and their colleagues have carried out over 1,000 observations of family triads (adult male–adult female–toddler) in public parks and zoos. Their data suggest that in such a homogeneous social environment patterns of interaction become more specifiable. They simply observed the means by which the child was transported through the park. They found a tendency for male toddlers to walk alone, a twofold increase in paternal over maternal carrying of toddlers (Mitchell, Obradovich, Herring, Tromborg, & Burns, 1992) and significantly more men carrying girls than boys (Burns, Mitchell, & Obradovich, 1989). A mother in a public park is more likely to push a stroller along, while the father cares for the child, carrying him or her and engaging his son particularly in a physical and interactive style. From a psychoanalytic perspective, Burlingham (1973) has highlighted the importance of such physical interactions as demonstrations of masculine power, but Mitchell et al. (1992, p. 329) are more concerned with the reproduction of norms and values. They write of men's "physical interactive style (holding, carrying) while adult females are left with empty strollers to push. These subtle behavioral differences, when taken in the context of the division of labour, offer insights into the methods by which parenting tasks themselves reproduce gender roles through the modeling of different behaviors for children."

If social representations are important in influencing children's understanding of what is "important" in adult norms and values, what other evidence is there to highlight how such reproduction takes place? There are data to suggest that fathers may make public gestures in a variety of settings which have a diversity of implications. One study concerned the interaction styles of parents when leaving their children at a day-care center (Noller, 1978). Mothers engaged in more interaction, particularly with their daughters, while there was significantly less father-son interaction. That father-son affection was very low may well underline the importance of communicating the stiff upper lip to preschool males. However, other research points to a more constructive role for fathers. In the study of hospitalized children discussed above it was found that under such circumstances men engage in both expressive actions, like comforting the child, and more stereotypically instrumental activities, like putting pressure on the physicians to discharge the child (Knafl & Dixon, 1984).

Public observations of fathers suggest that we know very little about the subtleties of father-child exchanges, particularly the transmission of cognitive skills. One moving study concerns the minute details of the interaction between men and children in the late preschool and early school years on a public fishing pier (Diamond & Bond, 1983). This research employed 88 clearly defined ethological categories of father and child behavior. It details just how in one specific, clearly defined context fathers and their children perform parallel activities in which the former gradually scaffolds the latter's maneuvers. Diamond and Bond found that parent-child interaction was heavily intertwined. A number of clusters of parent and child actions and gestures were apparent. For example, fathers spent time demonstrating a skill on their own line and then guiding the child's hand on his or her own line, while both describing what the activities involved and relating the joint action to their shared past activities. Diamond and Bond's analysis of interaction during fishing suggests, first, that distinctions between "instrumental" activities, like fishing, and "expressive" interaction, like showing affection, are not as clear as long-standing psychological assumptions have maintained (Parsons & Bales, 1955). Paternal instruction was often coupled with an affective gesture. So, when fathers described an action by analogy, they would accompany such a vocalization with a smile. Second, and by implication, their examination of the minute details of behavior reveal complexities of paternal-child interaction that appear to provide ample scope for the transfer of skills and understanding on both cognitive and affective levels.

The accumulated data on public displays of fathering appear to convey a complex impression of men's involvement with their preschoolers. On the one hand they suggest that men's interaction styles do not show as much sophistication as that of women. Liddell, Henzi, and Drew (1987) found that mothers adapted their interaction styles according to whether they were interacting with their preschoolers in a dyad or a mother-father-child triad. Fathers seemed to interact in the same way in both types of groups. On the basis of the above analysis (Russell et al., 1992), it may well be the case that men appear less flexible because they know that their "dyadic" interaction in a public place, like much of their play at home, is "triadic" since it is open to scrutiny from real or hypothetical others. On the other hand, there is sufficient evidence to show that within specific contexts like fishing, men appear to be highly attuned to the needs of their children, both in terms of instructing them and on more affective levels. Just what the child makes of such interactions will be the focus of the next and final section.

A ROLE FOR FATHERS IN PRESCHOOLERS' DEVELOPMENT?

Radin (1981) documents a wealth of data published since the Second World War suggesting that paternal involvement, particularly the relative amounts of nurturance the man provides for his offspring, has implications in terms of the child's intellectual and social development and that such correlations are evident in the preschool years. Yet she shows that the picture is not simple enough to discern cause-effect relationships. Just as mothers and fathers interact with their preschoolers in similar ways, so too do their styles appear to correlate with the child's behavior or attributions. Such common variance has been found in studies examining the impact of mothers' and fathers' styles upon the child's creativity (Bayard de Volo & Fiebert, 1977), exploration (Henderson, 1984), Type A propensity (Yamasaki, 1990), and peer interactions (Bhavnagri & Parke, 1991; Hart et al., 1992).

When mothers' and fathers' actions or child-rearing philosophies appear to relate to the child's psychosocial functioning in different ways, such differences are bounded by the father's social and socioeconomic circumstances. For example, Radin and Epstein's (1975) study of 180 preschoolers found complex interactions between sex of child, the family's social class membership, and paternal nurturance on the child's IQ. Boys seemed to be more influenced than girls by the amount of paternal involvement, but differentially in three social class groups. In middle-class families 30% of the variance in the son's IQ score was predicted by paternal cognitive stimulation and lower physical control, whereas in lower-class families the child's IQ was related to low paternal verbal restrictiveness. Such patterns are obviously interesting, but what they show is still not clear. Radin (1981) points out that since many studies have been cross-sectional it has been hard to separate paternal from other influences.

So, how successful has research since 1981 been in teasing apart the relative influence of paternal factors in the child's development? The answer to this question is not as clear as it might be. Many studies show that on measures like the child's intellectual competence it is hard to separate the relative effects of the father's interactional style and his socioeconomic circumstances (e.g., Roberts, 1987). Here the discussion will address first the topic of sex roles to examine the father's possible influence on the child's development, then the complex data on the child's social-cognitive functioning, and finally paternal influence on the child in longitudinal perspective.

Do Fathers Influence Preschoolers' Sex-Role Development?

By their third birthdays children appear to act in ways that confirm their ability to discriminate between others on the basis of their sex (Smith, 1985). Indeed, by two years of age children are above chance in their response to questions about gender labeling, sex-typing of toys, and adult roles (Weinraub et al., 1984). How do such skills emerge, and do fathers play their part in the development of such differences? If we consider the interpretative problems in understanding any differences between mothers' and fathers' interactional styles, the picture becomes complicated. Matters get even worse when we add the possible contributions of the child to any sex-linked patterns of parent-child interaction. In a study cited earlier, Ross and Taylor (1989) found that in dyadic play with their mother or father in one of two different playrooms, the son's gestures toward each parent were more influenced by the available toys than by the sex of the parent (Ross & Taylor, 1989). When surrounded by books and constructive play toys, boys demonstrated more constructive play, and they engaged in more pretence and physical play when the toys encouraged such interaction. So, perhaps parent-child interaction is sex stereotyped because of the nature of interaction each parent tends to engage in rather than as a result of qualities inherent in the parent or child. Rather than look for minute differences between parents, this analysis will examine general influences of parental work arrangements upon sex-role stereotyping in preschoolers.

By their fifth birthdays children appear to have highly stereotyped views of parental roles. Goldman and Goldman (1983) interviewed 838 5- to 15-year-olds across four different cultures. Even in more sexually liberated Sweden, 80% of five-year-olds could think of a distinct role for mothers in the home, whereas only half could think of such a role for fathers. However, there were cultural differences. Seventeen percent of children in the United States cited a functional social difference between mothers and fathers (as opposed to a nonsexual characteristic like an aspect of their personality), while the figure was only 3% in Sweden. Five-year-olds were less stereotyped than their older counterparts about the division of child-care responsibilities, yet they were still clear that mothers and fathers performed different domestic roles and were more stereotyped overall.

In keeping with Goldman and Goldman's survey, most studies over the past 40 years have revealed that from the preschool years children tend to perceive the home as the mother's domain and link the task of breadwinning with fathering (Dubin & Dubin, 1965; Hartley, 1960; Williams, Bennett, & Best, 1975). In one New Zealand study (Smith, Ballard, & Barham, 1989) mothers were twice as likely to be seen to engage in domestic activities than fathers, particularly household chores like cooking, cleaning, washing, and sewing. Fathers were associated with outdoor work and house repairs. What influences such understanding? A few studies have suggested that children's perceptions are influenced by their family circumstances. When their mothers work (Miller, 1975) or children are in day care (Mills & Stevens, 1985) there is a slight tendency to regard parental roles in less segregated ways. However, an equal proportion of studies has failed to find a relationship between maternal employment and children's perceptions (Marantz & Mansfield, 1977; Vener & Snyder, 1966). Perhaps children simply report what happens in the home in that mothers remain the main "homemakers" when they are employed outside the home and the parental roles described in these studies match what parents say they do (Horna & Lupri, 1987; Sandqvist, 1987)?

Studies that have attempted to delve into the relationship between parental domestic and employment commitments on the one hand and preschoolers' understanding on the other have suggested that three factors contribute to the child's understanding of parental gender roles. First, children's cognitive level correlates with their awareness of sex roles (Weinraub et al., 1984). Second, there is some evidence to suggest that the attitude of the employed mother is more important than that of her partner/husband in predicting whether or not the child appears to hold a sex-stereotyped view of adult roles (Baruch & Barnett, 1986). Given that women continue to provide most input even when they work, it seems plausible that their influence on children is greater. However, a third strand of evidence suggests that in families where the father is particularly nurturant and involved in child care, their preschoolers appear to attribute adults with fewer sex-role stereotypes (Carlson, 1984). Carlson found that boys were significantly more gendered in their attribution than girls, but not if their fathers shared in their care. Further work is needed to examine the relative contributions of the above three factors and other possible contributions to the child's understanding of adult gender. It must be emphasized that, despite a general increase in maternal employment when their children are young, preschoolers remain highly conservative about sex roles (Smith et al., 1989). In one intriguing study children were asked to pose for a photograph with a same-sex peer and an infant, either as themselves or as "mommy" or "daddy" (Reid, Tate, & Berman, 1989). When posing as a parent, girls stood closer to the infant while boys as "daddy" stood farther away than when each was simply asked to pose as themselves. Sex-role stereotypes concerning adult roles seem to be deeply ingrained.

FATHERS AND PRESCHOOLERS' SOCIAL AND COGNITIVE DEVELOPMENT

Researchers have long been divided over whether and how fathers might influence their children's intellectual functioning and their integration into the social world of relationships. As Radin's 1981 review suggests, much of the evidence in support of the argument that fathers have a major influence comes from studies where they are absent from the home, as a result of either death or divorce. Such studies have been controversial since, as Herzog and Sudia (1970) pointed out, single-parent families differ from two-parent families in a diversity of ways, particularly in terms of their financial solvency. Research since 1981 has tilted the balance in favor of the position advocated by Herzog and Sudia (1970; see also Chapter 11 of this volume). The clearest example with preschoolers is Eggebeen and Hawkins' analysis of a large data set, the U.S. National Longitudinal Survey of Youth, examining a group of over 1,500 preschoolers from a sample in which younger parents and members of ethnic minorities were overrepresented (Crockett, Eggebeen, & Hawkins, 1993; Hawkins & Eggebeen, 1991). They have dissected the minute details of "father absence" by breaking down the data set into finer subgroups, like families where the father has resided continuously through the child's life versus those where a father figure either resided for the child's early life or only in recent years, or never coresided. From Hawkins and Eggebeen's analyses it can be seen that the current coresidence of a father figure does not appear to influence the child's IQ or maternally reported behavioral problems (Hawkins & Eggebeen, 1991). More importantly, the effects of fathers' residence in the household are no longer in evidence when factors to do with the mother's social circumstances are employed in covariance analyses. When her age and the family's poverty are controlled for there appear to be no unique contributions to the child's development made by the father's presence or absence (Crockett et al., 1993). Such data on fatherless preschoolers are supported by meta-analytic research (Stevenson & Black, 1988).

Studies of intact families suggest that paternal involvement in families has an impact on the child. For example, in their analysis of 13,000 British families Osborn and Morris (1982) found that involvement in four aspects of paternal care (described above) related significantly to children's performance on a spatial motor task (copying designs) and verbal IQ. However, their sample was very large and, although not reported, the amount of predicted variance was obviously very low. In addition we still have little grasp on the causes of such relationships. They could reveal direct influences of the father in teaching the child, or indirect "effects" like family cohesion of which paternal involvement may be a marker. In Osborn and Morris's study increased child care by fathers was also associated with greater child neuroticism as reported by the mother. So we know that the picture is more complex than one whereby the father's involvement simply rubs off in positive ways on the preschooler.

There is some evidence that the quality and nature of paternal interaction relates to the level of the child's activities. For example, Clarke-Stewart (1980) found that paternal engagement in play with 30-month olds and also maternal warmth were related to children's intellectual test performance. Two-and-a-half-year old boys' social competence was correlated positively with both maternal and paternal warmth, while the relationship between parental warmth and girls' social functioning was significant, but negative. Research since 1981 has continued to show such patterns of paternal warmth relating to positive aspects of the child's social-cognitive development. for example, three-year-old boys in Bombay who share their candies with other children depict fathers (but not their mothers) as more nurturant (Pandit, 1988). In keeping with Gleason's (1975) claim concerning language development, MacDonald and Parke (1984) put forward the view that father-child play serves as a useful learning ground for the development of social skills in preschoolers, particularly their peer interactions. They examined the interactions of three-year-olds with their peers and found, particularly in boys, an association between peer competence and both maternal verbal interaction and paternal physical play. More directive fathers had children who were less popular. MacDonald's (1987) subsequent research examined boys who were neglected by their peers in nursery school. He found that when observed at home such boys engaged in less emotionally arousing and physical play with their fathers. Without longitudinal analyses of paternal and peer interactions, the direction of causality behind these patterns is difficult to pinpoint. The neglected boys may have had more difficult temperaments and kept their fathers at bay, although it is more likely that these data demonstrate that paternal style can influence the child by preparing him or her for the demands of peer relationships.

If obvious paternal effects are hard to discern, there has been sufficient evidence from a diversity of sources to suggest that fathers can influence their preschoolers in subtle ways that derive from their differential access to the child and as a result of their lifestyles. MacDonald and Parke's research is founded on the assumption that most men's involvement will be qualitatively different from that of mothers. This might arise from the bias toward men as secondary caregivers and primary providers, although there is little consistency in the literature on primary caregiver fathers to suggest that they treat their preschoolers in different ways. If fathers do interact with their children in different ways this might affect the child in terms of the values or styles that the father may wish to inculcate upon the child. Tentative support for such a claim comes from a diversity of sources. First, nursery-teacher-rated achievement motivation in preschool girls relates to fathers' but not mothers' achievement needs (Galejs, King, & Hegland, 1987). Second, preschoolers' understanding of the distinction between safety and danger has been found to relate to fathers' but not mothers' locus of control concerning accidents (Coppens, 1985). Third, how much children use technical equipment, like computers, in the preschool center relates to the amount they attribute their teachers and their fathers with an interest in them (McBride & Austin, 1986).

Some apparent influences of the father seem to result in part from the man's lifestyle, particularly his social and dietary habits. In one investigation, Sallis, Patterson, McKenzie, and Nader (1988) measured the amount of activity displayed by 33 children in a preschool center in relation to their own and their parents' body mass. A stereotype holds that children are active most of the time. In reality, they found that in 60% of observation time the preschoolers were sedentary. Moderate activity on their part was correlated with the amount of exercise their parents reporting doing and their fathers' (but neither their own or their mothers') lower body mass. So there seems to be a subtle relationship between a father's lifestyle and risk of cardiovascular disease on the one hand and his child's activity in a preschool setting on the other. A similar lifestyle influence is evident in families where the father acts in a deviant way. In one of a series of investigations Noll, Zucker, Fitzgerald, and Curtis (1992) examined the families of nontreated alcoholics, who were recruited through traffic convictions rather than alcohol dependency clinics. Noll et al. found that under such circumstances the son's social and personal adjustments, as measured by the Revised Yale Developmental Scales, were related to the quality of family life and the father's history of alcohol consumption. So alcoholism in the father was a risk factor alongside other influences, like the mother's personal problems, in influencing the child's intellectual performance.

The literature on paternal influences on the child's psychosocial functioning is thus complex. There is much about paternal influences that we have yet to grasp. This is partly because we do not know enough about the child's own contribution to the process by which parental influences are imparted upon him or her. The preschool years witness great strides in language and cognitive functioning. Greater attention should be paid to the child as an active agent in constructing an understanding of social and family relationships. This is demonstrated well in Springer's (1994) examinations of preschoolers' understanding of biological knowledge, particularly inheritance. Where children know about the development of the fetus in utero, they are more likely to attribute inheritance influences to the mother rather than the father. We have yet to know whether such induction processes spill over into the preschool child's understanding of parental behavior and responsibility, but Springer's finding serves to show that the child is an active agent who constructs a theoretical grasp of adult influence through biological knowledge. In addition to a general lack of consensus about how children develop an understanding of the social world (as opposed to well-worn research on children's understanding of the physical world), the research presented in this section suggests that the impact fathers have on their children is unclear. We know from studies of father absence and families where the man's individual psychological health is in question (e.g., as a result of excessive alcohol consumption) that their children are at risk. However, the role of the father is part of a more complex picture involving a range of social, economic, and psychological factors.

PATERNAL INFLUENCES OVER TIME

Longitudinal research on daily family interactions has suggested that the father becomes more involved as the child progresses from infancy to the preschool period. Clarke-Stewart's (1980) analysis of 14 children from 15 to 30 months showed that the amount of child care diminished, while playful interaction increased. As mothers were the major caregivers and fathers specialized in play, by 30 months the amounts of their respective interactions with the child were more equal. Analyses of the longitudinal patterns suggested that maternal stimulation and toy play at 15 months correlated with the child's IQ in the third year, while the child's developmental quotient at the earlier stage was related to the amount of father-child talk and play at 30 months. This might suggest that mothers are more influential upon the child's development, while fathers may simply be reactive once the child's skills are proficient. Subsequent research has produced similar patterns. For example, Hunter, McCarthy, MacTurk, and Vietze (1987) found that mother-child interaction around the child's first birthday predicted his or her IQ at 30 months, while father-infant interaction did not.

The data on parent-infant interactions play down a role for fathers in predicting the performance of preschoolers. Patterns of parent-infant attachment provide compatible data. In 1985 Main, Kaplan, and Cassidy presented longitudinal data showing that infant-mother attachment relationships, but not father-infant attachments, predict how confidently a child performs in a social setting (interaction with a strange adult) at age 5–6. They concluded that there is a "hierarchy of internal working models in which the mother stands foremost" (Main, Kaplan, & Cassidy 1985, p. 93). This pattern of findings has been extended in more recent studies (Suess, Grossman, & Sroufe, 1992; Youngblade & Belsky, 1992). Seuss et al. conducted a longitudinal analysis of 29 children when they were age five in a home observation. Strange Situation assessments of mother-infant attachments from infancy were stronger predictions of the child's play, conflict resolution, and fewer problem behaviors four years later. Some infant-father measures showed consistencies, but these correlations were less strong. While Suess et al.'s analyses replicated those of Main et al., they also found that the best predictions of the child's adjustment at age five were derived from mother- *and* father-infant attachment combined. If children had been securely attached to both parents in the second year, they were more likely to be self-reliant at the end of the preschool period. However, longitudinal analyses by Youngblade and Belsky (1992) of 73 families from 13 to 60 months suggested that paternal attachment at the earlier age predicted *less* synchronous interaction between the child and a friend at age five. So, in the light of such contradictory data we must assume either that the effects of father-infant attachment are complex or that the collective results need further exploration.

How does relative parental "influence" continue over the preschool period? In keeping with the findings on the predictions of parental attachment, the data suggest in the main that mothers continue to have a more obvious influence upon their children. For example, Pratt et al.'s (1992) study of parental speech to three-year-olds (discussed earlier) found that the child's linguistic proficiency later (at age five) was predicted by maternal conversational responsivity, but not paternal responsivity. The correlation held even when the child's linguistic capabilities at age three were controlled for. These results replicate previous work on mother-child language (Hess & McDevitt, 1984). Parallel findings come from a study of six-year-olds, which found that sibling conflict was predicted by maternal intrusiveness at age three and an insecure mother-child attachment at age one (Volling & Belsky, 1992). Such patterns suggest the primacy of maternal influence on positive and negative aspects of child performance at the end of the preschool period.

However, there are some strands of data that suggest that paternal styles might have an influence, even though the patterns are more diffuse. One study found that an authoritative paternal style at age three predicted the child's nonlinguistic skills at age five (Pratt et al., 1992). Other analyses appear to show that father-preschooler interaction predicts later prosocial skills. For example, Youngblade and Belsky's (1992) examination of five-year-olds' interactions with a close or best friend produced significant paternal predictions from parent-child interaction at age three. Negative peer interaction was related to less positive father-child interaction and greater paternal negativity at age three. Such findings may support MacDonald and Parke's (1984) claim that fathers serve a function of preparing the child for the outside world, but the amount of predicted variance accounted for was low, and such findings need replication and extension.

If the patterns of paternal influence are not completely clear across the first six years of the child's life, then the few analyses of the long-term correlates with paternal involvement from the preschool period onwards must be treated with even more caution. In the main they suggest that even high amounts of paternal involvement do not have a great influence on the child. The best demonstration of this comes from Radin's follow-up analysis of 32 children between ages 14 and 16, whose fathers had shared in their care during the preschool years (Williams et al., 1992). This study produced a few significant associations between parenting responsibilities in the preschool period, the primary school years, and the teenager's sex-role attitudes. For example, where parents had reversed roles for some time in the child's early life, the teenager had less sex-stereotyped attitudes toward employment, but not about sex roles in general.

Other investigations attest to the continuing primacy of maternal "influence," with paternal predictions contributing additional but not sufficient variance to the child's later psychosocial functioning. Gjerde, Block, and Block (1991) examined self-reported depression in 106 18-year-olds who had been observed in interaction with each parent at age five. Maternal interaction style in the late preschool period contributed significantly to teenage daughters' depression scores, even when the child's IQ at age five and parental education were controlled for. Women who expressed more warmth, resourcefulness in guidance, and control at age five had more depressed children 13 years later. Multiple regression analysis showed that paternal resourcefulness contributed additional variance to this relationship, suggesting that parental styles complement one another.

CONCLUSION

How far has research since 1976 represented a break from tradition, as suggested by Pedersen (1980)? In many respects we have made few if any methodological advances. Too much of the research reported in this chapter has been cross-sectional. We have traveled only a short distance from the 1970s researchers in terms of our readiness to use such designs and the relative scarcity of studies examining sequences of father-child interaction, longitudinal designs, and research on what the research process means to the "subjects" themselves. Nevertheless, changes in our understanding of the research process have come about. As a result of the studies on public displays of fatherhood, I have attempted to argue that children may learn more from such displays by fathers than they do in daily interactions within the home. In the latter the data are unclear, whereas in the former clear differences between mothers and fathers are apparent. Such a conclusion can only be speculative and suggests a need for comparisons of men's parenting in private and public settings and analyses of preschoolers' understanding of their father's actions in each.

In theoretical terms greater evidence of a break is in evidence. It seems as if we have had to modify theory to become more sophisticated about what parent-child interaction entails. If there are differences between mothers and fathers, these are not easy to measure and do not have demonstrable effects on the child's development, as was once simply assumed in the child development literature. The research on fathers has forced us to reconsider the nature of family relationships. Rather than looking for simple cause-effect patterns we have had to turn to examine the effects of a network of family relationships on the child's development. Such a network may or may not contain a father figure, and this figure may or may not be biologically related to the child (Furstenberg & Nord, 1985). The family is thus a sociological microcosm where negotiations between members and displays of affection, interest, and instruction may tell us more about the system than the individuals concerned. As members of that system fathers are important, but only in specific contexts do they have unique or specific effects on the development of preschoolers.

CHAPTER 8

The Father and the School-Aged Child

Henry B. Biller and Jon Lopez Kimpton
University of Rhode Island

ANY DISCUSSION of human behavior must take into account many different influences in addition to parent-child relationships. Thus, in the investigation of the father's influence of child development, we advocate a biopsychosocial perspective. In other words, we would argue that paternal behavior is affected by, and influences, the child's predispositions, maternal and other family variables, institutional forces, and cultural attitudes. Examples of child-specific characteristics include but are certainly not limited to genetically influenced talent or possible handicap. The traditional societal message that men are less capable of nurturing children than women is a cultural example of a powerful force that may influence the father's and mother's impact on their son or daughter.

With regard to parental influence, a major theme of this chapter is that children benefit from positive experiences with both parents, that the father and mother each have something special to offer to their son and daughter. Children who have *the two-parent advantage* (Biller, 1994) are exposed to a wider range of interests, activities, and adaptive behaviors, increasing the likelihood that they will have a broader repertoire of competencies than those with only one psychologically active parent (Biller, 1971, 1974c, 1993; Biller & Meredith, 1974; Biller & Solomon, 1986; Biller & Trotter, 1994).

This chapter focuses on the paternal role with the school-aged child, roughly covering research pertaining to the elementary school years, including kindergarten through the middle school period. For the most part, we concentrate on studies exploring father-child relations for children aged five up until adolescence. However, given our life-span perspective, there is also mention of research on younger children that predicts their later behavior during the elementary school years as well as of studies of adolescents and adults that reveal links between their present adjustment and paternal influences in earlier childhood.

By age five or six most children are at least starting to gain considerable experience in social settings outside of their home and immediate neighborhood. Father-mother cooperation and the quality of parent-child relationships continue to be influential in the boy's or girl's adaptation to new intellectual and social challenges. During the years between school entry and adolescence, the child increasingly tests self-competence with respect to peers and learns about rules and structures that exist outside of the family. The child is acquiring a tremendous amount of experience in dealing with different and progressively more challenging social situations. The support of a positively involved father can contribute much to the child's emotional security, confidence, and adaptability in meeting more complex intellectual, physical, and social challenges. Children with active, nurturant, and committed fathers are generally much more successful in their academic, athletic, and social pursuits and have higher self-esteem than do those who have been paternally deprived (Biller, 1993; Biller & Trotter, 1994; Warshak, 1993).

In Ericksonian terms, the beginning of the school-age period marks the psychosocial stage of industry versus inferiority. During this stage, children's cognitive capacities expand, allowing them to solve concrete problems. The child's cognitive development coupled with the social expectancy of school entry provide the child with the opportunity to meet this challenge of psychosocial development. Success during this stage helps children to develop the confidence to begin a project and carry it out well. However, if, during this period, children do not meet the expected standards they may be vulnerable to self-perceptions of inferiority or incompetence continuing into adulthood. The quality of the father's involvement during this period is a crucial factor in determining whether the child develops the confidence and competence to meet new challenges in a positive manner (Biller, 1993). According to Snarey (1993), "The mentorship of a good father during these years may give children a subsequent advantage in their ability to work hard, to think of themselves as industrious, and feel generally productive."

PREVIEW

We begin the chapter with a review of research concerning the father's role in the child's cognitive development. This is a widely studied area and represents a large proportion of the chapter. One may speculate as to why cognitive functioning has received so much attention with respect to family influences. Most obviously, academic competence is perceived as the major task to master in this phase of a child's life. Scholastic achievement in the early school years is often viewed as setting the foundation for future success. From a methodological perspective, it is also noteworthy that cognitive tests are the most reliable measures of psychological functioning typically available to researchers. It could be argued that tests of intellectual ability and academic achievement are utilized more often than other types of measures because they are more likely to yield clear-cut results. More than other assessment devices, they may reveal existing connections between the nature of the father's interactions and his influence on his child. It is also important to note that cognitive functioning is not something isolated from other aspects of the child's development, including social and moral growth (Biller, 1993; Biller & Trotter, 1994).

It has only been in the past few decades that researchers have even begun to look at how the quality of the father's involvement affects child and family development. It is interesting that prior to the 1970s, discussions of father-child relationships, when they occurred, tended to focus on the father's involvement beginning with the child's school-age years, especially in the case of sons (Biller, 1968a). However, somewhat ironically, father-oriented researchers in recent years have focused more on earlier childhood and adolescence than on the school-age period, especially with regard to emotional and social development.

One notable exception is provided by Snarey (1993). In a thought-provoking study, Snarey reported on a four-decade analysis on the parental generativity of fathers. Three types of childrearing participation were evaluated: (1) social-emotional, (2) intellectual-academic, and (3) physical-athletic. Various activities were measured to determine degree of involvement in these areas of generativity. Some examples include: social-emotional—takes to visit relatives, spends special time before bedtime, takes child with him during evening routine; intellectual-academic—provides educational toys, reads to child, takes to library or bookstore, consults with teacher; physical-athletic—takes to doctor, plays exercise games, teaches how to ride bike, demonstrates and encourages use of an erector set. During the childhood period, fathers seemed to devote more time to their child's social-emotional development, with physical-athletic development ranked second, and intellectual-academic ranked third. No significant correlation was found between the three types of childrearing support. Fathers who gave especially strong support in one area were not more likely to engage in other types of support.

In this chapter, the initial focus on cognitive functioning is followed by the discussion of the father's influence in the child's social and emotional development, including moral and sex-role functioning. Research is reviewed that connects the father-child relationship to the child's level of social competence and quality of peer interaction. There is also a consideration of data relating to the father's role in his child's self-esteem and later psychological adjustment.

COGNITIVE DEVELOPMENT

Each person is born with a unique patterning of intellectual potential. The child's potential is most likely to be realized provided he or she experiences positive interactions in the family environment. Evidence exists for a strong hereditary contribution to intellectual development (Dunn & Plomin, 1990). For instance, identical twins separated at birth and reared apart in different family environments nevertheless demonstrate remarkable similarities in their educational abilities and interests as adults. Additional evidence comes from adoption studies. The levels of intelligence for children adopted at birth tends to correlate more with the intelligence of their biological parents than with their adoptive parents. However, adoptive parents can also make a major contribution by providing an enriching and supportive social environment. Children adopted at birth have been found to be more successful academically than their counterparts who remain in less economically and socially stimulating environments (Scarr & Weinberg, 1976, 1980).

Data concerning the father's influence on cognitive development can also be seen as potentially relevant to the tremendous controversy surrounding the roots of individual and group differences in intelligence as exemplified by the intense reaction to *The Bell Curve* by Richard Herrnstein and Charles Murray. Much of the criticism of *The Bell Curve* was based on the implications of genetic differences in intellectual potential among various ethnic-racial groups (Jacoby & Glaberman, 1995). Neither the authors of *The Bell Curve* nor their critics seem to have considered variations in the average level of paternal involvement as a possible factor underlying average differences among ethnic-racial groups. There is evidence that the quality of father-child relationships varies among different subcultures during the school-age years as well as during earlier and later developmental periods (Biller, 1968b, 1974c). Such variations seem able to account for a significant proportion of the average differences in intellectual attainment among children growing up in different sociocultural environments (Biller, 1974a, 1974b, 1993, 1994).

Several studies have indicated that children, especially boys, who experience a nurturant and involved father receive cognitive advantages. For example, Radin (1976) conducted a study involving four-year-olds' interactions with their parents. She and her assistants conducted interviews and observations with fathers and their four-year-old sons. Sons remained in the room and played while fathers participated in the interview process. The sessions were tape-recorded and subsequently scored for how nurturant or restrictive each father was toward his son. Radin found that boys' intelligence test scores were positively related to the degree of father nurturance. In contrast, paternal restrictiveness was negatively associated with the children's test scores. A follow-up study when the children were five years old revealed that the level of father nurturance in the initial study was still related to the boys' intellectual functioning. The father's involvement in direct encouragement of such skills as counting and reading was associated with his son's test performance at both time 1 (age four) and time 2 (age five).

Father involvement appears to be an important factor in the school-aged child's academic performance. Although much of Biller's (1968a) early research focused on gender development in young boys, he also discovered that paternal nurturance was positively correlated with intellectual functioning, whereas father deprivation tended to lessen cognitive competence. Blanchard and Biller (1971) collected data on family background, grades, and achievement test scores for third-grade boys. Children were grouped according to level of father availability: early father absent (before age three), late father absent (after age five), low father present (less than six hours of contact per week), or high father present (more than two hours per day). Boys in the four groups were matched with respect to intelligence test scores, birth order, socioeconomic status, and maternal employment so as to control for the effects of these factors.

Results revealed that high father present boys had superior grades and scored approximately one year above their expected age level on the indexes of academic achievement. The late father absent and low father present boys scored slightly below their grade level on achievement tests; in addition, teachers evaluated their classroom performance as average or below. The lowest test scores and grades were obtained by boys in the early father absent group. Taken together, these results suggested that involved and available fathers can have an immense impact on their children's academic performance.

Other evidence suggests that father availability and involvement is a positive factor for children in other subcultures. Both Katz (1967) and Solomon (1969) reported data indicating a strong positive association between paternal interest and encouragement and academic achievement among lower-class black elementary school boys. Katz's findings were based on the boys' perceptions of their parents, whereas Solomon rated parent-child interactions while the boys were performing a series of intellectual tasks. Interestingly, in both studies, the father's behavior appeared to be a much more important factor in sons' academic achievement than did the mother's behavior. In a more recent study, Radin, Williams, and Coggins (1994) found that the more that Native American fathers were involved in childrearing, the more likely their children were to do well in school, both academically and socially.

PATERNAL DEPRIVATION

Whereas father involvement appears to be predictive of cognitive and academic success during middle childhood, paternal deprivation is likely to be a handicapping condition. Lessing, Zagorin, and Nelson (1970) examined the effects of father absence on cognitive functioning in a sample of 500 children (ages 9 to 15). Children from a child guidance center were administered the Wechsler Intelligence Scale for Children. Results indicated that, for both boys and girls, father absence (defined as two years of separation from father, not necessarily consecutive) was related to relatively low ability in perceptual—motor and manipulative—spatial tasks. In addition, boys who were father absent scored lower than their father present counterparts on the arithmetic subtest. These subtests involve skills that are traditionally thought of as male talents.

Another interesting finding from this study involved previously father absent children who had a father surrogate (such as a stepfather) in their home. These children did not have intelligence test scores that differed significantly from those of father present children. Taken together, these results suggest that a male role model present in the home is vital to the development of particular cognitive abilities.

Lessing et al. included a relatively detailed analysis of sex differences, social class, and specific areas of intellectual functioning. However, there are also a number of questionable aspects of this study. First, the authors only studied a clinical population and did not include a comparison group. Second, the variables of father presence and father absence were not clearly defined, a deficiency in methodology typical of most investigations of the effects of father involvement. Father absence was defined as two years of not necessarily consecutive separation from the father. No attempt was made to obtain age at onset of father absence. Furthermore, there was no consideration as to the amount or type of father-child interaction in intact homes (Biller & Solomon, 1986).

In a relatively well-controlled study, Santrock (1972) found that early father absence was associated with lowered intelligence test performance, especially for children growing up in relatively poor economic circumstances. Children who became father absent before the age of two generally scored significantly lower on measures of intelligence and achievement compared to those from two-parent homes. The strongest results were for father absence due to divorce, desertion, or separation rather than death.

Hetherington, Cox, and Cox (1978, 1982) also found evidence that father absence can have negative effects on cognitive functioning. They examined a sample of five-

and six-year-old boys who had been father absent for two years because of divorce and another group of boys of the same age from intact families. Results indicated that boys from intact families scored significantly higher on the block design, mazes, and arithmetic subtests of the WIPPSI and had higher Performance Scale Intelligence Scores and slightly higher Full Scale Intelligence Scores. In contrast, the results did not reveal any significant differences in cognitive functioning between girls who were father absent and those who were father present.

Shinn (1978) conducted an impressive review of research concerning father absence and intellectual performance. She focused her discussion on 28 studies that met some minimal methodological criteria: data were collected from nonclinical populations, some sort of father present comparison group was used, and an effort was made to control for socioeconomic status. Father absence due to divorce seemed particularly detrimental, and some evidence indicated that early, long-term, and complete father absence was especially likely to be related negatively to intellectual competence. More consistent results were reported from studies involving lower-class individuals and among males, but much evidence suggested that the cognitive functioning of females was also negatively affected by paternal deprivation. The family instability and financial difficulty often associated with divorce and father absence may be primary factors interfering with the child's cognitive functioning. However, the major disadvantage related to father absence for children is lessened parental attention, including fewer opportunities to model mature decision making and problem solving.

Berlinsky and Biller (1982) emphasized individual differences among children in their capacity to cope with family-related changes. Children below the age of seven or eight typically have not reached a stage of cognitive functioning at which they can realistically understand and confront the loss or absence of a parent. On the other hand, older children or those who are intellectually precocious may have a great advantage compared to their less able counterparts in dealing with the loss of a parent or some other type of radical change in family living circumstances.

Although paternal deprivation generally has a more immediate effect on the cognitive abilities of boys than girls, there is also much evidence that fathers can contribute both positively and negatively to their daughters' cognitive functioning. Radin (1981) suggests that the relationship between paternal behavior and girls' performance may not be as clear because the traditional father may feel uncomfortable with his daughter's intellectual achievement and may reinforce more gender stereotypic behavior. However, fathers who are highly committed to childrearing, have flexible views regarding sex roles for themselves and their children, and express interest, involvement, and encouragement likely will enrich their daughters' cognitive functioning (Radin, 1981). On the other hand, too much nurturance in the form of an overprotective, oversolicitous attitude by the father may actually inhibit intellectual development. This type of relationship would serve to foster dependence, not competence. This evidence is consistent with other findings which suggest that fathers who are too intrusive in solving problems for their children seem to inhibit the growth of self-sufficiency (Biller, 1971, 1974c; Biller & Meredith, 1974; Biller & Solomon, 1986).

ACADEMIC COMPETENCE

Variations in paternal involvement can also contribute to children's perceptions of their academic self-competence. In an intriguing study, Wagner and Phillips (1992) observed 74 high-achieving third-grade children working separately with their fathers and mothers on both solvable and unsolvable tasks. The 74 children varied on their levels of academic self-competence. The findings revealed that children's perceived academic competence was positively related to father warmth on tasks that involved consistent success (time 1) and tasks involving a mixture of success and failure (time 2). Also, children's perceived academic competence was positively related to their own behavior when working with their fathers on unsolvable tasks. Children who possessed high academic self-competence showed more emotional restraint and were more self-reliant when working on unsolvable tasks. Moreover, fathers of children possessing high perceptions of competence exhibited greater levels of warmth on tasks that involved failure. Because of the correlational nature of this study, direction of influence could not be determined. However, the results do indicate the importance of considering the role fathers play in the development and maintenance of their children's self-perceptions.

Further evidence for the father's influence on academic development is suggested from divorce-related studies investigating the linkages of variations in the amount of contact with the noncustodial parent (usually the father) and children's school performance. Bisnaire, Firestone, and Rynard (1990) examined the academic adjustment of children ranging in age from 9 to 15 (mean, 11 years, five months). At the time of parental separation these children were between the ages of 6 and 14. When data collection began, the children's parents had been separated an average of three years. Results revealed that one-third of the children suffered decreases in academic performance after parental separation. Children were divided into two groups: those experiencing decreases in performance (nonadjusted) and those not currently experiencing decreases in performance (adjusted). The two groups did not differ in terms of gender, age, grade at separation, number of friends, or amount of time spent at play.

However, the two groups differed significantly in regard to the amount of time they spent with their parents. The adjusted children spent much more time with their noncustodial parent (usually the father) than did the nonadjusted (seven days vs. two days per month). Bisnaire et al. suggest that the contact children receive from both parents is beneficial to their academic success by exposing them to a broad array of scholastic aptitudes and interests. They also emphasize the importance of the father's availability in the separation-individuation phase of a child's development. The absence of the father can lead to the emergence of an overly close relationship with the mother and difficulties in academic performance.

The decrease in father involvement typically associated with divorce can contribute to potentially serious problems in various developmental areas of a school-aged child's functioning including academic and cognitive deficits (Guidabaldi, Cleminshaw, Perry, Nastasi, & Lightel, 1986; Hetherington et al., 1978; Radin, 1986), as well as social adjustment and peer relationship handicaps (Guidabaldi et al., 1986) and mental and physical health difficulties (Beer, 1989; Emery, 1988; Guidabaldi et al., 1986). Problems for school-aged children have been found to be generally more severe for boys and girls growing up in lower socioeconomic circumstances, but even children from affluent families are at risk. Low socioeconomic status may be an additional stressor, but it by no means transcends the risks of inadequate father involvement (Biller & Solomon, 1986).

Using a longitudinal format, Guidabaldi et al. (1986) conducted a study investigating the home environment factors potentially associated with postdivorce child adjustment. The areas of adjustment studied included intellectual potential, academic achievement levels, social competence, and family and school environment. Data were collected for both intact and divorced families with children in first, third, and fifth grades. The children were then reevaluated two years later. The researchers found that the relationship of male children with the noncustodial parent (typically the father) predicted better performance in the WRAT Spelling test and better grades in spelling and math. For girls, a positive relationship with the father predicted better reading grades. For first-grade boys a better relationship with the noncustodial parent was associated with better adjustment on five social criteria including more productive interaction with peers, less irrelevant talk, less social overinvolvement, and better peer relations (as rated by peers and teachers). For boys, a positive relationship with their noncustodial fathers also predicted better performance on the WRAT Spelling test, better grades in spelling, and better performance in math two years later. For girls, a positive noncustodial father-child relationship at time 1 was associated with better reading grades and better sibling relationships at time 2. Guidabaldi et al. report that boys seemed to be consistently more handicapped both immediately after the divorce and in subsequent years. However, it is again important to point out that much research has revealed evidence of delayed impact of earlier paternal deprivation when daughters reach adolescence and adulthood (Biller, 1993; Biller & Solomon, 1986).

Although fathers have an influence on their child's cognitive development, it seems that in earlier development, they have more of a direct impact on their sons than on their daughters. In cognitive development as well as in other areas, sons as compared to daughters attempt to model their father's behavior in a much more explicit manner. The more time the child spends with a nurturant father the greater are the benefits to his problem-solving ability and intellectual functioning. In contrast, daughters' cognitive development seems not to be as directly influenced by amount of paternal nurturance. However, high paternal expectations in the context of warmth, moderate emotional distance, and sense of autonomy vis-à-vis their fathers tend to enhance daughters' intellectual functioning (Radin, 1986).

There are also data indicating that daughters who experienced abundant paternal interest and support during childhood are more likely as adults to actualize their intellectual potential (Biller, 1974a, 1974b; Snarey, 1993). Studies of young children do tend to reveal more linkages between paternal factors and behavioral functioning for boys than for girls, but in most families, fathers have tended to focus more of their attention on their sons than on their daughters. Studies of the family backgrounds of extremely successful women, in fact, indicate that they were much more likely than their female peers to have experienced a high level of paternal support, stimulation, and high expectations for competence during early childhood. Similarly, during the elementary school years, daughters seem less influenced by father absence than do sons, but again, by late adolescence and adulthood the experience of paternal deprivation during childhood is linked to increased risks for females as well as males (e.g., Biller, 1971, 1974c, 1982, 1993).

SCHOOL ADJUSTMENT

Schools tend to discriminate against boys and girls in varying ways at different grade levels. Most elementary schools are dominated by women, with a ratio of female teachers to male teachers at about 6:1—and more than 50:1 in the first few grades. As a result, boys may come to see academic achievement as a feminine pursuit, especially if they do not have an involved father or father figure who values education. There is also much evidence that a greater proportion of boys, as compared to girls, are likely to be biologically predisposed to handicaps interfering with their academic performance. In addition, during the elementary school period, more boys may be inhibited by the lack of other male role models (Biller, 1974a, 1974b, 1993).

Partially because of the feminized classroom, girls may learn to read more quickly than boys. Female teachers typically will pay more attention to girls, giving them more oral reading time than boys. Also, since girls are encouraged by a same-sex adult role model, they are likely to become more interested in reading. In Japan, where about 60% of elementary school teachers are male, reading scores for boys and girls are about equal. In Germany, where the majority of elementary school teachers are male, and reading is considered a masculine talent, boys consistently achieve significantly higher reading scores than girls and are less likely to suffer from severe reading problems (Biller, 1993).

Many researchers have obtained strong positive correlations between measurements of children's academic functioning and variables such as father's education, father's occupational status, and father's job satisfaction (Biller, 1971; Lynn, 1974; Radin, 1981). These findings suggest that fathers who value educational and occupational achievement have a positive influence on their children's cognitive development. As emphasized by Biller (1971, 1974c) and Radin (1976, 1981), however, it is crucial to consider the quality of the father-child relationship, not just the father's behavior outside the home.

In contrast, negative paternal behavior seems to be related to reduced academic competency. Harrington, Block, and Block (1978) conducted a longitudinal study in which they found a link between paternal emotional rigidity and impatience during their son's preschool years, and difficulties in the children's cognitive functioning and problem solving in second grade. However, as Biller (1976) and Radin (1981) emphasize, causation cannot be determined from such studies. For example, it may be that fathers' negative interactions were a reaction to the level of intellectual ability that their sons' possessed. Nevertheless, fathers who are overly intrusive and restrictive, and who attempt to impose their solutions on problems confronting their children, can certainly inhibit their sons' achievement motivation, cognitive competence, and creativity (Biller, 1974a, 1974b, 1974c, 1982; Biller & Solomon, 1986; Lynn, 1974; Radin, 1976, 1981).

Individual differences in the child's constitutional predispositions and behavior can greatly influence the quality of interactions between father and child (Biller, 1971, 1974c, 1982; Biller & Solomon, 1986). For example, fathers, compared to mothers, may not be as tolerant of a child with severe intellectual deficits (Farber, 1962). However, evidence indicates that the father's role is as important if not more important than the mother's in terms of a child's satisfaction with family life, including sibling relationships (Biller, 1971, 1982, 1993).

In a study involving children diagnosed with attention deficit hyperactivity disorder, Margalit (1985) assessed boys and girls in the fourth to sixth grades. One group was diagnosed hyperactive by a score of 15 or more on the Conners Abbreviated Symptom Questionnaire (ASQ). The other group was selected from the same classes and included children who scored from 0 to 4 on the ASQ. The two groups were matched on age and gender. The author administered a Life Satisfaction Scale. Results indicated that hyperactive children perceived their fathers to be more significant than their mothers in terms of familial satisfaction, with the boys who appeared to be the best adjusted reporting especially close relationships with their fathers. Other research indicates that boys and girls with a high level of paternal involvement have better initial adaptations to school (Barth & Parke, 1992) and that those children who experience problems in the first grade become more successful in the second grade if they have close relationships with their fathers (Elizur, 1986). These findings are also consistent with evidence indicating that mothers have more difficulties than fathers in dealing with hyperactive children (Barkley, 1981).

It is noteworthy that, although positive paternal involvement cannot prevent all school-related or other types of problems, children with initial handicaps have a much greater chance of coping constructively if they are the beneficiaries of close supportive relationships with their fathers. Among children who have temperamental difficulties or learning disabilities, those with involved fathers are still much more likely than those from paternally deprived families to develop self-esteem and a sense of well-being. In most cases, whatever the nature of their initial disadvantage (whether it be primarily intellectual, physical, emotional, or social), there is a much greater likelihood that children with attentive, encouraging fathers will eventually make relatively successful adjustments as compared to those who, additionally, suffer from a lack of paternal involvement (Biller, 1993).

SOCIAL AND EMOTIONAL DEVELOPMENT

The capacity to express positive concern for the feelings of others is an important dimension of successful intimate relationships. Longitudinal data analyzed by Koestner, Franz, and Weinberger (1990) suggest that a major early family predictor of both men's and women's capacity for empathy toward others is the extent of positive father involvement experienced during the preschool years. Father participation in child care (assessed from maternal interview data) when the subjects were age five was strongly related to a measure of empathic concern (derived from a complex self-report measure) when they were age 31. Other data have indicated that a secure attachment to the father during infancy is predictive of the child's capacity for empathy and positive emotional responsibility during later phases of development, including the elementary school years (Biller, 1993; Biller & Trotter, 1994).

Investigations involving the social competence of young children are relevant to the current discussion because they yield important connections between parental interactional style and the school-age child's later social competence with peers (Shulman, Collins, & Dital, 1993). Parent-child play has been viewed in the context of how it can afford children the opportunity to learn and develop skills necessary for positive social interaction. Cassidy, Parke, Butkovsky, and Braungart (1992) reported that a high level of peer acceptance was associated with a greater ability to identify emotions, to acknowledge emotional experience, and to describe the causes of emotion. Additionally, children who were more accepted by peers felt more confident that their parents would respond appropriately to emotional expression. Clearly, emotional development plays a crucial role in a child's successful peer relationships. Aspects of emotional development can be learned through parent-child interaction. The parent-child physical play situation has been shown to be a vehicle for positive emotional development. While there is evidence for this in the child's relationship with both parents, it has been found that fathers more often than mothers engage their children in physical play (Biller, 1993).

Russell and Russell (1987) studied 6- to 7-year-old Australian children. All the fathers were employed, and the majority of mothers were either full-time homemakers or were employed part-time. The researchers observed parent-child interactions during a 90-minute interview conducted in the family's home. Overall, a larger portion of fathers' time was spent interacting with their children in a playful manner, whereas mothers' time was more often involved with caregiving activities. When the amount of time during interactions was compared, mothers spent significantly more time interacting with their children and provided more directive responses to their children when compared with fathers. There was no difference between fathers and mothers in their amount of responsiveness, negativity, or restrictiveness with their children. Those patterns were similar for both sons and daughters, and there were no significant interactions between gender of parent and gender of child (Collins & Russell, 1991).

Observing Mexican families with school-aged children, Bronstein (1984) reported similar results. In another study, McBride-Chang and Jacklin (1993) found that fathers' earlier level of play, but not mothers' earlier level of play, was associated with sons' level of rough-and-tumble play in first grade. Thus, the father's role in emotional development, and therefore successful social development, appears to be at least as important as the mother's. The most clear-cut results from the research of Parke and his colleagues involved an association between the ability of the father to engage reciprocally in positively playful physical interactions with his son or daughter and the child's popularity (Parke, MacDonald, Beitel, & Bhavnagri, 1988). The father's ability to be responsive to the child's initiative, allowing for a nurturant give-and-take in their play, is especially important. However, when the father is dominating and controlling, the child is not learning effective social skills. Not surprisingly, Parke's research program has also revealed a linkage between paternal intrusiveness and over-directedness during play and the child's, especially the son's, being rejected or neglected by peers (Biller, 1993).

MORAL FUNCTIONING

Hoffman (1971) found that weak father identification was related to less adequate conscience development than was strong father identification. Hoffman asked middle-school-aged boys to respond to questions about the person to whom the boy felt most similar, whom he most admired, and whom he most wanted to resemble when he grew up. Hoffman's results indicated that boys who had strong identifications with their fathers scored higher on measures of internal moral judgment, moral values, and conformity to rules than did boys with weak father identification. The low father identification children scored lower on measures of internal moral judgment, guilt following transgressions, acceptance of blame, moral values, and rule conformity. In addition, they were rated as higher in aggression by their teachers, which may also reflect difficulties in self-control (Biller, 1993).

Other data presented by Hoffman (1981) support the father's role as an identification figure in the moral development process for both sons and daughters. He speculated that identification with the father may contribute to the acquisition of observable moral attributes but that the internalization of moral standards and values is a complex process in which the mother, because of her greater availability, usually plays a more primary role. He also discusses evidence suggesting that for fathers and their sons, achievement may become a moral imperative that obscures the learning of important values dealing with interpersonal sensitivity.

The role of both parents in the child's moral development is important. The kinds of moral decisions the mother and father make are often quite different, and each parent is likely to have a special perspective that can positively influence the child. A nurturant and involved father can have particular influence on the degree to which his child takes responsibility for his or her own actions (Biller & Solomon, 1986). By his example, a father who is actively committed to his children facilitates their development of responsible behavior. Radin (1982) and Sagi (1982) found that both boys and girls who experienced a high level of father participation were likely to have an internal locus of control and to take responsibility for their actions. In a study with elementary school children, Radin and Russell (1983) suggested that by actively choosing to be involved, the father presents his child with an especially salient model of responsible behavior. The father who exhibits a day-to-day interest in his child's activities is an excellent role model demonstrating commitment and positive family values. A father who is very involved can foster in his child a strong locus of control and sense of responsibility over his or her own actions. Through emulating their involved father, children are more likely to demonstrate moral behavior.

A multidimensional perspective is necessary to analyze moral behavior. An individual needs to develop self-control as well as consideration for the rights and feelings for others. The process of developing an increasingly differentiated time perspective is a key factor in the child's reaching progressively higher levels of moral functioning. To become a more responsible individual, it is important to gain the patience to delay gratification, to be able to resist the temptation of the moment (Biller, 1993).

Paternal deprivation has been found to interfere with a child's learning how to delay gratification. Mischel (1961) conducted a study with children in Trinidad in which they were given the choice between receiving a smaller piece of candy immediately or a much larger piece a week later. He found that, among the younger children, those who were father absent were much more likely to choose the smaller, immediate reward than those from two-parent families. Father-deprived children may be at risk to have less mature impulse control because of a difficulty in trusting adults to follow through on commitments (Biller, 1971). Paternal deprivation in the first few years of life can also interfere with the development of the child's comfort in dealing with adults outside of the family. Even in infancy, children who have positively involved fathers as well as mothers tend to display less anxiety and impulsivity in unfamiliar social situations (Biller, 1974c).

Inadequate fathering, especially when it begins early in the child's life, is often associated with delinquent behavior among both boys and girls. While it must be emphasized that delinquency typically stems from multiple factors, fathers should carefully reflect about the extent of their childrearing commitments. Certainly the inappropriate behavior of some mothers is a major negative influence contributing to their children's delinquent behavior patterns, but the lack of an adequate father-child relationship is a far more common factor in the backgrounds of troubled and acting-out sons and daughters. Among delinquents, even more common than an obviously abusive father is one who has been chronically neglectful. Delinquents have usually received very little positive attention or guidance from their fathers. Compared to fathers of nondelinquents, fathers of delinquents typically give little direction and share fewer plans, activities, and interests with their children. In a more general pattern of paternal neglect, any attention is accompanied by the father's intermittent verbal abuse and ridicule of the child (Biller, 1974c, 1993; Biller & Solomon, 1986; Haapasalo & Tremblay, 1994; Patterson, DeBaryshe, & Ramsey, 1989; Patterson & Stouthamer-Loeber, 1984; Phares & Compas, 1992; Stern, Northman, & VanSlyk, 1984).

In contrast, researchers have reported an association between children's having a nurturant father and their ability to confide in others and display empathy and altruism. Herman and McHale (1993) found that both paternal and maternal warmth were correlated with school-aged children's sharing their feelings and concerns with their parents. Hoffman's research (1975, 1981) has indicated school-aged girls who are rated as highly altruistic by their peers are especially likely to have been exposed to their fathers' expression of people-centered values, emphasizing how their behavior can affect the feelings of others.

McClelland, Constantian, Regalado, and Stone (1978) explored the possible connection between parenting practices when children were in kindergarten and their adjustment later in life. From maternal interview data they found that individuals who had involved fathers were much more likely to grow up to be tolerant and understanding than those whose fathers had been relatively uninvolved with them.

Provocative data collected by Speicher-Dubin (1982) suggested that the father's level of moral maturity, emotional warmth, and nurturance during his child's middle school years are actually more predictive of a son's or daughter's behavior on reaching late adolescence or early adulthood than during childhood. Other findings also suggest a connection between experiencing close, loving father involvement during kindergarten and successful relationships during midlife. Individuals who were reported to have warm and loving fathers when they were five were likely to have long-term marriages, successful parenthood, and close friendships as adults (Franz, McClelland, & Weinberger, 1991). A number of additional studies also suggest linkages among positive paternal involvement during childhood and the son's and daughter's adult capacity for empathic and responsible social behavior (Biller, 1993; Biller & Trotter, 1994).

SELF-CONCEPT

An atmosphere in which the father constructively shares parenting responsibilities with the mother allows the child to develop a healthier self-concept, gender identity, and perceived competence. In some of his earlier research, Biller (1968a, 1969a, 1969b) evaluated the parenting relationships of fathers and mothers by having them discuss various childrearing situations. Parental assertiveness in family decision making concerning children was found to be associated with the masculinity of kindergarten-aged sons' self-concepts, preferences, and interpersonal behavior. Moreover, interviews with the sons revealed that the boys' own perceptions of their fathers' relative family involvement was even more strongly related to their gender development. The boys' behavior was linked to their fathers' relative participation in day-to-day aspects of their lives. Consistent with findings from other studies, boys who were father absent during their preschool years were especially likely to have relatively unmasculine self-concepts.

However, several boys with relatively unmasculine self-concepts and rather passive personality styles had fathers who had a very dominant role in family interactions. Unfortunately, they had fathers who were controlling and restrictive of their children's behavior. For instance, this type of dominant father punished his son for disagreeing with him and generally demonstrated very rigid and authoritarian attitudes. A positive gender identity and social development are facilitated when the father is a competent model but also allows and encourages his child to be assertive. It is also interesting to note that data from several investigations have suggested that a high level of positive father caretaking involvement during childhood is associated with flexible and tolerant attitudes toward the sex-role related behavior of others, inside and outside of the family (Barnett & Baruch, 1988; Baruch & Barnett, 1986; Williams, Radin, & Allegro, 1992).

Some individuals, both during the middle school years and during later development continuing into adulthood, have self-concepts indicating a discomfort with, or rejection of, their biological sexuality. Certainly, constitutional predispositions, including levels of prenatal androgenic hormones, may be involved in the difficulties some children have in developing a secure gender identity. However, the father who remains interested and involved with his child, even in the face of seemingly atypical behavior, can, nevertheless, have a major role in fostering constructive sex-role development. Researchers have found that males and females who have insecure or negative gender identities are unlikely to have experienced any positive father involvement during childhood, whether due to paternal unavailability, neglect, or abusiveness (Biller, 1974c, 1993; Green, 1987).

Other researchers have found relationships between children's self-esteem and different aspects of paternal involvement. Sears (1970) reported on the strong relationship between mother-reported paternal warmth and a questionnaire measure of sixth-grade boys' self-esteem. Coopersmith (1967) discovered that the self-esteem of elementary school boys was highly influenced by the extent to which their fathers were involved in limit setting. Rosenberg (1965) found that adolescents who had become father absent in early childhood had particularly low self-esteem compared to their father present counterparts.

In a relatively extensive research project, Amato (1986) studied aspects of the father-child relationship and the child's self-esteem. His sample included boys and girls in middle childhood (ages 8–9) and adolescence (ages 15–16) divided among three different types of domestic situations (intact families, stepfamilies, and single-parent families). In order to assess father-child and mother-child relationships, children were asked four questions (e.g., "Does your father [mother] talk to you much?"). Children's self-esteem was measured by the Piers-Harris Children's Self-Concept Scale (Piers & Harris, 1969). Amato's results indicated that degree of parental involvement with children was moderately to strongly related to children's self-esteem. This was true of both the middle-school-aged boys and girls and the older adolescents. For eight- and nine-year-old boys and girls the father-child relationship measure was more strongly associated with self-esteem than was the mother-child relationship measure.

For adolescent males, the contribution of both parents to self-esteem was about the same, but among adolescent females the mother-child relationship seemed more salient.

Amato (1986) noted that most of the children and adolescents felt secure about the mother's positive availability, interest, and help. However, the interest, attention, and help provided by the father was less of a perceived constant, varying to a much greater extent among the children. Because of this, the father's level of involvement appeared to be an especially important factor in variations in self-esteem among children. Amato reported similar results for stepfamilies, with level of stepfather involvement also being related to children's self-esteem. In contrast, the divorced, noncustodial father-child relationship seems to contribute less to the child's self-esteem, possibly because of the relatively low level of paternal involvement in these mother-custody families. In several publications, Biller (e.g., 1971, 1974c, 1982, 1993) has pointed out that the greater overall variability in father involvement as compared to mother involvement may contribute to the stronger likelihood of statistically significant relationships between individual differences in child behavior and paternal relative to maternal factors.

LATER ADAPTATIONS

A number of researchers have compared adolescents and adults with varying levels of personal and social adaptations with respect to information concerning their family circumstances during middle childhood. In a retrospective study, Reuter and Biller (1973) investigated the relationship between various combinations of perceived paternal nurturance and availability during childhood and the personal adjustment among college males. They designed and administered a family background questionnaire to assess perceptions of the father-child relationship during the participants' childhood. The personal adjustment scale of Heilbrun's Adjective Checklist and the socialization scale of the California Personality Inventory were employed as measures of personality adjustment. High paternal nurturance combined with at least moderate paternal availability, and high paternal availability combined with at least moderate paternal nurturance, were associated with strongly positive scores on the personality adjustment measures. A male who experienced ample opportunities to observe a nurturant father is better able to imitate constructive paternal behavior and develop more positive personality characteristics (Biller, 1982, 1993).

In contrast, high paternal nurturance combined with low paternal availability, and high paternal availability combined with low paternal nurturance, were related to relatively low scores on the personality adjustment measures. The son who had a father who was highly nurturant but seldom home may feel frustrated that his father was not available more often or may find it difficult to imitate such an elusive figure. The males who reported that their fathers had been home often but spent little time with them seemed to be particularly deficient in social adjustment. The consistent presence of an inadequate, unnurturant father may lead to the development of feelings of negative self-worth and thus be detrimental to the male's personality functioning. Therefore, the boy with an unnurturant father may be better off if his father is not very available. This is consistent with evidence suggesting that father absent boys often have healthier personality adjustments than do boys with passive, ineffectual fathers (Biller, 1974c, 1982; Biller & Solomon, 1986).

In an intergenerational research project, Hansen and Biller (1992) investigated the father-related perceptions of young adult children and their parents. Middle-aged fathers who viewed themselves as having been the recipients of a high level of paternal nurturance during childhood tended to have sons and daughters who perceived them as being attentive and affectionate parents. Moreover, among the young adult sons and daughters, perceived nurturant father involvement during childhood was positively associated with self-reports of personal adjustment, emotional stability, and social competence. These findings are consistent with the notion that the earlier father-child relationship is a significant factor in the adult's personality functioning and potential to be an effective parent.

The research of John Snarey (1993) provides a particularly salient example of how a father's involvement in different dimensions of his school-aged child's life can have long-term consequences for his son's or daughter's later development. In his longitudinal analysis, he discovered that the educational and occupational mobility of young adult sons was predicted from level of paternal involvement in their intellectual-academic development during childhood. He also reported that the father's support of physical-athletic development during childhood was positively related to his son's occupational mobility during early adulthood. In addition, he found some evidence that the father's interest and involvement in his daughter's physical-athletic development was associated with her subsequent educational and occupational mobility during early adulthood.

It is important to emphasize that children can learn from their fathers in many different contexts. Important lessons, for example, are garnered in situations focusing on social relationships and athletic endeavors as well as in the help a father may provide in more structured school-related pursuits. It is clear that interactions between different aspects of a child's development need to be viewed holistically. The father's involvement with his son or daughter in a variety of activities can be at least as significant in the child's overall cognitive development as classroom experiences (Biller, 1993; Biller & Trotter, 1994).

The findings of Fish and Biller (1973) indicate that the father has a profound impact on his daughter's personality adjustment. An extensive family background questionnaire was administered to college women to assess the relationship with their fathers during childhood. The women who perceived their fathers as having been very nurturant and interested in them scored high on the Adjective Checklist personal adjustment scale. In contrast, the women who perceived their fathers as having been rejecting scored very low on personal adjustment. It is also interesting to note that Stattin and Klackenberg-Larsson (1991) found that fathers who had expressed a prenatal preference for a boy but then had a girl showed higher rates of conflict with their child during the middle school years and adolescence than did those who had originally desired a daughter.

Other data suggest that women benefit in terms of adjustment when they have the opportunity to observe a positive father-mother relationship. Block (1971) in his analysis of findings from the Berkeley Longitudinal Study emphasizes the importance of the father-mother as well as the father-daughter relationship in the development of a woman's healthy personality functioning. The group of women who were best adjusted as adults grew up in a home with two positively involved parents. Their mothers were described as affectionate, personable, and resourceful and their fathers as warm, competent, and firm. Another group of relatively well-adjusted women had mothers who were extremely bright, capable, and ambitious but fathers who were relatively warm but passive. The poorly adjusted women, however, were more likely to come from homes in which at least one if not both parents were grossly inadequate.

In a related research project, Block and his coworkers found that well-socialized and successful adult males typically had grown up in households with highly involved fathers and parents who had compatible relationships (Block, von der Lippe, & Block, 1973). In contrast, adult males who were relatively low in social skills and personal adjustment typically grew up in families in which the parents were incompatible and the fathers were either uninvolved, weak, or emotionally conflicted. The most well-adjusted females tended to come from families in which both parents had been positively involved with them. Their fathers were described as warm and accepting, and their mothers appeared to have been excellent role models with respect to intellectual competence. A variety of family patterns emerged among the less well-adjusted females, but it was clear that few if any had family backgrounds marked by a combination of a compatible father-mother relationship and a positively involved father.

Lozoff (1974), in her study involving upper-middle-class individuals, found that positive father-daughter relationships during childhood are crucial in the development of women who are able to be successful in their heterosexual relationships as well as in their career endeavors. These unusually competent women had accomplished fathers who had treated them with respect. They valued their daughters' basic femininity but at the same time encouraged and expected them to develop their competencies. The women exposed to a basic compatibility between their fathers and mothers developed positive identifications with both parents and comfortable feminine gender identities.

Inadequate father-child relationships were evident for a second group of women who displayed autonomy but had much personal conflict. Their fathers tended to be aloof perfectionists who had very high expectations for their daughters but did not provide enough emotional support for them to develop solid self-confidence. A third group of women who were very low in autonomy came from economically privileged but highly sex-typed family situations. The father in such a family seemed to offer his daughter little encouragement for intellectual competence, leaving her socialization mainly up to his wife. In contrast, women who had achieved a high level of success in intellectual and occupational endeavors were much more likely to have had a strong relationship with a father who accepted their femininity but expected them to be persistent and competent.

Appleton (1981) argued that the father remains a highly significant influence throughout his daughter's development. Using in-depth clinical interviews, he intensively studied the life histories and functioning of 81 middle-class women. These individuals, as compared to the hundreds he had dealt with in therapy, were not in treatment but nevertheless were willing to delve into their relationships with their fathers and other men in their lives. From these interviews as well as his clinical practice, Appleton emphasizes how the earlier father-daughter relationship may have a continuing impact on the development of adult women.

The father's attentiveness and support are crucial for the daughter's feelings of self-worth during childhood and for her potential to develop positive relationships with other men during adulthood. Unfortunately, fewer than 20% of the women reported having fathers who were able to be loving and supportive in a way that also enhanced their daughter's sense of individuality, competence, and ability to engage in mature intimate relationships with other men. Most of the women reported having experienced very inadequate relationships with their fathers. Almost 60% (48 of 81) described distant or nonexistent relationships with their fathers. Half of these (24) women had fathers who were very aloof, and a similar number (24) suffered from childhood paternal deprivation due to their father's death (12) or their parents' divorce (12). The remaining 22% (18 of 81) had overly intrusive, controlling, or restrictive fathers who enmeshed them in rather symbiotic relationships.

Whereas 60% (9 of 15) of the women who had positive relationships with their fathers during childhood reported healthy, satisfying marriages or attachments with men, this was true for less than 10% (6 of 61) of those who had suffered from inadequate or symbiotic paternal influence. For example, none of the women with symbiotic paternal relationships or divorced parents, and only three each in the deceased or aloof father groups, had yet achieved what Appleton considered a healthy heterosexual adjustment.

Appleton also reported other interview findings that supported a connection between a woman's perception of her childhood relationship with her father and her adult adjustment. More than 75% of the women who described their fathers as having been gentle to them considered themselves to be generally happy individuals. In contrast, among those who had viewed their fathers as stern, harsh, or cruel, more than 60% had experienced some form of paternal deprivation during childhood, whereas only 20% viewed their relationship with their father as having been positive.

Appleton's interview and clinical observations are quite provocative, but the richness of his speculations must be tempered with an awareness of the uncontrolled nature of his data collection. For example, he gives no detailed report of his subjects' characteristics or any objective assessment of their functioning—in fact, all observations and interpretations were made directly by him. Nevertheless, more systematic investigations support the notion that the quality of the early father-daughter relationship during middle childhood has a significant impact on the long-term adjustment of women (Biller, 1993; Block, 1971; Fish & Biller, 1973; Lozoff, 1974; Snarey, 1993).

OVERVIEW

This chapter has emphasized the importance of paternal influence during middle childhood with respect to the son's or daughter's long-term development as well as current functioning. This is not to say that an individual's level of psychological well-being is merely a function of the quality of paternal involvement experienced during childhood. Many different biological and social influences affect personality development. Some individuals who have been the recipients of attentive fathering still have serious developmental difficulties, while others function extremely well despite having had a history of paternal deprivation. Nevertheless, variations in the quality of fathering generally have a crucial impact on child development.

Children who experience positive father involvement are likely to develop their personal resources and social competence, whereas those who are paternally deprived are at risk to suffer from psychological problems. Biological predispositions and social circumstances have much to do with the details of how variations in paternal involvement affect particular children. Inadequate fathering may increase the vulnerability of a child to developing a poor self-concept, insecurity in peer relationships, and other types of dysfunction depending on the specific intermix of individual predispositions and social circumstances. In contrast, high-quality paternal involvement enhances a child's opportunity to live a satisfying and productive life. Effective fathering increases the child's chances of developing a positive body image, self-esteem, moral strength, and intellectual and social competence.

CHAPTER 9

Fathers and Adolescents

Cheryl A. Hosley and Raymond Montemayor
Ohio State University

IN THE PAST 30 YEARS, there has been much research exploring fathers' relationships with their children (Lamb & Oppenheim, 1989). Most of this research has examined the transition to fatherhood and characteristics of fathers' relationships with infants and young children. While our understanding of the fathering role and the nature of fathers' interactions with their small children was greatly furthered, little attention was paid to fathers of adolescents.

Since the mid-1980s, there have been a growing number of studies assessing characteristics of father-adolescent relationships. Most research in this area has been atheoretical and descriptive. These studies have utilized a variety of novel methods to provide a description of relationships between fathers and adolescents. We know much about what father-adolescent relationships are like, although as we shall see, we know less about the impact fathers have on their adolescents.

The study of father-adolescent relationships is still in its infancy. Many questions have not yet been asked, and many issues are not yet understood. The descriptive studies that have been conducted provide the foundation for future research exploring these questions. We must now begin to develop a comprehensive framework for understanding and explaining relationships between fathers and adolescents. By summarizing and integrating the available research on father-adolescent relationships, this chapter is a first step in providing that framework.

Two theoretical questions are particularly important in understanding father-adolescent relationships. First, are there differences between mothers' and fathers' relationships with their adolescent children? Second, is the father-adolescent relationship different from the father-child relationship? We answer these questions by describing what is currently known about relationships between fathers and adolescents. Particular attention is paid to those variables emphasized in the literature, namely, time spent together, communication patterns, closeness, conflict, and power. The impact of these relationships on adolescents is also explored. The chapter concludes with suggested explanations for the findings and recommendations for future research in this area.

THEORIES HYPOTHESIZING DIFFERENCES AND SIMILARITIES BETWEEN MOTHERS' AND FATHERS' RELATIONSHIPS WITH ADOLESCENT CHILDREN

Theoretical arguments suggest both difference and similarity between mothers' and fathers' relationships with their adolescent children. Arguments for gender differences in parenting styles have emerged from several theoretical perspectives. For example, psychoanalytic theory emphasizes the role of the mother as the primary attachment figure (e.g., Chodorow, 1978). Fathers are rarely mentioned in these theories, and when they are, the focus is on their distance and remoteness.

Role theory also suggests that there may be important differences between mothers' and fathers' parenting roles. The role of the father was traditionally defined as being a good provider and a firm disciplinarian (L. B. Feldman, 1990). As a result of this role definition, men have been socialized to be less involved than women in the day-to-day care and nurturance of their children. Evidence for this traditional father role definition is seen in the common use of fathers' educational and occupational status as the sole indicator of socioeconomic status for the family, a tendency that reflects the significance of the father's role as provider (Pederson, 1987). In addition, research has indicated that fathers typically report not only low levels of involvement with their children but also low levels of responsibility for child care (Barnett & Baruch, 1988; Pleck, 1983).

Role theory also allows for changes in role definitions through time. In recent decades, changes have been seen in the extent of fathers' involvement in the family. As a result of social changes, such as the growing prevalence of women in the workforce, men are increasingly pressured or permitted to join or relieve their wives in parenting (Daniels & Weingarten, 1988). As a result, fathers spend more time with and take more interest in their children (Stearns, 1991). It has been argued that one result of this increased family involvement is decreased differences between mothers' and fathers' orientations toward parenting.

THEORIES SUGGESTING CHANGE AND CONTINUITY IN FATHERS' RELATIONSHIPS WITH CHILDREN AND ADOLESCENTS

A second important question is whether there are differences between father-child and father-adolescent relationships. There are three views on this issue. First, some research indicates continuity through time in fathers' relationships with their children. For example, in one study, fathers' childrearing attitudes and goals remained relatively stable as their children grew, promoting stability in the nature of their interactions with their children (e.g., Roberts, Block, & Block, 1984).

However, one might also expect discontinuity in fathers' relationships with their children. A second view proposes that father-child relationships undergo constant, gradual change. Collins and Russell (1991) suggest that one reason to expect continual change in the relationship between fathers and their children is that children themselves are changing as they grow older. In their words, "To build a developmental theory, an account is needed that encompasses change over time in relationships, in terms of specific linkages to individual developmental changes in offspring" (p. 100). Seen in this way, one might expect the constant changes experienced by children to promote constant change in their relationships with their fathers.

Most of the research on parents and adolescents indicates a gradual transformation of the parent-child relationship as children enter adolescence rather than an abrupt alteration of this relationship (Collins, 1990). According to this view, relationships between fathers and their children are continuously transformed, with the changes that occur during adolescence built upon previous styles of interaction.

A third view suggests that there is a dramatic transformation in father-child relationships when children reach adolescence. Adolescence is often conceptualized as being a period of storm and stress, characterized by rapid and sweeping changes that lead to increased conflict and distance between adolescents and parents (Hall, 1904). These changes occur in many areas, including physical development, cognitive ability, and social relations (Montemayor, 1986). Among the most important changes for adolescents are pubertal development, cognitive advances, increasing peer orientation, strivings for autonomy, and emphasis on identity development.

Each of these developmental changes can lead to alterations in adolescents' relationships with fathers. For example, because peer relationships become more important, adolescents typically spend more time with their friends and show greater conformity to their peer group than do younger children (Berndt, 1979). As adolescents spend more time with their friends, they spend less time with their parents, possibly reducing the extent of the fathers' involvement in the adolescents' lives.

Recently, life-span theorists have stressed the importance of addressing not only the developmental changes that occur in children and adolescents but also the changes that occur in fathers. Age-related physical and psychological changes in fathers may influence and alter their relationships with their children (DeLuccie & Davis, 1991). Fathers of adolescents are typically middle aged. Some of the age-related changes that may be faced at this time include attempts to establish a sense of generativity and sex-role convergence (Montemayor, McKenry, & Julian, 1994).

Much theoretical attention has been paid to the concept of a period of midlife stress or crisis. A midlife crisis can result in physical, psychological, and social changes for middle-aged men. Physically, there are changes in hormonal levels and possible declines in health and strength. These changes may lead to heightened awareness of aging (Brim, 1976). Neugarten (1968) has suggested that one result of this physical decline is a shift in orientation from "time since birth" to "time left to live." Psychologically, in midlife men may reevaluate and modify their goals and identities (Levinson, 1978; Tamir, 1982). Socially, middle-aged men may experience changes in their relationships with wives, parents, and coworkers (Levinson, 1978).

The various changes associated with middle age and the possible midlife crisis may lead to changes in fathers' childrearing attitudes and behaviors. A father may become preoccupied with his own problems, reducing the time or energy he devotes to child care. Or, in contrast, a father may reappraise his previous level of involvement with childrearing and seek increased contact and interaction with his children.

In addition to being aware of the individual developmental changes experienced by fathers and adolescents, it is also informative to consider how these changes may interact with one another. For example, theorists have suggested that in middle age, men become more expressive and nurturant, a process known as sex-role convergence (Jung, 1933; Neugarten & Gutmann, 1958). Simultaneously, many men at this age feel a desire to guide and mentor the next generation, including their own children (Erikson, 1963). As a result of these two developmental changes, many fathers re-define their parenting role and attempt to become more involved in the daily lives of their adolescents. At the same time, however, their adolescent children are attempting to become more autonomous from the family, spending more time away from the home and establishing their own sense of identity. Thus, at this point in the family life cycle, the developmental issues of fathers and adolescents may be in conflict. The dynamics of this interaction may also lead to transformations in relationships between fathers and adolescents.

CHARACTERISTICS OF FATHER-ADOLESCENT RELATIONSHIPS

Researchers have focused on five major characteristics of the father-adolescent relationship: 1. time spent together, 2. communication and involvement, 3. closeness, 4. conflict, and 5. power. These characteristics are considered to be important dimensions of relationships in general, including relationships between parents and children (Hinde, 1979; Hinde & Stevenson-Hinde, 1987; Kelley et al., 1983; Reis & Shaver, 1988).

TIME SPENT TOGETHER

Time spent together has been used as one indicator of the nature of the father-adolescent relationship. Important factors include not only the actual amount of time spent together but also how that time is spent and each person's degree of satisfaction with this time. It is difficult to compare different studies on this topic, as they typically utilize different samples and methodologies. For instance, some studies rely on retro-spective estimates of the amount of time spent together, while others use direct ob-servational measurement. However, several consistent findings do emerge from the literature.

First, adolescents spend less time with both of their parents than do younger chil-dren. This decrease in time spent with parents has been found to correspond with the pubertal period (Csikszentmihalyi & Larson, 1984; Hill & Stafford, 1980; Youniss & Smollar, 1985). The reduction in time spent with parents may be related to an increas-ing peer orientation, with adolescents spending more time with their friends or in extracurricular activities. It may also be due to the adolescent's increased desire for autonomy from the family or to beginning after-school employment.

Research has indicated that fathers spend less time than mothers interacting with their preschool and school-aged children (Pleck, 1983; Russell & Russell, 1987). Simi-larly, research comparing the amount of time that adolescents spend with each parent finds that adolescents in high school and in college report spending less time alone with their fathers than with their mothers (Larson & Richards, 1994; Miller & Lane, 1991; Montemayor & Brownlee, 1987). For example, Montemayor (1982) found that adolescents spent an average of 84 minutes/day with their mothers but only 70 min-utes/day with their fathers.

The results of this study are somewhat modified when they are examined by gender of the adolescent and the parent. Adolescents typically report spending more time alone with their same-sex parent. In the Montemayor (1982) study, sons reported spending 53 minutes/day alone with their fathers and daughters spent 59 minutes/day alone with their mothers. In contrast, sons spent 26 minutes/day alone with their mothers, and daughters spent only 17 minutes/day alone with their fathers.

Not all time with parents is spent in face-to-face interaction. Larson and Richards (1994) found that adolescents spend more time physically close to their mothers than to their fathers but often engage in separate activities. When mutual activities are reported, differences are found regarding how adolescents spend time with each of their parents. Both males and females primarily spend free time with their fathers but spend equal amounts of leisure and work time with their mothers (Montemayor, 1982; Montemayor & Brownlee, 1987). This finding is consistent with the traditional stereo-type of the father as a playmate for his children.

The typical free time activity males and females engage in with their parents is watching TV (Larson & Richards, 1994; Montemayor, 1982). The predominance of this activity, especially with fathers, was also reported by Csikszentmihalyi and Lar-son (1984), who found that out of 1,000 self-reports, teenagers reported being alone with their fathers only 10 times, and on five of these occasions they were watching TV.

Adolescents of both genders experience more enjoyment and greater satisfaction when involved with activities with their fathers than when involved with activities with their mothers (Montemayor & Brownlee, 1987). One explanation for this parent preference is that adolescents engage in free time activities with their fathers but spend more time doing household chores with their mothers.

The quality of time adolescents spend with their fathers is influenced by several aspects of the relationship. For example, boys who feel understood by their fathers perceive time spent with fathers as pleasurable, with shared common interests. In contrast, boys who feel misunderstood by their fathers feel that time together is con-flictual and consists of activities that are forced and unwanted (Roll & Millen, 1978).

COMMUNICATION AND INVOLVEMENT

Communication is another important dimension of parent-adolescent relationships. One component of communication is the frequency of interactions between parents and adolescents. Miller and Lane (1991) found that college students reported commu-nicating with their mothers nearly once a week, but only once about every two weeks with fathers. The frequency of interactions provides very limited information about the nature of relationships, however. Not only is the frequency dependent upon the amount of time parents and adolescents spend together, but it may also vary depend-ing on the age of the adolescent, as many late adolescents leave home for college or employment.

Because of the limitations of using frequency to assess communication, patterns of communication between adolescents and their parents are a more informative reflec-tion of the nature of their relationship. Hauser and colleagues (1987) studied com-munication styles by observing adolescents and their parents discussing differences of opinion about Kohlberg's moral dilemmas. They coded these interactions as being either "constraining" (e.g., distancing and interrupting) or "enabling" (e.g., problem solving, focusing, and explaining). Their data indicated few differences in verbal communication between adolescent males and females, but dramatic differences between mothers and fathers. Both male and female adolescents spoke more to their fathers, engaged in more problem solving with them, and were more accepting of them. Fathers were also found to be more enabling and less constraining than mothers (Hauser et al., 1987). These findings suggest that for certain kinds of conversation, such as theoretical debates about morality, fathers are more talkative and more likely to facilitate talk in their adolescents than are mothers.

Other studies also point to the impact of content on mother-father differences in communication with their adolescents. Typically, fathers' involvement with teenagers has been found to be selective and restricted to instrumental and problem-solving discussions about topics such as academic performance and future educational and occupational plans (Noller & Bagi, 1985; Youniss & Smollar, 1985). More emotional topics such as relationships and personal feelings are rarely discussed, especially not with daughters (Larson & Richards, 1994; Noller & Callan, 1990; Youniss & Smollar, 1985). In contrast to fathers, mothers communicate with their adolescents about a broad range of instrumental and personal topics (Noller & Bagi, 1985).

In another area of communication, several researchers have explored parent differences in intimacy and self-disclosure. Adolescents report less intimacy with fathers than with mothers (LeCroy, 1988; Noller & Bagi, 1985; Youniss & Smollar, 1985). This is especially true for adolescent females. For example, Noller and Callan (1990) reported that females disclosed less to their fathers than to their mothers on every topic assessed. Male adolescents were more likely to disclose equally to both parents but disclosed more to fathers than did females about certain topics, such as sexuality, general problems, and plans.

Following from reports that adolescent females talk less openly with their fathers, Youniss and Ketterlinus (1987) found that females judged that their mothers knew them better than did their fathers. Daughters may assume that their fathers are either uninterested or judgmental (Youniss & Smollar, 1985). Sons felt that they were known better by their fathers than did daughters (Youniss & Ketterlinus, 1987). However, fathers were described as being less open to listen to problems and to help clarify feelings than were mothers, especially for daughters (Youniss & Smollar, 1985).

In terms of degree of satisfaction with their communication, adolescent males have reported moderate levels of satisfaction for discussions with both parents. Adolescent females, however, were less satisfied with discussions with their fathers on each topic they addressed (Youniss & Smollar, 1985). The likely explanation is that they perceive their mothers to be more understanding and accepting than their fathers.

Little work has explored changes in communication patterns through development. Several studies have examined changes in parental involvement, which is often defined by the topics parents discuss with their children. This research suggests a decline in paternal involvement during adolescence. DeLuccie and Davis (1991) found a steady decline in involvement from the preschool years through adolescence, with fathers of 16-year-olds less involved than fathers of young school-aged children or preschoolers. In this study, involvement included emotional support, school-related involvement, and religious or ethical involvement. The authors suggest several explanations for these findings. First, fathers may become less involved as adolescents attempt to gain autonomy and establish an identity separate from the family. Second, fathers may expect more maturity and independence through development. Finally, fathers may find it more rewarding to be involved with younger children, especially preschoolers who, unlike adolescents, are "small, nonthreatening, often charming, amusing, and immature" (p. 232).

There has been some research exploring the relationship between communication and the developmental changes faced by either fathers or adolescents. In one study, Montemayor et al. (1994) found a significant inverse correlation between fathers' midlife stress and the quality of communication with their adolescent children. One explanation for this finding is that fathers experiencing midlife stress are preoccupied with their own concerns, reducing their time or interest in communicating with their adolescents. It is also possible that midlife stress results from difficulties experienced within the father-adolescent relationship (Montemayor et al., 1994).

CLOSENESS

Closeness is often defined as feelings of warmth, acceptance, connectedness, attachment, and affection. Although many studies find that adolescents generally feel close to both parents, adolescents report feeling closer to their mothers than their fathers (e.g., Barnes & Olson, 1985; Kenny, 1987; Richardson, Galambos, Schulenberg, & Petersen, 1984). For example, Miller and Lane (1991) found that more than half of the college students in their sample reported feeling either "somewhat closer" or "much closer" to their mothers, while only 15% reported feeling "somewhat closer" or "much closer" to their fathers. Youniss and Ketterlinus (1987) also concluded that the father-adolescent relationship is more distant than the mother-adolescent relationship, especially in blue-collar households.

Differential ratings of parental closeness have also been obtained in several retrospective studies. In one study of male and female college students, it was found that 41% of the sample felt that their emotional needs were unmet during childhood. Although overall adolescent dissatisfaction with parental nurturance was high, dissatisfaction was significantly higher for fathers than for mothers (Zeidler, Nardin, Scolare, & Mich, 1987). Similarly, Youniss and Smollar (1985) reported that only 35% of adolescent females felt that their fathers met their emotional needs, compared with 72% for mothers.

Some researchers have defined closeness in terms of affectionate behaviors, such as compliments, praise, support, and love. Studies that use these criteria also report closer relationships between mothers and adolescents (Miller & Lane, 1991; Wright & Keple, 1981). Mothers do not differentiate between sons and daughters in their expression of closeness as much as fathers do. Fathers are less affectionate with their sons than with their daughters (Bronfenbrenner, 1961). The finding that mothers give more compliments and praise to their children is consistent with gender differences found for adolescents, with daughters expressing more affection to their parents than do sons (Savin-Williams & Small, 1986).

Gender differences in closeness also have been found. Fathers and sons express less affection toward each other than do mothers and daughters (Eberly, Montemayor, & Flannery, 1993). For example, fathers and sons are less likely to compliment and praise each other than are mothers and daughters. In addition, adolescents help their fathers around the home less than they help their mothers.

Some studies have explored differences in reported feelings of closeness depending on the age of the adolescent. Feelings of emotional closeness and attachment to parents decrease during the pubertal period (Papini, Roggman, & Anderson, 1991; Steinberg, 1987a, 1988). S. S. Feldman and Gehring (1988) reported a decrease in perceived cohesion to both parents between the 6th, 9th, and 12th grades. Sixth-graders perceived themselves as closer to their mothers than to their fathers, while 9th- and 12th-grade students perceived themselves as equally close to both parents. Although some authors have suggested that a decrease in perceived closeness is functional as adolescents attempt to gain greater autonomy from parents, S. S. Feldman and Gehring (1988) found that this decrease in cohesion was not perceived by adolescents as desirable, reporting that the relationship was not as close as they would like it to be.

Adolescents' perceptions of their parents as warm, affectionate, and nurturant are highly correlated with greater levels of disclosure by adolescents (Klos & Paddock, 1978; Snalk & Rothblum, 1979). Thus, lower levels of disclosure to fathers may lead to perceptions of more distant relationships. Similarly, decreases in feelings of closeness to fathers during adolescence may be associated with less intimacy.

CONFLICT

A number of studies have explored the nature and extent of conflict between adolescents and their parents. Montemayor (1982) reported that parents and adolescents experienced conflicts approximately twice per week, a high rate when compared to nondistressed marital couples. Both parents and adolescents report that adolescents have fewer arguments with fathers than with mothers, with mother-daughter conflict more frequent than mother-son conflict (Hill & Holmbeck, 1987; Montemayor, 1986; Smetana 1988a, 1988b, 1989).

One reason why adolescents report fewer conflicts with fathers than with mothers is that they spend less time with fathers. Another explanation is that fathers are less involved in setting limits and enforcing rules than are mothers, especially for daughters (Montemayor, 1983). The lower frequency of conflicts that adolescents report with fathers relative to mothers does not necessarily mean that father-adolescent relationships are more positive than mother-adolescent relationships. What this pattern may indicate is that fathers are more avoidant and less emotionally involved with their adolescents than are mothers, who play a more active role in childrearing and have closer relationships with their adolescents.

In contrast to popular conceptions of adolescents as rebelling against the values and beliefs of parents, most studies indicate that parents and adolescents do not typically have conflicts over major issues such as religion, politics, or sexuality. Instead, common areas of conflict are disagreements over rules, such as curfews or keeping one's room clean (Montemayor, 1983; Montemayor & Hanson, 1985; Smetana, 1989). Papini and Sebby (1988) also reported that most conflicts with parents occur over "everyday" issues. However, they also found adolescents reporting conflicts related to "Persistent Concerns and Issues," a factor defined as including sex, friends, and drinking. It was suggested that conflicts in this area may be related to receiving repetitive warnings about these issues, rather than having conflictual exchanges per se.

Most research exploring topics of conflict between adolescents and their parents has not explored differences between mothers and fathers. In one exception, Ellis-Schwabe and Thornburg (1986) found that adolescents reported more conflicts with their mothers related to personal issues, such as clothing choices, and more conflicts with their fathers related to practical issues, such as use of the phone. This finding is consistent with the literature on parent-adolescent communication, supporting the conceptualization of the mother as emotionally involved in the personal life of her adolescent children and the father as limiting his involvement to practical, instrumental issues.

The frequency of conflicts with mothers and fathers increases between childhood and early adolescence, with a subsequent decrease through late adolescence (Montemayor, 1982; Smetana, 1989). Pubertal development may be an important factor. Steinberg (1988) found that pubertal maturation increases the number of arguments that girls have with their mothers and increases the intensity of father-daughter conflict. For boys, pubertal maturation led to increases in the number of arguments reported with their mothers and to diminished father-son cohesion.

Several explanations have been proposed for the increase in parent-adolescent conflict during puberty. For example, undergoing the physical changes of puberty may prompt the adolescent to spend more time with peers rather than with parents. Hormonal changes associated with pubertal development may result in changes in the mood or behavior of the adolescent, leading to increased conflict (Susman et al., 1987). In addition, the timing of puberty may coincide with fathers' experiencing a decline in their own physical health. Observing their adolescents' growth and maturation may exacerbate parents' own feelings of midlife stress and lead to greater conflict (Montemayor et al., 1994). Finally, it has also been suggested that increased distance and conflict between adolescents and their parents may actually accelerate pubertal maturation (Steinberg, 1988).

Research has also indicated that fathers' exhibit increased negative affect as a function of adolescent pubertal status (Montemayor, Eberly, & Flannery, 1993). This increase in negative affect may be due to fathers' perceiving their adolescents' transition to puberty as a stressful event. In this same study, adolescents expressed greater negative affect with pubertal development only in conversations with their mothers (Montemayor et al., 1993). No relationship was found between adolescents' expression of negative affect with their fathers and pubertal development. This finding is consistent with findings that adolescents report greater conflict with their mothers (e.g., Montemayor, 1986).

Fathers' negative affect was found to be a strong predictor of adolescents' rating of communication quality and psychological autonomy (Flannery, Montemayor, & Eberly, 1994). Negative affect also predicted sons' rating of paternal control. Mothers' emotional expression did not consistently predict adolescent ratings of relationship quality. Because fathers spend less time interacting with their children, it is possible that any affective expression on their part is particularly salient to adolescents.

POWER

Power is often defined in terms of the amount of influence family members have in decision making or in the degree of control over other family members. In general, adolescents rate their fathers as being less egalitarian than their mothers (LeCroy, 1988; Noller & Bagi, 1985; Pipp, Jennings, Shaver, Lamborn, & Fischer, 1985; Youniss & Smollar, 1985). One reason why fathers are perceived as less egalitarian is that they are more likely to attempt to exert control over their adolescents, whereas mothers are more likely to relinquish control (e.g., Papini & Sebby, 1987; Steinberg, 1987a).

In addition to overall power differences between father and adolescents, there may be specific areas in which fathers retain or relinquish power. It has been suggested, for example, that fathers have considerably more power over adolescents' behavior only in areas involving economic decisions (McDonald, 1982). This is consistent with the role of the father as primarily engaged in instrumental, problem-centered interactions with his adolescent.

It is also informative to explore parental differences in the specific techniques used to maintain or assert power. Baranowski (1978) has suggested that fathers 1. have a greater need for dominance than mothers, 2. are more likely to be autocratic, and 3. are less likely to be permissive. Fathers typically report encouraging independence and assertiveness in their adolescents, whereas mothers report encouraging appropriate interpersonal behavior and child involvement in domestic chores (Power & Shanks, 1989). Fathers also report more use of physical punishment, whereas mothers report more material punishment (Power & Shanks, 1989). Mothers have also been found to use more coercive discipline practices than do fathers (Patterson, 1982; Patterson, Reid, & Dishion, 1992).

Power is an important topic during adolescence, as teenagers renegotiate their roles within the family to gain more relative power. This attempt to gain symmetry in the family has been detected by several researchers. For example, S. S. Feldman and Gehring (1988) found decreases in perceived power differences between parents and children between the 6th, 9th, and 12th grades. Age did not significantly influence the perception of either children's or mothers' power, but it did influence perception of fathers' power. Fathers of the older adolescents were perceived as less powerful than the fathers of the younger adolescents.

In this study, fathers were perceived as losing power not only in their relationships with their children but in their relationships with their wives as well. Younger adolescents consistently rated their fathers as being more powerful than their mothers. Among older adolescents, however, one-third rated the mother as having more power in the family than the father (S. S. Feldman & Gehring, 1988). According to these authors, it is surprising that younger adolescents report that their fathers are more powerful, given the role of the mother as more involved in setting limits and enforcing rules. Younger adolescents may rely more on cultural sex-role stereotypes of fathers as being powerful.

Across adolescence, there are decreases in parental unilateral power and increases in both children's and parents' use of mutual power strategies (Cowan, Drinkard, & MacGavin, 1984; Hunter, 1985; Youniss & Smollar, 1985). For father-son relationships, there is an increase in level of assertiveness on the part of the fathers as well as a decrease in assertiveness attempts by sons with increasing physical maturity (Steinberg, 1981; Steinberg & Hill, 1978).

IMPACT OF THE FATHER-ADOLESCENT RELATIONSHIP ON ADOLESCENTS

The literature reviewed above provides a consistent description of characteristics of relationships between fathers and adolescents. These relationships are described as distant and unemotional, with fathers primarily playing an instrumental role in the lives of their adolescent children. Not much research has explored the factors that may account for these patterns or for potential variability in these relationships. What individual or relationship variables explain the characteristics described above? For example, why do adolescents not report feeling close to their fathers? Are fathers uncomfortable discussing personal issues with their adolescents, or are adolescents uncomfortable discussing these issues with their fathers?

While these research questions are interesting in their own right, they become even more important when one considers the impact of the father-adolescent relationship. Relationship variables, such as those discussed above, are found to predict a number of behavioral outcomes for both fathers and adolescents. The same two questions that were used to explore characteristics of father-adolescent relationships can be applied to the exploration of the impact of these relationships. First, do mothers and fathers have different impacts on the lives of their adolescent children? Second, does the influence of the father change as his child develops?

DIFFERENCES BETWEEN FATHER-ADOLESCENT AND MOTHER-ADOLESCENT RELATIONSHIPS

While there is much research exploring the influence of parents on adolescent outcomes, fathers are underrepresented in these studies (Phares, 1992). Phares and Compas (1992) reviewed clinical child and adolescent research in eight journals between 1984 and 1991. They found that 48% of the studies dealt exclusively with mothers, and only 1% exclusively with fathers. When fathers are included in studies of impact, the possible unique contributions of mothers and fathers are often not assessed. For example, studies have reported the relative contribution of adolescents' attachment to parents and peers to a given outcome without distinguishing between attachment to mothers and to fathers (e.g., Armsden & Greenberg, 1987).

When studies do differentiate between the two parents, it is found that mothers and fathers have different effects on their adolescents. Because fathers spend less time with and have fewer conversations with their adolescent children, it may be expected that fathers have less impact on their adolescents. Some studies have found this to be true. For example, male and female adolescents report having attitudes that are more like their mothers' than their fathers'. Campbell, Adams, and Dobson (1984) reported that the amount of shared variance in attitudes between adolescents and mothers ranged from 9% to 24%, while only ranging from 1% to 15% for fathers.

While overall there is greater attitudinal similarity between adolescents and mothers, there are some specific content areas where fathers are more influential. Wilks and colleagues reported that adolescents' attitudes about alcohol are more like those of their fathers (Wilks, Callan, & Austin, 1989). These authors suggest that fathers may be the primary role models for adolescents because drinking is more prevalent among males. This finding indicates that fathers may have a greater impact on their adolescents in areas where they are more involved than mothers or where they serve as the primary role models.

These findings suggest that, overall, adolescent outcomes are predicted more by characteristics of their relationships with their mothers than with their fathers. Several studies, however, have highlighted the importance of the father. One study assessed the effect that closeness to parents has on female adolescents' expectations about making life course transitions, such as finishing school, beginning a job, becoming sexually active, and marrying (Crouter, Carson, Vicary, & Butler, 1988). Because fathers spend less time with and have fewer conversations with their adolescent daughters, it was expected that closeness to fathers would not significantly alter adolescents' expectations. Contrary to this hypothesis, closeness to fathers was related to expectations of postponing sexual activity but was not related to expectations about the timing of other important life transitions. Closeness to mothers predicted a number of additional expectations.

In some cases, fathers may have a greater impact than mothers. In one study, it was found that parents' strategies of exerting discipline and control can lead to differences in adolescent outcomes. Fathers' use of coercive discipline practices, though less frequent than mothers', appears to have a more powerful influence on their sons' antisocial behavior. Patterson and Dishion (1988) found that fathers' discipline accounted for about twice as much variance in antisocial behavior as mothers' discipline.

Overall, several conclusions can be drawn from comparisons of mothers' and fathers' impact on adolescent outcomes. First, the greater amount of time spent with mothers, as well as the greater intimacy, disclosure, and closeness that adolescents report with their mothers, makes mothers more influential in some respects. However, fathers are not unimportant. Their impact, like their involvement, is limited to specific areas. The influence of fathers on their adolescent children will be related to the areas they are most involved with, such as discipline.

DIFFERENCES BETWEEN FATHER-CHILD AND FATHER-ADOLESCENT RELATIONSHIPS

The lack of longitudinal studies that assess the relative impact of fathers on their children at different points in the life cycle makes it difficult to draw many conclusions on this topic. It is also a challenge to find studies that assess similar outcomes in children and adolescents. The difficulty is compounded by differences in how parental socialization is conceptualized across the life cycle. Studies of children often use a unidirectional socialization model, where parents are seen as exerting an influence on their children (Maccoby, 1992). In studies of adolescents, it is more common to see relationship variables, such as communication and closeness, used to explain adolescent outcomes.

Despite this shortage of comparable literature, it seems clear that the role of the father changes as his children age, as does the specific nature of his involvement. One model for envisioning changes in the father's influence is to expect his impact to decrease during adolescence. As children move into adolescence, they spend more time away from the family. Peers become more important. Outside forces, such as school and employment, play a greater role in socializing adolescents. Parents are no longer the dominant socializing agents. Thus, while fathers do not become unimportant, one could expect that the relative contribution of fathers in determining adolescent outcome decreases through time.

A second model for exploring potential changes in fathers' impact on children is to emphasize the changes in relevant outcomes to be assessed. As children move into and through adolescence, they encounter new experiences and face new decisions. What is important in childhood is different from what is important in adolescence;

thus in adolescence there are new outcomes to explore. Outcomes such as substance abuse and sexuality, for instance, gain relevance in adolescence. Fathers may have a different impact on adolescents than they have on children partly because adolescents are doing different things. Identity development, for example, also becomes particularly salient during adolescence (Erikson, 1963). Research indicates that fathers may play a unique role in the identity formation process. One study found that attachment to fathers was associated with identity foreclosure, while attachment to mothers was related to identity exploration (Benson, Harris, & Rogers, 1992).

Despite the changes in relevant outcomes and in other socializing agents, there may also be some stability in the impact of the father. Current conceptualizations of relationships emphasize that they are gradually coconstructed over time (Maccoby, 1992). The characteristics of father-adolescent relationships have their foundation in father-child relationships. Decisions made during adolescence will therefore be based on a lifetime of prior experiences and learning. Fathers who encouraged their younger children to explore their environments and try new things may have adolescents for whom identity exploration is more likely than identity foreclosure.

There may also be stability in fathers' childrearing goals across time. Longitudinal data indicate that there is some consistency in fathers' interactions with their children through time due to stability in childrearing attitudes and goals (Roberts et al., 1984). Thus, a father who encourages academic achievement in his younger children is likely to encourage it in his adolescents as well. The specific form that this encouragement takes may vary, however, depending on the skills and needs of the child. Therefore, while the overall impact may be stable, the specific mechanisms used to promote this impact may vary.

As seen, it is difficult to draw clear conclusions regarding stability and change in the father's impact on his children across time. It is likely, however, that there is both continuity and change in his impact. Continuity emerges as a result of stability in fathers' goals, attitudes, and patterns of interaction. At the same time, new experiences and issues encountered by adolescents will promote new mechanisms of impact, as well as different outcomes to assess.

CONCLUDING THOUGHTS AND DIRECTIONS FOR FUTURE RESEARCH

DIFFERENCES BETWEEN FATHER-ADOLESCENT AND MOTHER-ADOLESCENT RELATIONSHIPS

Overall, there are a number of differences between adolescents' relationships with their mothers and their fathers. Relationships with fathers are described as more distant and less intimate. Little time is spent with fathers, and when adolescents are with their fathers they are likely to be engaged in passive recreational activities. Fathers are often perceived as uninvolved, especially by their adolescent daughters. Adolescent reports of relationships with their mothers, in contrast, emphasize closeness, self-disclosure, and affection.

Taken as a whole, these findings paint a distinctly negative image of the father-adolescent relationship. Fathers are often portrayed as "the weak link in the companionate family" (Larson & Richards, 1994, p. 162). The conclusion, or at least the suggestion, is that fathers are naturally worse parents than mothers, who are characterized as superior caregivers. This recalls the deficit model once prevalent in multicultural studies, where differences between groups were simply attributed to weakness or failure on the part of one group.

Rather than take a deficit approach to explaining differences between mothers and fathers, with fathers described as less capable of, or less interested in, nurturant parenting, it is important to understand how fathers define parenting. Are fathers' child-rearing behaviors and attitudes consistent with their definition of quality caregiving, or do fathers today feel that they are distant and uninvolved parents?

Several studies have found that fathers perceive themselves as warm and involved parents who value their relationships with their children (Daniels & Weingarten, 1988). Fathers also report enjoying their parenting activities. For example, Larson and Richards (1994) found that fathers often expressed more enjoyment during activities shared with their adolescent children than the adolescents reported. This discrepancy between adolescents' and fathers' assessments of their relationships may be based on fathers' interpretation of the father role.

The fathering role has traditionally been defined as being the economic provider, the disciplinarian, and the playmate. In many families, the father continues to fulfill these roles. Men report that they are active and responsible parents because they support their families financially (Barnett & Baruch, 1988). As a result, many men feel that involved caregiving is a voluntary activity. Caregiving may be seen as a way to be a "mother's helper," rather than as a primary responsibility (Lamb & Oppenheim, 1989).

How a man defines his role within the family is important in shaping his interactions with his adolescents and his satisfaction with these relationships. For example, a father who views his role as the family breadwinner, rather than as an emotionally supportive caretaker, may have distant relationships with his adolescents and spend little time with them. In contrast, a father who defines his role as being an exciting playmate will engage in more recreational activities with his adolescents but may not have a deeply intimate relationship with them. These fathers may be equally satisfied with their relationships, however, as they are fulfilling their obligations as they or society define them.

Several explanations have been proposed for men's limited involvement in parenting. For example, some aspects of fathering may be strongly tied to traditional conceptions of masculinity and gender-role socialization. Men have not been socialized to be emotionally sensitive, leading some to have less intimate relationships with their children. These fathers may not perceive a lack of intimacy in their relationships with children to be negative. It has also been argued that men are conditioned to fear and avoid that which is perceived as "feminine," such as nurturing caregiving (L. B. Feldman, 1990). Thus, fathers may find displays of affection and emotions to be anxiety producing.

Attitudes and behavior toward caregiving are influenced by men's relationships with their own parents and wives. Most middle-aged men today grew up in the 1950s with traditional fathers who were distant and uninvolved with caregiving. Thus, these fathers did not have models of involved fathering on which to base their own behavior.

In addition, men may feel anxious if they act in ways that are substantially different from their own fathers; thus they may be reluctant to significantly alter their conceptions of fathering (L. B. Feldman, 1990).

Several studies have highlighted the importance of the marital relationship to fathering. Men's parenting behaviors are influenced in part by the quality of their marriages. For example, if a marriage is conflictual, spouses may attempt to undermine the parenting role of their partner (Yogman, Cooley, & Kindlon, 1988). Wives' attitudes toward the fathering role and experiences with their own fathers have been found to strongly predict the behavior of their husbands. Men are more likely to be highly involved caregivers if their wives view their own fathers as having been nurturant (Radin, 1981, 1982, 1988).

Fathers may not be as uninvolved and distant as the research suggests. Instead, the findings may be based somewhat on the instruments used. Researchers today need to better understand contemporary fathering in order to develop instruments. For example, scales assessing intimacy define intimacy from a traditionally feminine point of view (i.e., sharing feelings) rather than being sensitive to the ways in which fathers feel they are being intimate (Cancian, 1986). For example, fathers may express intimacy through shared activities and instrumental behaviors. Instruments and methodologies will need to be developed that are sensitive not only to the current views of fatherhood but also to variability in fathers' definitions of that role.

DIFFERENCES BETWEEN FATHER-ADOLESCENT AND FATHER-CHILD RELATIONSHIPS

There has not been much longitudinal research exploring continuity and change in the father-child and father-adolescent relationship. However, cross-sectional studies suggest that there may be important changes in this relationship through development. For example, fathers spend less time with their children through development and become progressively less involved in their children's lives. Adolescents and their fathers also report increased conflict and decreased feelings of closeness.

Many of these changes occur during early adolescence. A number of studies have reported significant relationships between these changes and adolescents' experiencing puberty. However, the actual amount of variance accounted for by pubertal development is often small, usually less than 8%. It is likely that changes in father-adolescent relationships are linked to developmental tasks faced by both the fathers and the adolescents. However, often these linkages are merely proposed as hypotheses. Future research in this area should explore these linkages in greater depth.

Little research has explored the nature of developmental changes faced during adulthood with developmental changes experienced in relationships with children. Middle age may be a period of stress and transition for men. The changes associated with this period can alter fathering attitudes and behaviors. It is also possible that changes experienced in the father-adolescent relationship may contribute to midlife stress. Silverberg and Steinberg (1990) found that a child's transition into adolescence contributed to feelings of midlife stress for fathers, especially for those with a weak orientation toward work.

Changes experienced through time in the father-child relationship may also be somewhat determined by a man's conception of his fathering role. A father who defines his role solely as a breadwinner may not experience change in his parenting role until the adolescent leaves home and becomes financially independent. However, a father who is emotionally involved in fathering may be more sensitive to the changes experienced by his child throughout adolescence.

FUTURE DIRECTIONS

Over the past several decades, there has been growing awareness of the importance of fathers and of the factors that contribute to or impede effective fathering. In addition to the areas of inquiry highlighted above, other important directions for future research include 1. an emphasis on relationships as a context for development, 2. the importance of understanding dyadic differences, and 3. the development of research programs that examine variation in fathers' roles and behaviors.

One recent development in the field of psychology that has promise for fostering greater understanding of the father-adolescent relationship is the emergence of an understanding of close relationships. In contrast to early theories of parent-child relationships that suggested a unidirectional socializing influence of parents on children and adolescents, the relationship approach emphasizes "the development of reciprocity and linked streams of behavior between the members of a familiar pair" (Maccoby, 1992, p. 1014). According to this approach, relationships are complex and multifaceted, have bidirectional influences, and are coconstructed by parents and children over time.

A consideration of multiple dimensions of relationships will lead to greater understanding of the father-adolescent relationship as dynamic and complex. Another strength of this model is the importance of bidirectionality. Father-adolescent relationships influence the development of both individuals. This approach will lead to increased research assessing the impact of this relationship on fathers.

A second direction for future research is greater exploration of dyadic differences. Research assessing the father-adolescent relationship has found a number of differences regarding the nature of fathers' relationships with sons and daughters. One sees dramatic differences in fathers' treatment of their sons and daughters. In fact, according to Steinberg (1987b), "the father-daughter relationship at adolescence is an outlier: It is distinguished from the other three parent-child dyads by its affective blandness and low level of interaction" (p. 196).

A number of reasons for these dyadic differences have been proposed. For example, as children get older fathers might find it easier to relate to a male child because they share more common interests and activities (Barnett & Baruch, 1988). A complete understanding of the factors contributing to fathers' differential treatment of their sons and daughters is a complex issue. These dyadic differences also highlight the importance of being aware of bidirectional influences within a relationship, with fathers responding differently to the development of their adolescent sons and daughters.

Finally, much research shows differences in family interaction styles based on socioeconomic or cultural background. These factors can lead to different attitudes toward fathering. The samples used thus far in studies of father-adolescent relationships have been almost entirely composed of white, middle-class families. Future research should systematically explore the impact that background factors have on fathering.

In this chapter we have highlighted the major research findings related to the father-adolescent relationship and have suggested some directions for future research. It is also important to be aware of historical transitions in society's conception of what it means to be a father. The past several years have seen a great deal of media attention directed toward "the new father" (Bronstein, 1988). No longer limited to serving merely as breadwinners or playmates, today's fathers are encouraged to be emotionally and actively involved in parenting. It is possible that with time fathers will become more nurturant and less distant. This, however, is an issue to be addressed by future research.

CHAPTER 10

Fathers of Children with Special Needs

Michael E. Lamb and Lisa A. Laumann Billings

National Institute of Child Health and Human Development

As this volume attests, the literature on the role of the father in normal children's development is now fairly rich. This is not the case, however, with respect to the development of mentally handicapped or chronically ill children. Over the past 20 years, much attention has been paid to the impact of disabled children on their parents' adjustment and marital satisfaction, but most researchers have only explored mothers' perspectives (Blacher, 1984). As a result, we do not yet know how much time fathers spend with children who are developmentally disabled, how they spend that time (Bristol & Gallagher, 1986), or how their psyches and relationships are affected by their children's disabilities. The few available studies of fathers whose children have disabilities support only the most limited conclusions because the findings are compromised in a variety of ways. First, few researchers have observed fathers whose children have disabilities. Instead, findings are often based on clinical impressions, ratings of parental attitudes, or maternal reports of their partners' emotional and behavioral reactions. Second, many studies are methodologically flawed, particularly with respect to sampling, and researchers often provide few details concerning the procedures used and the range of disabilities represented (Hornby, 1987). Third, most studies have focused on the fathers' reaction to the diagnosis and on their initial adaptation. Much less common are longitudinal studies following a disabled child through the developmental stages or studies and examining the impact on fathers of adolescent or adult-age offspring (Meyer, 1986a), even though parents of older children with mental retardation often feel more isolated than parents of young children with similar disabilities (Suelzle & Keenan, 1981). Fourth, most researchers have studied white, middle- and upper-middle-class families, thus limiting the generalizability of results to other socioeconomic and racial and ethnic groups. Finally, most researchers have examined the impact of organically caused mental retardation rather than chronic illness, sensory impairments, physical disabilities or even socioculturally caused mental retardation (Meyer, 1986b).

It is difficult to generalize about fathers whose children have special needs because many factors affect their experiences, including the type of disability, the health and behavioral characteristics of the children, and the fathers' education, personal characteristics, financial resources, and interpersonal supports. It certainly should not be assumed that handicapped children impose debilitating stress on fathers (Gallagher, Cross, & Scharfman, 1981). Fathers whose passive children have Down's syndrome may be affected quite differently than fathers whose children are chronically ill, physically disabled, and who display aggressive or autistic behaviors. Similarly, fathers whose marriage is sound and whose employment is stable may have different experiences than unemployed fathers whose marriages are unstable.

Three themes have dominated the literature on fathers of children with disabilities, and each is the focus of one section of this chapter. In the first section we discuss aspects of adaptation and coping that are specific to fathers of children with disabilities, and in the second, the effects of disabled children on marital relationships and family cohesion. In the final section we review some implications for intervention, summarizing what little is known about the ways in which programs can better serve fathers and look at the types of services these programs might provide.

FATHERS' REACTIONS

ADAPTATION AND ADJUSTMENT

According to Wikler (1981), the most disturbing crisis faced by parents during the lives of their handicapped children occurs when they first learn of the diagnosis. For many fathers, this tragedy is exacerbated by the insensitivity of professionals who treat them like second-class parents. Many of the fathers interviewed by Erickson (1974) reported that it was difficult to obtain information from physicians, and others only learned about disabilities after their wives had been informed. When disabilities are not evident soon after birth, fathers may later respond by denying their existence. According to Kanner (1953), a prolonged period of denial may be especially common among minimally involved fathers, who do not have enough interaction with their children to recognize the retardation and its effects.

According to health-care providers, mothers and fathers respond differently to the diagnosis of disabilities in ways that often mirror traditional parental roles (Gumz & Gubrium, 1972). Fathers tend to treat the diagnosis as an instrumental crisis and are thus especially concerned about the costs of providing for their children, whether their children will develop successfully, and whether their children will be able to support themselves in adulthood. Mothers, conversely, tend to perceive the diagnosis as an expressive crisis and are thus especially concerned about the emotional strain of caring for children with special needs and about the children's ability to be happy and to get along with others. Of course, some mothers are also concerned about the high costs of raising children with special needs, while some fathers are also concerned about the day-to-day demands. Some fathers may also experience an expressive crisis, harboring extremely intense positive and negative feelings toward their children (Hornby, 1992).

Much has been written about the stages parents pass through while adapting to their children's handicaps (see Blacher, 1984, for a review). According to some clinicians, many fathers pass through successive periods of disintegration—characterized by shock, denial, and emotional disorganization—adjustment—during which they partly accept and partly deny the existence of the handicap—and reintegration or mature adaptation—during which they begin to function more effectively and realistically. Following a period of reintegration, many parents assume a lifestyle not unlike that of families who do not have children with disabilities, although severe retardation can have a prolonged effect on the family's adjustment (Blacher, Nihira, & Meyers, 1987). In addition, Wikler (1981) contends that families are repeatedly subjected to stressful reminders of their children's disability. Some stresses are related to the hardships associated with mental retardation, such as social stigma and the prolonged burdens of care, while others are triggered by the lack of appropriate information, confusion concerning child care, and periodic grief occasioned by discrepancies between expectations and reality. Wikler's informants identified the ages at which children typically talk, walk, enter or graduate from school, and leave home as particularly stressful times, although next to the initial diagnosis, the child's 21st birthday was the most stressful crisis for parents of handicapped children. While this birthday signifies independence and adulthood for nondisabled children, it only reminds parents of special-needs children of the many barriers to independence. In addition, children over 21 are no longer eligible for school services, and services for adults are often inadequate (Meyer, 1986b). As a result, parents of older children with mental retardation often feel more isolated and more in need of services than do parents of younger children with mental retardation (Suelzle & Keenan, 1981).

To assess parents' needs during their disabled children's transition to adulthood, Brotherson and her colleagues (1988) interviewed 48 parents of disabled children aged 18 or older. These parents most commonly expressed concerns about residential options for their grown children, opportunities for socialization, and possibilities for employment. Positive family functioning was clearly associated with active planning for the future and with high levels of perceived social support.

Fathers are typically more concerned than mothers about the adoption of socially approved behavior by their children—especially their sons. Likewise, they are more concerned about the social status and occupational success of their offspring (Lamb, 1981). Not surprisingly, therefore, fathers are more concerned than mothers about the long-term implications of their children's disabilities. Similarly, fathers are more affected by the visibility of the handicap, presumably because they are more sensitive to socially defined norms and evaluations (Price-Bonham & Addison, 1978; Tallman, 1965) and performance outside the home (Gumz & Gubrium, 1972). Further, because fathers often have higher expectations for sons than for daughters, they are especially disappointed when a son is diagnosed as having mental retardation (Farber, 1959; Grossman, 1972). The behavioral consequences of this disappointment may take a wide variety of forms, however. Extremes of great involvement, on the one hand, and total withdrawal, on the other, have been observed in fathers of sons with mental retardation (Chigier, 1972; Tallman, 1965), whereas fathers tend to have limited, routine involvement with retarded daughters (Tallman, 1965) of whom they are more accepting (Grossman, 1972). Fathers also tend to become more involved with first-born handicapped children than with later-born children who have handicaps (Roth, 1985).

STRESS AND COPING

For many parents, children are a significant source of fulfillment and self-esteem, but when children clearly cannot live up to their parents' hopes and expectations, self-esteem suffers (Margalit, 1979; Margalit, Leyser, & Avraham, 1989; Ryckman & Henderson, 1965). Cummings (1976) noted reduced self-esteem in both the mothers and fathers of children with mental retardation, with fathers being especially concerned about their manifest "inferiority" as fathers. His survey revealed that these fathers were often depressed and preoccupied with their children's special needs, and that many felt inferior as fathers and were dissatisfied with their children and spouses. Cummings suggested that this may be because fathers have fewer opportunities than mothers to do things with and for children who are mentally retarded. Often fathers of handicapped children are afraid to engage in roughhouse play (Gallagher & Bristol, 1989). They thus have fewer concrete reminders of their own value and competence.

The need to seek help for their disabled children can further challenge parental self-esteem. Both mothers and fathers of special-needs children prefer to solicit professional help than to ask relatives or close friends for assistance (Nadler, Lewinstein, & Rahav, 1991), although fathers were more willing than mothers to seek outside help. According to Nadler et al., this difference exists because mothers of mentally retarded children view help-seeking as an indicator of personal failure, whereas fathers view help-seeking instrumentally, without implications for their egos.

This argument may help explain why fathers of handicapped children often report lower levels of stress than do mothers (Beckman, 1991; Darke & Goldberg, 1994; Kazak, 1987; Kazak & Marvin, 1984; although Rousey, Best, & Blacher, 1992; and Salisbury, 1987, found no difference between mothers and fathers) and sometimes report no more stress than fathers of nonhandicapped children (Darke & Goldberg, 1994; Houser, 1988; Kazak, 1987; Salisbury, 1987). Some have suggested that mothers and fathers experience substantively different types of stress. Krauss, Hauser-Cram, Upshur, and Shonkoff (1989) found that mothers were concerned about child-care responsibilities, whereas fathers were concerned about child attachment, behavior, and temperament. Similarly, Beckman (1991) found that mothers reported more problems with parenting, their spousal relationship, and their health, whereas fathers reported more problems with child attachment. Bailey, Blasco, and Simeonsson (1992) found that mothers reported significantly more needs than fathers, especially concerning family and social support, time for themselves, explanations to others, and child care.

Other researchers have suggested that mothers experience more stress because they are typically the primary sources of care for their handicapped children (Bristol, Gallagher, & Schopler, 1988; Darke & Goldberg, 1994; Gallagher, Scharfman, & Bristol, 1984; McLinden, 1990). They thus have less time for their own needs (Bailey et al., 1992) and experience more of their children's aversive behavior (Buhrmester, Camparo, Christensen, Gonzalez, & Hinshaw, 1992). Mothers may also be more realistic than fathers about the severity of their children's handicaps (Beckman & Bristol, 1987, as reported by McLinden, 1990).

As might be expected, levels of stress are related to the quality of interaction. Fathers who initially reported high levels of stress had much less positive interactions with their medically compromised infants (including both infants with cystic fibrosis and congenital heart disease) than fathers who reported little stress (Darke & Goldberg, 1994). Parental stress or unhappiness may also affect general perceptions of family life. Margalit et al. (1989) found that fathers of disabled children derived less satisfaction from family life, perceived fewer opportunities for independence, personal growth, and intellectual and recreational activities, and had less sense of coherence and confidence in themselves even though they lived on Israeli kibbutzim and thus did not have to worry about providing for the extra needs of disabled children and had substantial assistance with child care. In a later study comparing mothers and fathers along these lines, Margalit, Raviv, and Ankonina (1992) found that mothers reported even lower levels of coherence than fathers did.

Enjoyment of family life may be diminished by the extra burdens of caring for handicapped children. Parents of special-needs children feel their social mobility has been confined (Crnic, Friedrich, & Greenberg, 1983), and their leisure time curtailed (Blacher et al., 1987; Smith, 1986). Nearly one-third of the fathers studied by McLinden (1990) found it problematic that the family schedule revolved around the handicapped children, and over one-third said it was difficult to find reliable alternative care, which might allow parents more time alone. Thus, fathers of special-needs children could benefit both from learning how to include children in their favorite recreational activities and from access to reliable care providers.

An alternative perspective has been offered by professionals who claim that disabled children do not create additional stresses for families (Dunlap, 1976; Kazak & Marvin, 1984; Waisbren, 1980; Widerstrom & Dudley-Marling, 1986). Waisbren (1980) compared Danish and American parents of handicapped and nonhandicapped children and found that the two groups were remarkably similar with respect to family mental health and the influence of children on marriage. Indeed, many families report that handicapped children have a positive effect on family life (Dunlap, 1976; Dunlap & Hollingsworth, 1977), and some fathers speak of new values and personal growth as a result of successfully adapting to their children's disabilities: "Before Eric came along I was on what you might call a corporate fast track. That's not so important to me anymore. My family is more important to me now" (Meyer, 1986a). Unfortunately, it is difficult to extrapolate from these findings since they are either based on studies that failed to include comparison groups or on anecdotes.

The stressfulness of raising handicapped children may also vary depending on the parents' and children's characteristics. Children's handicaps may be especially hard for socially successful and intellectually talented parents (Holt, 1958; Michaels & Schuman, 1962; Ryckman & Henderson, 1965), who may view their children as extensions of their egos (Call, 1958; Illingsworth, 1967). This is not necessarily the case, however: Farber (1959) found that lower-class parents were more adversely affected by the birth of disabled children than middle- and upper-class parents were, and McConachie (1989) found that better educated fathers actually spent more time interacting with their handicapped children than less educated fathers did. The children's ages may be influential too: Fathers of older children with handicaps (9- to 13-year-olds) report slightly lower stress levels than fathers of younger children with handicaps (4- to 8-year-olds) do (Cummings, 1976). Fathers of older children also rated their depression slightly lower, enjoyment of their children higher, and their wives slightly higher than did fathers with younger children. By contrast, Gallagher, Beckman, and Cross (1983) suggested that the children's age and the parents' perceived stress were directly related because of the increasing difficulty of managing older children with increasingly visible disabilities. Fewer formal professional support services are available for older children as well (Meyer, 1986b; Suelzle & Keenan, 1981; Wikler, 1981), and this increases the burden of care.

The severity of the handicap may mediate the impact of age on family functioning

(Blacher et al., 1987; Boyce, Behl, Mortensen, & Akers, 1991). Blacher et al. (1987) found that the impact on daily life decreased with age for families of mildly retarded children, whereas age made no difference to families of moderately and severely retarded children, presumably because severely retarded children do not assume responsibility for their own care as they mature, whereas mildly disabled children often do.

Overall, the birth of a handicapped child presents additional stresses for both parents. Mothers and fathers tend to perceive the crisis differently and adopt different means of coping. Because mothers are usually responsible for most of the additional caretaking, they tend to report higher levels of stress, whereas fathers often report diminished satisfaction with family life as a result of the extra burdens of accommodating handicapped children.

Paternal Involvement

Research exploring paternal involvement in the care of children with disabilities paints a somewhat inconsistent picture. Tallman (1965) reported that some fathers became very involved in the care of sons who were mentally retarded, and Smith (1986) found that fathers of physically handicapped children devoted about 50% more time to child-care activities than did fathers of normal children. By contrast, other researchers have observed that fathers offer very little assistance even when their wives are overwhelmed by child-care burdens (Andrew, 1968; Bristol et al., 1988; Holt, 1958), and Shannon (1978) found that fathers were no more involved in the care of handicapped than nonhandicapped preschoolers. In fact, Bristol et al. (1988) found that fathers with disabled sons spent significantly less time than normal in both child-care and household tasks, whether or not the mothers were employed. Interestingly, parents of nondisabled children shared child-care duties almost equally. Gallagher et al. (1981, p. 13) concluded that "the traditional father roles of physical playmate and model for the male child are largely diminished or not present at all with the moderate to severely handicapped child."

Many researchers have shown that the severity of handicap affects paternal involvement (Baxter, 1989; Beckman, 1983; Bristol et al., 1988; Dunlap & Hollingsworth, 1977; Holroyd & McArthur, 1976), although some researchers report no such differences (Margalit et al., 1989; McConachie, 1989), and Blacher, Meyers, and Frame (1984) reported a high level of paternal involvement even in families with severely retarded children. Bristol et al. (1988) found that fathers were especially uninvolved in the care of disabled children whose speech, affect, and behavior were severely affected, and this may explain some of the inconsistencies. Presumably, levels of paternal involvement decline when fathers obtain less satisfaction from handicapped children than from nonhandicapped children (Cummings, 1976). Not surprisingly, therefore, fathers with handicapped children were no less (or more) involved with their nonhandicapped children than were fathers who had no handicapped children (Bristol et al., 1988). When fathers choose to withdraw from children who are mentally retarded, it is not only the children's development that is likely to be affected; the entire family is likely to suffer, as discussed in the next section.

Summary

Although findings in this area are remarkably inconsistent, a number of tentative conclusions can be offered. The initial identification of disabled children is extremely difficult for both parents, but because they have different expectations and are differentially sensitive to societal norms, fathers seem to experience the diagnosis as a greater crisis than mothers do. Because fathers are typically less involved in child care, however, they tend to report lower levels of stress than mothers do and may sometimes experience no more stress than normal. Some fathers complain that their social and recreational activities are curtailed by the additional child-care needs of disabled children and consequently obtain less satisfaction from family life. Increased paternal involvement is likely to benefit all members of families with disabled or handicapped children, but many fathers react to their children's disabilities by withdrawing from child-care and childrearing responsibilities.

MARITAL SATISFACTION AND FAMILY HAPPINESS

Marital satisfaction obviously has major implications for all aspects of family life: the well-being of the spouses, the quality of care for the children, and the family's general sense of cohesion and happiness (Belsky, 1981). For these reasons, much of the recent research on families with disabled children has focused on marital integration and family satisfaction. Some researchers have addressed this issue by studying the quality of marital relationships, using self-reports or observational measures, whereas others have compared divorce and separation rates in families with and without handicapped children. Unfortunately, many of these studies suffer from many of the same methodological flaws noted earlier, including 1. a lack of appropriate control groups, 2. extremely small samples, 3. a failure to control for demographic characteristics, such as socioeconomic status, birth order of the child, child's age, and family size, and 4. a lack of standardized measures (Benson & Gross, 1989). Longitudinal studies, especially studies in which marital satisfaction was assessed before the births of disabled children, are also lacking.

In his classic study, Farber (1959) studied 240 two-parent families, each comprising one child who was severely retarded and at least one other child. No comparison group was studied, so it was possible only to identify the correlates of marital disruption in the focal families, rather than whether these families differed from comparable families that did not have children who were mentally retarded. Boys who were mentally retarded appeared to have a greater negative impact on their families than girls did, especially in lower-class families. Presumably, this was because parents have higher expectations of boys than of girls, and so their expectations were most seriously violated by the disabilities of sons. Family disruption increased as the children with retardation grew older, probably because their inability to meet age-graded expectations became more noticeable with age. Even when both parents react adversely to their children's disabilities, differences in adaptation can place added stress on marriages (Price-Bonham & Addison, 1978). Opportunities to support one another effectively may be diminished if, for instance, one parent is grieving and the other is worried about the burden of care presented by the child's special needs.

Most researchers suggest that families with handicapped children experience higher levels of marital conflict than their matched counterparts do (Bristol et al., 1988; Cummings, 1976; Floyd & Zmich, 1991; Friedrich & Friedrich, 1981; Gath, 1977), although some report no differences in levels of marital satisfaction (Kazak,

1987; Kazak & Marvin, 1984; Waisbren, 1980). These discrepancies may be attributable to variations in age, sex, and severity of disability, although Blacher et al. (1987) found that severely retarded children and mildly or moderately retarded children had an equivalent impact on marital satisfaction. Bristol et al. (1988) found that parents (especially fathers) of handicapped children who had just enrolled in an intervention program reported significantly more marital difficulties than parents without retarded children did. Schonnell and Watts (1956) also found that fathers reported greater marital discord than mothers did. In contrast, Floyd and Zmich (1991) found no difference in reported marital satisfaction between parents of mentally retarded and nonretarded children, although the parents of the retarded children interacted more negatively with each other and with their children. This discrepancy raises questions about the validity of self-report measures of marital distress.

Farber (1959) and Gath (1977) found that marital integration in families with disabled children was related to marital integration prior to the child's birth, but Tew, Payne, and Lawrence (1974) reported otherwise. In one of the only studies to include a baseline measure of marital happiness, Tew et al. compared marital happiness in families of children with spina bifida and in families whose children had no medical problems. About 70% of the parents in both groups reported they were happy with their marriages when the focal children were born, but only 46% of the parents whose children had spina bifida reported happy marriages nine years later, compared with 79% of the parents with normal children.

Analyses of divorce rates yield similarly conflicting results. Reed and Reed (1965) reported that fathers whose children were mentally retarded were disproportionately likely to desert their families, and other researchers have found elevated divorce rates in these families (Gallagher & Bristol, 1989; Price-Bonham & Addison, 1978; Tew, Lawrence, Payne, & Rawnsley, 1977). Fowle (1968) failed to replicate these findings, however, and other researchers have reported that, when matched for social class, families with children who are mentally retarded are not more likely to divorce (Bristol & Schopler, 1984; Davis & MacKay, 1973; Schufiet & Wurster, 1976; Wikler, Haack, & Intagliata, 1984). Indeed, many parents claim that disabled children strengthened their marriages and brought the families closer together (Gath, 1977; Kramm, 1963), although disabilities can deliver the final blow to already-troubled marriages (Martin, 1975).

In addition to socioeconomic status, differences in the age of the focal children, the type of handicap, the small sample size, and the appropriateness of comparison groups may all contribute to the great variability in findings on divorce rates. In a study designed to overcome many of these shortcomings, Gallagher and Bristol (1989) reported that parents of children under five with autism or communication impairment ($n = 399$) had divorce rates 50% higher than a random sample of families with children under five either in North Carolina ($n = 8,882$) or the United States as a whole ($n = 6,767$). Similar results were obtained in a study of families with developmentally delayed children.

Severe paternal reactions can have profound second-order effects on other family members, especially mothers. When their involvement decreases, for example, fathers leave mothers to cope alone with the emotionally and physically draining tasks of attending to the children's many needs, and this may have adverse effects on their marriages. If fathers reacted by becoming more involved, their own satisfaction and family integration might both increase.

Tavormina, Ball, Dunn, Luscomb, and Taylor (1977; cited by Gallagher et al., 1981) identified four styles of parental adaptation and their possible consequences:

1. The father divorces himself from the child, absorbs himself in work or outside activities, and leaves the mother entirely responsible for the child's care;
2. Both parents reject the child, who is often institutionalized as a result;
3. The child becomes the center of the family's universe, and all family members subordinate their needs to those of the disabled child; or
4. Both parents jointly support the child and each other while maintaining their individual identities and an approximation of normal family life.

A major source of strength for many parents lies in the quality of informal social support received from spouses, relatives, and friends (Beckman, 1991; Bristol et al., 1988; Gallagher et al., 1981). Waisbren (1980) found that acceptance of the disabled child by the father's parents strongly influenced the father's acceptance of the child. Professional support also reduces familial stress (Bristol & Schopler, 1984; Wikler, Wasow, & Hatfield, 1981) and general life stress for fathers (Beckman, 1991). Indeed, low- and high-stress families with autistic children were best differentiated by the amount of training and support services the parents received (Bristol & Schopler, 1984). Unfortunately, support services for families with disabled children are inadequate. In their review of the literature, Byrne and Cunningham (1985) noted that the parents commonly desired better links between the family and educational, social, and health services for their handicapped children. In another study, many parents expressed a need for more information (Bailey et al., 1992).

Rather than focusing on the negative effects of disabled children on marital relationships and family integration, some researchers have focused on families that have made positive adaptations (Benson & Gross, 1989; Summers, Behr, & Turnbull, 1989). We have much to learn from this literature: By understanding the resources and coping styles of well-functioning families, we can perhaps design more effective interventions.

Despite many shortcomings, the majority of studies suggest that marital conflict and divorce are more common among families with disabled children than in families with normal children. Strong spousal and family support as well as access to professional services may both help families cope more successfully with the stresses and burdens imposed by disabled children.

IMPLICATIONS FOR INTERVENTION

As research on fathers with disabled children has proceeded, recognition of the need for appropriate programs has increased. Because mothers and fathers have different needs and coping styles (Crowley & Taylor, 1994), separate programs for mothers and fathers are ideal, but only a handful of such programs currently exist (Meyer, 1986b, 1993). Here we review recommendations concerning the design of effective programs for fathers and evaluate one comprehensive program of this sort.

STAFF ATTITUDE TOWARD FATHERS

According to Meyer (1986b), programs do not increase paternal participation unless staff members believe that fathers are important, expect them to be involved, and treat them as equal parents. This involves addressing correspondence to both parents (not just mothers), separately contacting fathers when parents are divorced or separated, adapting brochures, newsletters, and advertisements to attract fathers as well as mothers, and recruiting male staff members.

FLEXIBLE SCHEDULING

Programmatic attitudes toward fathers are reflected in staff's willingness to accommodate their schedules to employed parents whose work schedules may interfere with participation in weekday parent programs. A survey of 16 U.S. Handicapped Children's Early Education Program demonstration sites revealed that programs that held day meetings ($n = 4$) reported no paternal attendance; those that held both day and evening meetings ($n = 3$) reported an average of 2.6 fathers per 10 mothers; whereas programs offering evening meetings ($n = 9$) reported an average of 5.3 fathers per 10 mothers (Meyer, 1986b).

PROGRAMS SPECIFICALLY FOR FATHERS

A small but growing number of groups provide support and education programs specifically designed for fathers whose children have special needs (Meyer, 1986a, 1986b). One of the longer running of such programs is the Seattle-based SEFAM (Supporting Extended Family Members) Fathers Program, whose staff reached out to traditionally underserved family members by organizing workshops for fathers, siblings, and grandparents of children with special needs. The Fathers Program, a biweekly Saturday morning program, provided fathers with opportunities for peer support, information reflective of their interests, and involvement with their children (Meyer, Vadasy, Fewell, & Schell, 1985). Participating fathers reported less sadness, fatigue, pessimism, guilt, and stress due to the child's incapacitation, as well as more satisfaction, greater feelings of success, fewer problems, and better decision-making abilities than did fathers who did not participate (Vadasy, Fewell, Meyer, & Greenberg, 1985). After one to two years of participation, both mothers and fathers reported lower levels of depression, stress, and grief, more satisfaction with their spouses, and less need for information than in the pretest (Vadasy, Fewell, Greenberg, Dermond, & Meyer, 1986). In both the pretests and posttests, however, fathers' reports of satisfaction were inversely correlated with the ages of their handicapped children, and the fathers became more pessimistic over time, either because the intervention fostered more realistic expectations regarding their children's abilities and the resources available to them, or because the parents became increasingly aware of their children's limitations as they grew older. It is also possible that fathers had inflated hopes at the time of enrollment in the intervention program. Vadasy and her colleagues speculated that the participating fathers' problem-solving and advocacy skills would counter their pessimism over time.

Programs like SEFAM's Fathers Program meet on Saturday mornings or on evenings convenient to participants and attempt to provide the following:

1. *Information:* Parents need information about disabilities and their potential impact as well as about programs, services, and therapies, so that fathers and mothers can share the role of "expert" concerning their children. This not only helps fathers facilitate their children's development but provides support for mothers as well. Most such programs encourage the sharing of information among parti-

cipants and also arrange presentations by guest speakers (Meyer, Vadasy, Fewell & Schell, 1985).

2. *Opportunities for involvement:* Both mothers and fathers want fathers to be more involved (Gallagher et al., 1981), and 83% of the fathers (*n* = 152) interviewed by Linder and Chitwood (1984) thought that education was the joint responsibility of both parents and the school. By actively involving fathers, programs can foster increased father-child involvement outside the program and thus contribute to the child's cognitive and social development and foster attachment. In addition to learning how to care for their children, fathers would benefit from learning how to include their disabled children in recreational activities. This would help alleviate feelings that family schedules are dominated by the children's needs (Margalit, Leyser, & Avraham, 1989; McLinden, 1990). The Kennedy Foundation has adopted several games and sports, such as the Special Olympics, for families with handicapped children (Shriver, 1990).

3. *Support:* Programs that provide fathers with opportunities to discuss their concerns, joys, and interests with other men in similar situations can help decrease their sense of isolation and thereby benefit mothers as well (Bristol, 1984). Such support needs continue as children grow older, although parents of older children with mental retardation feel less supported and in greater need for services than do parents whose handicapped children are younger (Suelzle & Keenan, 1981), particularly when they realize the possible need to support their children financially and emotionally into adulthood (Price-Bonham & Addison, 1978).

The failure to recognize that fathers are emotionally affected by the birth of children with disabilities not only deprives them of potentially helpful counsel and support, but also conveys the implicit message that they do not matter and that they are not expected to behave or feel differently following major family crises. This may, in turn, have adverse effects on other family members (Vadasy et al., 1985, 1986). Programs that encourage fathers to participate more actively in caring for and educating their handicapped children not only help fathers feel more involved (Gallagher et al., 1981) but also give mothers respite from the burdens of child care (Bailey et al., 1992).

Despite the varied responses fathers may have to their children's disabilities, families—both traditional and nontraditional—are likely to be strengthened when fathers are emotionally and concretely involved with their families. The potential benefits of paternal involvement may even be greater when children have disabilities because family members need increased emotional support, understanding, and practical assistance in these circumstances.

SUMMARY

In this chapter we have sought to outline some of the more consistent findings concerning fathers of children with special needs, acknowledging the many contradictions and methodological problems that plague the literature. Fathers of disabled children may have very different stresses and needs than mothers in these families and fathers in families without disabled children. The traditional paternal worries concerning the success, social acceptance, and financial independence of their children lead fathers to experience the diagnosis of filial disability as a greater crisis than mothers do. However, because mothers tend to bear the brunt of child-care responsibility in these families, fathers often report lower levels of stress than mothers do, and the stress they do report has more to do with attachment issues than with child care. Whether or not fathers perceive high levels of stress, their self-esteem suffers and their enjoyment of family life is diminished by the presence of disabled children. As a result, the divorce rates in these families are disproportionately high. Both researchers and practitioners have stressed the importance of finding ways to increase paternal involvement, in both child-care and recreational activities, so as to reduce the burden on mothers and enhance family cohesion and happiness.

CHAPTER 11

The Effects of Divorce on Fathers and Their Children

E. Mavis Hetherington
University of Virginia

Margaret M. Stanley-Hagan
University of North Carolina at Charlotte

OVER THE PAST 30 years a rapid succession of social changes have dramatically affected the family. Perhaps the most salient in terms of their effects on marriage and marital dissolution are the greater education, economic independence, and employment of women. The role of the men's movement with its emphasis on shared parenting rights and responsibilities and a new parenting role for fathers, that of nurturer, has had a significant but less marked effect. As social attitudes and circumstances have changed, so have perceptions of marriage, divorce, and single-parent families. Marriage has become more optional and less permanent, and the structures, roles, and rules in families are becoming more diverse and discretionary and less socially proscribed. However, supported by a second generation of research interested in assessing the costs and benefits of different family forms rather than the model typical of earlier research that viewed all but the traditional two-parent family as deviant, family scientists and practitioners, court personnel and policy makers, and families themselves are coming to recognize that, for most children, divorced families can be positive environments in which to develop.

This chapter provides an overview of the complex and interactive factors that influence parent, child, and family adjustment during and following divorce. Summaries of the changing demographics of divorce and accompanying changes in legal and social policies provide a framework for understanding the current diversity in family structures and experiences and how family laws and policies simultaneously respond to and, in some cases, create problems in adaptation. Attention is given to an emerging line of research that views divorce as one stage in a family's development and that is beginning to examine how preexisting individual adjustment and family processes affect the decision to divorce and postdivorce adaptation. Throughout the chapter, special emphasis is given to differences in how men and women experience marriage and divorce, to children's postdivorce relationships with their resident and nonresident fathers, and to fathers who have primary physical custody of their children and fathers who do not. The experiences of parents who share custody of their children and the importance of the ongoing co-parenting relationship are briefly addressed. Finally, bringing the discussion full circle, recommendations are made for future legal and social policies that will be based on the growing understanding of the factors that put families at risk or protect them from the adverse consequences of divorce.

THE DEMOGRAPHICS OF DIVORCE

Almost half of all couples in first marriages divorce (Furstenberg & Seltzer, 1986; U.S. Bureau of Census, 1992), and an additional 17% separate but do not divorce (Castro-Martin & Bumpass, 1989). Furthermore, although 66% of divorced women and 75% of divorced men remarry, second marriages have a divorce rate 10% higher than first marriages (Bumpass, Sweet, & Castro-Martin, 1990; Cherlin & Furstenberg, 1994). As a consequence of their parents' conjugal successions, one of every 10 children will experience two divorces of their resident parent before turning 16 (Hetherington et al., 1992). However, even these figures are misleading in estimating the number of rearrangements in parental partnerships to which children are exposed. Rates of cohabitation have soared, and one out of seven divorced individuals live with a different partner between marriages (Cherlin & Furstenberg, 1994). These marital rates also mask significant racial differences. African American couples have a divorce rate higher than whites, are more likely to separate but not go through a legal divorce and to have a prolonged separation before divorce, and are less likely to remarry (Castro-Martin & Bumpass, 1989). Thus, the 48% overall national divorce rate masks the fact that 38% of white children but 75% of African American children will experience at least one parental divorce (National Center for Health Statistics, 1990).

Across racial groups, the overwhelming majority of children (86%) reside with their mothers following divorce (Loewan, 1988; Maccoby, Depner, & Mnookin, 1988; Seltzer, 1990; Shrier, Simring, Shapiro, Grief, & Lindethal, 1991; Sweet & Bumpass, 1987), and for many this arrangement is marked by decreased contact and involvement with their fathers. Only 25% of children see their fathers once a week or more, and over 33% do not see their nonresident fathers at all or see them only a few times a year (Seltzer, 1991). There is evidence that many nonresident fathers, even those who are involved initially, become increasingly uninvolved over time (Furstenberg, 1988; Furstenberg & Nord, 1985; Hetherington, Cox, & Cox, 1982). As fathers decrease contact, they also tend to decrease their financial support. Estimates of the number of nonresident fathers who pay the full amount of court-ordered child support range from 50% (Peterson & Nord, 1990; Weitzman, 1985) to 71% (Peters, Argys, Maccoby, & Mnookin, 1993) with a quarter paying nothing at all. It has been argued, however, that focusing on compliance with formal court-ordered support may give too pessimistic a picture of fathers' economic support. Many parents make informal agreements about support depending on the fathers' ability to pay support and the economic situations and needs of parents and children.

Despite indications of nonresident father withdrawal, Maccoby and her colleagues (1993) propose that recent changes in custody laws and changing gender norms are encouraging the continued involvement of nonresident fathers and are beginning to make continued involvement easier. Support for this proposal may be evident in the changing demographics of divorce. Although only 14% of divorcing fathers are awarded physical custody of their minor children, the proportion of father- to mother-headed families is changing. Since 1970, the number of single-father families has grown 300%, a growth rate significantly higher than that observed for single-mother families (Meyers & Garasky, 1991). It is now estimated that one in every six single-parent households in the United States is headed by a father (Aulette, 1994). In other words, 2.6% or 1.4 million single-parent families are headed by separated, divorced, or never married fathers. However, in divorce, as is found in many different kinds of social changes, changes in behavior precede changes in attitudes, which eventually lead to legal changes (Cherlin, 1992).

ACCOMPANYING CHANGES IN LEGAL AND SOCIAL POLICIES

The marked increase in divorce in the sixties and changes in attitudes toward divorce preceded the initiation of the no-fault divorce. In the United States no-fault divorce was initiated in California in 1970, and although all 50 states now have some form of no-fault divorce, no-fault criteria vary from state to state (Freed & Walker, 1991). The ability to file for divorce on the grounds of irreconcilable differences without the need to document that either adult was at fault meant that divorcing couples could potentially negotiate their own settlements in private without having to air their differences in open court (Mnookin, 1975). Although the no-fault divorce laws and the subsequent introduction of community property laws and gender-neutral custody guidelines may have reduced the adversarial nature of divorce for many couples, they did little to help couples in conflict over child custody and failed to address continuing gender inequities in custody decisions. Attorneys and judges continued to rely heavily on the myth of "maternal instinct" and the "tender years doctrine" when arguing for and making custody decisions (Neugubauer, 1989). Based on earlier psychological research that emphasized the importance of the mother-child bond, particularly for young children, the "best interests of the child" were interpreted to mean that custody should be granted to the primary or psychological parent, the mother (Emery, 1988b, 1994; Neugubauer, 1989).

Continuing changes in gender roles for both men and women and evidence that fathers can be no less competent parents than mothers countered the tender years doctrine (Ambert, 1982; Fry, 1983; Lowenstein & Koopman, 1978; Rosen, 1979; Schnayer & Orr, 1989; Warshak, 1986) and caused researchers, women's and fathers' rights advocates, and legislators to challenge how the best interests of the child were being defined (Arditti 1992; Emery, 1988b, 1994; Furstenberg & Morgan, 1987; Maccoby, Buchanan, Mnookin, & Dornbusch, 1993). Furthermore, there was a growing belief that if conflict could be constrained, children adjusted better to divorce when both parents remain actively involved in childrearing (Furstenberg & Morgan, 1987). In 1979, Kansas and Oregon introduced the first joint legal custody statutes (Folberg, 1984), and many other states soon followed with similar legislation. These laws vest both parents with equal legal authority for making important decisions pertaining to the welfare of their children regardless of residency arrangement and were passed with the hope that the rights and responsibilities of fathers would be expanded (Furstenberg & Morgan, 1987). Recent comparisons of the benefits of joint versus sole legal custody have found that when divorcing couples voluntarily seek or accept joint custody and are able to resolve custody questions without excessive conflict, the resulting shared parenting does facilitate nonresident parent involvement and appears to be positively related to parent adjustment (Arditti, 1992; Bender, 1994; Bowman & Ahrons, 1985; Greif, 1979; Kelly, 1993; Maccoby & Mnookin, 1992; Rothberg, 1983; Stephens, Freedman, & Hess, 1993). Most research indicates, however, that requiring hostile acrimonious parents to share legal custody increases conflict (Furstenberg, 1988) and litigation (Emery, 1994; Emery, Matthews, & Wyer, 1991; Johnston, Kline, & Tschann, 1989) and maintains dysfunctional family processes (Opie, 1993) which in turn leads to problems in child adjustment (Emery, 1994; Maccoby & Mnookin, 1992).

In response to concerns about the negative impact of adversarial litigation on already angry parents and their children, California implemented the first divorce mediation statute in 1980 and mandated that all parents who petition for a child custody or visitation court hearing must first attempt to resolve their dispute through mediation (Comeaux, 1983; Emery, 1988a, 1988b, 1994; Freed & Foster, 1984). By 1990, diverse statutes requiring or recommending mediation had been passed (Bruch, 1992). Although the content and quality of mediation programs vary, their primary goal usually is to provide the opportunity for couples to reach decisions about child custody and visitation in an environment less acrimonious and adversarial than a court setting. In general, the impact of the mediation movement has been positive. Mediation facilitates more rapid resolution of differences and decreases later court litigations (Emery, 1994; Emery et al., 1991). Since mediation is more likely to result in joint custody and litigation in sole maternal custody, it is not surprising that fathers are more likely than mothers to report that their rights have been best protected and the agreements more satisfactory in mediation than in litigation (Emery, 1994; Emery & Wyer, 1987; Emery et al., 1991).

In states that have not implemented mandatory mediation and in cases where parents are not able to agree with or without mediation, child custody and visitation arrangements still are resolved in the courts. Today, such disputes are resolved on a case-by-case determination of the best interest of the child often defined by a primary caregiver criteria based on which parent spends more time with the child and is more involved in routine child care. The use of time alone as a measure of parenting quality, especially given the number of mothers who work outside the home, is an indication of how ill-defined custody decision criteria remain. As Emery (1988b, 1994) notes, although the attempt to reduce gender bias in custody decisions has certainly been praiseworthy, current policies are almost impossible to implement consistently and fairly. The result is increased judicial bias and inconsistent decision criteria from court to court and state to state. In turn, this threatens the already angry parents' abilities to achieve satisfactory and workable agreements.

In summary, for some families joint legal custody, divorce mediation, and gender neutral decision processes have been advantageous. However, when couples are unable to resolve differences, when conflicts center around child custody and visitation arrangements, or when one or the other parent is unwilling to assume parenting responsibilities, forced shared custody and the resulting ongoing litigation can fuel existing conflict to the detriment of both parents and children (Goldstein, Freud, & Solnit, 1979; Hetherington & Stanley-Hagan, 1986; Johnston et al., 1989; Koel, Clark, Phear, & Hauser, 1988; Little, 1992; Opine, 1993; Richards & Goldenberg, 1985). At present, what can be said about judicial efforts is that great strides have been made to address and support divorcing families but that these efforts represent work in progress.

ADJUSTMENT TO DIVORCE

The evolution in legal and social policies witnessed over the past few decades has been accompanied by and at times influenced by an evolution in the focuses and guiding theoretical models of research on families in transition. Spurred on by a divorce rate that accelerated for more than two decades before leveling off in the mid-1980s, researchers initially approached the study of single-parent families with the expectation that divorce would be associated with long-term adverse outcomes for parents and children. This deficit model was sustained by evidence that children of divorce are overrepresented in antisocial and delinquent populations and that divorced parents are at risk for emotional and psychological problems and recurring physical disorders. However, many early studies were methodologically limited. Cross-sectional studies on small nonrepresentative samples and on clinical samples were common, and critical factors such as the developmental status of parents and children, time since separation and divorce, the availability of supports, and pre-existing pathology were often overlooked. Even with such limitations, early work revealed great diversity in the complex interacting factors that facilitate or impede postdivorce adjustment and in the adjustment of fathers, mothers, and children.

RISK AND RESILIENCY IN DIVORCE

The growing recognition that there are wide variations in parents' and children's responses to divorce has led investigators to focus on the diverse experiences and family processes that contribute to individual differences in adjustment (Bronfenbrenner, 1979; Elder, Caspi, & Nguyen, 1992; Furstenberg & Seltzer, 1986; Hetherington, 1989, 1991). The pathogenic model has been all but abandoned in favor of risk and resiliency models (Garmezy, 1983; Rutter, 1987) that incorporate developmental, family systems, and ecological theories. These models are proving to be effective and exciting frameworks for examining individual, family, and extrafamilial factors and processes that put families at risk or that protect them from the adverse adaptive consequences of divorce (Hetherington, 1995).

From a developmental perspective the normative challenges and the cognitive, social, and emotional capacities, resources, and vulnerabilities of children and parents characteristic of different developmental stages or points in the life cycle will influence how family members perceive and respond to experiences associated with divorce. For example, young children in contrast to older children may be more afraid of abandonment, less able to comprehend the realities of what precipitated the divorce, more likely to blame themselves for their parents' separation, and less able to utilize extrafamilial protective resources (Hetherington, Stanley-Hagan, & Anderson, 1989).

When a family transition such as divorce occurs concurrently with a normative developmental transition such as entry into adolescence, adaptive challenges and stresses may be compounded. On the other hand, certain normative developmental changes such as those associated with adolescence may trigger latent delayed effects of family transitions. Finally, both risk and protective factors change over the course of development and with time since divorce. Modifications in the balance between risk and protective factors continue over the years to alter the adjustment of family members and family functioning in the single-parent household.

The family systems perspective adds to the risk and resiliency model by providing a framework for understanding how characteristics of family members and interactions among family members and subsystems such as the divorced marital dyad, the parent-child, and the sibling subsystems affect individual and family adjustment. The family is an interdependent dynamic system wherein changes in family structure or in any family member or subsystem prompts changes throughout the system. Much of the work in divorce research has focused on the risks and protective factors associated with individual characteristics of the custodial parent and child and the parent-child interactions. More recently interest has shifted to the role of nonresident parents (Braver et al., 1993), the relationship between divorced spouses and their co-parenting (Maccoby, Buchanan, Mnookin, & Dornbusch, 1993), and to a lesser extent, the roles of siblings and grandparents in the adjustment of children of divorce (Hetherington, 1995; Cherlin & Furstenberg, 1986).

The ecological perspective recognizes that divorced families do not function in isolation but are affected by the larger historical and social contexts in which they operate. Neighborhoods, schools, the workplace, the church and religious affiliations, friends, formal and informal support networks, and changing attitudes and laws related to divorce may affect family functioning and directly or indirectly support or undermine family members' efforts to adjust to the experiences associated with divorce.

Risk and resiliency models are providing a framework for identifying the complex, changing interactions of risk and protective factors and processes that influence and predict diverse individual and family adaptation preceding, during, and following divorce. The picture emerging from this research is one not only of greater risks confronted by parents and children especially in the immediate aftermath of divorce but also of notable resiliency in adapting to the challenges and changes associated with divorce.

INDIVIDUAL ADJUSTMENT FOLLOWING DIVORCE

Parents and children must come to terms with many potentially stressful changes in the months immediately following divorce. Changing financial circumstances can lead to shifts in residences, new or second jobs and increased work hours for parents, and changes in schools and peer supports for children. The resident parent must assume responsibility for the house and child-care tasks that used to be shared. Children have to adjust to less frequent contact and involvement with both the nonresident parent and resident parent who may be overburdened, preoccupied, and emotionally withdrawn or irritable. Family environments often become chaotic as household routines and roles break down and are restructured. Thus, the stresses before, during, and after divorce place both parents and children at risk.

Parent Adjustment

The ability of divorcing parents to respond to the needs of their children and to establish a cooperative parenting relationship are important predictive factors in children's postdivorce adjustment. However, the stresses associated with family changes also place both resident and nonresident parents at risk for psychological and physical problems that may interfere with their abilities to be competent, responsive parents (Chase-Lansdale & Hetherington, 1990; Hetherington et al., 1982; Kiecolt-Glaser et al., 1987; Kitson & Holmes, 1992; Wallerstein & Kelly, 1980). Divorced adults often exhibit anger, anxiety and depression, and antisocial and impulsive behavior, and are overrepresented among suicides and homicides (Bloom, Asher, & White, 1978; Burman & Margolin, 1992). Furthermore, even controlling for factors such as initial health and health habits (Berkman & Breslow, 1983; Berkman & Syme, 1979), divorced men and women appear to experience disruptions in immune system functioning (Kiecolt et al., 1987) and a corresponding increased risk of recurring and severe physical disorders (Bloom et al., 1978; Burman & Margolin, 1992).

The long-term adjustment of divorced parents varies as a function of multiple factors including the degree of continuing attachment to their spouse and of ongoing conflict with their former spouse, economic security and employment situation, housing and neighborhood conditions, relationships with social support networks and family of origin, parenting stress, and most importantly the formation of a new supportive, intimate relationship. Parents and children in divorced families encounter more stressful life events than those in nondivorced families, and the more negative changes they experience the more problems in adjustment they exhibit (Hetherington, Cox, & Cox, 1985).

Recent evidence suggests that nonresident fathers may be at particular risk for long-term problems and that the lack of contact with children is associated with distress and psychological difficulties in nonresident fathers (Kitson, 1992). Nonresident fathers have been found to engage in impulsive and health-compromising behaviors such as excessive alcohol consumption to a greater extent and for a longer period of time than do fathers in any other family type (Umberson, 1987; Umberson & Williams, 1993), a fact that may be related to the stresses associated with separation and loss and the ambiguity and powerlessness often found in fathers' nonresident parenting role (Hughes, 1989; Umberson, 1987; Umberson & Williams, 1993). Most divorced parents, including nonresident fathers, do adapt. Over time, resident parents on average become less depressed, less anxious, and less likely to engage in impulsive or risky behavior. Moreover, although divorced, resident mother and resident father households continue to be more chaotic than nondivorced households, and although divorced, resident parents continue to report greater childbearing stress than that reported by their nondivorced counterparts, most divorced, resident mothers (Hetherington, 1993) and resident fathers (Nieto, 1990) also report that they are satisfied with their custody arrangements and are reasonably confident of their abilities to be effective parents.

Child Adjustment

There is ample evidence that children exposed to parental distress, conflict, and divorce initially experience a broad range of emotional and behavioral disorders (Allison & Furstenberg, 1989; Camara & Resnick, 1988; Cowan & Cowan, 1987, 1990;

Cowan, Cowan, Heming, & Miller, 1991; Easterbrooks, 1987; Emery, 1982, 1988a; Emery & O'Leary, 1982; Forehand, Brody, Long, Slotkin, & Fauber, 1986; Forehand et al., 1991; Gottman & Katz, 1989; Hetherington, 1989, 1991, 1993; Hetherington et al., 1992; Hetherington, Cox, & Cox, 1978, 1982, 1985; Howes & Markman, 1989; Katz & Gottman, 1991a, 1991b; McLanahan & Sandefur, 1994; Peterson & Zill, 1986; Porter & O'Leary, 1980; Shaw & Emery, 1987; Wallerstein & Kelly, 1980). Although these problems tend to diminish with time, children from divorced families on average exhibit more behavior problems and are less academically, socially, and psychologically well adjusted than those in never divorced families (Amato & Keith, 1991a, 1991b; Hetherington et al., 1992). Furthermore, in adolescence and young adulthood problems in adjustment, school dropout, teen pregnancy, work, family relations, and the formation of stable intimate relationships can emerge or intensify (Amato & Keith, 1991a; Hetherington, 1993; Hetherington et al., 1992; McLanahan & Sandefur, 1994; Zill, Morrison, & Coiro, 1993). It is important to recognize, however, that although severe psychological and behavioral problems are two to three times more prevalent in children from divorced families than from nondivorced families, 70% to 80% of children do not manifest severe or enduring problems in response to their parents' divorce and, after a period of readjustment, emerge as reasonably competent and well-adjusted individuals (Hetherington, 1993, 1995; Hetherington et al., 1992; McLanahan & Sandefur, 1994; Zill et al., 1993).

It is also important to note that most research has measured parent and child adjustment after the marital dissolution has occurred. Thus, the assumption is made that postdivorce problems in individual well-being or family relationships are caused by the stresses associated with divorce. This may be misleading, however; the degree to which postdivorce family interaction processes and adjustment problems are a reflection of ongoing predivorce problems have only recently become focuses of research.

PREEXISTING CONDITIONS AND POSTDIVORCE ADJUSTMENT

THEORIES OF DIVORCE

Despite limited longitudinal research on the relationships between pre- and postdivorce functioning, considerable research has focused on the factors that lead to marital dissolution. The target of much of this research has been the role of marital satisfaction, but marital satisfaction alone has not been found to be an accurate and powerful predictor of divorce (Kurdek, 1993; White, 1990). New theories of divorce have focused on problems in communication and conflict resolution in couples, but despite considerable overlap among theories, different theories have emphasized different aspects of the communication and problem-solving processes.

Social Exchange Theory

Social exchange theory proposes that spouses decide to end or stay in a relationship based on a perceived cost-benefit ratio (Braver et al., 1993; Levinger, 1979; Nye, 1979). If spouses perceive the ratio to be positive, if the relative emotional and practical benefits of their marriage significantly outweigh the perceived effort, psychological, social, and economic costs, divorce is less likely. When the converse is true, when a negative ratio exists with higher costs than benefits, divorce is more likely.

Attribution Theory

Some researchers have used attribution theory as a framework to explain how negative attributions contribute to divorce. Compared to couples in nondistressed marriages, those in distressed marriages are more likely to make negative attributions, to attribute their spouses' positive behaviors to short-term, situational causes and negative behaviors to stable, internal characteristics (Fincham, Bradbury, & Scott, 1990; Hotzworth-Monroe & Jacobson, 1985; Jacobson, McDonald, Follette, & Berley, 1985). Furthermore, distressed couples are more likely to spend time analyzing the reasons behind their spouse's actions and to develop attributional sets that maximize the negativity and minimize the positivity in their spouse's behaviors (Hotzworth-Monroe & Jacobson, 1985). These attributional sets can lead them to ignore behaviors that might disconfirm their beliefs and focus on behaviors that might confirm them (Jacobson et al., 1985) and make effective conflict and problem resolution difficult if not impossible, increasing the probability of marital dissolution.

Affective-Physiological Theory

John Gottman (1993, 1994) has developed a unique theory of how conflict resolution style, affect, physiological arousal, and attribution interact to propel couples down the pathway to divorce. Gottman notes that it is a couple's style of conflict resolution rather than their marital satisfaction or frequency of conflict that leads to divorce. He finds that what he calls the Four Horseman of the Apocalypse, that is, criticism, contempt, defensiveness, and withdrawal, are the most corrosive factors in marriage over time. Relatedly, a pursuer-distancer pattern where one spouse wants to confront and talk about problems and the other to avoid such discussions and conflict is a common precursor of divorce. Criticism and pushing husbands to talk about problems are more common in women, withdrawal and stonewalling more common in men. Gottman speculates that this may be because men experience more rapid and higher levels of discomfort, and more overwhelming autonomic arousal during conflicts than do women, and withdraw to deescalate their arousal and to gain self-control. He notes that a distressed spouse who feels emotionally flooded by the unexpected and unprovoked negative emotions expressed by the other spouse may experience an overwhelming need to escape or avoid flooding. This flooding can cause the person to become hypervigilant for potential negative cues in the partner's behavior and leads to the interpretation of even ambiguous or neutral cues as negative. Over time, the ongoing strain leads to emotional disengagement from the spouse and from the marriage itself.

GENDER DIFFERENCES IN THE DIVORCE EXPERIENCE

The gender differences in spouses' conflict resolution styles found by Gottman (1993, 1994) support the frequently made observation that the experiences of husbands and wives in marriage and their perceptions of their relationship are so divergent that we should talk of "his and her" marriages (Bernard, 1972). Research findings suggest that just as there are his and her marriages there may be his and her divorces (Hetherington & Tryon, 1989).

Women report having been dissatisfied and considering divorce for a longer period of time than do men (Hetherington & Tryon, 1989). Husbands are less sensitive to their wives' dissatisfaction in marriages, and many are surprised when their wife wishes to divorce. The main thing locking women into unsatisfying marriages is lack of financial resources; for fathers it is fear that they will lose their children. Although men and women often voice similar complaints about their marriage the salience of these complaints differ. Lack of communication, affection, and shared interests are the most common complaints of women, whereas for men their wives' nagging, whining, and fault finding followed closely by their immaturity and irresponsibility are prime grievances. Less important contributions to the decision to divorce for both men and women are economic factors, infidelity, alcoholism, and abuse. About one-third of men and women who later divorce also complain about their sexual relationship, but men are complaining about quantity and women about quality.

Although both men and women experience separation and divorce as stressful, the patterns of peaks of psychological distress vary. Women find the time before deciding to end the marriage and the actual separation and divorce most difficult, and it is then that they are most likely to suffer the most serious psychological and physical problems (Kiecolt-Glaser et al., 1987). Men are much less accepting than women of the end of their marriages (Emery, 1994), and thus for men, distress and psychological and health problems often increase following divorce (Emery, 1994; Hetherington & Tryon, 1989; Kiecolt-Glaser et al., 1987). Men frequently value their marriage and their relationships with their wives and children more after they have lost them, and men are more likely than women to sustain unrealistic fantasies of reconciliation (Emery, 1994; Hetherington & Tryon, 1989). Once women have decided to divorce they are more likely than men to face realistically the challenges of beginning a new single life. However, a substantial number of both men and women in the first year following divorce report wishing they had worked harder to solve their marital problems, and many have a secondary peak of distress at 12 to 18 months after divorce when their hopes for a better, new life are being tempered by recognition of the losses they have sustained and the new challenges confronting them (Hetherington & Tryon, 1989).

In summary, despite the research on family processes before and after divorce, there is little systematic research on how predivorce family processes affect postdivorce family relationships. However, it seems likely that personality characteristics that influence social relationships, communication and conflict resolution styles, the regulation and expression of affect, and attributions that contributed to dysfunctional family relations and marital dissolution will also influence postdivorce relationships and adjustment. Behaviors, emotions, and attributional sets established before the divorce may remain salient after the divorce, clouding former spouses' perceptions of each other's intentions, making conflict resolution and the establishment of a positive, co-parenting relationship difficult if not impossible.

Influence of Preexisting Adjustment Problems

Recent research suggests that many of the emotional, behavioral, and academic problems of children and problems of adjustment and in parenting skills in divorced adults may have anteceded the divorce (Block, Block, & Gjerde, 1989; Capaldi & Patterson, 1991; Cherlin et al., 1991). A review of the research on marriage and adult mental health concluded that preexisting psychological problems increase the risk for divorce and divorce increases the risk for psychological problems (Gottlieb & McCabe, 1990). Parents who are depressed, are low in impulse control, or have antisocial personalities are more likely to divorce, to go through multiple marital transitions, and to be unskilled parents and less adaptable in the face of stresses associated with marital transitions (Bentler & Newcomb, 1978; Block et al., 1989; Capaldi & Patterson, 1991). Correspondingly, children whose parents later divorce have been found to exhibit more behavior problems prior to divorce than their counterparts in nondivorced families (Block et al., 1989; Capaldi & Patterson, 1991; Cherlin et al., 1991). It may be that children who are troubled prior to divorce are responding to family problems, conflict, and inept parenting already evident. However, difficult children may also strain troubled marriages to the breaking point (Hetherington & Mekos, in press).

Regardless of whether postdivorce problems were evident before the divorce, the most marked disruptions in individual adjustment and family functioning following divorce are found in the first few months and years (Hetherington, 1991, 1993; Hetherington et al., 1992; Kitson & Holmes, 1992). Most families gradually establish new roles and relationships and achieve a new homeostasis within two years (Ahrons & Miller, 1993; Hetherington et al., 1978; Isaacs, 1988) and function reasonably well thereafter provided they are not faced with sustained or new adversities.

For children, the quality of the postdivorce parenting environment is a critical factor in their postdivorce adjustment (Baumrind, 1991; Fine & Kurdek, 1992; Forgatch, Patterson, & Ray, 1993; Hetherington, 1991, 1993; Hetherington et al., 1992). Parenting quality not only affects children directly but modifies the impact of many ecological stressors associated with divorce (Forgatch et al., 1993; Hetherington et al., 1992; Lempers, Clark-Lempers, & Simons, 1989; Patterson, 1991). Children adjust best when divorced parents are able to establish and maintain a cooperative, shared parenting relationship and when the resident parent is authoritative. Authoritative parenting is characterized by warmth, supportiveness, responsiveness to the child's needs, openness in communication, demands for mature behavior, monitoring of the child's activities, and firm, consistent control (Hetherington et al., 1992; Steinberg, Mounts, Lamborn, & Dornbusch, 1991).

FATHER-CHILD RELATIONSHIPS

A large body of research on postdivorce parent-child relationships has been accumulated over the past few decades. However, the target of most of this research has been the resident mother-child relationship. Substantially less research has targeted children's relationships with either their nonresident or resident fathers. What research is available supports the fact that fathers are competent parents and that although social norms and expectations can create unique challenges for fathers, many of the experiences of divorced fathers parallel those observed in mothers.

NONRESIDENT FATHERS

As noted in the section on legal and social policy changes, the joint legal custody movement has been based in part on the assumption that children fare better when both parents remain actively involved in childrearing (Emery, 1994; Furstenberg &

Morgan, 1987). However, empirical support for this assumption has been mixed. On the one hand, several researchers have found that the continuing involvement of non-resident fathers is associated with the well-being of mother custody children (Hess & Camara, 1979; Hetherington & Camara, 1984; Hetherington et al., 1978, 1979; Hetherington et al., 1989; Isaacs, 1988; Jacobson, 1978; Kelly, 1993; Koch & Lowery, 1985; Peterson & Zill, 1986; Tschann, Johnston, Kline, & Wallerstein, 1989; Wallerstein & Kelly, 1980). However, others have found little association between father involvement and child well-being (Baydar & Brooks-Gunn, 1991; Furstenberg, Morgan, & Allison, 1987; King, 1994a; Kurdek, 1986; Thomas & Forehand, 1993; Zill, 1988). Thomas and Forehand (1993) suggest that these apparent inconsistencies may result from differences among studies in the ages of the targeted children, time since divorce, and measures and informants used. However, these discrepant findings also may reflect whether it is the frequency of contact or the quality of the nonresident father-child relationship that is measured and whether moderating or mediating effects of the relationship are considered.

A warm relationship with an authoritative nonresident father has been found to be associated with higher self-esteem, better social and cognitive competencies, and fewer behavioral problems in children (Hetherington et al., 1978, 1979; Hetherington, 1991). Furthermore, such a warm, even if infrequent relationship with a nonresidential father may have more positive effects for African American than for white children (McLanahan & Sandefur, 1994). Furstenberg and Nord (1985) examined teenagers' perceptions of their relationships with their nonresident fathers and found that 76% reported that their fathers were interested in them and loved them even when contact was infrequent. Given such evidence, it has been proposed that children can identify with, and by extension establish a positive relationship with, their nonresident fathers even when contact is infrequent (Furstenberg et al., 1987).

A critical mediating factor, however, appears to be the parents' relationship. Under conditions of high parental conflict or when the parent is incompetent, rejecting, or psychologically impaired, frequent visitation can have adverse effects on children. Unfortunately, many divorced couples have a relationship that is more acrimonious than cooperative, and the necessary contact between former spouses during father visitations may actually fuel existing conflict (Furstenberg & Morgan, 1987). When this occurs, some fathers reduce contact with their children in order to avoid arguments with their ex-wives (Ahrons & Miller, 1993; Braver et al, 1993; Kelly, 1981; Seltzer, 1991; Umberson & Williams, 1993). Others maintain contact, but when ongoing battles are played out in front of the children and when children feel caught in the middle of parental conflict, the potential benefits of father-child contact for the children appear to be lost (Amato & Rezar, 1994; Hetherington & Camara, 1984; Hetherington et al, 1978, 1979; Hetherington, Stanley-Hagan, & Anderson, 1989; Maccoby et al., 1988).

Although in the absence of parental conflict, the quality of the father-child relationship appears to be more important than the frequency of contact, many nonresident fathers experience more problems than either resident or nonresident mothers in relating to their children after divorce (Amato & Keith, 1991a; Furstenberg, Nord, Peterson, & Zill, 1983; Peterson & Zill, 1986; Seltzer & Bianchi, 1988; White, Brinkerhoff, & Booth, 1985). For example, although research on the postdivorce relationships between nonresident mothers and children is scant, what evidence is available suggests that involvement with nonresident mothers appears to have a more positive impact on children's adjustment, particularly that of daughters, than does involvement with nonresident fathers (Brand, Clingempeel, & Bowen-Woodward, 1988; Gunnoe, 1993; Zill, 1988). This differential impact may reflect both the greater frequency of contact by nonresident mothers than nonresident fathers and differences in the quality in relationship with their children. Although nonresident mothers are poorer at monitoring and controlling their children's behaviors than are nondivorced mothers, they are better at it than are nonresident fathers (Gunnoe, 1993). Moreover, nonresident mothers are more sensitive to their children's emotional needs, communicate better, are more supportive in times of stress, and are more knowledgeable and interested in the children's activities (Furstenberg & Nord, 1985; Gunnoe, 1993).

Fathers who maintain contact tend to be more permissive than authoritative, and they are more likely to assume a recreational, companionate role than the role of teacher or disciplinarian (Furstenberg & Cherlin, 1991). In part, these parenting qualities may result from the pattern of intermittent and infrequent contact nonresident fathers tend to have with their children, the lesser experience and involvement of fathers than mothers in childrearing prior to divorce, and the pervasive "motherhood mystique" that mothers are more unique, central and competent in child care and promoting the well-being of children (Huffnung, 1989). Thus, many nonresidential and residential divorced fathers initially feel confused or apprehensive about their parenting role (Seltzer, 1991) and are not prepared to assume even part-time parenting responsibilities (Fox, 1985; Umberson & Williams, 1993). They report being uncertain about what to do during visitations, particularly with young children, and concerned about the extent to which they should assume a disciplinarian role during brief visits (Weiss, 1975). Nonresident fathers' discomfort with their parenting roles is associated with a more companionate parent-child relationship or with complete withdrawal, whereas a clear delineation of the parenting role and acceptance of its importance is related to the establishment and maintenance of high-quality parental involvement (Ihinger-Tallman, Pasley, & Buehler, 1993).

Factors other than perception of the paternal role influence continued involvement of the nonresident father, contact of the nonresident mother is related to higher education (Seltzer & Bianchi, 1988; Hetherington & Stanley-Hagan, 1986), close proximity (Furstenberg et al., 1983), and ethnicity with African American fathers more likely to maintain contact than whites, and Hispanic fathers least (McLanahan & Sandefur, 1994). However, the relationship with the noncustodial mother is the most salient factor in visitation (Ahrons & Miller, 1993; Hetherington et al., 1992; Isaacs, 1988; Koch & Lowrey, 1985; Tepp, 1983; Wallerstein & Kelly, 1980). When legal wranglings with their former wives are stressful, when fathers feel they have little control over court decisions or what will happen to their children, or when conflict is ongoing, they are less likely to remain involved or to pay child support (Arditti & Allen, 1993; Braver et al., 1993; Furstenberg et al., 1983; Kruk, 1992; Seltzer & Bianchi, 1988; Teachman, 1991; Wright & Price, 1986). Even when fathers would like to maintain contact, their former wives' residual anger or responses to ongoing conflict can make it difficult. Seltzer and Brandreth (1994) note that resident mothers act as gatekeepers after divorce, potentially limiting fathers' contact with children and determining the circumstances under which contact can occur. If conflict is high between former spouses, mothers are more likely to close and lock the gate.

The characteristics of the children also can affect the level of the nonresident father's involvement. Less contact is found with younger children than school-aged or adolescent children (Hetherington & Stanley-Hagan, 1986), and there is some inconsistent evidence of greater involvement with sons than daughters (Furstenberg et al., 1983; Hess & Camara, 1979; Hetherington et al., 1982; Mott, 1993; Seltzer, 1991; Seltzer & Bianchi, 1988). In addition, when children are adjusting well, fathers may be more likely to maintain contact. However, when children manifest behavioral and emotional problems, either of two extreme patterns of involvement emerge. Some fathers may feel their help is needed and sustain or increase their involvement, while others who may be having problems with their own postdivorce adjustment may withdraw (Furstenberg & Morgan, 1987).

There is some evidence that the first postdivorce year may be an especially salient period of reorganization when the patterns of father-child involvement are set. High conflict and low cooperation at this time can hinder the establishment of a positive father-child relationship. If a positive relationship is not established during the first postdivorce year, the father and child adjust to their loss, and future involvement becomes less likely and less important to either's well-being (Ahrons & Miller, 1993). This suggests that interventions aimed at increasing nonresident father involvement must occur early in the postdivorce or preferably postseparation period and must address the importance of a cooperative parenting relationship between former spouses.

Finally, the vast majority of both nonresidential and residential fathers marry. (See the chapter in this volume by Hetherington and Henderson on fathers in remarried families for a more detailed discussion of remarriage.) In contrast to nonresident mothers who are likely to remain involved with their children after the remarriage of the resident fathers, nonresident fathers tend to decrease involvement with their children when either they or their former spouse remarry. When the nonresident father remarries, new family responsibilities may take time and attention away from his earlier relationships (Furstenberg et al., 1983; Seltzer, 1991; Seltzer & Bianchi, 1988; Seltzer & Brandreth, 1994). Likewise, the remarriage of the resident mother may make it more complex and difficult for the nonresident father and his children to balance old and new relationships (Furstenberg et al., 1983; Seltzer & Bianchi, 1988). The likelihood of paternal withdrawal has also been found to be negatively related to the nonresident father's perception of family values. When the nonresident father, and in the case of his own remarriage his new wife, share strong family values that include a commitment to parental responsibilities, the father is less likely to disengage (Seltzer & Brandreth, 1994). When nonresident fathers do stay involved with their biological children, they are less likely than are nonresident mothers to find themselves in competition with their children's stepparent (Brand et al., 1988). In addition, authoritative, involved, divorced, nonresident fathers can to some extent attenuate the adverse effects of nonauthoritative residential mothers and stepfathers (Hetherington, 1993).

In summary, nonresidential divorced fathers often experience some difficulty in establishing a comfortable and effective parenting relationship and as their life situation changes may withdraw from their children's lives. Many nonresident fathers feel they have a right to disengage (Arendell, 1992) particularly when faced with difficult or conflictual relationships with their ex-wives or when they believe that they have lost their parental rights. When they do disengage, however, they often feel guilty and inadequate as parents (Reissman, 1990), and their children are denied an important source of support and stimulation. When parental conflict is low, when the fathers feel that they have some control over what is happening to their children, and when they are comfortable with their parenting role, the result is a more involved competent nonresident father and a positive relationship that benefits both father and child.

RESIDENT FATHERS AND THEIR CHILDREN

Although both joint legal and joint physical custody have become more common over the past few years, even when joint physical custody is awarded, most children reside almost full time with their mothers (Emery, 1988a; Hetherington & Stanley-Hagan, 1986; Maccoby & Mnookin, 1992; Shrier et al., 1991). Many physical custody decisions are made by the divorcing parents, not the courts, and the decisions may reflect concerns fathers themselves have about assuming full-time parenting (Maccoby & Mnookin, 1992). Many fathers report that they would like sole or joint physical custody of their children following divorce but choose not to pursue it because 1. they believe their children would benefit more from the closer relationships children are perceived to have with their mothers, 2. fathers' job responsibilities are not flexible enough to accommodate the time demands of single parenthood, and 3. fathers want to avoid exposing their children to prolonged negative custody battles (Hetherington & Stanley-Hagan, 1986; Maccoby et al., 1993).

Given that only about 14% of divorcing fathers are awarded sole custody, it is not surprising that relatively little is known about their parenting or the quality of their relationships with their children. Newly divorced resident fathers do appear to experience many of the same problems faced by resident mothers. They report feeling overloaded, socially isolated, and worried about their parenting competence and find that being a custodial father interferes with both their social life and work (Hetherington & Stanley-Hagan, 1986). However, many resident fathers have advantages less available to resident mothers; most notable are their greater economic resources and the concomitant better housing, neighborhood, schools, and child-care facilities available to them. In addition, there are gender differences in parenting strain. Fathers report more difficulty monitoring their children's health, school work, and behavior, whereas both resident and nonresident mothers report more problems with being firm and patient (Maccoby & Mnookin, 1992). Although resident fathers have problems in monitoring they do not seem to have the problems in control and discipline that are characteristic of divorced resident mothers, and they are more likely to assign household tasks to children (Chase-Lansdale & Hetherington, 1990). Less competent monitoring by resident fathers is associated with higher levels of delinquent activities in adolescents who are residing with divorced fathers than in those living with their mothers (Buchanan, Maccoby, & Dornbusch, 1992; Maccoby & Mnookin, 1992).

How well fathers cope with single-parenting may be related to whether they sought custody originally or assumed custody because the mother was incompetent or unwilling to parent (Hanson, 1988; Mendes, 1976a, 1976b). Physical custody seekers have been found to have had close relationships with their children prior to divorce, and the quality of their predivorce relationships may carry over into the new family unit (Parke & Tinsley, 1984). Moreover, custody seekers usually have more available resources and supports, are more highly educated, and are more likely to be parenting older children and adolescents (Hetherington & Stanley-Hagan, 1986). This is not to say that those who seek custody of their children adapt easily to the role of single parent. In one recent survey of new resident fathers who sought custody, Nieto (1993) found that only 18.2% felt comfortable and confident with their single-parent role. The balance felt varying degrees of discomfort with just under 25% reporting feeling extremely or fairly uncomfortable, frantic, frightened, and disoriented. However, despite their fears and concerns, virtually all of the men reported that they believed receiving primary custody was in the best interests of their children, that they were satisfied with having sought and won physical custody, and that they saw nothing unusual or pathological about heading single-parent families.

Despite any concerns the fathers may have, most measures of children's problem behaviors, social competencies, and self-esteem indicate that divorced, resident fathers are no less competent parents than mothers (Ambert, 1982; Fry, 1983; Lowenstein & Koopman, 1978; Rosen, 1979; Schnayer & Orr, 1989). In fact, when parents' reports are used to assess child well-being, resident mothers report better relations and fewer problems with their children than do resident mothers (Furstenberg, 1988; Schnayer & Orr, 1989). Given the higher economic status and greater resources typical of nonresident father households, however, the parents' ratings of their children's behavior problems may be more a reflection of the relative levels of stress and adverse living conditions associated with family finances for divorced women than the parenting of the custodial parent (Schnayer & Orr, 1989).

There is some evidence to suggest that children may fare better in the custody of their same-sex parent (Ambert, 1982; Camara & Resnick, 1988; Furstenberg, 1988; Lowenstein & Koopman, 1978; Zill, 1988). However, some recent evidence challenges these findings (Downey & Powell, 1993; Maccoby & Mnookin, 1992). Discrepant results may be due to the age of the child and methods of data collection, but the issue of such gender differences remains an open question. It has been reported that sons in resident father homes are more mature, socially outgoing and independent, and less demanding, and have higher self-esteem than do daughters living with their fathers (Santrock & Warshak, 1979). On the other hand, sons in resident father homes are also less communicative and less overtly affectionate, perhaps as a result of less exposure to female expressiveness. In contrast, compared to daughters living with their mothers, daughters living with their fathers have been found to exhibit more behavior problems and are more aggressive and less prosocial (Furstenberg, 1988).

Both boys and girls in divorced families, whether in mother or father custody, show more acting out behaviors than those in nondivorced families. However, boys in both divorced and nondivorced families show more externalizing behavior than girls (Furstenberg & Allison, 1985; Hetherington et al., 1982; Hetherington & Camara, 1984; Zeiss, Zeiss, & Johnson, 1980). It has been proposed that under stressful conditions boys are more likely to respond by externalizing and girls by internalizing (Emery, 1982). However, the form of acting out, externalizing behavior in response to divorce, may vary for boys and girls with precocious sexual activities and parenthood being more common in girls and aggressive delinquent activities in boys (Hetherington, 1993). In addition, boys may be more adversely affected by the conflict frequently associated with divorce. Parents fight more and their fights are longer in the presence of sons than daughters (Hetherington et al., 1982). Moreover, compared to couples with daughters, those with sons are more likely to delay divorcing and are 9% less likely to divorce (Morgan, Lye, & Condron, 1988). This may be because of greater involvement and attachment of fathers to sons or the reluctance of mothers to attempt raising sons alone. The apprehension of mothers may be well founded since divorced mothers of sons experience more childrearing stress than divorced mothers with daughters. These factors lead to sons being exposed to more conflict both before and after divorce. Since boys are less able than girls to talk about their feelings or seek help in times of stress they may have fewer protective resources available in dealing with the family dissension and divorce (Hetherington, 1989, 1991).

In summary, despite experiencing substantial changes in their lifestyles and being concerned initially about their parenting capabilities, most divorced, residential fathers establish positive, effective relationships with their children. Measures of parenting and of children's well-being indicate that residential fathers are as competent parents as residential mothers following divorce.

JOINT CUSTODY REVISITED

Thus far, discussions of joint custody have referred to joint legal custody, in which both parents are held responsible for the welfare of their children regardless of residency arrangements, as opposed to joint physical custody, in which parents share both legal and physical custody of their children. Although state laws vary with respect to physical custody and nonresident parent visitation guidelines, the joint custody arrangement required or recommended by most states refers to shared legal rather than shared physical custody. The goal has not been to have children shuttling back and forth between parents but to guarantee both mothers and fathers their parenting rights, facilitate parent involvement in childrearing decisions, and make access between nonresident parents and children frequent and easy. In practice, most children continue to reside with their mothers regardless of whether the mother has sole or shared custody. Thus, the question is whether or not joint legal custody statutes have facilitated nonresident father involvement to the benefit of his children.

Based on available research, the answer to this question is a qualified yes. When couples accept joint legal custody, most are able to resolve physical custody without conflict and can establish a workable if not cooperative parenting relationship. Joint legal custody appears to be advantageous, at least for parents. Fathers with joint custody are more comfortable with their parenting role, more involved in childcare (Arditti, 1991, 1992; Bowman & Ahrons, 1985; Stephens et al., 1993), and more compliant with child support orders (Bender, 1994; Stephens et al., 1993). Mothers appear to be better adjusted and less burdened by parenting responsibilities, which frees them to pursue other interests (Bender, 1994; Kelly, 1993; Rothberg, 1983; Stephens et al., 1993). Moreover, former spouses with joint custody are less likely to return to court to pursue alternative arrangements or resolve disagreements (Bender, 1994). Unfortunately, although there is evidence that the children establish close relationships with both parents (Bender, 1994), the superiority of joint over sole legal custody measured in terms of positive child adjustment has not been clearly demonstrated (Camara & Resnick, 1988; Depner & Bray, 1992; Furstenberg, 1990; Maccoby, Depner, & Mnookin, 1990). Additional longitudinal research is needed to explore the impact of joint legal custody arrangements on the children they are designed to benefit.

In rare cases families with joint custody also agree to or arrive at a shared physical custody arrangement. Although there are many variations in this arrangement, the most common is one where there are alternations of child care between parents on a weekly or biweekly basis, or a division of the week with either split or alternative weekends (Rosenthal & Keshet, 1981). In even rarer instances, the child may remain in one household and the parents move in and out. Several expectations are behind the pursuit for shared physical custody. Neither parent nor children need feel the loss of a family member, neither parent is relegated to the position of visitor, and the child is not placed in a situation in which he or she feels neglected by the nonresident parent. Moreover, parents have more time off from child-care responsibilities and are less likely to feel overloaded.

Although there is little evidence of the impact of such joint physical custody arrangements on children, it appears that those who alternate between mother and father residences fare better when the parents live in close geographic proximity so that the children's extrafamilial sources of support, school, and peer group memberships remain stable, and when in the absence of a cooperative relationship, parents are not acrimonious (Hetherington & Stanley-Hagan, 1986).

Like their counterparts who voluntarily share legal custody, parents who find joint physical custody satisfying are likely to report that they had positive relationships with their former spouses, especially over childrearing issues, prior to divorce and have experienced little conflict since the divorce. Moreover, they report significant congruence between their childrearing practices. When physical custody of their children is shared, neither residence is considered the primary residence and the schedule for the children's shifts in residence is formalized (Benjamin & Irving, 1990).

Parents dissatisfied with joint custody, whether it involves shared physical custody or not, are likely to have had acrimonious relationships before and since the divorce and to believe that they were coerced into the arrangement by the courts or the other parent. Mothers may have acquiesced out of guilt at denying their children access to their fathers or out of fear of loss of their children in a custody battle. Some parents may have believed that a shared parenting relationship that necessitates continued contact might lead to a reconciliation.

Unfortunately, for many divorcing couples the conflict that characterizes the period before the divorce does not end with the divorce but may escalate (Hetherington et al., 1985). Therefore, given ample evidence of the positive association between ongoing parent conflict (Amato & Rezac, 1994; Furstenberg & Morgan, 1987; Goldstein et al., 1979) and ongoing legal disputes (Johnston et al., 1989) and problems in children's adjustment, the practicality of joint custody in the face of continued conflict is questionable. Although children may benefit from the involvement of both their parents it is likely that only certain families can make joint legal custody a positive and relatively stress-free experience and even fewer families can make joint physical custody work (Hetherington & Stanley-Hagan, 1986; Koel et al., 1988; Steinman, 1981).

Shared Parenting

Whether children reside with their mothers or fathers or alternate parental residences, a critical factor in their postdivorce adjustment and long-term well-being is the quality of the co-parenting relationship. Maccoby and her colleagues (1990, 1993) have identified three parenting patterns to describe shared parenting in either sole or joint custody families. Cooperative parents talk with each other about their children, avoid arguments, and support rather than undermine each other's parenting efforts. Conflicted parents talk with each other about their children but with criticism, acrimony, defensiveness, and attempts to undermine each other's parenting (similar to the traits Gottman identified as predictive of divorce). Disengaged parents are both involved with their children but adopt what Furstenberg (1990) has termed a "parallel parenting" model. Each parent adopts his or her own style and does not interfere with the other's parenting. Communication with each other is avoided except perhaps through their children. This reduces the likelihood of direct conflict but also reduces cooperation.

Cooperative parenting is most satisfying to parents and children. When the biological parents are cooperative co-parents, their children adjust better to the divorce and adjust more easily to one or both parents' remarriages, and the children's relationship with their stepparents are more positive (Bray & Berger, 1993; Crosbie-Burnett, 1991). Parents are more likely to be cooperative when there are a small number of children who are school age, when there was little conflict at the time of divorce or since, and when both parents express an ongoing concern about the children's well-being (Maccoby et al., 1993).

Unfortunately, feelings of anger and resentment are difficult if not impossible for many divorced parents to control, and even two years after divorce about one-quarter of divorced parents are involved in conflicted parenting (Maccoby & Mnookin, 1992). Children suffer not only the adverse effects of exposure to parental conflict, but as a result of loyalty conflicts they often feel caught in the middle of warring parents (Buchanan et al., 1991; Hetherington, 1993). Children forced to serve as go-betweens may learn to exploit their parents and to play one off against the other, and when older escape careful monitoring of their activities (Hetherington, Law, & O'Connor, 1992). Even when conflict is encapsulated and children are neither directly exposed nor caught in the middle, the impact of ongoing parental conflict may be felt through changes in parental support and monitoring (Patterson, 1991).

Although coopperative co-parenting is associated with positive adjustment, in cases where both parents remain involved, the disengaged or parallel style of shared parenting is most common (Camara & Resnick, 1988; Debner & Bray, 1992; Furstenberg, 1990; Maccoby et al., 1990; Maccoby & Mnookin, 1992) particularly when parenting adolescents (Maccoby & Mnookin, 1992). Although a disengaged co-parenting style is not the ideal, children have been found to adjust well provided their parents do not interfere with each other's parenting, conflict is low, and the children are not asked to act as go-betweens.

IMPLICATIONS FOR SOCIAL AND LEGAL POLICIES

The encouragement of parental responsibility, the minimization of conflict and of getting the child caught in the middle of parental acrimony, and the encouragement of constructive involvement of both parents with the child should be the main goals of policy. With the introduction of no-fault divorce, state involvement in dissolving marital relationship decreased. However, the courts have become increasingly involved in determining child custody and financial settlements. This is because of poorly defined indeterminate laws relating to financial issues and childrearing, including custody and visitation, that promote acrimony and litigation and that allow a great deal of discretion and often bias in the decisions of judges (Emery, 1988b, 1994; Mnookin, 1975). Although sometimes legal coercion is necessary to protect the well-being and rights of the family members, contact with the legal system often promotes adversarial attitudes and behavior. Interventions that minimize legal involvement and conflict and that promote compromise and mutual parental responsibility for children should be facilitated. Although indeterminacy in divorce settlements was promoted as a means of being responsive to the diverse needs of different kinds of families it has also engendered conflict because of different expectations about rights and responsibilities in divorcing couples. In an attempt to resolve some of the conflicts associated with finances, federal legislation has been passed that contains incentives for states to adopt presumptive standards with specified amounts for child support (Landstreet & Takas, 1991). Although these schedules vary from state to state, their simplicity, clarity, and specificity have reduced some of the conflict in the determination of child support.

Enforcing compliance with child support has been more difficult and has included civil or criminal contempt proceedings, the garnishment of wages, and retention of tax refunds. However, compliance is still a serious problem. The earlier in the process accessing child support occurs, the more effective it seems to be. It has been suggested that child support should be automatically withheld from income just as are social security and income taxes.

Attempts to resolve issues of indeterminacy and bias in custody also have been problematic. Best interest standards are difficult to determine even by so-called experts (Mnookin, 1975; Emery, 1994), and the primary caretaker standard, although a clearer, determinative principle, presents problems. Although theoretically gender neutral, in practice it leads to a bias against father custody. Furthermore, it perpetuates traditional concepts of custody and visitation (Scott, 1992) and may be unfair when a parent who shared almost half of the parenting is treated the same as a parent who was uninvolved in parenting. Under the primary caretaker standard both of these parents would lose custody of the child and have limited visitation rights. The impact of recent changes in social gender norms are evident in the increasing numbers of fathers actively seeking joint legal and joint physical custody. More fathers consider sharing parenting responsibilities with their former wives to be not only a right but a responsibility they desire. For fathers who seek and are awarded physical custody and for nonresident fathers who remain involved, parenting can be a rewarding experience for both fathers and children.

It has been suggested that children's rights are not adequately protected in the divorce process and that children should be represented by guardians ad litem, lawyers or nonlawyers who support the child's interests independent from the parents. However, concerns have been raised about introducing a further adversary into the litigation process. Moreover, although greater consideration of children's wishes in custody decisions is sometimes advocated, forcing the child to choose between parents does make the child feel caught in the middle, an experience demonstrated to be detrimental to the child's well-being. Furthermore, there is little agreement about how old a child must be to participate in such a decision.

Joint custody and divorce mediation seem to be the most effective methods of maintaining involvement of the nonresident parent and sustaining child support (Emery, 1994). However, these mechanisms are not effective and may even be detrimental with highly conflictual, hostile couples. Conflict may escalate through increased spousal contact and children may be exposed to animosity between their parents and loyalty conflicts much greater than those found in sole custody.

Although research has led to a clear understanding of the divorce process, associated risk and protective factors, and their impact on the experiences and the adjustment of parents and their children, translating empirical findings into interventions and social and legal policy has proved difficult. Research findings may indicate how on the average various factors and legal arrangements may affect the well-being of parents and children but may not be directly relevant to individual cases. More clearly defined and enforced policies may reduce litigation but not fit the diverse circumstances and needs of different families. There are no easy universally applicable and just solutions, mechanisms, or laws for ensuring the rights of divorcing parents and their children. A major challenge is for the legal profession, policy makers, social scientists, and parents to work together on the difficult task of developing policies explicit enough to reduce litigation, promote parental responsibility, and ensure the economic support of parents and children during and following divorce, but flexible enough to respond to the varied needs and rights of different families and family members.

CHAPTER 12

Fathers in Stepfamilies

E. Mavis Hetherington and Sandra H. Henderson
University of Virginia

CHANGING PATTERNS of sexuality, cohabitation, marriage, separation, divorce, and childbearing have made marriage a more optional, less permanent institution and have led to instability and multiple transitions and reorganizations of the family. Many of the changes in family structure and family relationships have led to altered patterns of relationships with significant adult male figures in children's lives. Since mothers usually retain physical custody of children, as divorce and extramarital births have increased, many children experience limited, intermittent, or an absence of contact with biological fathers. Furthermore, with rising rates of repartnering, children often must adapt to their parent's cohabiting partner or, in the case of remarriage, to a stepparent.

Although there is now a substantial research literature on the unique place of fathers in children's lives and their contributions to the development of both competent, adaptive behavior and psychopathology in children and adolescents (Forehand & Nousiainen, 1993; Lamb, Chapter 1 of this volume; Parke, 1995), less is known about the role of stepfathers or biological fathers in remarried families.

In this chapter, recent research findings on stepfamilies will be reviewed with a particular emphasis on the relations of children in stepfamilies with their stepfathers and biological fathers and on the fathers' impact on child development. Several considerations must be kept in mind in examining remarriage and its consequences for families and family members.

First, the response to a remarriage will be determined not only by current circumstances but also by the experiences that have preceded it—by the quality of relationships in the previous marriage, by experiences in a single-parent household, and by cohabiting relationships.

Second, remarriage sets in motion a series of changes in economic circumstances, residential arrangements, family roles, and family process that affect the relationships and adjustment of family members. Adaptation in stepfamilies is a continuous process as the family confronts new challenges. The adaptive tasks and the relative balance between risk-potentiating factors and compensatory buffering factors is not static, but changes over time as the family, family members, their life circumstances, and the society in which they live change.

Third, changes associated with marital transitions must be considered from the perspective of changes in the entire family system. These experiences vary for husbands and wives, parents and children, and even among siblings in the same family. The functioning and adaptation of individuals and subsystems within the family interact and influence each other; however, adaptation and positive coping in one individual or family subsystem is not necessarily related to positive adjustment in others. Moreover, the model of optimal family relationships that promote well-being, based on studies of nondivorced families, may not be applicable to stepfamilies (Kurdek & Fine, 1995).

Fourth, the response of family members to remarriage and life in a stepfamily will be affected by other social systems, social networks, and family members outside of the stepfamily household and by the larger social context in which they function.

Finally, earlier simplistic stress and pathogenic models of stepfamilies are inappropriate. Remarriage confronts family members with unique adaptive challenges and some stressful life changes; however, it may also bring more resources to the family and the opportunity for new supportive, more fulfilling personal relationships. Marital transitions involve both negative and positive life changes that may undermine or promote the economic, psychological, and social well-being of parents and children. It is the diversity in patterns of change, family relationships, and the adjustment of family members in stepfamilies that is noteworthy.

We begin by reviewing the demographics of remarried families and the increasing occurrence of cohabiting unions prior to, or in place of, remarriage. A primary challenge to stepfathers is successfully integrating themselves into an already established mother-headed household; thus we continue with a discussion of the family environment in single-mother households. Next we turn to a summary of the empirical literature on stepfathers and their relationships with their new spouses and stepchildren. Finally, we end with a short review of children's adjustment in stepfather families.

DEMOGRAPHICS OF STEPFATHER FAMILIES

Sixty percent of couples in first marriages will separate or divorce (Castro-Martin & Bumpass, 1989), and of these two-thirds of women and three-quarters of men will remarry (Bumpass, Sweet, & Castro-Martin, 1990). It is estimated that one-third of children will spend some time in a stepfamily before they reach the age of 18 (Seltzer, 1994). The increase in the number of stepfamilies is due both to high rates of extramarital births and of divorce. One-quarter of children in recent cohorts will spend time in a single-parent family because of being born outside of marriage and one-quarter because of divorce (Seltzer, 1991).

One out of five white infants, one out of three Hispanic infants, and two out of three black infants are born to unmarried mothers. About 25% of nonmarital births are to couples who are cohabiting (Bumpass & Raley, 1993); however, these relationships show considerable instability, and only about two-thirds eventuate in marriage. Thus, even children born to single mothers may experience the dissolution of their parents' relationship.

Recently there has been an increase in the proportion of divorces to remarriages because of increasing rates of cohabitation. Statistically, the number of male-female pairs has remained similar over the past 20 years; however, legal marriage is being replaced by cohabiting unions. More than half of remarried stepfamilies have cohabited for an average of one year before remarriage (Thomson, 1994). Thus in considering duration of a remarriage, cohabitation should be included.

In the United States in 1994, half of all marriages were remarriages for one or both partners according to the National Center for Health Statistics 1994 survey. It has been suggested that reorganizations involving the entry of a family member, such as in cohabitation or remarriage, are more difficult and require a longer period of adjustment than those such as divorce that involve the exit of a family member (Hetherington, Stanley-Hagan, & Anderson, 1989). The challenges of re-creating families and establishing new family roles and relationships, however, prove to be overwhelming for some 54% of remarried women and 64% of remarried men who ultimately divorce again (Glick, 1983; Martin & Bumpass, 1989). The reasons for the dissolution of stepfamilies center around spousal and family relationships, such as roles and responsibilities in the marital relationship, parent-child relationships, and relationships with the divorced spouses and children from previous marriages. Frequent complaints involve conflicts over childrearing, children's behavior, and economic responsibilities. With these sequences of marriages, separations, repartnerings, and remarriages, many families become part of a chain of family transitions, requiring repeated adaptation to changing family structures, roles, and relationships.

The deinstitutionalization of marriage may be greater for blacks than for whites. Births to single mothers, cohabitation, separation, and divorce are higher for blacks than for whites. Black couples are less likely to marry, more likely to separate and to remain separated longer before obtaining a divorce or to never legally divorce, and less likely to remarry. Thus, black children are more likely than white children to spend longer periods of time in a household with a single or divorced mother often living with a cohabiting partner or with a grandmother or other kin (McLanahan & Sandefur, 1994).

The frequency of remarriage has produced what Furstenberg (1987) has called the new extended family. The complexity and variations in these families have caused researchers to struggle with labeling them in a way that accurately portrays family membership. The most common of remarried family structures is the simple stepfamily in which only one spouse has children from a previous marriage living at home (Bray, Berger, & Boethel, 1994). Approximately 86% of these families consist of a biological mother and stepfather (U.S. Bureau of the Census, 1989), although some simple stepfamilies are stepmother families. In addition, this may be the first marriage, the first remarriage, or one in a series of remarriages for the stepparent or biological parent.

More complex kinds of stepfamilies include families where 1. the stepparent also has nonresidential biological children, 2. both spouses bring children from previous marriages to live in a newly formed blended stepfamily, or 3. additional children are born to couples in stepfamilies with residential children from a previous marriage to create half siblings within the stepfamily. Further, noncustodial biological parents outside of the household may have remarried and had children in their new union. In addition, the structure of stepfamilies can change frequently as children leave to live with the other biological parent, children from a previous relationship enter the household, and new children are born into the family. Despite the diversity among stepfamilies, all share the tasks of incorporating outsiders in an established family system or blending two family systems, of simultaneously establishing close marital bonds and functional parent-child relationships, and of adapting relationships with family members outside of the household.

FAMILY RELATIONS IN HOUSEHOLDS HEADED BY A SINGLE MOTHER

Parent-child relationships in stepfather families can only be understood against the background of family experiences in a single-parent household following divorce or births to a single mother (see Hetherington & Stanley-Hagan, Chapter 11 of this volume, for more information on divorce). In the next section, first, differences in experiences in a household with a divorced mother versus a household with a never married mother are discussed. Second, differences in single-mother households versus two-parent households in the areas of finances and childrearing stability and in the quality of relationships that are built between mothers and their children are discussed. It is important to understand the quality of family relationships and family functioning in a single-mother household as this is the environment into which stepfathers must enter.

There are some defining differences between the two primary types of single-mother families—divorced and never married. The first is that all divorced families versus a minority of nonmarried mother families have involved a sustained period in a two-parent household that may have been terminated with considerable acrimony, conflict, and loss of an attachment figure. The second is that the child will be more aware of family reorganization, changes in roles and relationships, and separation and loss in a divorced family. Finally, the immediate decline in income following divorce is greater than following a birth to a single mother. Thus, conflict, loss, separation, and change may be more salient factors, at least in the short run, for mothers and children in divorced families.

The primary quality that characterizes single-mother households, both divorced and never married mothers, as compared to two-parent households, is more frequent and intense negative life experiences. In particular, these include greater economic duress, welfare dependency, work instability, and residence in poor, disorganized neighborhoods (McLanahan & Sandefur, 1994). In addition, both divorced and never married families manifest disruptions in family functioning with less authoritative, more coercive parenting by the custodial mother, diminished contact with the noncustodial father, and an increase in behavior problems in children (Hetherington, 1995).

The quality of mother-child relationships in single-mother families seem to differ by child gender. Single mothers and daughters can develop close, harmonious, companionate relationships. In contrast, single mothers with sons often experience greater childrearing stress (Belle, 1994) and are more likely to have problematic relationships involving high levels of coercive exchanges and poor maternal control (Hetherington, 1993; Hetherington & Clingempeel, 1992).

In general, though, mother-child relationships in single-mother families often become involved, intense, and self-sufficient (Hetherington, 1993; Hetherington & Clingempeel, 1992; Keshet, 1990). Children in mother-headed families have been described as maturing sooner than children in two-parent households. They are more autonomous, have less adult supervision, spend less time in the company of adults, and are more influential in family decision making (Hetherington, 1993; Steinberg, 1987) than children in nondivorced families. Society's portrayal of children in single-mother–headed families has characterized them as overburdened with household chores and responsibilities that force them to grow up faster (Weiss, 1984). If household tasks are beyond the competencies of the child or interfere with other activities, if the mother is making inappropriate emotional demands, or if role reversals between mother and child are occurring, the child may become resentful, anxious, angry, or depressed (Hetherington, 1989). However, although children's assigned chores in divorced families are greater than in remarried ones (Barber & Lyons, 1995), they usually do not perceive it to be a burden, but rather as an opportunity to contribute to their family's smooth functioning and may take pride in even mundane chores such as laundry, dishes, watching younger siblings, and yardwork (Barber & Lyons, 1995).

Finally, it might be expected that children's relationships with noncustodial fathers would also play a role in how new stepfathers are accepted into the family. After divorce, most noncustodial fathers become increasingly uninvolved with their children over time (Hetherington, 1993; Hetherington & Clingempeel, 1992; Hetherington & Stanley-Hagan, Chapter 11 of this volume), and the rates of contact by fathers with children of divorced and unwed mothers is similar (McLanahan & Sandefur, 1994). Although some recent estimates are more optimistic (Maccoby, Buchanan, Mnookin, & Dornbusch, 1993), most national surveys are in agreement with Seltzer (1991) in finding that over 33% of children do not see their fathers at all or see them only a few times a year, and only 25% see their fathers once a week or more, although contact is somewhat more frequent for black than white fathers (McLanahan & Sandefur, 1994). Contact is likely to diminish when fathers marry or remarry, if they or their wives relocate, if there is high conflict between spouses, and if fathers feel they have little control over their children's upbringing and well-being (Bray & Berger, 1993; Gunnoe, 1993; Maccoby et al., 1993). Given such low rates of meaningful contact between noncustodial fathers and children, it would seem that the roles of noncustodial father and stepfather do not typically compete with each other.

Directly after remarriage, contact with the noncustodial fathers seems more important than relations with stepfathers in children's adjustment (Bray & Berger, 1993; Hetherington, Cox, & Cox, 1982, 1985); however, over time it diminishes (Hetherington et al., 1982), and a recent study reported that effects disappear after 2.5 years for boys and 5–7 years for girls (Bray & Berger, 1993). Investigators have found relationships with stepfathers to be more salient than the noncustodial relationship in predicting children's adjustment with the importance of the stepfather relationship increasing with duration of the remarriage (Hetherington, 1993).

In summary, stepfathers enter into the single-mother family system with its shared history, close ties, and established roles and relationships. Never married families have had many years to establish family homeostasis, while divorced single-parent families have established a new equilibrium only to have family roles disrupted once again. The couples' expectations in the new marriage may be hopeful, but the children are frequently wary or resistant. The process of adjusting to the presence of a new family member and of building a stepfamily is often prolonged and difficult (Cherlin & Furstenberg, 1994).

FAMILY RELATIONSHIPS IN STEPFAMILIES

Although the focus here will be on the father-child relationship in stepfamilies, a family systems perspective would view that relationship as part of an interactional, interdependent system in which the behavior of each individual or family subsystem is mutually influential. From this perspective, the father-child relationship is linked to functioning in the marital, mother-child, and even the sibling subsystems. The question of whether these family subsystems are as integrated in stepfamilies as in nondivorced families or whether similar patterns of relationships lead to similar outcomes in the two types of families is open to question. Differences in cohesion in family relationships in the two-family structures may reflect normative differences rather than dysfunction in stepfamilies. The high rate of both positive and negative life changes following remarriage and the complex relationships between two or more families following remarriage may require less integrated relationships and more open family boundaries. Especially in binuclear families with children from previous marriages who make multiple exits from and entrances into the family, more flexibility and fluid boundaries, and less bonding and closeness, may be adaptive (Bray & Berger, 1993). Certainly both researchers and family clinicians have reported that stepfamilies in comparison to nondivorced families are more distant, less cohesive, less traditional, more lacking in clear role expectations, and more flexible in response to change (Bray, 1988; Cherlin, 1981; Visher & Visher, 1988). It seems likely that patterns of integration and of adaptation in stepfamilies will change over time as roles, resources, and the developmental status of family members change, and as the family has more opportunity to adjust in longer enduring remarriages; however, the few longitudinal studies of remarriage are not consistent in their findings in this regard (Bray & Berger, 1993; Hetherington & Clingempeel, 1992; Hetherington, Lindner, Miller, & Clingempeel, 1991).

MARITAL RELATIONSHIPS IN STEPFAMILIES

A primary challenge in building a stepfamily lies in developing and sustaining a marital bond in an instantly formed family with children, and in establishing the marital relationship in a family system within and outside of the home that is structurally more complex than that experienced by couples in a first marriage. Papernow (1984, p. 356) has remarked that the typical starting point for a remarried couple—"a weak couple subsystem, a tightly bonded parent-child alliance, and potential interference in family functioning from an outsider"—would be considered problematic in a first marriage.

Although there are some reports of positive honeymoon effects early in remarriages

(Hetherington & Clingempeel, 1992), most studies find few differences in marital satisfaction between couples in first marriages and those in longer established remarriages (Anderson & White, 1986; Pink & Wampler, 1985), although husbands report more satisfaction than wives in remarriages (Bray & Berger, 1993). Remarried couples view their relationship as more pragmatic and less romantic, more open in communication with a greater willingness to confront conflict, and more egalitarian with respect to decision-making (Coleman & Ganong, 1989; Furstenberg & Spanier, 1984; Hobart, 1991) and housekeeping roles (Furstenberg, 1990; Ganong & Coleman, 1994a, 1994b; Giles-Sims, 1987; Hetherington & Clingempeel, 1992; Ishii-Kuntz & Coltrane, 1992).

Observational studies indicate that in longer established remarriages compared to first marriages, greater negativity and less positivity may emerge in remarried women's interactions with their husbands (Bray & Berger, 1993; Hetherington, 1993), especially when they have adolescent children. Many parents find family relationships difficult when they are dealing with both the changes and concerns associated with their own middle age and with the challenges presented by adolescent offspring. These problems are often reflected in the marital relationship and seem to be exacerbated in remarried families.

In first marriages, a close marital relationship serves as the foundation for positive family relationships and promotes both the well-being and competent parenting of the spouse (Belsky, 1984; Bray & Berger, 1993; Cowan, Cowan, Heming, & Miller, 1991; Cox, Owen, Lewis, & Henderson, 1989; Hetherington & Clingempeel, 1992). These relationships among family subsystems are more closely linked in first marriages than in the early stages of a remarriage (Hetherington & Clingempeel, 1992; Hetherington et al., 1991). In longer established remarriages, however, positive marital adjustment has been found to be associated with competent parenting and with more positive, less negative behavior toward the stepfather by children (Bray & Berger, 1993; Hetherington, 1993).

The integration of the marital and parent-child system may differ based on who is reporting on the relationship (Kurdek & Fine, 1995). Different family members may have different perspectives on how the stepfamily functions. For example, a recent study (Kurdek & Fine, 1995) found that biological parents in stepfamilies separate conflict with spouses from difficulties with children, whereas stepparents perceive problems in one subsystem as linked to problems in another (Kurdek & Fine, 1995). However, the direction of effects in these relationships is open to question.

It is important to consider duration of marriage in comparing first marriages and remarriages. Rates of divorce are higher for remarried couples, and divorce occurs more rapidly in unhappy remarriages. The families that remain in stepfamilies after five years may be a select group with the most satisfying family relationships. Further, the underlying basis for marital satisfaction may differ in first marriages and later marriages. There is some indication that remarried spouses, especially remarried women with children (Kurdek, 1989b), may have a strong motivation to make the marriage work (Bray & Berger, 1993). They may be more concerned about the instrumental rewards they receive from marriage, such as economic security and the tangible things the spouse does for them, than about expressive and emotional rewards (Farrell & Markman, 1986).

REMARRIED MOTHERS

Remarriage is a transition that can alter patterns of mother-child functioning. Some mothers and children manage to make a relatively stress-free transition, some experience difficulties but are eventually able to restabilize their relationship, and some mothers and children experience a more permanent alteration in their relationship that may have long-term consequences for the development of the child. Both children's genders and their ages when the remarriage occurs appear to be important factors in predicting the ease of transition to stepfamily life and the quality of mother-child relations thereafter.

Mothers who remarry with young children, rather than with late preadolescents or adolescents, tend to experience fewer difficulties in maintaining positive parent-child relationships after remarriage. Although remarried mothers have initial difficulties in monitoring and control, most mothers of young children have regained control by two years after the remarriage (Hetherington & Clingempeel, 1992).

As noted previously, the relationship between daughters and their divorced mothers is more mutually supportive in contrast to that of sons and divorced mothers, which has been characterized by conflict, lack of maternal control, and reciprocally coercive exchanges, especially during preadolescence (Hetherington, 1989; Hetherington & Clingempeel, 1992). While initially both sons and daughters may fear interference in their autonomy by a stepfather after a remarriage, sons may have more to gain than daughters from the presence of a stepfather. A warm, involved stepfather may be a companion and role model and may buffer the son in acrimonious relationships with his mother. In contrast, daughters may see the stepfather as infringing on the closeness of the mother-daughter relationship and show more overt anger toward recently remarried mothers than do sons (Clingempeel, Ievoli, & Brand, 1984; Hetherington, 1993; Hetherington & Clingempeel, 1992; Hetherington & Jodl, 1994). In addition, preadolescent girls exhibit more intense and prolonged resistance to the stepfather than to preadolescent sons, and the severity of this resistance is directly related to the quality of the pre-remarriage mother-daughter relationship and the marital relationship. The closer the pre-remarriage relationship between the mother and her preadolescent daughter and the more satisfying the marital relationship, the greater the perceived threat and resistance by daughters (Hetherington, 1993). Conversely, the less cohesion in the new marriage, the better the adjustment of daughters (Brand, Clingempeel, & Bowen-Woodard, 1988; Bray, 1988).

Findings are mixed on the quality of mother-child relationships when mothers with adolescents remarry. Some studies report that mothers show lower monitoring and control of adolescents after remarriage, followed by a recovery, but not to levels equal to nondivorced families (Hetherington, 1995). In addition, adolescents in remarried families are observed to be less positive and more negative toward their remarried mothers in family problem-solving sessions (Bray, 1987; Hetherington et al., 1982, 1985; Hetherington & Stanley-Hagan, 1994). In contrast, other studies find few differences in the relationship between remarried mothers and adolescents two years after remarriage as compared to mother-child relationships in nondivorced households (Hetherington & Clingempeel, 1992; Pink & Wampler, 1985). Unlike when the remarriage occurs while children are in preadolescence, once children are in adolescence, a close marital relationship is associated with greater acceptance and more positive adjustment not only in sons but also in daughters (Hetherington & Clingempeel, 1992). It has been proposed that during adolescence, a close marital relationship is perceived as a protective buffer against inappropriate intimacy between stepfathers and adolescent stepdaughters (Hetherington, 1993). Also, adolescents may feel responsible, as companions and support, for their single mother, and as they become more independent and involved in intimate relations in their peer group, may be relieved to have a stepfather take over some of the emotional burden.

STEPFATHERS

THE LEGAL STATUS OF STEPPARENTS

Social and legal definitions of the family still center on biological connections (Hetherington & Stanley-Hagan, 1994; Mahoney, 1994), making traditional conceptions of family roles and structures too narrow to be applicable to the stepfamily (Pill, 1990). The role of the stepparent is not clearly delineated by social or legal norms; rather, it emerges as family members balance their family histories and sometimes contradictory expectations of stepfamily life and modify past roles and relationships to incorporate the stepparent into the family system.

In terms of legal status, stepparents have virtually none. Sarah Ramsey (1994) states that "biological parents [must] support, care for, educate and discipline their child, as well as [have] the right to the custody and control of the child. In contrast, the stepparent basically has no legal status in relation to the child: no right to discipline, consent to medical care, or access to school records, and no responsibility to support." Although there are exceptions to the premise that stepchildren and stepparents are "legal strangers" (Mahoney, 1994), they vary from state to state and are rare. Courts tend to look at the stepparent-child relationship on a case-by-case basis, recognizing that there is great diversity in stepparent-child relationships, and therefore that it would be inappropriate to grant full legal responsibility and rights to all stepparents. This puts stepparents in a legal limbo and also sends a strong societal message about the importance of stepparents in children's lives.

CO-PARENTING

Custody arrangements and co-parental relationships have an impact on stepparent-child relations. Specifically, the characteristics that are often viewed as assuring more positive postdivorce child adjustment—children's secure ties to both biological parents as well as minimal competition from others for relationships—unfortunately leave stepparents with ill-defined roles (Crosbie-Burnett, 1991). How does a stepparent begin finding a nonambiguous, appropriate place in the new stepfamily without interfering with biological parents' primary function as care providers for children?

For stepfathers, this challenge fits well with culturally defined expectations about performance of the fathers' childrearing role. Although father involvement in parenting has been demonstrated to be important, in many nondivorced families it primarily takes the form of emotional and economic support for the mother, rather than active involvement in child care and activities with the child (Parke, 1995). Typically, the preponderance of the day-to-day childrearing in the majority of U.S. households falls to mothers, who engage fathers only when necessary (Parke, 1995). Thus, stepfathers can ease themselves into the parenting role as a support to mothers without involving themselves in areas where children are not receptive to their input. In addition, unless there is conflict between the biological parents, a close relationship with a noncustodial father does not interfere with building a positive and salutary relationship with a stepfather (Hetherington, 1993; Hetherington & Jodl, 1994). This is in sharp contrast to the relationship between biological mothers and stepmothers.

Most remarried custodial fathers assume that stepmothers will become participants or even take over the major responsibility for child care and childrearing. However, residential stepmothers often have difficulty maintaining an active, constructive childrearing role when confronted with the noncustodial mother's continued involvement (White, 1994), and a rivalrous relationship often develops between the biological mother and stepmother (Hetherington et al., 1982). This is made especially difficult given noncustodial mothers' more frequent, intrusive contact with biological children relative to that of noncustodial fathers (Furstenberg & Nord, 1985; Gunnoe, 1993; White, 1994). Unlike noncustodial fathers, noncustodial mothers (Gunnoe, 1993; Santrock & Sitterle, 1987) continue to play a more active, traditional maternal role with children—setting limits, nagging, monitoring their behavior, and helping them solve problems with siblings and friends. Noncustodial mothers not only maintain two to three times more contact with their children than do noncustodial fathers but are also more likely to accommodate their living arrangements to facilitate visits from their children (Gunnoe, 1993; White, 1994). In fact, with respect to the quality of relationships, children perceive noncustodial mothers similarly to custodial mothers (Furstenberg & Nord, 1985; Gunnoe, 1993). Despite the fact that frequent contact with noncustodial mothers may interfere with stepmother-stepchild relationships, contact with the noncustodial mother does have salutary effects on children's adjustment, particularly on daughters' (Gunnoe, 1993; Zill, 1988). Noncustodial mothers' positivity and monitoring diminishes children's conduct problems and facilitates scholastic achievement (Gunnoe, 1993).

As is true with stepfathers, noncustodial stepmothers have also found their place within the stepfamily difficult and ill defined, but their active role elicits more stress and problems in their relationship with stepchildren (Brand et al., 1988). A majority of nonresidential stepmothers feel their stepchildren interfere with their marital happiness (Ambert, 1986), dread or have ambivalent feelings about stepchildren's visits (Ganong & Coleman, 1994a, 1994b), and experience more stress than residential stepmothers (Ambert, 1986). In addition, although some researchers have found that nonresidential stepmother-stepdaughter relationships can become more positive over time (Clingempeel & Segal, 1986), findings are generally mixed (Guisinger, Cowan, & Schuldberg, 1989) and are probably mediated by several factors that have not been assessed empirically. Factors such as number of stepchildren, number of stepmother's biological children, age and gender of stepchildren, and frequency of stepchildren's visits, as well as individual characteristics of stepchildren and stepmothers such as temperament, attitude, and willingness to build a relationship (Ganong & Coleman, 1994a, 1994b), are likely to be important variables to consider when studying the quality of stepmother-child relationships over time.

Finally, the success that stepparents achieve in integrating themselves smoothly into a new family and their satisfaction with their situation may to a large extent depend on their own expectations and conceptions of stepfamily life and the goals they set for themselves and for relationships with new family members. Stepparents who believe that stepfamily life should mirror a traditional nuclear family are likely to encounter difficulties (Burchardt, 1990; Keshet, 1990; Visher & Visher, 1990); stepparents with realistic expectations and a more flexible family model fare better in the remarriage (Keshet, 1990; Marsiglio, 1992; Pill, 1990).

STEPFATHERS' PARENTING

Time since remarriage, child gender, and age of the child at remarriage and at assessment interact to make predicting the quality of stepfather-child relationships difficult. In the immediate aftermath of remarriage, stepfathers have been characterized as behaving like polite strangers with their stepchildren, exhibiting low to moderate positive affect, low negative affect, and low monitoring and control as compared with fathers in nondivorced families (Amato, 1987; Astone & McLanahan, 1991; Fine, Voydanoff, & Donnelly, 1993; Hetherington, 1989; Hetherington & Clingempeel, 1992; Hetherington & Jodl, 1994; Kurdek & Fine, 1995). Biological nondivorced, nonresidential fathers are more likely to be actively involved and interested in their children's lives, to feel close to their children and express affection, but also to discipline their children and criticize them for homework, chores not done, poor grades, and unacceptable behavior toward family members.

Although authoritative parenting, defined by moderate to high warmth and control, is almost universally accepted as the preferred mode of childrearing among nondivorced, two-parent families (Baumrind, 1991), equal efficacy of other less directly controlling styles of parenting by stepfathers has been suggested (Maymi et al., 1991). Both preadolescent and adolescent stepchildren often initially do not accept the stepfather and recognize his authority in the family. Younger children, especially daughters, may resist both authoritative control accompanied by warmth and authoritarian control accompanied by coercion and punitiveness by the stepfather. The path to establishing authoritative control by the stepfather with younger children seems to be one of supporting the mother's parenting and discipline, building a positive supportive relationship with the child, and gradually becoming more authoritative (Hetherington, 1993). With highly resistant children, this mode of indirect control through support of the mother and a companionate relationship with children may be the best that can be attained. Although about one-third of stepfathers with younger children may eventually be able to establish an authoritative relationship, particularly with stepsons, many stepfathers retreat in the face of hostile, defiant, contemptuous behavior from stepchildren (Hetherington & Clingempeel, 1992; Maymi et al., 1991). As a result, disengaged parenting is the predominant parenting style of stepfathers (Hetherington, 1988, 1989; Hetherington & Clingempeel, 1992). Moreover, even stepfathers who are able to become authoritative parents to younger children may confront additional conflict as children approach adolescence, especially daughters.

Early adolescence is a period in which it is not only difficult to have successful stepfather-stepchild relations occur in a new remarriage, but it is also a time in which problems may emerge in longer established remarriages. Fathers and daughters often have difficulty in realigning their relationships, especially in the area of affection, as girls move through puberty. These ambivalent feelings are more likely to be exacerbated in the relationships between nonbiologically related stepfathers and stepdaughters (Hetherington, 1993, 1995; Hetherington & Clingempeel, 1992), when girls are particularly sensitive about physical and sexual changes associated with puberty.

Generally, when remarriage occurs when children are in early adolescence, as contrasted with preadolescence or very late adolescence, prospects for high-quality stepfather-stepchild relationships diminish (Hetherington, 1989, 1995). Hetherington and Clingempeel (1992) found stepfathers in recent remarriages to be more disengaged and both adolescent boys and girls, aged 11–15, to be more coercive and less warm and affectionate with stepfathers than adolescents in nondivorced families. A study of long-established stepfamilies remarried a minimum of five years with a mean length of marriage of nine years (Reiss et al., 1993) supports Hetherington's earlier findings. Even in these long-married stepfamilies, stepfathers were less warm and more coercive to residential stepchildren than to their own residential, biologically related children (Henderson & Dalton, 1995). Similarly, stepchildren showed less warmth and more negativity toward stepfathers than children did to biological fathers (Henderson & Dalton, 1995). In addition, these patterns appear in adolescence in some stepfather-stepchild relationships that previously were relatively nonconflictual (Hetherington, 1989, 1993). That this pattern of behavior occurs among stepfathers and children in long-term, restabilized, relatively successful stepfamilies suggests that many stepfather-child relationships may never attain the kind of closeness, warmth, and rapport associated with biological parents and children.

As we turn to an examination of children's adjustment in stepfamilies, we must consider the direction of effects in the relationship between parenting and children's behavior. There is now accumulating evidence to indicate that in comparison to nondivorced families, the behavior of children in stepfamilies, especially adolescents, is more likely to influence parents' behavior than the reverse. Children's externalizing behavior influences later negativity in stepfathers, and children's social competence influences later positivity in both remarried mothers and stepfathers (Hetherington, 1993; Hetherington & Clingempeel, 1992; Hetherington & Jodl, 1994). The parenting of both biological and stepparents in stepfamilies in comparison to nondivorced families seems to be more responsive and contingent on the behavior of children, especially adolescents.

CHILD ADJUSTMENT

EFFECT ON CHILDREN OF LIVING IN STEPFAMILIES VERSUS SINGLE-MOTHER FAMILIES AND NONDIVORCED FAMILIES

Do children fare better in remarried families than in single mother families? The transition to a single-parent family sets in motion a series of changes for parents and children. Single parenthood is associated with increased negative life events and family processes such as decreased socioeconomic status, mother's diminished parenting competence, and coercive mother-child relationships (Hetherington & Stanley-Hagan, 1994).

Children in single parent, mother-headed families face more of the hardships related to living in poverty than do children in remarried families. Remarriage is the most effective way out of poverty for single women. After divorce, women's yearly income drops substantially—approximately half live below the poverty line as compared to only 8% of mother-stepfather families (Bachrach, 1983). Custodial mothers retain only 67% of their predivorce income as compared to 90% for fathers (McLanahan & Booth, 1989). Divorced mothers' attempt to cope with declines in income necessitate making decisions that often have adverse effects on children: moving into less expensive housing, often in poorer neighborhoods (McLanahan, 1983; Rogers & Emery, 1992), going back to work or working longer hours (Duncan & Hoffman, 1985), and often applying for public assistance (Select Committee on Children, Youth and Families [SCCYF], 1989).

It might be expected that the economic and emotional support stepfathers can offer mothers and children would promote better adjustment in children in remarried families. However, on average, the empirical data indicate that the adjustment of children living with single parents is fairly similar to children living with stepfamilies (Cherlin & Furstenberg, 1994; Dawson, 1991; Hetherington & Clingempeel, 1992; Zill, 1988). There are few or no differences in incidence of children's behavioral and emotional problems (Hetherington & Clingempeel, 1992; Kurdek & Sinclair, 1988; Santrock, Sitterle & Warshak, 1988; Zill, 1988), children's use of professional psychological intervention (Zill, 1988), children's likelihood of repeating a grade in school (Zill, 1988), and incidence of high school dropout. The most notable difference between children in divorced and remarried families is that children in remarried families leave the home earlier (Cherlin & Furstenberg, 1994), perhaps in response to a tense or unsatisfying family situation. These findings suggest that the stresses associated with a remarriage and the additional transition into a stepfamily create problems that counter the salutary effects—greater economic stability and possible support for the mothers and stepchildren—that stepfathers bring.

Outcomes for children living in divorced and remarried families vary with the child's sex, temperament, age at the time of parental remarriage, the length of time in a stepfamily, and other factors. Intelligent children with easy temperaments, high self-esteem and an internal locus of control are more likely to adapt in both divorced and remarried families (Hetherington, 1989, 1993, Hetherington & Jodl, 1994). In addition, although there are some findings that preadolescent boys may have more problems in adjusting to divorce and living in a mother custody household and preadolescent girls in adjusting to remarriage (Hetherington, 1989, 1993; Hetherington et al., 1985), newer studies and studies of adolescents rarely find gender differences (Amato & Keith, 1991; Hetherington & Clingempeel, 1992). Children are more likely to adapt to and benefit from a remarriage when they are younger, with early adolescence being an especially turbulent and difficult time in which to have a remarriage occur (Hetherington, 1989, 1993; Hetherington & Clingempeel, 1992; Hetherington & Jodl, 1994). In addition, family resources such as the number of adults available to supervise children, time parents spend in childrearing, number of siblings who compete for parental time, education level of parents, family income, and books, computers, and educational resources in the home (Hetherington & Jodl, 1994) also may affect children's developmental outcomes. These structural and resource variables, along with the varying degrees of risk and protective factors in individuals, families, and the larger social ecology, combine to produce great diversity in the adjustment of children in response to remarriage (Hetherington & Jodl, 1994).

A notable exception to lack of positive outcomes for children with stepfathers is found in black families. McLanahan and Sandefur (1994) report that black male teenagers who live with stepfathers are significantly less likely to drop out of school and black female teenagers with stepfathers are significantly less likely to become teen mothers than those in single-parent households. Furthermore, their rates of school dropout and teenaged childrearing were equivalent to those in two-parent households and were superior to those in mother-grandmother households. The authors speculate that the income, supervision, and role models that black stepfathers bring to black children may be even more important than to young whites since more blacks tend to live in communities with fewer resources and less social control. However, the National Survey of Families and Children-Cohort I, from which these conclusions were drawn by the authors, indicate that remarriage rates are low among blacks, and in the sample only about 33% of black children lived with stepfathers compared to over half in white families. Moreover, the authors alert us to the fact that black women who remarry may already be more advantaged before they marry than other single mothers. Unfortunately, most studies of stepfamilies have involved white samples or samples of mixed or unidentified ethnicity. It seems critical to examine ethnicity and cultural contexts in studying single parenting and remarriage.

While children from single parent and remarried families look fairly similar in terms of adjustment, they do not look similar to children from nondivorced families. When compared to children in nondivorced families, children in stepfamilies, from early elementary years through adolescence, on the average have more difficulties. They have more problems with social relations and academic achievement, and with both internalizing and externalizing behaviors (Amato & Keith, 1991; Bray, 1988; Bray & Berger, 1993; Hetherington, 1993; Hetherington & Clingempeel, 1992; Hetherington & Jodl, 1994; Zill, 1993). Further, as compared to children living with nondivorced parents, children in mother-stepfather families are 80% more likely to repeat a grade, twice as likely to be suspended or expelled, one-quarter more likely to be in the bottom half of their class, and 50% more likely to have their parents contacted regarding their behavior problems in school in the last year (Zill, 1993), with few differences found between step- and single-parent families.

In general, children living in continuously intact two-parent families will encounter fewer risks, and are buffered by more protective factors, than children in divorced and remarried families (Hetherington & Jodl, 1994). It is important to note that, as is true in divorced families, the majority of children living in remarried families do not suffer from severe or prolonged behavior disorders. Only about 25%, in comparison to 10% of nondivorced families, have severe problems, and some of these problems may have been present before the remarriage or even before the divorce (Block, Block, & Gjerde, 1988; Bray & Berger, 1993; Capaldi & Patterson, 1991; Cherlin et al., 1991); thus, most children are not demonstrating serious emotional and behavioral maladjustment. In the end, the response of most children to the challenges of life in a stepfamily is characterized by resiliency and adaptability.

CONCLUSIONS AND SUMMARY

Remarriage leads to a series of reorganizations in family roles and relationships and to stresses and challenges that put children at risk for developing behavior problems. However, it also can offer parents and children additional supports and resources and an escape from some of the risks in single-parent households. A positive marital relationship and a constructive, supportive relationship with a stepparent can benefit both parents and stepchildren. Negotiating a remarriage and building a stepfamily is a more difficult challenge than establishing a marriage without stepchildren; yet, the large number of successful stepfamilies suggests that it can be done. The accumulating research literature on both strengths and problems in stepfamilies can serve as a foundation for interventions and social and legal policies that will ease the transition into remarriage and help promote the well-being of children and parents in stepfamilies.

CHAPTER 13

Young Fathers and Child Development

William Marsiglio and Mark Cohan
University of Florida, Gainesville

YOUNG PERSONS in the United States continue to have unplanned children at a much higher rate than persons in other Western, industrialized countries despite the American public's growing concern about this phenomenon (Jones et al., 1986). During the past few decades, researchers and policymakers have diligently studied and debated the consequences of these types of unplanned births for the parents and their children (Furstenberg, 1991; Geronimus, 1991; Hayes, 1987; National Institute of Child Health and Human Development [NICHD], 1992). In this chapter we review some of the key issues that pertain specifically to young fathers and how their circumstances and actions may affect their children's development. Our discussion of young fathers and their children is one relatively small, but significant, piece of the larger public discourse about single-parent families (Hanson, Heims, Julian, & Sussman, 1995).

We focus on the population of young men who beget children when they are adolescents or in their early 20s. From both a life course and developmental perspective, many of the circumstances surrounding young fathers' paternity differ from those related to the more general population of fathers. We are concerned primarily, then, with those young men who have become fathers in an "off-time" manner because they have not finished their formal education or have not secured steady employment that would permit them to support their children in a reasonable fashion. The overwhelming majority of these young men and their partners do not plan to have children together; the pregnancies are unintended. Thus, whatever type of relationship the young men eventually develop with their child may be tainted because these fathers did not desire or anticipate assuming paternal roles at this time. Moreover, we assume that young fathers in their early 20s may in some instances encounter problems simi-

Some sections of this chapter are based on the first author's 1995 article "Young Nonresident Biological Fathers," in *Marriage and Family Review, 20*(3/4), 325–48.

lar to those of their younger counterparts and that their amount and type of involvement with their children may be similar as well (Marsiglio, 1995b). Because our chapter focuses only on young fathers, our observations apply to fathers' involvement with young children, whereas Hosley and Montemayor (Chapter 9 of this volume) address fathers' relationships with their adolescent children. For simplicity, we also examine only biological fathers, even though growing numbers of men are assuming fatherlike roles toward children (Larson, 1992).

It is well known that researchers interested in adolescent childbearing issues define their sample populations in diverse ways. Some studies of fathers (Lerman, 1986) include but others (Marsiglio, 1987) exclude fathers who are in their early 20s without taking into account the mother's age at birth. Meanwhile, there are those researchers (Furstenberg & Harris, 1993; Hardy, Duggan, Masnyk, & Pearson, 1989) who define their sample in terms of the mother's age irrespective of the father's age. The fact that young men are often a few (or more) years older than their female partners complicates efforts to simplify sample definitions (Adams & Pittman, 1988; Hardy et al., 1989; Lamb, Elster, Peters, Kahn, & Tavaré, 1986). This review, for the most part, focuses on adolescent fathers and young adult males who have fathered children with adolescent mothers.

The primary objective here is to explore how young fathers affect (or might affect) their children's development and well-being. The discussion begins by highlighting issues of personal development that tend to occupy young fathers at the time they become fathers. The preponderance of concerns related to emotional and psychological maturity as well as gender role development at this time in the men's (or adolescents') lives foregrounds the fact that fathering is often seen as an "off-time" life course event for these men. These concerns create a context for father-child relations that may differ substantially from that associated with many adult fathers and their children.

After distinguishing the young father-child context from one that involves adult fathers, we develop a descriptive profile of young fathers. We depict trends in their paternal history, their socioeconomic status, the socioeconomic status of their families of origin, and their financial contributions to their children. Next, we focus on factors that affect young fathers' paternal conduct. We modify Lamb and Elster's (1990) conceptual framework to discuss, in turn, influential factors that relate to 1. the father's personal characteristics and stress-related factors, 2. social support and disincentives, and 3. the characteristics of the child. Finally, we turn our attention to the array of past and present programs designed to improve young fathers' relationships with their children. These programs address the father-child relationship on either a cultural, institutional, or individual level. At each program level, we examine what specific initiatives promise and, where possible, what results they have been able to deliver. We also speculate on what future innovative programs at each level might look like.

UNIQUE DIMENSIONS OF THE YOUNG FATHER-CHILD CONTEXT

The first issue to be addressed in terms of young fathers and child development is how young fathers' involvement in this process might differ from that of adult fathers. Many of these potential differences result from the ways in which young fathers' personal development shapes how they view their paternal roles and their conduct with their children. In this regard, Hawkins, Christiansen, Sargent, and Hill (1993) recently discussed the *generativity* theme in connection with adult fathers' involvement with their children. This phase of adult male (and female) development refers to individuals' need to care for younger generations and to transmit their values to them. Adult men may thus grow to value the idea that children need and depend upon them for their wisdom and guidance. Since this developmental phase tends to be associated with other aspects of the larger maturation process than men seldom experience prior to their mid- or late 20s, young fathers, especially those who are still adolescents (Montemayor, 1986), will probably not view their paternal roles in the same way as do older fathers. The extent to which older fathers are more supportive parents than very young fathers is an important empirical question. Older fathers will at the very least tend to have a greater wealth of experience and personal discipline than younger fathers. They typically will have had time to accumulate more financial and educational resources as well. Consequently, when compared to older fathers, the begetting of children is more likely to be perceived as an "off-time" life course event for young fathers. This is particularly the case when a young man begets a child prior to finishing his high school degree or when he is not employed full time.

Young fathers' emotional and psychological immaturity may also negatively affect their children. When young men become parents, they are often still developing the capacity for abstract and logical thought that is necessary to cope with complex social and psychological situations. Thus, they may be confronted with parental responsibilities before they have the cognitive and emotional maturity to handle them effectively. Furthermore, adolescent boys and young men will often experience a self-centeredness that may prevent them from putting the needs of their children ahead of their own (Lamb & Elster, 1986).

Young fathers' immaturity affects the expectations they have for their children because they are often unaware of young children's (especially infants') developmental stages. This lack of awareness may reflect social as much as cognitive immaturity since boys and young men may have little experience being around and caring for children. Young fathers may have unrealistically high expectations of their children's abilities because they are unfamiliar with the stages of child development (Lamb & Elster, 1986; Pirog-Good, 1993). Consequently, their parenting effectiveness may be hindered. To date, however, little research has been done to test this hypothesis. While researchers have begun to attend to the parenting behavior of fathers, most studies of young parents still focus exclusively on mothers (Lamb & Elster, 1990).

The typical path of males' gender role development represents another instance in which young men's developmental course and the responsibilities of parenthood interact to the detriment of young fathers' children. Adolescent boys are often confused as they confront their newfound sexual maturity and struggle to form their own adult male identity. This anxiety prompts many boys to cling to traditional masculine gender roles by aggressively distancing themselves from feminine activities (Teti & Lamb, 1986). To the extent that young men adopt traditional gender roles and devalue feminine qualities, they are likely to be ambivalent about childrearing responsibilities. This type of ambivalence is illustrated by research that shows that 14- and 15-year-old males are more likely than same-age females to ignore social bids by infants (Frodi & Lamb, 1978; Nash & Feldman, 1981).

Adolescent boys' ambivalence toward parenthood might also result from their need to establish their autonomy. Many young fathers may resist the restrictions to their autonomy that a partner and child could impose. Research based on a sample of high school students in a metropolitan city in 1985 revealed that adolescent males were quite concerned about how living with a hypothetical partner and child at this point in their life would limit their chances to spend time with their friends, a finding that was more pronounced for whites than blacks (Marsiglio, 1988). The social and psychological demands of adolescent males' gender role development, such as the avoidance of feminine behavior and the assertion of autonomy, may help account for young fathers' lack of preparation for, or willingness to assume, parental responsibilities. It may thus limit their potential to make a positive contribution to their children's development. However, aspects of the culture of fatherhood and family life promulgated in some young fathers' immediate environments may serve as a counterbalancing force that helps to foster their readiness for fatherhood and increase their potential to contribute positively to their children's development. For instance, a community may extend its informal support to fathers who make a concerted effort to fulfill their obligations to their children, or young fathers may be rewarded for taking part in the care and nurturing of siblings.

Unfortunately, little research has assessed how individual fathers' beliefs about fatherhood affect their children's development. One study suggests, however, that social factors have a greater impact than chronological age on fathers' perceptions about fatherhood. Adult fathers (older than 19 years) with adolescent partners were found to be more similar to adolescent fathers in their beliefs about fatherhood than to adult fathers with adult partners (Elster, Lamb, & Kimmerly, 1989).

Both psychological and sociological research suggest, then, that young fathers' readiness for and acceptance of paternal responsibilities may be hindered by male youths' developmental experiences. Given their level of development they are unlikely to have acquired a sense of generativity toward children. In fact, they may show signs of cognitive, emotional, psychological, and social immaturity that affect, among other things, their knowledge of children's developmental stages and their ability to put their child's needs ahead of their own. Many young fathers may repudiate the "feminine" world of children and abdicate their paternal responsibilities because they adhere to the traditional masculine gender roles often associated with adolescent males' development. Young fathers will also have a difficult time developing a sense of paternal commitment because they probably did not plan their child's conception and birth.

A DESCRIPTIVE PORTRAIT OF YOUNG FATHERS

Prior to exploring the role young fathers play in their children's development, it is useful to present a brief description of these young men (for other reviews see Adams & Pittman, 1988; Kiselica, 1995; Marsiglio, 1995b; Parke & Neville, 1987; Smollar & Ooms, 1987). Unfortunately, it is difficult to present an accurate portrait of young fathers and their children because reliable national demographic data on young fathers (or children with young fathers) are not readily available. It was estimated in the early 1980s that 32% of unwed mothers (many of whom were adolescents) did not report the age of the father on the birth certificate (National Center for Health Statistics [NCHS], 1983). In a more recent study of 334 unwed couples, Wattenberg (1993) reported that only slightly more than half of the fathers signed a "declaration of parentage"—the means by which a father's name is placed on the birth certificate. Wattenberg blames this poor rate of male acknowledgment of paternity, in part, on hospital staff for failing to provide young fathers with information on paternity establishment (see also Rozie-Battle, 1989; Wattenberg, 1988; Wattenberg, Brewer, & Resnick, 1991). Data on young fathers are also limited because a significant number of men are unable or unwilling to provide an accurate report of their paternity history (Mott, 1983).

Notwithstanding these limitations, national survey data collected in the 1980s do provide some basic demographic information on young fathers and more specifically on those young fathers who do or do not live with their children shortly after the children's births. Data based on male respondents interviewed in 1979 and 1984 from the youth cohort (20–27 years of age in 1984) of the National Longitudinal Survey of Labor Market Experience (NLSY) indicated that 6.8% reported fathering children while they were teenagers and 5.5% (1.7% were between 11 and 17 years of age) were responsible for nonmaritally conceived first births (Marsiglio, 1987). This study also documented the living arrangements of fathers of nonmaritally conceived first-born children. Among teenagers, about 23% of whites who were not disadvantaged economically, 42% of disadvantaged whites, 52% of Hispanics, and 85% of blacks were not living with their first-born child at the initial observation date after the births.

In another analysis of NLSY data, Lerman (1986) focused on fathers who were 18–25 years of age in 1983 and had fathered at least one child at some point in their lives who were not living with them for reasons other than death and schooling (the mothers were not always teenagers). He found that about one-third of all fathers aged 18–25 lived away from at least one of their children irrespective of whether the children were conceived within or outside of marriage. In addition, 5% of 18–21-year-old and about 20% of 22–25-year-old "absent" fathers, lived with some, but not all, of their children, a pattern that was most pronounced among Hispanic men. While these data actually document patterns for men who are currently in their 30s, we suspect that they are still reasonably representative of current patterns, although they may overestimate slightly the extent to which young fathers live with their partners and children.

Additional analyses have revealed that young fathers are often disadvantaged economically and have completed fewer years of schooling than their childless peers (Lerman, 1986, 1993a, 1993b; Marsiglio, 1987). In an analysis of data from the NLSY (cohort of young men 23–27 in 1987), Lerman (1993a) found that young men who were unwed fathers as of 1984 (not controlling for the age of the mothers) worked fewer hours and earned considerably less than their peers in 1983. This disparity continued to increase by 1987, at which time unwed fathers were working 400–500 fewer hours and earning $5,000–$9,000 less per year than counterparts who were either single without children, married without children, or married fathers.

Young fathers' ability to make financial contributions to their children and partners will tend to be influenced by their families of origin's socioeconomic status. Lerman (1986) found that young men 18–25 years of age who became nonresident fathers by 1983 were more likely to have been raised in families that were economically disadvantaged; 27% of nonresident fathers lived in families that received welfare in 1978, whereas only about 9% of other young men (resident fathers and childless peers) in 1983 had lived in impoverished families in 1978.

Although data are not available to document the extent to which young fathers' parents financially support their grandchildren, it is assumed that more advantaged grandparents, on average, will provide more assistance to their grandchildren than grandparents who are less advantaged financially. Furthermore, young fathers who work (especially full time), compared to their school-attending peers who do not work, may in some instances be in a better position to support their children financially in the short term when their children are very young. But young fathers who are not working may be in a better position to provide financial assistance later in life if they are able to complete their high school degrees in a timely fashion and perhaps graduate from a technical school or college as well.

Our description of young fathers is clearly sketchy. This rough portrait is largely due to reporting problems that reflect the relative newness of researchers' interest in young fathers. Nonetheless, certain important, broad features stand out. The survey data suggest that the proportion of young fathers who live away from their children is high and differs greatly by race. Regardless of race, however, young fathers tend to be disadvantaged economically and educationally compared to their childless peers. They are also more likely to come from economically disadvantaged families.

FACTORS AFFECTING YOUNG FATHERS' PATERNAL CONDUCT

Personal Characteristics and Stress-related Factors

Do young fathers tend to possess personal characteristics (including attitudes and behavioral tendencies) that exacerbate the difficulties they face as parents and distinguish them from other young men? In general, the answer is yes, although research on these kinds of issues remains sparse. Young fathers, in addition to experiencing economic and educational disadvantages, are more likely than other young men to be involved in a host of problem behaviors. These interrelated disadvantages and problem behaviors can represent both a source and consequence of young fathers' stress and anxiety about their paternal roles. Using NLSY data, Lerman (1993b) found higher rates of hard drug use and criminal behavior among young unwed fathers (14–21 years of age) than among other young men (never married, married with children, married without children). He also found that, within racial groups, the difference in the incidence of problem behaviors between unwed fathers and other adolescents was typically larger among whites than among blacks or Hispanics.

In another study, Elster and his colleagues (1987) found a high incidence of criminal involvement among a sample of predominantly white lower-middle- and middle-class partners of adolescent mothers who participated in a university-based program for pregnant teenagers. Compared to other male adolescents, these fathers also had significantly higher rates of involvement in noncriminal problem behaviors, such as previous pregnancy, drinking behavior, and behavior problems at school. The authors of this study interpret these findings as evidence that some, though not all, young fathers may be psychosocially maladjusted even before they become involved in a teen pregnancy.

Although research has not yet documented a direct link between young fathers' problem behaviors and their children's development, it is reasonable to assume that children will experience adverse consequences if their fathers are hard drug users or imprisoned, or if their fathers are not psychosocially well adjusted. At the very least, young fathers with these problems will generally be limited in their ability to contribute financially to their children's support, or they may feel that the only way they can make a significant financial contribution is by resorting to criminal behavior. These illegal income-producing activities in some cases may actually benefit their children financially in the short term. Many young men will be able to acquire more money through these means than through legitimate employment (Achatz & MacAllum, 1994).

It should come as no surprise that many young fathers are apprehensive and frustrated about being parents because they feel as though they are unable to secure legitimate jobs that would enable them to fulfill the breadwinner role. Although the provider role is generally considered one of the most important indicators of adult masculinity, young fathers with slim job prospects may shirk this responsibility rather than risk being "emasculated" by their failed attempt to assume it. Alternatively, as alluded to above, they may turn to illegal activities to help fulfill their financial obligations. Young fathers' sentiments regarding their limited employment prospects are forcefully conveyed by two participants in a recent ethnographic study of inner-city youth:

> I mean the main thing to being a good parent is the money part. . . . I get stressed out . . . a lot of people do, and then take it out on the kids cuz I ain't got a job, you know. . . . One of the worst stresses in the world is not to have no money when you need it . . . when you wanna do right for your people, you know, your family and you know you can't.
>
> I've been like really, really, really searching and trying, I've been trying to find any kind of job. . . . I even called a job to work on a cruise ship, just a summer job, but they told me you have to pay a fee. I called employment agencies, I've been everywhere. . . . I talked to friends and all that . . . to get tips on jobs and I go down there and it be like, shh, fill out applications we'll call you. . . . And like it used to be I'd feel excited when they say they hirin . . . but everything I feel excited about just like tumbles down. So I'm like it must be it wasn't meant for me to, you know, work . . . maybe I'm one of them people that just have to live by selling drugs. (Achatz & MacAllum, 1994, p. 72)

The fact that the breadwinner role is so inextricably linked to adult masculinity and fatherhood is a source of stress for these fathers. Indeed, their efforts to fulfill the role and act in a masculine fashion may encourage them to seek illegal sources of income in the face of weak prospects for legal employment.

In summary, young fathers' handling of paternal responsibilities is often complicated by a variety of factors, including personal characteristics and stress factors that are unique to their developmental age cohort. As many young fathers develop their sense of adult masculinity they recognize that fulfilling the breadwinner role for a family or child is a key emblem of that masculinity. However, because these men typically have limited educational and work skills, they often experience anxiety about their perceived inability to provide for a family and thereby "prove" their masculinity. While some young fathers cope with this stress and provide for their families (or at least their children) through legal employment, others may turn to more lucrative, illegal income-producing activities, and still others may reject their paternal responsibilities altogether. An additional complication is that young fathers are more likely than other young men to be involved in a host of problem behaviors (e.g., criminal behavior or hard drug use), although this distinction between fathers and men who are not fathers tends to be greater among whites than nonwhites. How a young father responds to various stressors and the degree to which he is involved in problem behaviors may have important consequences for the development of his children.

SOCIAL SUPPORT AND DISINCENTIVES

A number of interpersonal relationships and institutional factors mediate how young fathers affect their children. Typically, the most important of these include the father's relationship with the mother, the involvement of the maternal and paternal grandparents of the child, peer pressures, and community or institutional supports and disincentives (Achatz & MacAllum, 1994; Barth, Claycomb, & Loomis, 1988; Cervera, 1991; Christmon, 1990; Freeman, 1989; Kiselica, 1995; Lamb & Elster, 1986, 1990; Leitch, Gonzalez, & Ooms, 1993; Smith, 1989; Sullivan, 1993; Teti, Lamb, & Elster, 1987). Each of these factors can exacerbate or minimize the stress young fathers experience in connection with their life circumstances as we noted above, or they may create additional dilemmas for fathers.

The connection between a young father's relationship with his adolescent partner and his impact on his child's development parallels that between "adult" fathers and their partners and children. In a study involving home observations of adolescent mothers, their partners (16–29 years of age), and their six-month-old infants, Lamb and Elster (1985) found that the quality of father-infant interaction was significantly correlated with all measures of mother-father interaction. A similar connection was *not* found between mother-infant interaction and mother-father interaction. These findings indicate that in couples comprised of adolescent mothers and young fathers, just as in older couples, the father's but not the mother's involvement with the child varies with the status of the mother-father relationship. If the couple's relationship is good and the father has stable employment, the father's presence may help alleviate some of the mother's stress and positively affect the child by indirectly facilitating quality maternal care. Conversely, the father's continued presence in a bad situation may detract from the child's development (Lamb & Elster, 1986).

Though this dynamic has been found among young and adult fathers alike, the potential for detrimental effects on child development may be exacerbated by conditions more commonly found among young fathers. Young fathers' partners are likely to act as "gatekeepers" and either facilitate or impede young fathers' opportunities to spend time with their children. While it is not known whether these partners tend to have any more leverage than older mothers, it is clear that men who marry as adolescents (a group that includes a substantial portion but not all of those considered young fathers) experience a significantly greater rate of marital dissolution than do men who marry as adults (Teti et al., 1987). To the extent that fathers' involvement with their children is contingent on positive mother-father interactions, the instability commonly found within marriages involving adolescent fathers is likely to mean that the children of these marriages have fewer opportunities to experience their fathers in a positive fashion than do children of adult marriages.

The involvement of the paternal and maternal grandparents of young fathers' children (young fathers' parents and those of their partners) may play an important role in shaping fathers' involvement with and influence on their children (Leitch et al., 1993). For example, qualitative research in urban black neighborhoods reveals that adolescent mothers' parents and other female kin may restrict young fathers' access to their children if the fathers' prospects for employment are uncertain (Achatz & MacAllum, 1994; Sullivan, 1993). Young mothers' relatives sometimes impose such restrictions because they assume that they can provide for the mother and child more effectively through their kinship network than the young fathers can alone. The attitudes of the young mothers' parents may also be one reason why young mothers often seek a "good cause exemption" from legally establishing the child's paternity (Wattenberg, 1993).

The involvement of the child's paternal grandparents seems to be less common than the involvement of his or her maternal grandparents. A pilot study of teen pregnancy programs that were targeted at young fathers revealed that fathers' parents were most likely to become involved in the program if there was a dispute between the families about keeping the baby or placing the child for adoption (Leitch, Gonzalez, & Ooms, 1993). The same study also indicated that, in rural programs, the young couples' parents often worked together to aid their children and their new grandchildren. Patterns of grandparents' involvement in the children's lives exert a direct influence on fathers' access to their children and thus indirectly affect paternal influence on child development—for better or for worse.

The impact of young fathers' peers on their involvement with their children is open to question. On the one hand, qualitative data suggest that peers show little respect for fathers who abdicate paternal responsibilities (Achatz & MacAllum, 1994; Sullivan, 1993). This type of negative sanction may indirectly encourage fathers to provide for their children at least informally. On the other hand, young fathers' peer groups are likely to be dominated by adolescent boys, and these youth often exert enormous pressure on their peers to adhere to stereotypically masculine gender roles. Since these gender roles are constructed around a devaluation of femininity, they may draw some young fathers away from their partners and their familial responsibilities (Teti & Lamb, 1986), especially if norms associated with men assuming the primary breadwinner role are not well established.

Grandparents' and peers' expectations of young fathers are likely to be associated with the norms of the larger community, which may vary from place to place. Community norms will therefore shape the social expectations applied to young fathers and the social supports extended to them. A qualitative study of unwed fathers in two poor urban neighborhoods—one predominantly black, the other Puerto Rican—revealed important differences in "folk" norms related to teenage pregnancy (Sullivan, 1993). In both neighborhoods, the adolescent peers of teenage fathers expressed condemnation for boys who fathered children and then neglected paternal responsibilities. Responsibility was defined differently in each neighborhood, however. In the predominantly black neighborhood, the young partners were discouraged from marrying or cohabitating (see also Achatz & MacAllum, 1994; Furstenberg, 1995). Young fathers' decisions to stay in school were usually supported by both their parents and their partner's parents, even though, in the short run, the decision would limit their ability to contribute to their families. In the Puerto Rican neighborhood, on the other hand, teenage pregnancy norms stressed the importance of young women's virginity. Pregnant adolescent girls were pressured to leave their parents' houses, marry the fathers of the children, and cohabitate with them. Fathers who wished to support their partners and children were expected to leave school and find full-time work.

While it is difficult to generalize from these ethnographic data, they suggest that community-based norms may mediate young unwed fathers' influence on their children's development. Young fathers' contributions might be defined largely or only remotely in terms of monetary support, with a lesser or greater degree of importance placed on their willingness to provide child care directly. Young fathers may encounter additional impediments to their involvement in their children's lives through the types of institutional obstacles we discuss in a subsequent section on policies and programs relevant to young fathers.

In considering young fathers' role in child development, attention must be paid to the larger social and interpersonal context in which a young father's relationship with his child is embedded. As noted above, "folk" norms sometimes play an important role in affecting how young fathers' responsibilities to their children are defined in a given community. This process may be evident in the ways that young fathers' relatives and friends, as well as others in the community, facilitate certain patterns of paternal involvement while discouraging others. For example, a father may have a minimal or negative effect if the mother acts as a gatekeeper to the father's access to the child, or the mother and father are struggling with an unstable relationship. Similarly, the child's maternal grandparents may limit the father's influence on his child by restricting the father's contact with his son or daughter. Conversely, both paternal and maternal grandparents may work together to assist their children and new grandchildren. In these types of situations, which have been observed in rural teen pregnancy programs (Leitch et al., 1993), the young father's influence on his child is likely to be more sustained and, perhaps, more positive.

The young father's peer group can affect his involvement with his child in contradictory ways. On the one hand, peers often say they have little respect for adolescents or young men who abdicate their responsibilities as fathers. The promise of negative sanctions for behavior deemed irresponsible may influence the young father and indirectly benefit his child. On the other hand, of all the people with whom a young father shares close ties, the members of his peer group are most likely to encourage him to adhere to a traditional masculine gender role. The devaluation of roles and activities considered feminine (the role of caregiver to children being one of these) and the emphasis on autonomy that this gender role brings is likely to deter a young father's involvement with his child.

CHARACTERISTICS OF THE CHILD

Certain characteristics of young fathers' children may be associated with father-child interactions. While in most cases the characteristics of the child are likely to affect young fathers' actions in the same ways they would an older father's behavior, there may be occasions where young fathers respond differently.

The age, gender, and personality of children may mediate young fathers' influence on their children's development. Young nonresident fathers tend to see their children less often as their children get older. NLSY data from 1986 indicated that 57% of nonresident young fathers with a child two years of age or younger visited more than once a week (Lerman, 1993b). This percentage decreased, however, for each progressively older age group of children. Nearly one-third of fathers with children at least 7 ½ years of age reported never visiting their children. This pattern is largely a function of the timing and quality of fathers' romantic relationships with the mothers of their children, rather than the age of the children per se. While children's ages may seldom represent a major causal factor that impedes young nonresident fathers' interaction with their children, the father-child relationships in these situations will nevertheless often grow weaker as the children age (assuming of course that there were any relationships to begin with).

Furstenberg and Harris's (1993) 20-year longitudinal study of how father figures affect children's well-being in early adulthood revealed some important consequences associated with children's gender. In the initial interviews and in follow-up interviews conducted 17 and 20 years later, the children of adolescent mothers rated their *degree of closeness* and the *extent to which they identified* with their biological fathers. Responses to these two items were combined to form an index of attachment. Boys consistently reported being closer to their fathers than did girls; however, girls who were strongly attached to father figures reported higher rates of successful adjustment in early adulthood than did similarly attached boys. These correlations between children's gender and fathers' influence over their children's well-being are important given the general finding of this study—fathers' influence on their children's development is weak unless fathers and their children share stable and close relationships. If boys do in fact generally establish closer relationships with their fathers than do girls, they may be more likely than girls to be affected positively by their fathers.

Additional evidence relevant to young fathers' possible differential involvement with sons and daughters can be gleaned from Mott's (1994) study of the home environments that boys and girls experience when fathers are present in the household. Unfortunately, this research is not ideal for our purposes because the female sample of the NLSY, and the Child Supplement data associated with it, did not focus specifically on families headed by young adults or adolescents. Only 13% of the 1,686 children in the research sample were born to mothers who were 18 years or younger, so the proportion of children sired by young fathers can be assumed to be even smaller.

It is noteworthy that among white families in this sample, fathers were more likely to be present if the children were male. Also, results from the Home Observation for Measurement of the Environment (HOME) scale—which considers environmental aspects, such as family interaction patterns, parental control, child task expectations, and intellectual input to the child from the family—suggest that white boys enjoy an advantage over white girls in their home environment in households where fathers are present. In households where fathers are present, girls are more likely than boys to be responsible for chores, and boys are more likely to be given special lessons or to belong to organizations. When fathers are absent, however, these advantages decline; in white, father-absent (female-headed) households, the home environment for children tends to be more egalitarian. Among black families, systematic patterns are less distinct, but there is some suggestion that girls experience home environment advantages over boys in father-present households, advantages which do not appear in black father-absent households. (The finding that children in father-absent households experience a more egalitarian environment should not, however, obscure the fact that these households are typically poorer than father-present [two-parent] households, with the economic difference between father-present and father-absent households being more pronounced among white than among black families.)

Although Mott's research does not specifically target the children of men whom we have defined as young fathers, his findings, taken in light of the work by Furstenberg and Harris, provide the rudimentary basis for meaningful speculation about the relationship between a child's gender and a father's impact on child development. There may be substantial differences between the home environments that black and white children experience when their fathers live with them. Young black fathers may favor girl children slightly; young white fathers may favor boy children to the extent that the boy's presence is an inducement for the father to remain with the family. If such gender-based favoritism exists, it may manifest in the home environment through preferential treatment with regard to task expectations, issues of punishment and parental control, interaction patterns, and the like. Since young fathers are more likely than adult fathers to adhere to traditional or even hypermasculine gender roles, it is possible that young (white?) fathers may introduce into the home environment even more bias toward male children than do adult fathers. This hypothesis has yet to be tested empirically.

Finally, young fathers' contribution to their children's development may be affected by their children's personality. Young fathers may have less patience than older fathers with children they perceive to be temperamentally difficult (Lamb & Elster, 1986). The issue of temperament may be particularly salient for infants since some are much easier to be around and less demanding than others. Because young fathers tend to be less knowledgeable about child development and less emotionally mature than older fathers, they are more likely to have difficulty interpreting infant behavior and responding in a constructive manner to it. This difficulty increases the probability that young fathers will experience infants as temperamentally difficult.

We have noted several characteristics of children that may be associated with or directly influence how children's fathers affect their development. While a child's age probably does not directly influence a young nonresident father's paternal involvement, the net effect of fathers distancing themselves from their nonresident children over time is that these fathers may play only a marginal, indirect role in shaping their children's character and behavior. In some respects, their unwillingness or inability to provide financial support may be felt most when the children are young because the children's mothers will have had less time to either improve their own financial opportunities or develop relationships with other men who financially provide for her children. Young fathers' involvement with their children may also be affected in some ways by their children's gender. Boys tend to report being closer to fathers than do girls, and this closeness *may* enable fathers to more easily have a positive influence on their sons than daughters. Finally, a young father's involvement with his child can be affected by the father's perception of the child's personality. Young fathers, more so than older fathers, are prone to see their children as temperamentally difficult, particularly when the children are infants. This perception is likely to have a negative effect on father-child interaction and, ultimately, child development. The long-term significance of the previously mentioned patterns for children's development is not well understood.

POLICIES AND PROGRAMS FOR YOUNG FATHERS AND THEIR CHILDREN

We now turn our attention to the various intervention strategies that have been developed and implemented in response to concern about young fathers' lack of involvement with and support of their children. Although it is an arduous task to improve young fathers' relationships with their children, there is some room for optimism given the public's growing awareness of and concern for adolescent pregnancy issues and children's well-being. Furthermore, social interventions designed to improve young fathers' relationships with their children are more likely to be successful because of the increased attention policymakers, social service providers, scholars, and the media have given to this issue (Adams & Pittman, 1988; Freeman, 1989; Hendricks & Solomon, 1987; Joshi & Battle, 1990; Kiselica, 1995; Marsiglio, 1995a, 1995b; Parke & Neville, 1987; Sander & Rosen, 1987; Smollar & Ooms, 1987; Vinovskis, 1986; Westney, Cole, & Munford, 1988). The combination of social interventions most likely to be successful is one that is theoretically informed and addresses issues at the cultural, institutional, and individual levels.

At the cultural level, it appears that the U.S. media have played a role in creating public fatherhood images along the lines of Furstenberg's (1988) "good dad–bad dad complex" and in the process have helped to clarify normative standards for responsible fatherhood. While these cultural images are typically used to describe fathers in a general way, irrespective of their age, they are sometimes used to convey images of young fathers in particular. The "bad dad" or "deadbeat dad" imagery is perceived to be relevant in many instances because a large proportion of young fathers beget children who are unplanned and perceived to be "off-time" from a life course perspective (Marsiglio, 1987). One of the typical stereotypes of many young fathers during the 1970s and 1980s was that they were uninterested in their children and unable to provide for them financially. In recent years, though, social policies and programs have been introduced that acknowledge that some young fathers are indeed interested in their children—even if many of them were unplanned. Moreover, as we noted earlier, there is a growing awareness that it is in the public's best interest to relax expectations of young fathers in some cases when their children are very young if doing so helps to strengthen these fathers' financial contributions to their children in the long run. Social interventions that emphasize these themes are noteworthy because they underscore more positive, proactive fatherhood images.

Institutional changes are thus necessary if more young men who do become fathers are to assume responsible roles toward their children. Unfortunately, current U.S. social policies do not adequately address young fathers' needs. With respect to inner-city fathers in particular, Achatz and MacAllum (1994, p. 99; see also Freeman, 1989) conclude that "The nation's major social policies do not promote effective programming for these young men, and do not act to support or sustain the fathers' desire to do the right thing by their children." Mounting qualitative evidence reveals that some young fathers are clearly eager to be responsible "good dads," but many are unable to forge ahead without assistance because they are hindered by either their gang connections and criminal past, poor employment record, or weak educational background. These fathers indicate that their commitment to parental responsibilities is also hindered because the child support enforcement system does not connect fulfillment of support obligations with visitation rights. Some young fathers feel that the government is doing them an injustice when it demands that they provide financial support for their children but does not guarantee them access to their children or provide them with legal representation so they can petition for access. As is illustrated by one young father's comments, awareness of this situation may prompt fathers to resist or avoid establishing paternity: "It's not fair. . . . Why bother with paternity if you can't see your child? I don't know anybody who could afford no lawyer. It just ain't fair" (Achatz & MacAllum, 1994, p. 97). Disadvantaged fathers are likely to resent the child support enforcement system if they feel that they can be denied access to their children even though they make what they consider to be significant sacrifices to meet their child support obligations. This type of resentment will probably diminish their commitment to their father roles.

A number of policy analysts and scholars have concluded that innovative strategies are needed that enable young fathers to develop an interpersonal commitment to their children from the outset without alienating them from their children simply because they are unable to provide for them financially. The viability of these interventions is likely to be enhanced if they are informed by applying identity theory to young fathers' paternal attitudes and conduct (see Marsiglio, 1995a, 1995b). This theory, which provides a meaningful way of interpreting why some fathers are more likely than others to have a strong commitment to particular paternal roles, can inform specific efforts to improve the quality of fathers' involvement in their children's lives. In general, both the child support enforcement system, with its emphasis on securing immediate monetary contributions, and the legal process of establishing paternity frequently discourage young, economically disadvantaged fathers from being more involved with their children. Young fathers and their partners often experience these legal processes as complex, punitive, and fraught with bureaucratic barriers (Achatz & MacAllum, 1994; Danzinger, Kastner, & Nickel, 1993; Pirog-Good, 1993; Wattenberg, 1993). Critics of the current policy that emphasizes legal paternity are also concerned that it reduces paternity to a financial obligation. To the extent that the child support system emphasizes immediate financial contributions, it restricts young fathers' opportunities for developing a self-identity as competent, loving, and involved fathers. This system also discourages young fathers from investing in education and increasing their long-term earning potential for the sake of their children (Lamb, 1988; Marsiglio, 1995b; Sullivan, 1993). Many of these fathers have not yet completed high school, so the child support demands come when their prospects for employment are the poorest. Fathers must choose to either quit school and seek full-time employment, stay in school and struggle to support their children, or engage in illegal activities to procure money. While the choice to quit school and find work may satisfy the child's immediate needs for financial support, the father's lifelong earning potential and the child's access to adequate child support may be irrevocably depressed as a consequence.

In addition, one of the most significant legislative disincentives that curbs young parents' willingness to establish paternity stipulates that children receiving AFDC will receive only $50 of the father's child support payment regardless of its size while the remainder is used to offset the costs of AFDC. Under this scenario, many young fathers (and mothers) make the rational choice to avoid the legal system. Given this set of circumstances, it should not be surprising that young fathers' participation in the system is so low.

Children born to unwed mothers appear to be particularly hurt by this lack of participation. In 1991, only 16.8% of never-married mothers reported receiving any child support during the previous year, and the amount they received was generally much less than that received by separated or divorced mothers (U.S. Bureau of the Census, 1995). Thus, failures in the legal process of paternity establishment may be constricting the flow of financial support from young fathers to their children, especially in the long term.

A number of researchers have studied innovative paternity establishment and child support enforcement programs in an effort to determine how these federal and state efforts can better support, rather than hinder, young fathers' involvement with their children. Danzinger et al. (1993) identify three components of promising paternity establishment programs: education and job training, public outreach and education, and support and assistance for responsible parenting (see also Achatz & MacAllum, 1994; Sullivan, 1993). Young men have shown an expressed interest in those fatherhood programs that provide them with an opportunity to improve their employment prospects. In addition, the recruitment and retention of young men is likely to be increased if male staff play a visible role in public outreach and programmatic efforts. Many researchers also insist that child support programs need to recognize in-kind support and introduce flexible levels of support (Danzinger et al., 1993; Marsiglio, 1995a, 1995b; Sullivan, 1993; Wattenberg, 1993). By broadening the definition of child support contributions to include the provision of food and clothes, time spent with the child, even participation in job-training programs and parenting classes, it is believed that young fathers—especially those who are poor—will be more inclined and capable of making positive contributions to their children's long-term development.

Evidence from a program that recognized in-kind support is not promising, however. In her evaluation of the Teen Alternative Parenting Program (TAPP, now called "On Track"), Pirog-Good (1993, p. 263) found that "the innovative effort to encourage young fathers by providing credits for parenting, education, and training achieved meager results." Though there is some evidence that fathers in the program had more contact with their children than fathers who were not in the program, overall participation of TAPP fathers in activities that provided child support credit was much less than anticipated. Furthermore, fathers did not increase their overall compliance with support obligations by supplementing financial contributions with in-kind activities. Thus, the discouraging results from this innovative program suggest that it is a formidable task to increase young fathers' involvement in their children's lives. This task is made difficult because young fathers encounter both institutional and interpersonal obstacles. Notwithstanding these difficulties, the lessons learned from the many promising programs across the country that are designed to increase men's involvement in early childhood programs, and others designed to promote responsible fatherhood, should provide social service providers with creative ideas to serve young fathers more efficiently (Levine, Murphy, & Wilson, 1993; Levine & Pitt, 1995). In addition, innovative strategies that either encourage or require parents to utilize formal mediation services to negotiate their co-parental roles might prompt some young, disgruntled fathers and mothers to negotiate acceptable compromises that would allow their children's best interests to be served (Marsiglio, 1995a).

At the individual level, one of the important objectives of social agents interested in young men and paternity issues is to alter young men's personal views about fathering unplanned children. Efforts need to focus on young men who are not yet fathers as well as men who have already fathered children. Clearly the most logical way of improving young fathers' involvement in their children's lives is to make sure that only men who are prepared to be committed to their father identity and roles will actually become fathers. The intent of some ongoing efforts is to dissuade young fathers from thinking that begetting unplanned children is a legitimate way to demonstrate their manliness, or an acceptable way to add meaning to their lives (National Urban League, 1987; see also Marsiglio, 1993). Ironically, masculine imagery has also been used sometimes to promote a nurturing style of fatherhood among young fathers. For example, media images that depict bare-chested young men cradling their infant children in their muscular arms are designed to break down young men's views that child care is a feminine activity (Knijn, 1995). These images are consistent with the emerging need some fathers have to create an impression in the minds of others that they are being "good fathers" by spending time with their children in public. One of the crucial challenges for social agents in the years ahead will be to strengthen community norms about responsible fathering while developing strategies that increase young men's willingness and opportunities to assimilate and act upon these messages.

Policy and programmatic responses to the needs of young fathers and their children appear to be evolving on all levels. At the cultural level, though the "deadbeat dad" imagery of young fathers still predominates, it appears to be sharing the stage with more positive images that acknowledge many fathers' desire to be involved with their children, despite financial and other obstacles. On the institutional level, there is a growing awareness that policies targeted at fathers do not address young fathers' needs and difficulties. For many young fathers, the fact that fulfillment of child support obligations is not rewarded with guaranteed access to their children makes them reluctant to establish paternity and may undermine their commitment to their children. Many are also disillusioned with the prospects of their children directly receiving a maximum of $50 in official child support from them if the children are receiving AFDC benefits. This policy can further erode a young father's precarious commitment to his child. Compounding young fathers' difficulty (and hardening their resistance to the child support program) is the fact that many young fathers have little or no understanding of the benefits of paternity establishment; many experience the process as complex and punitive. In response to these problems, a number of experimental programs have been tested that accept in-kind support from young fathers in lieu of monetary child support payments. To date, the results of these programs have been mixed. On the individual level, young men are being encouraged to accept community norms regarding responsible parenting. In the process they are being discouraged from thinking that fathering unplanned children is an acceptable way to demonstrate their masculinity.

CONCLUSIONS

Although a major objective of the present review was to highlight young fathers' role in children's development, understanding of this process remains limited because little research has focused on it directly, and much of the informative ethnographic data about young fathers are restricted to inner-city fathers. Nevertheless, policymakers, scholars, social service providers, and the general public have become much more aware in recent years that attempts to address the social problem of adolescent pregnancy and childbearing should include young fathers. This focus on young fathers is also connected to the growing public concern about children's well-being in single-parent families. Given this level of interest, our understanding of young fathers' lives will probably continue to increase in the near future, and it is likely that a greater effort will be made to understand how children's lives are affected when they are sired by young fathers. We have already learned quite a bit about how to develop programs that are designed to increase male involvement in child development and promoting young fathers' efforts in particular (Achatz & MacAllum, 1994; Levine et al., 1993; Sander & Rosen, 1987). Previous ethnographic studies of inner-city fathers have also provided policymakers and program developers with a rich source of data upon which multifaceted policies and programs can be tailored for this group of young fathers. The overriding objective of those efforts designed to assist young men who have already become fathers should be to ensure that they develop a genuine sense of commitment to their father roles, as well as the requisite knowledge, skills, and opportunities to be a positive force in their children's lives.

Many observers believe that children will stand to benefit emotionally and financially if young fathers are exposed to early childbearing programs that facilitate paternity establishment and encourage fathers to be more involved in their children's lives. Policymakers' interest in helping children by enforcing child support obligations is especially relevant in this regard. Other advocates of a more comprehensive approach to early childbearing issues that would include young fathers assume that fathers who want to be involved with their children have legitimate rights and needs that should be honored if at all possible. According to this view, young fatherhood programs should be available so that fathers can enrich their lives and be responsible, involved fathers during all stages of their children's development. In an ideal context, programs should serve fathers' needs and advance children's well-being at the same time.

As our earlier discussion suggests, however, these programs must be sensitive to a multitude of factors that shape the context within which young fathers try to fulfill their fatherhood roles. Cultural and subcultural norms regarding a father's role in childrearing, a father's employment opportunities, the relationship between a young father and his partner, and the level of economic and practical support offered by the child's grandparents all affect the father's sense of commitment and, in many ways, his ability to commit himself to his child. The unwed prospective father who lives in a community where he is expected to leave school and set up a separate household with his new wife and child, the father who has limited employment opportunities, the father whose access to his child is being restricted by the mother's kinship group, and the father whose peer group encourages him to reject his parental role all present very different challenges to policymakers who want to help these fathers develop and demonstrate a commitment to their children. Policy efforts will be most effective if they are flexible enough to respond to variations in these contextual factors.

Legal efforts to increase fathers' involvement with their children must also be sensitive to contextual factors. In one sense, this condition means recognizing that exacting child support from fathers without addressing their interest in visitation rights is likely to reduce their long-term commitment to their children. In another sense, it means that efforts to legislate increased contact between young fathers and their children should be sensitive to the fact that a father's influence on his child's development may be positive only if the father enjoys a stable relationship with the child's mother.

While we have focused on young fathers and their children's development, it is important to recognize that initiatives relevant to young fathers and their children will evolve alongside the larger public discourse about fathers' rights and obligations in general. Thus, an understanding of the broader issues associated with fatherhood in the late 20th century will inform the way society views the specific strategies and outcomes associated with facilitating young fathers' involvement with their children.

CHAPTER 14

Gay Fathers

Charlotte J. Patterson and Raymond W. Chan
University of Virginia

THE CONCEPTS of heterosexuality and parenthood are intertwined so deeply in cultural history and in contemporary thought that, at first glance, the idea of gay fatherhood can seem exotic or even impossible. Undeniably, however, some men identify themselves both as fathers and as gay. Most of these men have been able to avoid media attention, but some have become the subjects of intense public discussion and controversy (Campbell, 1994; Ricks, 1995). For instance, when Ross and Luis Lopton, a gay couple living in Seattle, attempted in 1993 to complete a legal adoption of their young foster son, the boy's biological mother, Megan Lucas, raised objections and attempted to halt the adoption process. Even though the Loptons refused to discuss the case in public, considerable controversy nevertheless ensued. Eventually, the men were allowed to complete the adoption (Ricks, 1995). Although this was by no means the first adoption of its kind (Seligmann, 1990), and although the Loptons are by no means the first gay men to become fathers by means of adoption (Patterson, 1995a), the publicity surrounding their case brought more attention to the issue of gay fatherhood than ever before.

In the wake of the Lopton matter, a number of questions about gay fatherhood have emerged more clearly into public awareness than in previous years. Who are gay fathers, and how do they become parents? What kinds of parents do gay men make, and how do their children develop? What special challenges and stresses do gay fathers and their children face in daily life, and how do they cope with them? And what can acquaintance with gay fathers and their children offer to the understanding of parenthood, child development, and family life more generally? Although the research literatures bearing on such questions are still quite new and relatively sparse, existing studies do allow us to begin consideration of some relevant issues raised by the existence of gay fathers.

In this chapter, we review the social science literature on gay fathers and their children. We begin by considering sources of heterogeneity among gay fathers and examining estimates about the prevalence of gay fatherhood in the United States today. We then describe the results of research on gay fathers, both as individuals and in their roles as parents. Finally, we outline findings from studies of the offspring of gay fathers, and describe ways in which such findings are relevant to popular stereotypes. Research on these issues is just beginning to emerge, and much remains to be done; accordingly, we end with a discussion of directions for future research on gay fathers and their families.

WHO ARE GAY FATHERS AND HOW DO THEY BECOME PARENTS?

Gay fathers are a varied group. In addition to diversity engendered by age, education, race, ethnicity, and other demographic factors, some of the issues specific to gay fathers also create important distinctions among them, and among their families. To illustrate the diversity of gay father families, we begin by considering some of the ways in which a man might become a gay father. We then consider some of the ambiguities that arise in deciding whether a particular man should be considered a gay father, and we end with a discussion of estimates of the prevalence of gay fatherhood in the United States today.

DIVERSITY AMONG GAY FATHERS

Probably the largest group of gay fathers are those who are divorced (Bozett, 1982, 1989; Green & Bozett, 1991). Men in this category generally have entered into a heterosexual marriage and had children before declaring a public gay identity. After coming out, many say that they got married because they wanted to have children, because they loved their wives, because they wanted a domestic, married life, or because of social and cultural pressures. Some of these men report that they married despite their knowledge of being attracted to other men, sometimes in the hope that marriage would dispel such desires. Other men explain that they were not fully aware of their sexual desires for other men until well into their marriages. Although some men remain married after coming out, most separate from their wives and eventually divorce (Bozett, 1982, 1989).

When couples divorce after a husband comes out as gay, custody of children is likely to be granted to the wife (Editors of the Harvard Law Review, 1990; Rivera, 1991). If the courts have biases about which parent should be given custody of minor children, they are likely to favor mothers over fathers and heterosexual over homosexual parents (Thompson, 1983). Together, these two factors usually combine to ensure that primary physical custody of children goes to the mother in such cases. Thus, the largest group of divorced gay fathers are nonresidential parents (Strader, 1993). Visitation arrangements may vary across a wide range of possibilities. One divorced gay father's children may visit with him every other weekend (Fadiman, 1983), while another man's children may visit only rarely and be forbidden to stay in his home overnight (Campbell, 1994). A divorced gay father without primary custody is likely to encounter issues related to grieving the loss of daily contact with his children while adjusting to his new life as a gay man.

A smaller group of divorced gay fathers have custody of their children and act as their primary caregivers. Although heterosexual mothers tend to be preferred custodians in the eyes of the judiciary (Editors of the Harvard Law Review, 1990; Rivera, 1991), extenuating circumstances may place one or more children in the father's custody. For instance, in one family, the mother felt that she could care for two of the couple's three children, but believed that bearing responsibility as a single parent for the third, a 10-year-old who had been diagnosed with Downs syndrome and mental retardation, would overwhelm her; this family agreed that the gay father would take custody of the 10-year-old (Fadiman, 1983). In another instance, a mother's serious illness precluded her taking custody of the couple's child during a period of chemotherapy (*Roe v. Roe,* 1985). Divorced gay fathers with primary custody of their child or children may need time to adjust to being the primary caregiver for children, often as a single parent, while also striving to accommodate to their new social circumstances as gay men.

Another group of gay fathers have become foster or adoptive parents after coming out as gay. At this writing, two states (Florida and New Hampshire) have laws forbidding the adoption of minor children by gay or lesbian adults, but foster placements with and adoptions by gay adults have taken place in many jurisdictions (Ricketts, 1991; Ricketts & Achtenberg, 1990). Foster or adoptive placements may involve children who are biological relatives of the adoptive father, or they may involve unrelated children (Patterson, 1995a). Gay men have also legally adopted the biological children of their gay partners (Patterson, 1995a; Seligmann, 1990). Because of antigay prejudices in adoption and foster-care circles as well as in the courts, gay men have often had to fight for the right to adopt or to become foster parents (Ricketts, 1991), with cases sometimes remaining in the courts for years (Patterson, 1995a); others who have been given the opportunity to become foster or adoptive parents have been offered only children who are considered difficult to place due to age, mixed ethnicity, illness, or disability. Gay foster and adoptive families may thus include older children of mixed racial backgrounds, those with illnesses or disabilities, or sibling groups. A number of gay men have also completed interracial or international adoptions (Martin, 1993). Foster and adoptive gay families themselves are thus a very diverse group.

Another way in which gay men have become parents is by fathering biological children with a surrogate mother (Martin, 1993; McPherson, 1993; Sbordone, 1993). For instance, a gay couple might make a contract with a woman to bear a child or children conceived using the sperm of one member of the couple. Upon the child's birth, the woman legally relinquishes parental rights and responsibilities, and the biological father becomes the sole legal parent. The child is then reared by the two men (McPherson, 1993; Sbordone, 1993) and may eventually be adopted by the nonbiological father (e.g., *In re W.S.D.,* 1992).

Yet another route to parenthood taken by some gay men is to conceive and raise children jointly with a woman or women with whom the men are not sexually involved (Martin, 1993; Van Gelder, 1991). In one common scenario, a gay couple and a lesbian couple might undertake parenthood together, with sperm from one of the men being used to inseminate one of the women. In an arrangement sometimes called "quadra-parenting," the child or children might spend part of the time in one, and part of the time in the other, home. Of course, gay men can undertake such arrangements with women who are heterosexual as well as lesbian, or who are single as well as in relationships with partners. The details of child custody and visitation may also vary considerably from family to family, and over time. Contrary to stereotypes about children growing up in gay households, children in such circumstances may grow up from birth not only with two fathers but also with two mothers and two homes (Van Gelder, 1991).

There is thus considerable diversity among gay fathers and among their families. Despite the variety of family forms described above, however, there is little question about whether each of the children in such families has a gay father. In other instances, however, it can be much less clear whether or not a particular man should be regarded as a gay father. In these cases, the dispute can revolve around the definitions of "gay" or of "father"; in what follows, we consider each type of dispute briefly.

One ambiguity in the definition of the term "gay father" involves the term "gay." Many men who have sexual relations with other men do not identify themselves as gay (Matteson, 1987; Ross, 1978, 1983). In a pioneering study of same-sex sexual behavior, the majority of men engaging in sex in public meeting places were married and did not regard themselves as gay or homosexual (Humphreys, 1975). In other cases, men in confined settings such as jails or prisons have sex with other men but do not define themselves as gay or homosexual. If such men have children, should they be regarded as gay fathers, regardless of their self-identification as heterosexual? Although it may be useful for purposes of public health planning to consider the behavior of such men, for purposes of this article we limit our use of the term "gay" to those who identify themselves as such. For purposes of the present discussion, we thus regard "gayness" neither as a fantasy nor as an activity, but as an identity acknowledged to the self and, most often, to others as well. Even while acknowledging the possibilities of changes in identities over time, we refer to men as gay only when they identify themselves as gay.

Another of the ambiguities surrounding definitions of gay fatherhood involves the degree to which biological linkages should be regarded as central in establishing parenthood. In the context of lesbian and gay families, one issue concerns the status of sperm donors. Is a gay male sperm donor properly considered as the father of children who may be conceived through donor insemination using his sperm? In some states, when donor insemination is supervised by a medical doctor, and unless the sperm donor is the recipient's husband, the sperm donor is legally considered to have relinquished both parental rights (e.g., to child custody) and parental responsibilities (e.g., to provide economic support for the child). In some instances, however, a gay male sperm donor may be known to the prospective mother or the insemination may not be supervised by a physician. Sperm donors who set out to be anonymous may eventually become known to the child or to the mother. In some cases, sperm donors have sought greater contact with the child or legal standing as a parent. For example, in a recent New York case, a gay sperm donor was granted legal standing as a child's father, despite the fact that the child was 13 years old and had never lived in the man's household (Dunlap, 1994).

Another way in which ambiguities in the definition of parenthood may arise in gay families concerns the status of a gay father's partner. Regardless of how a gay man became a parent, he may begin a relationship with a gay partner after children are already a part of his life; what, then, is the role of the new partner, vis-à-vis the children? Some have argued that the issues of gay partners are similar in many respects to those of heterosexual stepparents (Baptiste, 1987; Crosbie-Burnett & Helmbrecht, 1993). A gay partner who moved in when a child was 12 months old and who lives in the household throughout the childhood years is probably more likely to be regarded as a parent figure than one who joins the household when a youngster is already in high school. Although the first man would be more likely than the second to be considered a parent by the child and by other members of the family, neither would be likely to be granted parental standing by the courts (Editors of the Harvard Law Review, 1990; Rivera, 1991). Thus, legal and psychological definitions of parenthood may often be at odds with one another in gay and lesbian families.

PREVALENCE OF GAY FATHERHOOD

In light of the diversity of gay parenthood, it is easy to appreciate the difficulties of providing accurate estimates of the numbers of gay fathers in the United States today. In response to widespread prejudice and discrimination, many gay and lesbian individuals believe that they must conceal their sexual identities in many environments. This is especially true of gay fathers and lesbian mothers, who may fear that child custody or visitation will be curtailed or even terminated if their sexual identities become known (e.g., Campbell, 1994). For these and other reasons, many gay fathers attempt to conceal their gay identities, sometimes even from their own children (Dunne, 1987; Robinson & Barret, 1986).

Despite acknowledged difficulties in making them, estimates of the numbers of gay parents in the United States today have been made by a number of authors (e.g., Bozett, 1987; Miller, 1979). One common way in which such estimates can be developed is by extrapolating from what is known or believed about base rates in the population. For instance, some estimates begin from the assumption (drawn from the work of Kinsey and his colleagues, 1948) that 10% of the male population is predominantly gay in sexual orientation. According to results of large-scale survey studies (Bell & Weinberg, 1978; Bryant & Demian, 1994; Saghir & Robins, 1973), about 10% of gay men are parents. Results of calculations based on figures like these generally suggest that there are between one and two million gay fathers in the United States today (Bozett, 1987; Miller, 1979). If each of these fathers has, on average, two children, then one might estimate that there are between two and four million children of gay fathers.

Like any such estimates, these are only as good as the figures on which they are based, and there are a number of reasons to question the estimates given above. On the one hand, recent research has suggested that the gay-identified population may be smaller than previously believed, perhaps in the range of 3%–5%, rather than the much-cited 10% figure attributed to Kinsey (Gagnon, Laumann, Michael, & Michaels, 1994). The accuracy of survey sampling techniques with respect to gay fathers remains unknown, and it is therefore impossible to determine whether surveys may over- or underrepresent gay fathers among their respondents.

In addition, the numbers of some kinds of gay fathers may be on the rise even while the numbers of other types are falling. In view of increasing openness about sexual identities, it would appear that fewer gay men feel the need to marry in order to have children (Martin, 1993). In one recent survey of gay couples (Bryant & Demian, 1994), one-third of respondents under the age of 35 were either planning or considering the idea of having children. In another recent study, a majority of gay men who were not fathers said that they would like to rear a child, and those who said they wanted children were, on average, younger than those who did not (Sbordone, 1993). Secular trends may thus influence both the prevalence of gay fatherhood and characteristics of gay fathers, making any numerical estimates unstable at best.

Gay fathers are thus a diverse group whose circumstances and experiences vary in many respects. Some have been married and become fathers in the context of heterosexual marriages that ended in divorce, while others were never heterosexually married and have become fathers only after assuming gay identities. Some are the primary caregivers for children who live with them on a full-time basis, while others are nonresidential parents. Some gay fathers conceal their sexual identities in public to avoid possible discrimination against them or against their children, whereas others are entirely open about their identities. There are also some areas of controversy about which men should or should not be counted as gay, or as fathers. For all these reasons, the reliability of estimates of the numbers of gay fathers in the United States today remains unknown. Whatever the correct estimates may be, however, it is clear that the numbers of gay fathers are substantial and that their visibility is on the rise (Patterson, 1995a).

GAY FATHERS AS PARENTS

In this section we will review the available social science research on gay fathers, considering descriptive material on gay fathers themselves as well as comparisons between gay fathers and heterosexual fathers, between gay fathers and gay men who are not fathers, and between gay and lesbian parents. We first discuss research on divorced gay fathers, then studies relevant to gay men who have become fathers after assuming gay identities. Other reviews of this literature can be found in Barret and Robinson (1990, 1994), Bigner and Bozett (1990), Bozett (1980, 1989), and in Patterson (1992, 1994b, 1995c, 1995d).

Despite the diversity of gay fatherhood, research to date has with few exceptions been conducted with relatively homogeneous groups of participants, and using a relatively narrow range of methodological approaches. Samples of gay fathers have been mainly Caucasian, well-educated, affluent, and living in major urban centers. Although recent evidence suggests that self-identified gay men are much more likely to live in large cities than elsewhere (Gagnon et al., 1994), the representativeness of the samples of gay fathers studied to date cannot be established. Most research has been cross-sectional in nature and has involved information provided through interviews and questionnaires by gay fathers themselves. Although valuable information has been collected in this way, the degree to which data from observational and other methodologies would converge with existing results is not known. Caution in the interpretation of findings from research in this new area of work is thus required.

DIVORCED GAY FATHERS

Research on gay fathers was initiated by two investigators, one in Canada (Miller, 1979) and one in the United States (Bozett, 1980, 1981a, 1981b, 1987), and focused on concerns about gay father identities and their transformations over time. Both Miller and Bozett sought to provide conceptualizations of the steps through which a man who considers himself to be a heterosexual father may begin to identify himself, in public as well as in private, as a gay father. Based on extensive interviews with gay fathers, these authors emphasized the centrality of identity disclosure and of the reactions to disclosure by significant people in a man's life in the process of identity acquisition. By disclosing his status as a gay man to those in the heterosexual world, by disclosing his status as a father to members of the gay community, and by receiving validating responses from significant others, Bozett argued that a gay father is gradually able to integrate these previously separate aspects of his identity.

Miller's (1979) conceptualization of the acquisition of gay father identities, based on his interviews with 50 gay fathers, consists of a four-step model. In the first step, a married man who desires sexual contact with other men engages in "covert behavior," seeking secretive and frequently anonymous sexual encounters with men, often employing excuses such as drunkenness to explain away his behavior (Ortiz & Scott, 1994). A man engaging in covert behavior of this kind is likely, according to Miller, to see his children and family life as "duties" and not to see life as a gay man as a viable option.

In Miller's next step, a man may have "marginal involvement" in the gay community. Although the man continues to live with his wife and children and generally presents himself in public as heterosexual, he may have occasional contact with gay men, either sexually or in gay community meeting places or organizations. At this point, a man is likely to feel guilty about his growing need to conceal important aspects of his identity from his wife and children, perhaps compensating by showering them with gifts. A man may begin to think about living separately from his wife and children during this period.

In the third step of Miller's model, the "transformed participation" step, a man begins to assume a gay identity for the first time. Many move away from their wives and children and begin to disclose their sexual orientation to people outside the family. It is at this stage, Miller argues, that men begin to worry about possible interventions by the courts into their relationships with their children, and about the possibility that the legal system may curtail or deny their visitation with children. With the demise of pretense, however, many men feel better and experience heightened self-esteem and more favorable mental health.

The fourth and final step in Miller's model is called "open endorsement." At this point, gay fathers have solidified their identities as gay men and are often working for various gay causes, whether professionally or in volunteer capacities. Miller describes the lives of these men as organized around gay communities, very often involving a gay partner. By this time, men have disclosed their gay identities to exwives and to children, and these relationships are now unencumbered by the psychological distance that was once involved in keeping secrets about their sexual orientation. Concerns mentioned by gay fathers at this point revolve around the difficulties of integrating identities as fathers and as gay men in a world that valorizes one identity but denigrates the other.

Some ideas about what propels a man through the steps of acknowledging an identity as a gay father, both to himself and to others, have been proposed. Miller and Bozett concur that, although a number of factors such as occupational autonomy and amount of access to gay communities may affect how rapidly a man acquires a gay identity and discloses it to others, the most important of these is likely to be the experience of falling in love with another man. It is this experience, more than any other, Miller and Bozett suggested, that is likely to lead a man to integrate the otherwise compartmentalized parts of his identity as a gay father. This hypothesis is open to empirical evaluation, but to date such research has not been reported.

The contributions of Miller and Bozett to research on gay fathers have been substantial, and Miller's model is apparently an accurate compilation of the retrospective reports of men he interviewed. On the other hand, approaches of this kind are not useful for prospective purposes. For instance, these models do not provide any basis for predicting which married men who engage in covert sexual relations with other men will eventually divorce and identify themselves as gay fathers. Similarly, these kinds of models do not account for diversity due to race, ethnicity, geographic locale, and other variables that may be crucial to understanding the experiences of gay fathers. They also explain little about gay fathers' actual behavior in parenting and other roles.

Research on the parenting attitudes of gay versus heterosexual divorced fathers has, however, been conducted (Barret & Robinson, 1990). Bigner and Jacobsen (1989a, 1989b, 1992) compared 33 gay and 33 heterosexual divorced fathers, each of whom had at least two children. With one exception, results showed no differences between motives for parenthood among gay and heterosexual men. The single exception was the greater likelihood of gay than heterosexual fathers to cite the higher status accorded to parents as compared with nonparents in the dominant culture as a motivation for parenthood (Bigner & Jacobsen, 1989b). The best interpretation of this finding is by no means clear. One possibility is that gay fathers were more candid and hence more likely to acknowledge that their desire for children might have been driven at least in part by self-serving motives. Another possibility is that, because of the stigma associated with gay identity, gay fathers were less likely to take for granted the respect accorded to parents. Further research will be necessary in order to clarify these and other possibilities.

Bigner and Jacobsen (1989a) also asked gay and heterosexual fathers in their sample to report on their own behavior with their children. Although no differences emerged in the fathers' reports of involvement or intimacy, gay fathers reported that their behavior was characterized by greater responsiveness, more reasoning, and more limit-setting than did heterosexual fathers. These reports by gay fathers of greater warmth and responsiveness, on the one hand, and greater control and limit-setting, on the other, are strongly reminiscent of findings from research with heterosexual families and would seem to raise the possibility that gay fathers are more likely than their heterosexual counterparts to exhibit authoritative patterns of parenting behavior such as those described by Baumrind (1967; Baumrind & Black, 1967). Caution must be exercised, however, in the interpretation of results such as these, which stem entirely from paternal reports about their own behavior.

Similar results were, however, reported in an early study by Scallen (1982; cited in Flaks, 1994). Scallen collected self-report information from 60 gay and heterosexual fathers, all of whom were divorced. In areas of problem solving, providing recreation for children, and encouraging children's autonomy, no differences were reported as a function of sexual orientation. In concert with Bigner and Jacobsen's (1989a) findings, gay fathers placed greater emphasis than did heterosexual fathers on paternal nurturance. At the same time, gay fathers also placed less importance upon their role as economic providers for children. Although the study thus revealed many similarities in the responses of gay and heterosexual divorced fathers, the gay fathers seemed to be somewhat less traditional in their views of the paternal role.

In addition to research comparing gay and heterosexual fathers, a few studies have made other comparisons. For instance, Robinson and Skeen (1982) compared sex-role orientations of gay fathers with those of gay men who were not fathers, and found no differences. Similarly, Skeen and Robinson (1985) found no evidence to suggest that gay men's retrospective reports about relationships with their own parents varied as a function of whether or not they were parents themselves. Harris and Turner (1985/86) compared gay fathers and lesbian mothers, reporting that, although gay fathers had higher incomes and were more likely to report encouraging their children to play with sex-typed toys, lesbian mothers were more likely to believe that their children received positive benefits such as increased tolerance for diversity from growing up with lesbian or gay parents. Studies like these begin to suggest a number of issues for research on gender, sexual orientation, and parenting behavior, and it is clear that there are many valuable directions that future work in this area could take.

Although little research has examined the sources of individual differences within gay father families, one recent study by Crosbie-Burnett and Helmbrecht (1993) is notable in this regard. These authors focused on a group of 48 gay stepfamilies—that is, families composed of a gay father, his lover or partner, and at least one child who either lives in or visits the gay father's household. In assessing the aspects of step-family functioning that were associated with family happiness, Crosbie-Burnett and Helmbrecht found that, both for the gay father and the child, the best predictors of family happiness were concerned with the integration and inclusion of gay stepfathers. Interestingly, however, integration of the stepfather did not predict his own ratings of family happiness. Another finding of interest from this study was that gay fathers reported greater openness about their sexual orientation than did their children; whereas only 4% of gay fathers reported that they were not open with heterosexual friends about being gay, fully 54% of adolescents reported that their heterosexual friends did not know about the father's sexual orientation. Thus, children were more closeted than their gay fathers about their status as members of a gay family, and they reported receiving less support from nongay friends. Given negative societal attitudes toward same-sex sexual relationships, it is not surprising that some adolescent offspring of gay fathers felt the need to monitor disclosures about their fathers' gay identities.

GAY MEN CHOOSING TO BECOME PARENTS

Although for many years, gay fathers were generally assumed to have become parents only in the context of previous heterosexual relationships, both men and women are believed increasingly to be undertaking parenthood in the context of already established lesbian and gay identities (Patterson, 1994a, 1995d). A sizable research literature describes the transition to parenthood among heterosexual couples (e.g., Cowan & Cowan, 1992), but no research has addressed the transition to parenthood among gay men. Many issues that arise for heterosexual individuals are also faced by lesbians and gay men (e.g., worries about how children will affect couple relationships or economic concerns about supporting children), but gay men and lesbians must also cope with additional issues because of their situation as members of stigmatized minorities (Martin, 1993; Patterson, 1994a; Weston, 1991).

A number of interrelated issues are often faced by gay men who wish to become parents (Martin, 1993; Patterson, 1994a), for whom the sheer logistics of becoming parents can seem quite daunting. One of the first needs among prospective gay parents is for accurate, up-to-date information about how they could become parents, how their children are likely to develop, and what supports are likely to be available in the community where they live. Will they seek to father biological children in a co-parenting or surrogacy arrangement, or will they seek to become foster or adoptive parents, and what are the likely paths through which any of these aims can be accomplished? Gay men who are seeking biological parenthood are also likely to encounter various health concerns, such as medical screening of prospective birthparents and assistance with techniques for donor insemination, among others. As matters progress, a number of legal concerns about the rights and responsibilities of all parties are likely to emerge. Associated with all of these will generally be financial issues; in addition to the support of a child, auxiliary costs of medical and legal assistance can be considerable. Finally, social and emotional concerns of various kinds are also likely to be significant (Patterson, 1994a).

As this overview suggests, numerous questions are posed by the emergence of prospective gay parents (Patterson, 1994a). What are the factors that influence gay men's inclinations to make parenthood a part of their lives? What impact does parenting have on gay men who undertake it, and how do the effects compare with the ones experienced by heterosexuals? How effectively do special services such as support groups serve the needs of the gay fathers and prospective gay fathers for whom they were designed? What are the elements of a social climate that is supportive for gay and lesbian parents and their children? As yet, little research has addressed such questions.

At the time of this writing, only two psychological studies of men who have become fathers after identifying themselves as gay have been reported. Sbordone (1993) studied 78 gay men who had become parents through adoption or through surrogacy arrangements and compared them with 83 gay men who were not fathers. Consistent with Skeen and Robinson's (1985) findings with divorced gay fathers, there were no differences between fathers and nonfathers on reports about relationships with the men's own parents. Gay fathers did, however, report higher self-esteem and fewer negative attitudes about homosexuality than did gay men who were not fathers.

An interesting result of Sbordone's (1993) study was that most gay men who were not fathers indicated that they would like to rear a child. Those who said that they wanted children were younger than those who said they did not, but the two groups did not differ on income, education, race, self-esteem, or attitudes about homosexuality. Given that fathers had higher self-esteem and fewer negative attitudes about homosexuality than either group of nonfathers, Sbordone speculated that gay fathers' higher self-esteem might have been a result, not a cause or simple correlate of parenthood. Longitudinal research could be useful in evaluating this idea, but such work has yet to be reported.

A study of gay couples choosing parenthood was conducted by McPherson (1993), who assessed division of labor, satisfaction with division of labor, and satisfaction with couple relationships among 28 gay and 27 heterosexual parenting couples. Consistent with evidence from lesbian parenting couples (Hand, 1991; Osterweil, 1991; Patterson, 1995b), McPherson found that gay couples reported a more even division of responsibilities for household maintenance and child care than did heterosexual couples. Gay couples also reported greater satisfaction with their division of child-care tasks than did heterosexual couples. Finally, gay couples also reported greater satisfaction with their couple relationships, especially in the areas of cohesion and expression of affection.

As this brief discussion has revealed, research on gay men who have chosen to become parents is as yet quite sparse. Existing research is limited in scope, and many important issues have yet to be addressed. Existing work suggests, however, that although the source of such a difference is not well understood, gay fathers are likely to have higher self-esteem than gay men who are not parents. Results to date also suggest that gay parenting couples are more likely than heterosexual couples to share tasks involved in child care relatively evenly, and also to be more satisfied than heterosexual couples with their arrangements. Much remains to be learned about the determinants of gay parenting, about its impact on gay parents themselves, and about its place in contemporary communities. In the next section, we summarize what is known about the impact of gay fatherhood on members of the gay father's family.

RESEARCH ON CHILDREN OF GAY FATHERS

Gay fathers are by definition members of families; they have children and often have wives or exwives as well as gay partners. Of course, gay fathers most often have other family members as well, including parents, aunts, uncles, siblings, nieces, nephews, and cousins. Since research on other family members has scarcely begun (for exceptions, see Buxton, 1994; Hays & Samuels, 1989), we focus in this section on the children of gay fathers. We consider first the results of research on children's sexual identity, then that on other aspects of children's personal and social development. All of the research to date has focused on children of divorced gay fathers. Other reviews of this material can be found in Bozett (1987), Gottman (1990), Green and Bozett (1991), and Patterson (1992, 1995d).

Sexual Orientation

Much research on the offspring of gay fathers has examined the development of sexual identity. In response to the popular stereotype that children of gay fathers may grow up to become gay themselves, a number of researchers have studied sexual orientation among the offspring of gay fathers. In contrast to popular notions, research has revealed that the vast majority of both sons and daughters of gay fathers grow up to become heterosexual adults.

The earliest findings about sexual orientation among children of gay fathers were reported by Miller (1979) and by Bozett (1980, 1982, 1987, 1989). Their research involved interviews with gay fathers, during which fathers were asked to report on the sexual orientation of their adolescent and young adult children. In Miller's (1979) sample, 4 of 48 children were said by their fathers to be gay or lesbian. In Bozett's two samples (1980, 1982, 1987, 1989), zero of 25 and 2 of 19 children were described by their fathers as gay or lesbian. Although the precise numbers are not available in published reports, it would seem that at least some of the children in Bozett's research had not yet reached adolescence, so these figures must be interpreted with caution. In addition, small sample sizes and varied sampling procedures also suggest that interpretations should be made with care. If, however, the findings from these three studies are combined, the results reveal that 6 of 92 offspring, or 6.5%, were reported by their fathers to be gay or lesbian.

In the largest study of sexual orientation among the offspring of gay fathers to date, Bailey, Bobrow, Wolfe, and Mikach (1995) studied 82 adult sons of 55 gay fathers. They obtained self-reports from the majority of sons as well as reports about the sons' sexual orientation from fathers, which allowed them to assess the reliability of fathers' reports in cases where both father and son had been interviewed. Bailey and his colleagues reported that, in the 41 cases in which fathers said they were "virtually certain" or "entirely certain" of their son's orientation, and in which sons also provided information, fathers and sons agreed in all but one case; the lone disagreement occurred when a father described his son as heterosexual and the son described himself as bisexual. Fathers' reports were thus very accurate overall, allowing the confident use of paternal reports when sons could not be contacted. Of sons whose sexual orientation could be rated with confidence, 68 of 75 were said by their fathers to be heterosexual, indicating that about 9% were reported to be gay or bisexual.

An interesting aspect of the Bailey et al. (1995) study was its assessment of environmental factors relevant to the experience of the sons. If exposure to gay fathers increases the likelihood that their sons grow up to be gay men, then sons who have lived in their gay fathers' households over longer periods of time might be expected to show greater likelihood of being gay. In contrast to such an expectation, Bailey and his colleagues reported that the sexual orientation of sons was unrelated to the number of years spent living in the gay fathers' households, to frequency of current contact with the gay fathers, or to the rated quality of current father-son relationships. For instance, gay sons had actually lived with their fathers, on average, only about six years, whereas heterosexual sons had lived with their fathers, on average, for about 11 years. Although this difference was not statistically significant, it was clear that no evidence for environmental transmission of sexual orientation was provided by these data. As Bailey and his colleagues concluded, these findings suggest that any environmental contributions to sexual orientation must be small.

The available data thus suggest that, while the great majority of children of gay fathers grow up to be heterosexual, a minority—perhaps 5%–10%—are gay or bisexual. Appropriate interpretation of these results rests heavily upon estimates of the population base rates for homosexuality, and as noted above these are the subject of considerable controversy at the present time (Bailey, 1995; Bailey et al., 1995). Estimates of male homosexuality range from 1%–2% up to approximately 5% or more, depending upon the details of sampling, assessment, and other aspects of methodology (Bailey, 1995). If the lower estimates are adopted, then the 5%–10% rates of nonheterosexuality observed among sons of gay fathers seem to be elevated over the base rates. If, on the other hand, the higher population estimates of approximately 5% are used, then rates for the offspring of gay fathers would appear to be only slightly elevated, if at all, and probably remain within the range of chance variation. At this time, the data do not allow unambiguous interpretation on this point. What is clear on the basis of existing research, however, is that the great majority of children of gay fathers grow up to be heterosexual adults.

OTHER ASPECTS OF PERSONAL AND SOCIAL DEVELOPMENT

Many aspects of the personal and social development of children of gay fathers have gone unstudied to date, but there is some evidence about relationships between parents and their children. Harris and Turner (1985/86) studied 10 gay fathers, 13 lesbian mothers, 2 heterosexual fathers, and 14 heterosexual mothers, most of whom had custody of their children. In all, the respondents had 39 children, who ranged from 5 to 31 years of age. Parents described relationships with their children in generally positive terms, and there were no differences among gay, lesbian, and heterosexual parents in this regard. Most gay and lesbian parents did not report that their sexual identities had created special problems for their children, and it was heterosexual parents who were more likely to report that their children's visits with the other parents presented problems for them.

One long-standing cultural stereotype about gay fathers suggests that they may be more likely than other parents to perpetrate sexual abuse upon their children. In contrast to the stereotype, however, the great majority of sexual abuse can be characterized as heterosexual in nature, with an adult male abusing a young female (Jones & McFarlane, 1980). Available evidence reveals that gay men are no more likely than heterosexual men to perpetrate child sexual abuse (Groth & Birnbaum, 1978; Jenny, Roesler, & Poyer, 1994; Sarafino, 1979).

For example, in a recent study, Jenny and her colleagues found that of all children seen for sexual abuse during a one-year period at a large urban hospital, only 2 of 269—or fewer than 1%—of adult offenders could be identified as gay or lesbian. In particular, of the 219 sexually abused girls, one attack (0.4%) was attributed to an identifiably lesbian woman; of the 50 sexually abused boys, one attack (2%) was attributed to an identifiably gay man. In contrast, 77% of abuse against girls and 74% of abuse against boys was perpetrated by the adult male heterosexual partners of the girls' family members (e.g., mothers, foster mothers, and grandmothers). There was thus no evidence whatever for the belief that gay men are more likely than other men to perpetrate sexual abuse against children.

Much of what is known about the peer relations of the children of gay fathers comes from the work of Bozett (1980, 1987). From his interviews with adolescent and young adult offspring of gay fathers, Bozett concluded that although children affirmed their fathers in parental roles and generally considered their relationships with gay fathers as positive ones, they nevertheless expressed some concerns. Prominent among the children's concerns was that, if their fathers' sexual identities were widely known, then the children too might be seen as nonheterosexual.

To avoid problems, children reported that they employed a number of strategies. These included selective disclosure of the fathers' sexual identities, nondisclosure, and what Bozett termed "boundary control," in which children attempted to limit their fathers' expressions of gay identity. For instance, adolescents might avoid bringing friends home when the gay father and his partner were likely to be there, or an adult son might ask his father not to bring his lover or partner to a party at the son's house. Some gay fathers were reported to have accommodated to children's requests in this regard, by putting away gay publications during the visits of children's friends or by avoiding expressions of affection for a gay partner when in the company of their adolescent or adult children. Bozett suggested that these kinds of negotiations were affected by the age of the child, by the nature of the father-child relationship, by the perceived obtrusiveness of the father's sexual orientation (i.e., how visible it appeared to the child), and by a number of other factors. Systematic research on the ways in which children of gay fathers cope with the potentially stigmatizing nature of their fathers' sexual orientation could make important contributions toward the understanding of children's coping with prejudice as well as toward the understanding of gay family dynamics.

Overall, then, research on children of gay fathers, though still sparse, has produced some important information. First, contrary to popular stereotypes, there is little evidence to suggest that children of gay fathers are any more likely to encounter difficulties in the development of their own sexual identities, to be the victims of sexual abuse, or for that matter, to be placed at any significant disadvantage relative to otherwise similar children of heterosexual fathers. Although children of gay fathers do appear to encounter some special challenges (e.g., in learning how to cope with potentially stigmatizing information about their fathers' sexual orientations), there is every indication that most children surmount these without undue difficulty. Probably the most important finding in the literature on children of gay fathers is that, despite the undoubted prejudice and discrimination against their fathers, children nevertheless described relationships with their gay fathers as generally warm and supportive.

DIRECTIONS FOR FURTHER RESEARCH

As the preceding discussion makes clear, research on gay fathers and their families is relatively recent and still relatively sparse. Many important questions remain to be addressed, and there is much for future researchers to accomplish in this area.

In considering the substantive issues for future research on gay fathers, we distinguish between normative questions, on the one hand, and individual differences questions, on the other. Normative questions concern the central tendencies of a population, whereas individual differences questions concern differences among members of a population. In the present context, these include questions about gay fathers considered as a group, on the one hand, and about diversity among gay fathers, on the other. We discuss directions for research on the normative questions first, then examine avenues for research on individual differences.

One important task for research is to provide normative information about actual parenting behaviors of gay fathers with infants, children, adolescents, and adult children. As contemporary research on heterosexual families attests (Lamb, 1981, 1986), relationships with fathers are significant aspects of a child's family environment, yet very little is known about the qualities of children's relationships with their gay fathers, or about how these may compare to those of children's relationships with heterosexual fathers at different points in the life course. Is there any correlation between fathers' sexual orientation and their involvement in parenting, or style of parenting? And what effects, if any, might such differences have on children's development?

Another significant direction for future research is to identify patterns of family organization and family climate that may be characteristic of gay father families. Are there distinctive ways in which gay father families differ from heterosexual families, or from lesbian families, and if so, what are they? In studies of lesbian, gay, and heterosexual couples without children, Kurdek (1995) has reported that many issues for couples depend more upon the length of time that a couple has been together than upon the gender or sexual orientation of partners. Similar research on couples with children has not, however, been reported. A number of recent studies have suggested that gay and lesbian couples are more likely than heterosexual couples to divide the labor involved in child care evenly between the partners (Hand, 1991; McPherson, 1993; Patterson, 1995d); what impact, if any, does this egalitarian tendency have on the overall family climate in gay, lesbian, and heterosexual families?

Yet a third major direction for research involves exploration of interfaces between gay father families and major educational, religious, and cultural institutions with which they have contact. What are the most common issues and concerns for gay father families in their contacts with settings such as children's schools or parents' work environments, and how are they usually addressed? Are gay father family issues the same as, or different from, those of lesbian mother families or of members of other stigmatized minorities (e.g., ethnic or religious minorities)?

It will also be valuable to examine in a normative spirit the issues of subgroups of gay fathers. For instance, building on the work of Bozett (1980, 1981a, 1981b) and Miller (1979), research could examine the normative life trajectories of nonresidental gay fathers following divorce, examining the challenges and stresses of such life transitions and of noncustodial parenting. In the same vein, one might examine the issues of gay stepfathers over time, comparing them with those of both heterosexual stepfathers and with lesbian stepmothers.

From an individual difference perspective, a central concern is to identify and examine factors that add to or detract from the quality of life in gay father families. For instance, using different levels of analysis, one might examine individual, family, community, and cultural factors for evidence of their impact on the well-being of individual gay fathers as well as that of their family members. Drawing on results of research with heterosexual families (e.g., Lewis, Feiring & Weinraub, 1981), one would expect psychologically healthy men, living in supportive families and communities, in a favorable cultural milieu, to cope in more favorable ways with the challenges of life in gay father families. The relative importance of various levels of analysis is, however, far from clear, and there is much to be done in this area.

It will also be important to examine issues of contemporary relevance to gay communities, as these may influence the experience of life in gay father families. Prejudice and discrimination against gay men and lesbians is, of course, one of the important factors that must be considered. Another is the special health concerns faced by gay men, especially the long illnesses and premature deaths attributable to HIV disease (Paul, Hays, & Coates, 1995). More often than heterosexual families, gay father families may be faced with caretaking responsibilities for family members and friends who are ill, and with grieving the loss of loved ones to a stigmatized illness. How do these special challenges, and the environments in which they occur, affect the experiences of those who live in gay father families?

The advent of gay father and lesbian mother families also provides an opportunity to assess the long-assumed significance both of gender and of sexual orientation in parenting. It will be as interesting to compare the dynamics of gay and lesbian families as it is to compare those of gay and heterosexual families. The results of such work should clarify the significance of fundamental assumptions about the significance of gender and sexual orientation in parenting that have long been taken for granted but rarely if ever subjected to rigorous test. The results of this process should be not only a better understanding of gay families in particular, but also a better understanding of families and parenting in general.

From a methodological perspective, we can also offer a number of suggestions for future research. The first of these concerns sampling methods. Existing research has tended to involve small, unsystematic samples of unknown representativeness. Larger, more representative samples of individuals and families would be helpful. Also valuable would be longitudinal research, with observational and other varied assessment procedures. Multisite studies that systematically assess the impact of environmental as well as personal and familial processes hold great promise. Except in the case of qualitative work, rigorous statistical procedures should be employed. Methodological directions of these kinds would maximize the likelihood that future research has a major impact on understanding in this area (Patterson, 1995d).

SUMMARY AND OVERVIEW

Social science research on gay fathers is a relatively recent phenomenon. Because the research has arisen in the context of widespread prejudice and discrimination against members of sexual minorities, much research has been concerned to evaluate negative stereotypes about gay father families. Although a great deal in this regard remains to be done, the results of existing research fail to provide evidence for any of the prevailing stereotypes about gay fathers or about their children. On the basis of existing research, we can conclude that there is no reason for concern about the development of children living in the custody of gay fathers; on the contrary, there is every reason to believe that gay fathers are as likely as heterosexual fathers to provide home environments in which children grow and flourish. Additional research is, however, certainly needed.

As researchers seek to expand the evidence relevant to traditional stereotypes, it will also be important to begin to examine individual differences among gay fathers and among their children. In this regard, it will be important for researchers to remember that, despite widespread prejudice, many gay fathers and many of their children are competent, well-functioning members of society. Having begun to address negative assumptions embodied in psychological theory as well as in popular opinion, researchers are now in a position also to explore a broader range of issues, examining the personal, social, community, and cultural factors that affect the quality of life for gay father families. Much important work remains to be done in order to understand the structure and functioning of gay father families.

CHAPTER 15

Psychological Adjustment, Maladjustment, and Father-Child Relationships

Vicky Phares

University of South Florida

T HE STUDY of father-child relationships related to the development of psychopathology has lagged behind the study of father-child relationships related to
normative development (Phares, 1996). Although some researchers throughout the years have argued that fathers' roles in their children's maladjustment should
be investigated (e.g., Lidz, Parker, & Cornelison, 1956; Nash, 1965; Sanua, 1961, 1963),
comparatively little work has been completed in this area. Historically, children's maladjustment has been explored in relation to paternal absence rather than paternal
presence (Biller & Solomon, 1986), and paternal presence has been all but ignored in
relation to children's maladjustment. A number of factors have been delineated that
may be related to the lack of attention to paternal influences in children's nonnormative development, including a tendency toward blaming mothers for their children's
problematic behavior, practical issues of participant recruitment with the concomitant assumption that fathers are more difficult to recruit into research than mothers,
and base rates of paternal and maternal psychopathology that influence the types of
parental psychopathology that are investigated in relation to children's maladjustment
(Phares, 1992).

Before exploring causal mechanisms related to developmental psychopathology
and fathers' roles in the development of psychopathology, the historical tendency for
researchers to blame mothers for their children's maladjustment and the concomitant
exclusion of fathers from clinical research are discussed.

Preparation of this chapter was supported in part by National Institute of Mental Health Grant R29
49601–02.

MOTHER BLAMING AND THE LACK OF FATHERS
IN CLINICAL RESEARCH

A number of writers have noted the preponderance of mother blaming in clinical practice (Chess, 1964, 1982) and in clinical research (Caplan & Hall-McCorquodale, 1985). Mother blaming reflects the tendency to consider and investigate maternal contributions to the development of psychopathology in children while not considering or investigating paternal contributions to the same phenomena (Caplan & Hall-McCorquodale, 1985). In addition to the primary focus on maternal influences in the development of psychopathology in children, there has also been a parallel focus on maternal culpability (i.e., blame) for children's maladjustment.

Throughout the history of clinical psychology and psychiatry, examples of direct and indirect mother blaming are pervasive (Bateson, Jackson, Haley, & Weakland, 1956; Freud, 1949; Fromm-Reichmann, 1948; Mahler, 1952; Rheingold, 1967; Wylie, 1946). More recent investigations suggest that mothers continue to be overrepresented in comparison to fathers in studies of children's maladjustment. Caplan and Hall-McCorquodale (1985; reviewed in Caplan, 1989) found that articles published in clinical journals used mothers at a 5:1 ratio to fathers in descriptions of case examples. In addition, 82% of the studies they evaluated included data on mothers' psychological functioning, whereas only 54% of the studies collected these data for fathers. Phares and Compas (1992) found similar patterns in empirical research related to child and adolescent psychopathology. They found that of the 577 articles reviewed, 48% included mothers only, 1% included fathers only, 26% included both mothers and fathers and analyzed for effects of parental gender, and 25% included "parents" without defining whether they were mothers or fathers.

Even more striking differences were found in unpublished doctoral dissertation research that investigated child, adolescent, and family functioning. In their review of *Dissertation Abstracts* from 1986 through 1994, Silverstein and Phares (1996) found that 59% of dissertation research included mothers only, 11% included fathers only, and 30% used both parents. This distribution differed significantly from that found by Phares and Compas (1992) and suggested that doctoral students were more likely to include mothers only or fathers only in their dissertation projects. Interestingly, male graduate students were more likely than female graduate students to include fathers in their doctoral research. No other differences in the likelihood of including fathers were found when advisor gender, type of doctoral degree, or research topic were analyzed. Although doctoral students were more likely to use mother only or fathers only than were published researchers, the rationales for these procedures were rarely provided.

Research is considered sexist when only one gender is investigated without good reason (Denmark, Russo, Frieze, & Sechzer, 1988). Although there are some legitimate areas of research that focus on mothers (e.g., the psychosocial and physical effects of prenatal exposure to teratogenergic substances during pregnancy), there are surprisingly few areas that cannot also be investigated for fathers or father figures. For example, although maternal cigarette smoking has been linked to low birthweight, which is associated with decreased cognitive abilities and increased behavioral problems in children (Behrman, 1992), paternal cigarette smoking has also been implicated in fetal nicotine exposure in nonsmoking mothers (T. R. Martin & Bracken,

1986; Schwartz-Bickenbach, Schulte-Hobein, Abt, Plum, & Nau, 1987). In addition, postpartum depression in fathers has been identified as similar to maternal postpartum depression in putting the infant at risk for the development of later emotional/behavioral problems (Atkinson & Rickel, 1984; Carro, Grant, Gotlib, & Compas, 1993), as well as being linked to paternal postpartum anxiety (Ballard, Davis, Handy, & Mohan, 1993).

Given that most areas of clinical research could investigate fathers in similar ways as mothers, why do clinical researchers continue to neglect fathers in their research designs? It may be that many clinical and family researchers assume that fathers are rarely involved in the lives of their children. As noted earlier in this volume, a substantial number of children in the United States and around the world continue to live with both of their parents. For those children and adolescents who do not live with both of their biological parents, a substantial number (estimated at 61% by Seltzer & Bianchi, 1988) continue to have contact with the "absent" parent (Danziger & Radin, 1990; Seltzer, 1991). In addition, it is logical to assume that the way in which children and adolescents feel about their truly absent and uninvolved fathers may influence their psychosocial functioning; however, there are few investigations into this area.

When researchers are interested in including fathers in their research design, there is equivocal evidence as to the difficulty in recruiting fathers into family research. In their comprehensive review of participants and nonparticipants in psychological research, Rosenthal and Rosnow (1975) found that women were more likely than men to volunteer for research unless the research was perceived to be stressful, anxiety provoking, or physically harmful. Unfortunately, they did not provide the same set of analyses for mothers and fathers. A number of studies have investigated maternal and paternal involvement in research more directly. In a comprehensive epidemiological study of depression in adolescents, Hops and Seeley (1992) found that fathers were significantly less likely than mothers to participate. Out of 500 two-parent families, 92% of the mothers participated (either in completion of questionnaires through the mail or in clinic-based behavioral observations) as compared to 40% of the fathers. When only one parent from the family participated, interesting effects emerged. Mothers who participated without their husbands were less satisfied with their marriage and felt less family cohesion than did mothers whose husbands participated. Fathers who participated without their wives showed greater depressive symptoms. In addition, when fathers do participate in direct observational research, different behavioral information emerges than when only mother-adolescent dyads are involved. Hops and Seeley (1991) found that when fathers from two-parent families were present for behavioral observations, mothers and adolescents were less distressed but more aggressive than when fathers were not present for the interactions. It appears that the mother-adolescent relationship was adversely influenced by the absence of the father from the direct observations, and this was especially true for the mother-daughter relationship. Overall, the work by Hops and colleagues suggests that fathers are more difficult to recruit into research, but that they are important to include because of the greater complexity and breadth of information that can be collected when both parents are involved in research.

Two other studies suggest that fathers from two-parent families of older adolescents are not significantly more difficult to recruit than are mothers. In a study of perceived social support within families of older adolescent and young adult college students, Sarason, Pierce, Bannerman, and Sarason (1993) found that 65% of mothers and 55% of fathers of college students completed questionnaires and returned them through the mail. Strikingly similar response rates were found at a different university by Phares (1995) who found that 65% of mothers and 58% of fathers completed measures and returned them through the mail. These data suggest that, although mothers of college students are somewhat more likely to participate in research, fathers were also willing to participate. These findings need to be explored in groups of younger children as well as in more culturally diverse samples.

The topic of recruitment of participants and the differences between participants and nonparticipants is especially important in clinical child and adolescent research. A number of studies suggest that children and adolescents who participate in research are more psychologically and socially well-adjusted than those who do not participate (e.g., Beck, Collins, Overholser, & Terry, 1984; Frame & Strauss, 1987; Weinberger, Tublin, Ford, & Feldman, 1990). This pattern appears to be more evident in nonminority children, whereas few differences have been found between participating and nonparticipating children who represent an ethnic minority (La Greca & Silverman, 1993). The next level of investigation should focus on differences in the characteristics of mothers and fathers who participate in clinically oriented research in children, adolescents, and families in comparison with those parents who choose not to participate.

CAUSAL MECHANISMS

Before exploring research on fathers' and children's psychopathology, causal mechanisms and theoretical models must be explored in order to put research findings into context. Although it is beyond the scope of this chapter to review every possible etiology of psychopathology, there are certain common characteristics related to fathers that appear to be involved in the development and maintenance of many types of psychopathology in children and adolescents. It is also important to acknowledge the reciprocity of effects between fathers and their children. Although there are common themes that relate to causal mechanisms across different disorders, it is important to remain cognizant of the possibility of different causal mechanisms for different types of psychopathology in children as well as in parents.

GENETIC EFFECTS

There is differing support for genetic linkages of psychopathology between fathers and their offspring. Based on adoption and twin studies, alcoholism appears to be more strongly linked through the Y chromosome (from father to son) than through the X chromosome (Delong & Roy, 1993; Pihl, Peterson, & Finn, 1990). Hawkins, Catalano, and Miller (1992) reviewed this literature and surmised that approximately 30% of sons of alcoholic fathers become alcoholic themselves. There is also significant support for genetic linkages of paternal and maternal schizophrenia and bipolar affective disorder (Vandenberg, Singer, & Pauls, 1986; Wachs & Weizmann, 1992). Autism and attention-deficit/hyperactivity disorder (AD/HD) in children have been strongly linked to genetic and biological factors (Vandenberg et al., 1986; Wachs &

Weizmann, 1992). Other disorders have less consistent support for genetic and biological contributions to the development of psychopathology.

Any discussion of genetic effects would be incomplete without a discussion of more recent investigations in the area of behavioral genetics. For example, Plomin and Daniels (1987) reviewed twin adoption studies that showed genetic factors accounted for approximately 40% of the variance in the development of schizophrenia, whereas environmental factors (both shared and nonshared environmental factors as well as measurement error) accounted for 60% of the variance. The study of behavioral genetics emphasizes that even with strong empirical support for genetic linkages, environmental and biological influences can serve to lessen or to exacerbate a child's genetic predisposition to develop a particular disorder (Plomin, DeFries, & McClearn, 1990; Plomin, Reiss, Hetherington, & Howe, 1994).

Based on both genetic and environmental factors, some children are at increased risk for maladjustment because both of their parents experience psychopathology. Assortative mating, which is the tendency for a psychologically distressed person to have children with another psychologically distressed person, has been documented for depression, alcohol abuse, and anxiety disorders, as well as for psychiatric disorders as a group (McLeod, 1993; Merikangas, Weissman, Prusoff, & John, 1988). Merikangas and colleagues found that 58% of the offspring who had one psychiatrically disturbed parent were themselves diagnosed with a psychiatric disorder, whereas 75% of the offspring with two disturbed parents were themselves diagnosed. These results highlight the need to evaluate both maternal and paternal psychopathology when conducting research on risk factors and protective factors in the development of psychopathology.

ENVIRONMENTAL EFFECTS

As suggested by the work in behavioral genetics, there is evidence that environmental influences are related to the development and maintenance of psychopathology in children in addition to genetic contributions. The two environmental factors that have received the majority of support are parenting behavior and interparental conflict.

Paternal Behavior

The investigation into paternal behavior has found connections between a vast array of father and child behaviors, including relations between fathers' and children's aggression (Bjorkqvist & Osterman, 1992), fathers' and adolescents' alcohol consumption (Ullman & Orenstein, 1994), fathers' lower use of rewards and adolescents' negative personality traits (Gussman & Harder, 1990), fathers's coercive parenting behavior and children's coercive or antisocial behavior (Patterson, 1990), and fathers' parenting behavior and child adjustment (Abidin, 1992).

In a comprehensive review of factors influencing child adjustment, Lee and Gotlib (1991) identified parental emotional availability and responsivity to children's needs as central themes that cut across many situations in which children are at risk for the development of psychopathology (e.g., parental divorce, parental conflict, and parental psychopathology). They argued that fathers' and mothers' emotional unavailability and unresponsiveness to their children may mediate the impact of disruptive family situations on children's adjustment. Paternal emotional availability appears to be a fruitful topic of investigation in an attempt to investigate mediating factors and additional etiological factors related to children's risk for the development of psycho-pathology.

Paternal behavior has also been investigated with retrospective reports of psychiatrically disturbed adult clients' recollections of the parenting behavior they received during their youth. Gerlsma, Emmelkamp, and Arrindell (1990) conducted a meta-analysis and found that depressed adults recalled their fathers as more controlling and less affectionate than did nondepressed adults. Adult clients who experienced a specific phobia also reported greater affectionless control from their fathers than did nonphobic adults, but there were no differences in the retrospective reports of clients who experienced obsessive/compulsive disorder (OCD) when compared with controls. Overall, the investigation of paternal parenting behavior has highlighted possible factors related to the development and maintenance of psychopathology in children and adolescents. In addition to the direct interactions between father and child that have been investigated, a great deal of research has focused on the maladaptive interactions between fathers and mothers in relation to child maladjustment.

Interparental Conflict

The association between interparental conflict and children's and adolescents' emotional/behavioral problems is well established (Cummings & O'Reilly, Chapter 4 of this volume; Emery, 1988; Erel & Burman, 1995; Grych & Fincham, 1990; Hetherington & Clingempeel, 1992). Overt parental conflict appears to be more strongly related to child maladjustment than lack of marital satisfaction or other aspects of parental disharmony (Jenkins & Smith, 1991). Reid and Crisafulli (1990) found that the association between interparental conflict and children's maladjustment is similar for clinical and nonclinical samples of children and adolescents. Interestingly, B. Martin (1987) argues that mothers are more adversely affected by their husband's conflict and psychopathology than vice versa. Based on Martin's review, it is necessary to investigate the directionality of dyadic and triadic relationships within the family regarding conflict and psychopathology. Interested readers are referred to Cummings's excellent work on interparental conflict and conflict resolution (Cummings & Davies, 1994; Cummings & O'Reilly, Chapter 4 of this volume).

Overall, there is only partial support for any of these etiological mechanisms. As each disorder is discussed, additional information is provided with regard to causal mechanisms and differential linkages between fathers' and children's maladjustment.

FATHERS AND DEVELOPMENTAL PSYCHOPATHOLOGY

Although fathers have been underrepresented in research on the development of psychopathology in children, there are a growing number of studies that have investigated paternal factors related to the adjustment and maladjustment of children and adolescents. Two methodologies dominate this area of research. First, the investigation of paternal psychopathology as a risk factor for later development of problems in children focuses on fathers who exhibit problematic adjustment and then investigates the level of adjustment evidenced by their offspring. This line of research has a rich history in the investigation of risk and protective factors related to maternal psycho-pathology (Rolf, Masten, Cicchetti, Neuchterlein, & Weintraub, 1990). The second methodology focuses on children and adolescents who have shown problematic adjustment and then investigates the functioning level of fathers of these children and adolescents. This methodology has also been used extensively to investigate maternal characteristics in relation to child and adolescent psychopathology. Too many different disorders have been investigated in relation to the father-child relationship to cover adequately in this chapter. However, the disorders of conduct disorder/antisocial personality disorder, alcohol abuse, depression, anxiety disorders, schizophrenia, autism, attention-deficit/hyperactivity disorder, and eating disorders are reviewed in order to cover a broad spectrum of psychopathology in fathers and their offspring. A more extensive review is provided by Phares (1996). In addition, the effects of paternal abuse are reviewed by Sternberg (Chapter 16 of this volume). Note that research on fathers is highlighted, and research on mothers will be mentioned only briefly.

CONDUCT DISORDER AND ANTISOCIAL PERSONALITY DISORDER

Conduct disorder (CD) and antisocial personality disorder (APD) are both characterized by overt transgressions against social norms and by activities that violate the basic rights of others (American Psychiatric Association, 1994). The diagnosis of APD cannot be given to anyone younger than 18 years old, but the diagnosis of CD can be given at any age. Epidemiological studies suggest that between 6% and 18% of boys and approximately 2% to 9% of girls under 18 meet diagnostic criteria for CD. In adults, APD is present in about 3% of men and 1% of women.

Paternal Antisocial Personality Disorder and Criminality

It is surprising to find that little research has been conducted with the offspring of fathers who evidence APD or criminality. The majority of research linking paternal criminality and delinquency in children and adolescents has identified troubled youth and then investigated paternal characteristics (reviewed below). The few studies that have investigated criminality in fathers have attempted to establish the type of contact that incarcerated fathers have with their children.

One-third of the incarcerated fathers in a maximum-security prison reported visits from their children while they were incarcerated (Hairston, 1989), and 78% reported that they had been in phone contact with their children since being incarcerated (Lanier, 1991). Hairston (1989) found that 91% of the incarcerated fathers reported that they were interested in receiving educational training in order to improve their parenting skills. Unfortunately, these studies did not investigate the psychosocial functioning of the offspring of incarcerated fathers, nor did these studies explore the impact of the father-child relationship on incarcerated fathers or on their children.

Child and Adolescent Conduct Disorder

As just noted, the majority of research on delinquency and criminality has focused on troubled youth and their fathers. Overall, there is strong evidence that delinquent behavior in children and adolescents is associated with paternal antisocial behavior (Goetting, 1994; Loeber, 1990; Loeber & Dishion, 1987). When compared with fathers of nonclinical children, fathers of children diagnosed with CD showed greater likelihood of experiencing APD and alcohol abuse (Reeves, Werry, Elkind, & Zametkin, 1987; Schachar & Wachsmuth, 1990). Similar results were found when fathers of children diagnosed with CD and children diagnosed with another disorder were compared. Fathers of offspring diagnosed with CD showed greater levels of APD and alcohol abuse than fathers of offspring diagnosed with AD/HD, depression, or an anxiety disorder (Frick, Lahey, Christ, Loeber, & Green, 1991; Jary & Stewart, 1985; Lahey et al., 1988; Reeves et al., 1987). Delinquency in adolescents is associated with a poor father-child relationship (Atwood, Gold, & Taylor, 1989), defensive and unsupportive paternal communication (Alexander, Waldron, Barton, & Mas, 1989; Borduin, Pruitt, & Henggeler, 1986), and low levels of paternal supervision (Goetting, 1994).

Paternal aggression also appears to be linked to children's and adolescents' level of aggression. Paternal physical abuse was more prevalent in groups of homicidally aggressive children (Lewis, Shanok, Grant, & Ritvo, 1983), delinquent adolescents (Lewis, Pincus, Lovely, Spitzer, & Moy, 1987), adjudicated male adolescent offenders (Truscott, 1992), and adolescents who ran away from home (Warren, Gary, & Moorhead, 1994) than in clinical and nonclinical control groups. Severe aggressive behavior (evidenced by rape and murder) also appears to be linked to a maladaptive father-child relationship (Heide, 1992; Lisak, 1991; Lisak & Roth, 1990; Singhal & Dutta, 1990).

The connection between CD or aggression in children and paternal characteristics may be stronger for boys than girls. Note that the studies finding strong connections between conduct problems in children and psychiatric problems in fathers used samples of boys primarily (Frick et al., 1991; Jary & Stewart, 1985; Lahey et al., 1988; Reeves et al., 1987). In a study of girls diagnosed with CD, Johnson and O'Leary (1987) found stronger associations between maternal characteristics (such as overt hostility and aggression) and conduct problems in daughters than between paternal characteristics and conduct problems in daughters. However, two other studies (Henggeler, Edwards, & Borduin, 1987; Kavanagh & Hops, 1994) found few differences between fathers and mothers of boys and girls who evidenced delinquent behavior. Overall, there is not enough research to conclude whether there are stronger associations between paternal characteristics and sons' or daughters' CD behavior. However, there is consistent evidence that paternal aggression, APD, and alcohol abuse are associated with problems of conduct and aggression in children and adolescents (for comprehensive reviews, see Goetting, 1994; Loeber & Dishion, 1987).

An important area of investigation is the study of possible mechanisms and etiological factors related to the onset of conduct disorder and juvenile delinquency. In a comprehensive review of risk factors related to juvenile antisocial behavior, Loeber (1990) suggested that no one risk factor is associated with the development of conduct disorder or juvenile delinquency. Rather, a combination of biological and social factors that occur at different developmental stages are related to the development of antisocial behavior in children and adolescents. Loeber argued that the combination of poor parental childrearing practices, parental uninvolvement, parental criminality, parental aggressiveness, and deviant peers were strong predictors of the development of juvenile delinquency. In addition, higher interparental discord is associated with poorer childrearing practices that are linked to greater levels of externalizing problems in children (Dadds, Sheffield, & Holbeck, 1990). According to Loeber, factors that received less empirical support were poor discipline, parental absence, socioeconomic status, and poor parental health. Based on a comprehensive review of the research literature, Yoshikawa (1994) surmised that risk factors interact to create greater likelihood of the development of antisocial behavior. There appears to be a multiplicative, rather than additive, effect for the number of risk factors and the likelihood of development of antisocial behavior.

ALCOHOL ABUSE

Abuse of alcohol is characterized by a maladaptive pattern of alcohol use that interferes with personal functioning and results in adverse personal, social, medical, or legal consequences (American Psychiatric Association, 1994). Prevalence rates appear to be about 5% in adults and adolescents. Of all of the types of parental psychopathology, alcohol abuse is the primary area in which researchers have focused on fathers almost to the exclusion of mothers (West & Prinz, 1987).

Paternal Alcohol Abuse

When compared with children of nonclinical fathers, children of alcoholic fathers are at increased risk for alcohol and substance abuse (Cavell, Jones, Runyan, & Constantin-Page, 1993; Chassin, Rogosch, & Barrera, 1991; Merikangas, Weissman, Prusoff, Pauls, & Leckman, 1985; Weinberg, Dielman, Mandell, & Shope, 1994), delinquency and conduct problems (Maguin, Zucker, & Fitzgerald, 1994; Rimmer, 1982), hyperactivity (Fitzgerald, Sullivan, Ham, & Zucker, 1993), depression and anxiety (Berkowitz & Perkins, 1988; Callan & Jackson, 1986; Wellner & Rice, 1988), and personality problems (Whipple & Noble, 1991). Family stress (Dumka & Roosa, 1993) and detrimental discipline practices (Tarter, Blackson, Martin, & Loeber, 1993) are also more evident in families with alcoholic fathers. It appears that African American children and adolescents may be at even greater risk for the development of substance abuse in relation to paternal alcohol abuse than Caucasian children (Luthar, Merikangas, & Rounsaville, 1993). Across all ethnicities and races, there is strong evidence that children of alcoholic fathers are at greater risk for maladjustment than children of fathers who do not evidence any psychopathology. Notably, children's academic functioning has been identified as not showing adverse effects due to paternal alcoholism. When compared with the offspring of fathers in a nonclinical control group, young adolescents of alcoholic fathers showed comparable school attendance and grade point average (Murphy, O'Farrell, Floyd, & Connors, 1991).

When offspring of alcoholic fathers are compared with offspring of fathers who evidence other types of psychopathology, few differences are found. Children and adolescents of fathers who abuse alcohol appear to be at similar risk for the development of psychopathology as children and adolescents of fathers who are depressed (Jacob, Krahn, & Leonard, 1991; Jacob & Leonard, 1986) or who are schizophrenic (el-Guebaly, Offord, Sullivan, & Lynch, 1978).

Somewhat equivocal results emerge when considering the adult offspring of alcoholic fathers. A number of researchers have found increased psychopathology and alcohol abuse (Alford, Jouriles, & Jackson, 1991; el-Guebaly et al., 1991; Jarmas & Kazak, 1992; Knop, Goodwin, Jensen, & Penick, 1993; Mathew, Wilson, Blazer, & George, 1993; Mutzell, 1994; Sher, Walitzer, Wood, & Brent, 1991), decreased personality adjustment (E. D. Martin & Sher, 1994), and decreased cognitive functioning (Peterson, Finn, & Pihl, 1992) in adult offspring of alcoholic fathers. However, more rigorous and large-scale studies should be conducted before concluding that a strong link exists between adult functioning and paternal alcohol abuse (Sher, 1991; Velleman, 1992). In addition, greater attention should be paid to comparing the risk status of offspring of alcoholic fathers with those whose fathers experience other types of psychopathology. Research on children and adolescents would suggest that paternal alcohol abuse is associated with similar levels of psychopathology in offspring when compared with other types of paternal psychopathology.

Because most of this research focused on male offspring, it is noteworthy to mention that alcoholism in women appears to be about equally related to paternal and maternal alcoholism (Kendler, Neale, Heath, & Kessler, 1994). In addition, even when adult women of alcoholic fathers do not abuse alcohol themselves, they are more likely to marry an alcoholic man (Schuckit, Tipp, & Kelner, 1994).

With regard to mechanisms, there is evidence that early temperamental factors and other social and familial factors may serve as mediating factors in relation to paternal alcohol abuse. Specifically, the risk for maladjustment appears to be mediated by fathers' and children's temperament, with negative temperament being more highly associated with risk for development of maladjustment in children and adolescents (Blackson, Tarter, Martin, & Moss, 1994a, 1994b). When families with alcoholic fathers are characterized by high levels of interparental anger and conflict, children and adolescents appear to be at greater risk of developing maladjustment than are children and adolescents who are not exposed to high levels of interparental anger and conflict (Cummings & Davies, 1994).

Child and Adolescent Alcohol Abuse

Surprisingly little research has been conducted with children and adolescents who abuse alcohol. Some research studies have grouped together adolescents who abuse alcohol with adolescents who abuse other substances, such as marijuana and heroin, in order to investigate paternal characteristics (e.g., Downs & Robertson, 1991; Klinge & Piggott, 1986; Tarter, Laird, & Bukstein, 1991). These studies failed to find significant associations between adolescents' substance abuse and their fathers' self-reported substance abuse, but there do appear to be associations between adolescents' abuse of substances and their reports of poor relationships with their fathers (Jiloha, 1986), problematic family boundaries (Marett, Sprenkle, & Lewis, 1992), and family conflict (Downs & Robertson, 1991).

The majority of studies of paternal characteristics of alcoholic offspring have focused on retrospective reports by adults who abuse alcohol. A meta-analysis of 32 of these studies suggested that both male and female alcoholics were more likely to have fathers who abused alcohol than to have mothers who were alcoholics (Pollock, Schneider, Gabrielli, & Goodwin, 1987).

The overreliance on retrospective studies with adults who abuse alcohol may be related to the onset of this disorder. A study by DeJone, Harteveld, and van de Wielen (1991) suggested that the average age of alcohol abuse onset was 23.2 years. Because alcohol use and abuse are evident in children and adolescents, researchers should also investigate the paternal characteristics associated with alcohol abuse while it is occurring in children and adolescents rather than waiting to investigate the retrospective reports once these children reach adulthood.

In an attempt to elucidate the mechanisms related to the development of alcohol problems in adolescents and young adults, Hawkins and colleagues (1992) reviewed a number of contextual, individual, and interpersonal risk factors associated with alcohol problems. They found that parental alcohol abuse, perceived parental permissiveness toward alcohol and drug use, and extreme poverty in association with antisocial behavior were all predictive of alcohol problems in adolescents and young adults. With regard to physiological and genetic linkages to alcoholism, there is evidence that sensation seeking and low harm avoidance in early childhood are predictive of alcohol abuse in young adulthood (Cloniger, Sigvardsson, & Bohman, 1988), and there is stronger evidence of a genetic linkage from father to son for alcoholism based on twin and adoption studies (Hrubec & Omenn, 1981).

DEPRESSION

There are a variety of different ways to conceptualize depression, from a depressive mood to a depressive syndrome to a major depressive disorder (Petersen et al., 1993). Prevalence rates differ greatly depending on which definition is used. Because most of the research related to fathers has focused on the diagnosis of major depressive disorder (MDD), research based on fathers with major depression is reviewed in this section. MDD, and specifically unipolar depression, is evident when an individual experiences a two-week period of either depressed mood or loss of interest in nearly all formerly enjoyable activities, with concomitant psychomotor agitation, disruption of appetite, disruption of sleeping habits, and feelings of worthlessness or suicidality (American Psychiatric Association, 1994). In children, MDD is often characterized by irritable mood and somatic complaints rather than depressed mood per se. Prevalence rates suggest that between 5% and 12% of men and 10% to 25% of women will experience MDD in their lifetime. A review of epidemiological studies suggested that about 7% of children and adolescents meet criteria for MDD (Petersen et al., 1993).

Paternal Depression

Depression has been studied extensively in mothers but has been all but ignored in fathers. In their reviews of parental depression, Downey and Coyne (1990) and Kaslow, Deering, and Racusin (1994) noted that the majority of studies focused only on maternal depression with little or no attention paid to paternal depression. Even with this caveat, there are enough studies of paternal depression to suggest that it serves as a risk factor in the development of maladjustment in children and adolescents.

Out of the 17 studies that have investigated paternal depression and child adjustment, 12 have found significant associations between paternal depression and child maladjustment (Atkinson & Rickel, 1984; Beardslee, Schultz, & Selman, 1987; Billings & Moos, 1983, 1985; Carro et al., 1993; el-Guebaly et al., 1978; Forehand & Smith, 1986; Harjan, 1992; Jacob & Leonard, 1986; Klein, Clark, Dansky, & Margolis, 1988; Orvaschel, Walsh-Allis, & Ye, 1988; Thomas & Forehand, 1991). These studies encompassed 10 different samples. The five studies that did not find significant associations between paternal depression and child maladjustment (Keller et al., 1986; Klein, Depue, & Slater, 1985; Radke-Yarrow, Cummings, Kuczynski, & Chapman, 1985; Radke-Yarrow, Nottelman, Martinez, Fox, & Belmont, 1992; Zahn-Waxler, Cummings, McKnew, & Radke-Yarrow, 1984) encompassed three different samples.

Overall, there appears to be stronger evidence than not that depression in fathers serves as a risk factor for the development of psychopathology in their offspring.

Children of depressed fathers show increased levels of psychopathology (Billings & Moos, 1983, 1985; Orvaschel et al., 1988) and increased levels of both internalizing and externalizing emotional and behavioral problems (Jacob & Leonard, 1986) when compared with children of fathers in a nonclinical control group. Note also that post-partum paternal depression is related to children's increased emotional and behavioral problems at two or three years of age (Carro et al., 1993).

Paternal functioning in relation to maternal depression has also received attention. Hops and colleagues (1987) found that husbands of depressed women showed more caring and nurturant behavior toward their children than did husbands of mothers who were not psychologically distressed. Conrad and Hammen (1993) found that having a "healthy" father (i.e., a father who did not meet any psychiatric diagnostic criteria) in the home served as a resource factor for children of mothers with unipolar depression. Similarly, Tannenbaum and Forehand (1994) found that a good father-adolescent relationship served to buffer adolescents from maternal depression, which resulted in a lower likelihood of adolescent emotional and behavioral problems.

Overall, paternal depression appears to serve as a risk factor for a wide variety of problems in children and adolescents. The increased risk does not appear to be linked to only one type of disorder in offspring. With regard to mechanisms of transmission, Downey and Coyne (1990) suggested that parental depression in the absence of inter-parental conflict was linked to internalizing problems (such as depression and anxiety) in children, whereas parental depression in the presence of interparental conflict was linked to externalizing problems (such as oppositional and conduct problems) in children. Further, when children of depressed fathers are compared with children of depressed mothers, few differences are found (Beardslee et al., 1987; Billings & Moos, 1983, 1985; Harjan, 1992; Orvaschel et al., 1988). That is, paternal and maternal depression both serve as risk factors to approximately the same degree in the development of psychopathology in children and adolescents.

Child and Adolescent Depression

As with alcohol abuse, little research has been conducted with the fathers of children and adolescents who are depressed. Many more retrospective studies have been conducted with depressed adults reporting on their relationships with their fathers when they were younger. These two methodologies yield conflicting results.

When depressed children and adolescents are studied, few paternal characteristics emerge as significantly associated with the depression. For example, Cole and Rehm (1986) did not find differences in father-child interactions when comparing groups of depressed children, nondepressed clinically referred children, and nonclinical children. Similar null results were found by Puig-Antich and colleagues (1985a, 1985b). Rates of paternal depression were not elevated in groups of depressed children (Cole & Rehm, 1986; Jensen, Bloedau, Degroot, Ussery, & Davis, 1990; Kaslow, Rehm, Pollack, & Siegel, 1988). Rates of APD were higher in fathers of depressed children, but there were no differences in rates of paternal unipolar depression, bipolar depression, alcohol abuse, drug abuse, anxiety disorder, somatization disorder, or schizophrenia (Weller et al., 1994). Most of these studies found significant associations for maternal characteristics and depression in children. Although Hops (1992) found a link between fathers' and sons' depressive symptoms, he found a stronger link between mothers' and daughters' depressive symptoms. The few studies that did show significant paternal associations with children's depression showed that depressed children reported more maladaptive relationships with their father (John, Gammon, Prusoff, & Warner, 1987), depressed children who reported a problematic relationship with their father were more likely to report problems with their mother and their peers (Puig-Antich, Kaufman, Ryan, & Williamson, 1993), and father-adolescent conflict was more predictive of depression in adolescents than was mother-adolescent conflict (Cole & McPherson, 1993). Fathers of suicidal-mood-disordered adolescents reported greater levels of depressive symptoms and greater levels of problems in the family unit than did fathers of nonsuicidal-mood-disordered and nondisturbed adolescents (King, Segal, Naylor, & Evans, 1993).

In contrast to research on depressed children and adolescents, retrospective research on depressed adults has found relatively consistent associations between fathers' characteristics and their adult offsprings' depression. In a comprehensive meta-analysis, Gerlsma and colleagues (1990) found that depressed adults were more likely to report affectionless control (i.e., low levels of affection combined with high levels of control) from their fathers when they were growing up than did nondepressed adults. In addition, Kendler, Silberg, et al. (1991) found that depressed adult women were significantly more likely to report paternal psychiatric disturbance than their nondepressed counterparts. An interesting caveat to this study was that their "counterparts" were their own twin sisters. Given that twins would be recalling the psychiatric status of the same father, Kendler, Silberg, et al. (1991) argued that the presence of depression may increase the likelihood that an adult will recall parental psychopathology. The same pattern was found for adults with generalized anxiety disorder but not for adults who abuse alcohol. Given the tenuous nature of retrospective reports of parental psychopathology and parental behavior, these studies suggest a need for more research with children and their fathers rather than relying on retrospective reports of adults who experience depression. There is evidence, however, to suggest that psychiatrically disturbed clients are no less likely to provide reliable retrospective reports than their nondisturbed counterparts (Brewin, Andrews, & Gotlib, 1993).

Because of the different research findings regarding fathers of depressed children and fathers of depressed adults, it has been difficult for researchers to establish the etiological mechanisms related to depression. Although there is more evidence for mother-child correspondence of major depression in childhood, there is more support for both mother-child and father-child correspondence of major depression in young adulthood. Kaslow and colleagues (1994) argued that a variety of factors put children and young adults at risk for the development of depression, including genetic contributions, parental psychopathology, conflicted and disengaged family environment, and negative life events.

ANXIETY DISORDERS

The term anxiety disorders actually encompasses a number of separate disorders that appear to have anxiety as a primary component in the disorder. In adulthood, anxiety disorders include panic disorder with or without agoraphobia, specific and social phobias, OCD, posttraumatic stress disorder (PTSD), and generalized anxiety disorder (American Psychiatric Association, 1994). All of these disorders are evident in children and adolescents, with the addition of separation anxiety disorder. Although the diagnostic criteria and prevalence rates are quite different for these disorders (e.g., lifetime prevalence of panic disorder is approximately 2.5%, whereas lifetime prevalence for a specific phobia is about 10.5%), most of the studies on family factors have grouped these disorders together. The primary exception has been PTSD, which has received a noticeable amount of attention separate from other anxiety disorders.

Paternal Anxiety Disorders

Although anxiety disorders are relatively common in adult men, few studies have explored fathers who experience an anxiety disorder. Weissman and colleagues (1984) compared children of fathers who showed an anxiety disorder in addition to depression with children of fathers who did not evidence any psychopathology. Children of anxious-depressed fathers showed higher rates of psychopathology than children of nonclinical fathers. Unfortunately, separate analyses of the different types of anxiety disorders (such as panic disorder and generalized anxiety disorder) were not conducted.

Although not a formal diagnostic category, a recent study on paternal anxiety related to separation from young children is worthy of mention. Deater-Deckard, Scarr, McCartney, and Eisenberg (1994) investigated fathers and mothers in dual-earner households who placed their children (aged one to five) in a center-based child care facility during the day. They found that fathers and mothers reported similar levels of separation anxiety. Unfortunately, no outcome measure of child well-being was collected, so it is unclear how fathers' separation anxiety relates to their children's emotional and behavioral functioning. This study represents a step toward understanding paternal processes that have previously only been investigated in mothers.

Regarding other anxiety disorders, more extensive research has been conducted on fathers who experienced PTSD as a result of combat exposure. Overall, the offspring of fathers experiencing PTSD showed elevated levels of maladjustment. This was true for children and adolescents of Vietnam veterans (Jordan et al., 1992; Parsons, Kehle, & Owen, 1990) as well as the adult offspring of World War II veterans (Rosenheck, 1986). It is unclear whether the symptoms of PTSD were directly associated with greater maladjustment in offspring, given that children of parents in the military are exposed to a variety of risk factors other than PTSD, such as prolonged parental absence, geographic instability, and the authoritarian military structure (Jensen, Lewis, & Xenakis, 1986).

Child and Adolescent Anxiety Disorders

Only a handful of researchers have investigated child and adolescent anxiety disorders in relation to the father-child relationship. Clark and Bolton (1985) found that fathers of children with OCD showed greater levels of obsessional thoughts than nonclinical controls. Similarly, fathers of OCD children and adolescents were more likely to receive a diagnosis of OCD than would be expected in the general population (Lenane et al., 1990). However, in a study of children experiencing panic disorder, Last and Strauss (1989) did not find greater rates of paternal panic disorder. In an investigation of children who evidenced school phobia, fathers of school-phobic children showed elevated dysfunction on only two of seven subscales related to family functioning (role performance and values or norms) when compared with men in the normative sample (Bernstein, Svingen, & Garfinkel, 1990).

In a study that combined children with a variety of anxiety disorders (including overanxious disorder, separation anxiety disorder, avoidant disorder, and phobic disorder), Reeves and colleagues (1987) did not find any greater likelihood of paternal psychopathology. Approximately 10% of fathers of children with an anxiety disorder and 10% of fathers of children in a nonclinical control group showed evidence of APD or alcohol abuse.

Two retrospective studies of adults diagnosed with an anxiety disorder provide evidence of a connection between paternal functioning and later development of an anxiety disorder in offspring. Fathers of undergraduate and graduate students who experienced subclinical levels of OCD were more overprotective, critical, and perfectionistic than fathers of students who did not develop OCD (Frost, Steketee, Cohn, & Griess, 1994). In a sample of male Vietnam veterans who were diagnosed with PTSD, recollections of negative paternal behaviors were more predictive of PTSD symptoms than the type and amount of combat exposure (McCranie, Hyer, Boudewyns, & Woods, 1992). Overall, there appears to be some support for a link between anxiety disorders in children and greater psychopathology or negative parenting in fathers. However, the small number of studies in this area make these conclusions tentative at best. In addition, because there are so few comprehensive studies in this area, it is difficult to speculate on the etiological factors that are most strongly associated with the development of different anxiety disorders.

SCHIZOPHRENIA

Schizophrenia is a severe psychopathology that is characterized by hallucinations, delusions, lack of self-care, and nonnormative emotional expressions (such as blunted affect or labile affect). Although the lifetime prevalence is relatively low (less than 1%), schizophrenia warrants attention because of the disruption that it causes for diagnosed individuals and their families. Childhood schizophrenia is extremely rare, and the onset of the first psychotic episode is usually in the early to mid-20s for men and in the late 20s for women (American Psychiatric Association, 1994).

Paternal Schizophrenia

Not surprisingly, there is little research on schizophrenic fathers. Schizophrenic men are unlikely to marry and take part in the parenting of their offspring (Watt, 1986). In a sample of psychiatric outpatients (most of whom were diagnosed with schizophrenia), Coverdale, Schotte, Ruiz, Pharies, and Bayer (1994) found that 18 of the 35 participants (51%) had fathered children. There were 41 offspring born to these 18 fathers, and approximately half of the children were younger than 16 years old. Of the children who were younger than 16, 30% were being raised by their fathers and mothers together, 60% were being raised by their mothers alone, and the whereabouts of 10% were not known by their fathers. Coverdale and colleagues argued that more attention must be given to help schizophrenic men learn to prevent unwanted pregnancies and to engage in safer sex methods in order to prevent sexually transmitted diseases.

Findings from research on schizophrenic fathers are equivocal. Silverton, Mednick, Schulsinger, Parnas, and Harrington (1988) found that offspring of schizophrenic fathers had brain abnormalities (such as cerebral ventricular enlargement) and lower birthweight than offspring of fathers in a nonclinical control group. However, Itil, Huque, Shapiro, Mednick, and Schulsinger (1983) found that children of schizophrenic fathers differed from children of fathers in a nonclinical control group on only 4 out of 22 EEG measures.

With regard to the adjustment of children of schizophrenic fathers, very little is known. A number of large-scale prospective studies have followed offspring of schizophrenic parents (reviewed in Rolf et al., 1990; Watt, Anthony, Wynne, & Rolf, 1984). However, the majority of reports combined analyses of fathers and mothers who were schizophrenic or only investigated the offspring of schizophrenic mothers. Erlenmeyer-Kimling and colleagues (1984) found that children had the same likelihood of needing psychological services whether their fathers or their mothers were schizophrenic. Similar results were found by el-Guebaly and colleagues (1978). Children of schizophrenic fathers reported less acceptance and less involvement from their fathers when compared with children of fathers without a psychiatric disorder.

Overall, there are too little data to draw firm conclusions on the adjustment level of the offspring of schizophrenic fathers. Even if it is rare that men with schizophrenia interact with their children, the mothers of these children are also likely to be psychologically disturbed given the prevalence of assortative mating (Merikangas et al., 1988). With regard to mechanisms of transmission, it appears that children of schizophrenic fathers may be at risk for greater levels of brain abnormalities and psychological maladjustment, presumably due to a combination of genetic and environmental factors related to their functioning.

Schizophrenia in Offspring

Although a strong genetic predisposition to schizophrenia is evident, a number of studies have investigated environmental and familial characteristics, such as expressed emotion and communication deviance, that are associated with increased risk for the development of schizophrenia (e.g., Hahlweg et al., 1989; Miklowitz et al., 1989; Strachan, Feingold, Goldstein, Miklowitz, & Nuechterlein, 1989). Although these studies usually include fathers and mothers in their samples, few analyses have investigated paternal and maternal characteristics separately.

The few studies that investigated paternal and maternal characteristics separately seemed to focus on characteristics associated with behavior related to therapeutic progress of the offspring who were schizophrenic. Severe discipline (Yesavage et al., 1983), hostility (Angermeyer, 1982), and overprotection (Onstad, Skre, Torgersen, & Kringlen, 1993) from fathers were associated with increased symptoms and decreased treatment gains in adults with schizophrenia.

AUTISM

Research on the rare disorder of autism has only focused on fathers (or mothers) of autistic children and not on autistic fathers (or mothers). Due to the nature of autism, it is extremely rare that individuals with severe autism would have offspring. With regard to fathers of autistic children, there is relatively consistent evidence that these fathers do not differ significantly from other fathers. Sanua reviewed studies conducted in England (1986a) and the United States (1986b) and found that fathers of autistic children do not show differences in personality characteristics or psychological adjustment when compared to fathers of children in nonclinical and clinical control groups.

An interesting line of research has emerged that investigates the impact of having a child who experiences autism. Freeman, Perry, and Factor (1991) argued that due to the potentially stressful nature of having a child with such special needs, researchers should focus on the level of stress in parents of autistic children in order to find ways to decrease the stress. Konstantareas and Homatidis (1989) found that autistic children's level of self-abuse was related to their father's level of stress, whereas Freeman et al. (1991) found that fathers' reports of child-related stress were associated with their overall level of stress as a parent. When comparing fathers and mothers, one study (Konstantareas & Homatidis, 1989) did not find a difference in levels of stress, but two studies (Freeman et al., 1991; Moes, Koegel, Schreibman, & Loos, 1992) found that mothers of autistic children reported significantly more stress than fathers. Findings from the Moes et al. study suggested that the greater amount of stress experienced by mothers was related to the greater amount of maternal child-care duties. Overall, recent research on parents of autistic children firmly contradict Kanner's (1943) notion of "refrigerator" parents.

ATTENTION-DEFICIT/HYPERACTIVITY DISORDER

Like autism, the majority of research on AD/HD has been conducted with fathers of children with AD/HD rather than with fathers who experience AD/HD. This trend may change in the future, given the relatively recent interest in adults who experience AD/HD (e.g., Kane, Mikalac, Benjamin, & Barkley, 1990). Longitudinal studies of AD/HD children who are now moving into adulthood (e.g., Barkley, Fischer, Edelbrock, & Smallish, 1990; see Weiss & Hechtman, 1986, for a review) should provide a wealth of information about the fathering behavior of men who had experienced or who continue to experience AD/HD. Because the preponderance of children diagnosed with AD/HD are boys (between 4:1 and 9:1 boys to girls), this area will be especially interesting for researchers on fathering and psychopathology. The prevalence of AD/HD in school-aged children is estimated at 3% to 5% (American Psychiatric Association, 1994).

Relatively clear patterns emerge in studies that have explored characteristics of the fathers of AD/HD children. When investigating paternal psychopathology in samples of AD/HD and nonclinical children, few differences are found. Fathers of AD/HD children do not show higher levels of depression (Cunningham, Benness, & Siegel, 1988) or higher rates of alcohol abuse or APD (Reeves et al., 1987) when compared with fathers of children in a nonclinical control group. Similarly, fathers of AD/HD children were no different than fathers of conduct-disordered children in their likelihood of experiencing APD or substance abuse (Lahey et al., 1988). In fact, fathers of AD/HD children were less likely than fathers of conduct-disordered children to have experienced a major depressive episode within the past year. When exploring childhood psychiatric histories, fathers of AD/HD children were more likely than fathers of other clinically referred children to have been diagnosed with AD/HD during their own childhood (Frick et al., 1991). There were no differences in childhood histories of antisocial behavior or substance abuse when fathers of AD/HD children were compared with fathers of children in a clinical control group. Overall, Barkley (1990) suggested that there is more evidence for genetic and biological linkages to the development of AD/HD, although parental and psychosocial factors can increase the likelihood of development of AD/HD for those at risk.

An interesting area of research relates to the level of alcohol consumption of fathers who have a child diagnosed with AD/HD. Cunningham and colleagues (1988) found that fathers of AD/HD children reported significantly more drinks of alcohol per week than did fathers of children in the nonclinical control group. A laboratory-based study by Lang, Pelham, Johnston, and Gelernter (1989) provided evidence that fathers' drinking may be influenced by their child's heightened level of behavioral activity. Male and female young adult participants in the study were randomly assigned to interact with a child confederate who was either role playing a "normal" child or an "AD/HD conduct-disordered" child. After interacting with the child for approximately 18 minutes, the participants were allowed to drink as much alcohol as they desired while waiting to interact with the child again. Both men and women showed greater distress in response to the "AD/HD conduct-disordered" child, but only men showed a propensity to consume more alcohol as a result of their interactions with the child. Based on blood-alcohol levels, men who had interacted with the "AD/HD conduct-disordered" child and who thought they would be interacting with him again drank significantly more than men who had interacted with the "normal" child. Lang and colleagues suggested that this laboratory-based study may help put into context the greater consumption of alcohol by fathers of AD/HD children. When stress level is considered, mothers of AD/HD children reported more parenting stress than fathers (Baker, 1994).

EATING DISORDERS

Research on eating disorders has focused on the fathers of disordered children and adolescents. Because bulimia nervosa and anorexia nervosa primarily occur in females (more than 90% of those with an eating disorder are female), it is unlikely that research will ever focus on children of eating-disordered fathers. Although full-blown eating disorders are fairly rare (less than 1% and 3% of the population meet criteria for anorexia nervosa and bulimia nervosa, respectively), a significant portion of girls and women have subthreshold levels of eating disorders and body image disturbance that cause distress and result in the need for therapeutic intervention (American Psychiatric Association, 1994).

The findings on paternal characteristics related to eating disorders in daughters are complex, depending on the specific disorder that is investigated, the type of methodology that is used, and the specific informant who is questioned. For example, Calam, Waller, Slade, and Newton (1990) found that anorexic and bulimic young women were more likely than nonclinical controls to report lower levels of paternal care and higher levels of paternal overprotection during childhood. Kendler, MacLean, et al. (1991) also found lower levels of paternal care reported by bulimic women when compared to nonbulimic women but did not find higher levels of overprotectiveness. Fathers of daughters with anorexia were also found to be less emotionally involved with their daughters than were fathers of daughters without an eating disorder (Telerant, Kronenberg, Rabinovitch, & Elman, 1992).

These findings did not hold up when a clinical control group was utilized. Russell, Kopec-Schrader, Rey, and Beumont (1992) found that anorexic adolescents reported their fathers as more caring than adolescents referred for other psychiatric problems. Overall, anorexic adolescents were more similar to the adolescents in the nonclinical control group than adolescents in the clinical control group.

Humphrey and her colleagues (Humphrey, 1986, 1987, 1989; Humphrey, Apple, &

Kirschenbaum, 1986) have conducted a series of complex investigations of families of adolescents with or without an eating disorder. Using structural analysis of social behavior, and based on direct observations of family interactions, Humphrey (1989) found that fathers of bulimic daughters were more hostilely enmeshed with their daughters, and they appeared to undermine their daughters' attempts at self-assertion and separation. More consistent associations were found for the father-daughter relationship than for the mother-daughter relationship in a sample of bulimic adolescents (Humphrey, 1986).

Overall, the father-daughter relationship appears to be problematic when families with an eating-disordered daughter are compared with families in a nonclinical control group. However, these differences may not be as strong when families with an eating-disordered daughter are compared with families in which a daughter meets criteria for a psychiatric diagnosis other than an eating disorder. More research is needed to clarify the similarities and differences in the father-daughter relationship with regard to different types of eating disorders and with regard to other types of maladjustment.

Given that there are a number of strong associations between paternal characteristics and child characteristics related to maladjustment, it is disheartening to find that there is not more known about the mechanisms related to the development and maintenance of psychopathology in children and fathers. Although a thorough understanding of etiology would be ideal before attempting amelioration of psychopathology, a number of interventions have been attempted and have been found successful in the treatment of psychopathology in children and adolescents (see Weisz & Weiss, 1993, for review). With regard to the investigation of paternal involvement in therapeutic interventions, research into fathers' involvement in therapy has lagged behind the consideration of mothers' involvement in therapy. However, enough information has been collected to provide a template for research that is needed.

EFFECTIVENESS OF FATHERS' INVOLVEMENT IN THERAPY

Clinical psychologists have pursued two primary avenues in considering paternal involvement in therapy. Clinical researchers have conducted empirical investigations into the effectiveness of paternal involvement in child- and family-oriented treatment. Concomitantly, clinicians have written about their experiences in engaging fathers in therapy and about the outcome of fathers' involvement in therapy.

CLINICAL RESEARCH

Although the overall efficacy of a variety of therapeutic interventions for children and adolescents has been investigated (e.g., Barrnett, Docherty, & Frommelt, 1991; Casey & Berman, 1985; Hazelrigg, Cooper, & Borduin, 1987; Kazdin, 1991; Weisz & Weiss, 1993), only behavioral parent training interventions have been investigated to establish directly the possible impact of paternal involvement in the therapeutic process. Note that "involvement" for both fathers and mothers is operationalized as attendance in therapy rather than as active participation or motivation within the therapeutic process. In the four studies completed in this area (Adesso & Lipson, 1981; Firestone, Kelly, & Fike, 1980; B. Martin, 1977; Webster-Stratton, 1985), father involvement, mother involvement, or both father and mother involvement in behavioral parent training resulted in approximately equal therapeutic benefits for the child. As is appropriate for behavioral parent training (Barkley, 1987), all of these studies investigated families of children aged 11 and younger who evidenced emotional/behavioral problems that were primarily externalizing in nature. Two studies (Firestone et al., 1980; B. Martin, 1977) randomly assigned families to a mother-only, a mother and father, or a no-treatment control condition. In addition to random assignment to these three conditions, Adesso and Lipson (1981) also had a fourth condition of father-only treatment. The fourth study (Webster-Stratton, 1985) did not randomly assign families to different conditions, but rather placed families in the father-involved condition if the father was present in the household and placed families in the father-absent condition if the father was not present in the household.

Overall, the results of these four studies were consistent. Behavioral parent training was more effective than no treatment in decreasing problematic child behavior, and there were no differences between treatment groups (i.e., mother involved, father involved, or both mother and father involved) after treatment based on parental reports of child behavior. The two caveats to this summary were that Firestone and colleagues (1980) only found decreased child behavior problems as a result of treatment when parent reports of child behavior problems were utilized. When teacher reports were utilized, there were no differences between the treatment and control groups. The other additional finding was that Webster-Stratton (1985) found superior maintenance of treatment gains in the father-involved families at one-year follow-up when compared with the father-absent families. However, this result may have been due to factors other than who was involved in treatment, given that the father-absent families may have had increased stressors and economic hardship due to the mothers' status as single parents.

Overall, the inclusion of fathers in behavioral parent training is no more advantageous or disadvantageous for improvement of children's behavior than the inclusion of mothers in the treatment. This leads to the next topic of the differential benefits for mothers and fathers when they are both involved in treatment. The majority of studies (Alexander et al., 1989; Dadds, Sanders, Behrens, & James, 1987; Mann, Borduin, Henggeler, & Blaske, 1990; Nicol et al., 1988; Webster-Stratton, 1992; Webster-Stratton, Hollinsworth, & Kolpacoff, 1989; Webster-Stratton, Kolpacoff, & Hollinsworth, 1988) have found similar levels of improvement for mothers and fathers when they are involved in a variety of types of therapy. In a study of mothers involved in behavioral parent training, Reisinger (1982) found that fathers also learned similar skills (e.g., differential attention skills in order to ignore maladaptive behavior and pay attention to adaptive behavior) as mothers even though they were not involved in therapy directly. Fathers' improvements in parenting skills were attributed to unprogrammed learning that the mother transferred from the treatment setting to the father at home. Only one study was identified (Henggeler et al., 1986) in which more improvements in the mother-adolescent relationship than the father-adolescent relationship were found in conjunction with a significant decrease in problematic behavior by the adolescent.

Overall, there is no evidence that either parent is superior to the other in their involvement in therapy. This conclusion is limited to behavioral parent training and should be investigated for other types of therapy (Coplin & Houts, 1991). When both mothers and fathers are involved in a wide variety of child- and family-oriented therapy, similar benefits occur for each parent.

CLINICAL WRITINGS

Although the increased efficacy of paternal involvement in therapy has not been established, a number of clinicians who practice therapeutic techniques other than behavioral parent training have made suggestions for how to ensure paternal involvement in child- and family-oriented therapy. Because fathers are somewhat less likely to be involved in child or adolescent therapy (Churven, 1978; Szapocznik et al., 1988), a number of clinicians have suggested techniques for increasing the likelihood of paternal involvement in psychological treatment. For example, Doherty (1981) suggested that fathers' participation in treatment should be explained as "automatic" at the time of the first intake phone call. Similarly, Feldman (1990) argued that therapists are often responsible for paternal uninvolvement because they do not include fathers in the initial stages of the therapeutic process. There is empirical evidence to support the claim that therapists often serve as gatekeepers for fathers' participation in therapy. For example, Lazar, Sagi, and Fraser (1991) found that therapist characteristics were significantly related to their inclusion of fathers in therapy. Specifically, therapists were significantly more likely to include both mothers and fathers in treatment when they were male, newer to the profession, more educated in family therapy techniques through coursework, and more likely to espouse egalitarian beliefs about family responsibilities. In addition, when the agency or practice in which therapists provided therapy was supportive of family involvement, offered child welfare services, and offered flexible appointment times such as evening and weekend hours, therapists were more likely to include fathers in treatment.

Given that clinical researchers often do not include fathers in empirical investigations of therapeutic effectiveness (Budd & O'Brien, 1982), it is not surprising that clinicians may be reluctant to include fathers in treatment. There may also be reluctance on the part of fathers to get involved in child or family therapy. Guillebeaux, Storm, and Demaris (1986) found that men were more likely to participate in marriage and family therapy if they had nontraditional gender role orientation, if they perceived their family problems to be quite serious, and if they had prior experience in therapy. Men who were initially reluctant to attend therapy were rated by therapists as less resistant after attending the initial intake session. Once fathers are involved in therapy, emotional expression (Liddle, 1994), ethnic and cultural values (McGoldrick, Pearce, & Giordano, 1982; Yaccarino, 1993), and paternal psychopathology (Jacobsen, Sweeney, & Racusin, 1993; Maguin et al., 1994) must be considered.

Because fathers are often not in the family household, a number of clinicians and researchers have commented on the importance of considering the inclusion of "absent" fathers in the therapeutic process. For example, Feldman (1990) suggested that therapists should at least consider whether or not to include noncustodial fathers in treatment. These decisions will obviously be dictated by the clinical issues that are of concern to the child and the family, but too often therapists seem to assume that they cannot even invite a noncustodial father into child- or family-oriented treatment. Frieman (1994) provided recommendations for how school counselors could involve noncustodial fathers in school-based therapy and home-based academic activities of their children.

A number of writers have also highlighted the psychological needs of fathers who no longer live with their children (Halperin & Smith, 1983; Jacobs, 1982, 1983; Richards & Goldenberg, 1985; Tillitski, 1992). For example, Greif and Kristall (1993) conducted group therapy sessions for noncustodial parents and identified a number of clinically relevant issues. Fathers who did not have primary parental responsibility for their children struggled with their children's rejection of them as parents, their own psychological rejection of their children, emotional triangulation, holiday visitation schedules, children's adjustment to divorce, and difficulties with their own parents' grandparent-grandchild relationship with their children. Tillitski (1992) argued that therapists must become conversant in these issues, even if they do not focus on child-oriented treatment. In addition, teen fathers have been identified as having unique and often neglected psychological needs in relation to their children (Kiselica, Stroud, Stroud, & Rotzien, 1992). Many men and older adolescents in individual therapy may need help with their parental role, whether or not they have primary residential responsibilities for their children.

FUTURE DIRECTIONS

Throughout this chapter, areas in need of research have been highlighted. The topic of the father-child relationship and children's abnormal adjustment has lagged behind the study of the father-child relationship and children's normative adjustment. A number of areas deserve further attention.

The areas that Phares and Compas (1992) delineated continue to require attention. They argued that researchers of developmental psychopathology should focus on conducting separate analyses of maternal and paternal factors, identifying mechanisms through which paternal characteristics influence children's well-being, identifying moderating variables between father-child relationships in relation to the development of psychopathology, and exploring risk and protective factors in relation to the risk associated with children's maladjustment. In addition, researchers should be more clear about the theoretical model they are testing and should put their studies in a broader context in order to help understand the relations between paternal characteristics and children's adjustment. Just as in the study of normative developmental processes (Starrels, 1994; Steinberg, 1987), it will be important to explore gender differences of both parents and children (e.g., father-son, father-daughter, mother-son, and mother-daughter relations) in the study of nonnormative developmental processes.

Phares (1992, 1996) also noted the importance of questioning sexist and mother-blaming research. Similarities among maternal and paternal factors in relation to children's maladjustment should be explored as well as the differences between these factors. Researchers should also move toward the investigation of common themes within contemporary families, regardless of whether these themes were once thought to be more traditionally a mother's concern or a father's concern. For example, the investigation of paternal separation anxiety, in addition to maternal separation anxiety, by Deater-Deckard and colleagues (1994) is a step in the right direction given that "parental" separation anxiety used to be considered the mothers' domain. Similarly, the work by Greenberger and colleagues (e.g., Greenberger & Goldberg, 1989;

Greenberger & O'Neil, 1990) has extended the investigation of employment satisfaction and family functioning to both fathers and mothers.

As more individual empirical studies of child maladjustment and the father-child relationship are published, the next step will be to conduct meta-analyses of the individual findings in order to arrive at higher order conclusions. Rothbaum and Weisz (1994) conducted a meta-analysis of studies that investigated the relation between parental caregiving and externalizing behavior problems in children and adolescents from nonclinical samples. Based on the analysis of effect sizes in 15 studies, they found that maternal caregiving was more strongly associated with children's externalizing problems than was paternal caregiving. This finding was in direct conflict with Loeber and Stouthamer-Loeber's (1986) meta-analysis that suggested paternal caregiving was more crucial than maternal caregiving in relation to delinquency in clinically referred samples of youth. The different methodologies of these two meta-analyses may point to different processes within families of children and adolescents with externalizing problems. Whereas the Loeber and Stouthamer-Loeber (1986) meta-analysis focused on referred samples of adolescents who evidenced delinquency, the Rothbaum and Weisz (1994) meta-analysis focused on nonreferred samples of both children and adolescents. It may be that paternal caregiving is more strongly associated with extreme levels of externalizing problems (as is evident in delinquency), while maternal caregiving is more strongly associated with elevated, but less severe, levels of externalizing problems in children and adolescents. These meta-analyses illustrate the usefulness of conducting empirical reviews of large numbers of studies in order to provide more firm conclusions than are possible with only one single study. The different conclusions of these two meta-analyses also point to the need for investigations into a variety of different dimensions, including developmental level, severity of maladjustment, and clinical referral status. In addition, only through comprehensive studies, reviews, and meta-analyses can researchers begin to establish etiological mechanisms associated with the development of psychopathology in children and adolescents.

Overall, when fathers and mothers are both assessed, relatively similar patterns emerge in relation to children's adjustment for most types of developmental psychopathology. However, clinical researchers still appear to be hesitant to include fathers in their research designs to the same extent as they include mothers. Although this tendency may be due to the perceptions of difficulty in recruitment of fathers, the enormous literature that is reviewed in this book attests to fathers' willingness to be involved in research related to their children. It is time that clinical researchers and clinical therapists stop serving as gatekeepers who prevent fathers' involvement in research and therapy.

CHAPTER 16

Fathers, the Missing Parents in Research on Family Violence

Kathleen J. Sternberg

National Institute of Child Health and Human Development

O VER THE PAST 30 YEARS there has been increased public awareness about child and spouse abuse and their impact on children's development. These concerns have fostered research that began with case studies and clinical reports and is developing into a field characterized by more careful scientific inquiry. Unfortunately, however, the study of violence in the family has been hampered by a number of logistical, ethical, and sociopolitical issues that have made it difficult and very expensive to conduct large-scale experimental studies. This reality has led to an empirical literature characterized by a number of methodological compromises. Although there have been considerable improvements in research design in this field, a number of problems still exist, including failure to carefully document all types of abuse in the family, lack of specificity about who is the perpetrator of the various types of violence in the family, and reliance on single informants for information about family history and outcome measures for parents and children.

A review of the literature on children's victimization and observation of violence in the family reveals a conspicuous lack of information from and about fathers in these families. Although fathers are frequently portrayed as the perpetrators of family violence (Silverstein, 1996), little is actually known about the roles played by fathers and other male figures in these families. The purpose of this chapter is to review the limited available data about fathers in violent families and to explore some of the reasons why empirical data about fathers are so sparse in the family violence literature. Recent statistics suggest that a significant proportion of males involved in violence against women and children are not biologically related to the children or married to the women (Bachman & Salzman, 1995; Blankenhorn, 1995). It seems reasonable to assume that the effects on children of witnessing or being victims of domestic violence

I am grateful to Jeffrey Edelson, Richard Gelles, Ernest Jouriles, and Michael Lamb for their helpful comments on earlier versions of this chapter.

may differ depending on the relationships between the men and children in question. Abuse by transient male figures may be less harmful to children than abuse by men with whom the children and their mothers have meaningful and enduring relationships, but these issues have not been explored systematically. In this chapter I include all men in protoparental roles when I speak of "fathers," the inadequacies and inaccuracies of this term notwithstanding.[1] Violence by transient male figures needs to be distinguished from violence by family members or individuals who have more than transient relationships with mothers and their children.

The chapter begins with a description of how child and spouse abuse came to be recognized as social problems and how the sociopolitical process has influenced research on family violence in general, and as it relates to fathers in particular. This is followed by a section in which I review incidence and prevalence statistics related to child maltreatment and spouse abuse and describe what is known about the differences in the rates and patterns of abuse by mothers and fathers. In this section, statistics concerning the co-occurrence of child and spouse abuse are discussed.

The chapter continues with an overview of the major theoretical attempts to explain the etiology of maltreatment and to develop reliable ways of identifying perpetrators of abuse and predicting which parents are likely to abuse their children or spouses. This is followed by an overview of studies that have focused on comparing parent-child interactions in violent and nonviolent families. In this context, I illustrate how rare it is to include fathers in these studies. Research depicting children's perceptions of their parents is described, and the methodological implications of failing to discriminate between perpetrating and nonperpetrating parents are highlighted. Several recent studies that explore the role of the father in violent families using maternal reports about children's behavior problems and the limitations inherent in relying on maternal reports in violent families are also discussed. Directions and recommendations for future research are presented.

WHY AREN'T FATHERS INCLUDED IN STUDIES OF FAMILY VIOLENCE?

Although a number of researchers have emphasized the importance of collecting data about the role of the father in violent families (Cicchetti & Toth, 1993; Geffner, Rosenbaum, Hughes, & O'Leary, 1988; Mash, 1991; National Research Council, Panel on Child Abuse and Neglect, 1993; Sternberg et al., 1993; Wolfe, 1987), only a handful of researchers have explored the father's role in a comprehensive fashion. A review of the literature reveals that the field has evolved without much information about fathers. The unspoken assumption has been that information from mothers is sufficient.

There are a number of reasons why research on fathers from violent families is so sparse. Because of the difficulties in collecting data on family violence from middle- and upper-middle-class families, most researchers have collected data about child and spouse abuse from social service agencies like child protective services and battered women's shelters. This dependence constrains the generalizability of many published

---

1. Because of space limitations, the focus of this chapter is confined to physically violent families; I do not address families in which sexual abuse has occurred.

findings. In addition, the goals and structure of these settings have important implications for collecting information about fathers in violent families. Traditionally, child protection agencies have not routinely involved fathers in their diagnostic and treatment programs (Jaffe, 1983; Wolins, 1983). These agencies tend to be staffed primarily by women, to be open during routine business hours when fathers might be working, and to have mother-headed families as their primary (though not exclusive) clientele. These agencies have made limited efforts to reach out to fathers. They consider mothers rather than fathers largely responsible for their children's well-being and rely on mothers as the primary source of information about the family. In some jurisdictions, keeping fathers and father figures out of the picture is reinforced by the fact that benefits like AFDC are terminated when father figures live with their wives or female partners. Low-income women are thus encouraged to hide or distort the role played by fathers or male partners for fear of losing financial support for their children. This practice decreases researchers' access to fathers and father figures who are afraid to demonstrate their involvement in these families (Cicchetti & Toth, 1993). The lack of empirical data about the involvement of these men reflects an implicit assumption that men do not play meaningful roles in children's lives. Unfortunately, this assumption has not been addressed empirically.

With respect to children who witness spousal violence, the empirical data about fathers is even more sparse. Because of limited funding and the difficulty inherent in identifying community samples of children who observe spousal violence, researchers interested in this topic tend to recruit samples from battered women's shelters. Heavily sponsored by women's advocacy organizations, the primary role of these shelters is to protect women from violent spouses. Children are viewed as secondary clients, and the fathers of these children are viewed as spouse abusers. Because of the advocacy role assumed by many of these shelters, researchers have had to be very careful about the types of information they collect from women and children. In some cases, shelter staff have been reluctant to cooperate with researchers (Walker, 1995) and have raised concerns about researchers who ask questions about fathers and the roles they play. The shelter staff perceive their primary role as the protection of women from batterers, and they are unwilling to put their clients at risk for the sake of research. Even when shelters permit researchers to collect data about the effects of witnessing family violence, therefore, it is important to recognize that the quality and comprehensiveness of information collected in these settings may be compromised by the inability to collect information about the fathers' roles in these families. In an attempt to rectify the need for more information about the role of fathers in violent families, some researchers have recently begun to interview women about the roles their husbands or exhusbands played as fathers. Although it is extremely important to learn more about the roles played by fathers from families in which marital violence was reported, one must question the validity of information about father-child relationships provided by women who were battered by these men. Fortunately, some researchers have attempted, in the past few years, to identify battered women living in the community (e.g., McCloskey, Figueredo, & Koss, 1995). Although these studies eliminate confounds associated with shelter life, most of these researchers have not considered paternal roles and perspectives. A few researchers have even identified nonclinical samples in the community and have asked both partners about spousal disagreements and violence (e.g., O'Brian, Margolin, & John, 1995; Sternberg et al., 1994).

Recent research exploring the discrepant information obtained from different informants about violence in the family and its effects on children underscores some of the methodological problems that result when mothers are the primary or sole informants (see Sternberg, Lamb, & Dawud-Noursi, 1996, for a review of this topic). In a recent study, for example, Kaufman and her colleagues (Kaufman, Jones, Stieglitz, Vitulano, & Mannarino, 1994) reported that it was possible to obtain a more comprehensive picture of the frequency and severity of child abuse by collecting information from multiple sources (mothers, medical records, and observations in the home) than by relying solely on data from protective service workers. Similarly, researchers comparing husbands' and wives' reports of marital violence report that the apparent incidence of spousal violence may vary depending on whether the husband or wife is the reporter, particularly when agreement about specific violent incidents is of interest (Jouriles & O'Leary, 1985; Szinovacz, 1983). Interestingly, approximately 40% of the incongruities between spouses' reports about their aggressive behaviors may be the result of underreporting of aggression by both men and women (Langhinrichsen-Rohling & Vivian, 1994; see O'Brien, John, Margolin, & Erel, 1994, for a review of this topic). Similar concerns about informant unreliability have been raised with respect to reliance on single informants for information about the effects of child and spouse abuse on children (Sternberg et al., 1993; Sternberg et al., 1996).

Together, the results of these studies raise serious questions about the exclusive reliance on mothers for information about the history of family violence and its effects on children. They highlight the methodological risks of relying on single informants concerning family violence and make clear the importance of including information from multiple sources, including fathers.

Although there are many reasons why fathers and father figures are usually not included in research on family violence—including cost and the difficulties of locating and interviewing these men—there is now ample evidence that fathers are unique sources of information, whose perspectives may be of great importance to both researchers and clinicians.

THE EVOLUTION OF CHILD ABUSE AND SPOUSE ABUSE AS SOCIAL PROBLEMS

Although historical records suggest that domestic violence has existed from at least biblical times (Radbill, 1968; Starr, 1987), professionals in North America did not recognize abuse as a social problem until recently (Pfohl, 1977). Even after radiologists demonstrated that many of the injuries presented by children in emergency rooms could not have happened by accident (Caffey, 1946), pediatricians avoided considering parents as potential perpetrators and continued to focus on "accidental injuries" (Starr, 1987). Only in 1955, when Wooley and Evans severely criticized pediatricians for their refusal to recognize their responsibilities, did Kempe and his colleagues begin to evaluate the pattern of injuries systematically, coining the term "battered child syndrome" (Helfer & Kempe, 1987; Kempe, Silverman, Steele, Droegemueller, & Silver, 1962).

In the 30 years that have passed since the emergence of the "battered child syndrome," a number of attempts have been initiated to improve our understanding of the extent, antecedents, and consequences of physical child abuse. We have discovered that the etiology of abuse is multifaceted and complicated, and that the effects, too, are much more complex than originally believed.

In the meantime, another social problem—spouse abuse—was "discovered," and many have become concerned about the effects on children who witness marital violence (Straus, Gelles, & Steinmetz, 1980). Women's organizations and feminist groups were the first to direct attention to spousal violence and coined the term "battered women." It is only in the past 10 years that spousal violence has gained wider public recognition as a social problem, with public and professional attention focused on the way conjugal violence may affect the physical and psychological well-being of children. As in the case of the battered child syndrome, the etiology of spousal abuse is very complex. As Margolin, Sibner, and Gleberman (1988) pointed out, competing theories of spousal violence have little empirical evidence to support them. Even fewer empirical studies have tested the relative explanatory power of different theories in explaining conjugal violence.

Recognizing the complexities of family violence has not been an easy task for clinicians, researchers, or the public at large, but within the last decade psychologists, sociologists, social workers, physicians, historians, and anthropologists have improved our understanding of the antecedents and effects of domestic violence on children. Perhaps because different advocacy groups and professional organizations were responsible for drawing attention to child and spouse abuse, these social problems have for the most part been investigated as unrelated phenomena (Edelson, 1995). Even today, researchers studying the effects of witnessing spousal violence remain somewhat isolated from the child abuse research community even though children who witness violence appear to behave quite like children who were physically or psychologically abused. The coordination of research on child abuse and marital violence would greatly benefit the field.

Unfortunately, the media have and continue to play an important role in defining social perceptions of child and spouse abuse. By focusing on sensational accounts of family violence, such as the O. J. Simpson trial, media attention fosters the development of "folk theories" about family violence, and these theories play an important role in shaping policy and intervention. Social scientists are often drawn into this process and inadvertently contribute to the promulgation of these theories by providing professional opinions that are only partially based on empirical findings.

THE INCIDENCE OF FAMILY VIOLENCE

In attempting to grapple with the problem of violence in the family, and to develop prevention and intervention programs, demographers have attempted to establish how many children are victims of child abuse or witnesses of spousal violence. The patterns of perpetration of violence by gender of parent and in different family constellations have also been explored by theorists. Researchers who have hypothesized that child abuse can be predicted by sociobiological theory, which focuses on the efficient allocation of resources as a means of enhancing inclusive fitness, have designed studies to test predictions about the differential propensities of men and women or of related and nonrelated caretakers to abuse children (Daly & Wilson, 1984; Malkin & Lamb, 1994). Other researchers have used varying rates of child abuse in different segments of the population to help understand the specific circumstances that place children at risk for child abuse or witnessing violence. In this section such data are used to illustrate the difficulties involved in developing estimates of the incidence of abuse, as well as of their co-occurrence; My primary goal here is to describe the problems in assessing the number of children potentially exposed to harm by virtue of their parents' violent behavior.

It is important to acknowledge that estimates of the incidence of child and spouse abuse differ as a function of how these behaviors are defined, the source of information (e.g., victim, parent, and service records), the research design, and a variety of other factors. Statistics can be used to paint very different pictures of any given phenomenon, and they have often been used to buttress specific points that authors wish to convey. These issues become particularly important in estimating the frequency with which fathers are identified as perpetrators of physical abuse, perpetrators of spousal violence witnessed by children, and partners of women who behave violently toward their children or their husbands.

INCIDENCE OF PHYSICAL CHILD ABUSE

The National Center on Child Abuse and Neglect commissioned two studies to assess the incidence of child maltreatment: NIS-1 in 1980 and NIS-2 in 1986 (Office of Human Development Services, 1988; a third study has been completed and data will soon be released). Information was collected from county service agencies (schools, CPS agencies, etc.) in a research design that was nationally representative. In the NIS-1, the definition of maltreatment was based on a "standard of harm" (whether the child was actually injured), whereas in NIS-2 the definition was based on "standard of harm and endangerment" (whether the child was at risk of harm). Based on the "harm standard" of the NIS-2, it was estimated in 1986 that approximately 0.4% of children under age 18 were physically abused, 0.2% were sexually abused, and 0.3% were neglected.

Arguing that data collected from agency records provide only a partial picture of the prevalence of family violence, researchers at the Universities of Rhode Island and New Hampshire have conducted nationally representative telephone surveys to explore the prevalence of family violence (Gelles & Straus, 1988; Straus & Gelles, 1986, 1990). In a large nationally representative survey ($n = 6002$) conducted in 1985, 2.3% of the parents (one parent from each household) reported that they had punched, kicked, bit, burned, beat, or threatened a child (3 to 17 years old) in their household with a knife or gun in the preceding 12 months. If one considers incidents in which children were hit with objects (sticks, belts, etc.) as abuse, 11% of the children were reported to have been abused (Straus & Gelles, 1990). These statistics reflect much higher rates of violence than estimates based on CPS records. In attempting to explain discrepancies between these estimates and their own, Straus and Gelles (1986) emphasized that the NIS estimates represent the number of cases referred for intervention, whereas their surveys assess the admitted incidents of physical maltreatment, many of which may be unknown to service agencies. They argue that the design of their Family Violence Surveys, particularly the anonymous nature of data collection, fosters more accurate estimates of violence in the family. Researchers at the Family Research Laboratory recently extended the survey paradigm developed by Straus and Gelles and conducted phone interviews using children as informants about family violence. Two thousand 10- to 16-year-old children participated in a random telephone survey designed to obtain a comprehensive picture of victimization within and outside the family (Finkelhor & Dziuba-Leatherman, 1994). Twenty-seven percent of the girls and 30% of the boys reported that their parents had used corporal punishment in the last year, whereas 71% percent of the girls and 78% percent of the boys had experience corporal punishment at some time in their lives. With respect to more serious parent-child maltreatment, 0.9% of the children reported an incident (punching, slapping, kicking, hitting with an object, or threatening with a weapon) in the last year, and 2.2% reported at least one incident of maltreatment ever. Interestingly, children were more likely to have been assaulted by nonparent family perpetrators (5%) and nonfamilial perpetrators (22%) than by a parent. In addition, it was interesting to find that although two-thirds of the youth interviewed disclosed the assault to someone, only 25% reported the assaults to authorities.

It is difficult to compare the results of these different studies because the age of the target children, the source of data, and the definitions of abusive events vary across studies. Children in the Finkelhor and Dziuba-Leatherman sample reported lower rates of parent-child violence than parents in the Straus and Gelles surveys, for example, but the children's ages differed substantially. Gelles and Straus focused on violence toward 0- to 17-year-old children, whereas Finkelhor and Dziuba-Leatherman focused on 10- to 17-year-old children. The discrepancies nonetheless show how difficult it is to develop accurate estimates of child abuse and underscore the importance of "reading the fine print" when evaluating statistics about child abuse and other types of violence in the family. Clearly, differences in sampling methodologies influence the estimates obtained.

Are There Differences in the Rates of Physical Child Abuse Perpetrated by Mothers and Fathers?

Evaluation of the relative prevalence of abuse by mothers and fathers requires a careful examination of the survey data. In some of the major surveys, researchers have concluded that female caretakers are more likely than male caretakers to be identified as perpetrators of physical child abuse (American Association for Protecting Children [AAPC], 1986; Gil, 1973; National Center on Child Abuse and Neglect [NCAN], 1988; Straus et al., 1980; Wolfner & Gelles, 1993). All of these researchers acknowledge that these estimates are somewhat biased because female caretakers spend more time with children than male caretakers do, and some have estimated that fathers are more likely to be perpetrators of abuse than mothers when such differences in availability are taken into account (Lennington, 1981; Lightcap, Kurland, & Burgess, 1982; Malkin & Lamb, 1994). In an attempt to test several predictions of sociobiological theory, for example, Malkin and Lamb (1994) studied statistics collected from 11 states by the American Humane Society. In their sample, fathers were identified as perpetrators in more cases of physical abuse than mothers were. A closer examination of the data revealed that fathers engaged in more minor acts of abuse, while mothers engaged in more serious acts of abuse. These findings suggest that it is difficult to determine whether children are at greater risk of abuse by mothers or fathers and that the severity of abusive acts should also be considered.

Is Physical Child Abuse More Prevalent in Single-Parent Families?

Although clinicians have long argued that child abuse is more prevalent in single-parent than in dual-parent families, there was little empirical data to address this hypothesis until recently. Results of the Second Family Violence Survey suggest that, while overall rates of violence are the same in single- and dual-parent households, single parents ($n = 512$) were significantly more likely to engage in serious violence toward their children than were parents from dual-parent families ($n = 2,705$; Gelles, 1989). In evaluating mother-father differences in the prevalence of violence in these families, severity of violence emerges as an important dimension. While single fathers ($n = 58$) and single mothers ($n = 454$) were equally likely to behave violently toward their children, single fathers reported higher rates of severe violence than single mothers. Gelles conducted further analyses to explore some of the hypothesized explanations for heightened rates of severe violence in single-parent families. For households headed by single mothers, abuse was significantly correlated with poverty but was unrelated to maternal age and to residing with other adults in the household. For fathers, no clear pattern of association emerged, although the small number of single fathers earning less than $10,000 a year were at highest risk for severe child abuse.

Are Children Who Live with Nonbiological Caretakers at Heightened Risk for Physical Abuse?

For both practical and theoretical reasons, a number of researchers have asked whether nonrelated male careproviders (e.g., stepfathers or boyfriends) are more likely to abuse children than are biological fathers. Data from the study conducted by Daly and Wilson (1984) are often cited as alarming evidence of the risks of involving nonrelated males in the family. Daly and Wilson reported that children living with stepfathers were significantly more likely to be abused than children living with their biological fathers. However, because these researchers were not able to identify the perpetrators of abuse in these families, it was not possible to determine whether children were at heightened risk of being abused by their biological mothers, their stepfathers, or both. In order to address this concern, Malkin and Lamb (1994) included information about gender, relationship, and identity of perpetrator in their study. They found that biological caretakers were more likely to engage in major physical and fatal acts of child abuse whereas nonrelated caretakers were more likely to engage in minor acts of abuse. Although they reported that 28% of the children in this sample lived in families with one biological parent and one stepparent, Malkin and Lamb did not discuss differences between family units which included biological mothers and stepfathers as opposed to biological fathers and stepmothers.

In sum, the available data suggest that between 1% and 10% of the children in the United States may be victims of physical abuse. Questions about the relative risks of abuse by mothers and fathers, nonrelated caretakers, and single parents are not easy to answer, however. In order to improve our understanding of the prevalence of child abuse, it is obviously important to specify the identity of the perpetrator and their relationship to the child and not simply indicate that child abuse occurred. Unless researchers distinguish between perpetrating and nonperpetrating parents in child abuse statistics, our understanding of the phenomenon will continue to be limited. In addition, specificity about the severity of violence appears crucial.

INCIDENCE OF SPOUSAL VIOLENCE

Between 10% and 30% of the families living in the United States are believed to experience spouse abuse, depending on the definitions and the methodology (Geffner & Pagelow, 1990; Hughes, in press; Straus & Gelles, 1986). In the Second National Violence Study (Straus & Gelles, 1986), for example, approximately 3.4% of the women in the sample reported being severely assaulted (e.g., punched, bitten, burned, kicked, or choked) by their partners. Equivalent numbers of men reported being assaulted by their partners, although the survey methodology made it impossible to determine whether these assaults occurred in response to provocations or assaults, and whether the acts had similar effects on male and female victims (see Kurz, 1993, and Straus, 1993, for a discussion of this topic).

Defining spousal violence has proved to be very difficult, and this has influenced the conceptualization of spouse abuse as a social, legal, and research problem. Issues such as mutual violence between spouses, the use of violence as a tactic, as well as the frequency and duration of violence need to be considered when attempting to define and measure spouse abuse. Discussions focused on defining and estimating the incidence of spousal violence underscore the fact that it is not a simple undimensional phenomena but a very complex issue.

The National Crime Victimization Survey conducted by the Department of Justice (Bachman & Salzman, 1995) showed that women are more likely to be abused by boyfriends or exhusbands than by husbands. In the 1992–93 survey, approximately 29% of simple and aggravated assaults were committed by "intimates": spouses, 5% and 11%; exspouses, 5% and 4%; and boy- or girlfriends, 17% and 15%, respectively. Interestingly, most simple (41%) and aggravated (36%) assaults were committed by acquaintances or friends. This survey raises questions about whether fathers or father figures are the most probable perpetrators of violence against women and children or whether the men involved in abuse are more transient figures. From a child's perspective, the distinction between being abused by or observing your mother being abused by a permanent male figure as compared to a transient figure may have important implications for child adjustment. Researchers have only recently begun to address the phenomenon of transient versus more permanent male figures, and much more research is needed on this issue (see Margolin, 1992).

Although researchers did not systematically ask about the whereabouts of children during violent fights between their parents in most of the early studies, there is now accumulating evidence that children are present during these interactions. In one study, researchers reported that children were either in the same room or a room adjacent to the assault in 90% of the cases (Hughes, 1988). In another study, researchers reported that 25% of 8- to 11-year-old children described having witnessed husband-wife violence and wife-husband violence at least once in their lives (O'Brien et al., 1994). Dobash and Dobash (1984) found that 58% of the women in their study reported that children were present during assaults by their husbands. Although spouse abuse has traditionally been considered a social problem faced by women, these data suggest that a significant number of children are directly exposed to spousal violence. This reality has begun to foster serious concern about the impact of family violence on children, although it remains extremely difficult to estimate how many children are exposed to or are aware of spousal violence. Because "witnessing violence" does not leave clear signs of impact like some forms of child abuse, researchers must rely on verbal reports of participants and bystanders who were present.

Do Spouse and Child Abuse Co-occur in Families?

Although it is widely believed that men who abuse their wives are also likely to abuse their children, research exploring the co-occurrence of child and spouse abuse is sparse. While researchers have articulated several important questions related to the co-morbidity of child and spouse abuse, empirical data addressing these questions are only beginning to appear. Are children who live in families where there is abuse between the parents at heightened risk of child abuse? If so, are children at heightened risk of being abused by the same parent who perpetrated violence against a spouse, the parent who was the victim of spouse abuse, or both? Theoretical models focusing on the cultural acceptance of violent behavior as a means of problem solving could lead to a hypothesis that individuals who are in violent relationships with their partners are also likely to use violence as parents. Models concentrating on parental stress (e.g., being abused by a spouse) as explanations of abusive parenting would suggest that victims of spouse abuse would be more likely to abuse their children as well.

Data from two national surveys offer some support for each of these predictions. The data from the First National Family Violence Survey conducted in 1975 suggested that different types of violence within the family were linked to one another (Straus et al., 1980). "Ordinary marital violence" (pushing, slapping, or shoving) by husbands toward their wives was associated with an increase in violence by both fathers and mothers toward their children. Children whose mothers were abused by their husbands were approximately twice as likely to be abused by both their mothers and fathers than children whose mothers were not abused by their husbands. Furthermore, mothers who experienced more serious acts of abuse once or twice in the survey year were four times more likely to abuse their children than were fathers who perpetrated serious spousal violence once or twice. For fathers, those few who seriously abused their wives frequently (three or more times a year) were more likely than victims of frequent and serious spouse abuse to abuse their children. Fathers who frequently and severely abused their wives were five times more likely to abuse their children than fathers who did not abuse their partners.

A somewhat different picture emerged from the Second National Family Violence Survey (Straus & Gelles, 1990). Gelles reported that men who abused their wives were four and a half times more likely to abuse their children than men who did not behave violently with their partners. Women who were physically abused by their husbands were two and a half times more likely to abuse their children than women who were not abused by their partners. In order to understand how child and spouse abuse are related it is also necessary to explore the association between wife-husband violence and violence toward children. Data from the Second Family Violence Survey suggested that women who abused their husbands were 29% more likely to abuse their children than women who did not abuse their husbands (R. J. Gelles, personal communication, December 1995). When severe violence was examined, women who abused their husbands were more than twice as likely to abuse their children. When men were abused by their wives, they were 4% more likely to abuse their children than men who were not abused by their partners. Men who were abused by their partners were one and a half times more likely to abuse their children severely.

The data from the First and Second National Family Violence Surveys indicate that the statistical association between spouse and child abuse is more complex than often portrayed, perhaps depending on the perpetrators' and victims' sexes and the severity and frequency of the violence concerned. The data from these two surveys collectively suggest that children of women who are abused by their husbands are at heightened risk of child abuse by both their mothers and fathers, when compared with children of nonabused women. The association between male violence toward women and children is strongest for the small number of cases where women were severely abused by their partners. Children of men who were abused by their wives were somewhat more likely to be abused by both mothers and fathers, when compared with children of men who were not abused by their wives.

These data suggest that when there is violence in the spousal relationship, there is a significantly greater risk of child abuse. Nevertheless, most of the children whose parents were violent with each other were not victims of child abuse.

In sum, a review of the statistics about the incidence of child and spouse abuse suggests that questions about the relative risk of abuse by mothers as compared with fathers and related or nonrelated perpetrators are not simple to answer. The results of the studies reviewed in this section suggest that any discussion of the incidence of violence in the family should differentiate between minor and severe acts of violence. Additional research is needed to explore the co-occurrence of child and spouse abuse within families.

ADVOCACY ORGANIZATIONS AND RESEARCH ON FAMILY VIOLENCE

Advocacy organizations often use research to buttress their philosophies and advance the interests of their constituents. Unfortunately, this process often involves selecting only those findings that support a specific approach and ignoring other important findings (cf. Gilbert, 1993). Neither the radical "feminists" nor the "right-wing fathers' movement" have systematically used empirical research to inform the policy recommendations they espouse regarding family violence. Feminist scholars emphasize the risks of father-child contact in families where domestic violence has occurred, suggesting that fathers' primary or sole motivation for obtaining shared custody or visitation is to continue exerting power over their ex-wives. Although some of these scholars cite clinical research and case studies, these theories have not been submitted to careful scientific scrutiny and their scientific implications are thus limited (Margolin et al., 1988). By contrast, some members of the fathers' rights movement argue that an abusive father is better than no father at all. Again, although there are case studies demonstrating that men who abuse their partners can be good parents, these data offer inadequate support for the more radical position summarized here. Empirical studies are needed to assess the quality of parenting skills evinced by fathers who are violent toward their partners.

Although advocacy organizations have an important role to play in focusing public attention on children who live in violent families, the simplistic and selective way that they report research findings sometimes hampers the development of empirical research and its implications for policies related to children who are victims and witnesses of violence. When certain research questions become "politically incorrect" our understanding of important social issues like father-child relationships in violent families is impeded. Children's interests would be better served if these agencies were more careful in their presentation of research findings and more open to the complexities of violence and its impact on family relationships.

LEGISLATION, SOCIAL POLICY, AND RESEARCH

According to a recent report from the American Bar Association (Howard Davidson, Reporter, 1994), 38 states and the District of Columbia have enacted laws making domestic violence a relevant factor in the awarding of custody and visitation rights. In light of data suggesting that adults who abuse each other are more likely to abuse their children, and the growing body of evidence suggesting that witnessing spousal violence can have detrimental effects on children, this legislation appears consistent with empirical research. The fact that these states have laws that make domestic violence a factor for consideration but refrain from any more restrictive presumption (a policy adopted by 10 other states) about domestic violence is probably the ideal arrangement given what is known about family violence and its effects on children. Because "domestic violence" may refer to a diverse array of acts that differ in frequency and severity, the latitude offered by a "consideration" rather than a "presumption" appears preferable. We also know that not all violent spouses are violent parents and that their openness to treatment varies as well. Thus, knowing that a person has been violent with a spouse is only somewhat informative with respect to their parenting behavior and the quality of their relationship with their children.

In developing policies for violent families it is important to distinguish between children's needs for contact with their fathers and women's needs for protection from their violent partners. Custody negotiations are often used as a means of exerting power over ex-partners, and this issue is of particular concern in cases where a history of spousal abuse places women at continued risk of being abused by their ex-husbands. These women deserve protection and arrangements need to be made whereby their children can have access to their fathers without placing their mothers at risk. Protecting women from violent ex-spouses, however, is not necessarily at odds with fostering contact between children and their fathers. In her recent paper entitled "Fathering Is a Feminist Issue," Silverstein (1996) summarizes the complexities and biases involved in weighing the importance of the father-child relationship in violent families.

Our human tendency toward dualistic thinking has too often resulted in the conception of mothers as the protectors of children, and fathers as their abusers. Yet simply separating fathers from families often increases the danger for women; most murders of battered wives take place during separation. Furthermore, we know that mothers as well as fathers neglect and abuse children. Although abusive mothers are separated from their children, repairing the mother-child relationship usually remains a social policy priority. Abusive fathers who are sincere in their motivation to establish positive relationships with their children should be treated in a similar fashion. (p. 11)

In the past 10 years, institutes like the shelter in Duluth, Minnesota (McMahon & Pence, 1996), have begun to address children's needs for contact with their fathers while simultaneously protecting their mothers from contact with their ex-spouses. The expansion and development of innovative social programs like this one will continue to play an important role in addressing the needs of children, mothers, and fathers from violent families.

Just as there is no uniform picture of batterers (Gottman et al., 1995) or victims, there is no formulaic solution for deciding custody and visitation questions in families where violence has occurred. Instead, legal decisions about custody and child placement should be based on the individual merits of each case, taking into consideration the quality of the children's relationship with each of their parents. After evaluating the quality of children's relationships with each of their parents, all options need to be considered. Depending on the circumstances, it may be wise to have transitions between parents (for either custody or visitation) supervised by third parties. If there is reason to believe that the child's welfare is at risk while being supervised by either the mother or father, it may be wise to recommend supervised visitation, and in some extreme cases, it may be necessary to terminate contact between violent parents and their children.

PREDICTORS OF ABUSIVE BEHAVIOR TOWARD CHILDREN

In an effort to understand the etiology of child maltreatment, a number of researchers have attempted to develop models to explain abusive behavior by parents. The earliest theoretical model, the psychiatric model, used individual psychopathology of the abusive parent to explain child maltreatment. The initial psychiatric model was abandoned in the early 1970s as a number of researchers found that only 10% of the reported child abusers had identifiable psychiatric disorders (Parke & Collmer, 1975). These data, in combination with the changing sociopolitical climate, led researchers concerned with the etiology of maltreatment to focus on sociological models emphasizing the roles of factors such as unemployment, poverty, and social isolation in the etiology of abuse (e.g., Gil, 1975; Pelton, 1978). Sociologists have enriched our understanding of the etiology of abuse by demonstrating that child and spouse abuse occur in all social classes, not merely among the impoverished segments of society, and that family violence is not restricted to the parental mistreatment of children or to husbands' mistreatment of their wives. Stressful life circumstances are now widely recognized as major contributors to abuse, taxing the resources of parents who appear to have "normal" personalities and predisposing them to behave abusively. Sociologists have argued that wife-to-husband, adolescent-to-parent, and sibling-to-sibling abuse merit attention as well (Kalmuss, 1984; Straus & Gelles, 1986).

One popular paradigm for exploring the etiology of maltreatment has been the ecological model proposed by Belsky (1980, 1993). According to this model, the potential for abusing a child is affected by a number of proximal and distal variables ranging from individual parent and child characteristics to factors such as stress or support in the workplace, community resources, and cultural attitudes about the appropriateness of physical punishment and violence in the family. Although there is wide agreement about the importance of these factors, few researchers have included measures of all these ecological factors in their studies.

As the scientific community has grown to understand the complexity of child abuse, attempts have been made to develop more sophisticated models for explaining the etiology and effects of child maltreatment. A review of these approaches reveals that these models have advanced beyond the exploration of main effects and have been expanded to include interactions between individual characteristics of the perpetrators, characteristics of victims, and sources of stress and support in the family. As researchers improve their measurement strategies, it may be possible to sharpen the focus of these theoretical models and develop a better understanding of the complex roles played by fathers in these families. In the meantime, practitioners are forced to make decisions about children at risk for abuse. Stimulated by both practical and theoretical concerns, researchers continue to search for measures to help predict which parents will come to abuse their children and spouses, and what the effects are likely to be. In the next section, studies attempting to characterize abusive parents are described.

THE PROFILE OF THE ABUSIVE PARENT AND SPOUSE

DEVELOPMENT OF SCREENING TOOLS TO IDENTIFY ABUSIVE PARENTS

Although the sole emphasis on psychopathology as the explanation of child abuse was abandoned over 15 years ago, researchers and practitioners have continued to seek profiles of "typical" abusive parents. This persistence stems partially from the heavy caseloads handled by child protection workers, and the resulting need to identify children who are at greatest risk of being abused. The desire to find simple explanations coupled with the reality of limited resources has provoked several attempts to develop psychometrically sound tools for identifying abusive parents (for reviews, see Kaufman & Zigler, 1989; Starr, 1982).

Because of the severe implications of misclassification, the development of screening tools to identify potential perpetrators of child abuse is very complex. In order to be useful, a diagnostic instrument must be sensitive enough to detect real cases of abuse and discriminating enough to exclude nonabuse cases. Because child abuse is a low baserate phenomenon and appears to have a complex set of predictors, it is methodologically very difficult to develop such an instrument (see Kaufman & Zigler, 1989, for a review). Kaufman and Zigler (1989) argue that attempts to predict individual cases are so impractical that they should be abandoned in place of efforts to identify high-risk populations. Given the limited resources in child protection agencies across the country, however, the development of tools is very important (Starr, 1987).

One of the most commonly used screening measures is the Child Abuse Potential Inventory (CAPI; Milner, 1994). The CAPI is a 160-item self-report questionnaire containing six factor-analyzed scales (distress, rigidity, unhappiness, problems with child and self, problems with family and others, and physical abuse), as well as three validity scales. Although the CAPI has impressive psychometric properties (internal consistency and temporal stability), additional research is needed to evaluate its predictive validity. Although a number of fathers have been included in studies using the CAPI (Milner & Robertson, 1989), researchers have not systematically explored whether the risk profiles for mothers and fathers are different. In one study (Holden, Willis, & Foltz, 1989), researchers reported that fathers referred for abuse obtained lower scores on the CAPI and the PSI than mothers referred for abuse. Another study exploring differences between male and female perpetrators is currently underway using data from a large number of U.S. Air Force personnel and their families (B. Mollerstrom, personal communication, 1995).

Further research is needed to improve the reliability of screening tools for identifying abusive parents and spouses (Gottman et al., 1995) and to determine whether the patterns of risk factors differ for mothers and fathers. Researchers need to work with practitioners to develop useful strategies for identifying families at risk while sensitizing them about the methodological limitations and potential dangers of these instruments. In the next section, I examine how being a victim or witness of violence in childhood predicts subsequent spousal and parental behavior.

Intergenerational Transmission of Violence

In an attempt to understand how parents come to abuse their spouses and children, researchers and practitioners have wondered whether the parents' own childhood experiences influence their subsequent parenting. The popular notion "violence begets violence" suggests that abused children become abusive parents or perpetrators or victims of spousal violence; in this way, violence in the family is transmitted from one generation to the next. This belief has become so widely accepted that researchers often refer to "breaking the cycle of violence" as if the "cycle of violence" is a well-established empirical phenomenon. In fact, this widely circulated belief is based on an informal aggregation of media reports and findings from clinical samples characterized by many methodological shortcomings (e.g., Curtis, 1963; Steele & Pollack, 1968).

Because of the widespread belief that violence in early childhood fosters subsequent abusive parenting, however, researchers interested in child abuse now have begun to routinely ask adults (usually mothers) about their childhood experiences. After reviewing several studies, Kaufman and Zigler (1989) concluded that approximately one-third of the individuals who are abused or neglected as children will abuse their own children. The spouse abuse literature is also characterized by a belief in the cycle-of-violence hypothesis. Hotaling and Sugarman (1986) reported that witnessing spousal violence as children was a characteristic of both male batterers and female victims in most of the studies they reviewed. In several recent studies, researchers have used community samples to explore the cycle-of-violence hypothesis and to examine whether the experiences predicting violent adult behavior differ for men and women.

Because these reports are based on retrospective accounts of violence in childhood, a number of concerns have been raised about their validity. These include respondents' tendency to alter reports about previous life experiences to fit current needs as well as the possibility of forgetting or not wanting to report unpleasant experiences from the past. In her review, Widom discusses at length other methodological problems that characterize research on the cycle of violence and concludes that "empirical evidence demonstrating that abuse leads to abuse is fairly sparse" (Widom, 1989b, p. 23).

In order to determine whether violence is transmitted across generations, prospective longitudinal studies examining children's exposure to different types and intensity of violence are needed. By taking an epidemiological approach, and evaluating whether exposure to violence as children increases the likelihood of using violence in the family during adulthood, it would be possible to critically evaluate this hypothesis. It would be equally important to examine the childrearing experiences of children who were not victims or witnesses of violence as children but who subsequently were involved in child or spouse abuse as adults. In her research program, Widom (1989b) has attempted to address the intergenerational hypothesis by following large cohorts of children who were reported to authorities for child abuse and neglect. Using a prospective design, Widom compared children who had been reported to the authorities for abuse or neglect (*n* = 908) with comparison children located through county records (*n* = 667). At the time data were collected the subjects averaged 26 years of age. Information about childhood abuse and neglect, juvenile delinquency, and adult criminal behavior including child abuse were collected from official records. Results revealed that rates of arrests for child abuse and neglect were almost identical for both groups (approximately 1%), and this failed to confirm the simplistic prediction about the intergenerational transmission of violence. Because this study relies on official records and is skewed to include more serious cases, however, Widom warns that the findings cannot be generalized to the broader population. In addition, the follow-up took place when the "victims" had at best only just begun parenting.

In spite of 30 years of intensive efforts by researchers and practitioners, we have only a limited understanding of how parents come to abuse their children. Existing data suggest that a wide array of factors can contribute to abusive parental behavior. Attempts to develop screening tools to predict abusive behavior in clinical populations have failed to meet conventional psychometric standards of discrimination between abusive and nonabusive parents.

EFFECTS OF DOMESTIC VIOLENCE ON CHILDREN'S RELATIONSHIPS WITH THEIR FATHERS

Although there is consensus among clinicians that children who are victims of child abuse or witnesses of spouse abuse are at heightened risk for developmental problems, the pattern of symptomatology evinced by children from violent families is not as consistent as researchers would have predicted. Researchers have emphasized that individual differences in children's responses to maltreatment are partially attributable to the fact that children respond differently to stressful situations. Although this is certainly true, there are a number of possible methodological reasons why researchers have not been able to identify a pattern of symptoms that is unique to or distinguishes victims of child abuse and witnesses of spouse abuse from comparison children. Variations in the definitions of child abuse, the failure to account for multiple types of maltreatment (e.g., neglect or witnessing violence), and the failure to account for protective factors in children's lives may also contribute to the inconsistent symptom pictures displayed by children who are abused. Finally and most pertinent to this chapter, the failure to include information obtained from fathers about their children's adjustment and behavior may be partially responsible for these inconsistencies. Without information about children's relationships with fathers who abuse them or live with women who abuse them, we cannot expect to make reliable predictions about the effects of abuse on children.

OBSERVATIONS OF FATHER-CHILD INTERACTIONS IN PHYSICALLY ABUSIVE FAMILIES

Prompted by beliefs that inappropriate parenting fosters deviant relationships and problematic developmental outcomes, investigators began examining the effects of physical abuse on children's relationships with their parents more than a decade ago. Researchers who have studied the quality of infant-mother attachment have reported that abused infants are often insecurely attached to their mothers (Carlson, Cicchetti, Barnett, & Braunwald, 1989; Crittenden, 1988; Lamb, Gaensbauer, Malkin, & Schultz, 1985). Concerns have been voiced about the extent to which children generalize the internal representations of their primary attachment relationships to relationships with other attachment figures (Cicchetti & Toth, 1993; Lamb et al., 1985). Although there is some evidence that abused infants develop secure attachment relationships with nonabusive foster mothers (Lamb et al., 1985), little is known about abused infants' attachments to their fathers. Given the current theoretical interest in how early working models of parent-child interactions affect the subsequent ability to develop relationships, information about abused children's attachment relationships with their fathers is invaluable.

With older abused children, observations of parent-child interactions have focused on disciplinary tactics, attempts to achieve compliance, and the mutual solution of problem-solving tasks. Only a few studies have included fathers, and they are described here. Approximately 20 years ago, Burgess and Conger (1978) reported the first study comparing mothers' and fathers' interactions with their children in physically abusive and neglectful families. They found that abusive mothers had fewer verbal interactions with their children than did comparison mothers but did not differ from them in rates of physical interactions, positive and negative behaviors, and maternal compliance with child requests. Although the fathers of abused children complied with their children's requests less frequently than comparison fathers did, they spoke to their children more often than comparison fathers and more often than their mothers did. Although this study was conducted almost 20 years ago, it remains one of the few studies in which differences between mothers and fathers in abusive families were systematically explored. Unfortunately, Burgess and Conger did not distinguish between perpetrators and nonperpetrators, and it was thus not possible to examine differences between abusive and nonabusive parent-child dyads within the same families.

Herrenkohl, Herrenkohl, Toedter, and Yanushefski (1984) examined whether abused children interacted more provocatively with their parents than control children did and whether abusive parents responded more aggressively to their children's behavior. Their analyses revealed that maltreating parents ($n = 350$ mothers, $n = 89$ fathers) directed more hostile and negative behaviors, and fewer positive verbal behaviors, toward their children than parents in the comparison group. Interestingly, Herrenkohl et al. reported that socioeconomic status accounted for a greater proportion of the variance in their sample than child abuse did. Although fathers or father figures were included in this study, Herrenkohl et al. have not reported differences between mother-child (*n* = 350) and father-child (*n* = 89) interactions. These analyses are currently underway and may provide additional information about the interactional styles of mothers and fathers (Herrenkohl & Herrenkohl, 1995).

In reviewing the observational studies of parent-child interaction in abusive families, Mash (1991) underscored how much more we need to learn about the differences between abusive and nonabusive parent-child interactions: "It is not yet known whether the primary interactional risks to the child stem from a lack of affectionate care, actively hostile, cruel, or punitive parenting, the general effects of social impoverishment or, as is likely, from some combination of all of these factors" (p. 204).

The studies reviewed in this section are unique in that researchers included observations of fathers in their research design. By including fathers and father figures in future observational studies of parent-child interactions, and specifying whether they are perpetrators, we can learn more about the quality of their relationships with their children.

OBSERVATIONS OF FATHER-CHILD INTERACTIONS IN FAMILIES WITH MARITAL CONFLICT

Despite ample scientific evidence that infants and young children are affected by angry outbursts between their parents (Cummings, Zahn-Waxler, & Radke-Yarrow, 1981, 1984), researchers have not studied how spousal violence affects the development of infants' and young children's attachment relationships with their fathers and mothers. Although researchers have suggested that conflict in the family reduces the psychological availability of parents, thus placing their children at risk for attachment disorders, this hypothesis has not been adequately explored. Research on the interactional styles of men who behave violently toward their wives and of men whose wives are violent would provide valuable theoretical and policy-relevant information. By observing father-child dyads with younger and older children in families where marital conflict is present, it would be possible to learn the strengths and weaknesses of these men's parenting behaviors and how their interactional style compares with that of fathers in nonviolent families. Unfortunately, there have been no empirical observational studies of children who are witnesses of spousal violence.

DISCIPLINARY STYLES AND CONFLICT OVER CHILDREARING

In spite of the fact that abusive interactions often take place in the context of discipline (Gil, 1973; Martin, 1983; Parke & Colmer, 1975) and the use of corporal punishment is related to physical abuse (Gelles, 1991), surprisingly few attempts have been made to examine differences in the disciplinary styles of abusive and nonabusive parents. Although a number of researchers have argued that by studying disciplinary tactics in nonreferred community samples it is possible to learn more about the association between discipline and abuse (e.g., Hemenway, Solnick, & Carter, 1994; Lenton, 1990; Nicholas & Bieber, 1994), these studies are not reviewed in this chapter. Because they lack independent confirmation of child abuse status and often rely on retrospective reports of parental disciplinary practices, their validity and relevance is somewhat questionable.

Only one experimental study included information about childrearing and disciplinary practices obtained from fathers whose children were abused. Trickett and Sussman (1988) explored differences between maternal and paternal perceptions of childrearing practices in abusive ($n = 28$) and nonabusive ($n = 28$) families. Their study focused on two domains of parenting (parental control and parental nurturance) in a sample of children from 4 to 11 years old. Several important differences emerged between abusive and nonabusive parents. Abusive parents used verbal prohibitions and removal of privileges more often and reasoning less often when their children misbehaved. Abused parents differed from comparison parents in their perceptions of the most effective disciplinary techniques. Interestingly, abusive mothers from abusive families endorsed spanking as a more effective disciplinary technique than did fathers from abusive families and parents in a comparison group. Abusive parents also reported less satisfaction with their children and a generally more negative childrearing context.

Although there is some evidence that incidents of spousal abuse occur in the context of discipline and other childrearing disagreements (Dobash & Dobash, 1984; Walker, 1979), the disciplinary tactics of abused spouses have seldom been studied. This is particularly surprising in light of reports that spousal conflict reduces the quality of parenting behavior in a number of ways (Fauber, Forehand, Thomas, & Wierson, 1990) and that conflict over child-related issues is particularly distressing for children (Grych & Fincham, 1993).

Although clinicians report that many battered women are dissatisfied with the extent to which their husbands are involved in childrearing, disciplinary practices in spouse-abusing families have received little attention from researchers. Holden and Ritchie (1991) compared maternal reports of the quality of childrearing in a sample of women in a battered women's shelter ($n = 37$) and in a matched comparison group ($n = 37$). Clear differences emerged between their own and their husbands' disciplinary styles. Abused mothers reported greater discrepancies between the disciplinary styles of mothers and fathers. They also reported that they altered their disciplinary practices when their husbands were present and that fathers spanked children too frequently and too harshly. Finally, abused women reported that their husbands were less involved in childrearing tasks than were fathers in the comparison families and that they were less affectionate toward the children and less likely to use inductive reasoning when disciplining the children. According to mothers, children in this sample received less consistent discipline.

Meanwhile, Eisikovits and his colleagues (Eisikovits, Guttman, Sela-Amit, & Edelson, 1993) explored marital satisfaction, conflict over childrearing, and several aspects of social support using data from 120 Israeli couples who had been referred to social welfare agencies for husband-to-wife violence ($n = 60$) and a comparison group for whom no violence was reported in the last year ($n = 60$). Analyses revealed that conflict over childrearing and the unavailability of attachment relationships were the most important predictors of men's violent relationships with their wives. For women, overall marital satisfaction followed by conflict over childrearing was the most important predictor of being victims of abuse by their husbands. Collectively, these data suggest that disciplinary styles are an important domain of inquiry in families with marital violence and child abuse. Given that disciplinary actions often precede acts of child or spousal abuse, more extensive research is needed on this topic.

Although observations of parent-child interactions and parental reports of childrearing can provide us with some insight into the style and quality of interactions within abusive and nonabusive dyads, they do not help us understand how children who are victims of child abuse or witnesses of spousal violence interpret their parents' behavior. For this reason, some researchers have turned their attention to children's and adolescents' perceptions of their relationships with their parents.

CHILDREN'S PERCEPTIONS OF FATHERS

Considerable disagreement exists over the optimal way to assess children's relationships with their parents, and special concerns arise when we focus on children and parents from violent families. Although not without biases, children's perceptions and interpretations of their relationships with their parents provide unique insights that can be overlooked when researchers focus only on observational data or reports by others (e.g., Bryant, 1985; Dubin & Dubin, 1965; Finkelhor & Dziuba-Leatherman, 1994; Garbarino, Sebes, & Schellenbach, 1984; Grych & Fincham, 1993).

In one study, Hertzberger, Potts, and Dillon (1981) asked abused boys living in a group home to describe their parents' disciplinary techniques and their feelings about acceptance and rejection. The responses of boys who had been abused by one or both parents ($n = 14$) were compared with those of comparison children ($n = 10$). The authors reported that abused children were more fearful of and negative in their descriptions of their parents than comparison children were. Approximately 40% of the father-abused and 70% of the mother-abused children believed that the punishments were not deserved. The authors concluded that "perceptions of abusive and nonabusive fathers did not differ from each other as strongly or as often as did perceptions of abusive and nonabusive mothers" (p. 88). Although the sample is small, the authors were careful to document whether children were abused by one or both parents, a methodological precaution often overlooked by other researchers. Discriminating between perpetrating and nonperpetrating parents is crucial in improving our understanding of how child abuse affects children's adjustment. It is particularly important to learn more about how children's relationships with their nonabusive parents buffer the negative impact of abuse.

In our longitudinal study of 8- to 12-year-old Israeli children, we examined a variety of measures related to children's psychosocial adjustment, including perceptions of their parents (Sternberg et al., 1994). Children who were victims of physical abuse ($n = 33$), witnesses of spousal violence ($n = 16$), or victims and witnesses of abuse ($n = 30$) were compared with each other and with a comparison group ($n = 31$) using positive and negative descriptors of relationships with their mothers and fathers using the Family Relations Test (Bene & Anthony, 1957). Physically abused children more frequently reported negative perceptions of their perpetrating parents but did not differ from comparison children in the number of positive items reported. This finding suggested that while they were able to express negative feelings about the perpetrating parent, abused children also acknowledged some positive features of their relationship with abusive parents. More detailed analyses comparing fathers ($n = 31$) and mothers ($n = 13$) who were sole perpetrators of abuse with their nonabusive spouses revealed that children differentiated between their perpetrating and nonperpetrating parents. Abused children rated the quality of their relationships with the nonperpetrating parent like children in the comparison group viewed the parent of the same gender. Interestingly, fathers were assigned more positive *and* negative descriptors than mothers, highlighting the salience of fathers from their children's perspective. When the children averaged 14 years old, we again examined their relationships with their mothers and fathers using the Inventory for Peer and Parent Attachment (IPPA; Armsden & Greenberg, 1987). Because four years had passed since we conducted our first interviews, we needed to collect information about current patterns of child and spouse abuse in these families, and in order to obtain the most comprehensive picture of violence in the family, the adolescents, their mothers, and their fathers were independently asked about experiences of child and spouse abuse since they were last interviewed. Responses are being analyzed to create new group assignments based on child and spouse abuse that occurred in the past year. Preliminary analyses suggest that child abuse at time 1 had little impact on these adolescents' current relationships with their parents, whereas current child abuse appeared to have an important influence on the adolescents' perceptions of their parents. Because of the importance we placed on understanding the role of fathers in these violent families, qualitative interviews focusing on fathers' relationships with the target children were conducted with fathers in this study. We hope that they will enhance our understanding of how men in violent families perceive their roles as fathers.

Very few researchers have explored children's perceptions of their relationship with father figures in families where spouse abuse has occurred. Although we know that spousal violence is a painful experience for adults, we do not know how witnessing violence affects children's relationships with their fathers. Motivated by concerns to include information about fathers, researchers have recently begun to explore the father's role in families where marital violence occurs by asking women to provide information about their spouses' parental behavior (e.g., O'Keefe, 1994). In several studies, researchers have also asked children about their perceptions of their fathers. Interestingly, children are usually asked to comment on dimensions related to negative aspects of parenting, such as paternal disciplinary practices and aggression, and almost never asked about neutral or positive dimensions of parent-child relationships as though it is inconceivable that such dimensions might exist when violence has occurred.

CHILDREN'S REPORTS OF PATERNAL AGGRESSION AND OTHER DIMENSIONS OF FATHER-CHILD RELATIONSHIPS

In a recent study, Jouriles and Norwood (1995) explored mothers' and children's reports of mothers' and fathers' aggressive behavior toward children. Forty-eight mothers who lived in battered women's shelters were asked to complete the Conflict Tactics Scale (CTS) and the externalizing scale of the Child Behavior Checklist (CBCL; Achenbach & Edelbrock, 1983) about a male and female child. In families where the target children were eight years and older ($n = 20$), children completed the parent-child version of the CTS for themselves and a sibling from the opposite gender. According to the children's and mothers' reports, fathers were more aggressive with their children than mothers were. Some interesting differences emerged, however, when mothers' and children's reports were compared. Boys whose mothers reported less severe violence from their husbands reported higher rates of abuse by their mothers than boys whose mothers were more severely abused by their husbands. In contrast, mothers in the more severe abuse group reported they were more aggressive with their sons than were mothers in the less severe group. Although it is interesting to note the discrepancies between mothers' and sons' perspectives, interpreting these discrepancies is difficult and limited by the fact that information about marital violence was only collected from the mothers.

In another study, researchers touched on children's perceptions of nonviolent aspects of their relationships with their fathers by asking a few questions about paternal warmth and support. McCloskey and her colleagues (McCloskey et al., 1995) interviewed children living in shelters for battered women ($n = 64$), children of battered women living at home ($n = 102$), and a community comparison group ($n = 199$) using the Parent Perception Inventory (Hazzard, Christensen, & Margolin, 1983) to assess positive aspects of their relationships with their mothers and siblings. Only a subset of the questions focusing on warmth and support from family members was also asked about fathers. Although this study improves on others by including battered women and their children who continue to live in the community rather than in shelters, it fails in the attempt to explore whether supportive features of parent-child and sibling affiliation serve to "buffer the children from the effects of families" (p. 1242). By only superficially exploring nonaggressive aspects of children's relationships with their fathers, researchers reduced their chances of obtaining a coherent picture of the father-child relationship and its association with the children's adjustment.

In the longitudinal study described in the previous section (Sternberg et al., 1994), we found that children who were witnesses of spouse abuse ($n = 16$) but not victims of physical abuse did not differ from comparison children with respect to perceptions of their parents. Children who were victims of child abuse and witnesses of spousal violence ($n = 30$) were similar to abused children in the way they perceived their parents. Although it appears that observing parental violence did not affect children's perceptions of their parents as perpetrators or victims of marital violence, the size of our sample warrants caution in drawing such conclusions.

Recently, researchers have begun asking children who witness spousal violence about their father's abusive behavior toward them and their mothers, yet children have seldom been asked about potentially positive and nonaggressive aspects of father-child relationships. By systematically refraining from asking children who witness spousal violence about their relationships with their fathers, researchers preclude learning more about how children's adjustment to violence is mediated by the role these men play as fathers. Additional research is needed to explore how children who have witnessed spousal violence perceive their relationships with their fathers.

EFFECTS OF DOMESTIC VIOLENCE ON CHILDREN'S BEHAVIOR PROBLEMS

Most researchers believe that children who are victims or witnesses of domestic violence have more social and emotional problems than nonabused counterparts, but there are considerable inconsistencies across studies. Few researchers have carefully distinguished among types of domestic violence and among informants regarding the behavior problems, and few have distinguished the effects of domestic violence from the effects of the many traumatic or pathogenic experiences that children suffer. Interestingly, in spite of the fact that both child abuse and spouse abuse are believed to affect children's behavior problems and psychological well-being, a surprising number of researchers do not systematically inquire about both types of family violence in their studies. It is plausible that some of the inconsistencies across studies reflect the failure to account for the co-occurrence of child abuse and witnessing spousal violence in the families that have been studied.

There is a growing body of research emphasizing the impact of marital conflict on children's short-term adjustment and coping (Cummings & Davies, 1994; Cummings & O'Reilly, Chapter 4 of this volume), and many attempts have been made to explain how marital conflict can affect children's mental health and behavior. These models differ in their relative emphasis on how direct (e.g., observing arguments or violent fights between parents) and indirect (e.g., living in stressful and chaotic family circumstances that are the outcome of marital conflict; Faeber & Long, 1991) exposure to conflict affect children's mental health (see Fincham, Grych, & Osborne, 1994, and Cummings & O'Reilly, Chapter 4 of this volume, for a more detailed discussion of these models). Researchers have demonstrated that conflict involving verbal hostility, conflict that focuses on issues related to children (e.g., Grych & Fincham, 1993), and conflict that is not resolved (Cummings, Ballard, El-Sheikh, & Lake, 1991) are extremely distressing to children, whereas nonaggressive conflicts that are fully resolved appear to have little impact on children (Cummings et al., 1991; Cummings, Simpson, & Wilson, 1993).

Finally, I review three studies that focus on families where domestic violence has occurred and in which fathers' perspectives on their children's behavior problems have been included. In a recent study, mothers, fathers, and children ranging in age from 8 to 11 years were interviewed about spousal violence, behavior problems, and coping strategies. O'Brien et al. (1995) interviewed intact families from the community ($n = 86$) in order to learn more about how children's distancing strategies affects their ability to cope with marital conflict. Twenty-one children reported witnessing spousal violence. Marital conflict was not related to either mothers' or fathers' reports of their children's behavior problems.

Feldman and his colleagues (Feldman, Salzinger, & Kaplan, 1995) combined data from two studies to compare mothers' and fathers' perceptions of their children's behavior problems using the CBCL (Achenbach & Edelbrock, 1987) in families where child abuse was confirmed by social services. The researchers reported that fathers in both the comparison and child abuse groups assigned their children higher behavior problem scores than did mothers; however, these differences were statistically different only for the control group. Interestingly, neither spouse abuse nor perpetrator status influenced mothers' ratings of their children's behavior problems.

In the first phase of our longitudinal study (Sternberg et al., 1993, 1994), the CBCL and Youth Self-Report were completed by mothers, fathers, and their 8- to 12-year-old children in order to assess the effects of various types of domestic violence on children's behavior problems (see earlier in this chapter for a description of the sample). According to their mothers ($n = 110$), children had high levels of problematic behavior when spouse abuse had occurred, whereas children ($n = 110$) reported higher levels of problematic behavior when they themselves had been abused. For fathers ($n = 85$) there were no significant differences across the four groups. Although fathers in the comparison group viewed their children as considerably less problematic than fathers in the three violence groups, these differences were not statistically different.

These three studies are unique in the field because they include fathers' reports of their children's behavior problems. It is difficult to synthesize data from these studies because their samples and methodologies vary. We hope that, as researchers begin to ask fathers about their children's behavior problems, our understanding of the impact of domestic violence on children will become richer.

CONCLUSION

In this chapter I have attempted to illustrate how the lack of information about fathers and father figures has hampered our efforts to understand the etiology of abuse by parents and its impact on children's development. In spite of numerous reports suggesting how important it is to collect data from fathers, a review of the research on children as victims and witnesses of family violence suggests that the role of the father is seriously understudied. Although many abstracts of empirical articles indicate that the research report is about parents, a closer examination reveals that the actual focus is on mothers. Even in more recent studies, in which researchers have begun to include reports from wives and children about men's behavior as fathers, the measures they have used focus almost exclusively on aggressive aspects of father-child relationships. By failing to assess other facets of children's relationships with their fathers, researchers have implicitly ruled out the possibility that children may have more positive interactions or perceptions of their fathers. It is almost as though researchers feel that by inquiring about positive or neutral dimensions, they are endorsing violence by fathers. In addition, researchers have yet to design studies that take into consideration the fact that fathers are sometimes involved not as perpetrators of violence but as the spouses of perpetrators. Researchers also must explore how the quality of relationships with nonperpetrating fathers affects the development of abused children.

By including information from and about fathers in studies focused on domestic violence, it should be possible to improve the overall quality of research on child and spouse abuse. Because of the potential biases of different informants, it is important to collect data about family violence and its effects from multiple sources, including fathers. Likewise, distinguishing between perpetrating and nonperpetrating parents should make it possible to learn more about parent-child relationships in these families. In addition, a variety of data collection methods—observations of fathers and children, standardized questionnaires, and subjective accounts of father-child relationships—could provide us with comprehensive information about the roles of fathers in violent families.

Although I have acknowledged the many difficulties involved in locating and interviewing fathers in violent families, I would like to conclude this chapter by emphasizing the importance of overcoming these difficulties and developing more innovative ways of including paternal perspectives in research on family violence. In light of what has been learned about the methodological and practical implications of ignoring the roles played by fathers in violent families, the price of overlooking their influence is too high. In our longitudinal study, for example, it was three to four times more difficult and costly to interview fathers than to interview either mothers or children. We nevertheless insisted on collecting these data; without them our understanding of the impact of violence and sexual abuse within the family cannot be complete. Given our investment in locating and interviewing fathers, we were disappointed in the initial data (from phase I) suggesting that fathers in violent families did not report the predicted differences in children's behavior problems. Rather than abandoning our efforts to incorporate fathers' perspectives, however, we decided to expand our interviews with fathers, developing a qualitative approach in attempting to understand what fatherhood means to them. A preliminary review of the data suggests that fathers are willing to discuss both violent and nonviolent aspects of their relationships with their children and to share their perspectives and beliefs (Sternberg, Lamb, Dawud-Noursi, 1996). These data may begin to provide us with a better understanding of the father's role in violent families and suggest new directions for future research.

REFERENCES

CHAPTER 1

Adams, P. L., Milner, J. R., & Schrepf, N. A. (1984). *Fatherless children.* New York: Wiley.

Amato, P. R. (1993). Children's adjustment to divorce: Theories, hypotheses, and empirical support. *Journal of Marriage and the Family, 55,* 23–38.

Amato, P. R., & Keith, B. (1991). Parental divorce and the well-being of children: A meta-analysis. *Psychological Bulletin, 110,* 26–46.

Barnett, R. C., & Baruch, G. K. (1988). Correlates of father's participation in family work. In P. Bronstein & C. P. Cowan (Eds.), *Fatherhood today* (pp. 76–78). New York: Wiley.

Baruch, G. K., & Barnett, R. C. (1983). *Correlates of fathers' participation in family work: A technical report.* Wellesley, MA: Wellesley College Center for Research on Women.

Belsky, J. (1990). Parental and nonparental child care and children's socioemotional development: A decade in review. *Journal of Marriage and the Family, 52,* 885–903.

Biller, H. B. (1971). *Father, child, and sex role.* Lexington, MA: Heath.

Biller, H. B. (1974). *Paternal deprivation: Family, school, sexuality, and society.* Lexington, MA: Heath.

Biller, H. B. (1981). Father absence, divorce, and personality development. In M. E. Lamb (Ed.), *The role of the father in child development* (2nd ed., pp. 489–552). New York: Wiley.

Biller, H. B. (1993). *Fathers and families.* Westport, CT: Auburn House.

Blankenhorn, D. (1995). *Fatherless America.* New York: Basic Books.

Cherlin, A. J. (1992). *Marriage, divorce, remarriage.* Cambridge, MA: Harvard University Press.

Cherlin, A. J., Furstenberg, F., Chase-Lansdale, P. L., Kiernan, K. E., Robins, P. K., Morrison, D. R., & Teitler, J. O. (1991). Longitudinal studies of effects of divorce on children in Great Britain and the United States. *Science, 252,* 1386–1389.

Cowan, C. P., Cowan, P. A., Heming, G., Garrett, E., Coysh, W. S., Curtis-Boles, H., & Boles, A. J. (1985). Transitions to parenthood: His, hers, and theirs. *Journal of Family Issues, 6,* 451–481.

Cowan, P. A., Cowan, C. P., & Kerig, P. K. (1993). Mothers, fathers, sons, and daughters: Gender differences in family formation and parenting style. In P. A. Cowan, D. Field, D. Hansen, A. Skolnick, & G. Swanson (Eds)., *Family, self and society: Toward a new agenda for family research* (pp. 165–195). Hillsdale, NJ: Erlbaum.

Cummings, E. M., & Davies, P. (1994). *Children and marital conflict.* New York: Guilford.

Elster, A. B., & Lamb, M. E. (Eds.) (1986). *Adolescent fatherhood.* Hillsdale, NJ: Erlbaum.

Emery, R. E. (1982). Interparental conflict and the children of discord and divorce. *Psychological Bulletin, 92,* 310–330.

Gerson, K. (1993). *No man's land: Man's changing commitment to family and work.* New York: Basic Books.

Glick, P. C., & Norton, A. J. (1979). Marrying, divorcing, and living together in the U.S. today [Special issue]. *Population Bulletin, 32*(5).

Goldman, J. D. G., & Goldman, R. J. (1983). Children's perceptions of parents and their roles: A cross-national study in Australia, England, North America, and Sweden. *Sex Roles, 9,* 791–812.

Griswold, R. L. (1993). *Fatherhood in America.* New York: Basic Books.

Grossman, F. R., Pollack, W. S., & Golding, E. (1988). Fathers and children: Predicting the quality and quantity of fathering. *Developmental Psychology, 24,* 82–91.

Guidubaldi, J., & Perry, J. D. (1985). Divorce and mental health sequelae for children: A two-year follow-up of a nationwide sample. *Journal of the American Academy of Child Psychiatry, 24,* 531–537.

Haas, L. (1992). *Equal parenthood and social policy.* Albany, NY: State University of New York Press.

Herzog, R., & Sudia, C. E. (1973). Children in fatherless families. In B. M. Caldwell & H. N. Ricciuti (Eds.), *Review of child development research* (Vol. 3, pp. 141–232). Chicago: University of Chicago Press.

Hess, R. D., & Camara, K. A. (1979). Post-divorce family relationships as mediating factors in the consequences of divorce for children. *Journal of Social Issues, 35,* 79–96.

Hetherington, E. M., Cox, M., & Cox, R. (1982). Effects of divorce on parents and children. In M. E. Lamb (Ed.), *Nontraditional families* (pp. 233–288). Hillsdale, NJ: Erlbaum.

Hetherington, E. M., Cox, M., & Cox, R. (1985). Long-term effects of divorce and remarriage on the adjustment of children. *Journal of the American Academy of Child Psychiatry, 24,* 518–530.

Hochschild, A. R. (1995). Understanding the future of fatherhood: The "daddy hierarchy" and beyond. In M. C. P. van Dongen, G. A. B. Frinking, & M. J. G. Jacobs (Eds.), *Changing fatherhood: An interdisciplinary perspective* (pp. 219–230). Amsterdam: Thesis.

Horn, W. F. (1995). *Father facts.* Lancaster, PA: National Fatherhood Initiative.

Jacobs, M. (1995). The wish to become a father: How do men decide in favor of parenthood? In M. C. P. van Dongen, G. A. B. Frinking, & M. J. G. Jacobs (Eds.), *Changing fatherhood: An interdisciplinary perspective* (pp. 67–83). Amsterdam: Thesis.

Johnson, L. C., & Abramovitch, R. (1985). *Unemployed fathers: Parenting in a changing labour market.* Toronto: Social Planning Council.

Johnson, L. C., & Abramovitch, R. (1988). Parental unemployment and family life. In A. Pence (Ed.), *Ecological research with children and families: From concepts to methodology* (pp. 49–75). New York: Teachers College Press.

Klinman, D. (1986). Fathers and the educational system. In M. E. Lamb (Ed.), *The father's role: Applied perspectives* (pp. 413–428). New York: Wiley.

Knibiehler, Y. (1995). Fathers, patriarchy, paternity. In M. C. P. van Dongen, G. A. B. Frinking, & M. J. G. Jacobs (Eds.), *Changing fatherhood: An interdisciplinary perspective* (pp. 201–214). Amsterdam: Thesis.

Koestner, R., Franz, C., & Weinberger, J. (1990). The family origins of empathic concern: A 26-year longitudinal study. *Journal of Personality and Social Psychology, 58,* 709–717.

Kurdek, L. A. (1986). Custodial mothers' perceptions of visitation and payment for child support by noncustodial fathers in families with low and high levels of preseparation interparent conflict. *Journal of Applied Developmental Psychology, 7,* 307–323.

Lamb, M. E. (Ed.). (1976). *The role of the father in child development.* New York: Wiley.

Lamb, M. E. (1980). What can "research experts" tell parents about effective socialization? In M. D. Fantini & R. Cardenas (Eds.), *Parenting in a multicultural society* (pp. 160–169). New York: Longman.

Lamb, M. E. (1981a). The development of father-infant relationships. In M. E. Lamb (Ed.), *The role of the father in child development* (Rev. ed., pp. 459–488). New York: Wiley.

Lamb, M. E. (1981b). Fathers and child development: An integrative overview. In M. E. Lamb (Ed.), *The role of the father in child development.* (Rev. ed., pp. 1–70). New York: Wiley.

Lamb, M. E. (Ed.). (1981c). *The role of the father in child development* (Rev. ed.). New York: Wiley.

Lamb, M. E. (Ed.). (1986). *The father's role: Applied perspectives.* New York: Wiley.

Lamb, M. E. (Ed.). (1987). *The father's role: Cross-cultural perspectives.* Hillsdale, NJ: Erlbaum.

Lamb, M. E., Elster, A. B., Peters, L. J., Kahn, J. S., & Tavaré, J. (1986). Characteristics of married and unmarried adolescent mothers and their partners. *Journal of Youth and Adolescence, 13,* 487–496.

Lamb, M. E., Frodi, M., Hwang, C. P., & Frodi, A. M. (1983). Effects of paternal involvement on infant preferences for mothers and fathers. *Child Development, 54,* 450–452.

Lamb, M. E., & Levine, J. A. (1983). The Swedish parental insurance policy: An experiment in social engineering. In M. E. Lamb & A. Sagi (Eds.), *Fatherhood and family policy* (pp. 39–51). Hillsdale, NJ: Erlbaum.

Lamb, M. E., Pleck, J. H., Charnov, E. L., & Levine, J. A. (1987). A biosocial perspective on paternal behavior and involvement. In J. B. Lancaster, J. Altmann, A. S. Rossi, & L. R. Sherrod (Eds.), *Parenting across the lifespan: Biosocial perspectives* (pp. 111–142). Hawthorne, NY: Aldine.

Lamb, M. E., Pleck, J. H., & Levine, J. A. (1985). The role of the father in child development: The effects of increased paternal involvement. In B. B. Lahey & A. E. Kazdin (Eds.), *Advances in clinical child psychology* (Vol. 8, pp. 229–266). New York: Plenum.

Larson, R., & Richards, M. (1994). *Divergent lives: The emotional lives of mothers, fathers, and adolescents.* New York: Basic Books.

Lee, R. A. (1983). Flexitime and conjugal roles. *Journal of Occupational Behavior, 4,* 297–315.

Levine, J. A., Murphy, D. T., & Wilson, S. (1993). *Getting men involved.* New York: Scholastic.

Levine, J. A., & Pitt, E. (1995). *New expectations: Community strategies for responsible fatherhood.* New York: Families and Work Institute.

Lewis, M., & Weinraub, M. (1976). The father's role in the child's social network. In M. E. Lamb (Ed.), *The role of the father in child development* (pp. 157–184). New York: Wiley.

Maccoby, E. E. (1977, September). *Current changes in the family and their impact upon the socialization of children.* Paper presented at the meetings of the American Sociological Association, Chicago.

Mosely, J., & Thomson, E. (1995). Fathering behavior and child outcomes: The role of race and poverty. In W. Marsiglio (Ed.), *Fatherhood: Contemporary theory, research, and social policy* (pp. 148–165). Thousand Oaks, CA: Sage.

Mussen, P. H., & Rutherford, E. (1963). Parent-child relations and parental personality in relation to young children's sex-role preferences. *Child Development, 34,* 589–607.

O'Hare, W. P. (1995). *KIDS COUNT data book.* New York: Annie Casie Foundation.

Parke, R. D., Power, T. G., & Gottman, J. (1979). Conceptualizing and quantifying influence patterns in the family triad. In M. E. Lamb, S. J. Suomi, & G. R. Stephenson (Eds.), *Social interaction analysis: Methodological issues* (pp. 231–252). Madison, WI: University of Wisconsin Press.

Payne, D. E., & Mussen, P. H. (1956). Parent-child relations and father identification among adolescent boys. *Journal of Abnormal and Social Psychology, 52,* 358–362.

Pearson, J., & Thoennes, N. (1990). Custody after divorce: Demographic and attitudinal patterns. *American Journal of Orthopsychiatry, 60,* 233–249.

Pleck, J. H. (1981). *The myth of masculinity.* Cambridge, MA: MIT Press.

Pleck, J. H. (1982). *Husbands' and wives' paid work, family work, and adjustment.* Wellesley, MA: Wellesley College Center for Research on Women.

Pleck, J. H. (1983). Husbands' paid work and family roles: Current research issues. In H. Lopata & J. H. Pleck (Eds.), *Research in the interweave of social roles: Vol. 3. Families and jobs* (231–333). Greenwich, CT: JAI.

Pleck, J. H. (1984). *Working wives and family well-being.* Beverly Hills, CA: Sage.

Pleck, J. H. (1986). Employment and fatherhood: Issues and innovative policies. In M. E. Lamb (Ed.), *The father's role: Applied perspectives* (pp. 385–412). New York: Wiley.

Polatnick, M. (1973–74). Why men don't rear children: A power analysis. *Berkeley Journal of Sociology, 18,* 44–86.

Popenoe, D. (1989). The family transformed. *Family Affairs, 2 (2–3),* 1–5.

Popenoe, D. (1996). *Life without father.* New York: Free Press.

Pruett, K. D. (1983). Infants of primary nurturing fathers. *Psychoanalytic Study of the Child, 38,* 257–277.

Pruett, K. D. (1985). Children of the fathermothers: Infants of primary nurturing fathers. In J. D. Call, E. Galenson, & R. L. Tyson (Eds.), *Frontiers of infant psychiatry* (Vol. 2, pp. 375–380). New York: Basic Books.

Quinn, R. P., & Staines, G. L. (1979). *The 1977 Quality of Employment survey.* Ann Arbor, MI: Survey Research Center.

Radin, N. (1981). The role of the father in cognitive, academic, and intellectual development. In M. E. Lamb (Ed.), *The role of the father in child development* (Rev. ed., pp. 379–428). New York: Wiley.

Radin, N. (1982). Primary caregiving and role-sharing fathers. In M. E. Lamb (Ed.), *Nontraditional families: Parenting and child development* (pp. 173–204). Hillsdale, NJ: Erlbaum.

Radin, N. (1994). Primary-caregiving fathers in intact families. In A. E. Gottfried & A. W. Gottfried (Eds.), *Redefining families: Implications for children's development* (pp. 11–54). New York: Plenum.

Radin, N., & Goldsmith, R. (1985). Caregiving fathers of preschoolers: Four years later. *Merrill-Palmer Quarterly, 31,* 375–383.

Robinson, J. P., Andreyenkov, V. G., & Patrashev, V. D. (1988). *The rhythm of everyday life: How Soviet and American citizens use time.* Boulder, CO: Westview.

Russell, G. (1983). *The changing roles of fathers?* St. Lucia, Queensland: University of Queensland Press.

Russell, G. (1986). Primary caretaking and role-sharing fathers. In M. E. Lamb (Ed.), *The father's role: Applied perspectives* (pp. 29–57). New York: Wiley.

Sears, R. R., Maccoby, E. E., & Levin, H. (1957). *Patterns of child rearing.* Evanston, IL: Peterson.

Thompson, R. A. (1986). Fathers and the child's "best interests": Judicial decision making in custody disputes. In M. E. Lamb (Ed.), *The father's role: Applied perspectives* (pp. 61–102). New York: Wiley.

Thompson, R. A. (1994). Fathers and divorce. In L. S. Quinn (Ed.), *The future of children* (pp. 210–235). Palo Alto, CA: Packard Foundation.

van Dongen, M. (1995). Men's aspirations concerning child care: The extent to which they are realized. In M. C. P. van Dongen, G. A. B. Frinking, & M. J. G. Jacobs (Eds.), *Changing fatherhood: An interdisciplinary perspective* (pp. 91–105). Amsterdam: Thesis.

Wallerstein, J. S., & Kelly, J. B. (1980). *Surviving the breakup: How children and parents cope with divorce.* New York: Basic Books.

Whitehead, B. D. (1993, April). Dan Quayle was right. *Atlantic Monthly,* pp. 47–84.

Winett, R. A., & Neale, M. S. (1980, November). Results of experimental study of flexitime and family life. *Monthly Labor Review, 113,* 29–32.

Yankelovich, D. (1974). The meaning of work. In J. Rosow (Ed.), *The worker and the job.* Englewood Cliffs, NJ: Prentice-Hall.

CHAPTER 2

Abramovitch, H. H. (1994a). *The first father. Abraham: The psychology and culture of a spiritual revolutionary.* Lanham, MD: University Press of America.

Abramovitch, H. H. (1994b). The relation between fathers and sons in biblical narrative: Toward a new interpretation of the akeda. In *Proceedings of the Eleventh World Congress of Jewish Studies,* division a: The Bible and its world (pp. 31–36). Jerusalem: World Union of Jewish Studies.

Abramovitch, H. H. (1995). Ethics: A Jewish Perspective. In L. Ross & M. Roy (Eds.), *Cast the first stone: The ethics of analytical therapy* (pp. 34–41). Boston: Shambhala.

Baker, M. (1992). *What men really think: About women, love, sex, themselves.* New York: Pocket.

Beebe, J. (1985). The Father's anima. In Andrew Samuels (Ed.), *The father: Contemporary Jungian perspectives* (pp. 95–109). London: Free Association.

Berry, P. (Ed.). (1993). *Fathers and mothers.* Dallas: Spring.

Blaise, C. (1993). *I had a father: A post-modern autobiography.* Reading, MA: Addison-Wesley.

Bly, R. (1990). *Iron John: A book about men.* Reading, MA: Addison-Wesley.

Bolen, J. B. (1989). *Gods in everyman: A new psychology of men's lives and loves.* San Francisco: Harper and Row.

Carvalho, P. (1982). Paternal deprivation in relation to narcissistic damage. *Journal of Analytical Psychology 27,* 341–356.

Cath, S., Gurwitz, A., & Ross, J. (Eds.). (1982). *Father and child.* Boston: Little, Brown.

Coleman, A., & Coleman, L. (1981). *Earth father-sky father: The changing concept of fathering.* New York: Prentice-Hall; reprinted as *The father* (1988). New York: Avon.

Collins, A. (1994). *Fatherson: A self psychology of the archetypal masculine.* Wilmette, IL: Chiron.

Edwards, O. D. (1992). Druids, priests, bards, and other fathers. In S. French (Ed.), *Fatherhood: Men writing about fathering* (pp. 63–70). London: Virago.

French, S. (Ed.). (1992). *Fatherhood: Men writing about fathering.* London: Virago.

Gurian, M. (1992). *The prince and the king: Healing the father-son wound.* New York: Putnam.

Henderson. J. (1967). *Thresholds of initiation.* Middleton, CT: Wesleyan University Press.

Hewlett, B. S. (1992). *Intimate fathers: The nature and context of Aka pygmy paternal infant care.* Ann Arbor, MI: University of Michigan Press.

Homer. (1937). *The Odyssey* (W. H. D. Rouse, trans.). New York: Mentor.

Hopcke, R. (1991). *Men's dreams, men's healing.* Boston: Shambhala.

The Jerusalem Bible. (1968). Garden City, NY: Doubleday.

Jones, M. (1992). Learning to be a father. In S. French (Ed.), *Fatherhood: Men writing about fathering* (pp. 23–30). London: Virago.

Jung, C. J. (1977). *Collected works.* Princeton, NJ: Princeton University Press.

Kaplan, J., & Sadock, A. (1994). *Synopsis of psychiatry* (7th ed.). Baltimore: Williams and Wilkins.

Leonard, L. S. (1983). *The wounded woman: Healing the father/daughter relationship.* Cleveland, OH: Ohio University Press/Swallow Press.

Levinson, D. J. (1978). *The seasons of a man's life.* New York: Knopf.

Maeder, T. (1989). *Children of psychiatrists and other psychotherapists.* New York: Harper and Row.

Mahdi, L., Foster, S., & Little, M. (Eds.). (1987). *Betwixt and between: Patterns of masculine and feminine initiation.* LaSalle, IL: Open Court.

Mitscherlich, A. (1969). *Society without father.* London: Tavistock.

Monick, E. (1987). *Phallos.* Toronto: Inner City.

Moore, R., & Gillette, D. (1990). *King, warrior, magician, lover: Rediscovering masculine potential.* San Francisco: HarperCollins.

Osherson, S. (1986). *Finding our fathers: How a man's life is shaped by his relationship with his father.* New York: Fawcet Columbine.

Pedersen, L. E. (1991). *Dark hearts: The unconscious forces that shape men's lives.* Boston: Shambhala.

Pirani, A. (1989). *The absent father: Crisis and creativity.* London: Arkana.

Ross, J. M. (1982). Oedipus revisited: Laius and the Laius complex. *The psychoanalytic study of the child 37,* 169–200.

Ross, J. M. (1986). The darker side of fatherhood. *International Journal of Psychoanalytic Psychotherapy 11,* 117–144.

Ross, J. M. (1992). *The male paradox.* New York: Simon and Schuster.

Samuels, A. (Ed.). (1985). *The father: Contemporary Jungian perspectives.* London: Free Association.

Samuels, A. (Ed.). (1989). *The plural psyche: Personality, morality and the father.* London: Routledge.

Samuels, A. (Ed.). (1993). *The political psyche.* London: Routledge.

Samuels, A. (1995). The good-enough father of whatever sex. *Feminism and Psychology, 5,* 511–530.

Shapiro, S. A. (1984). *Manhood: A new definition.* New York: Putnam.

Tatham, P. (1992). *The making of maleness: Men woman and the flight of Daedalus.* London: Karnac.

Vogt, G. M. (1992). *Return to the father: Archetypal dimensions of the patriarch.* Dallas: Spring.

CHAPTER 3

Bailey, B. (1988). *From front porch to back seat: Courtship in twentieth century America.* Baltimore: Johns Hopkins University Press.

Bederman, G. (1995). *Manliness and civilization: A cultural history of gender and race in the United States, 1880–1917.* Chicago: University of Chicago Press.

Bernard, J. (1981). The good provider role. *American Psychologist, 36,* 1–12.

Berry, V. T. (1992). From *Good Times* to *The Cosby Show:* Perceptions of changing televised images among black fathers and sons. In S. Craig (Ed.), *Men, masculinity, and the media* (pp. 111–123). Newbury Park, CA: Sage.

Blankenhorn, D. (1995). *Fatherless America: Confronting our most urgent social problem.* New York: Basic Books.

Bloom-Feshbach, J. (1981). Historical perspectives on the father's role. In M. E. Lamb (Ed.), *The role of the father in child development* (2nd ed., pp. 71–112). New York: Wiley.

Bumpass, L. L., & Sweet, J. A. (1989). Children's experience in single-parent families: Implications of cohabitation and marital transitions. *Family Planning Perspectives, 21*(6e), 256–260.

Caplow, R., Bahr, H. M., Chadwick, B. A., Hill, R., & Williamson, M. H. (1982). *Middletown families: Fifty years of change and continuity.* Minneapolis, MN: University of Minnesota Press.

Carnes, M. (1989). *Secret ritual and manhood in Victorian America.* New Haven, CT: Yale University Press.

Carnes, M. C., & Griffen, C. (Eds.). (1990). *Meanings for manhood: Constructions of masculinity in Victorian America.* Chicago: University of Chicago Press.

Chauncey, G. (1995). *Gay New York: Gender, urban culture, and the making of the gay male world, 1890–1940.* New York: Basic Books.

Chodorow, N. (1978). *The reproduction of mothering: Psychoanalysis and the sociology of gender.* Berkeley, CA: University of California Press.

Clawson, M. A. (1989). *Constructing brotherhood: Class, gender, and fraternalism.* Princeton, NJ: Princeton University Press.

Cody, C. A. (1982). Naming, kinship and estate dispersal: Notes on slave family life on a South Carolina plantation, 1786 to 1833. *William and Mary Quarterly, 39,* 192–211.

Cohen, M. (1988). *The sisterhood: True story of the women who changed the world.* New York: Simon and Schuster.

Cole, D. (1963). *Immigrant city.* Chapel Hill, NC: University of North Carolina Press.

Coltrane, S., & Allan, K. (1994). "New" fathers and old stereotypes: Representations of masculinity in 1980s television advertising. *Masculinities, 2,* 1–25.

Coontz, S. (1992). *The way we never were: American families and the nostalgia trap.* New York: Basic Books.

Cott, N. F. (1977). *The bonds of womanhood: "Woman's Sphere" in New England, 1780–1835.* New Haven, CT: Yale University Press.

Covello, L. (1967). *The social background of the Italo-American school child.* Leiden: Brill.

Day, R. D., & Mackey, W. C. (1986). The role image of the American father: An examination of a media myth. *Journal of Comparative Family Studies, 27*(3), 377–388.

DeMause, L. (1974). The evolution of childhood. In L. DeMause (Ed.), *The history of childhood* (pp. 1–74). New York: Harper and Row.

Demos, J. (1970). *A little commonwealth: Family life in Plymouth Colony.* New York: Oxford University Press.

Demos, J. (1986). *Past, present and personal: The family and the life course in American history.* New York: Oxford University Press.

Diner, H. (1983). *Erin's daughters in America: Irish immigrant women in the nineteenth century.* Baltimore: Johns Hopkins University Press.

Dinnerstein, D. (1976). *The mermaid and the minotaur: Sexual arrangements and the human malaise.* New York: Harper and Row.

Ehrenreich, B. (1983). *The hearts of men: American dreams and the flight from commitment.* New York: Anchor/Doubleday.

Epstein, B. (1981). *The politics of domesticity: Women, evangelism, and temperance.* Middletown, CT: Wesleyan University Press.

Evans, S. M. (1979). *Personal politics: The roots of women's liberation in the civil rights movement and the new left.* New York: Knopf.

Ewen, E. (1985). *Immigrant women in the land of dollars: Life and culture on the Lower East Side 1890–1925.* New York: Monthly Review.

Faludi, S. (1992). *Backlash: The undeclared war against American women.* New York: Crown.

Fein, R. (1978). Research on fathering. *Journal of Social Issues, 34*(1), 122–135.

Frank, S. M. (1992). "Rendering aid and comfort": Images of fatherhood in the letters of Civil War soldiers from Massachusetts and Michigan. *Journal of Social History, 26,* 5–32.

Frazier, E. F. (1939). *The Negro family in the United States.* Chicago: University of Chicago Press.

Friedan, B. (1963). *The feminine mystique.* New York: Norton.

Furstenberg, F. F., Jr. (1988). Good dads—bad dads: Two faces of fatherhood. In A. Cherlin (Ed.), *The changing American family and public policy* (pp. 193–218). Washington, DC: Urban Institute.

Furstenberg, F. F., Jr. (1990). Divorce and the American family. *American Review of Sociology, 16,* 379–403.

Furstenberg, F. F., Jr. (1995). Fathering in the inner city: Paternal participation and public policy. In W. Marsiglio (Ed.), *Fatherhood: Contemporary theory, research, and social policy* (pp. 119–147). Thousand Oaks, CA: Sage.

Genovese, E. D. (1974). *Roll, Jordan, roll: The world the slaves made.* New York: Random House.

Gerson, K. (1993). *No man's land: Men's changing commitments to family and work.* New York: Basic Books.

Gilbert, J. B. (1986). *A cycle of outrage: America's reaction to the juvenile delinquent in the 1950s.* New York: Oxford University Press.

Gilligan, C. (1982). *In a different voice: Psychological theory and women's development.* Cambridge, MA: Harvard University Press.

Glenn, S. (1990). *Daughters of the shtetl: Life and labor in the immigrant generation.* Ithaca, NY: Cornell University Press.

Greven, P. J., Jr. (1972). *Four generations: Population, land, and family in colonial Andover, Massachusetts.* Ithaca, NY: Cornell University Press.

Greven, P. J., Jr. (1977). *The protestant temperament: Patterns of child-rearing, religious experience, and self in early America.* New York: Knopf.

Griswold, R. L. (1993). *Fatherhood in America: A history.* New York: Basic Books.

Grossberg, M. (1983). Who gets the child? Custody, guardianship, and the rise of a judicial patriarchy in nineteenth-century America. *Feminist Studies, 9,* 235–260.

Gutierrez, R. (1991). *When Jesus came, the corn mothers went away.* Stanford, CA: Stanford University Press.

Gutman, H. G. (1976). *The black family in slavery and freedom, 1750–1925.* New York: Pantheon.

Handlin, O. (1951). *The uprooted.* Boston: Little, Brown.

Haralovich, M. B. (1992). Sit-coms and suburbs: Positioning the 1950s homemaker. In L. Spigel & D. Mann (Eds.), *Private screenings: Television and the female consumer* (pp. 111–142). Minneapolis, MN: University of Minnesota Press.

Hochschild, A. (1989). *The second shift: Working parents and the revolution at home.* New York: Viking.

Hondagneu-Sotelo, P., & Messner, M. A. (1994). Gender displays and men's power: The "new man" and the Mexican immigrant man. In H. Brod & M. Kaufman (Eds.), *Theorizing masculinities* (pp. 200–218). Thousand Oaks, CA: Sage.

Hood, J. C. (1983). *Becoming a two-job family: Role bargaining in dual worker households.* New Yorker: Praeger.

Howe, I. (1989). *World of our fathers.* New York: Schocken.

Jensen, J. M. (1977). Native American women and agriculture: A Seneca case study. *Sex Roles, 3,* 423–440.

Jones, J. (1985). *Labor of love, labor of sorrow: Black women, work and family from slavery to the present.* New York: Basic Books.

Karp, A. (1976). *Golden door to America.* New York: Viking.

Komarovsky, M. (1940). *The unemployed man and his family—The effect of unemployment upon the status of the man in fifty-nine families.* New York: Dyden.

Lamb, M. E., Pleck, J. H., Charnov, E. L., & Levine, J. A. (1985). Paternal behavior in humans. *American Zoologist, 25,* 883–894.

LaRossa, R. (1988). Fatherhood and social change. *Family Relations, 36,* 451–458.

LaRossa, R., Gordon, B. A., Wilson, R. J., Bairan, A., & Jaret, C. (1991). The fluctuating image of the 20th century American father. *Journal of Marriage and the Family, 53,* 987–997.

LaRossa, R., & Reitzes, D. (1993). Continuity and change in middle class fatherhood: 1925–1939: The culture-conduct connection. *Journal of Marriage and the Family, 55,* 455–468.

Leavitt, J. R. (1988). *Brought to bed: Childbearing in America, 1750–1950.* New York: Oxford University Press.

Liebow, E. (1967). *Tally's corner.* Boston: Little, Brown.

Litwack, L. (1979). *Been in the storm so long: The aftermath of slavery.* New York: Knopf.

Lynd, R. S., & Lynd, H. M. (1929). *Middletown: A study in American culture.* New York: Harcourt, Brace, and World.

Marsh, M. (1990). Suburban men and masculine domesticity, 1870–1915. In M. C. Carnes & C. Griffen (Eds.), *Meanings for manhood: Constructions of masculinity in Victorian America* (pp. 111–127). Chicago: University of Chicago Press.

Mason, M. A. (1994). *From father's property to children's rights: The history of child custody in the United States.* New York: Columbia University Press.

May, E. T. (1988). *Homeward bound: American families in the Cold War.* New York: Basic Books.

Mintz, S., & Kellogg, S. (1988). *Domestic revolutions: A social history of the American family life.* New York: Free Press.

Morgan, E. S. (1966). *The Puritan family.* New York: Harper and Row.

Norton, M. B. (1980). *Liberty's daughters: The revolutionary experience of American women, 1750–1800.* Boston: Little, Brown.

Okin, S. M. (1989). *Justice, gender and the family.* New York: Basic Books.

Parke, R. D., & Tinsley, B. (1984). Fatherhood: Historical and contemporary perspectives. In K. A. McCloskey & H. W. Reese (Eds.), *Life-span developmental psychology: Historical and generational effects* (pp. 429–457). New York: Academic.

Perdue, T. (1985). Southern Indians and the cult of true womanhood. In W. J. Fraser, J., F. Saunders, Jr., & J. L. Wakelyn (Eds.), *The web of southern social relations: Women, family and education* (pp. 35–51). Athens, GA: University of Georgia Press.

Pettigrew, T. F. (1964). *A profile of the Negro American.* Princeton: NJ: Van Nostrand.

Pleck, E. (1983). Challenges to traditional authority in immigrant families. In M. Gordon (Ed.), *The American family in social-historical perspective* (pp. 504–517). New York: St. Martin's.

Pleck, E. (1987). *Domestic tyranny: The making of American social policy against family violence from colonial times to the present.* New York: Oxford University Press.

Pleck, J. (1981). *The myth of masculinity.* Cambridge, MA: MIT Press.

Pleck, J. (1983). The theory of male sex role identity: Its rise and fall, 1936–present. In M. Lewin (Ed.), *In the shadow of the past: Psychology views the sexes* (pp. 205–225). New York: Columbia University Press.

Pleck, J. (1985). *Working wives/Working husbands.* Newbury Park, CA: Sage.

Pleck, J. (1987). American fathering in historical perspective. In M. Kimmel (Ed.), *Changing men: New directions in research on men and masculinity* (pp. 83–97). Newbury Park, CA: Sage.

Pollock, L. A. (1983). *Forgotten children: Parent-child relations from 1500 to 1900.* Cambridge: Cambridge University Press.

Rothman, E. K. (1984). *Hands and hearts: A history of courtship in America.* Cambridge, MA: Harvard University Press.

Rotundo, E. A. (1985). American fatherhood: A historical perspective. *American Behavioral Scientist, 29,* 7–25.

Rubel, A. (1966). *Across the tracks: Mexican-Americans in a Texas city.* Austin, TX: University of Texas Press.

Ruddick, S. (1989). *Maternal thinking: Toward a politics of peace.* Boston: Beacon.

Ryan, M. P. (1981). *Cradle of the middle class: The family in Oneida County, New York, 1790–1865.* Cambridge: Cambridge University Press.

Sanchez, G. (1993). *Becoming Mexican American: Ethnicity, culture, and identity in Chicano Los Angeles, 1900–1945.* New York: Oxford University Press.

Shorter, E. (1975). *The making of the modern family.* New York: Basic Books.

Skolnick, A. (1991). *Embattled paradise: The American family in an age of uncertainty.* New York: Basic Books.

Smith-Rosenberg, C. (1975). The female world of love and ritual. *Signs, 1,* 1–29.

Spock, B., & Rothenberg, M. B. (1992). *Dr. Spock's baby and child care.* New York: Pocket.

Stack, C. B. (1974). *All our kin: Strategies for survival in a black community.* New York: Harper and Row.

Stansell, C. (1986). *City of women: Sex and class in New York, 1789–1860.* New York: Knopf.

Stearns, P. N. (1991). Fatherhood in historical perspective: The role of social change. In F. W. Bozett & S. M. Hanson (Eds.), *Fatherhood and families in cultural context* (pp. 28–52). New York: Springer.

Stone, L. (1977). *The family, sex and marriage in England 1500–1800.* New York: Harper and Row.

Stowe, S. M. (1987). *Intimacy and power in the Old South: Rituals in the lives of the planters.* Baltimore: Johns Hopkins University Press.

Terman, L., & Miles, C. (1936). *Sex and personality.* New York: McGraw-Hill.

Thomas, W. I., & Znaniecki, F. (1918). *The Polish peasant in Europe and America: Monograph of an immigrant group.* Chicago: University of Chicago Press.

Thornton, A. (1989). Changing attitudes toward family issues in the United States. *Journal of Marriage and the Family, 51,* 873–893.

Ulrich, L. T. (1983). *Good wives: Image and reality in the lives of women in Northern New England, 1650–1750.* New York: Oxford University Press.

U.S. Department of Labor. (1965). *The Negro family: The case for national action.* Washington, DC: U.S. Government Printing Office.

Vinovskis, M. A. (1988). *An "epidemic" of adolescent pregnancy: Some historical and policy considerations.* New York: Oxford University Press.

Wilkie, J. R. (1993). Changes in U.S. men's attitudes toward the family provider role 1972–1989. *Gender and Society, 1,* 261–279.

Wilson, W. J. (1987). *The truly disadvantaged: The inner city, the underclass and public policy.* Chicago: University of Chicago Press.

Wyatt-Brown, B. (1982). *Southern honor.* New York: Oxford University Press.

Wylie, P. (1942). *A generation of vipers.* New York: Rinehart.

Yans-McLaughlin, V. (1981). *Family and community: Italian immigrants in Buffalo, 1880–1930.* Urbana, IL: University of Illinois Press.

Zinaldin, J. S. (1979). The emergence of a modern American family law: Child custody, adoption, and the courts, 1796–1851. *Northwestern University Law Review, 73,* 1038–1039.

CHAPTER 4

Amato, P. R. (1986). Marital conflict, the parent-child relationship, and child self-esteem. *Family Relations, 35,* 403–410.

Amato, P. R., & Booth, A. (1991). Consequences of parental divorce and marital unhappiness for adult well-being, *Social Forces, 69,* 895–914.

Amato, P. R., & Keith, B. (1991). Consequences of parental divorce for children's well-being: A meta-analysis. *Psychological Bulletin, 110,* 26–46.

Amato, P. R., Rezac, S. J., & Booth, A. (in press). Helping between parents and young adult offspring: The role of parental marital quality, divorce, and remarriage. *Journal of Marriage and the Family.*

Ballard, M. E., Cummings, E. M., & Larkin, K. (1993). Emotional and cardiovascular responses to adults' angry behavior and to challenging tasks in children of hypertensive and normotensive parents. *Child Development, 64,* 500–515.

Baruch, D. W., & Wilcox, J. A. (1944). A study of sex differences in preschool children's adjustment coexistent with interparental tensions. *Journal of Genetic Psychology, 64,* 281–303.

Beach, B. (1995). *The relation between marital conflict and child adjustment: An examination of parental and child repertoires.* Unpublished doctoral dissertation, West Virginia University, Morgantown.

Beach, S. R. H., Arias, I., & O'Leary, K. D. (1987). The relationship of marital satisfaction and social support to depressive symptomology. *Journal of Psychopathology and Behavioral Assessment, 8,* 305–316.

Beach, S. R. H., & Nelson, G. M. (1990). Pursuing research on major psychopathology from a contextual perspective: The example of depression and marital discord. In G. Brody and I. Sigel (Eds.), *Methods of family research: Biographies of research projects: Vol. 2. Clinical populations.* Hillsdale, NJ: Erlbaum.

Belsky, J. (1981). Early human experience: A family perspective. *Developmental Psychology, 17,* 3–23.

Belsky, J. (1984). The determinants of parenting: A process model. *Child Development, 55,* 83–96.

Belsky, J. (1990). Parental and nonparental child care and children's socioemotional development: A decade in review. *Journal of Marriage and the Family, 52,* 885–903.

Belsky, J., Gilstrap, B., & Rovine, M. (1984). The Pennsylvania Infant and Family Development Project: I. Stability and change in mother-infant and father-infant interaction in a family setting at one, three, and nine months. *Child Development, 55,* 692–705.

Belsky, J., Rovine, M., & Fish, M. (1989). The developing family system. In M. Gunnar (Ed.), *Minnesota Symposia on Child Psychology: Vol. 22. Systems and development* (pp. 119–166). Hillsdale, NJ: Erlbaum.

Belsky, J., Youngblade, L., Rovine, M., & Volling, B. (1991). Patterns of marital change and parent-child interaction. *Journal of Marriage and the Family, 53,* 487–498.

Benoit, D., & Parker, K. (1994). Stability and transmission of attachment across three generations. *Child Development, 65,* 1444–1456.

Block, J. H., Block, J., & Gjerde, P. (1986). The personality of children prior to divorce: A prospective study. *Child Development, 52,* 965–974.

Booth, A., & Amato, P. R. (1994). Parental marital quality, parental divorce, and relations with parents. *Journal of Marriage and the Family, 56,* 21–34.

Bradbury, T. N., & Fincham, F. D. (1987). Affect and cognition in close relationships: Towards an integrative model. *Cognition and Emotion, 1,* 59–87.

Bradbury, T. N., & Fincham, F. D. (1990). Attributions in marriage: Review and critique. *Psychological Bulletin, 107,* 3–33.

Brennan, K. A., & Shaver, P. R. (1995). Dimensions of adult attachment: Affect regulation and romantic relationship functioning. *Personality and Social Psychology Bulletin, 21,* 267–283.

Bretherton, I. (1985). Attachment theory: Retrospect and prospect. In I. Bretherton & E. Waters (Eds.), Growing points of attachment theory and research. *Monographs of the Society for Research in Child Development, 50* (1–2, Serial No. 209), 167–193.

Broder, D. S. (1993, March 24). Quayle: Right on the family. *Washington Post,* p. 21.

Brody, G., Pelligrini, A., & Sigel, I. (1986). Marital quality and mother-child and father-child interactions with school-aged children. *Developmental Psychology 22,* 291–296.

Brody, G. H., Stoneman, Z., McCoy, J. K., & Forehand, R. (1992). Contemporaneous and longitudinal associations of sibling conflict with family relationships assessments and family discussions about sibling problems. *Child Development, 63,* 391–400.

Bugental, D. B., Mantyla, S. M., & Lewis, J. (1989). Parental attributions as moderators of affective communication to children at risk for physical abuse. In D. Cicchetti & V. Carlson (Eds.), *Child maltreatment: Theory and research on the causes and consequences of child abuse and neglect* (pp. 254–279). New York: Cambridge University Press.

Christensen, A., & Heavey, C. L. (1990). Gender and social structure in the demand/withdraw pattern of marital conflict. *Journal of Personality and Social Psychology, 59,* 73–81.

Christensen, A., & Margolin, G. (1988). Conflict and alliance in distressed and nondistressed families. In R. A. Hinde & J. Stevenson-Hinde (Eds.), *Relationships within families* (pp. 263–282). New York: Oxford University Press.

Christensen, A., & Shenk, J. L. (1991). Communication, conflict, and psychological distance in nondistressed, clinic, and divorcing couples. *Journal of Consulting and Clinical Psychology, 59,* 458–463.

Clark, J., & Barber, B. L. (1994). Adolescents in postdivorce and always-married families: Self-esteem and perceptions of fathers' interest. *Journal of Marriage and the Family, 56,* 608–614.

Cohn, D. A., Cowan, P. A., Cowan, C. P., & Pearson, J. (1992). Mothers' and fathers' working models of childhood attachment relationships, parenting styles, and child behavior. *Development and Psychopathology, 4,* 417–431.

Cohn, D. A., Silver, D. H., Cowan, C. P., Cowan, P. A., & Pearson, J. (1992). Working models of childhood attachment and couple relationships. *Journal of Family Issues, 13,* 432–449.

Cooney, T. M. (1994). Young adults' relations with parents: The influence of recent parental divorce. *Journal of Marriage and the Family, 56,* 45–56.

Cox, A. D., Puckering, C., Pound, A., & Mills, M. (1987). The impact of maternal depression in young people. *Journal of Child Psychology and Psychiatry, 28,* 917–928.

Cox, M. J., & Owen, M. T. (1993, March). Marital conflict and conflict negotiation: Effects on infant-mother and infant-father relationships. In M. Cox & J. Brooks-Gunn (Chairs), *Conflict in families: Causes and consequences.* Symposium conducted at the meeting of the Society for Research in Child Development, New Orleans.

Cox, M. J., Owen, M. T., Lewis, J. M., & Henderson, V. K. (1989). Marriage, adult adjustment and early parenting. *Child Development, 60,* 1015–1024.

Coyne, J. C., Burchill, S. A. L., & Stiles, W. B. (1991). An interactional perspective on depression. In C. R. Snyder & D. O. Forsyth (Eds.), *Handbook of social and clinical psychology: The health perspective* (pp. 327–348). New York: Pergamon.

Crockenberg, S., & Forgays, D. K. (1996). The role of children's emotion in children's understanding and emotional reactions to marital conflict. *Merrill-Palmer Quarterly, 42,* 22–47.

Cummings, E. M. (1987). Coping with background anger in early childhood. *Child Development, 58,* 976–984.

Cummings, E. M. (1994). Marital conflict and children's functioning. *Social Development, 3,* 16–36.

Cummings, E. M. (1995a). Security, emotionality, and parental depression. *Developmental Psychology, 31,* 425–427.

Cummings, E. M. (1995b). The usefulness of experiments for the study of the family. *Journal of Family Psychology, 9,* 175–185.

Cummings, E. M., & Davies, P. T. (1994a). *Children and marital conflict: The impact of family dispute and resolution.* New York: Guilford.

Cummings, E. M., & Davies, P. T. (1994b). Maternal depression and child development [Annual research review]. *Journal of Child Psychology and Psychiatry, 35,* 73–112.

Cummings, E. M., & Davies, P. T. (1995). The impact of parents on their children: An emotional security hypothesis. *Annals of Child Development, 10,* 167–208.

Cummings, E. M., & Davies, P. T. (1996). Emotional security as a regulatory process in normal development and the development of psychopathology. *Development and Psychopathology, 8,* 123–139.

Cummings, E. M., Davies, P. T., & Simpson, K. (1994). Marital conflict, gender, and children's appraisal and coping efficacy as mediators of child adjustment. *Journal of Family Psychology, 8,* 141–149.

Cummings, E. M., & el-Sheikh, M. (1991). Children's coping with angry environments: A process-oriented approach. In M. Cummings, A. Greene, & K. Karraker (Eds.), *Life-span developmental psychology: Perspectives on stress and coping* (pp. 131–150). Hillsdale, NJ: Erlbaum.

Cummings, E. M., Hennessy, K., Rabideau, G., & Cicchetti, D. (1994). Responses of physically abused boys to interadult anger involving their mothers. *Development and Psychopathology, 6,* 31–41.

Cummings, E. M., Iannotti, R., & Zahn-Waxler, C. (1985). The influence of conflict between adults on the emotions and aggression of young children. *Developmental Psychology, 21,* 495–507.

Cummings, E. M., Simpson, K., & Wilson, A. (1993). Children's responses to interadult anger as a function of information about resolution. *Developmental Psychology 29,* 978–985.

Cummings, E. M., & Smith, D. (1993). The impact of anger between adults on siblings' emotions and social behavior. *Journal of Child Psychology and Psychiatry, 34,* 1425–1433.

Cummings, E. M., Vogel, D., Cummings, J. S., & El-Sheikh, M. (1989). Children's responses to different forms of expression of anger between adults. *Child Development, 60,* 1392–1404.

Cummings, E. M., Zahn-Waxler, C., & Radke-Yarrow, M. (1981). Young children's responses to expressions of anger and affection by others in the family. *Child Development, 52,* 1274–1282.

Cummings, E. M., Zahn-Waxler, C., & Radke-Yarrow, M. (1984). Developmental changes in children's reactions to anger in the home. *Journal of Child Psychology and Psychiatry, 25,* 63–75.

Cummings, J. S., Pelligrini, D., Notarius, C., & Cummings, E. M. (1989). Children's responses to angry adult behavior as a function of marital distress and history of interparent hostility. *Child Development, 60,* 1035–1043.

Davies, P. T., & Cummings, E. M. (1994). Marital conflict and child adjustment: An emotional security hypothesis. *Psychological Bulletin, 116,* 387–411.

Dawson, G., Hessl, D., & Frey, K. (1994). Social influences on early developing biological and behavioral systems related to risk for affective disorder. *Development and Psychopathology 6,* 759–780.

Dickstein, S., & Parke, R. D. (1988). Social referencing in infancy: A glance at fathers and marriage. *Child Development, 59,* 506–511.

Downey, G., & Coyne, J. C. (1990). Children of depressed parents: An integrative review. *Psychological Bulletin, 108,* 50–76.

Easterbrooks, M. A., Cummings, E. M., & Emde, R. N. (1994). Young children's responses to constructive marital disputes. *Journal of Family Psychology, 8,* 160–169.

Easterbrooks, M. A., & Emde, R. N. (1988). Marital and parent-child relationships: The role of affect in the family system. In R. Hinde & J. Stevenson-Hinde (Eds.), *Relationships within families* (pp. 83–103). Oxford: Clarendon.

El-Sheikh, M., & Cummings, E. M. (1995). Children's responses to angry adult behavior as a function of experimentally manipulated exposure to resolved and unresolved conflict. *Social Development, 4,* 75–91.

Emery, R. E. (1982). Interparental conflict and the children of discord and divorce. *Psychological Bulletin, 92,* 310–330.

Emery, R. E. (1994, December). *Children and divorce.* Paper presented at the NICHD Consensus Conference on the Effects of Divorce and Custody Arrangements on Children's Development, Middleburg, VA.

Emery, R. E., & O'Leary, K. D. (1984). Marital discord and child behavior problems in a non-clinic sample. *Journal of Abnormal Child Psychology, 12,* 411–420.

Feldman, S., & Downey, G. (1994). Rejection sensitivity as a mediator of the impact of childhood exposure to family violence on adult attachment behavior. *Development and Psychopathology, 6,* 231–247.

Fincham, F. D. (1994). Understanding the association between marital conflict and child adjustment: An overview. *Journal of Family Psychology, 8,* 123–127.

Folkman, S. (1991). Coping across the lifespan: Theoretical issues. In E. M. Cummings, A. Greene, & K. Karraker (Eds.), *Lifespan developmental psychology: Perspectives on stress and coping* (pp. 3–20). Hillsdale, NJ: Erlbaum.

Fox, N., Calkins, S. D., & Bell, M. A. (1994). Neural plasticity and developments in the first two years of life. Evidence from cognitive and socioemotional domains of research. *Development and Psychopathology, 6,* 677–696.

Gjerde, P. F. (1988). Parental concordance on childrearing and the interactive emphases of parents: Sex differentiated relationships during the preschool years. *Developmental Psychology, 24,* 700–706.

Goldberg, W. A. (1990). Marital quality, parental personality, and spousal agreement about perceptions and expectations for children. *Merrill-Palmer Quarterly, 36,* 531–556.

Goldberg, W. A., & Easterbrooks, M. A. (1984). The role of marital quality in toddler development. *Developmental Psychology, 20,* 504–514.

Goth-Owens, T. L., Stollak, G. E., Messe, L. A., Peshkess, I., & Watts, P. (1982). Marital satisfaction, parenting satisfaction, and parenting behavior in early infancy. *Infant Mental Health Journal, 3,* 187–198.

Gotlib, I. H., & Whiffen, V. E. (1989). Depression and maternal functioning: An examination of specificity and gender differences. *Journal of Abnormal Psychology, 98,* 23–30.

Gottman, J. M. (1994). *Why marriages succeed or fail.* New York: Simon and Schuster.

Gottman, J. M., & Levenson, R. W. (1988). Assessing the role of emotion in marriage. *Behavioral Assessment, 8,* 31–48.

Grych, J. H., & Fincham, F. (1990). Marital conflict and children's adjustment: A cognitive-contextual framework. *Psychological Bulletin, 108,* 267–290.

Grych, J. H., & Fincham, F. (1993). Children's appraisals of marital conflict: Initial investigations of the cognitive-contextual framework. *Child Development, 64,* 215–230.

Hazen, C., & Shaver, P. R. (1987). Romantic love conceptualized as an attachment process. *Journal of Personality and Social Psychology, 52,* 511–524.

Hershorn, M., & Rosenbaum, A. (1985). Children of marital violence: A closer look at the unintended victims. *American Journal of Orthopsychiatry, 55,* 260–266.

Hetherington, E. M., & Clingempeel, W. G. (1992). Coping with marital transitions: A family systems perspective. *Monographs of the Society for Research in Child Development, 57* (2–3, Serial No. 227).

Hetherington, E. M., & Parke, R. D. (1993). *Child psychology: A contemporary viewpoint.* New York: McGraw-Hill.

Hill, M. S. (1988). Marital stability and spouses' shared time: A multidisciplinary hypothesis. *Journal of Family Issues, 9,* 427–451.

Holden, G. W., & Ritchie, K. L. (1991). Linking extreme marital discord, child rearing, and child behavior problems: Evidence from battered women. *Child Development, 62,* 311–327.

Howes P., & Markman, H. J. (1989). Marital quality and child functioning: A longitudinal investigation. *Child Development, 60,* 1044–1051.

Hubbard, R. M., & Adams, C. F. (1936). Factors affecting the success of child guidance clinic treatment. *American Journal of Orthopsychiatry, 6,* 81–103.

Hughes, H. (1988). Psychological and behavioral correlates of family violence in child witnesses and victims. *American Journal of Orthopsychiatry, 6,* 81–103.

Jaffe, P., Wolfe, D., & Wilson, S. K. (1990). *Children of battered women.* London: Sage.

Jaffe, P., Wolfe, D., Wilson, S. K., & Zak, L. (1986). Family violence and child adjustment: A comparative analysis of girls' and boys' behavioral symptoms. *American Journal of Psychiatry, 143,* 74–77.

Jenkins, J. M., & Smith, M. A. (1991). Marital disharmony and children's behavior problems: Aspects of poor marriages that affect children adversely. *Journal of Child Psychology and Psychiatry, 32,* 793–810.

Jouriles, E. N., Barling, J., & O'Leary, K. D. (1987). Predicting child behavior problems in maritally violent families. *Journal of Abnormal Child Psychology, 15,* 165–173.

Jouriles, E. N., & Farris, A. M. (1992). Effects of family research designs: A model of interdependence. *Communications Research, 17,* 462–482.

Kagan, J. (1994). On the nature of emotion. In N. Fox (Ed.), The development of emotion regulation. *Monographs of the Society for Research in Child Development, 59* (2–3, Serial 240), 7–24.

Katz, L. F., & Gottman, J. (1993). Patterns of marital conflict predict children's internalizing and externalizing disorders. *Development Psychology, 29,* 940–950.

Katz, L. F., & Gottman, J. M. (1995a). *Marital conflict and child adjustment: Father's parenting as a mediator of children's negative peer play.* Paper presented at the meetings of the Society for Research in Child Development, Indianapolis.

Katz, L. F., & Gottman, J. M. (1995b). Vagal tone predicts children from marital conflict. *Development and Psychopathology, 7,* 83–92.

Katzev, A. R., Warner, R. L., & Adcock, A. C. (1994). Girls or boys? Relationship of child gender to marital instability. *Journal of Marriage and the Family, 56,* 89–100.

Kerig, P. K., Cowan, P. A., & Cowan, C. P. (1993). Marital quality and gender differences in parent-child interaction. *Developmental Psychology, 29,* 931–939.

Klaczynski, P. A., & Cummings, E. M. (1989). Responding to anger in aggressive and non-aggressive boys. *Journal of Child Psychology and Psychiatry, 30,* 309–314.

Lamb, M. E. (1976). The role of the father: An overview. In M. E. Lamb (Ed.), *The role of the father in child development* (pp. 3–70). New York: Wiley.

Lamb, M. E., & Elster, A. B. (1985). Adolescent mother-infant-father relationships. *Developmental Psychology, 21,* 768–773.

Lazarus, R. S., & Folkman, S. (1984). *Stress, coping, and appraisal.* New York: Springer.

Lee, C. L., & Bates, J. E. (1985). Mother-child interaction at two years and perceived difficult temperament. *Child Development, 56,* 1314–1325.

Levenson, R. W., & Gottman, J. M. (1983). Marital interaction: Physiological linkage and affective exchange. *Journal of Personality and Social Psychology, 49,* 85–94.

Mangelsdorf, S., Gunnar, M., Kestenbaum, R., Lang, S., & Andreas, D. (1990). Infant-proneness-to-distress temperament, maternal personality, and mother-infant attachment: Associations and goodness-of-fit. *Child Development, 61,* 820–831.

Margolin, G., & Wampold, B. (1981). Sequential analysis of conflict and accord in distressed and nondistressed marital partners. *Journal of Consulting and Clinical Psychology, 49,* 554–567.

Markman, H. J., & Kraft, S. (1989). Men and women in marriage: Dealing with gender differences in marital therapy. *Behavior Therapist, 12,* 51–56.

McLanahan, S., & Sandefur, G. (1994). *Growing up with a single parent: What hurts, what helps.* Cambridge, MA: Harvard University Press.

Minuchin, P. (1985). Families and individual development: Provocations from the field of family therapy. *Child Development, 56,* 289–302.

National Institute of Child Health and Human Development. (in press). Consensus statement on the effects of divorce and custody arrangements.

Notarius, C., & Markman, H. (1993). *We can work it out: Making sense of marital conflict.* New York: Putnam.

Olweus, D. (1980). Familial and temperamental determinants of aggressive behavior in adolescent boys: A casual analysis. *Developmental Psychology, 16,* 644–660.

Parke, R. D., & Tinsley, B. (1987). Family interaction in infancy. In J. Osofsky (Ed.), *Handbook of infant development* (2nd ed., pp. 579–641). New York: Wiley.

Pedlow, R., Sanson, A., Prior, M., & Oberklaid, F. (1993). Stability of maternally reported temperament from infancy to 8 years. *Developmental Psychology, 29,* 998–1007.

Peterson, J. L., & Zill, N. (1986). Marital disruption, parent-child relationships, and behavior problems in children. *Journal of Marriage and the Family, 48,* 295–307.

Pratt, M. W., Kerig, P. K., Cowan, P. A., & Cowan, C. P. (1992). Family worlds: Couple satisfaction, parenting style, and mothers' and fathers' speech to young children. *Merrill-Palmer Quarterly, 38,* 245–262.

Pruchno, R., Burant, C., & Peters, N. D. (1994). Family mental health: Marital and parent-child consensus as predictors. *Journal of Marriage and the Family, 56,* 747–758.

Rossi, A., & Rossi, P. (1990). *Of human bonding: Parent-child relations across the life course.* New York: de Gruyter.

Rothbart, M. K., Posner, M. I., & Rosicky, J. (1994). Orienting in normal and pathological development. *Development and Psychopathology, 6,* 635–652.

Rutter, M. (1970). Sex differences in response to family stress. In E. J. Anthony & C. Koupernick (Eds.), *The child in his family* (pp. 165–196). New York: Wiley.

Rutter, M. (1980). *Changing youth in a changing society.* Cambridge, MA: Harvard University Press.

Simons, R. L., Whitbeck, L. B., Beaman, J., & Conger, R. D. (1994). The impact of mothers' parenting, involvement by nonresidential fathers, and parental conflict on the adjustment of adolescent children. *Journal of Marriage and the Family, 56,* 356–374.

Simpson, K., & Cummings, E. M. (1996). Mixed message resolution and children's responses to interadult conflict. *Child Development, 67,* 437–448.

Sroufe, L. A., & Rutter, M. (1984). The domain of developmental psychopathology. *Child Development, 48,* 1184–1199.

Sternberg, K. J., Lamb, M. E., Greenbaum, C., Cicchetti, D., Dawud, S., Cortes, R. M., Krispin, O., & Lorey, F. (1993). Effects of domestic violence on children's behavior problems and depression. *Developmental Psychology, 29,* 44–52.

Thompson, E., & Walker, A. (1989). Gender in families: Women and men in marriage, work, and parenthood. *Journal of Marriage and the Family, 51,* 845–872.

Thompson, R. A. (1991). Emotional regulation and emotional development. *Educational Psychology Review, 3,* 269–307.

Thompson, R. A. (1994). The role of the father after divorce. *The Future of Children, 4,* 211–235.

van den Boom, D., & Hoeksma, J. (1994). The effect of infant irritability on mother-infant interaction: A growth curve analysis. *Developmental Psychology, 30,* 581–590.

Volling, B. L., & Belsky, J. (1992). Infant, father and marital antecedents of infant-father attachment security in dual-earner and single-earner families. *International Journal of Behavioral Development, 15,* 83–100.

Vuchinich, S., Emery, R. E., & Cassidy, J. (1988). Family members as third parties in dyadic family conflict: Strategies, alliances, and outcomes. *Child Development, 59,* 1293–1302.

Vuchinich, S., Wood, B., & Vuchinich, R. (1994). Coalitions and family problem solving with preadolescents in referred, at-risk, and comparison families. *Family Process, 33,* 409–424.

Watson, J. B. (1925). *Behaviorism.* New York: Norton.

West, M. O., & Prinz, R. J. (1987). Parental alcoholism and childhood psychopathology. *Psychological Bulletin, 102,* 204–218.

White, L., Brinkerhoff, D., & Booth, A. (1985). The effects of marital disruption on child's attachment to parents. *Journal of Family Issues, 6*, 5–22.

Wilson, B. J., & Gottman, J. M. (1995). Marital interaction and parenting: The role of repair of negativity in families. In M. H. Bornstein (Ed.), *Handbook of parenting: Vol. 4. Applied and practical considerations of parenting*. Hillsdale, NJ: Erlbaum.

Wolfe, D. A, Jaffe, P., Wilson, S. K., & Zak, L. (1985). Children of battered women: The relation of child behavior to family violence and maternal stress. *Journal of Consulting and Clinical Psychology, 53*, 657–665.

CHAPTER 5

Abidin, R. R. (1992). The determinants of parenting behavior. *Journal of Clinical Child Psychology, 21*, 407–412.

Ahmeduzzaman, M., & Roopnarine, J. L. (1992). Sociodemographic factors, functioning style, social support, and fathers' involvement with preschoolers in African-American families. *Journal of Marriage and the Family, 54*, 699–707.

Allen, W. R. (1981). Moms, dads, and boys: Race and sex differences in the socialization of male children. In L. E. Gary (Ed.), *Black men* (pp. 99–114). Beverly Hills, CA: Sage.

Almeida, D. M., & Galambos, N. L. (1991). Examining father involvement and the quality of father-adolescent relations. *Journal of Research on Adolescence, 1*, 155–172.

Almeida, D. M., Maggs, J. L., & Galambos, N. L. (1993). Wives' employment hours and spousal participation in family work. *Journal of Family Psychology, 7*, 233–244.

Amato, P. R. (1987). *Children in Australian families: The growth of competence*. New York: Prentice-Hall.

Bailey, W. T. (1991). Fathers' involvement in their children's health care. *Journal of Genetic Psychology, 152*, 289–293.

Bailey, W. T. (1992). Psychological development in men: Generativity and involvement with young children. *Psychological Reports, 71*, 929–930.

Bailey, W. T. (1993). Fathers' knowledge of development and involvement with preschool children. *Perceptual and Motor Skills, 77*, 1032–1034.

Bailey, W. T. (1994). Fathers' involvement and responding to infants: "More" may not be "better." *Psychological Reports, 74*, 92–94.

Barnett, R. C., & Baruch, G. B. (1987). Determinants of father's participation in family work. *Journal of Marriage and the Family, 49*, 29–40.

Barnett, R. C., Marshall, N. L., & Pleck, J. H. (1992). Men's multiple roles and their relationship to men's psychological distress. *Journal of Marriage and the Family, 54*, 358–367.

Baruch, G. K., & Barnett, R. C. (1981). Fathers' involvement in the care of their preschool children. *Sex Roles, 7*, 1043–1059.

Baruch, G. K., & Barnett, R. C. (1986a). Consequences of fathers' participation in family work: Parents' role strain and well-being. *Journal of Personality and Social Psychology, 51*, 983–992.

Baruch, G. K., & Barnett, R. C. (1986b). Father's participation in family work and children's sex-role attitudes. *Child Development, 57*, 1210–1223.

Belsky, J. (1981). Early human experience: A family perspective. *Developmental Psychology, 17*, 3–23.

Belsky, J. (1984). The determinants of parenting: A process model. *Child Development, 55*, 83–96.

Belsky, J., & Volling, B. L. (1987). Mothering, fathering, and marital interaction in the family triad during infancy: Exploring family systems processes. In P. W. Berman & F. A. Pederson (Eds.), *Men's transitions to parenthood: Longitudinal studies of early family experience* (pp. 37–64). Hillsdale, NJ: Erlbaum.

Belsky, J., Youngblood, L., Rovine, M., & Volling, B. (1991). Patterns of marital change and parent-child interaction. *Journal of Marriage and the Family, 53,* 487–498.

Berman, P. W., & Pedersen, F. A. (1987). Research on men's transitions to parenthood: An integrative discussion. In P. W. Berman & F. A. Pedersen (Eds.), *Men's transitions to parenthood: Longitudinal studies of early family experience* (pp. 217–242). Hillsdale, NJ: Erlbaum.

Biller, H. B. (1981). The father and personality development: Paternal deprivation and sex-role development. In M. E. Lamb (Ed.), *The role of the father in child development* (pp. 89–156). New York: Wiley.

Blair, S. L., & Hardesty, C. (1994). Parental involvement and the well-being of fathers and mothers of young children. *Journal of Men's Studies, 3,* 49–68.

Blair, S. L., Wenk, D., & Hardesty, C. (1994). Marital quality and paternal involvement: Interconnections of men's spousal and parental roles. *Journal of Men's Studies, 2,* 221–237.

Blankenhorn, D. (1995). *Fatherless America: Confronting our most urgent social problem.* New York: Basic Books.

Bohen, H., & Viveros-Long, A. (1981). *Balancing jobs and family life: Do flexible schedules help?* Philadelphia: Temple University Press.

Bolger, N., DeLongis, A., Kessler, R. C., & Wethington, E. (1989). The contagion of stress across multiple roles. *Journal of Marriage and the Family, 51,* 175–183.

Bond, J. T., Galinsky, E., Lord, M., Staines, G. L., & Brown, K. R. (1991). *Beyond the parental leave debate: The impact of laws in four states.* New York: Families and Work Institute.

Brody, G. H., Pellegrini, A. D., & Sigel, I. E. (1986). Marital quality and mother-child and father-child interactions with school-aged children. *Developmental Psychology 22,* 291–296.

Caplow, T., Bahr, S., Chadwick, B. A., Hill, R. E., & Williamson, M. H. (1982). *Middletown families.* Minneapolis: University of Minnesota Press.

Carlson, B. E. (1984). The father's contribution to child care: Effects on children's perceptions of parental roles. *American Journal of Orthopsychiatry, 54,* 123–136.

Cath, S. H., Gurwitt, A. R., & Ross, J. M. (1988). *Father and child: Developmental and clinical perspectives.* New York: Blackwell.

Coltrane, S. (1990). Birth timing and the division of labor in dual-earner families. *Journal of Family Issues, 11,* 157–181.

Cooney, T. M., Pedersen, F. A., Indelicato, S., & Palkovitz, R. (1993). Timing of fatherhood: Is "on-time" optimal? *Journal of Marriage and Family, 55,* 205–215.

Cowan, C. P. (1988). Working with men becoming fathers: The impact of a couples group intervention. In P. Bronstein & C. P. Cowan (Eds)., *Fatherhood today: Men's changing role in the family* (pp. 276–298). New York: Wiley.

Coysh, W. S. (1983, August). *Predictive and concurrent factors related to fathers' involvement in childrearing.* Paper presented to the American Psychological Association, Anaheim, CA.

Crouter, A. C., Perry-Jenkins, M., Huston, T., & McHale, S. M. (1987). Processes underlying father involvement in dual-earner and single-earner families. *Developmental Psychology, 23,* 431–440.

Daly, K. (1993). Reshaping fatherhood: Finding the models. *Journal of Family Issues, 14,* 510–530.

DeFrain, J. (1979). Androgynous parents tell who they are and what they need. *Family Coordinator, 28,* 237–243.

Dickie, J. R. (1987). Interrelationships within the mother-father-infant triad. In P. W. Berman & F. A. Pederson (Eds.), *Men's transitions to parenthood: Longitudinal studies of early family experience* (pp. 113–144). Hillsdale, NJ: Erlbaum.

Dubnoff, S. (1978, August). *Class, class contradictions within the family, and husbands' child care time.* Paper presented to the American Sociological Association.

Ehrensaft, D. (1987). *Parenting together: Men and women sharing the care of their children.* New York: Free Press.

Eiduson, B. T. & Alexander, J. W. (1978). The role of children in alternative family styles. *Journal of Social Issues, 34,* 149–167.

Ember, C. R. (1973). The effect of feminine task assignment on the social behavior of boys. *Ethos, 1,* 424–439.

Emlen, A. A. (1987, August). *Panel on child care, work and family.* Paper presented at the American Psychological Association, New York.

Essex, M. J., & Klein, M. H. (1991). The Wisconsin parental leave study: The roles of fathers. In J. S. Hyde and M. J. Essex (Eds.), *Parental leave and child care: Setting a research and policy agenda.* Philadelphia: Temple University Press.

Feldman, S. S., & Aschenbrenner, B. (1983). Impact of parenthood on various aspects of masculinity and femininity: A short-term longitudinal study. *Developmental Psychology, 19,* 278–289.

Feldman, S. S., Nash, S. C., & Aschenbrenner, B. G. (1983). Antecedents of fathering. *Child Development, 54,* 1628–1636.

Forsyth, B. H., Lessler, J. T., & Hubbard, M. L. (1992). Cognitive evaluation of the questionnaire. In C. F. Turner, J. T. Lessler, & J. C. Groerer (Eds.), *Survey measurement of drug use: Methodological studies* (pp. 13–52). Rockville, MD: DHHS Publication.

Gerson, K. (1993). *No man's land: Men's changing commitments to family and work,* New York: Basic Books.

Glueck, S., & Glueck, E. (1950). *Unravelling juvenile delinquency,* New York: Commonwealth Fund.

Goldscheider, F. K., & Waite, L. J. (1991). *New families, no families: The transformation of the American home.* Berkeley, CA: University of California Press.

Gottfried, A. E., Bathurst, K. & Gottfried, A. W. (1994). Role of maternal and dual-earner employment status in children's development. In A. E. Gottfried & A. W. Gottfried (Eds.), *Redefining families: Implications for children's development* (pp. 55–97). New York: Plenum.

Gottfried, A. E., Gottfried, A. W., & Bathurst, K. (1988). Maternal employment, family environment, and children's development: Infancy through the school years. In A. E. Gottfried & A. W. Gottfried (Eds.), *Maternal employment and children's development: Longitudinal research* (pp. 11–58). New York: Plenum.

Greenberger, E., & O'Neil, R. (1990). Parents' concerns about their child's development: Implications for fathers' and mothers' well-being and attitudes toward work. *Journal of Marriage and the Family, 52,* 621–635.

Grossman, F. K., Pollack, W. S., & Golding, E. (1988). Fathers and children: Predicting the quality and quantity of fathering. *Developmental Psychology, 24,* 82–91.

Haas, L. (1988, November). *Understanding fathers' participation in childcare: A social constructionist perspective.* Paper presented to the National Council on Family Relations, Philadelphia.

Haas, L. (1992). *Equal parenthood and social policy: A study of parental leave in Sweden.* Albany, NY: State University of New York Press.

Haas, L. (1993). Nurturing fathers and working mothers: Changing gender roles in Sweden. In J. C. Hood (Ed.), *Men, work, and family roles* (pp. 238–261). Newbury Park, CA: Sage.

Harold-Goldsmith, R., Radin, N., & Eccles, J. S. (1988). Objective and subjective reality: The effects of job loss and financial stress on fathering behaviors. *Family Perspective, 22,* 309–325.

Harris, K. H., & Morgan, S. P. (1991). Fathers, sons, and daughters: Differential paternal involvement in parenting. *Journal of Marriage and the Family, 53,* 531–544.

Hawkins, A. J., & Belsky, J. (1989). The role of father involvement in personality change in men across the transition to parenthood. *Family Relations, 38,* 378–384.

Hawkins, A. J., Christiansen, S. L., Sargent, K. P., & Hill, E. J. (1993). Rethinking fathers' involvement in child care: A developmental perspective. *Journal of Family Issues, 14,* 531–549.

Hawkins, J. D., Catalano, R. F., & Miller, J. Y. (1992). Risk and protective factors for alcohol and other drug problems in adolescence and early adulthood: Implications for substance abuse prevention. *Psychological Bulletin, 112,* 64–105.

Heath, D. H. (1978). What meaning and effects does fatherhood have for the maturing of professional men? *Merrill-Palmer Quarterly, 24,* 265–278.

Heath, D. H. (with Heath, H. E). (1991). *Fulfilling lives: Paths to maturity and success.* San Francisco: Jossey-Bass.

Hochschild, A., & Machung, A. (1989). *The second shift: Working parents and the revolution at home.* New York: Viking.

Hoffman, M. L. (1981). The role of the father in moral internalization. In M. E. Lamb (Ed.), *The role of the father in child development* (pp. 359–378). New York: Wiley.

Hwang, C. P. (1987). The changing role of Swedish fathers. In M. E. Lamb (Ed.), *The father's role: Cross cultural perspectives* (pp. 115–138). Hillsdale, NJ: Erlbaum.

Hwang, C. P., Eldén, G., & Frannson, A. (1984). *Employers' and co-workers' attitudes toward father taking parental leave.* Sweden: University of Goteborg, Department of Psychology, Report 31.

Hyde, J. S., Essex, M. J., & Horton, F. (1993). Fathers and parental leave: Attitudes and experiences. *Journal of Family Issues, 14,* 616–638.

Ihinger-Tallman, M., Pasley, K., & Buehler, C. (1993). Developing a middle-range theory of father involvement postdivorce. *Journal of Family Issues, 14,* 550–571.

Ishii-Kuntz, M. (1994). Paternal involvement and perception toward fathers' roles: A comparison between Japan and the United States. *Journal of Family Issues, 15,* 30–48.

Ishii-Kuntz, M., & Coltrane, S. (1992). Predicting the sharing and household labor: Are parenting and housework distinct? *Sociological Perspectives, 35,* 629–647.

Jump, T. L., & Haas, L. (1987). Fathers in transition: Dual-career fathers participating in childcare. In M. Kimmel (Ed.), *Changing men: New research on men and masculinity* (pp. 98–114). Beverly Hills, CA: Sage.

Juster, F. T. (1985). A note on recent changes in time use. In F. T. Juster and F. Stafford (Eds)., *Time, goods, and well-being* (pp. 313–332). Ann Arbor, MI: Institute for Social Research.

Klinman, D. G. (1986). Fathers and the educational system. In M. E. Lamb (Ed.), *The father's role: Applied perspectives* (pp. 413–428). New York: Wiley.

Koestner, R., Franz, C., & Weinberger, J. (1990). The family origins of empathic concern: A 26-year longitudinal study. *Journal of Personality and Social Psychology, 58,* 709–717.

Krampe, E. M., & Fairweather, P. D. (1993). Father presence and family formation: A theoretical reformulation. *Journal of Family Issues, 14,* 572–591.

Labor Letter. (1991, April 30). *Wall Street Journal,* p. 1.

Lamb, M. E. (1987). Introduction: The emergent American father. In M. E. Lamb (Ed.), *The father's role: Cross-cultural perspectives* (pp. 3–25). Hillsdale, NJ: Erlbaum.

Lamb, M. E., Frodi, A. M., Hwang, C. P., & Frodi, M. (1982). Varying degrees of paternal involvement in infant care: Attitudinal and behavioral correlates. In M. E. Lamb (Ed.), *Nontraditional families: Parenting and child development* (pp. 117–138). Hillsdale, NJ: Erlbaum.

Lamb, M. E., Hwang, P., Broberg, A., Bookstein, F., Hult, G., & Frodi, M. (1988). The determinants of paternal involvement in a representative sample of primiparous Swedish families. *International Journal of Behavior and Development, 11,* 433–449.

Lamb, M. E., Pleck, J. H., Charnov, E. L., & Levine, J. A. (1985). Paternal behavior in humans. *American Zoologist, 25,* 883–894.

Lamb, M. E., Pleck, J. H., Charnov, E. L., & Levine, J. A. (1987). A biosocial perspective on paternal behavior and involvement. In J. B. Lancaster, J. Altman, A. Rossi, & L. R. Sherrod (Eds.), *Parenting across the lifespan: Biosocial perspectives* (pp. 11–42). New York: Academic.

Lamb, M. E., Pleck, J. H., & Levine, J. A. (1985). The role of the father in child development: The effects of increased paternal involvement. In B. Lahey & A. Kazdin (Eds.), *Advances in clinical child psychology* (Vol. 8; pp. 229–266). New York: Plenum.

LaRossa, R. (1988). Fatherhood and social change. *Family Relations, 37,* 451–457.

Larson, R. W. (1993). Finding time for fatherhood: The emotional ecology of adolescent-father interactions. *New Directions for Child Development, 62,* 7–25.

Lee, R. A. (1983). Flexitime and conjugal roles. *Journal of Occupational Behaviour, 4,* 297–315.

Lein, L. (1979). Male participation in home life: Impact of social supports and breadwinner responsibility on the allocation of tasks. *Family Coordinator, 28,* 489–495.

Lenney, E. (1991). Sex roles: The measurement of masculinity, femininity, and androgyny. In J. P. Robinson, P. R. Shaver, & L. S. Wrightsman (Eds.), *Measures of personality and social psychological attitudes* (pp. 573–660). New York: Academic.

Leslie, L. A., Anderson, E. A., & Branson, M. P. (1991). Responsibility for children: The role of gender and employment. *Journal of Family Issues, 12,* 197–210.

Levant, R. F., & Doyle, G. F. (1983). An evaluation of a parent education program for fathers of school-aged children. *Family Relations, 32,* 29.

Levant, R. F., Slattery, S. C., & Loiselle, J. E. (1987). Fathers' involvement in housework and child care with school-aged daughters. *Family Relations, 36,* 152–157.

Levy-Shiff, R., & Israelashvili, R. (1988). Antecedents of fathering: Some further exploration. *Developmental Psychology, 24,* 434–440.

MacDonald, K., & Parke, R. D. (1984). Bridging the gap: Parent-child play interaction and peer interactive competence. *Child Development, 55,* 1265–1277.

Maklan, D. (1977). *The four-day workweek.* New York: Praeger.

Manion, J. (1977). A study of fathers and infant caretaking. *Birth and the Family Journal, 4,* 174–179.

Marsiglio, W. (1991a). Male procreative consciousness and responsibility: A conceptual analysis and research agenda. *Journal of Family Issues, 12,* 268–290.

Marsiglio, W. (1991b). Paternal engagement activities with minor children. *Journal of Marriage and the Family,* 53, 973–986.

Marsiglio, W. (1992). Stepfathers with minor children living at home. *Journal of Family Issues, 13* (2), 195–214.

Marsiglio, W. (1994). Contemporary scholarship on fatherhood: Culture, identity, and conduct. *Journal of Family Issues, 14,* 484–450.

McAdoo, J. L. (1988). The roles of Black fathers in the socialization of Black children. In H. P. McAdoo (Ed.), *Black family* (pp. 257–269). Newbury Park, CA: Sage.

McBride, B. A. (1990). The effects of a parent education/play group program on father involvement in child rearing. *Family Relations, 39,* 250–256.

McBride, B. A., & Mills, G. (1993). A comparison of mother and father involvement with their preschool age children. *Early Childhood Research Quarterly, 8,* 457–477.

McHale, S. M., & Huston, T. L. (1984). Men and women as parents: Sex role orientations, employment, and parental roles with infants. *Child Development, 55,* 1349–1361.

McKenry, P. C., Price, S. J., Fine, M. A., & Serovich, J. (1991). Predictors of single, noncustodial fathers' physical involvement with their children. *Journal of Genetic Psychology, 153,* 305–319.

McLoyd, V. C. (1989). Socialization and development in a changing economy: The effects of paternal job and income loss on children. *American Psychologist, 44,* 293–302.

Mosley, J., & Thomson, E. (1995). Fathering behavior and child outcomes: The role of race and poverty. In W. Marsiglio (Ed.), *Fatherhood: Contemporary theory, research, and social policy* (pp. 148–165). Thousand Oaks, CA: Sage.

Ninio, A., & Rinott, N. (1988). Fathers' involvement in the care of their infants and their attributions of cognitive competence to infants. *Child Development, 59,* 652–663.

Nock, S. L., & Kingston, P. W. (1988). Time with children: The impact of couples' work-time commitments. *Social Forces, 67,* 59–85.

Nugent, J. K. (1991). Cultural and psychological influences on the father's role in infant development. *Journal of Marriage and the Family, 53,* 475–485.

O'Connell, M. (1993). *Where's papa? Fathers' role in child care.* Washington, DC: Population Reference Bureau.

O'Neil, R., & Greenberger, E. (1994). Patterns of commitment to work and parenting: Implications for role strain. *Journal of Marriage and the Family, 56,* 101–112.

Palkovitz, R. (1984). Parental attitudes and father's interactions with their 5-month-old infants. *Developmental Psychology, 20,* 1054–1060.

Palkovitz, R. (1985). Fathers' birth attendance, early contact, and extended contact with their newborns: A critical review. *Child Development, 56,* 392–406.

Parke, R. D., & Anderson, E. R. (1987). Fathers and their at-risk infants: Conceptual and empirical analyses. In P. W. Berman & F. A. Pederson (Eds.), *Men's transitions to parenthood: Longitudinal studies of early family experience* (pp. 197–216). Hillsdale, NJ: Erlbaum.

Pederson, F. A. (1976). Does research on children reared in father-absent families yield information on father influences? *Family Coordinator, 25,* 459–464.

Peterson, R. R., & Gerson, K. (1992). Determinants of responsibility for child care arrangements among dual-earner couples. *Journal of Marriage and the Family, 54,* 527–536.

Pleck, J. H. (1977). The work-family role system. *Social Problems, 24,* 417–427.

Pleck, J. H. (1983). Husbands' paid work and family roles: Current research issues. In H. Lopata & J. Pleck (Eds.), *Research in the interweave of social roles: Vol. 3. Families and jobs* (pp. 231–333). Greenwich, CT: JAI.

Pleck, J. H. (1985). *Working wives, working husbands.* Beverly Hills, CA: Sage.

Pleck, J. H. (1992a). Families and work: Small changes with big implications. *Qualitative Sociology, 15,* 427–432.

Pleck, J H. (1992b). Work-family policies in the United States. In H. Kahne & J. Z. Giele (Eds.), *Women's work and women's lives: The continuing struggle worldwide* (pp. 248–275). Boulder, CO: Westview.

Pleck, J. H. (1993). Are "family-supportive" employer policies relevant to men? In J. C. Hood (Ed.), *Men, work, and family* (pp. 217–237). Newbury Park, CA: Sage.

Pleck, J. H., Lamb, M. E., & Levine, J. A. (1986). Epilogue: Facilitating future change in men's family roles. In R. A. Lewis & M. Sussman (Eds.), *Men's changing roles in the family* (pp. 11–16). New York: Haworth.

Pleck, J. H., Sonenstein, F. L., & Ku, L. C. (1994a). Attitudes toward male roles among adolescent males: A discriminant validity analysis. *Sex Roles, 30,* 481–501.

Pleck, J. H., Sonenstein, F. L., & Ku, L. C. (1994b). Problem behaviors and masculinity ideology in adolescent males. In R. Ketterlinus & M. E. Lamb (Eds.), *Adolescent problem behaviors* (pp. 165–186). Hillsdale, NJ: Erlbaum.

Pleck, J. H., & Staines, G. (1985). Work schedules and family life in two-earner couples. *Journal of Family Issues, 6,* 61–81.

Pleck, J. H., Staines, G., & Lang, L. (1980). Conflict between work and family life. *Monthly Labor Review, 102,* 29–32.

Plomin, R. (1989). Environment and genes: Determinants of behavior. *American Psychologist, 44,* 105–111.

Presser, H. B. (1989). Can we make time for children? The economy, work schedules, and child care. *Demography, 26,* 523–543.

Pruett, K. D. (1987). Shining a new light on the fatherhood role [Review of *The nurturing father*]. *Yale*, 46.

Radin, N. (1981). The role of the father in cognitive, academic, and intellectual development. In M. E. Lamb (Ed.), *The role of the father in child development* (pp. 379–428). New York: Wiley.

Radin, N. (1994). Primary-caregiving fathers in intact families. In A. E. Gottfried & A. W. Gottfried (Eds.), *Redefining families: Implications for children's development* (pp. 55–97). New York: Plenum.

Rane, T. R., & Draper, T. W. (1995). Negative evaluations of men's nurturant touching of young children. *Psychological Reports, 76*, 811–818.

Rebelsky, F., & Hanks, C. (1971). Fathers' verbal interaction with infants in the first three months of life. *Child Development, 42*, 63–68.

Regional Research Institute for Human Services. (1987). *Employee profiles: 1987 dependent care survey*, Unpublished report, Portland State University.

Reuter, M. W., & Biller, H. B. (1973). Perceived paternal nurturance availability and personality adjustment among college males. *Journal of Consulting and Clinical Psychology, 40*, 339–342.

Robinson, J. P. (1977a). *Changes in Americans' use of time, 1965–75: A progress report*. Cleveland, OH: Cleveland State University, Communications Research Center.

Robinson, J. P. (1977b). *How Americans use time: A social-psychological analysis*. New York: Praeger.

Robinson, J. P., Andreyenkov, V. G., & Patrushev, V. D. (1988). *The rhythm of everyday life: How Soviet and American citizens use time*. Boulder, CO: Westview.

Roopnarine, J. L., & Ahmeduzzaman, M. (1993). Peurto Rican fathers' involvement with their preschool-age children. *Hispanic Journal of Behavioral Science*, pp. 96–107.

Rosenwasser, S. M., & Patterson, W. (1984–85). Nontraditional male: Men with primary child care/household responsibilities. *Psychology and Human Development, 1*, 101–111.

Russell, G. (1983). *The changing role of fathers*. St. Lucia, Queensland: University of Queensland Press.

Russell, G. (1986). Primary caretakers and role sharing fathers. In M. E. Lamb (Ed.), *The father's role: Applied perspectives* (pp. 29–60). New York: Wiley.

Rustia, J. G., & Abbott, D. (1993). Father involvement in infant care: Two longitudinal studies. *International Journal of Nursing Studies, 30*, 467–476.

Sagi, A. (1982). Antecedents and consequences of various degrees of paternal involvement in child rearing: The Israeli project. In M. E. Lamb (Ed.), *Nontraditional families: Parenting and child development* (pp. 205–222). Hillsdale, NJ: Erlbaum.

Sears, R. R., Maccoby, E. E., & Levin, H. (1957). *Patterns of childrearing*. Evanston, IL: Row Peterson.

Shinn, M., Ortiz-Torres, B., Morris, A., & Simko, P. (1987, August). *Child care patterns, stress, and job behaviors among working parents*. Paper presented to the American Psychological Association, New York.

Skow, J. (1989, August 7). The myth of male housework. *Time*, p. 62.

Small, S. A., & Eastman, G. (1991). Rearing adolescents in contemporary society: A conceptual framework for understanding the responsibilities and needs of parents. *Family Relations, 40*, 455–462.

Smith, H. L., & Morgan, S. P. (1994). Children's closeness to father as reported by mothers, sons and daughters: Evaluating subjective assessments with the Rasch Model. *Journal of Family Issues, 15*, 3–29.

Snarey, J. (1993). *How fathers care for the next generation: A four-decade study*. Cambridge, MA: Harvard University Press.

Spence, J. T., Helmreich, R. L., & Holanan, C. T. (1979). Negative and positive components of psychological masculinity and femininity and their relationships to self-reports of neurotic and acting out behaviors. *Journal of Personality and Social Psychology 37*, 1673–1682.

Staines, G. L., & Pleck, J. H. (1983). *The impact of work schedules on the family.* Ann Arbor, MI: Institute for Social Research.

Staines, G., & Pleck, J. H. (1986). Work schedule flexibility and family life. *Journal of Occupational Behaviour, 7*, 147–153.

Thomas, E. (1988, December 18). The reluctant father. *Newsweek*, pp. 64–66.

Trost, C. (1988, November 1). Men, too, wrestle with career-family stress. *Wall Street Journal*, p. 33.

Tulananda, O., Young, D. M., & Roopnarine, J. L. (1994). Thai and American fathers' involvement with preschool-age children. *Early Child Development and Care, 97*, 123–133.

Volling, B. L., & Belsky, J. (1991). Multiple determinants of father involvement during infancy in dual-earner and single earner families [Abstract]. *Journal of Marriage and the Family, 53*, 461–474.

Volling, B. L., & Belsky, J. (1992). The contribution of mother-child and father-child relationships to the quality of sibling interaction: A longitudinal study. *Child Development, 63*, 1209–1222.

Vondra, J., & Belsky, J. (1993). Developmental origins of parenting: Personality and relationship factors. In T. Luster & L. Okagaki (Eds.), *Parenting: An ecological perspective* (pp. 1–33). Hillsdale, NJ: Erlbaum.

Vrazo, D. (1990, October 15). Paternity leaves offered more often. *Providence Journal*, p. 17.

Whiting, B., & Edwards, C. P. (1973). A cross-cultural analysis of sex difference in the behavior of children aged 3 through 11. *Journal of Social Psychology, 91*, 171–188.

Williams, E., Radin, N., & Allegro, T. (1992). Sex-role attitudes of adolescents raised primarily by their fathers. *Merrill-Palmer Quarterly, 38*, 457–476.

Winett, R. A., & Neale, M. S. (1980). Results of experimental study on flexitime and family life. *Monthly Labor Review, 113*, 29–32.

Yogman, M. W. (1987). Father-infant caregiving and play with preterm and full-term infants. In P. W. Berman & F. A. Pederson (Eds.), *Men's transitions to parenthood: Longitudinal studies of early family experience* (pp. 175–196). Hillsdale, NJ: Erlbaum.

CHAPTER 6

Ainsworth, M. D. S. (1973). The development of infant-mother attachment. In B. M. Caldwell & H. N. Ricciuti (Eds.), *Review of child development research* (Vol. 3, pp. 1–94). Chicago: University of Chicago Press.

Ainsworth, M. D. S., Blehar, M. C., Waters, E., & Wall, S. (1978). *Patterns of attachment.* Hillsdale, NJ: Erlbaum.

Anderson, B. J., & Standley, K. (1976, September). *A methodology for observation of the childbirth environment.* Paper presented at the meeting of the American Psychological Association, Washington, DC.

Ban, P., & Lewis, M. (1974). Mothers and fathers, girls and boys: Attachment behavior in the one-year-old. *Merrill-Palmer Quarterly, 20*, 195–204.

Belsky, J. (1979). Mother-father-infant interaction: A naturalistic observational study. *Developmental Psychology, 15*, 601–607.

Belsky, J. (1980). A family analysis of parental influence on infant exploratory competence. In F. A. Pedersen (Ed.), *The father-infant relationship: Observational studies in a family setting* (pp. 87–110). New York: Praeger.

Belsky, J. (1981). Early human experience: A family perspective. *Developmental Psychology 17*, 3–19.

Belsky, J. (1985). Experimenting with the family in the newborn period. *Child Development, 56*, 407–414.

Belsky, J., Fish, M., & Isabella, R. (1991). Continuity and discontinuity in infant negative and positive emotionality: Family antecedents and attachment consequences. *Developmental Psychology, 27,* 421–431.

Belsky, J., Gilstrap, B., & Rovine, M. (1984). The Pennsylvania Infant and Family Development Project: I. Stability and change in mother-infant and father-infant interaction in a family setting at one, three, and nine months. *Child Development, 55,* 692–705.

Blount, G. B., & Padgug, E. J. (1976). Mother and father speech: Distribution of parental speech features in English and Spanish. *Papers and Reports on Child Language Development, 12,* 47–59.

Bowlby, J. (1969). *Attachment and loss: Vol. 1. Attachment.* New York: Basic Books.

Brachfeld-Child, S. (1986). Parents as teachers: Comparisons of mothers' and fathers' instructional interactions with infants. *Infant Behavior and Development, 9,* 127–131.

Brazelton, T. B. (1973). *Neonatal Behavioral Assessment Scale.* Philadelphia: Lippincott.

Brazelton, T. B., Yogman, M. W., Als, H., & Tronick, E. (1979). The infant as a focus for family reciprocity. In M. Lewis & L. A. Rosenblum (Eds.), *The child and its family* (pp. 29–43). New York: Plenum.

Bridges, L. J., Connell, J. P., & Belsky, J. (1988). Similarities and differences in infant-mother and infant-father interaction in the Strange Situation: A component process analysis. *Developmental Psychology, 24,* 92–100.

Bronstein, P. (1988). Father-child interaction: Implications for gender role socialization. In P. Bronstein & G. P. Cowan (Eds.), *Fatherhood today: Men's changing role in the family* (pp. 107–124). New York: Wiley.

Bronstein, P., & Cowan, G. P. (Eds.). 1988. *Fatherhood today: Men's changing role in the family.* New York: Wiley.

Brooks-Gunn, J., & Lewis, M. (1979). "Why Mama and Papa?" The development of social labels. *Child Development, 50,* 1203–1206.

Caldera, Y. M., Huston, A. C., & O'Brien, M. (1989). Social interactions and play patterns of parents and toddlers with feminine, masculine, and neutral toys. *Child Development, 60,* 70–76.

Clarke-Stewart, K. A. (1978). And daddy makes three: The father's impact on mother and young child. *Child Development, 49,* 466–478.

Clarke-Stewart, K. A. (1980). The father's contribution to children's cognitive and social development in early childhood. In F. A. Pedersen (Ed.), *The father-infant relationship: Observational studies in a family setting* (pp. 111–146). New York: Praeger.

Cleaves, W., & Rosenblatt, P. (1977, March). *Intimacy between adults and children in public places.* Paper presented at the meeting of the Society for Research in Child Development, New Orleans.

Cohen, L. J., & Campos, J. J. (1974). Father, mother, and stranger as elicitors of attachment behaviors in infancy. *Developmental Psychology, 10,* 146–154.

Cox, M. J., & Owen, M. T. (1991). *The origin of fathering.* Unpublished manuscript.

Cox, M. J., Owen, M. T., Henderson, V. K., & Margand, N. A. (1992). Prediction of infant-father and infant-mother attachment. *Developmental Psychology, 28,* 474–483.

Cox, M. J., Owen, M. T., Lewis, J. M., & Henderson, U. K. (1989). Marriage, adult adjustment, and early parenting. *Child Development, 60,* 1015–1024.

Crawley, S. B., & Sherrod, R. B. (1984). Parent-infant play during the first year of life. *Infant Behavior and Development, 7,* 65–75.

Crouter, A. C., Perry-Jenkins, M., Huston, T. L., & McHale, S. M. (1987). Processes underlying father-involvement in dual-earner and single-earner families. *Developmental Psychology, 23,* 431–440.

Dalton-Hummel, D. (1982). Syntactic and conversational characteristics of fathers' speech. *Journal of Psycholinguistic Research, 11,* 465–483.

Darke, P. R., & Goldberg, S. (1994). Father-infant interaction and parent stress with healthy and medically compromised infants. *Infant Behavior and Development, 17,* 3–14.

Deater-Deckard, K., Scarr, S., McCartney, K., & Eisenberg, M. (1994). Paternal separation anxiety: Relationships with parenting stress, child-rearing attitudes, and maternal anxieties. *Psychological Science, 5,* 341–346.

Dickie, J., & Matheson, P. (1984, August). *Mother-father-infant: Who needs support?* Paper presented at the meeting of the American Psychological Association Convention, Toronto.

Dickstein, S., & Parke, R. D. (1988). Social referencing in infancy: A glance at fathers and marriage. *Child Development, 59,* 506–511.

Donate-Bartfield, D., & Passman, R. H. (1985). Attentiveness of mothers and fathers to their baby's cries. *Infant Behavior and Development, 8,* 385–393.

Durrett, M. E., Otaki, M., & Richards, P. (1984). Attachment and the mothers' perception of support from the father. *International Journal of Behavioral Development, 7,* 167–176.

Durrett, M., Richards, P., Otaki, M., Pennebaker, J., & Nyquist, L. (1986). Mother's involvement with infant and her perception of spousal support, Japan and America. *Journal of Marriage and the Family, 68,* 187–194.

Easterbrooks, M. A., & Emde, R. N. (1988). Marital and parent-child relationships: The role of affect in the family system. In R. Hinde & J. Stevenson-Hinde (Eds)., *Relationships within families* (pp. 83–103). New York: Oxford University Press.

Easterbrooks, M. A., & Goldberg, W. A. (1984). Toddler development in the family: Impact of father involvement and parenting characteristics. *Child Development, 53,* 740–752.

Engfer, A. (1988). The interrelatedness of marriage and the mother-child relationship. In R. A. Hinde & J. Stevenson-Hinde (Eds.), *Relationships within families: Mutual influences* (pp. 104–118). New York: Oxford University Press.

Fagot, B. I. (1974). Sex differences in toddler's behavior and parental reaction. *Developmental Psychology, 10,* 554–558.

Fagot, B. L., & Hagan, R. (1991). Observations of parent reactions to sex-stereotyped behaviors: Age and sex effects. *Child Development, 62,* 617–628.

Fagot, B. L., & Kavanagh, K. (1993). Parenting during the second year: Effects of children's age, sex, and attachment classification. *Child Development, 64,* 258–271.

Feiring, C. (1976, March). *The preliminary development of a social systems model of early infant-mother attachment.* Paper presented at the meeting of the Eastern Psychological Association, New York.

Feldman, S. S., & Ingham, M. E. (1975). Attachment behavior: A validation study in two age groups. *Child Development, 46,* 319–330.

Feldman, S. S., & Nash, S. C. (1977). The effect of family formation on sex stereotypic behavior: A study of responsiveness to babies. In W. Miller & L. Newman (Eds.), *The first child and family formation* (pp. 51–63). Chapel Hill, NC: University of North Carolina Press.

Feldman, S. S., & Nash, S. C. (1978). Interest in babies during young adulthood. *Child Development, 49,* 617–622.

Feldman, S. S., & Nash, S. C. (1985). Antecedents of early parenting. In A. D. Fogel & G. F. Nelson (Eds.), *Origins of nurturance* (pp. 1–33). Hillsdale, NJ: Erlbaum.

Feldman, S. S., Nash, S. C., & Aschenbrenner, B. G. (1983). Antecedents of fathering. *Child Development, 54,* 1628–1636.

Feldman, S. S., Nash, S. C., & Cutrona, C. (1977). The influence of age and sex on responsiveness to babies. *Developmental Psychology, 13,* 675–676.

Field, T. (1978). Interaction behaviors of primary versus secondary caretaker fathers. *Developmental Psychology, 14,* 183–184.

Field, T., Gewirtz, J. L., Cohen, D., Garcia, R., Greenberg, R., & Collins, K. (1984). Leave-takings and reunions of infants, toddlers, preschoolers, and their parents. *Child Development, 55,* 628–635.

Field, T., Vega-Lahr, N., Goldstein, S., & Scafidi, F. (1987). Interaction behavior of infants and their dual-career parents. *Infant Behavior and Development, 10,* 371–377.

Fox, N. A., Kimmerly, N. L., & Schafter, W. D. (1991). Attachment to mother/attachment to father: A meta-analysis. *Child Development, 62,* 210–225.

Frascarolo-Moutinot, F. (1994). *Engagement paternal quotidien et relations parents-enfant* [Daily paternal involvement and parent-child relationships]. Unpublished doctoral dissertation, University of Geneva.

Frodi, A. M., & Lamb, M. E. (1978). Sex differences in responsiveness to infants: A developmental study of psychophysiological and behavioral responses. *Child Development, 49,* 1182–1188.

Frodi, A. M., Lamb, M. E., Hwang, C. P., & Frodi, M. (1983). Father-mother-infant interaction in traditional and nontraditional Swedish families: A longitudinal study. *Alternative Lifestyles, 5,* 142–163.

Frodi, A. M., Lamb, M. E., Leavitt, L. A., & Donovan, W. L. (1978). Fathers' and mothers' responses to infant smiles and cries. *Infant Behavior and Development, 1,* 187–198.

Frodi, A. M., Lamb, M. E., Leavitt, L. A., Donovan, W. L., Neff, C., & Sherry, D. (1978). Fathers' and mother's responses to the faces and cries of normal and premature infants. *Developmental Psychology, 14,* 490–498.

Frodi, A. M., Murray, A. D., Lamb, M. E., & Steinberg, J. (1984). Biological and social determinants of responsiveness to infants in 10- to 15-year-old girls. *Sex Roles, 10,* 639–649.

Gable, S., Crnic, K., & Belsky, J. (1994). Coparenting within the family system: Influences on children's development. *Family Relations, 43,* 380–386.

Gewirtz, H. B., & Gewirtz, J. L. (1968). Visiting and caretaking patterns for kibbutz infants: Age and sex trends. *American Journal of Orthopsychiatry, 38,* 427–443.

Gleason, J. B. (1975). Fathers and other strangers: Men's speech to young children. In D. P. Dato (Ed.), *Language and linguistics* (pp. 289–297). Washington, DC: Georgetown University Press.

Goldberg, W. A., & Easterbrooks, M. A. (1984). The role of marital quality in toddler development. *Developmental Psychology, 20,* 504–514.

Golinkoff, R. M., & Ames, G. J. (1979). A comparison of fathers' and mothers' speech with their young children. *Child Development, 50,* 28–32.

Gottfried, A. E., Gottfried, A. W., & Bathurst, K. (1988). Maternal employment, family environment, and children's development: Infancy through the school years. In A. E. Gottfried & A. W. Gottfried (Eds.), *Maternal employment and children's development: Longitudinal research* (pp. 11–58). New York: Plenum.

Greenberg, M., & Morris, N. (1974). Engrossment: The newborn's impact upon the father. *American Journal of Orthopsychiatry, 44,* 520–531.

Grossmann, K. E., & Volkmer, H. J. (1984). Fathers' presence during birth of their infants and paternal involvement. *International Journal of Behavioral Development, 7,* 157–165.

Haas, L. (1992). *Equal parenthood and social policy: A study of parental leave in Sweden.* Albany, NY: State University of New York Press.

Haas, L. (1993). Nurturing fathers and working mothers: Changing gender roles in Sweden. In J. C. Hood (Ed.), *Men, work, and family* (pp. 238–261). Newbury Park, CA: Sage.

Heermann, J. A., Jones, L. C., & Wikoff, R. L. (1994). Measurement of parent behavior during interactions with their infants. *Infant Behavior and Development, 17,* 311–321.

Heinicke, C. M. (1984). Impact of prebirth parent personality and marital functioning on family development: A framework and suggestions for future study. *Developmental Psychology, 20,* 1044–1053.

Heinicke, C. M., Diskin, S. D., Ramsey-Klee, D. M., & Oates, D. S. (1986). Pre- and postbirth antecedents of two-year-old attention, capacity for relationships, and verbal expressiveness. *Developmental Psychology, 22,* 777–787.

Heinicke, C. M., & Guthrie, D. (1992). Stability and change in husband-wife adaptation and the development of the positive parent-child relationship. *Infant Behavior and Development, 15,* 109–127.

Heinicke, C. M., & Lampl, E. (1988). Pre- and postbirth antecedents of 3- and 4-year-old attention, IQ, verbal expressiveness, task orientation, and capacity for relationships. *Infant Behavior and Development, 11,* 381–410.

Henneborn, W. J., & Cogan, R. (1975). The effect of husband participation in reported pain and the probability of medication during labor and birth. *Journal of Psychosomatic Research, 19,* 215–222.

Hewlett, B. S. (1987). Intimate fathers: Patterns of paternal holding among Aka pygmies. In M. E. Lamb (Ed.), *The father's role: Cross-cultural perspectives* (pp. 295–330). Hillsdale, NJ: Erlbaum.

Hewlett, B. S. (Ed.) (1990). *Father-child relations: Cultural and biosocial contexts.* New York: de Gruyter.

Hirshberg, L. M., & Svejda, M. (1990). When infants look to their parents: I. Infants' social referencing of mothers compared to fathers. *Child Development, 61,* 1175–1186.

Hossain, Z., & Roopnarine, J. L. (1994). African-American fathers' involvement with infants: Relationship to their functional style, support, education, and income. *Infant Behavior and Development, 17,* 175–184.

Hunter, F. T., McCarthy, M. E., MacTurk, R. H., & Vietze, P. M. (1987). Infants' social-constructive interactions with mothers and fathers. *Developmental Psychology, 23,* 249–254.

Hwang, C. P. (1986). Behavior of Swedish primary and secondary caretaking fathers in relation to mothers' presence. *Developmental Psychology, 22,* 749–751.

Hwang, C. P. (1987). The changing role of Swedish fathers. In M. E. Lamb (Ed.), *The father's role: Cross-cultural perspectives* (pp. 115–138). Hillsdale, NJ: Erlbaum.

Hyde, J. S., Essex, M. J., & Horton, F. (1993). Fathers and parental leave: Attitudes and expectations. *Journal of Family Issues, 14,* 616–641.

Hyde, B. L., & Texidor, M. S. (1988). A description of the fathering experience among black fathers. *Journal of Black Nurses Association, 2,* 67–78.

Jackson, S. (1987). Great Britain. In M. E. Lamb (Ed.), *The father's role: Cross-cultural perspectives* (pp. 29–57). Hillsdale, NJ: Erlbaum.

Jarvis, P. A., & Creasey, G. L. (1991). Parental stress, coping, and attachment in families with an 18-month-old infant. *Infant Behavior and Development, 14,* 383–395.

Jouriles, E. N., Pfiffner, L. J., & O'Leary, S. G. (1988). Marital conflict, parenting, and toddler conduct problems. *Journal of Abnormal Psychology, 16,* 197–206.

Kaitz, M., Lapidot, P., Bronner, R., & Eidelman, A. L. (1992). Parturient women can recognize their infants by touch. *Developmental Psychology, 28,* 35–39.

Kaitz, M., Meirov, H., Landman, I., & Eidelman, A. L. (1993). Infant recognition by tactile cues. *Infant Behavior and Development, 16,* 333–341.

Kaitz, M., Shiri, S., Danziger, S., Hershko, Z., & Eidelman, A. L. (1994). Fathers can also recognize their newborns by touch. *Infant Behavior and Development, 17,* 205–207.

Kauffman, A. L. (1977, April). *Mothers' and fathers' verbal interactions with children learning language.* Paper presented at the meeting of the Eastern Psychological Association, Boston.

Keller, W. D., Hildebrandt, K. A., & Richards, M. E. (1985). Effects of extended father-infant contact during the newborn period. *Infant Behavior and Development, 8,* 337–350.

Klaus, M., Kennell, J., Plumb, N., & Zuehlke, S. (1970). Human maternal behavior at the first contact with her young. *Pediatrics, 46,* 862–866.

Kotelchuck, M. (1972). *The nature of the child's tie to his father.* Unpublished doctoral dissertation, Harvard University.

Kotelchuck, M. (1975, September). *Father caretaking characteristics and their influence on infant father interaction.* Paper presented at the meeting of the American Psychological Association, Chicago.

Kotelchuck, M. (1976). The infant's relationship to the father: Experimental evidence. In M. E. Lamb (Ed.), *The role of the father in child development* (pp. 329–344). New York: Wiley.

Lamb, M. E. (1975). Fathers: Forgotten contributors to child development. *Human Development, 18,* 245–266.

Lamb, M. E. (1976a). Effects of stress and cohort on mother- and father-infant interaction. *Developmental Psychology, 12,* 435–443.

Lamb, M. E. (1976b). Interaction between eight-month-old children and their fathers and mothers. In M. E. Lamb (Ed.), *The role of the father in child development* (pp. 307–327). New York: Wiley.

Lamb, M. E. (1976c). Interactions between two-year-olds and their mothers and fathers. *Psychological Reports, 38,* 447–450.

Lamb, M. E. (1976d). Parent-infant interaction in eight-month-olds. *Child Psychiatry and Human Development, 7,* 56–63.

Lamb, M. E. (1976e). Twelve-month-olds and their parents: Interaction in a laboratory playroom. *Developmental Psychology, 12,* 237–244.

Lamb, M. E. (1977a). The development of mother-infant and father-infant attachments in the second year of life. *Developmental Psychology, 13,* 637–648.

Lamb, M. E. (1977b). The development of parental preferences in the first two years of life. *Sex roles, 3,* 495–497.

Lamb, M. E. (1977c). Father-infant and mother-infant interaction in the fist year of life. *Child Development, 48,* 167–181.

Lamb, M. E. (1978). Infant social cognition and "second-order" effects. *Infant Behavior and Development, 1,* 1–10.

Lamb, M. E. (1979). The effects of the social context on dyadic social interaction. In M. E. Lamb, S. J. Suomi, & G. R. Stephenson (Eds.), *Social interaction analysis: Methodological issues* (pp. 253–268). Madison, WI: University of Wisconsin Press.

Lamb, M. E. (1981). The development of social expectations in the first year of life. In M. E. Lamb & L. R. Sherrod (Eds.), *Infant social cognition: Empirical and theoretical considerations* (pp. 155–175). Hillsdale, NJ: Erlbaum.

Lamb, M. E. (1986). The changing roles of fathers. In M. E. Lamb (Ed.), *The father's role: Applied perspectives* (pp. 3–27). New York: Wiley.

Lamb, M. E. (1987). Predictive implications of individual differences in attachment. *Journal of Consulting and Clinical Psychology, 55,* 817–824.

Lamb, M. E., Chase-Lansdale, L., & Owen M. T. (1979). The changing American family and its implications for infant social development: The sample case of maternal employment. In M. Lewis & L. A. Rosenblum (Eds.), *The child and its family* (pp. 267–291). New York: Plenum.

Lamb, M. E., & Easterbrooks, M. A. (1981). Individual differences in parental sensitivity: Origins, components and consequences. In M. E. Lamb & L. R. Sherrod (Eds.), *Infant social cognition: Empirical and theoretical considerations* (pp. 127–153). Hillsdale, NJ: Erlbaum.

Lamb, M. E., & Elster, A. B. (1985). Adolescent mother-infant-father relationships. *Developmental Psychology, 21,* 768–773.

Lamb, M. E., Frodi, A. M., Frodi, M., & Hwang, C. P. (1982). Characteristics of maternal and paternal behavior in traditional and nontraditional Swedish families. *International Journal of Behavioral Development, 5,* 131–141.

Lamb, M. E., Frodi, A. M., Hwang, C. P., & Frodi, M. (1982). Varying degrees of paternal involvement in infant care: Attitudinal and behavioral correlates. In M. E. Lamb (Ed.), *Nontraditional families: Parenting and child development* (pp. 117–137). Hillsdale, NJ: Erlbaum.

Lamb, M. E., Frodi, M., Hwang, C. P., & Frodi, A. M. (1983a). Effects of paternal involvement on infant preferences for mothers and fathers. *Child Development, 54,* 450–458.

Lamb, M. E., Frodi, A. M., Hwang, C. P., & Frodi, M. (1983b). Interobserver and test retest reliability of Rothbart's Infant Behavior Questionnaire. *Scandinavian Journal of Psychology, 24,* 153–156.

Lamb, M. E., Frodi, A. M., Hwang, C. P., Frodi, M., & Steinberg, J. (1982a). Effects of gender and caretaking role on parent-infant interaction. In R. N. Emde & R. J. Harmon (Eds.), *Development and attachment and affiliative systems* (pp. 109–118). New York: Plenum.

Lamb, M. E., Frodi, A. M., Hwang, C. P., Frodi, M., & Steinberg, J. (1982b). Mother- and father-infant interaction involving play and holding in traditional and nontraditional Swedish families. *Developmental Psychology, 18,* 215–221.

Lamb, M. E., & Gilbride, R. (1985). Compatibility in parent-infant relationships: Origins and processes. In W. Ickes (Ed.), *Compatible and incompatible relationships* (pp. 33–60). New York: Springer.

Lamb, M. E., Hwang, C. P., Broberg, A., Bookstein, F. L., Hult, G., & Frodi, M. (1988). The determinants of paternal involvement in primiparous Swedish families. *International Journal of Behavioral Development, 11,* 433–449.

Lamb, M. E., Hwang, C. P., Frodi, A. M., & Frodi, M. (1982). Security of mother- and father-infant attachment and its relation to sociability with strangers in traditional and nontraditional Swedish families. *Infant Behavior and Development, 5,* 355–367.

Lamb, M. E., & Levine, J. A. (1983). The Swedish parental insurance policy: An experiment in social engineering. In M. E. Lamb & A. Sagi (Eds.), *Fatherhood and family policy* (pp. 39–51). Hillsdale, NJ: Erlbaum.

Lamb, M. E., Owen, M. T., & Chase-Lansdale, L. (1980). The working mother in the intact family: A process model. In R. R. Abidin (Ed.), *Parent education and intervention handbook* (pp. 59–81). Springfield, IL: Thomas.

Lamb, M. E., & Sherrod, L. R. (Eds). (1981). *Infant social cognition: Empirical and theoretical considerations.* Hillsdale, NJ: Erlbaum.

Lamb, M. E., & Stevenson, M. B. (1978). Father-infant relationships: Their nature and importance. *Youth and Society, 9,* 277–298.

Lamb, M. E., Thompson, R. A., Gardner, W., & Charnov, E. L. (1985). *Infant-mother attachment: The origins and developmental significance of individual differences in Strange Situation behavior.* Hillsdale, NJ: Erlbaum.

Lester, B. M., Kotelchuck, M., Spelke, E., Sellers, M. J., & Klein, R. E. (1974). Separation protest in Guatemalan infants: Cross-cultural and cognitive findings. *Developmental Psychology, 10,* 79–85.

Levy-Shiff, R., Goldschmidt, I., & Har-Even, D. (1991). Transition to parenthood in adoptive families. *Developmental Psychology, 27,* 131–140.

Levy-Shiff, R., & Israelashvili, R. (1988). Antecedents of fathering: Some further exploration. *Developmental Psychology, 24,* 434–440.

Levy-Shiff, R., Sharir, H., & Mogilner, M. B. (1989). Mother- and father-preterm infant relationship in the hospital preterm nursery. *Child Development, 60,* 93–102.

Lewis, C. (1984, September). *Men's involvement in fatherhood: Historical and gender issues.* Paper presented at the meeting of the British Psychological Society (Developmental Section), Lancaster.

Lewis, C. (1986). *Becoming a father.* Milton Keynes, UK: Open University Press.

Lewis, M., & Ban, P. (1971, April). *Stability of attachment behavior: A transformational analysis.* Paper presented at the meeting of the Society for Research in Child Development, Minneapolis.

Lewis, M., Feiring C., & Weinraub, M. (1981). The father as a member of the child's social network. In M. E. Lamb (Ed.), *The role of the father in child development* (pp. 259–294). New York: Wiley.

Lewis, M., & Kreitzberg, V. S. (1979). Effects of birth order and spacing on mother-infant interactions. *Developmental Psychology, 15,* 617–625.

Lewis, M., & Weinraub, M. (1974). Sex of parent × sex of child: Socioemotional development. In R. Richart, R. Friedman, & R. Vande Wiele (Eds.), *Sex differences in behavior* (pp. 165–189). New York: Wiley.

Lewis, M., Weinraub, M., & Ban, P. (1972). Mothers and fathers, girls and boys: Attachment behavior in the first two years of life. *Educational Testing Service Research Bulletin,* Princeton, NJ.

Liddell, C., Henzi, S. P., & Drew, M. (1987). Mothers, fathers, and children in an urban park playground: A comparison of dyads and triads. *Developmental Psychology, 23,* 262–266.

Lind, R. (1974, October). *Observations after delivery of communications between mother-infant-father.* Paper presented at the meeting of the International Congress of Pediatrics, Buenos Aires.

Lytton, H. (1979). Disciplinary encounters between young boys and their mothers and fathers: Is there a contingency system? *Developmental Psychology, 15,* 256–268.

Lytton, H., & Romney, D. M. (1991). Parents' differential socialization of boys and girls: A meta-analysis. *Psychological Bulletin, 109,* 267–296.

MacDonald, K., & Parke, R. D. (1984). Bridging the gap: Parent-child play interaction and peer interactive competence. *Child Development, 55,* 1265–1277.

Main, M., & Weston, D. (1981). The quality of the toddler's relationship to mother and to father: Related to conflict behavior and the readiness to establish new relationships. *Child Development, 52,* 932–940.

Marsiglio, W. (Ed.). (1993). Fatherhood [Special issue]. *Journal of Family Issues, 14*(4).

Marsiglio, W. (Ed.). (1994). Fatherhood: Results from national surveys [Special issue]. *Journal of Family Issues, 15*(1).

Marton, P. L., & Minde, K. (1980, April). *Paternal and maternal behavior with premature infants.* Paper presented at the meeting of the American Orthopsychiatric Association, Toronto.

Marton, P., Minde, K., & Perrotta, M. (1981). The role of the father for the infant at risk. *American Journal of Orthopsychiatry, 51,* 677–679.

McConachie, H. (1989). Mothers' and fathers' interaction with their young mentally handicapped children. *International Journal of Behavioral Development, 12,* 239–255.

McGuire, J. (1982). Gender-specific differences in early childhood: The impact of the father. In N. Beail & J. McGuire (Eds.), *Fathers: Psychological aspects* (pp. 95–125). London: Junction.

McHale, S. M., & Huston, T. L. (1984). Men and women as parents: Sex role orientations, employment, and parental roles with infants. *Child Development, 55,* 1349–1361.

Mebert, C. J. (1989). Stability and change in parents' perceptions of infant temperament: Early pregnancy to 13.5 months post-partum. *Infant Behavior and Development, 12,* 237–244.

Meyer, H. J. (1988). Marital and mother-child relationships: Developmental history, parent personality, and child difficultness. In R. A. Hinde & J. Stevenson-Hinde (Eds.), *Relationship within families: Mutual influences* (pp. 119–139). Oxford: Clarendon.

Minde, K., Marton, P., Manning, D., & Hines, B. (1980). Some determinants of mother-infant interaction in the premature nursery. *Journal of the Academy of Child Psychiatry, 19,* 1–21.

Myers, B. J. (1982). Early intervention using Brazelton training with middle-class mothers and fathers of newborns. *Child Development, 53,* 462–471.

Nash, S. C., & Feldman, S. S. (1981). Sex role and sex-related attributions: Constancy and change across the family life cycle. In M. E. Lamb & A. L. Brown (Eds.), *Advances in developmental psychology* (Vol. 1, pp. 1–35). Hillsdale, NJ: Erlbaum.

New, R. S., & Benigni, L. (1987). Italian fathers and infants: Cultural constraints on paternal behavior. In M. E. Lamb (Eds.), *The father's role: Cross-cultural perspectives* (pp. 139–167). Hillsdale, NJ: Erlbaum.

Nickel, H., & Köcher, E. M. T. (1987). West Germany and the German-speaking countries.

In M. E. Lamb (Ed.), *The father's role: Cross-cultural perspectives* (pp. 89–114). Hillsdale, NJ: Erlbaum.

Ninio, A., & Rinott, N. (1988). Fathers' involvement in the care of their infants and their attributions of cognitive competence to infants. *Child Development, 59,* 652–663.

Nugent, J. K. (1987). The father's role in early Irish socialization: Historical and empirical perspectives. In M. E. Lamb (Ed.), *The father's role: Cross-cultural perspectives* (pp. 169–193). Hillsdale, NJ: Erlbaum.

Oppenheim, D., Sagi, A., & Lamb, M. E. (1988). Infant-adult attachments on the kibbutzim and their relation to socioemotional development 4 years later. *Developmental Psychology, 24,* 427–433.

Owen, M. T., Easterbrooks, M. A., Chase-Lansdale, L., & Goldberg, W. A. (1984). The relation between maternal employment status and the stability of attachments to mother and to father. *Child Development, 55,* 1894–1901.

Palkovitz, R. (1984). Parental attitudes and fathers' interactions with their 5-month-old infants. *Developmental Psychology, 20,* 1054–1060.

Palkovitz, R. (1985). Fathers' birth attendance, early contact, and extended contact with their newborns: A critical review. *Child Development, 56,* 392–406.

Pannabecker, B., Emde, R. N., & Austin, B. (1982). The effect of early extended contact on father-newborn interaction. *Journal of Genetic Psychology, 141,* 7–17.

Parke, R. D. (1979). Perspectives on father-infant interaction. In J. D. Osofsky (Ed.), *Handbook of infant development* (pp. 549–590). New York: Wiley.

Parke, R. D., & Beitch, A. (1986). Hospital-based intervention for fathers. In M. E. Lamb (Ed.), *The father's role: Applied perspectives* (pp. 293–323). New York: Wiley.

Parke, R. D., & O'Leary, S. E. (1976). Family interaction in the newborn period: Some findings, some observations and some unresolved issues. In K. Riegel & J. Meacham (Eds.), *The developing individual in a changing world: Vol. 2. Social and environmental issues* (pp. 653–663). The Hague: Mouton.

Parke, R. D., O'Leary, S. E., & West, S. (1972). Mother-father-newborn interaction: Effects of maternal medication, labor and sex of infant. *Proceedings of the Annual Convention of the American Psychological Association, 7,* 85–86.

Parke, R. D., & Sawin, D. B. (1975, April). *Infant characteristics and behavior as elicitors of maternal and paternal responsivity in the newborn period.* Paper presented at the meeting of the Society for Research in Child Development, Denver.

Parke, R. D., & Sawin, D. B. (1977, March). *The family in early infancy: Social interactional and attitudinal analyses.* Paper presented at the meeting of the Society for Research in Child Development, New Orleans.

Parke, R. D., & Sawin, D. B. (1980). The family in early infancy: Social interactional and attitudinal analyses. In F. A. Pedersen (Ed.), *The father-infant relationship: Observational studies in a family setting* (pp. 44–70). New York: Praeger.

Parke, R. D., & Tinsley, B. R. (1985). Fathers as agents and recipients of support in the postnatal period. In Z. Boukydis (Ed.), *Research on support for parents and infants in the postnatal period* (pp. 84–113). Norwood, NJ: Ablex.

Pedersen, F. A. (1975, September). *Mother, father, and infant as an interactive system.* Paper presented at the meeting of the American Psychological Association, Chicago.

Pedersen, F. A., Anderson, B., & Cain, R. (1977, March). *An approach to understanding linkages between the parent-infant and spouse relationships.* Paper presented at the meeting of the Society for Research in Child Development, New Orleans.

Pedersen, F. A., Anderson, B., & Cain, R. (1980). Parent-infant and husband-wife interactions observed at age 5 months. In F. A. Pedersen (Ed.), *The father-infant relationship: Observational studies in a family setting* (pp. 71–86). New York: Praeger.

Pedersen, F. A., Cain, R., Zaslow, M., & Anderson, B. (1982). Variation in infant experience associated with alternative family roles. In L. Laosa & I. Siegel (Eds.), *Families as learning environments for children* (pp. 203–221). New York: Plenum.

Pedersen, F. A., & Robson, K. (1969). Father participation in infancy. *American Journal of Orthopsychiatry, 39,* 466–472.

Pedersen, F. A., Rubinstein, J. L., & Yarrow, L. J. (1979). Infant development in father-absent families. *Journal of Genetic Psychology, 135,* 51–61.

Phillips, P., & Parke, R. D. (1979). *Father and mother speech to prelinguistic infants.* Unpublished manuscript, University of Illinois.

Power, T. G. (1985). Mother- and father-infant play: A developmental analysis. *Child Development, 56,* 1514–1524.

Power, T. G., & Parke, R. D. (1979, March). *Toward a taxonomy of father-infant and mother-infant play patterns.* Paper presented to the Society for Research in Child Development, San Francisco.

Power, T. G., & Parke, R. D. (1983). Patterns of mother and father play with their 8-month-old infant: A multiple analyses approach. *Infant Behavior and Development, 6,* 453–459.

Power, T. G., & Parke, R. D. (1986). Patterns of early socialization: Mother- and father-infant interaction in the home. *International Journal of Behavioral Development, 9,* 331–341.

Price, G. (1977, March). *Factors influencing reciprocity in early mother-infant interaction.* Paper presented at the meeting of the Society for Research in Child Development, New Orleans.

Pruett, K. (1985). Oedipal configurations in young father-raised children. *Psychoanalytic Study of the Child, 40,* 435–460.

Pruett, K., & Litzenberger, B. (1992). Latency development in children of primary nurturing fathers: Eight-year follow-up. *Psychoanalytic Study of the Child, 4,* 85–101.

Radin, N. (1994). Primary-caregiving fathers in intact families. In A. E. Gottfried & A. W. Gottfried (Eds.), *Redefining families: Implications for children's development* (pp. 11–54). New York: Plenum.

Rendina, I., & Dickerscheid, J. D. (1976). Father involvement with first-born infants. *Family Coordinator, 25,* 373–379.

Richards, M. P. M., Dunn, J. F., & Antonis, B. (1975). *Caretaking in the first year of life: The role of fathers' and mothers' social isolation.* Unpublished manuscript, Cambridge University.

Rödholm, M., & Larsson, K. (1979). Father-infant interaction at the first contact after delivery. *Early Human Development, 3*(1), 21–27.

Rödholm, M., & Larsson, K. (1982). The behavior of human male adults at their first contact with a newborn. *Infant Behavior and Development, 5,* 121–130.

Rondal, J. A. (1980). Fathers' and mothers' speech in early language development. *Journal of Child Language, 7,* 353–369.

Rosenblatt, P. C. (1974). Behavior in public places: Comparison of couples accompanied and unaccompanied by children. *Journal of Marriage and the Family, 36,* 750–755.

Ross, G., Kagan, J., Zelazo, P., & Kotelchuck, M. (1975). Separation protest in infants in home and laboratory. *Developmental Psychology, 11,* 256–257.

Sagi, A., Lamb, M. E., & Gardner, W. (1986). Relations between Strange Situation behavior and stranger sociability among infants on Israeli kibbutzim. *Infant Behavior and Development, 9,* 271–282.

Sagi, A., Lamb, M. E., Shoham, R., Dvir, R., & Lewkowicz, K. S. (1985). Parent-infant interaction in families on Israeli kibbutzim. *International Journal of Behavioral Development, 8,* 273–284.

Schaffer, H. R. (1963). Some issues for research in the study of attachment behaviour. In B. M. Foss (Ed.), *Determinants of infant behaviour* (Vol. 2, pp. 179–196). London: Methuen.

Schaffer, H. R., & Emerson, P. E. (1964). The development of social attachments in infancy [Special issue]. *Monographs of the Society for Research in Child Development, 29*(94).

Siegel, A. U. (1987). Are sons and daughters treated more differently by fathers than by mothers? *Developmental Review, 7,* 183–209.

Snow, M. E., Jacklin, C. N., & Maccoby, E. E. (1983). Sex-of-child differences in father-child interaction at one year of age. *Child Development, 54,* 227–232.

Spelke, E., Zelazo, P., Kagan, J., & Kotelchuck, M. (1973). Father interaction and separation protest. *Developmental Psychology, 9,* 83–90.

Stevenson, M. B., & Lamb, M. E. (1981). The effects of social experience and social style on cognitive competence and performance. In M. E. Lamb & L. R. Sherrod (Eds.), *Infant social cognition: Theoretical and empirical considerations* (pp. 375–394). Hillsdale, NJ: Erlbaum.

Stoneman, Z., & Brody, G. H. (1981). Two's company, three makes a difference: An examination of mothers' and fathers' speech to their young children. *Child Development, 52,* 705–707.

Teti, D. M., Bond, L. A., & Gibbs, E. D. (1988). Mothers, fathers, and siblings: A comparison of play styles and their influence upon infant cognitive level. *International Journal of Behavioral Development, 11,* 415–432.

Wachs, T., Uzgiris, I., & Hunt, J. (1971). Cognitive development in infants of different age levels and from different environmental backgrounds. *Merrill-Palmer Quarterly, 17,* 283–317.

Warren-Leubecker, A., & Bohannon, J. N., III. (1984). Intonation patterns in child-directed speech: Mother-father differences. *Child Development, 55,* 1379–1385.

Weinraub, M., & Frankel, J. (1977). Sex differences in parent-infant interaction during free play, departure, and separation. *Child Development, 48,* 1240–1249.

West, M. M., & Konner, M. J. (1976). The role of the father: An anthropological perspective. In M. E. Lamb (Ed.), *The role of the father in child development* (pp. 185–216). New York: Wiley.

Willemsen, E., Flaherty, D., Heaton, C., & Ritchey, G. (1974). Attachment behavior of one-year-olds as a function of mother vs. father, sex of child, session, and toys. *Genetic Psychology Monographs, 90,* 305–324.

Woollett, A., White, D., & Lyon, L. (1982). Observations of fathers at birth. In N. Beail & J. McGuire (Eds.), *Fathers: Psychological perspectives* (pp. 72–94). London: Junction.

Yarrow, L. J., MacTurk, R. H., Vietze, P. M., McCarthy, M. E., Klein, R. P., & McQuiston, S. (1984). Developmental course of parental stimulation and its relationship to mastery motivation during infancy. *Developmental Psychology, 20,* 492–503.

Yogman, M. (1981). Games fathers and mothers play with their infants. *Infant Mental Health Journal, 2,* 241–248.

Yogman, M. J., Dixon, S., Tronick, E., Als, H., Adamson, L., Lester, B., & Brazelton, T. B. (1977, March). *The goals and structure of face-to-face interaction between infants and their fathers.* Paper presented at the meeting of the Society for Research in Child Development, New Orleans.

Zelazo, P. R., Kotelchuck, M., Barber, L., & David, J. (1977, March). *Fathers and sons: An experimental facilitation of attachment behaviors.* Paper presented at the meeting of the Society for Research in Child Development, New Orleans.

CHAPTER 7

Amato, P. R. (1989). Who cares for children in public places? *Journal of Marriage and the Family, 51,* 981–990.

Austin, A. M., & Braeger, T. J. (1990). Gendered differences in parents' encouragement of sibling interaction: Implications for the construction of a personal premise system. *First Language, 10,* 181–197.

Backett, K. C. (1982). *Mothers and fathers: A study of the development and negotiation of parental behaviour.* London: Macmillan.

Baruch, G. K., & Barnett, R. C. (1986). Fathers' participation in family work and children's sex-role attitudes. *Child Development, 57,* 1210–1223.

Bayard de Volo, C. L., & Fiebert, M. S. (1977). Creativity in the preschool child and its relationship to parental authoritarianism. *Perceptual and Motor Skills, 45,* 170.

Bell, R. G. (1968). A reinterpretation of the direction of effects in studies of socialisation. *Psychological Review, 75,* 81–95.

Belsky, J. (1981). Early human experience: A family perspective. *Developmental Psychology, 21,* 244–268.

Belsky, J. (1990). Parental and nonparental care and children's socio-emotional development: A decade review. *Journal of Marriage and the Family, 52,* 885–903.

Bentley, K. S., & Fox, R. A. (1991). Mothers and fathers of young children: Comparison of parenting styles. *Psychological Reports, 69,* 320–322.

Berger, P. R. L., & Kellner, H. (1964). Marriage and the construction of reality. *Diogenes, 46,* 1–25.

Berman, P., & Pedersen, F. (Eds.). (1987). *Men's transition to parenthood.* Hillsdale, NJ: Erlbaum.

Bhavnagri, N. P., & Parke, R. D. (1991). Parents as direct facilitators of children's peer relationships: Effects of age of child and sex of parent. *Journal of Social and Personal Relationships, 8,* 423–440.

Biller, H. B. (1981). The father and sex role development. In M. E. Lamb (Ed.), *The role of the father in child development* (2nd ed.). Chichester: Wiley.

Block, J. (1976). Issues, problems and pitfalls in assessing sex differences: A critical review of "The Psychology of Sex Differences." *Merrill-Palmer Quarterly, 22,* 283–340.

Blurton Jones, N. (1972). Characteristics of ethological studies of human behaviour. In N. Blurton Jones (Ed.), *Ethological studies of human behaviour.* Cambridge: Cambridge University Press.

Bright, M. C., & Stockdale, D. F. (1984). Mothers', fathers' and preschool children's interactive behaviours in a play setting. *Journal of Genetic Psychology, 144,* 219–232.

Burlingham, D. (1973). The pre-oedipal infant-father relationship. *Psychoanalytic Study of the Child, 28,* 23–47.

Burns, A. L., Mitchell, G., & Obradovich, S. (1989). Of sex roles and strollers: Female and male attention to toddlers at the zoo. *Sex Roles, 20,* 309–315.

Carlson, B. (1984). The father's contribution to child care: Effects on children's perceptions of parental roles. *American Journal of Orthopsychiatry, 54,* 123–136.

Clarke-Stewart, K. A. (1977). *Child care in the family: A review of research and some propositions for policy.* New York: Academic.

Clarke-Stewart, K. A. (1980). The father's contribution to children's cognitive and social development in early childhood. In F. A. Pedersen (Ed.), *The father-infant relationship: Observational studies in the family setting.* New York: Praeger.

Coppens, N. (1985). Cognitive development and locus of control as predictors of preschoolers' understanding of safety and protection. *Journal of Applied Developmental Psychology, 6,* 43–55.

Coverman, S., & Sheley, J. F. (1986). Change in men's housework and child care time. *Journal of Marriage and the Family, 48,* 413–422.

Crockett, L. J., Eggebeen, D. J., & Hawkins, A. J. (1993). Fathers' presence and young children's behavioural and cognitive adjustment. *Journal of Family Issues, 14,* 355–377.

De Frain, J. (1979). Androgynous parents tell who they are and what they need. *Family Coordinator, 28,* 237–243.

Diamond, J., & Bond, A. B. (1983). The transmission of learned behaviour: An observational study of father-child interaction during fishing. *Ethology and Sociobiology, 4*, 95–110.

Dubin, R., & Dubin, E. (1965). Children's social perceptions. *Child Development, 36*, 238–255.

Fagot, B. (1985). Beyond the reinforcement principle: Another step toward understanding sex role development. *Developmental Psychology, 21*, 1092–1104.

Fagot, B. I., & Hagan, R. (1991). Observations of parent reactions to sex-stereotyped behaviour. *Child Development, 62*, 617–628.

Fash, D. S., & Madison, C. L. (1981). Parents' language interaction with young children: A comparative study of mothers and fathers. *Child Study Journal, 11*, 137–152.

Frankell, M. T., & Rollins, H. A. (1983). Does mother know best? Mothers and fathers interacting with preschool sons and daughters. *Developmental Psychology, 19*, 694–702.

Furstenberg, F. F., & Nord, C. W. (1985). Parenting apart: Patterns of childrearing after marital disruption. *Journal of Marriage and the Family, 47*, 893–904.

Galejis, I., King, A., & Hegland, S. M. (1987). Antecedents of achievement motivation in preschool children. *Journal of Genetic Psychology, 148*, 333–348.

Gjerde, P. F., Block, J., & Block, J. H. (1991). The family context of 18 year olds with depressive symptoms: A prospective study. *Journal of Research on Adolescence, 1*, 63–91.

Gleason, J. B. (1975). Fathers and other strangers: Men's speech to young children. In I. D. P. Dato (Ed.), *Developmental psycholinguistics: Theory and applications* (pp. 289–297). Washington, DC: Georgetown University Press.

Goldman, J. D. G., & Goldman, R. J. (1983). Children's perceptions of parents and their roles: A cross-national study in Australia, England, North America and Sweden. *Sex Roles, 9*, 791–812.

Grossman, F. K., Pollack, W. S., & Golding, E. (1988). Fathers and children: Predicting the quality and quantity of fathering. *Developmental Psychology, 24*, 82–91.

Hart, C. H., De Wolfe, D. M., Wozniak, P., & Burts, D. C. (1992). Maternal and paternal disciplinary styles: Relations with preschoolers' playground behavioral orientations and peer status. *Child Development, 63*, 879–892.

Hartley, R. (1960). Children's concepts of male and female roles. *Merrill-Palmer Quarterly, 6*, 83–91.

Hawkins, A. J., & Eggebeen, D. J. (1991). Are fathers fungible? Patterns of coresident adult men in maritally disrupted families and young children's well-being. *Journal of Marriage and the Family, 53*, 958–972.

Haynes, S. N., & Horn, W. F. (1982). Reactivity in behavioural observation: A review. *Behavioural Assessment, 4*, 369–385.

Henderson, B. B. (1984). Parents and exploration: The effect of context on individual differences in exploratory behaviour. *Child Development, 55*, 1237–1245.

Herzog, E., & Sudia, C. (1970). *Boys in fatherless families.* Washington, DC: U.S. Department of Health, Education and Welfare.

Hess, R., & McDevitt, T. (1984). Some cognitive consequences of maternal intervention techniques: A longitudinal study. *Child Development, 55*, 2017–2030.

Hewlett, B. S. (1987). Intimate fathers: Patterns of holding among Aka pygmies. In M. E. Lamb (Ed.), *The father's role: Cross-cultural perspectives* (pp. 295–320). Hillsdale, NJ: Erlbaum.

Hladik, E. G., & Edwards, H. T. (1984). A comparative analysis of mother-father speech in the naturalistic home environment. *Journal of Psycholinguistic Research, 13*, 321–332.

Horna J., & Lupri, E. (1987). Fathers' participation in work, family life and leisure. In C. Lewis & M. O'Brien (Eds.), *Reassessing fatherhood* (pp. 54–73). London: Sage.

Hunter, F. T., McCarthy, M. E., MacTurk, R. H., & Vietze, P. N. (1987). Infants' social-constructive interactions with mothers and fathers. *Developmental Psychology, 23*, 249–254.

Idle, T., Wood, E., & Desmaris, S. (1993). Gender role socialization in toy play situations: Mothers and fathers with their sons and daughters. *Sex Roles, 28*, 679–691.

Johnson, M. M. (1982). Fathers and "femininity" in daughters: A review of the research. *Sociology and Social Research, 67* (1), 1–17.

Knafl, K. A., & Dixon, D. M. (1984). The participation of fathers in their children's hospitalisation. *Issues in Comprehensive Pediative Nursing, 7,* 269–281.

Lamb, M. E. (1975). Fathers: Forgotten contributors to child development. *Human Development, 18,* 245–266.

Lamb, M. E. (Ed.). (1981a). *The role of the father in child development* (2nd ed.). Chichester: Wiley.

Lamb, M. E. (1981b). Fathers and child development: An integrative overview. In M. E. Lamb (Ed.), *The role of the father in child development* (2nd ed., pp. 1–70). Chichester: Wiley.

Lamb, M. E. (Ed.). (1987). *The father's role: Cross-cultural perspectives.* Hillsdale, NJ: Erlbaum.

LaRossa, R. (1977). *Conflict and power in marriage: Expecting the first child.* Beverly Hills: Sage.

Layman, E. M. (1961). Discussion of International Council of Psychologists' Symposium on Fathers' Influence in the Family. *Merrill-Palmer Quarterly, 7,* 107–111.

Lewis, C. (1982). The observation of father-infant relationships: An attachment to outmoded concepts? In L. McKee & M. O'Brien (Eds.), *The father figure.* London: Tavistock.

Lewis, C. (1985). Early sex role socialisation. In D. Hargreaves & A. Colley (Eds.), *The psychology of sex roles* (pp. 95–117). Milton Keynes: Open University Press.

Lewis, C. (1986). *Becoming a father.* Milton Keynes: Open University Press.

Lewis, C., & Gregory, S. (1987). Parents' talk to their infants: The importance of context. *First Language, 7,* 201–216.

Lewis, C., & O'Brien, M. (1987). *Reassessing fatherhood: New observations on the modern man.* London: Sage.

Lewis, M., Feiring C., & Weinraub, M. (1981). The father's role in the child's social network. In M. E. Lamb (Ed.), *The role of the father in child development* (2d ed.). Chichester: Wiley.

Lewis, M., & Weinraub, M. (1976). The father's role in the child's social network. In M. E. Lamb (Ed.), *The role of the father in child development.* Chichester: Wiley.

Lewis, R. A., & Salt, R. E. (1986). *Men in families.* Beverly Hills, CA: Sage.

Liddell, C., Henzi, S. P., & Drew, N. (1987). Mothers, fathers and children in an urban park playground: A comparison of dyads and triads. *Developmental Psychology, 23,* 262–266.

Lytton, H., & Romney, D. M. (1991). Parents' differential socialisation of boys and girls: A meta-analysis. *Psychological Bulletin, 109,* 267–296.

Maccoby, E., & Jacklin, C. (1974). *The psychology of sex roles.* Stanford, CA: Stanford University Press.

MacDonald, K. (1987). Parent-child physical play with rejected, neglected and popular boys. *Developmental Psychology, 23,* 705–711.

MacDonald, K., & Parke, R. D. (1984). Bridging the gap: Parent-child play interaction and peer interactive competence. *Child Development, 55,* 1265–1277.

MacDonald, K. B., & Parke, R. D. (1986). Parent-child physical play: The effects of sex and age of children and parents. *Sex Roles, 15,* 367–378.

Mackey, W. C. (1985). *Fathering behaviors: The dynamics of the man-child bond.* New York: Plenum.

Main, M., Kaplan, N., & Cassidy, J. (1985). Security of infancy, childhood and adulthood. In I. Bretherton (Ed.), *Growing points of attachment theory and research. Monographs of the Society for Child Development, 50*(12, Serial No. 209).

Mannle, S., & Tomasello, M. (1987). Fathers, siblings and the bridge hypothesis. In K. E. Nelson & A. van Kleeck (Eds.), *Children's language.* Hillsdale, NJ: Erlbaum.

Marantz, S., & Mansfield, A. (1977). Maternal employment and the development of sex-role stereotypes in five to eleven-year-old children. *Child Development, 48,* 668–673.

Masur, E. F. (1982). Cognitive content of parents' speech to preschoolers. *Merrill-Palmer Quarterly, 28,* 471–484.

McBride, K. M., & Austin, A. M. (1986). Computer affect of preschool children and perceived affect of their parents, teachers and peers. *Journal of Genetic Psychology, 147,* 497–506.

McGillicuddy-deLisi, A. V. (1988). Sex differences in parental teaching behaviours. *Merrill-Palmer Quarterly, 34,* 147–162.

McKee, L. (1982). Fathers' participation in infant care: A critique. In L. McKee & M. O'Brien (Eds.), *The father figure.* London: Tavistock.

McLoughlin, B., Schutz, C., & White, D. (1980). Parental speech to five-year-old children in a game-playing situation. *Child Development, 51,* 580–582.

Miller, S. (1975). Effect of maternal employment on sex-role perceptions, interests and self-esteem in kindergarten girls. *Developmental Psychology, 11,* 405–406.

Mills, B. C. (1985). Four year old day care and home care children's parental perceptions. *Early Child Care and Development, 21,* 27–34.

Mitchell, G., Obradovich, S., Herring, F., Tromborg, C., & Burns, A. L. (1992). Reproducing gender in public places: Adults' attention to toddlers in three public locales. *Sex Roles, 26,* 323–330.

Mott, F. L. (1990). When is a father really gone? Parental-child contact in father absent homes. *Demography, 27,* 499–517.

Newson, J., & Newson, E. (1968). *Four years old in an urban community.* London: Allen and Unwin.

Newson, J., & Newson, E. (1976). *Seven years old in the home environment.* London: Allen and Unwin.

Noll, R. B., Zucker, R. S., Fitzgerald, H. E., & Curtis, W. J. (1992). Cognitive and motoric functioning of sons of alcoholic fathers and controls. The early childhood years. *Developmental Psychology, 28,* 665–675.

Noller, P. (1978). Sex differences in the socialisation of affectionate expression. *Developmental Psychology, 14,* 317–319.

Osborn, A. F., & Morris, A. C. (1982). Fathers and child care. *Early Child Development and Care, 8,* 279–307.

Pakizegi, B. (1978). The interaction of mothers and fathers with their sons. *Child Development, 49,* 479–482.

Pandit, M. (1988). Generosity in nursery school boys. *Child Psychiatry Quarterly, 21,* 13–17.

Parsons, T., & Bales, R. F. (1955). *Family socialisation and interaction process.* New York: Free Press.

Patterson, G. R. (1980). Mothers: The unacknowledged victims. *Monographs of the Society for Child Development, 45*(Serial No. 186).

Pedersen, F. A. (1980). *The father-infant relationship: Observational studies in the family setting.* New York: Praeger.

Pellegrini, A. D., Brody, G. H., & Stoneman, Z. (1987). Children's conversational competence with their parents. *Discourse Processes, 10,* 93–106.

Power, T. (1981). Sex typing in infancy: The role of the father. *Infant Mental Health Journal, 2,* 226–240.

Pratt, M. W., Kerig, P. K., Cowan, P. A., & Cowan, C. P. (1992). Family worlds: Couple satisfaction, parenting style, and mothers' and fathers' speech to young children. *Merrill-Palmer Quarterly, 38,* 245–262.

Presser, H. B. (1988). Shift work and child care among young American parents. *Journal of Marriage and the Family, 50,* 133–148.

Radin, N. (1981). The role of the father in cognitive, academic and intellectual development. In M. E. Lamb (Ed.) *The role of the father in child development* (2nd ed.). Chichester: Wiley.

Radin, N., & Epstein, A. (1975). *Observed paternal behavior and the intellectual functioning of preschool boys and girls.* Paper presented at the Society for Research in Child Development, Denver.

Radin, N., & Goldsmith, R. (1985). Caregiving fathers of preschoolers: Four years later. *Merrill-Palmer Quarterly, 31,* 375–383.

Radin, N., & Goldsmith, R., (1989). The involvement of selected unemployed and employed men with their children. *Child Development, 60,* 454–459.

Reese, E., & Fivush, R. (1993). Parental styles of talking about the past. *Developmental Psychology, 29,* 596–606.

Reid, P. T., Tate, C. S., & Berman, P. W. (1989). Preschool children's self-presentations in situations with infants: Effects of sex and race. *Child Development, 60,* 710–714.

Roberts, W. L. (1987). Two-career families: Demographic variables, parenting, and competence in young children. *Canadian Journal of Behavioural Science, 19,* 347–356.

Rosenthal, R. (1966). *Experimenter effects in behavioural research.* New York: Appleton-Century-Crofts.

Ross, H., & Taylor, H. (1989). Do boys prefer daddy or his physical style of play? *Sex Roles, 20,* 23–33.

Russell, A., Russell, G., & Midwinter, D. (1992). Observer influences on mothers and fathers: Self-reported influence during a home observation. *Merrill-Palmer Quarterly 38,* 263–283.

Russell, G. (1978). The father role and its relation to masculinity, femininity and adrogyny. *Child Development, 49,* 1174–1181.

Russell, G. (1983). *The changing role of fathers.* Milton Keynes: Open University Press.

Russell, G., & Radojevic, M. (1992). The changing role of fathers? Current understandings and future directions for research and practice. *Infant Mental Health Journal, 13,* 296–311.

Sallis, J. F., Patterson, T. L., McKenzie, T. L., & Nader, P. R. (1988). Family variables and physical activity in preschool children. *Developmental and Behavioural Pediatrics, 9,* 57–61.

Sandqvist, K. (1987). Swedish family policy and the attempt to change paternal roles. In C. Lewis & M. O'Brien (Eds.), *Reassessing fatherhood* (pp. 144–160). London: Sage.

Siegal, A. U. (1987). Are sons and daughters more differently treated by fathers than by mothers? *Developmental Review, 7,* 183–209.

Smith, A. B., Ballard, K. D., & Barham, L. J. (1989). Preschool children's perceptions of parent and teacher roles. *Early Childhood Research Quarterly, 4,* 523–532.

Smith, P. K. (1985). Exploration, play and social development in boys and girls. In D. Hargreaves & A. Colley (Eds.), *The psychology of sex roles* (pp. 118–141). Milton Keynes: Open University Press.

Springer, K. (1994, July). *Do children believe mothers or fathers contribute more to inheritance?* Post session presented at the 13th biennial meeting of the International Society for the Study of Behavioural Development, Amsterdam.

Stevenson, M. B., Leavitt, L. A., Thompson, R. H., & Roach, M. (1988). A social relations model analysis of parent and child play. *Developmental Psychology, 24,* 101–107.

Stevenson, M. R., & Black, K. N. (1988). Paternal absence and sex-role development: A meta-analysis. *Child Development, 59,* 793–814.

Suess, G. J., Grossmann, K. E., & Sroufe, L. A. (1992). Effects of infant attachment to mother and father on quality of adaptation in preschool: From dyadic to individual organisation of self. *International Journal of Behavioural Development, 15,* 43–65.

Underwood, V. V. M. (1949). Student fathers with their children. *Marriage and Family Living, 11,* 101–106.

Vener, A., & Snyder, C. (1966). The preschool child's awareness and anticipation of adult sex roles. *Sociometry, 29,* 159–168.

Volling, B. L, & Belsky, J. (1991). Multiple determinants of father involvement during infancy in dual-earner and single-earner families. *Journal of Marriage and the Family, 53,* 461–474.

Volling, B., & Belsky, J. (1992). The contribution of mother-child and father-child relationships to the quality of sibling interaction: A longitudinal study. *Child Development, 63,* 1209–1222.

Weinraub, M. (1978). Fatherhood: The myth of the second class parent. In J. H. Stevens & M. Matthews (Eds.) *Mother/child and father/child relationships.* Washington, DC: National Association for the Education of Young Children.

Weinraub, M., Clemens, L. P., Sockloff, A., Ethridge, T., Gracely, E., & Myers, B. (1984). The development of sex-role stereotypes in the third year: Relationships to gender labelling, gender identity, sex-types toy preference, and family characteristics. *Child Development, 55,* 1493–1503.

Welkowitz, J., Bond, R. N., Feldman, L., & Tota, M. E. (1990). Conversational time patterns and mutual influence in parent-child interactions: A time series approach. *Journal of Psycholinguistic Research, 19,* 221–243.

Williams, E., Radin, N., & Allegro, T. (1992). Sex role attitudes of adolescents reared primarily by their fathers: An 11-year follow up. *Merrill-Palmer Quarterly, 38,* 457–476.

Williams, J., Bennett, S., & Best, D. (1975). Awareness and expression of sex stereotypes in young children. *Developmental Psychology, 11,* 635–642.

Worden, P. E., Kee, D. W., & Ingle, M. J. (1987). Parental teaching strategies with preschoolers: A comparison of mothers and fathers within different alphabet tasks. *Contemporary Educational psychology, 12,* 95–109.

Yamasaki, K. (1990). Parental child-rearing attitudes associated with Type A behaviours in children. *Psychological Reports, 67,* 235–239.

Youngblade, L. M., & Belsky, J. (1992). Parent-child antecedents of 5-year-olds' close friendships: A longitudinal analysis. *Developmental Psychology, 28,* 700–713.

CHAPTER 8

Amato, P. (1986). Father involvement and the self-esteem of children and adolescents. *Australian Journal of Sex, Marriage, and Family, 7,* 6–16.

Appleton, W. S. (1981). *Fathers and daughters.* New York: Doubleday.

Barkley, R. A. (1981). *Hyperactive children: A handbook for diagnosis and treatment.* New York: Guilford.

Barnett, R. C., & Baruch, G. (1988). Correlates of father's participation in family work. In P. Bronstein and C. P. Cowan (Eds.), *Fatherhood today: Men's changing role in the family* (pp. 66–78). New York: Wiley.

Barth, J. M. & Parke, R. D. (1992). Parent-child relationship influences on children's transition to school. *Merrill-Palmer Quarterly, 39,* 173–195.

Baruch, G., & Barnett, R. C. (1986). Father's participation in family work and children's sex role attitudes. *Child Development, 57,* 1210–1223.

Beer, W. R. (1989). *Strangers in the house: The world of stepsiblings and half-stepsiblings.* New Brunswick, NJ: Transaction.

Berlinsky, E. B., & Biller, H. B. (1982). *Parental death and psychological development.* Lexington, MA: Lexington.

Biller, H. B. (1968a). A multiaspect investigation of masculine development in kindergarten-age boys. *Genetic Psychology Monographs, 76,* 89–139.

Biller, H. B. (1968b). A note on father-absence and masculine development in young lower class Negro and white boys. *Child Development, 39,* 1001–1006.

Biller, H. B. (1969a). Father-absence, maternal encouragement, and sex-role development in kindergarten-age boys. *Child Development, 40,* 539–546.

Biller, H. B. (1969b). Father dominance and sex-role development in kindergarten-age boys. *Developmental Psychology, 1,* 87–94. (Reprinted in slightly abridged form in D. R. Heise [Ed.], *Personality and socialization* [pp. 73–78]. New York: Rand-McNally, 1972.)

Biller, H. B. (1971). *Father, child, and sex role.* Lexington, MA: Lexington.

Biller, H. B. (1974a). Paternal and sex-role factors in cognitive and academic functioning. In J. K. Cole & R. Dienstbier (Eds.), *Nebraska Symposium on Motivation* (pp. 83–123). Lincoln, NE: University of Nebraska Press.

Biller, H. B. (1974b). Paternal deprivation, cognitive functioning and the feminized classroom. In A. Davids (Ed.), *Child personality and psychopathology: Current topics* (pp. 11–52). New York: Wiley.

Biller, H. B. (1974c). *Paternal deprivation: Family, school, sexuality, and society.* Lexington, MA: Lexington.

Biller, H. B. (1976). The father and personality development: Paternal deprivation and sex-role development. In M. E. Lamb (Ed.), *The role of the father in child development* (pp. 89–156). New York: Wiley.

Biller, H. B. (1982). Fatherhood: Implications for child and adult development. In B. B. Wolman (Ed.), *Handbook of developmental psychology* (pp. 702–725). Englewood Cliffs, NJ: Prentice-Hall.

Biller, H. B. (1993). *Fathers and families: Paternal factors in child development.* Westport, CT: Auburn.

Biller, H. B. (1994). Paternal deficit poses serious problem. *Brown University Child and Adolescent Letter, 11,* 1–6.

Biller, H. B., & Meredith, D. L. (1974). *Father power.* New York: David McKay; reprinted, New York: Doubleday/Anchor, 1975.

Biller, H. B., & Solomon, R. S. (1986). *Child maltreatment and paternal deprivation: A manifesto for research, prevention, and treatment.* Lexington, MA: Lexington.

Biller, H. B., & Trotter, R. J. (1994). *The father factor.* New York: Simon and Schuster.

Bisnaire, L., Firestone, P., & Rynard, D. (1990). Factors associated with academic achievement in children following parental separation. *American Journal of Orthopsychiatry, 60,* 67–76.

Blanchard, R. W., & Biller, H. B. (1971). Father availability and academic performance among third grade boys. *Developmental Psychology, 4,* 301–305.

Block, J. (1971). *Lives through time.* Berkeley, CA: Bancroft.

Block, J., von der Lippe, A., & Block, J. H. (1973). Sex role and socialization: Some personality concomitants and environmental precursors. *Child Development, 59,* 336–355.

Bronstein, P. (1984). Difference in mothers' and fathers' behaviors toward children: A cross-cultural comparison. *Developmental Psychology, 20,* 995–1003.

Cassidy, J., Parke, R. D., Butkovsky, L., & Braungart, J. (1992). Family-peer connections: The roles of emotional expressiveness within the family and children's understanding of emotions. *Child Development, 63,* 603–618.

Collins, W. A., & Russell, G. (1991). Mother-child and father-child relationships in middle childhood and adolescence: A developmental analysis. *Developmental Review, 11,* 99–136.

Coopersmith, S. (1967). *The antecedents of self-esteem.* San Francisco: Freeman.

Dunn, J., & Plomin, R. (1990). *Separate lives: Why siblings are so different.* New York: Basic Books.

Elizur, J. (1986). The stress of school entry: Parental coping behaviors and children's adjustment to school. *Journal of Child Psychology and Psychiatry, 27,* 625–638.

Emery, R. E. (1988). *Marriage, divorce, and children's adjustment.* Beverly Hills, CA: Sage.

Farber, B. (1962). Effects of a severely mentally retarded child on the family. In E. P. Trapp & P. Himelstein (Eds.), *Readings on the exceptional child* (pp. 227–246). New York: Appleton-Century-Crofts.

Fish, K. D., & Biller, H. B. (1973). Perceived childhood paternal relationships and college females' personal adjustment. *Adolescence, 8,* 415–420.

Franz, C. E., McClelland, D. C., & Weinberger, J. (1991). Childhood antecedents of conventional social accomplishment in mid-life adults: A 35-year prospective study. *Journal of Personality and Social Psychology, 60,* 586–595.

Green, R. (1987). *The "sissy-boy-syndrome" and the development of homosexuality.* New Haven, CT: Yale University Press.

Guidabaldi, J., Cleminshaw, H. K. Perry, J. D., Nastasi, B. K., & Lightel, J. (1986). The role of selected family environment factors in children's post-divorce adjustment. *Family Relations, 35,* 141–151.

Haapasalo, J., & Tremblay, R. E. (1994). Physically aggressive boys from ages 6 to 12: Family background, parenting behavior, and prediction of delinquency. *Journal of Consulting and Clinical Psychology, 62,* 1044–1052.

Hansen, M., & Biller, H. B. (1992). *Intergenerational perceptions of paternal nurturance and personality adjustment among young adult sons and daughters.* Unpublished study, University of Rhode Island.

Harrington, D. M., Block, J. H., & Block, J. (1978). Intolerance of ambiguity in preschool children: Psychometric considerations, behavioral manifestations, and parental correlates. *Developmental Psychology, 14,* 242–256.

Herman, M. A., & McHale, S. M. (1993). Coping with parental negativity: Links with parental warmth and child adjustment. *Journal of Applied Developmental Psychology, 14,* 121–130.

Herrnstein, R. J., & Murray, C. (1994). *The bell curve: Intelligence and class in American life.* New York: Free Press.

Hetherington, E. M., Cox, M., & Cox, R. (1978). Family interaction and the social, emotional, and cognitive development of children following divorce. In V. Vaughn & B. Brazelton (Eds.), *The family: Setting priorities.* New York: Science and Medicine Publishing.

Hetherington, E. M., Cox, M., & Cox, R. (1982). Effects of divorce on parents and children. In M. E. Lamb (Ed.), *Nontraditional families* (pp. 233–288). Hillsdale, NJ: Erlbaum.

Hoffman, M. L. (1971). Father absence and conscience development. *Child Development, 4,* 400–406.

Hoffman, M. L. (1975). Altruistic behavior and the parent-child relationship. *Journal of Personality and Social Psychology, 31,* 937–943.

Hoffman, M. L. (1981). The role of the father in moral internalization. In M. E. Lamb (Ed.), *The role of the father in child development* (2nd ed., pp. 359–378). New York: Wiley.

Jacoby, R., & Glaberman, N. (Eds.). (1995). *The bell curve debate: History, documents, opinions.* New York: Times.

Katz, I. (1967). Socialization of academic motivation in minority group children. In D. Levine (Ed.), *Nebraska Symposium on Motivation* (pp. 133–191). Lincoln, NE: University of Nebraska Press.

Koestner, R., Franz, C., & Weinberger, J. (1990). The family origins of empathic concerns: A 26-year longitudinal study. *Journal of Personality and Social Psychology, 58,* 709–717.

Lessing, E. E., Zagorin, S. W., & Nelson, D. (1970). WISC subtest and IQ correlates of father absence. *Journal of Genetic Psychology, 67,* 181–195.

Lozoff, M. M. (1974). Fathers and autonomy in women. In R. B. Kundsin (Ed.), *Women and success* (pp. 103–109). New York: Morrow.

Lynn, D. B. (1974). *The father: His role in child development.* Belmont, CA: Brooks/Cole.

Margalit, M. (1985). Perception of parents' behavior, familial satisfaction, and sense of coherence in hyperactive children. *Journal of School Psychology, 23,* 355–364.

McBride-Chang, C., & Jacklin, C. N. (1993). Early play arousal, sex-typed play, and activity level as precursors to later rough-and-tumble play. *Early Education and Development, 4,* 99–108.

McClelland, D. C., Constantian, C. A., Regalado, D., & Stone, C. (1978). Making it to maturity. *Psychology Today, 12,* 42–46.

Mischel, W. (1961). Father absence and delay of gratification. *Journal of Abnormal and Social Psychology, 62,* 116–124.

Mullis, R. L., & Mullis, A. K. (1990). The effects of context on parent-child interactions. *Journal of Genetic Psychology, 15,* 1573–1585.

Parke, R. D., MacDonald, K. D., Beitel, A., & Bhavnagri, N. (1988). The role of the family in the development of peer relationships. In R. D. Peters and R. J. McMahon (Eds.), *Marriages and families: Behavioral treatments and processes.* New York: Brunner/Mazel.

Patterson, G. R., DeBaryshe, B. D., & Ramsey, F. (1989). A developmental perspective on antisocial behavior. *American Psychologist, 44,* 325–329.

Patterson, G. R., & Stouthamer-Loeber, M. (1984). The correlation of family management practices and delinquency. *Child Development, 55,* 1299–1307.

Phares, V., & Compas, B. E. (1992). The role of fathers in child and adolescent psychopathology: Make room for daddy. *Psychological Bulletin, 111,* 387–412.

Piers, E. V., & Harris, D. B. (1969). *Manual for the Piers-Harris children's self-concept scale.* Nashville: Counselor Recordings and Tests.

Radin, N. (1976). The role of the father in cognitive, academic, and intellectual development. In M. E. Lamb (Ed.), *The role of the father in child development* (pp. 237–276). New York: Wiley.

Radin, N. (1981). The role of the father in cognitive, academic, and intellectual development. In M. E. Lamb (Ed.), *The role of the father in child development* (2nd ed., pp. 379–427). New York: Wiley.

Radin, N. (1982). Primary caregiving and rolesharing fathers of preschoolers. In M. E. Lamb (Ed.), *Nontraditional families: Parenting and child development* (pp. 173–208). Hillsdale, NJ: Erlbaum.

Radin, N. (1986). The influence of fathers on their sons and daughters and the implications for social work. *Social Work in Education, 8,* 77–91.

Radin, N., & Russell, G. (1983). Increased father participation and child development outcomes. In M. E. Lamb & A. Sagi (Eds.), *Fatherhood and family policy* (pp. 191–218). Hillsdale, NJ: Erlbaum.

Radin, N., Williams, E., & Coggins, K. (1994). Paternal involvement in childrearing and the school performance of Native American Children: An exploratory study. *Family Perspectives, 27,* 375–391.

Reuter, M. W., & Biller, H. B. (1973). Perceived paternal nurturance-availability and personality adjustment among college males. *Journal of Consulting and Clinical Psychology, 40,* 339–342.

Rosenberg, M. (1965). *Society and the adolescent self-image.* Princeton, NJ: Princeton University Press.

Russell, G., & Russell, A. (1987). Mother-child and father-child relationships in middle childhood. *Child Development, 58,* 1573–1585.

Sagi, A. (1982). Antecedents and consequences of various degrees of paternal involvement in childrearing: The Israeli Project. In M. E. Lamb (Ed.), *Nontraditional families: Parenting and child development.* Hillsdale, NJ: Erlbaum.

Santrock, J. (1972). Relation of type and onset of father-absence to cognitive development. *Child Development, 43,* 455–469.

Scarr, S., & Weinberg, R. A. (1976). IQ test performance of black children adopted by white parents. *American Psychologist, 31,* 726–739.

Scarr, S., & Weinberg, R. A. (1980). Calling all camps! The war is over. *American Sociological Review, 45,* 859–865.

Sears, R. R. (1970). Relations of early socialization experiences to self-concepts and gender role in middle childhood. *Child Development, 41,* 267–289.

Shinn, M. (1978). Father absence and children's cognitive development. *Psychological Bulletin, 85*, 295–324.

Shulman, S., Collins, W. A., & Dital, M. (1993). Parent-child relationships and peer-perceived competence during middle childhood and preadolescence in Israel. *Journal of Early Adolescence, 13*, 204–218.

Snarey, J. (1993). *How fathers care for the next generation: A four decade study.* Cambridge, MA: Harvard University Press.

Solomon, D. (1969). The generality of children's achievement-related behavior. *Journal of Genetic Psychology, 114*, 393–409.

Speicher-Dubin, B. (1982). Relationships between parent moral judgment, child moral judgment and family interaction: A correlational study. *Dissertation Abstracts International, 434*, 1600B.

Stattin, H., & Klackenberg-Larsson, I. (1991). The short-and long-term implications for parent-child relations of parents' prenatal preferences for their child's gender. *Developmental Psychology, 27*, 141–147.

Stern, M., Northman, J. E., & Van Slyk, M. R. (1984). Father-absence and adolescent "problem behaviors": Alcohol consumption, drug use, and sexual activity. *Adolescence, 19*, 301–312.

Wagner, B. M., & Phillips, D. A. (1992). Beyond beliefs: Parent and child behaviors and children's perceived academic competence. *Developmental Psychology, 63*, 1380–1391.

Warshak, R. A. (1993). *The custody revolution: The father factor and the motherhood mystique.* New York: Poseidon.

Williams, E., Radin, N., & Allegro, T. (1992). Sex-role attitudes of adolescents reared primarily by their fathers: An 11 year follow-up. *Merrill-Palmer Quarterly, 38*, 457–476.

CHAPTER 9

Armsden, G. C., & Greenberg, M. T. (1987). The Inventory of Parent and Peer Attachment: Individual differences and their relationship to psychological well-being in adolescence. *Journal of Youth and Adolescence, 16*, 427–453.

Baranowski, M. D. (1978). Adolescents' attempted influence on parental behaviors. *Adolescence, 13*, 585–604.

Barnes, H., & Olson, D. (1985). Parent-adolescent communication and the circumplex model. *Child Development, 56*, 438–447.

Barnett, R. C., & Baruch, G. K. (1988). Correlates of fathers' participation in family work. In P. Bronstein & C. P. Cowan (Eds.), *Fatherhood today: Men's changing role in the family* (pp. 66–78). New York: Wiley.

Benson, M. J., Harris, P. B., & Rogers, C. S. (1992). Identity consequences of attachment to mothers and fathers among late adolescents. *Journal of Research on Adolescence, 2*, 187–204.

Berndt, T. J. (1979). Developmental changes in conformity to peers and parents. *Developmental Psychology 15*, 608–616.

Brim, O. G., (1976). Theories of the male mid-life crisis. *Counseling Psychologist, 6*, 2–9.

Bronfenbrenner, U. (1961). Some familial antecedents of responsibility and leadership in adolescents. In L. Petrullo & B. M. Boss (Eds.), *Leadership and interpersonal behavior.* New York: Holt, Rinehart, and Winston.

Bronstein, P. (1988). Marital and parenting roles in transition: An overview. In P. Bronstein & C. P. Cowan (Eds।)., *Fatherhood today: Men's changing role in the family* (pp. 3–10). New York: Wiley.

Campbell, E., Adams, G. R., & Dobson, W. R. (1984). Familial correlates of identity formation in late adolescence: A study of the predictive utility of connectedness and individuality in family relations. *Journal of Youth and Adolescence, 13*, 509–525.

Cancian, F. M. (1986). The feminization of love. *Signs: Journal of Women in Culture and Society, 11,* 692–709.

Chodorow, N. (1978). *The reproduction of mothering: Psychoanalysis and the sociology of gender.* Berkeley, CA: University of California Press.

Collins, W. A. (1990). Parent-child relationships in the transition to adolescence: Continuity and change in interaction, affect, and cognition. In R. Montemayor, G. R. Adams, & T. P. Gulotta (Eds.), *From childhood to adolescence: A transitional period?* (pp. 85–106). Newbury Park, CA: Sage.

Collins, W. A., & Russell, G. (1991). Mother-child and father-child relationships in middle childhood and adolescence: A developmental analysis. *Developmental Review, 11,* 99–136.

Cowan, G., Drinkard, J., & MacGavin, L. (1984). The effects of target, age, and gender on the use of power strategies. *Journal of Personality and Social Psychology, 47,* 1391–1398.

Crouter, A. C., Carson, J. H., Vicary, J. R., & Butler, J. (1988). Parent-child closeness as an influence on the projected life course of rural adolescent girls. *Journal of Early Adolesence, 8,* 345–355.

Csikszentmihalyi, M., & Larson, R. (1984). *Being adolescent: Conflict and growth in the teenage years.* New York: Basic Books.

Daniels, P., & Weingarten, K. (1988). The fatherhood click: The timing of parenthood in men's lives. In P. Bronstein & C. P. Cowan (Eds.), *Fatherhood today: Men's changing role in the family* (pp. 36–52). New York: Wiley.

DeLuccie, A., & Davis, A. (1991). Do men's adult life concerns affect their fathering orientations? *Journal of Psychology, 125,* 175–188.

Eberly, M. B., Montemayor, R., & Flannery, D. J. (1993). Variation in adolescent helpfulness toward parents in a family context. *Journal of Early Adolescence, 13,* 228–244.

Ellis-Schwabe, M., & Thornburg, H. D. (1986). Conflict areas between parents and their adolescents. *Journal of Psychology, 120,* 59–68.

Erikson, E. (1963). *Childhood and society* (2nd ed.). New York: Norton.

Feldman, L. B. (1990). Fathers and fathering. In R. L. Meth & R. S. Pasick (Eds.), *Men in therapy: The challenge of change* (pp. 88–107). New York: Guilford.

Feldman, S. S., & Gehring, T. M. (1988). Changing perceptions of family cohesion and power across adolescence. *Child Development, 59,* 1034–1045.

Flannery, D. J., Montemayor, R., & Eberly, M. B. (1994). The influence of parent negative emotional expression on adolescents' perceptions of their relationships with their parents. *Personal Relationships, 1,* 259–274.

Hall, G. S. (1904). *Adolescence, Vols. 1 and 2.* Englewood Cliffs, NJ: Prentice-Hall.

Hauser, S. T., Book, B. K., Houlihan, J., Powers, S., Weiss-Perry, B., Follansbee, D., Jacobson, A. M., & Noam, G. G. (1987). Sex differences within the family: Studies of adolescent and parent family interactions. *Journal of Youth and Adolescence, 16,* 199–220.

Hill, J. P., & Holmbeck, G. (1987). Disagreements about rules in families with seventh graders. *Journal of Youth and Adolescence, 16,* 312–319.

Hill, J. P., & Stafford, F. (1980). Parental care of children: Time diary estimate of quantity, predictability, and variety. *Journal of Human Resources, 15,* 219–239.

Hinde, R. A. (1979). *Toward understanding relationships.* London: Academic.

Hinde, R. A., & Stevenson-Hinde, J. (1987). Interpersonal relationships and child development. *Developmental Review, 7,* 1–21.

Hunter, F. T. (1985). Individual adolescents' perceptions of interactions with friends and parents. *Journal of Early Adolescence, 5,* 295–305.

Jung, C. G. (1933). *Modern man in search of a soul.* New York: Harcourt, Brace, Jovanovich.

Kelley, H. H., Berscheid, E., Christensen, A., Harvey, J. H., Huston, T. L., Levinger, G., McClintock, E., Peplau, L. A., & Peterson, D. R. (Eds.). (1983). *Close relationships.* New York: Freeman.

Kenny, M. E. (1987). The extent and function of parental attachment among first year college students. *Journal of Youth and Adolescence, 16,* 17–29.

Klos, D., & Paddock, J. (1978). Relationship status: Scales for assessing the vitality of late adolescents' relationships with their parents. *Journal of Youth and Adolescence, 7,* 353–368.

Lamb, M. E., & Oppenheim, D. (1989). Fatherhood and father-child relationships: Five years of research. In S. H. Cath et al. (Eds.), *Fathers and their families* (pp. 11–26). Hillsdale, NJ: Analytic.

Larson, R., & Richards, M. (1994). *Divergent lives: The emotional lives of mothers, fathers, and adolescents.* New York: Basic Books.

LeCroy, C. W. (1988). Parent-adolescent intimacy: Impact on adolescent functioning. *Adolescence, 23,* 137–147.

Levinson, D. J. (1978). *The seasons of a man's life.* New York: Knopf.

Maccoby, E. E. (1992). The role of parents in the socialization of children: An historical overview. *Developmental Psychology, 28,* 1006–1017.

McDonald, G. W. (1982). Parental power perceptions in the family. *Youth and Society, 14,* 3–31.

Miller, J. B., & Lane, M. (1991). Relations between young adults and their parents. *Journal of Adolescence, 14,* 179–194.

Montemayor, R. (1982). The relationship between parent-adolescent communciation and the amount of time adolescents spend alone with parents and peers. *Child Development, 53,* 1512–1519.

Montemayor, R. (1983). Parents and adolescents in conflict: All families some of the time and some families most of the time. *Journal of Early Adolescence, 3,* 83–103.

Montemayor, R. (1986). Family variation in parent-adolescent storm and stress. *Journal of Adolescent Research, 1,* 15–31.

Montemayor, R., & Brownlee, J. (1987). Fathers, mothers, and adolescents: Gender-based differences in parental roles during adolescence. *Journal of Youth and Adolescence, 16,* 281–291.

Montemayor, R., Eberly, M., & Flannery, D. J. (1993). Effects of pubertal status and conversation topic on parent and adolescent affective expression. *Journal of Early Adolescence, 13,* 431–447.

Montemayor, R., & Hanson, E. (1985). A naturalistic view of conflict between adolescents and their parents and siblings. *Journal of Early Adolescence, 5,* 23–30.

Montemayor, R., McKenry, P. C., & Julian, T. (1994). Men in mid-life and the quality of father-adolescent communication. In S. Shulman & W. A. Collins (Eds.), *Father-adolescent relationships: Development and context* (pp. 59–72). San Francisco: Jossey-Bass.

Neugarten, B. L. (1968). *Middle age and aging.* Chicago: University of Chicago Press.

Neugarten, B. L., & Gutmann, D. L. (1958). Age-sex roles and personality in middle-age: A thematic apperception study. *Psychology Monographs, 72,* 1–33.

Noller, P., & Bagi, S. (1985). Parent-adolescent communication. *Journal of Adolescence, 8,* 125–144.

Noller, P., & Callan, V. J. (1990). Adolescents' perceptions of the nature of their communication with parents. *Journal of Youth and Adolescence, 19,* 349–362.

Papini, D. R., Roggman, L. A., & Anderson, J. (1991). Early-adolescent perceptions of attachment to mother and father: A test of the emotional-distancing and buffering hypotheses. *Journal of Early Adolescence, 11,* 258–275.

Papini, D., & Sebby, R. (1987). Adolescent pubertal status and affective family relationships: A multivariate assessment. *Journal of Youth and Adolescence, 16,* 1–15.

Papini, D., & Sebby, R. (1988). Variations in conflictual family issues by adolescent pubertal status, gender, and family member. *Journal of Early Adolescence, 8,* 1–16.

Patterson, G. R. (1982). *Coercive family process.* Eugene, OR: Castalia.

Patterson, G. R., & Dishion, T. J. (1988). Multilevel family process models: Traits, interactions, and relationships. In R. A. Hinde & J. Stevenson-Hinde (Eds.), *Relationships within families.* Oxford: Clarendon.

Patterson, G. R., Reid, J. B., & Dishion, T. J. (1992). *Antisocial boys.* Eugene, OR: Castalia.

Pederson, F. A. (1987). Introduction: A perspective on research concerning fatherhood. In P. W. Berman & F. A. Pederson (Eds.), *Men's transitions to parenthood: Longitudinal studies of early family experience* (pp. 1–12). Hillsdale, NJ: Erlbaum.

Phares, V. (1992). Where's Poppa? The relative lack of attention to the role of fathers in child and adolescent psychopathology. *American Psychologist, 47,* 656–664.

Phares, V., & Compas, B. E. (1992). The role of fathers in child and adolescent psychopathology: Make room for daddy. *Psychological Bulletin, 111,* 387–412.

Pipp, S., Jennings, S., Shaver, P., Lamborn, S., & Fischer, K. W. (1985). Adolescent theories about the development of their relationships with parents. *Journal of Personality and Social Psychology, 48,* 991–1001.

Pleck, J. H. (1983). Husbands' paid work and family roles: Current research issues. In H. Z. Lopata & J. H. Pleck (Eds.), *Research in the interweave of social roles and family jobs* (pp. 251–333). Greenwich, CT: JAI.

Power, T. G., & Shanks, J. (1989). Parents as socializers: Maternal and paternal views. *Journal of Youth and Adolescence, 18,* 203–220.

Radin, N. (1981). Childrearing fathers in intact families: I. Some antecedents and consequences. *Merrill-Palmer Quarterly, 27,* 489–514.

Radin, N. (1982). Primary caregiving and role-sharing fathers. In M. E. Lamb (Ed.), *Nontraditional families: Parenting and child development.* Hillsdale, NJ: Erlbaum.

Radin, N. (1988). Primary caregiving fathers of long duration. In P. Bronstein & C. P. Cowan (Eds.), *Fatherhood today: Men's changing role in the family* (pp. 127–143). New York: Wiley.

Reis, H. T., & Shaver, P. (1988). Intimacy as an interpersonal process. In S. W. Duck (Ed.), *Handbook of personal relationships* (pp. 367–389). New York: Wiley.

Richardson, R. A., Galambos, N. L., Schulenberg, J. E., & Petersen, A. C. (1984). Young adolescents' perceptions of the family environment. *Journal of Early Adolescence, 4,* 131–153.

Roberts, G., Block, J. H., & Block, J., (1984). Continuity and change in parents' child rearing practices. *Child Development, 55,* 586–597.

Roll, S., & Millen, L. (1978). Adolescent males' feeling of being understood by their fathers as revealed through clinical interviews. *Adolescence, 13,* 83–94.

Russell, G., & Russell, A. (1987). Mother-child and father-child relationships in middle childhood. *Child Development, 58,* 1573–1585.

Savin-Williams, R. C., & Small, S. A. (1986). The timing of puberty and its relation to adolescent and parent perceptions of family interactions. *Developmental Psychology, 22,* 342–347.

Silverberg, S. B., & Steinberg, L. (1990). Psychological well-being with early adolescent children. *Developmental Psychology, 26,* 658–666.

Smetana, J. G. (1988a). Adolescents' and parents' conceptions of parental authority. *Child Development, 59,* 321–335.

Smetana, J. G. (1988b). Concepts of self and social convention: Adolescents' and parents' reasoning about hypothetical and actual family conflicts. In M. R. Gunnar & W. A. Collins (Eds.), *21st Minnesota Symposium on Child Psychology: Development during the transition to adolescence* (pp. 79–122). Hillsdale, NJ: Erlbaum.

Smetana, J. G. (1989). Adolescents' and parents' reasoning about actual family conflict. *Child Development, 60,* 1052–1067.

Snalk, D., & Rothblum, E. (1979). Self-disclosure among adolescents in relation to parental affection and control patterns. *Adolescence, 14,* 333–340.

Stearns, P. N. (1991). Fatherhood in historical perspective: The role of social change. In F. W. Bozett & S. M. H. Hanson (Eds.), *Fatherhood and families in cultural context* (pp. 28–52). New York: Springer.

Steinberg, L. (1981). Transformations in family relations at puberty. *Developmental Psychology, 17,* 833–840.

Steinberg, L. (1987a). The impact of puberty on family relations: Effects of pubertal status and pubertal timing. *Developmental Psychology, 23,* 451–460.

Steinberg, L. (1987b). Recent research on the family at adolescence: The extent and nature of sex differences. *Journal of Youth and Adolescence, 16,* 191–197.

Steinberg, L. (1988). Reciprocal relation between parent-child distance and pubertal maturation. *Developmental Psychology, 24,* 122–128.

Steinberg, L., & Hill, J. (1978). Patterns of family interaction as a function of age, the onset of puberty, and formal thinking. *Developmental Psychology, 14,* 683–684.

Susman, E. J., Inoff-Germain, G., Nottelmann, E. D., Loriaux, D. L., Cutler, G. B., Jr., & Chrousos, G. P. (1987). Hormones, emotional dispositions, and aggressive attributes in young adolescents. *Child Development, 58,* 1114–1134.

Tamir, L. B. (1982). *Men in their forties: The transition to middle age.* New York: Springer.

Wilks, J., Callan, V. J., & Austin, D. A. (1989). Parent, peer and personal determinants of adolescent drinking. *British Journal of Addiction, 84*(6), 619–630.

Wright, H., & Keple, W. (1981). Friends and parents of a sample of high school juniors: An explanatory study of relationship intensity and interpersonal rewards. *Journal of Marriage and the Family, 43,* 559–570.

Yogman, M. W., Cooley, J., & Kindlon, D. (1988). Fathers, infants, and toddlers: A developing relationship. In P. Bronstein & C. P. Cowan (Eds.), *Fatherhood today: Men's changing role in the family* (pp. 53–65). New York: Wiley.

Youniss, J., & Ketterlinus, R. D. (1987). Communication and connectedness in mother- and father-adolescent relationships. *Journal of Youth and Adolescence, 16,* 191–197.

Youniss, J., & Smollar, J. (1985). *Adolescent relations with mothers, fathers, and friends.* Chicago: University of Chicago Press.

Zeidler, A., Nardine, F., Scolare, C., & Mich, P. (1987). *Adult perceptions of parent-child relations: Implications for families as educators.* Paper presented at the annual meeting of the American Educational Research Association, Washington, DC.

CHAPTER 10

Andrew, G. (1968). Determinants of Negro family decisions in management of retardation. *Journal of Marriage and the Family, 30,* 612–617.

Bailey, D. B., Jr., Blasco, P. M., & Simeonsson, R. J. (1992). Needs expressed by mothers and fathers of young children with disabilities. *American Journal of Mental Retardiation, 97,* 1–10.

Baxter, C. (1989). Investigating stigma as stress in social interactions of parents. *Journal of Mental Deficiency Research, 33,* 455–466.

Beckman, P. J. (1983). Influences of selected child characteristics on stress in families of handicapped infants. *American Journal of Mental Deficiency, 88,* 150–156.

Beckman, P. J. (1991). Comparison of mothers' and fathers' perceptions of the effect of young children with and without disabilities. *American Journal of Mental Retardiation, 95,* 585–595.

Belsky, J. (1981). Early human experience: A family perspective. *Developmental Psychology, 17,* 3–23.

Benson, B. A., & Gross, A. M. (1989). The effect of a congenitally handicapped child upon the marital dyad: A review of the literature. *Clinical Psychology Review, 9,* 747–758.

Blacher, J. (1984). Sequential stages of parental adjustment to the birth of a child with handicaps: Fact or artifact? *Mental Retardation, 22,* 55–68.

Blacher, J., Meyers, C. E., & Frame, E. G. (1984). *Relationship between use of respite, perceived need for respite, and social support networks.* Paper presented at the annual meeting of the American Association on Mental Deficiency, Minneapolis.

Blacher, J., Nihira, K., & Meyers, C. E. (1987). Characteristics of home environment of families with mentally retarded children: Comparison across levels of retardation. *American Journal of Mental Deficiency, 91,* 313–320.

Boyce, G. C., Behl, D., Mortensen, L., & Akers, J. (1991). Child characteristics, family demographics and family processes: Their effects on the stress experienced by families of children with disabilities. *Counseling Psychology Quarterly, 4,* 273–288.

Bristol, M. M. (1984). Family resources and successful adaptation to autistic children. In E. Schopler & G. Mesibov (Eds.), *The effects of autism on the family* (pp. 289–309). New York: Plenum.

Bristol, M. M., & Gallagher, J. J. (1986). Research on fathers of young handicapped children: Evolution, review, and some future direction. In J. J. Gallagher & P. M. Vietze (Eds.), *Families of handicapped persons: Research, programs, and policy issues* (pp. 81–100). Baltimore: Brookes.

Bristol, M. M., Gallagher, J. J., & Schopler, E. (1988). Mothers and fathers of developmentally disabled and nondisabled boys: Adaptation and spousal support. *Developmental Psychology, 24,* 441–451.

Bristol, M. M., & Schopler, E. (1984). A developmental perspective of stress and coping in families of autistic children. In J. Blacher (Ed.), *Severely handicapped children and their families: Research in review* (pp. 91–134). New York: Academic.

Brotherson, M. J., Turnbull, A. P., & Bronicki, G. J. (1988). Transition into adulthood: Parental planning for sons and daughters with disabilities. *Education and Training in Mental Retardation, 23,* 165–174.

Buhrmester, D., Camparo, L., Christensen, A., Gonzalez, L. S., & Hinshaw, S. P. (1992). Mothers and fathers interacting in dyads and triads with normal and hyperactive sons. *Developmental Psychology, 28,* 500–509.

Byrne, E. A., & Cunningham, C. C. (1985). The effects of mentally handicapped children on families—A conceptual review. *Journal of Child Psychology and Psychiatry, 26,* 847–864.

Call, J. (1958). Psychological problems of the cerebral palsied child, his parents and siblings as revealed by a dynamically oriented small group discussion with parents. *Cerebral Palsy Review, 10,* 3–15.

Chigier, E. (1972). *Down's syndrome.* Lexington, MA: Heath.

Crnic, K. A., Friedrich, W. N., & Greenberg, M. T. (1983). Adaptation of families with mentally retarded children: A model of stress, coping, and family ecology. *American Journal of Mental Deficiency, 88,* 125–138.

Crowley, S. L., & Taylor, M. J. (1994). Mothers' and fathers' perceptions of family functioning in families having children with disabilities. *Early Education and Development, 5,* 213–225.

Cummings, S. T. (1976). The impact of the child's deficiency on the father: A study of fathers of mentally retarded and chronically ill children. *American Journal of Orthopsychiatry, 46,* 246–255.

Darke, P. R., & Goldberg, S. (1994). Father-infant interaction and parent stress with healthy and medically compromised infants. *Infant Behavior and Development, 17,* 3–14.

Davis, M., & McKay, D. (1973, October 27). Mentally subnormal children and their families. *Lancet,* pp. 974–975.

Dunlap, W. R. (1976). Services for families of the developmentally disabled. *Social Work, 21,* 220–223.

Dunlap, W. R., & Hollingsworth, J. S. (1977). How does a handicapped child affect the family? Implications for practitioners. *Family Coordinator, 26,* 286–293.

Erickson, M. (1974). Talking with fathers of young children with Down Syndrome. *Children Today, 3,* 22–25.

Farber, B. (1959). Effects of a severely mentally retarded child on family integration [Special issue]. *Monographs of the Society for Research in Child Development, 24*(71).

Floyd, F. J., & Zmich, D. E. (1991). Marriage and the parenting partnership: Perceptions and interactions of parents with mentally retarded and typically developing children. *Child Development, 62,* 1434–1448.

Fowle, C. M. (1968). The effect of the severely mentally retarded child on his family. *American Journal of Mental Deficiency, 73,* 468–473.

Friedrich, W. N., & Friedrich, W. L. (1981). Psychosocial assets of parents of handicapped and nonhandicapped children. *American Journal of Mental Deficiency, 85,* 551–553.

Gallagher, J. J., Beckman, P., & Cross, A. H. (1983). Families of handicapped children: Sources of stress and its amelioration. *Exceptional Children, 50,* 10–19.

Gallagher, J. J., & Bristol, M. M. (1989). Families of young handicapped children. In M. C. Wang, M. C. Reynolds, & H. J. Walberg (Eds.), *Handbook of special education: Research and practice* (pp. 295–317). Oxford: Pergamon.

Gallagher, J. J., Cross, A. H., & Sharfman, W. (1981). Parental adaptation to a young handicapped child: The father's role. *Journal of the Division for Early Childhood, 3,* 3–14.

Gallagher, J. J., Scharfman, W., & Bristol, M. M. (1984). The division of responsibilities in families with preschool handicapped and non-handicapped children. *Journal for the Division of Early Childhood, 8,* 3–11.

Gath, A. (1977). The impact of an abnormal child upon the parents. *British Journal of Psychiatry, 130,* 405–410.

Grossman, F. (1972). *Brothers and sisters of retarded children: An exploratory study.* Syracuse, NY: Syracuse University Press.

Gumz, E. J., & Gubrium, J. F. (1972). Comparative parental perceptions of a mentally retarded child. *American Journal of Mental Deficiency, 77,* 175–180.

Holroyd, J., & McArthur, D. (1976). Mental retardation and stress on the parents: A contrast between Down's Syndrome and childhood autism. *American Journal of Mental Deficiency, 80,* 431–436.

Holt, K. S. (1958). The influence of a retarded child upon family limitation. *Journal of Mental Deficiency Research, 2,* 28–34.

Hornby, G. (1987). *Fathers of handicapped children: A review.* Unpublished manuscript, University of Manchester, Peter Adrian Research Center, England.

Hornby, G. (1992). A review of fathers' accounts of their experiences of parenting children with disabilities. *Disability, Handicap, and Society, 7,* 363–374.

Houser, R. A. (1988). A comparison of stress and coping by fathers of mentally retarded and non-retarded adolescents. *Dissertation Abstracts International, 48,* 2244-A.

Illingworth, R. S. (1967). Counseling the parents of the mentally handicapped child. *Clinical Pediatrics, 6,* 340–348.

Kanner, L. (1953). Parents' feelings about retarded children. *American Journal of Mental Deficiency, 57,* 375–383.

Kazak, A. E. (1987). Families with disabled children: Stress and social networks in three samples. *Journal of Abnormal Child Psychology, 15,* 137–146.

Kazak, A. E., & Marvin, R. (1984). Differences, difficulties, and adaptation: Stress and social networks in families with a handicapped child. *Family Relations, 33,* 67–77.

Kramm, E. R. (1963). *Families of mongoloid children.* Washington, DC: Children's Bureau.

Krauss, M. W., Hauser-Cram, P., Upshur, C. C., & Shonkoff, J. P. (1989). *Parenting a child with disabilities: Differences between mothers and fathers in reported stress.* Poster session presented at the biennial meeting of the Society for Research in Child Development, Kansas City, MO.

Lamb, M. E. (1981). Fathers and child development: An integrative overview. In M. E. Lamb (Ed.), *The role of the father in child development* (rev. ed., pp. 1–70). New York: Wiley.

Linder, T., & Chitwood, D. (1984). The needs of fathers of young handicapped children. *Journal of the Division for Early Childhood, 7,* 133–139.

Margalit, M. (1979). Ethnic differences in expressions of shame feeling by mothers of severely handicapped children. *International Journal of Social Psychology, 17,* 57–67.

Margalit, M., Leyser, Y., & Avraham, Y. (1989). Classifications and validation of family climate subtypes in kibbutz fathers of disabled and nondisabled children. *Journal of Abnormal Child Psychology, 17,* 91–107.

Margalit, M., Raviv, A., & Ankonina, D. B. (1992). Coping and coherence among parents with disabled children. *Journal of Child Clinical psychology, 21,* 202–209.

Martin, P. (1975). Marital breakdown in families of patients with spina bifida cystica. *Developmental Medicine and Child Neurology, 17,* 557–564.

McConachie, H. (1989). Mothers' and fathers' interaction with their young mentally handicapped children. *International Journal of Behavioral Development, 12,* 239–255.

McLinden, S. (1990). Mothers' and fathers' reports of the effects of a young child with special needs on the family. *Journal of Early Intervention, 14,* 249–259.

Meyer, D. J. (1986a). Fathers of children with handicaps: Developmental trends in fathers' experiences over the family life cycle. In R. R. Fewell & P. F. Vadasy (Eds.), *Families of handicapped children: Needs and supports across the lifespan* (pp. 35–73). Austin, TX: Pro-Ed.

Meyer, D. J. (1986b). Fathers of children with mental handicaps. In M. E. Lamb (Ed.), *The father's role: Applied perspectives* (pp. 227–254). New York: Wiley.

Meyer, D. J. (1993). Lessons learned: Cognitive coping strategies of overlooked family members. In A. P. Turnbull, J. M. Patterson, S. K. Behr, D. L. Murphy, J. G. Marquis, & M. J. Blue-Banning (Eds.), *Cognitive coping, families, and disabilities.* Baltimore: Brookes.

Meyer, D. J., Vadasy, P. F., Fewell, R. R., & Schell, G. (1985). *A handbook for the Fathers Program: How to organize a program for fathers and their handicapped children.* Seattle, WA: University of Washington Press.

Michaels, J., & Schueman, H. (1962). Observations on the psychodynamics of retarded children. *American Journal of Mental Deficiency, 66,* 568–573.

Nadler, A., Lewinstein, E., & Rahav, G. (1991). Acceptance of mental retardation and help-seeking by mothers and fathers of children with mental retardation. *Mental Retardation, 29,* 17–23.

Price-Bonham, S., & Addison, S. (1978). Families and mentally retarded children: Emphasis on the father. *Family Coordinator, 3,* 221–230.

Reed, E. W., & Reed, S. C. (1965). *Mental retardation: A family study.* Philadelphia: Saunders.

Roth, S. I. (1985). Fathers of special needs infants and toddlers enrolled in early intervention programs: Patterns of involvement. *Dissertation Abstracts International, 45,* 3115.

Rousey, A., Best, S., & Blacher, J. (1992). Mothers' and fathers' perceptions of stress and coping with children who have severe disabilities. *American Journal on Mental Retardation, 97,* 99–109.

Ryckman, D. B., & Henderson, R. A. (1965). The meaning of a retarded child for his parents: A focus for counselors. *Mental Retardation, 3,* 4–7.

Salisbury, C. (1987). Stressors of parents with young handicapped and nonhandicapped children. *Journal of the Division for Early Childhood, 11,* 154–160.

Schonnell, F. J., & Watts, B. H. (1956). A first survey of the effects of a subnormal child on the family unit. *American Journal of Mental Deficiency, 61,* 210–219.

Schufiet, L. J., & Wurster, S. R. (1976). Frequency of divorce among parents of handicapped children. *Resources in Education, 11,* 71–78.

Shannon, L. B. (1978). *Interactions of fathers with their handicapped preschoolers.* Unpublished doctoral dissertation, University of Kentucky.

Shriver, E. K. (1990). *Let's play to grow.* Washington, DC: J. P. Kennedy Foundation.

Smith, R. (1986). Physically disabled children and parental time use. *Journal of Leisure Research, 18,* 284–299.

Suelzle, M., & Keenan, V. (1981). Changes in family support networks over the lifecycle of mentally retarded persons. *American Journal of Mental Deficiency, 86,* 267–274.

Summers, J. A., Behr, S. K., & Turnbull, A. P. (1989). Positive adaptation and coping strengths of families who have children with disabilities. In G. H. Singer & L. K. Irvin (Eds.), *Support for caregiving families: Enabling positive adaptation to disability* (pp. 27–40). Baltimore: Brookes.

Tallman, I. (1965). Spousal role differentiation and the socialization of severely retarded children. *Journal of Marriage and the Family, 27,* 37–42.

Tavormina, J., Ball, N. J., Dunn, R. C., Luscomb, B., & Taylor, J. R. (1977). *Psychosocial effects of raising a handicapped child on parents.* Unpublished manuscript, University of Virginia.

Tew, B., Payne, H., & Lawrence, K. (1974). Must a family with a handicapped child be a handicapped family? *Developmental Medicine and Child Neurology, 16,* 32–35.

Tew, B. J., Lawrence, K. M., Payne, H., & Rawnsley, K. (1977). Marital stability following the birth of a child with spina bifida. *British Journal of Psychiatry, 131,* 79–82.

Vadasy, P. F., Fewell, R. R., Greenberg, M. T., Dermond, N. L., & Meyer, D. J., (1986). Follow-up evaluation of the effects of involvement in the father's program. *Topics in Early Childhood Education, 6,* 16–31.

Vadasy, P. F., Fewell, R. R., Meyer, D. J., & Greenberg, M. T. (1985). Supporting fathers of handicapped young children: Preliminary findings of program effects. *Analysis and Intervention in Developmental Disabilities, 5,* 151–164.

Waisbren, S. (1980). Parents' reactions to the birth of a developmentally disabled child. *American Journal of Mental Deficiency, 84,* 345–351.

Widerstrom, A. H., & Dudley-Marling, C. (1986). Living with a handicapped child: Myth and reality. *Childhood Education, 62,* 359–367.

Wikler, L. (1981). Chronic stresses of families of mentally retarded children. *Family Relations, 30,* 281–288.

Wikler, L., Haack, J., & Intagliata, J. (1984). *Bearing the burden alone? Helping divorced mothers of children with developmental disabilities.* Monograph on families with handicapped members, Family Therapies Collection.

Wikler, L., Wasow, M., & Hatfield, E. (1981). Chronic sorrow revisited: Parent vs. professional depiction of adjustment of parents of mentally retarded children. *American Journal of Orthopsychiatry, 51,* 63–70.

CHAPTER 11

Ahrons, C. R., & Miller, R. B. (1993). The effect of the post-divorce relationship on paternal involvement: A longitudinal analysis. *American Journal of Orthopsychiatry, 63,* 441–450.

Allison, P. D., & Furstenberg, F. F. (1989). How marital dissolution affects children: Variations by age and sex. *Developmental Psychology, 25,* 540–549.

Amato, P. R., & Keith, B. (1991a). Parental divorce and the well-being of children: A meta-analysis. *Psychological Bulletin, 110,* 26–46.

Amato, P. R., & Keith, B. (1991b). Parental divorce and adult well-being: A meta-analysis. *Journal of Marriage and the Family, 53,* 43–58.

Amato, P. R., & Rezac, S. J. (1994). Contact with nonresident parents, interparental conflict, and children's behavior. *Journal of Family Issues, 15,* 191–207.

Ambert, A. (1982). Differences in children's behaviour toward custodial mothers and custodial fathers. *Journal of Marriage and the Family, 44,* 73–86.

Arditti, J. A. (1991). Child support noncompliance and divorced fathers: Rethinking the role of paternal involvement. *Journal of Divorce and Remarriage, 14,* 107–114.

Arditti, J. A. (1992). Differences between fathers with joint custody and noncustodial fathers. *American Journal of Orthopsychiatry, 62,* 186–195.

Arditti, J. A., & Allen, K. R. (1993). Understanding distressed fathers' perceptions of legal and relational inequities post-divorce. *Family and Conciliation Courts Review, 31,* 461–476.

Arendell, T. (1992). After divorce: Investigations into father absence. *Sociologists for Women in Society, 6,* 562–586.

Aulette, J. R. (1994). *Changing families.* Belmont, CA: Wadsworth.

Baumrind, D. (1991). Effective parenting during the early adolescent transition. In P. A. Cowan & E. M. Hetherington (Eds.), *Family transitions* (pp. 111–163). Hillsdale, NJ: Erlbaum.

Baydar, N., & Brooks-Gunn, J. (1991, December). *The dynamics of child support and its consequences for children.* Paper presented at the Conference on Child Support Reform, Arlie House, VA.

Bender, W. N. (1994). Joint custody: The option of choice. *Journal of Divorce and Remarriage, 21,* 115–131.

Benjamin, M., & Irving, H. H. (1990). Comparison of the experience of satisfied and dissatisfied shared parents. *Journal of Divorce and Remarriage, 14,* 43–61.

Bentler, P. M., & Newcomb, M. D. (1978). Longitudinal study of marital success and failure. *Journal of Consulting and Clinical Psychology, 46,* 1053–1070.

Berkman, L. F., & Breslow, L. (1983). *Health and the ways of living: The Alameda County Study.* New York: Oxford University Press.

Berkman, L. F., & Syme, S. L. (1979). Social networks, host resistance, and mortality: A nine-year follow-up study of Alameda County residents. *American Journal of Epidemiology, 109,* 186–204.

Bernard, J. (1972). *The future of marriage.* New York: Bantam.

Block, J. H., Block, J., & Gjerde, P. F. (1989). The personality of children prior to divorce: A prospective study. *Child Development, 57,* 827–840.

Bloom, B. L., Asher, J. A., & White, S. W. (1978). Marital disruption as a stressor: A review and analysis. *Psychological Bulletin, 85,* 867–894.

Bowman, M., & Ahrons, C. (1985). Impact of legal custody status on fathers' parenting post-divorce. *Journal of Marriage and the Family, 47,* 481–488.

Brand, E., Clingempeel, W. G., & Bowen-Woodward, K. (1988). Family relationships and children's psychosocial adjustment in stepmother and stepfather families. In E. M. Hetherington & J. D. Arasteh (Eds.), *Impact of divorce, single-parenting, and stepparenting on children* (pp. 299–324). Hillsdale, NJ: Erlbaum.

Braver, S. L., Wolchik, S. A., Sandler, I. N., Sheets, V. L., Fogas, B., & Bay, R. C. (1993). A longitudinal study of noncustodial parents: Parents without children. *Journal of Family Psychology, 6,* 1–16.

Bray, J. H., & Berger, S. H. (1993). Developmental issues in stepfamilies research project: Family relationships and parent-child interactions. *Journal of Family Psychology, 7,* 1–17.

Bronfenbrenner, U. (1979). *The ecology of human development.* Cambridge, MA: Harvard University Press.

Bruch, C. S. (1992). And how are the children? The effects of ideology and mediation on child custody law and children's well-being in the United States. *Family and Conciliation Courts Review, 30,* 112–134.

Buchanan, C. M., Maccoby, E. E., & Dornbusch, S. M. (1992). Adolescents and their families after divorce: Three residential arrangements compared. *Journal of Research on Adolescence, 2,* 261–291.

Bumpass, L. L., Sweet, J. A., & Castro-Martin, T. (1990). Changing patterns of remarriage. *Journal of Marriage and the Family, 52,* 747–756.

Burman, B., & Margolin, G. (1992). Analysis of the association between marital relationships and health problems. *Psychological Bulletin, 112,* 39–63.

Camara, K. A., & Resnick, G. (1988). Interparental conflict and cooperation: Factors moderating children's post-divorce adjustment. In E. M. Hetherington & J. D. Arasteh (Eds.), *Impact of divorce, single parenting, and stepparenting on children* (pp. 169–195). Hillsdale, NJ: Erlbaum.

Capaldi, D. M., & Patterson, G. R. (1991). Relation of parental transitions to boys' adjustment problems: I. A linear hypothesis. II. Mothers at risk for transitions and unskilled parenting. *Developmental Psychology, 27,* 489–504.

Castro-Martin, T., & Bumpass, L. (1989). Recent trends and differentials in marital disruption. *Demography, 26,* 37–51.

Chase-Lansdale, P. L., & Hetherington, E. M. (1990). The impact of divorce on life-span development: Short and long term effects. In P. B. Baltes, D. L. Featherman, & R. M Lerner (Eds.), *Life-span development and behavior* (Vol. 10, pp. 105–150). Hillsdale, NJ: Erlbaum.

Cherlin, A. (1992). *Marriage, divorce, remarriage: Social trends in the U.S.* Cambridge, MA: Harvard University Press.

Cherlin, A., & Furstenberg, F. F. (1986). Grandparents and family crisis. *Generations, 10*(4), 26–28.

Cherlin, A. J., & Furstenberg, F. F. (1994). Stepfamilies in the United States: A reconsideration. In J. Blake & J. Hagen (Eds.), *Annual review of sociology* (pp. 359–381). Palo Alto, CA: Annual Reviews.

Cherlin, A. J., Furstenberg, F. F., Chase-Lansdale, P. L., Kiernan, K. E., Robins, P. K., Morrison, D. R., & Teitler, J. O. (1991). Longitudinal studies of the effects of divorce on children in Great Britain and the United States. *Science, 252,* 1386–1389.

Comeaux, E. A. (1983). A guide to implementing divorce mediation in the public sector. *Conciliation Courts Review, 21,* 1–25.

Cowan, C. P., Cowan, P. A., Heming, G., & Miller, N. B. (1991). Becoming a family: Marriage, parenting and child development. In P. A. Cowan & M. Hetherington (Eds.), *Family transitions* (pp. 79–110). Hillsdale, NJ: Erlbaum.

Cowan, P. A., & Cowan, C. P. (1987, April). *Couple's relationships, parenting styles and the child's development at three.* Paper presented at the Society for Research in Child Development, Baltimore.

Cowan, P. A., & Cowan, C. P. (1990). Becoming a family: Research and intervention. In I. Sigel & G. A. Brody (Eds.), *Family research* (pp. 246–279). Hillsdale, NJ: Erlbaum.

Crosbie-Burnett, M. (1991). Impact of joint versus sole custody and quality of co-parental relationship on adjustment of adolescents in remarried families. *Behavioral Sciences and the Law, 9,* 439–449.

Debner, C. E., & Bray, J. H. (1992). *Nonresidential parenting: New vistas in family living.* Newbury Park, CA: Sage.

Downey, D. B., & Powell, B. (1993). Do children in single-parent households fare better living with same-sex parents? *Journal of Marriage and the Family, 55,* 55–71.

Easterbrooks, M. A. (1987, April). *Early family development: Longitudinal impact of marital quality.* Paper presented at the meeting of the Society for Research in Child Development, Baltimore.

Elder, G. H., Jr., Caspi, A., & Nguyen, T. V. (1992). Resourceful and vulnerable children: Family influences in stressful times. In R. K. Silbereisen & K. Eyferth (Eds.), *Development in context: Integrative perspectives on youth development* (pp. 266–304). New York: Springer.

Emery, R. E. (1982). Interparental conflict and the children of discord and divorce. *Psychological Bulletin, 92,* 310–330.

Emery, R. E. (1988a). *Marriage, divorce, and children's adjustment.* Newbury Park, CA: Sage.

Emery, R. E. (1988b). Mediation and the settlement of divorce disputes. In E. M. Hetherington & J. D. Arasteh (Eds.), *Impact of divorce, single parenting, and stepparenting on children* (pp. 53–71). Hillsdale, NJ: Erlbaum.

Emery, R. E. (1994). *Renegotiating family relationships: Divorce, child custody and mediation.* New York: Guilford.

Emery, R. E., Matthews, S. G., & Wyer, M. M. (1991). Child custody mediation and litigation: Further evidence on the differing views of mothers and fathers. *Journal of Consulting and Clinical Psychology, 59,* 410–418.

Emery, R. E., & O'Leary, K. D. (1982). Children's perceptions of marital discord and behavior problems of boys and girls. *Journal of Abnormal Child Psychology, 10,* 11–24.

Emery, R. E., & Wyer, M. M. (1987). Child custody mediation and litigation: An experimental evaluation of the experience of parents. *Journal of Consulting and Clinical Psychology, 55,* 179–186.

Fincham, F. F., Bradbury, T. N., & Scott, C. K. (1990). Cognition in marriage. In F. D. Fincham & T. N. Bradbury (Eds.), *The psychology of marriage* (pp. 118–149). New York: Guilford.

Fine, M. A., & Kurdek, L. A. (1992). Adjustment of adolescents in stepfather and stepmother families. *Journal of Marriage and the Family, 54,* 725–736.

Folberg, J. (1984). Stress and trends in the law of joint custody. In J. Folberg (Ed.), *Joint custody and shared parenting* (pp. 159–167). Washington, DC: Bureau of National Affairs and Association of Family and Conciliation Courts.

Forehand, R., Brody, G., Long, N., Slotkin, J., & Fauber, R. (1986). Divorce/divorce potential and interparental conflict: The relationship to early adolescent social and cognitive functioning. *Journal of Adolescent Research, 1,* 389–397.

Forehand, R., Wierson, M., Thomas, A. M., Fauber, R., Armistead, L., Kemptom, T., & Long, N. (1991). A short-term longitudinal examination of young adolescent functioning following divorce: The role of family factors. *Journal of Abnormal Child Psychology, 19,* 97–111.

Forgatch, M. S., Patterson, G. R., & Ray, J. A. (1993). Divorce and boys' adjustment problems: Two paths with a single model. In E. M. Hetherington (Ed.), *Stress, coping, and resiliency in children and the family* (pp. 195–218). Hillsdale, NJ: Erlbaum.

Fox, G. L. (1985). Noncustodial fathers. In S. Hanson & F. Bozett (Eds.), *Dimensions of fatherhood* (pp. 393–415). Beverly Hills, CA: Sage.

Freed, D. J., & Foster, H. H. (1984). Divorce in the fifty states: An overview. *Family Law Quarterly, 17,* 365–447.

Freed, D. J., & Walker, T. B. (1991). Family law in the fifty states: An overview. *Family Law Quarterly, 24,* 309–405.

Fry, P. S. (1983). The kid's eye view: The OPF and children's perceptions of personal needs and concerns for the future. *Journal of Child Care, 1,* 31–50.

Furstenberg, F. F., Jr. (1988). Child care after divorce and remarriage. In E. M. Hetherington & J. D. Arasteh (Eds.), *Impact of divorce, single parenting, and stepparenting on children* (pp. 245–261). Hillsdale, NJ: Erlbaum.

Furstenberg, F. F. (1990). Divorce and the American family. *Annual Review of Sociology, 16,* 379–403.

Furstenberg, F. F., Jr., & Allison, P. D. (1985). *How marital dissolution affects children: Variations by age and sex.* Unpublished manuscript.

Furstenberg, F. F., Jr., & Cherlin, A. J. (1991). *Divided families: What happens to children when parents part.* Cambridge, MA: Harvard University Press.

Furstenberg, F. F., Jr., & Morgan, S. P. (1987). Paternal participation and children's well-being after marital dissolution. *American Sociological Review, 52,* 695–701.

Furstenberg, F. F., Jr., Morgan, S. P., & Allison, P. D. (1987). Paternal participation and children's well-being after marital dissolution. *American Sociological Review, 52,* 695–701.

Furstenberg, F. F., Jr., & Nord, C. W. (1985). Parenting apart: Patterns of childbearing after marital disruption. *Journal of Marriage and the Family, 47,* 893–904.

Furstenberg, F. F., Jr., Nord, C. W., Peterson, J., & Zill, N. (1983). The life course of children of divorce: Marital disruption and parental contact. *American Sociological Review, 48,* 656–668.

Furstenberg, F. F., Jr., & Seltzer, J. A. (1986). Divorce and child development. *Sociological Studies of Child Development, 1,* 137–160.

Garmezy, N. (1983). Stressors of childhood. In N. Garmezy & M. Rutter (Eds.), *Stress, coping, and development in children* (pp. 43–84). New York: McGraw-Hill.

Goldstein, J., Freud, A., & Solnit, A. (1979). *Beyond the best interests of the child.* New York: Free Press.

Gottlieb, I. H., & McCabe, S. B. (1990). Marriage and psychopathology. In F. D. Fincham & T. N. Bradbury (Eds.), *The psychology of marriage* (pp. 226–257). New York: Guilford.

Gottman, J. M. (1993). A theory of marital dissolution and stability. *Journal of Family Psychology, 7,* 1–19.

Gottman, J. M. (1994). *What predicts divorce? The relationship between marital processes and marital outcomes.* Hillsdale, NJ: Erlbaum.

Gottman, J. M., & Katz, L. (1989). Effects of marital discord on young children's peer interaction and health. *Developmental Psychology, 25,* 373–381.

Greif, J. (1979). Fathers, children, and joint custody. *American Journal of Orthopsychiatry, 49,* 311–319.

Gunnoe, M. L. (1993). *Noncustodial mothers' and fathers' contributions to the adjustment of adolescent stepchildren.* Unpublished doctoral dissertation, University of Virginia.

Hanson, S. M. H. (1988). Single custodial fathers and the parent-child relationship. *Nursing Research, 30,* 202–204.

Hess, R. D., & Camara, K. A. (1979). Post-divorce family relationships as mediating factors in the consequences of divorce for children. *Journal of Social Issues, 35,* 79–98.

Hetherington, E. M. (1989). Coping with family transitions: Winners, losers and survivors. *Child Development, 60,* 1–14.

Hetherington, E. M. (1991). The role of individual differences and family relationships in children's coping with divorce and remarriage. In P. A. Cowan & E. M. Hetherington (Eds.), *Family transitions* (pp. 165–194). Hillsdale, NJ: Erlbaum.

Hetherington, E. M. (1993). An overview of the Virginia longitudinal study of divorce and remarriage with a focus on early adolescence. *Journal of Family Psychology, 7,* 1–18.

Hetherington, E. M. (1995, March). *Teenaged childbearing and divorce.* Paper presented at the Biennial Meetings of the Society for Research in Child Development, Indianapolis.

Hetherington, E. M., & Camara, K. A. (1984). Families in transition: The process of dissolution and reconstitution. In R. D. Parke (Ed.), *Review of child development research* (pp. 398–439). Chicago: University of Chicago Press.

Hetherington, E. M., Clingempeel, W. G., Anderson, E. R., Deal, J. E., Stanley-Hagan, M., Hollier, E. A., & Lindner, M. S. (1992). Coping with marital transitions: A family systems perspective. *Monographs of the Society for Child Development, 57* (Serial No. 227, Nos. 2–3).

Hetherington, E. M., Cox, M., & Cox, R. (1978). The aftermath of divorce. In J. H. Stevens, Jr., & M. Matthews (Eds.), *Mother-child, father-child relations* (pp. 149–176). Washington, DC: National Association for the Education of Young Children.

Hetherington, E. M., Cox, M., & Cox, R. (1979). Family interactions and the social, emotional, and cognitive development of children following divorce. In V. C. Vaughn & T. B. Brazelton (Eds.), *The family: Setting priorities* (pp. 26–49). New York: Science and Medicine Publishers.

Hetherington, E. M., Cox, M., & Cox, R. (1982). Effects of divorce on parents and children. In M. Lamb (Ed.), *Nontraditional families* (pp. 233–288). Hillsdale, NJ: Erlbaum.

Hetherington, E. M., Cox, M., & Cox, R. (1985). Long-term effects of divorce and remarriage on the adjustment of children. *Journal of American Academy of Psychiatry, 24* (5), 518–830.

Hetherington, E. M., Law, T. C., & O'Connor, T. G. (1992). Divorce: Challenges, changes, and new chances. In F. Walsh (Ed.), *Normal family processes* (2nd ed., pp. 219–246). New York: Guilford.

Hetherington, E. M., & Mekos, D. (in press). Alterations in family life following divorce: Effects on children and adolescence. In N. Alessi (Ed.), *Handbook of child and adolescent psychiatry.* New York: Wiley.

Hetherington, E. M., & Stanley-Hagan, M. (1986). Divorced fathers: Stress, coping, and adjustment. In M. E. Lamb (Ed.), *The father's role: Applied perspectives* (pp. 103–134). New York: Wiley.

Hetherington, E. M., Stanley-Hagan, M., & Anderson, E. (1989). Marital transitions: A child's perspective. *American Psychologist, 44,* 303–312.

Hetherington, E. M., & Tryon, A. S. (1989, November/December). His and her divorces. *The Family Therapy Network,* 1–16.

Hotzworth-Monroe, A., & Jacobson, N. S. (1985). Causal attributions of married couples: When do they search for causes? What do they conclude when they do? *Journal of Personality and Social Psychology, 48,* 1398–1412.

Howes, P., & Markman, H. J. (1989). Marital quality and child functioning: A longitudinal investigation. *Child Development, 60,* 1044–1051.

Huffnung, M. (1989). Motherhood: Contemporary conflict for women. In J. Freeman (Ed.), *Women: A feminist perspective* (pp. 147–175). Mountain View, CA: Mayfield.

Hughes, M. (1989). Parenthood and psychological well-being among the formerly married: Are children the primary source of psychological distress? *Journal of Family Issues, 10,* 463–481.

Ihinger-Tallman, M., Pasley, K., & Buehler, C. (1993). Developing a middle-range theory of father involvement post-divorce. *Journal of Family Issues, 14,* 550–571.

Isaacs, M. (1988). The visitation schedule and child adjustment: A three-year study. *Family Process, 27,* 251–256.

Jacobson, D. (1978). The impact of marital separation/divorce on children: II. Interparental hostility and child adjustment. *Journal of Divorce, 2,* 3–19.

Jacobson, N. S., McDonald, D. W., Follette, W. C., & Berley, R. A. (1985). Attributional process in distressed and nondistressed married couples. *Cognitive Therapy and Research, 9,* 35–50.

Johnston, J. R., Kline, M., & Tschann, J. M. (1989). Ongoing post-divorce conflict: Effects on children of joint custody and frequent access. *American Journal of Orthopsychiatry, 59,* 576–592.

Katz, L. F., & Gottman, J. M. (1991a). Marital discord and child outcomes: A social psychophysiological approach. In K. Dodge & J. Garber (Eds.), *The development of emotion regulation and disregulation* (pp. 111–164). New York: Cambridge University Press.

Katz, L. F., & Gottman, J. M. (1991b, April). *Marital interaction process and preschool children's peer interactions and emotional development.* Paper presented at the meeting of the Society for Research in Child Development, Seattle.

Kelly, J. (1981). The visiting relationship after divorce: Research findings and clinical implications. In I. R. Stuart & L. D. Abt (Eds.), *Children of separation and divorce: Management and treatment* (pp. 338–361). New York: Van Nostrand Reinhold.

Kelly, J. (1993). Current research on children's post-divorce adjustment. *Family and Conciliation Courts Review, 31,* 29–49.

Kiecolt-Glaser, J. K., Fisher, B. S., Ogrocki, P., Stout, J. C., Speicher, C. E., & Glaser, R. (1987). Marital quality, marital disruption, and immune function. *Psychosomatic Medicine, 49,* 13–33.

King, V. (1994a). Nonresident father involvement and child well-being: Can dads make a difference? *Journal of Family Issues, 15,* 78–96.

King, V. (1994b). Variation in the consequences of nonresident father involvement for children's well-being. *Journal of Marriage and the Family, 56,* 963–972.

Kitson, G. C., & Holmes, W. M. (1992). *Portrait of divorce: Adjustment to marital breakdown.* New York: Guilford.

Koch, M., & Lowery, C. (1985). Visitation and the noncustodial father. *Journal of Divorce, 8*, 47–65.

Koel, A., Clark, S. C., Phear, W. P. C., & Hauser, B. B. (1988). A comparison of joint and sole legal customary agreements. In E. M. Hetherington & J. D. Arasteh (Eds.), *Impact of divorce, single parenting, and stepparenting on children* (pp. 72–90). Hillsdale, NJ: Erlbaum.

Kruk, E. (1992). Psychological and structural factors contributing to the disengagement of noncustodial fathers after divorce. *Family and Conciliation Courts Review, 30*, 81–101.

Kurdek, L. A. (1986). Children's reasoning about parental divorce. In R. D. Ashmore & D. M. Brodinsky (Eds.), *Thinking about the family: Views of parents and children* (pp. 233–276). Hillsdale, NJ: Erlbaum.

Kurdek, L. A. (1993). Predicting marital dissolution: A 5-year prospective study of newlywed couples. *Journal of Personality and Social Psychology, 64*, 221–242.

Landstreet, R., & Tokas, M. (1991). *Developing effective procedures for pro se modification of child support awards.* Washington, DC: U.S. Department of Health and Human Resources.

Lempers, J. D., Clark-Lempers, D., & Simons, R. (1989). Economic hardship, parenting and distress in adolescence. *Child Development, 60*, 25–39.

Levinger, G. (1979). A social psychological perspective on marital dissolution. In G. Levinger & O. C. Moles (Eds.), *Divorce and separation: Conditions, causes and consequences* (pp. 37–60). New York: Basic Books.

Little, M. A. (1992). The impact of the custody plan on the family: A five-year follow-up: Executive summary. *Family and Conciliation Courts Review, 30*, 243–251.

Loewan, J. W. (1988). Visitation fatherhood. In P. Bornstein & C. P. Cowan (Eds.), *Fatherhood today: Men's changing role in the family* (pp. 195–213). New York: Wiley.

Lowenstein, J. S., & Koopman, E. J. (1978). A comparison of self-esteem between boys living with single-parent mothers and single-parent fathers. *Journal of Divorce, 2*, 195–207.

Maccoby, E. E., Buchanan, C. M., Mnookin, R. H., & Dornbusch, S. M. (1993). Post-divorce roles of mothers and fathers in the lives of their children. *Journal of Family Psychology, 7*, 1–15.

Maccoby, E. E., Depner, C. E., & Mnookin, R. H. (1988). Custody of children following divorce. In E. M. Hetherington & J. Arasteh (Eds.), *Impact of divorce, single parenting, and stepparenting on children* (pp. 91–114). Hillsdale, NJ: Erlbaum.

Maccoby, E. E., Depner, C. E., & Mnookin, R. H. (1990). Co-parenting in the second year after divorce. *Journal of Marriage and the Family, 52*, 141–155.

Maccoby, E. E., & Mnookin, R. H. (1992). *Dividing the child: Social and legal dilemmas of custody.* Cambridge, MA: Harvard University Press.

Marsiglio, W. (1992). Stepfathers with minor children living at home. *Journal of Family Issues, 13*, 195–214.

McLanahan, S., & Sandefur, G. (1994). *Growing up with a single parent: What hurts, what helps.* Cambridge, MA: Harvard University Press.

McLanahan, S., Seltzer, J., Hanson, T., & Thomson, E. (1991, December). *Child support enforcement and child well-being: Greater security or greater conflict?* Paper presented at the Conference on Child Support Reform, Arlie House, VA.

Mendes, H. A. (1976a). Single-fatherhood. *Social Work, 21*, 308–312.

Mendes, H. A. (1976b). Single fathers. *Family Coordinator, 25*, 439–444.

Meyers, D., & Garasky, S. (1991). *Custodial fathers: Myths, realities and child support policy.* U.S. Department of Health and Human Services. Washington, DC: U.S. Government Printing Office.

Mnookin, R. H. (1975). Child-custody adjudication: Judicial functions in the face of indeterminacy. *Law and Contemporary Problems, 39*, 226–292.

Morgan, P. S., Lye, D. N., & Condron, G. A. (1988). Sons, daughters and the risk of marital disruption. *American Journal of Sociology* (DHHS Publication No. PHS-90-1100). Washington, DC: U.S. Government Printing Office.

National Center for Health Statistics (1990). *Vital statistics of the United States, 1988: Vol. 1. Natality* (DHHS Publication No. PHS-90-1100). Washington, DC: U.S. Government Printing Office.

Neugubauer, R. (1989). Divorce, custody, and visitation: The child's point of view. *Journal of Divorce, 12,* 153–168.

Nieto, D. S. (1990). The custodial single father: Who does *he* think he is? *Journal of Divorce, 13,* 27–43.

Nye, F. I. (1979). Choice, exchange, and the family. In W. Burr, R. Hill, F. I. Nye, & I. Reiss (Eds.), *Contemporary theories about the family* (Vol. 2, pp. 567–614). New York: Free Press.

Office of Child Support Enforcement. (1990). *Child support enforcement: Fifteenth Annual Report to Congress, For the Period Ending September 30, 1990.* Washington, DC: U.S. Department of Health and Human Services, Administration for Children and Families, Office of Child Support Enforcement.

Opie, A. (1993). Ideologies of joint custody. *Family and Conciliation Courts Review, 31,* 313–326.

Parke, R. D., & Tinsley, B. R. (1984). Historical and contemporary perspectives on fathering. In K. A. McCluskey & H. W. Reese (Eds.), *Life span developmental psychology: Historical and generational effects in life span development* (pp. 231–252). New York: Academic.

Patterson, G. R. (1991, April). *Interaction of stress and family structure and their relation to child adjustment.* Paper presented at the Biennial Meetings of the Society for Research on Child Development, Seattle.

Peters, H. E., Argys, L. M., Maccoby, E. E., & Mnookin, R. H. (1993). Enforcing divorce settlements: Evidence from child support compliance and award modification. *Demography, 30,* 719–735.

Peterson, J. L., & Nord, C. W. (1990). The regular receipt of child support: A multistep process. *Journal of Marriage and the Family, 52,* 539–551.

Peterson, J., & Zill, N. (1986). Marital disruption, parent-child relationships, and behavior problems in children. *Journal of Marriage and the Family, 48,* 295–307.

Pleck, J. (1987). The theory of male sex role identity: Its rise and fall 1936 to the present. In H. Brod (Ed.), *The making of masculinities* (pp. 21–38). Boston: Allen and Unwin.

Porter, B., & O'Leary, K. D. (1980). Marital discord and childhood behavior problems. *Journal of Abnormal Child Psychology, 8,* 287–295.

Reissman, C. K. (1990). *Divorce talk: Women and men make sense of personal relationships.* New Brunswick, NJ: Rutgers University Press.

Richards, C. A., & Goldenberg, I. (1985). Joint custody: Current issues and implications for treatment. *American Journal of Family Therapy, 13,* 33–40.

Rosen, R. (1979). Some crucial issues concerning children of divorce. *Journal of Divorce, 3,* 19–25.

Rosenthal, K. M., & Keshet, H. F. (1981). *Fathers without partners: A study of fathers and the family after marital separation.* Totowa, NJ: Rowman and Littlefield.

Rothberg, B. (1983). Joint custody: Parental problems and satisfaction. *Family Process, 22,* 43–52.

Rutter, M. (1987). Psychosocial resilience and protective mechanisms. *American Journal of Orthopsychiatry, 57,* 316–331.

Santrock, J. W., & Warshak, R. A. (1979). Father custody and social development in boys and girls. *Journal of Social Issues, 35* (4), 112–125.

Schnayer, R., & Orr, R. R. (1989). A comparison of children living in single-mother and single-father families. *Journal of Divorce, 12,* 171–184.

Scott, E. S. (1992). Pluralism, parental preference and child custody. *California Law Review, 80*, 615–712.

Seltzer, J. A. (1990). Legal and physical custody in recent divorces. *Social Science Quarterly, 71*, 250–266.

Seltzer, J. A. (1991). Relationships between fathers and children who live apart: The father's role after separation. *Journal of Marriage and the Family, 53*, 79–101.

Seltzer, J. A., & Bianchi, S. M. (1988). Children's contact with absent parents. *Journal of Marriage and the Family, 50*, 663–677.

Seltzer, J. A., & Brandreth, Y. (1994). What fathers say about involvement with children after separation. *Journal of Family Issues, 15*, 49–77.

Shaw, D. S., & Emery, R. E. (1987). Parental conflict and other correlates of the adjustment of school-age children whose parents have separated. *Journal of Abnormal Child Psychology, 15*, 269–281.

Shrier, D. K., Simring, S. K., Shapiro, E. T., Grief, J. B., & Lindenthal, J. J. (1991). Level of satisfaction of fathers and mothers with joint or sole custody arrangements. *Journal of Divorce and Remarriage, 16*, 163–169.

Steinberg, L., Mounts, N. S., Lamborn, S. D., & Dornbusch, S. M. (1991). Authoritative parenting and adolescent adjustment across varied ecological niches. *Journal of Research on Adolescence, 1*, 19–36.

Steinman, S. (1981). The experience of children in a joint-custody arrangement: A report of a study. *American Journal of Orthopsychiatry, 51*, 403–414.

Stephens, E. H., Freedman, V. A., & Hess, J. (1993). Near and far: Contact of children with their non-residential fathers. *Journal of Divorce and Remarriage, 20*, 171–191.

Sweet, J. A., & Bumpass, L. L. (1987). *American families and households.* New York: Russell Sage.

Teachman, J. D. (1991). Contributions to children by divorced fathers. *Social Problems, 38*, 358–371.

Tepp, A. (1983). Divorced fathers: Predictors of continued paternal involvement. *American Journal of Psychiatry, 24*, 545–553.

Thomas, A. M., & Forehand, R. (1993). The role of paternal variables in divorced and married families: Predictability of adolescent depression. *American Journal of Orthopsychiatry, 63*, 126–135.

Tschann, J., Johnston, J., Kline, M., & Wallerstein, J. (1989). Family process and children's functioning during divorce. *Journal of Marriage and the Family, 51*, 431–444.

Umberson, D. (1987). Family status and health behaviors: Social control as a dimension of social integration. *Journal of Health and Social Behavior, 28*, 306–319.

Umberson, D., & Williams, C. L. (1993). Divorced fathers: Parental role strain and psychological distress. *Journal of Family Issues, 14*, 378–400.

U.S. Bureau of the Census. (1992). Studies in marriage and the family: Married couple families with children. In *Current populaton reports* (Series P-23, No. 162). Washington, DC: U.S. Government Printing Office.

Wallerstein, J. S., & Kelly, J. B. (1980). *Surviving the breakup.* New York: Basic Books.

Warshak, R. A. (1986). Father custody and child development: A review and analysis of psychological research. *Behavioral Sciences and the Law, 4*, 185–202.

Weiss, R. S. (1975). *Marital separation.* New York: Basic Books.

Weitzman, L. (1985). *The divorce revolution.* Chicago: Free Press.

White, L. K. (1990). Determinants of divorce: Review of research in the eighties. *Journal of Marriage and the Family, 50*, 45–51.

White, L. K., Brinkerhoff, D. B., & Booth, A. (1985). The effect of marital disruption on child's attachment to parents. *Journal of Family Issues, 6*, 5–22.

Wright, D., & Price, S. (1986). Court-ordered child support payment: The effect of the former spouse relationship on compliance. *Journal of Marriage and the Family, 48,* 869–874.

Zeiss, A., Zeiss, R. A., & Johnson, S. W. (1980). Sex differences in initiation of and adjustment to divorce. *Journal of Divorce, 4,* 21–33.

Zill, N. (1988). Behavior, achievement, and health problems among children in stepfamilies: Findings from a national survey of child health. In E.M. Hetherington & J. D. Arasteh (Eds.), *Impact of divorce, single parenting, and stepparenting on children* (pp. 325–368). Hillsdale, NJ: Erlbaum.

Zill, N., Morrison, D. R., & Coiro, M. J. (1993). Long-term effects of parental divorce on parent-child relationships, adjustment, and achievement in young adulthood. *Journal of Family Psychology, 7,* 1–13.

CHAPTER 12

Amato, P. R. (1987). Family process in one-parent, step-parent, and intact families: The child's point of view. *Journal of Marriage and the Family, 49,* 327–337.

Amato, P. R., & Keith, B. (1991). Parental divorce and the well-being of children: A meta-analysis. *Psychological Bulletin, 110,* 26–46.

Ambert, A. M. (1986). Being a stepparent: Live-in and visiting stepchildren. *Journal of Marriage and the Family, 48,* 795–804.

Anderson, J. Z., & White, G. D. (1986). An empirical investigation of interaction and relationship patterns in functional and dysfunctional nuclear families and stepfamilies. *Family Process, 25,* 407–422.

Astone, M. N., & McLanahan, S. S. (1991). Family structure, parental practices and high school completion. *American Sociological Review, 56,* 309–320.

Bachrach, C. (1983). Children in families: Characteristics of biological, step- and adopted children. *Journal of Marriage and the Family, 45,* 171–179.

Barber, B. L., & Lyons, J. M. (1995, April). *Chores in divorced and remarried families: A burden or an opportunity to contribute?* Paper presented at the biennial meetings of the Society for Research in Child Development, Indianapolis.

Baumrind, D. (1991). Effective parenting during the early adolescent transition. In P. A. Cowan & E. M. Hetherington (Eds.), *Family transitions* (pp. 111–163). Hillsdale, NJ: Erlbaum.

Belle, D. (1994). Social support issues for "latchkey" and supervised children. In F. Nestmann & K. Hurrelmann (Eds.), *Social networks and social support in childhood and adolescence: Prevention and intervention in childhood and adolescence* (pp. 293–304). Berlin: de Gruyter.

Belsky, J. (1984). The determinants of parenting: A process model. *Child Development, 55,* 83–96.

Block, J., Block, J. H., & Gjerde, P. R. (1988). Parental functioning and the home environment in families of divorce: Prospective and concurrent analyses. *Journal of the American Academy of Child and Adolescent Psychiatry, 27,* 207–213.

Brand, E., Clingempeel, W. E., & Bowen-Woodard, K. (1988). Family relationships and children's psychological adjustment in stepmother and stepfather families: Findings and conclusions for the Philadelphia Stepfamily Research Project. In E. M. Hetherington & J. D. Arasteh (Eds.), *Impact of divorce, single-parenting, and stepparenting on children* (pp. 299–324). Hillsdale, NJ: Erlbaum.

Bray, J. H. (1987, August). *Becoming a stepfamily.* Paper presented at the meeting of the American Psychological Association, New York.

Bray, J. H. (1988). Children's development during early remarriage. In E. M. Hetherington &

J. D. Arasteh (Eds.), *Impact of divorce, single parenting and stepparenting on children* (pp. 279–298). Hillsdale, NJ: Erlbaum.

Bray, J. H., & Berger, S. H. (1993). Developmental issues in Stepfamilies Research Project: Family relationships and parent-child interactions. *Journal of Family Psychology, 7,* 1–17.

Bray, J. H., Berger, S. H., & Boethel, C. L. (1994). Role integration and marital adjustment in stepfather families. In K. Pasley & M. Ihinger-Tallman (Eds.), *Stepparenting: Issues in theory, research and practice* (pp. 69–86). Westport, CT: Greenwood.

Bumpass, L., & Raley, R. K. (1993). *Trends in the duration of single-parent families* (NSFH Working Paper No. 58). Madison, WI: University of Wisconsin, Center for Demography and Ecology.

Bumpass, L. L., Sweet, J. A., & Castro-Martin, T. C. (1990). Changing pattern of remarriage. *Journal of Marriage and the Family, 52,* 747–756.

Burchardt, N. (1990). Stepchildren's memories: Myth, understanding, and forgiveness. In R. Samuel & P. Thompson (Eds.), *The myths we live by* (pp. 239–251). London: Routledge.

Capaldi, D. M., & Patterson, G. R. (1991). Relation of parental transition to boys' adjustment problems: I. A linear hypothesis. II. Mothers at risk for transitions and unskilled parenting. *Developmental Psychology, 27,* 489–504.

Castro-Martin, T., & Bumpass, L. (1989). Recent trends and differentials in marital disruption. *Demography, 26,* 37–51.

Cherlin, A. J. (1981). *Marriage, divorce, remarriage: Changing patterns in the postwar United States.* Cambridge, MA: Harvard University Press.

Cherlin, A. J., & Furstenberg, F. F. (1994). Stepfamilies in the United States: A reconsideration. *Annual Review of Sociology, 20,* 359–381.

Cherlin, A. J., Furstenberg, F. F., Chase-Lansdale, P. L., Kiernan, K. E., Robings, P. K., Morrison, D. R., & Teitler, J. O. (1991). Longitudinal studies of effects of divorce on children in Great Britain and the United States. *Science, 252,* 1386–1389.

Clingempeel, W. G., Ievoli, R., & Brand, E. (1984). Structural complexity and the quality of stepfather-stepchild relationships. *Family Process, 23,* 547–560.

Clingempeel, W. G., & Segal, S. (1986). Stepparent-stepchild relationships and the psychological adjustment of children in stepmother and stepfather families. *Child Development, 57,* 474–484.

Coleman, M., & Ganong, L. H. (1989). Financial management in stepfamilies. *Lifestyles, 10,* 217–232.

Cowan, C. P., Cowan, P. A., Heming, G., & Miller, N. B. (1991). Becoming a family: Marriage, parenting, and child development. In P. A. Cowan & E. M. Hetherington (Eds.), *Family transitions* (pp. 79–109). Hillsdale, NJ: Erlbaum.

Cox, M. J., Owen, M. T., Lewis, J. M., & Henderson, V. K. (1989). Marriage, adult adjustment, and early parenting. *Child Development, 60,* 1015–1024.

Crosbie-Burnett, M. (1991). Impact of joint versus sole custody and quality of co-parental relationship on adjustment of adolescents in remarried families. *Behavioral Sciences and the Law, 9,* 439–449.

Dawson, D. A. (1991). Family structure and children's health and well-being: Data from the 1988 National Health Interview Survey on Child Health. *Journal of Marriage and the Family, 53,* 573–584.

Duncan, G. J., & Hoffman, S. D. (1985). A reconsideration of the economic consequences of marital dissolution. *Demography, 22,* 485–497.

Farrell, J., & Markman, H. (1986). Individual and interpersonal factors in the etiology of marital distress: The example of remarital couples. In R. Glimour & S. Duck (Eds.), *The emerging field of personal relationships* (pp. 251–263). Hillsdale, NJ: Erlbaum.

Fine, M. A., Voydanoff, P., & Donnelly, B. W. (1993). Relations between parental control and warmth and child well-being in stepfamilies. *Journal of Family Psychology, 7,* 222–232.

Forehand, R., & Nousiainen, S. (1993). Maternal and paternal parenting: Critical dimensions in adolescent functioning. *Journal of Family Psychology, 7,* 213–221.

Furstenberg, F. F. (1981). Remarriage and intergenerational relations. In R. W. Fogel, E. Hatfield, S. B. Kiesler, & E. Shanas (Eds.), *Aging: Stability and change in the family* (pp. 115–142). New York: Academic.

Furstenberg, F. F. (1987). The new extended family: The experience of parents and children after remarriage. In K. Pasley & M. Ihinger-Tallman (Eds.), *Remarriage and stepparenting: Current research and theory* (pp. 42–61). New York: Guilford.

Furstenberg, F. F. (1990). Divorce and the American family. *Annual Review of Sociology, 16,* 379–403.

Furstenberg, F. F., & Nord, C. W. (1985). Parenting apart: Patterns of childrearing after marital disruption. *Journal of Marriage and the Family, 47,* 893–904.

Furstenberg, F. F., & Spanier, G. (1984). *Recycling the family: Remarriage after divorce.* Beverly Hills, CA: Sage.

Ganong, L., & Coleman, M. (1994a). Adolescent-stepchild-stepparent relationships: Changes over time. In K. Pasley & M. Ihinger-Tallman (Eds.), *Stepparenting: Issues in theory, research, and practice* (pp. 87–104). Westport, CT: Greenwood.

Ganong, L. H., & Coleman, M. (1994b). *Remarried family relationships.* Thousand Oaks, CA: Sage.

Giles-Sims, J. (1987). Social exchange in remarried families. In K. Pasley & M. Ihinger-Talman (Eds.), *Remarriage and stepparenting today: Current research and theory* (pp. 141–163). New York: Guilford.

Glick, P. C. (1983). Prospective changes in marriage, divorce, and living arrangements. *Journal of Family Issues, 33,* 7–26.

Guisinger, S., Cowan, P., & Schuldberg, D. (1989). Changing parent and spouse relations in the first years of remarriage of divorced fathers. *Journal of Marriage and the Family, 51,* 445–456.

Gunnoe, M. L. (1993). *Noncustodial mothers' and fathers' contribution to the adjustment of adolescent stepchildren.* Unpublished doctoral dissertation, University of Virginia, Charlottesville.

Henderson, S. H., & Dalton, R. P. (1995, April). *Parent-child relationships in simple-step, complex-step and nondivorced families.* Paper presented at the biennial meeting of the Society for Research in Child Development, Indianapolis.

Hetherington, E. M. (1988). Parents, children and siblings six years after divorce. In R. Hinde & J. Stevenson-Hinde (Eds.), *Relationships within families: Mutual influences* (pp. 311–331). Oxford: Clarendon.

Hetherington, E. M. (1989). Coping with family transitions: Winners, losers and survivors. *Child Development, 60,* 1–15.

Hetherington, E. M. (1993). An overview of the Virginia Longitudinal Study of Divorce and Remarriage with a focus on early adolescence. *Journal of Family Psychology, 7,* 39–56.

Hetherington, E. M. (in press). Teenaged childbearing and divorce. In S. Luthar (Ed.), *Developmental psychopathology.* New York: Cambridge University Press.

Hetherington, E. M., & Clingempeel, W. G., in collaboration with Anderson, E. R., Deal, J. E., Stanley-Hagan, M., Hollier, E. A., & Lindner, M. S. (1992). Coping with marital transitions: A family systems perspective. *Monographs of the Society for Research in Child Development, 57*(2–3, Serial No. 227).

Hetherington, E. M., Cox, M., & Cox, R. (1982). Effects of divorce on parents and children. In M. Lamb (Ed.), *Nontraditional families* (pp. 233–288). Hillsdale, NJ: Erlbaum.

Hetherington, E. M., Cox, M., & Cox, R. (1985). Long-term effects of divorce and remarriage on the adjustment of children. *Journal of the American Academy of Psychiatry, 34*(5), 518–530.

Hetherington, E. M., & Jodl, K. M. (1994). Stepfamilies as settings for child development. In A. Booth & J. Dunn (Eds.), *Stepfamilies: Who benefits? Who does not?* (pp. 55–79). Hillsdale, NJ: Erlbaum.

Hetherington, E. M., Lindner, M., Miller, N. B., & Clingempeel, W. G. (1991, April). *Work, marriage and parenting in nondivorced and remarried families.* Paper presented at the Biennial meetings of the Society for Research in Child Development, Seattle.

Hetherington, E. M., & Stanley-Hagan, M. (1994). Parenting in divorced and remarried families. In M. H. Bornstein (Ed.), *Handbook of parenting.* Hillsdale, NJ: Erlbaum.

Hetherington, E. M., Stanley-Hagan, M., & Anderson, E. R. (1989). Marital transitions: A child's perspective. *American Psychologist, 44,* 303–312.

Hobart, C. (1991). Conflict in remarriages. *Journal of Divorce and Remarriage, 15,* 69–86.

Ishii-Kuntz, M., & Coltrane, S. (1992). Remarriage, stepparenting, and household labor. *Journal of Family Issues, 13,* 215–233.

Keshet, J. K. (1990). Cognitive remodeling of the family: How remarried people view stepfamilies. *American Journal of Orthopsychiatry, 60,* 196–203.

Kurdek, L. A. (1989a). Social support and psychological distress in first-married and remarried newlywed husbands and wives. *Journal of Marriage and the Family, 51,* 1047–1052.

Kurdek, L. A. (1989b) Relationship quality for newly married husbands and wives: Marital history, stepchildren, and individual-difference predictors. *Journal of Marriage and the Family, 51,* 1053–1064.

Kurdek, L. A., & Fine, M. A. (1995). Mothers, fathers, stepfathers, and siblings as providers of supervision, acceptance, and autonomy to young adolescents. *Journal of Family Psychology, 9,* 95–99.

Kurdek, L. A., & Sinclair, R. J. (1988). Adjustment of young adolescents in two-parent nuclear, stepfather, and mother-custody families. *Journal of Consulting and Clinical Psychology, 56,* 91–96.

Maccoby, E. E., Buchanan, C. M., Mnookin, R. H., & Dornbusch, S. M. (1993). Postdivorce roles of mother and fathers in the lives of their children: Special section. Families in transition. *Journal of Family Psychology, 7,* 24–38.

Mahoney, M. M. (1994). Reformulating the legal definition of the stepparent-child relationship. In A. Booth & J. Dunn (Eds.), *Stepfamilies: Who benefits: Who does not?* (pp. 191–196). Hillsdale, NJ: Erlbaum.

Marsiglio, W. M. (1992). Stepfathers with minor children living at home: Parenting perceptions and relationship quality. *Journal of Family Issues, 13,* 195–214.

Martin, T. C., & Bumpass, L. L. (1989). Recent trends in marital disruption. *Demography, 26,* 37–51.

Maymi, J. R., Bray, J. H., Berger, S. H., Boethel, C. L., Higgenbotham, L., & Corazao, L. N. (1991, August). *Behavioral observations of developing stepfamilies.* Paper presented at the annual meeting of the American Psychological Association, San Francisco.

McLanahan, S. (1983). Family structure and stress: A longitudinal comparison of two-parent and female-headed families. *Journal of Marriage and the Family, 45,* 347–357.

McLanahan, S., & Booth, D. (1989). Mother-only families: Problems, prospects, and politics. *Journal of Marriage and the Family, 51,* 557–580.

McLanahan, S., & Sandefur, G. (1994). *Growing up with a single parent.* Cambridge, MA: Harvard University Press.

Papernow, P. L. (1984). The stepfamily cycle: An experimental model of stepfamily development. *Family Relations, 33,* 355–363.

Parke, R. D. (1995). Fathers and families. In M. Bornstein (Ed.), *Handbook of parenting.* Hillsdale, NJ: Erlbaum.

Pill, C. J. (1990). Stepfamilies: Redefining the family. *Family Relations, 39,* 186–193.

Pink, J., & Wampler, K. (1985). Problem areas in stepfamilies: Cohesion, adaptability and the stepparent-adolescent relationship. *Family Relations, 34,* 327–335.

Ramsey, S. H. (1994). Stepparents and the law: A nebulous status and need for reform. In K. Pasley & M. Ihinger-Tallman (Eds.), *Stepparenting: Issues in theory, research and practice* (pp. 217–237). Westport, CT: Greenwood.

Reiss, D., Plomin, R., Hetherington, E. M., Howe, G. W., Rovine, M., Tryon, A., & Stanley-Hagan, M. (1993). The separate worlds of teenage siblings: An introduction to the study of nonshared environment and adolescent development. In E. M. Hetherington, D. Reiss, & R. Plomin (Eds.), *Separate social worlds of siblings: The impact of nonshared environment on development* (pp. 63–110). Hillsdale, NJ: Erlbaum.

Rogers, K. C., & Emery, R. E. (1992). *Economic consequences of divorce and children's adjustment.* Unpublished manuscript, University of Virginia, Department of Psychology.

Santrock, J. W., & Sitterle, K. (1987). Parent-child relationships in step-mother families. In K. Pasley & M. Ihinger-Tallman (Eds.), *Remarriage and stepparenting today: Current research and theory* (pp. 273–299). New York: Guilford.

Santrock, J. W., Sitterle, K. A., & Warshak, R. A. (1988). Parent-child relationships in step-father families. In P. Bronstein & C. P. Cowan (Eds.), *Fatherhood today: Men's changing role in the family* (pp. 144–165). New York: Wiley.

Select Committee on Children, Youth and Families (SCCYF) of the United States House of Representatives (1989). *U.S. children and their families: Current conditions and trends.* Washington, DC: U.S. Government Printing Office.

Seltzer, J. A. (1991). Relationships between fathers and children who live apart: The father's role after separation. *Journal of Marriage and the Family, 53,* 79–101.

Seltzer, J. A. (1994). Intergenerational ties in adulthood and childhood experience. In A. Booth & J. Dunn (Eds.), *Stepfamilies: Who benefits? Who does not?* (pp. 153–166). Hillsdale, NJ: Erlbaum.

Steinberg, L. (1987). Single parents, stepparents, and the susceptibility of adolescents to antisocial peer pressure. *Child Development, 58,* 269–275.

Thomson, E. (1994). "Settings" and "development" from a demographic point of view. In A. Booth & J. Dunn (Eds.), *Stepfamilies: Who benefits? Who does not?* (pp. 89–96). Hillsdale, NJ: Erlbaum.

U.S. Bureau of the Census (1989). *Studies in marriage and the family* (Current Population Reports, Series P-23, No. 162, pp. 27–38). Washington, DC: U.S. Government Printing Office.

Visher, E. B., & Visher, J. S. (1988). *Old loyalties, new ties: Therapeutic strategies with stepfamilies.* New York: Brunner/Mazel.

Visher, E. B., & Visher, J. S. (1990). Dynamics of successful stepfamilies. *Journal of Divorce and Remarriage, 14,* 3–12.

Weiss, R. S. (1984). The impact of marital dissolution on income and consumption in single-parent households. *Journal of Marriage and the Family, 46,* 115–127.

White, L. (1994). Stepfamilies over the life course: Social support. In A. Booth & J. Dunn (Eds.), *Stepfamilies: Who benefits? Who does not?* (pp. 109–137). Hillsdale, NJ: Erlbaum.

Zill, N. (1988). Behavior, achievement, and health problems among children in stepfamilies. In E. M. Hetherington & J. Arasteh (Eds.), *Impact of divorce, single parenting, and stepparenting on children* (pp. 325–368). Hillsdale, NJ: Erlbaum.

Zill, N. (1993). Long-term effects of parental divorce on parent-child relationships, adjustment, and achievement in young adulthood. Special section: Families in transition. *Journal of Family Psychology, 7,* 91–103.

CHAPTER 13

Achatz, M., & MacAllum, C. A. (1994). *The young unwed fathers demonstration project: A status report.* Philadelphia: Public/Private Ventures.

Adams, G., & Pittman, K. (1988). *Adolescent and young adult fathers: Problems and solutions.* Washington, DC: Children's Defense Fund, Adolescent Pregnancy Prevention Clearinghouse Report.

Barth, R. P., Claycomb, M., & Loomis. A. (1988). Services to adolescent fathers. *Health and Social Work, 13,* 277–287.

Cervera, N. (1991). Unwed teenage pregnancy: Family relationships with the father of the baby. *Families in Society: The Journal of Contemporary Human Services, 72,* 29–37.

Christmon, K. (1990). Parental responsibility of African-American unwed adolescent fathers. *Adolescence, 25,* 645–653.

Danzinger, S. K., Kastner, C. K., & Nickel, T. J. (1993). The problems and promise of child support policies. In R. I. Lerman & T. J. Ooms (Eds.), *Young unwed fathers: Changing roles and emerging policies* (pp. 235–250). Philadelphia: Temple University Press.

Elster, A. B., Lamb, M. E., & Kimmerly, N. (1989). Perceptions of parenthood among adolescent fatherhood. *Pediatrics, 83,* 758–765.

Elster, A. B., Lamb, M. E., Peters, L., Kahn, J., & Tavaré, J. (1987). Judicial involvement and conduct problems of fathers of infants born to adolescent mothers. *Pediatrics, 79,* 230–234.

Freeman, E. (1989). Adolescent fathers in urban communities: Exploring their needs and role in preventing pregnancy. *Journal of Social Work and Human Sexuality, 8,* 113–131.

Frodi, A. M., & Lamb, M. E. (1978). Sex differences in response to infants: A developmental study of psychophysiological and behavioral responses. *Child Development, 49,* 1182–1188.

Furstenberg, F. F., Jr. (1988). Good dads—bad dads: Two faces of fatherhood. In A. Cherlin (Ed.), *The changing American family and public policy* (pp. 193–218). Washington, DC: Urban Institute.

Furstenberg, F. F., Jr. (1991). As the pendulum swings: Teenage childbearing and social concern. *Family Relations, 40,* 127–138.

Furstenberg, F. F., Jr. (1995). Fathering in the inner-city: Paternal participation and public policy. In W. Marsiglio (Ed.), *Fatherhood: Contemporary theory, research, and social policy* (pp. 119–147). Newbury Park, CA: Sage.

Furstenberg, F. F., Jr., & Harris, K. M. (1993). When and why fathers matter: Impacts of father involvement on the children of adolescent mothers. In R. I. Lerman & T. J. Ooms (Eds.), *Young unwed fathers: Changing roles and emerging policies* (pp. 117–138). Philadelphia: Temple University Press.

Geronimus, A. T. (1991). Teenage childbearing and social and reproductive disadvantage: The evolution of complex questions and the demise of simple answers. *Family Relations, 40,* 463–471.

Hanson, S. M. H., Heims, M. C., Julian, D. J., & Sussman, M. B. (1995). *Single parent families: Diversity, myths and realities.* New York: Haworth.

Hardy, J. B., Duggan, A. K., Masnyk, K., & Pearson, C. (1989). Fathers of children born to young urban mothers. *Family Planning Perspectives, 21,* 159–163, 187.

Hawkins, A. J., Christiansen, S. L., Sargent, K. P., & Hill, E. J. (1993). Rethinking fathers' involvement in child care. *Journal of Family Issues, 14,* 531–549.

Hayes, C. (1987). *Risking the future: Adolescent sexuality, pregnancy, and childbearing.* Washington, DC: National Academy Press.

Hendricks, L. E., & Solomon, A. M. (1987). Reaching black male adolescent parents through nontraditional techniques. *Child and Youth Services, 9,* 111–124.

Jones, E. F., Forrest, J. D., Goldman, N., Henshaw, S., Lincoln, R., Rosoff, J. I., Westoff, C. F., & Wulf, D. (1986). *Teenage pregnancy in industrialized countries.* New Haven, CT: Yale University Press.

Joshi, N. P., & Battle, S. F. (1990). Adolescent fathers: An approach for intervention. *Journal of Health & Social Policy, 1,* 17–33.

Kiselica, M. S. (1995). *Multicultural counseling with teenage fathers: A practical guide.* Thousand Oaks, CA: Sage.

Knijn, T. (1995). Towards post-paternalism? Social and theoretical changes in fatherhood. In G. A. B. Frinking, M. van Dongen, & M. J. G. Jacobs (Eds.), *Changing fatherhood: An interdisciplinary perspective* (pp. 1–20). Amsterdam: Thesis.

Lamb, M. E. (1988). The ecology of adolescent pregnancy and parenthood. In A. R. Pence (Ed.), *Ecological research with children and families: From concepts to methodology* (pp. 99–121). New York: Teachers College Press.

Lamb, M. E., & Elster, A. B. (1985). Adolescent mother-infant-father relationships. *Developmental Psychology, 21,* 768–773.

Lamb, M. E., & Elster, A. B. (1986). Parental behavior of adolescent mothers and fathers. In A. B. Elster & M. E. Lamb (Eds.), *Adolescent fatherhood* (pp. 89–106). Hillsdale, NJ: Erlbaum.

Lamb, M. E., & Elster, A. B. (1990). Adolescent parenthood. In G. H. Brody & I. E. Sigel (Eds.), *Methods of family research: Biographies of research projects* (pp. 159–190). Hillsdale, NJ: Erlbaum.

Lamb, M. E., Elster, A. B., Peters, L. J., Kahn, J. S., & Tavaré, J. (1986). Characteristics of married and unmarried adolescent mothers and their partners. *Journal of Youth and Adolescence, 15,* 487–496.

Larson, J. (1992, July). Understanding stepfamilies. *American Demographics,* pp. 36–40.

Leitch, M. L., Gonzalez, A. M., & Ooms, T. J. (1993). Involving unwed fathers in adoption counseling and teen pregnancy programs. In R. I. Lerman & T. J. Ooms (Eds.), *Young unwed fathers: Changing roles and emerging policies* (pp. 267–287). Philadelphia: Temple University Press.

Lerman, R. I. (1986). Who are the young absent fathers? *Youth & Society, 18,* 3–27.

Lerman, R. I. (1993a). Employment patterns of unwed fathers and public policy. In R. I. Lerman & T. J. Ooms (Eds.), *Young unwed fathers: Changing roles and emerging prospects* (pp. 316–334). Philadelphia: Temple University Press.

Lerman, R. I. (1993b). A national profile of young unwed fathers. In R. I. Lerman & T. J. Ooms (Eds.), *Young unwed fathers: Changing roles and emerging policies* (pp. 27–51). Philadelphia: Temple University Press.

Levine, J. A., Murphy, D. T., & Wilson, S. (1993). *Getting men involved: Strategies for early childhood programs.* New York: Scholastic.

Levine, J. A., & Pitt, E. W. (1995). *New expectations: Community strategies for responsible fatherhood.* New York: Families and Work Institute.

Marsiglio, W. (1987). Adolescent fathers in the United States: Their initial living arrangements, marital experience and educational outcomes. *Family Planning Perspectives, 19,* 240–251.

Marsiglio, W. (1988). Commitment to social fatherhood: Predicting adolescent males' intentions to live with their child and partner. *Journal of Marriage and the Family, 50,* 427–441.

Marsiglio, W. (1993). Adolescent males' orientation toward paternity and contraception. *Family Planning Perspectives, 25,* 22–31.

Marsiglio, W. (1995a). Fathers' diverse life course patterns and roles: Theory and social interventions. In W. Marsiglio (Ed.), *Fatherhood: Contemporary theory, research, and social policy* (pp. 78–101). Thousand Oaks, CA: Sage.

Marsiglio, W. (1995b). Young nonresident biological fathers. *Marriage and Family Review, 20* (3/4), 325–348.

Montemayor, R. (1986). Boys as fathers: Coping with the dilemmas of adolescence. In A. B. Elster & M. E. Lamb (Eds.), *Adolescent fatherhood* (pp. 1–18). Hillsdale, NJ: Erlbaum.

Mott, F. L. (1983). *Fertility-related data in the 1982 National Longitudinal Surveys of Work Experience of Youth: An evaluation of data quality and some preliminary analytical results.* Columbus, OH: Ohio State University, Center for Human Resource Research.

Mott, F. L. (1994). Sons, daughters and fathers' absence: Differentials in father-leaving probabilities and in home environment. *Journal of Family Issues, 15,* 97–128.

Nash, S. C., & Feldman, S. S. (1981). Sex-role and sex-related attributions: Constancy and change across the family life cycle. In M. E. Lamb & A. L. Brown (Eds.), *Advances in developmental psychology* (Vol. 1; pp. 1–35). Hillsdale, NJ: Erlbaum.

National Center for Health Statistics [NCHS]. (1983). Advance report of final natality statistics, 1981. *Monthly Vital Statistics Report, 32*(9).

National Institute of Child Health and Human Development [NICHD]. (1992). *Outcomes of early childbearing: An appraisal of recent evidence.* Bethesda, MD: Author.

National Urban League. (1987). *Adolescent male responsibility pregnancy prevention and parenting program: A program development guide.* New York: Author.

Parke, R. D., & Neville, B. (1987). Teenage fatherhood. In S. Hofferth & C. Hayes (Eds.), *Risking the future: Adolescent sexuality, pregnancy and childbearing* (Vol. 2; pp. 145–173). Washington, DC: National Academy Press.

Pirog-Good, M. A. (1993). In-kind contributions as child support: The teen alternative parenting program. In R. I. Lerman & T. J. Ooms (Eds.), *Young unwed fathers: Changing roles and emerging policies* (pp. 251–266). Philadelphia: Temple University Press.

Rozie-Battle, J. L. (1989). Adolescent fathers: The question of paternity. *National Urban League Review, 12,* 129–137.

Sander, J., & Rosen, J. (1987). Teenage fathers: Working with the neglected partner in adolescent childbearing. *Family Planning Perspectives, 19,* 107–110.

Smith, A. (1989). Responsibility of the African-American church as a source of support for adolescent fathers. *Urban League Review, 12,* 83–90.

Smollar, J., & Ooms, T. (1987). *Young unwed fathers: Research, review, policy dilemmas and options.* Summary report to U.S. Department of Health and Human Services. Washington, DC: Catholic University of America, Family Impact Seminar.

Sullivan, M. L. (1993). Young fathers and parenting in two inner-city neighborhoods. In R. I. Lerman & T. J. Ooms (Eds.), *Young unwed fathers: Changing roles and emerging policies* (pp. 52–73). Philadelphia: Temple University Press.

Teti, D. M., & Lamb, M. E. (1986). Sex-role learning and adolescent fatherhood. In A. B. Elster & M. E. Lamb (Eds.), *Adolescent fatherhood* (pp. 19–30). Hillsdale, NJ: Erlbaum.

Teti, D. M., Lamb, M., & Elster, A. B. (1987). Long-range socioeconomic and marital consequences of adolescent marriage in three cohorts of adult males. *Journal of Marriage and the Family, 49,* 499–506.

U.S. Bureau of the Census. (1995). *Child support for custodial mothers and fathers: 1991* (Current Population Reports, Series P60–187). Washington, DC: U.S. Government Printing Office.

Vinovskis, M. A. (1986). Young fathers and their children: Some historical and policy perspectives. In A. B. Elster & M. E. Lamb (Eds.), *Adolescent fatherhood* (pp. 171–192). Hillsdale, NJ: Erlbaum.

Wattenberg, E. (1988, Summer). Establishing paternity for nonmarital children. *Public Welfare,* pp. 9–48.

Wattenberg, E. (1993). Paternity actions and young fathers. In R. I. Lerman & T. J. Ooms (Eds.), *Young unwed fathers: Changing roles and emerging policies* (pp. 213–234). Philadelphia: Temple University Press.

Wattenberg, E., Brewer, R., & Resnick, M. (1991, February 12). *A study of paternity decisions of young unmarried parents.* Final report to the Ford Foundation.

Westney, O. E., Cole, J., & Munford, T. L. (1988). The effects of prenatal education intervention on unwed prospective adolescent fathers. *Journal of Adolescent Health Care, 9,* 214–218.

CHAPTER 14

Bailey, J. M. (1995). Biological perspectives on sexual orientation. In A. R. D'Augelli & C. J. Patterson (Eds.), *Lesbian, gay and bisexual identities over the lifespan: Psychological perspectives* (pp. 102–135). New York: Oxford University Press.

Bailey, J. M., Bobrow, D., Wolfe, M., & Mikach, S. (1995). Sexual orientation of adult sons of gay fathers. *Developmental Psychology, 31,* 124–129.

Baptiste, D. A. (1987). Psychotherapy with gay/lesbian couples and their children in "stepfamilies": A challenge for marriage and family therapists. In E. Coleman (Ed.), *Integrated identity for gay men and lesbians: Psychotherapeutic approaches for emotional well-being* (pp. 223–238). New York: Harrington Park.

Barret, R. L., & Robinson, B. E. (1990). *Gay fathers.* Lexington, MA: Lexington.

Barret, R. L., & Robinson, B. E. (1994). *Gay dads.* In A. E. Gottfried & A. W. Gottfried (Eds.), *Redefining families: Implications for children's development* (pp. 157–170). New York: Plenum.

Baumrind, D. (1967). Child care practices anteceding three patterns of preschool behavior. *Genetic Psychology Monographs, 75,* 43–88.

Baumrind, D., & Black, A. E. (1967). Socialization practices associated with dimensions of competence in preschool boys and girls. *Child Development, 38,* 291–327.

Bell, A. P., & Weinberg, M. S. (1978). *Homosexualities: A study of diversity among men and women.* New York: Simon and Schuster.

Bigner, J. J., & Bozett, F. W. (1990). Parenting by gay fathers. In F. W. Bozett & M. B. Sussman (Eds.), *Homosexuality and family relations* (pp. 155–176). New York: Harrington Park.

Bigner, J. J., & Jacobsen, R. B. (1989a). Parenting behaviors of homosexual and heterosexual fathers. In F. W. Bozett (Ed.), *Homosexuality and the family* (pp. 173–186). New York: Harrington Park.

Bigner, J. J., & Jacobsen, R. B. (1989b). The value of children to gay and heterosexual fathers. In F. W. Bozett (Ed.), *Homosexuality and the family* (pp. 163–172). New York: Harrington Park.

Bigner, J. J., & Jacobsen, R. B. (1992). Adult responses to child behavior and attitudes toward fathering: Gay and nongay fathers. *Journal of Homosexuality, 23,* 99–112.

Bozett, F. W. (1980). Gay fathers: How and why they disclose their homosexuality to their children. *Family Relations, 29,* 173–179.

Bozett, F. W. (1981a). Gay fathers: Evolution of the gay father identity. *American Journal of Orthopsychiatry, 51,* 552–559.

Bozett, F. W. (1981b). Gay fathers: Identity conflict resolution through integrative sanctioning. *Alternative Lifestyles, 4,* 90–107.

Bozett, F. W. (1982). Heterogeneous couples in heterosexual marriages: Gay men and straight women. *Journal of Marital and Family Therapy, 8,* 81–89.

Bozett, F. W. (1987). Children of gay fathers. In F. W. Bozett (Ed.), *Gay and lesbian parents* (pp. 39–57). New York: Praeger.

Bozett, F. W. (1989). Gay fathers: A review of the literature. In F. W. Bozett (Ed.), *Homosexuality and the family* (pp. 137–162). New York: Harrington Park.

Bryant, A. S., & Demian. (1994). Relationship characteristics of American gay and lesbian couples: Findings from a national survey. In L. A. Kurdek (Ed.), *Social services for gay and lesbian couples* (pp. 101–117). New York: Haworth.

Buxton, A. P. (1994). *The other side of the closet: The coming out crisis for straight spouses and families* (2nd ed.). New York: Wiley.

Campbell, K. (1994, November 18). A gay father's quiet battle. *Washington Blade,* p. 5.

Cowan, C. P., & Cowan, P. A. (1992). *When partners become parents: The big life change for couples.* New York: Basic Books.

Crosbie-Burnett, M., & Helmbrecht, L. (1993). A descriptive empirical study of gay male stepfamilies. *Family Relations, 42,* 256–62.

Dunlap, D. W. (1994, November 19). Gay sperm donor awarded standing as girl's father. *New York Times,* p. B-27.

Dunne, E. J. (1987). Helping gay fathers come out to their children. *Journal of Homosexuality, 13,* 213–222.

Editors of the Harvard Law Review. (1990). *Sexual orientation and the law.* Cambridge, MA: Harvard University Press.

Fadiman, A. (May, 1983). The double closet: How two gay fathers deal with their children and ex-wives. *Life,* pp. 76ff.

Flaks, D. (1994). Gay and lesbian families: Judicial assumptions, scientific realities. *William and Mary Bill of Rights Journal, 3,* 345–372.

Gagnon, J. H., Laumann, E. O., Michael, R. T., & Michaels, S. (1994). *The social organization of sexuality.* Chicago: University of Chicago Press.

Gottman, J. S. (1990). Children of lesbian and gay parents. In F. W. Bozett & M. B. Sussman (Eds.), *Homosexuality and family relations* (pp. 177–196). New York: Harrington Park.

Green, G. D., & Bozett, F. W. (1991). Lesbian mothers and gay fathers. In J. C. Gonsiorek & J. D. Weinrich (Eds.), *Homosexuality: Research implications for public policy* (pp. 197–214). Thousand Oaks, CA: Sage.

Groth, A. N., & Birnbaum, H. J. (1978). Adult sexual orientation and attraction to underage persons. *Archives of Sexual Behavior, 7,* 175–181.

Hand, S. I. (1991). *The lesbian parenting couple.* Unpublished doctoral dissertation, Professional School of Psychology, San Francisco.

Harris, M. B., & Turner, P. H. (1985/86). Gay and lesbian parents. *Journal of Homosexuality, 12,* 101–113.

Hays, D., & Samuels, A. (1989). Heterosexual women's perceptions of their marriages to bisexual or homosexual men. In F. W. Bozett (Ed.), *Homosexuality and the family* (pp. 81–100). New York: Harrington Park.

Humphreys, L. (1975). *Tearoom trade: Impersonal sex in public places.* Chicago: Aldine.

In re W.S.D., No. A-308-90 (D.C. Superior Ct. Fam. Div. April 30, 1992).

Jenny, C., Roesler, T. A., & Poyer, K. L. (1994). Are children at risk for sexual abuse by homosexuals? *Pediatrics, 94,* 41–44.

Jones, B. M., & McFarlane, K. (Eds.). (1980). *Sexual abuse of children: Selected readings.* Washington, DC: National Center on Child Abuse and Neglect.

Kinsey, A. C., Pomeroy, W. B., & Martin, C. E. (1948). *Sexual behavior in the human male.* Philadelphia: Saunders.

Kurdek, L. (1995). Lesbian and gay couples. In A. R. D'Augelli & C. J. Patterson (Eds.), *Lesbian, gay and bisexual identities across the lifespan: Psychological perspectives* (pp. 243–261). New York: Oxford University Press.

Lamb, M. E. (Ed.). (1981). *The role of the father in child development* (2nd ed.). New York: Wiley.

Lamb, M. E. (Ed.). (1986). *The father's role: Cross-cultural perspectives.* Hillsdale, NJ: Erlbaum.

Lewis, M., Feiring, C., & Weinraub, M. (1981). The father as a member of the child's social network. In M. E. Lamb (Ed.), *The role of the father in child development* (2nd ed., pp. 259–294). New York: Wiley.

Martin, A. (1993). *The lesbian and gay parenting handbook.* New York: HarperCollins.

Matteson, D. R. (1987). The heterosexually married gay and lesbian parent. In F. W. Bozett (Ed.), *Gay and lesbian parents* (pp. 138–161). New York: Praeger.

McPherson, D. (1993). *Gay parenting couples: Parenting arrangements, arrangement satisfaction, and relationship satisfaction.* Unpublished doctoral dissertation, Pacific Graduate School of Psychology.

Miller, B. (1979). Gay fathers and their children. *Family Coordinator, 28,* 544–552.

Ortiz, E. T., & Scott, P. S. (1994). Gay husbands and fathers: Reasons for marriage among homosexual men. *Journal of Gay and Lesbian Social Services, 1,* 59–71.

Osterweil, D. A. (1991). *Correlates of relationship satisfaction in lesbian couples who are parenting their first child together.* Unpublished doctoral dissertation, California School of Professional Psychology, Berkeley/Alameda.

Patterson, C. J. (1992). Children of lesbian and gay parents. *Child Development, 63,* 1025–1042.

Patterson, C. J. (1994a). Lesbian and gay couples considering parenthood: An agenda for research, service, and advocacy. *Journal of Gay and Lesbian Social Services, 1,* 33–55.

Patterson, C. J. (1994b). Lesbian and gay families. *Current Directions in Psychological Science, 3,* 62–64.

Patterson, C. J. (1995a). Adoption of minor children by lesbian and gay adults: A social science perspective. *Duke Journal of Gender Law and Policy, 2,* 191–205.

Patterson, C. J. (1995b). Families of the lesbian baby boom: Parents' division of labor and children's adjustment. *Developmental Psychology, 31,* 115–123.

Patterson, C. J. (1995c). Lesbian and gay parenthood. In M. H. Bornstein (Ed.), *Handbook of parenting, Vol. 3. Status and social conditions of parenting* (pp. 255–274). Hillsdale, NJ: Erlbaum.

Patterson, C. J. (1995d). Lesbian mothers, gay fathers, and their children. In A. R. D'Augelli & C. J. Patterson (Eds.), *Lesbian, gay and bisexual identities over the lifespan: Psychological perspectives* (pp. 262–290). New York: Oxford University Press.

Paul, J. P., Hays, R. B., & Coates, T. J. (1995). The impact of the HIV epidemic on U.S. gay male communities. In A. R. D'Augelli & C. J. Patterson (Eds.), *Lesbian, gay and bisexual identities over the lifespan: Psychological perspectives* (pp. 347–397). New York: Oxford University Press.

Ricks, I. (1995, February 7). Fathers and sons. *The Advocate,* No. 674, pp. 27–28.

Ricketts, W. (1991). *Lesbians and gay men as foster parents.* Portland, ME: University of Southern Maine, National Child Welfare Resource Center.

Ricketts, W., & Achtenberg, R. (1990). Adoption and foster parenting for lesbians and gay men: Creating new traditions in family. In F. W. Bozett & M. B. Sussman (Eds.), *Homosexuality and family relations* (pp. 83–118). New York: Harrington Park.

Rivera, R. (1991). Sexual orientation and the law. In J. C. Gonsiorek & J. D. Weinrich (Eds.), *Homosexuality: Research implications for public policy* (pp. 81–100). Newbury Park, CA: Sage.

Robinson, B. E., & Barret, R. L. (1986). Gay fathers. In B. E. Robinson & R. L. Barret (Eds.), *The developing father: Emerging roles in contemporary society* (pp. 145–168). New York: Guilford.

Robinson, B. E., & Skeen, P. (1982). Sex-role orientation of gay fathers versus gay nonfathers. *Perceptual and Motor Skills, 55,* 1055–1059.

Roe v. Roe, 324 S.E.2d 691, 228 Va. 722 (1985).

Ross, M. W. (1978). Modes of adjustment of married homosexuals. *Social Problems, 18,* 385–393.

Ross, M. W. (1983). *The married homosexual man.* London: Routledge and Kegan Paul.

Saghir, M. T., & Robins, E. (1973). *Male and female homosexuality: A comprehensive investigation.* Baltimore: Williams and Wilkins.

Sarafino, E. P. (1979). An estimate of nationwide incidence of sexual offenses against children. *Child Welfare, 58,* 127–134.

Sbordone, A. J. (1993). *Gay men choosing fatherhood.* Unpublished doctoral dissertation, City University of New York, Department of Psychology.

Seligmann, J. (1990). Variations on a theme: Gay and lesbian couples. *Newsweek* [Special issue on the 21st century family], pp. 38–39.

Skeen, P., & Robinson, B. (1985). Gay fathers' and gay nonfathers' relationships with their parents. *Journal of Sex Research, 21,* 86–91.

Strader, S. C. (1993). *Non-custodial gay fathers: Considering the issues.* Paper presented at the 101st annual convention of the American Psychological Association, Toronto.

Thompson, R. A. (1983). The father's case in child custody disputes: The contributions of psychological research. In M. E. Lamb & A. Sagi (Eds.), *Fatherhood and family policy* (pp. 53–100). Hillsdale, NJ: Erlbaum.

Van Gelder, L. (1991, March/April), A lesbian family revisited. *Ms. Magazine,* pp. 44–47.

Weston, K. (1991). *Families we choose: Lesbian, gays, kinship.* New York: Columbia University Press.

CHAPTER 15

Abidin, R. R. (1992). The determinants of parenting behavior. *Journal of Clinical Child Psychology, 21,* 407–412.

Adesso, V. J., & Lipson, J. W. (1981). Group training of parents as therapists for their children. *Behavior Therapy, 12,* 625–633.

Alexander, J. F., Waldron, H. B., Barton, C., & Mas, C. H. (1989). The minimizing of blaming attributions and behaviors in delinquent families. *Journal of Consulting and Clinical Psychology, 57,* 19–24.

Alford, G. S., Jouriles, E. N., & Jackson, S. C. (1991). Differences and similarities in development of drinking behavior between alcoholic offspring of alcoholics and alcoholic offspring of non-alcoholics. *Addictive Behaviors, 16,* 341–347.

American Psychiatric Association. (1994). *Diagnostic and statistical manual of mental disorders IV.* Washington, DC: American Psychiatric Press.

Angermeyer, M. C. (1982). The association between family atmosphere and hospital career of schizophrenic patients. *British Journal of Psychiatry, 141,* 1–11.

Atkinson, A. K., & Rickel, A. U. (1984). Postpartum depression in primiparous parents. *Journal of Abnormal Psychology, 93,* 115–119.

Atwood, R., Gold, M., & Taylor, R. (1989). Two types of delinquents and their institutional adjustment. *Journal of Consulting and Clinical Psychology, 57,* 68–75.

Baker, D. B. (1994). Parenting stress and ADHD: A comparison of mothers and fathers. *Journal of Emotional and Behavioral Disorders, 2,* 46–50.

Ballard, C. G., Davis, R., Handy, S., & Mohan, R. N. (1993). Postpartum anxiety in mothers and fathers. *European Journal of Psychiatry, 7,* 117–121.

Barkley, R. A. (1987). *Defiant children: A clinician's manual for parent training.* New York: Guilford.

Barkley, R. A. (1990). *Attention Deficit Hyperactivity Disorder: A handbook for diagnosis and treatment.* New York: Guilford.

Barkley, R. A., Fischer, M., Edelbrock, C. S., & Smallish, L. (1990). The adolescent outcome of hyperactive children diagnosed by research criteria: I. An 8 year prospective follow-up study. *Journal of the American Academy of Child and Adolescent Psychiatry, 29,* 546–557.

Barrnett, R. J., Docherty, J. P., & Frommelt, G. M. (1991). A review of child psychotherapy research since 1963. *Journal of the American Academy of Child and Adolescent Psychiatry, 30,* 1–14.

Bateson, G., Jackson, D. D., Haley, J., & Weakland, J. (1956). Toward a theory of schizophrenia. *Behavioral Science, 1,* 251–264.

Beardslee, W. R., Schultz, L. H., & Selman, R. L. (1987). Level of social-cognitive development, adaptive functioning, and DSM-III diagnoses in adolescent offspring of parents with affective disorders: Implications of the development of the capacity for mutuality. *Developmental Psychology, 23,* 807–815.

Beck, S., Collins, L., Overholser, J., & Terry, K. (1984). A comparison of children who receive and who do not receive permission to participate in research. *Journal of Abnormal Child Psychology, 12,* 573–580.

Behrman, R. E. (1992). *Nelson textbook of pediatrics* (14th ed.). Philadelphia: Saunders.

Berkowitz, A., & Perkins, H. W. (1988). Personality characteristics of children of alcoholics. *Journal of Consulting and Clinical Psychology, 56,* 206–209.

Bernstein, G. A., Svingen, P. H., & Garfinkel, B. D. (1990). School phobia: Patterns of family functioning. *Journal of the American Academy of Child and Adolescent Psychiatry, 29,* 24–30.

Biller, H. B., & Solomon, R. S. (1986). *Child maltreatment and paternal deprivation: A manifesto for research, prevention, and treatment.* Lexington, MA: Lexington.

Billings, A. G., & Moos, R. H. (1983). Comparisons of children of depressed and nondepressed parents: A social-environmental perspective. *Journal of Abnormal Child Psychology, 11,* 463–486.

Billings, A. G., & Moos, R. H. (1985). Children of parents with unipolar depression: A controlled 1-year follow-up. *Journal of Abnormal Child Psychology, 14,* 149–166.

Bjorkqvist, K., & Osterman, K. (1992). Parental influence on children's self-estimated aggressiveness. *Aggressive Behavior, 18,* 411–423.

Blackson, T. C., Tarter, R. E., Martin, C. S., & Moss, H. B. (1994a). Temperament-induced father-son family dysfunction: Etiological implications for child behavior problems and substance abuse. *American Journal of Orthopsychiatry, 64,* 280–292.

Blackson, T. C., Tarter, R. E., Martin, C. S., & Moss, H. B. (1994b). Temperament mediates the effects of family history of substance abuse on externalizing and internalizing child behavior. *American Journal on Addictions, 3,* 58–66.

Borduin, C. M., Pruitt, J. A., & Henggeler, S. W. (1986). Family interactions in Black, lower-class families with delinquent and nondelinquent adolescent boys. *Journal of Genetic Psychology, 147,* 333–342.

Brewin, C. R., Andrews, B., & Gotlib, I. H. (1993). Psychopathology and early experience: A reappraisal of retrospective reports. *Psychological Bulletin, 113,* 82–98.

Budd, K. S., & O'Brien, T. P. (1982). Father involvement in behavioral parent training: An area in need of research. *Behavior Therapist, 5,* 85–89.

Calam, R., Waller, G., Slade, P. D., & Newton, T. (1990). Eating disorders and perceived relationships with parents. *International Journal of Eating Disorders, 9,* 479–485.

Callan, V. J., & Jackson, D. (1986). Children of alcoholic fathers and recovered alcoholic fathers: Personal and family functioning. *Journal of Studies on Alcohol, 47,* 180–182.

Caplan, P. J. (1989). *Don't blame mother: Mending the mother-daughter relationship.* New York: Harper and Row.

Caplan, P. J., & Hall-McCorquodale, I. (1985). Mother-blaming in major clinical journals. *American Journal of Orthopsychiatry, 55,* 345–353.

Carro, M. G., Grant, K. E., Gotlib, I. H., & Compas, B. E. (1993). Postpartum depression and child development: An investigation of mothers and fathers as sources of risk and resilience. *Development and Psychopathology, 5,* 567–579.

Casey, R. J., & Berman, J. S. (1985). The outcome of psychotherapy with children. *Psychological Bulletin, 98,* 388–400.

Cavell, T. A., Jones, D. C., Runyan, R. D., & Constantin-Page, L. P. (1993). Perceptions of attachment and the adjustment of adolescents with alcoholic fathers. *Journal of Family Psychology, 7,* 204–212.

Chassin, L., Rogosch, F., & Barrera, M. (1991). Substance use and symptomatology among adolescent children of alcoholics. *Journal of Abnormal Psychology, 100,* 449–463.

Chess, S. (1964). Mal de mere. *American Journal of Orthopsychiatry, 34,* 613–614.

Chess, S. (1982). The "blame the mother" ideology. *International Journal of Mental Health, 11,* 95–107.

Churven, P. G. (1978). Families: Parental attitudes to family assessment in a child psychiatry setting. *Journal of Child Psychology and Psychiatry,19,* 33–41.

Clark, D. A., & Bolton, D. (1985). Obsessive-compulsive adolescents and their parents: A psychometric study. *Journal of Child Psychology and Psychiatry, 26,* 267–276.

Cloninger, C. R., Sigvardsson, S., & Bohman, M. (1988). Childhood personality predicts alcohol abuse in young adults. *Alcoholism, 12,* 494–503.

Cole, D. A., & McPherson, A. E. (1993). Relation of family subsystems to adolescent depression: Implementing a new family assessment strategy. *Journal of Family Psychology, 7,* 119–133.

Cole, D. A., & Rehm, L. P. (1986). Family interaction patterns and childhood depression. *Journal of Abnormal Child Psychology, 14,* 297–314.

Conrad, M., & Hammen, C. (1993). Protective and resource factors in high- and low-risk children: A comparison of children with unipolar, bipolar, medically ill, and normal mothers. *Development and Psychopathology, 5,* 593–607.

Coplin, J. W., & Houts, A. C. (1991). Father involvement in parent training for oppositional child behavior: Progress or stagnation? *Child and Family Behavior Therapy, 13,* 29–51.

Coverdale, J. H., Schotte, D., Ruiz, P., Pharies, S., & Bayer, T. (1994). Family planning needs of male chronic mental patients in the general hospital psychiatry clinic. *General Hospital Psychiatry, 16,* 38–41.

Cummings, E. M., & Davis, P. (1994). *Children and marital conflict: The impact of family dispute and resolution.* New York: Guilford.

Cunningham, C. E., Benness, B. B., & Siegel, L. S. (1988). Family functioning, time allocation, and parental depression in the families of normal and AD/HD children. *Journal of Clinical Child Psychology, 17,* 169–177.

Dadds, M. R., Sanders, M. R., Behrens, B. C., & James, J. E. (1987). Marital discord and child behavior problems: A description of family interactions during treatment. *Journal of Clinical Child Psychology, 16,* 192–203.

Dadds, M. R., Sheffield, J. K., & Holbeck, J. F. (1990). An examination of the differential relationship of marital discord to parents' discipline strategies for boys and girls. *Journal of Abnormal Child Psychology, 18,* 121–129.

Danziger, S. K., & Radin, N. (1990). Absent does not equal uninvolved: Predictors of fathering in teen mother families. *Journal of Marriage and the Family, 52,* 636–642.

Deater-Deckard, K., Scarr, S., McCartney, K., & Eisenberg, M. (1994). Paternal separation anxiety: Relationships with parenting stress, child-rearing attitudes, and maternal anxieties. *Psychological Science, 5,* 341–346.

DeJong, C. A. J., Harteveld, F. M., & van de Wielen, G. E. M. (1991). Memories of parental rearing in alcohol and drug addicts: A comparative study. *International Journal of the Addictions, 26,* 1065–1076.

Delong, J. A., & Roy, A. (1993). Paternal lineage of alcoholism, cohort effects, and alcoholism criteria. *Addiction, 88,* 623–629.

Denmark, F., Russo, N. F., Frieze, I. H., & Sechzer, J. A. (1988). Guidelines for avoiding sexism in psychological research: A report of the ad hoc committee on nonsexist research. *American Psychologist, 43,* 582–585.

Doherty, W. J. (1981). Involving the reluctant father in family therapy. In A. S. Gurman (Ed.), *Questions and answers in the practice of family therapy* (Vol. 1, pp. 23–26). New York: Brunner/Mazel.

Downey, G., & Coyne, J. C. (1990). Children of depressed parents: An integrative review. *Psychological Bulletin, 108,* 50–76.

Downs, W. R., & Robertson, J. F. (1991). Random versus clinical samples: A question of inference. *Journal of Social Service Research, 14,* 57–83.

Dumka, L. E., & Roosa, M. W. (1993). Factors mediating problem drinking and mothers' personal adjustment. *Journal of Family Psychology, 7,* 333–343.

El-Guebaly, N., Offord, D. R., Sullivan, K. T., & Lynch, G. W. (1978). Psychosocial adjustment of the offspring of psychiatric inpatients: The effect of alcoholic, depressive and schizophrenic parentage. *Canadian Psychiatric Association Journal, 23,* 281–289.

El-Guebaly, N., Staley, D., Rockman, G., Leckie, A., Barkman, K., O'Riordan, J., & Koensgen, S. (1991). The adult children of alcoholics in a psychiatric population. *American Journal of Drug and Alcohol Abuse, 17,* 215–226.

Emery, R. E. (1988). *Marriage, divorce, and children's adjustment.* Newbury Park, CA: Sage.

Erel, O., & Burman, B. (1995). Interrelatedness of marital relations and parent-child relations: A meta-analytic review. *Psychological Bulletin, 118,* 108–132.

Erlenmeyer-Kimling, L., Marcuse, Y., Cornblatt, B., Friedman, D., Rainer, J. D., & Rutschmann, J. (1984). The New York High-Risk Project. In N. F. Watt, E. J. Anthony, L. C. Wynne, & J. E. Rolf (Eds.), *Children at risk for schizophrenia: A longitudinal perspective* (pp. 169–189). New York: Cambridge University Press.

Feldman, L. B. (1990). Fathers and fathering. In R. L. Meth & R. S. Pasick (Eds.), *Men in therapy: The challenge of change* (pp. 88–107). New York: Guilford.

Firestone, P., Kelly, M. J., & Fike, S. (1980). Are fathers necessary in parent training groups? *Journal of Clinical Child Psychology, 9,* 44–47.

Fitzgerald, H. E., Sullivan, L. A., Ham, H. P., & Zucker, R. A. (1993). Predictors of behavior problems in three-year-old sons of alcoholics: Early evidence for the onset of risk. *Child Development, 64,* 110–123.

Forehand, R., & Smith, K. A. (1986). Who depresses whom? A look at the relationship of adolescent mood to maternal and paternal mood. *Child Study Journal, 16,* 19–23.

Frame, C. L., & Strauss, C. C. (1987). Parental informed consent and sample bias in grade-school children. *Journal of Social and Clinical Psychology, 5,* 227–236.

Freeman, N. L., Perry, A., & Factor, D. C. (1991). Child behaviours as stressors: Replicating and extending the use of the CARS as a measure of stress: A research note. *Journal of Clinical Psychology and Psychiatry, 32,* 1025–1030.

Freud, S. (1949). *A general introduction to psychoanalysis.* New York: Garden City.

Frick, P. J., Lahey, B. B., Christ, M. A. G., Loeber, R., & Green, S. (1991). History of childhood behavior problems in biological relatives of boys with attention-deficit hyperactivity disorder and conduct disorder. *Journal of Clinical Child Psychology, 20,* 445–451.

Frieman, B. B. (1994). Children of divorced parents: Action steps for the counselor to involve fathers. *Elementary School Guidance and Counseling, 28,* 197–205.

Fromm-Reichmann, F. (1948). Notes on the development of treatment of schizophrenics by psychoanalytic psychotherapy. *Psychiatry, 11,* 263–273.

Frost, R. O., Steketee, G., Cohn, L., & Griess, K. (1994). Personality traits in subclinical and non-obsessive-compulsive volunteers and their parents. *Behavior Research and Therapy, 32,* 47–56.

Gerlsma, C., Emmelkamp, P. M. G., & Arrindell, W. A. (1990). Anxiety, depression, and perception of early parenting: A meta-analysis. *Clinical Psychology Review, 10,* 251–277.

Goetting, A. (1994). The parenting-crime connection. *Journal of Primary Prevention, 14,* 169–186.

Greenberger, E., & Goldberg, W. A. (1989). Work, parenting, and the socialization of children. *Developmental Psychology, 25,* 22–35.

Greenberger, E., & O'Neil, R. (1990). Parents' concerns about their child's development: Implications for fathers' and mothers' well-being and attitudes toward work. *Journal of Marriage and the Family, 52,* 621–635.

Greif, G. L., & Kristall, J. (1993). Common themes in a group for noncustodial parents. *Families in Society, 74,* 240–245.

Grych, J. H., & Fincham, F. D. (1990). Marital conflict and children's adjustment: A cognitive-contextual framework. *Psychological Bulletin, 108,* 267–290.

Guillebeaux, F., Storm, C. L., & Demaris, A. (1986). Luring the reluctant male: A study of males participating in marriage and family therapy. *Family Therapy, 13,* 215–225.

Gussman, K., & Harder, D. (1990). Offspring personality and perceptions of parental use of reward and punishment. *Psychological Reports, 67,* 923–930.

Hahlweg, K., Goldstein, M. J., Nuechterlein, K. H., Magana, A. B., Mintz, J., Doane, J. A., Miklowitz, D. J., & Snyder, K. S. (1989). Expressed emotion and patient-relative interaction in families of recent onset schizophrenics. *Journal of Consulting and Clinical Psychology, 57,* 11–18.

Hairston, C. F. (1989). Men in prisons: Family characteristics and parenting views. *Journal of Offender Counseling, Services and Rehabilitation, 14,* 23–30.

Halperin, S. M., & Smith, T. A. (1983). Differences in stepchildren's perceptions of their step-fathers and natural fathers: Implications for family therapy. *Journal of Divorce, 7,* 19–30.

Harjan, A. (1992). Children of parents with affective disorders: The role of an ill mother or an ill father. *European Journal of Psychiatry, 6,* 74–87.

Hawkins, J. D., Catalano, R. F., & Miller, J. Y. (1992). Risk and protective factors for alcohol and other drug problems in adolescence and early adulthood: Implications for substance abuse prevention. *Psychological Bulletin, 112,* 64–105.

Hazelrigg, M. D., Cooper, H. M., & Borduin, C. M. (1987). Evaluating the effectiveness of family therapies: An integrative review and analysis. *Psychological Bulletin, 101,* 428–442.

Heide, K. M. (1992). *Why kids kill parents: Child abuse and adolescent homicide.* Columbus, OH: Ohio State University Press.

Henggeler, S. W., Edwards, J., & Borduin, C. M. (1987). The family relations of female juvenile delinquents. *Journal of Abnormal Child Psychology, 15,* 199–209.

Henggeler, S. W., Rodick, J. D., Borduin, C. M., Hanson, C. L., Watson, S. M., & Urey, J. R. (1986). Multisystemic treatment of juvenile offenders: Effects on adolescent behavior and family interaction. *Developmental Psychology, 22,* 132–141.

Hetherington, E. M., & Clingempeel, W. G. (1992). Coping with marital transitions: A family systems perspective. *Monographs of the Society for Research in Child Development, 57,* (Serial No. 227).

Hops, H. (1992). Parental depression and child behavior problems: Implications for behavioural family intervention. *Behaviour Change, 9,* 126–138.

Hops, H., Biglan, A., Sherman, L., Arthur, J., Friedman, L., & Osteen, V. (1987). Home observations of family interactions of depressed women. *Journal of Consulting and Clinical Psychology, 55,* 341–346.

Hops, H., & Seeley, J. R. (1991, November). *Father-presence effects in studies of mother-adolescent interaction: Methodological and substantive considerations.* Paper presented at the convention of the Association for Advancement of Behavior Therapy, New York.

Hops, H., & Seeley, J. R. (1992). Parent participation in studies of family interaction: Methodological and substantive considerations. *Behavioral Assessment, 14,* 229–243.

Hrubec, Z., & Omenn, G. S. (1981). Evidence of genetic predisposition to alcoholic cirrhosis and psychosis: Twin concordances for alcoholism and its biological end points by zygosity among male veterans. *Alcoholism, 5,* 207–215.

Humphrey, L. L. (1986). Structural analysis of parent-child relationships in eating disorders. *Journal of Abnormal Psychology, 95,* 395–402.

Humphrey, L. L. (1987). Comparison of bulimic-anorexic and nondistressed families using structural analysis of social behavior. *Journal of the American Academy of Child and Adolescent Psychiatry, 26,* 248–255.

Humphrey, L. L. (1989). Observed family interactions among subtypes of eating disorders using structural analysis of social behavior. *Journal of Consulting and Clinical Psychology, 57,* 206–214.

Humphrey, L. L., Apple, R. F., & Kirschenbaum, D. S. (1986). Differentiating bulimic-anorexic from normal families using interpersonal and behavioral observational systems. *Journal of Consulting and Clinical Psychology, 54,* 190–195.

Itil, T. M., Huque, M. F., Shapiro, D. M., Mednick, S. A., & Schulsinger, F. (1983). Computer-analyzed EEG findings in children of schizophrenic parents ("high risk" children). *Integrative Psychiatry, 1,* 71–79.

Jacob, T., Krahn, G. L., & Leonard, K. (1991). Parent-child interactions in families with alcoholic fathers. *Journal of Consulting and Clinical Psychology, 59,* 176–181.

Jacob, T., & Leonard, K. (1986). Psychosocial functioning in children of alcoholic fathers, depressed fathers and control fathers. *Journal of Studies on Alcohol, 47,* 373–380.

Jacobs, J. W. (1982). The effect of divorce on fathers: An overview of the literature. *American Journal of Psychiatry, 139,* 1235–1241.

Jacobs, J. W. (1983). Treatment of divorcing fathers: Social and psychotherapeutic considerations. *American Journal of Psychiatry, 140,* 1294–1299.

Jacobsen, L. K., Sweeney, C. G., & Racusin, G. R. (1993). Group psychotherapy for children of fathers with PTSD: Evidence of psychopathology emerging in the group process. *Journal of Child and Adolescent Group Therapy, 3,* 103–120.

Jarmas, A. L., & Kazak, A. E. (1992). Young adult children of alcoholic fathers: Depressive experiences, coping styles, and family systems. *Journal of Consulting and Clinical Psychology, 60,* 244–251.

Jary, M. L., & Stewart, M. A. (1985). Psychiatric disorder in the parents of adopted children with aggressive conduct disorder. *Neuropsychobiology, 13,* 7–11.

Jenkins, J. M., & Smith, M. A. (1991). Marital disharmony and children's behaviour problems: Aspects of a poor marriage that affect children adversely. *Journal of Child Psychology and Psychiatry, 32,* 793–810.

Jensen, P. S., Bloedau, L., Degroot, J., Ussery, T., & Davis, H. (1990). Children at risk: I. Risk factors and child symptomatology. *Journal of the American Academy of Child and Adolescent Psychiatry, 29,* 51–59.

Jensen, P. S., Lewis, R. L., & Xenakis, S. N. (1986). The military family in review: Context, risk, and prevention. *Journal of the American Academy of Child Psychiatry, 25,* 225–234.

Jiloha, R. C. (1986). Psycho-social factors in adolescent heroin addicts. *Child Psychiatry Quarterly, 19,* 138–142.

John, K., Gammon, G. D., Prusoff, B. A., & Warner, V. (1987). The Social Adjustment Inventory for Children and Adolescents (SAICA): Testing of a new semistructured interview. *Journal of the American Academy of Child and Adolescent Psychiatry, 26,* 898–911.

Johnson, P. L., & O'Leary, K. D. (1987). Parental behavior patterns and conduct disorders in girls. *Journal of Abnormal Child Psychology, 15,* 573–581.

Jordan, B. K., Marmar, C. R., Fairbank, J. A., Schlenger, W. E., Kulka, R. A., Hough, R. L., & Weiss, D. S. (1992). Problems in families of male Vietnam veterans with posttraumatic stress disorder. *Journal of Consulting and Clinical Psychology, 60,* 916–926.

Kane, R., Mikalac, C., Benjamin, S., & Barkley, R. A. (1990). Assessment and treatment of adults with ADHD. In R. A. Barkley (Ed.), *Attention-deficit hyperactivity disorder: A handbook for diagnosis and treatment.* New York: Guilford.

Kanner, L. (1943). Autistic disturbances of affective contact. *Nervous Child, 2,* 217–250.

Kaslow, N. J., Deering, C. G., & Racusin, G. R. (1994). Depressed children and their families. *Clinical Psychology Review, 14,* 39–59.

Kaslow, N. J., Rehm, L. P., Pollack, S. L., & Siegel, A. W. (1988). Attributional style and self-control behavior in depressed and nondepressed children and their parents. *Journal of Abnormal Child Psychology, 16,* 163–175.

Kavanagh, K., & Hops, H. (1994). Good girls? Bad boys? Gender and development as contexts for diagnosis and treatment. In T. H. Ollendick & R. J. Prinz (Eds.), *Advances in clinical child psychology* (Vol. 16, pp. 45–79). New York: Plenum.

Kazdin, A. E. (1991). Effectiveness of psychotherapy with children and adolescents. *Journal of Consulting and Clinical Psychology, 59,* 785–798.

Keller, M. B., Beardslee, W. R., Dorer, D. J., Lavori, P. W., Samuelson, H., & Klerman, G. R. (1986). Impact of severity on chronicity of parental affective illness and adaptive functioning and psychopathology in children. *Archives of General Psychiatry, 43,* 930–937.

Kendler, K. S., MacLean, C., Neale, M. C., Kessler, R. C., Heath, A. C., & Eaves, L. (1991). The genetic epidemiology of bulimia nervosa. *American Journal of Psychiatry, 148,* 1627–1637.

Kendler, K. S., Neale, M. C., Heath, A. C., & Kessler, R. C. (1994). A twin-family study of alcoholism in women. *American Journal of Psychiatry, 151,* 707–715.

Kendler, K. S., Silberg, J. L., Neale, M. C., Kessler, R. C., Heath, A. C., & Eaves, L. (1991). The family history method: Whose psychiatric history is measured? *American Journal of Psychiatry, 148,* 1501–1504.

King, C. A., Segal, H. G., Naylor, M., & Evans, T. (1993). Family functioning and suicidal behavior in adolescent inpatients with mood disorders. *Journal of the American Academy of Child and Adolescent Psychiatry, 32,* 1198–1206.

Kiselica, M. S., Stroud, J., Stroud, J., & Rotzien, A. (1992). Counseling the forgotten client: The teen father. *Journal of Mental Health Counseling, 14,* 338–350.

Klein, D. N., Clark, D. C., Dansky, L., & Margolis, E. T. (1988). Dysthymia in the offspring of parents with primary Unipolar Affective Disorder. *Journal of Abnormal Psychology, 97,* 265–274.

Klein, D. N., Depue, R. A., & Slater, J. F. (1985). Cyclothymia in the adolescent offspring of parents with Bipolar Affective Disorder. *Journal of Abnormal Psychology, 94,* 115–127.

Klinge, V., & Piggott, L. R. (1986). Substance use by adolescent psychiatric inpatients and their parents. *Adolescence, 21,* 323–331.

Knop, J., Goodwin, D. W., Jensen, P., & Penick, E. (1993). A 30-year follow-up study of the sons of alcoholic men. *Acta Psychiatrica Scandinavica, 87,* 48–53.

Konstantareas, M. M., & Homatidis, S. (1989). Assessing child symptom severity and stress in parents of autistic children. *Journal of Child Psychology and Psychiatry, 30,* 459–470.

La Greca, A. M., & Silverman, W. K. (1993). Parent reports of child behavior problems: Bias in participation. *Journal of Abnormal Child Psychology, 21,* 89–101.

Lahey, B. B., Piacentini, J. C., McBurnett, K., Stone, P., Hartdagen, S., & Hynd, G. (1988). Psychopathology in the parents of children with Conduct Disorder and Hyperactivity. *Journal of the American Academy of Child and Adolescent Psychiatry, 27,* 163–170.

Lang, A. R., Pelham, W. E., Johnston, C., & Gelernter, S. (1989). Levels of adult alcohol consumption induced by interactions with child confederates exhibiting normal versus externalizing behaviors. *Journal of Abnormal Psychology, 98,* 294–299.

Lanier, C. S. (1991). Dimensions of father-child interactions in a New York state prison population. *Journal of Offender Rehabilitation, 16,* 27–42.

Last, C. G., & Strauss, C. C. (1989). Panic disorder in children and adolescents. *Journal of Anxiety Disorders, 3,* 87–95.

Lazar, A., Sagi, A., & Fraser, M. W. (1991). Involving fathers in social services. *Children and Youth Services Review, 13,* 287–300.

Lee, C. M., & Gotlib, I. H. (1991). Family disruption, parental availability and child adjustment. In R. J. Prinz (Ed.), *Advances in behavioral assessment of children and families* (Vol. 5, pp. 171–199). London: Jessica Kingsley.

Lenane, M. C., Swedo, S. E., Leonard, H., Pauls, D. L., Sceery, W., & Rapoport, J. L. (1990). Psychiatric disorders in first degree relatives of children and adolescents with Obsessive Compulsive Disorder. *Journal of the American Academy of Child and Adolescent Psychiatry, 29,* 407–412.

Lewis, D. O., Pincus, J. H., Lovely, R., Spitzer, E., & Moy, E. (1987). Biopsychosocial characteristics of matched samples of delinquents and nondelinquents. *Journal of the American Academy of Child and Adolescent Psychiatry, 26,* 744–752.

Lewis, D. O., Shanok, S. S., Grant, M., & Ritvo, E. (1983). Homicidally aggressive young children: Neuropsychiatric and experiential correlates. *American Journal of Psychiatry, 140,* 148–153.

Liddle, H. A. (1994). The anatomy of emotions in family therapy with adolescents. *Journal of Adolescent Research, 9,* 120–157.

Lidz, T., Parker, B., & Cornelison, A. (1956). The role of the father in the family environment of the schizophrenic patient. *American Journal of Psychiatry, 113,* 126–132.

Lisak, D. (1991). Sexual aggression, masculinity, and fathers. *Signs: Journal of Women in Culture and Society, 16,* 238–262.

Lisak, D., & Roth, S. (1990). Motives and psychodynamics of self-reported, unincarcerated rapists. *American Journal of Orthopsychiatry, 60,* 268–280.

Loeber, R. (1990). Development and risk factors of juvenile antisocial behavior and delinquency. *Clinical Psychology Review, 10,* 1–41.

Loeber, R., & Dishion, T. J. (1987). Antisocial and delinquent youths: Methods for their early identification. In J. D. Burchard & S. N. Burchard (Eds.), *Prevention of delinquent behavior* (pp. 75–89). Newbury Park, CA: Sage.

Loeber, R., & Stouthamer-Loeber, M. (1986). Family factors as correlates and predictors of juvenile conduct problems and delinquency. In M. Tonry & N. Morris (Eds.), *Crime and justice* (Vol. 7, pp. 219–339). Chicago: University of Chicago Press.

Luthar, S. S., Merikangas, K. R., & Rounsaville, B. J. (1993). Parental psychopathology and disorders in offspring: A study of relatives of drug abusers. *Journal of Nervous and Mental Disease, 181,* 351–357.

Maguin, E., Zucker, R. A., & Fitzgerald, H. E. (1994). The path to alcohol problems through conduct problems: A family based approach to early intervention with risk. *Journal of Research on Adolescence, 4,* 249–269.

Mahler, M. (1952). On child psychosis in schizophrenia: Autistic and symbiotic infantile psychosis. In R. S. Eissler, H. Hartmann, A. Freud, & E. Kris (Eds.), *Psychoanalytic study of the child* (Vol. 7, pp. 286–305). New York: International Universities Press.

Mann, B. J., Borduin, C. M., Henggeler, S. W., & Blaske, D. M. (1990). An investigation of systemic conceptualizations of parent-child coalitions and symptom change. *Journal of Consulting and Clinical Psychology, 58,* 336–344.

Marett, K. M., Sprenkle, D. H., & Lewis, R. A. (1992). Family members' perceptions of family boundaries and their relationship to family problems. *Family Therapy, 19,* 233–242.

Martin, B. (1977). Brief family intervention: Effectiveness and the importance of including the father. *Journal of Consulting and Clinical Psychology, 45,* 1002–1010.

Martin, B. (1987). Developmental perspectives on family theory and psychopathology. In T. Jacob (Ed.), *Family interaction and psychopathology: Theories, methods, and findings* (pp. 163–202). New York: Plenum.

Martin, E. D., & Sher, K. J. (1994). Family history of alcoholism, alcohol use disorders and the five-factor model of personality. *Journal of Studies on Alcohol, 55,* 81–90.

Martin, T. R., & Bracken, M. B. (1986). Association of low birth weight with passive smoke exposure in pregnancy. *American Journal of Epidemiology, 124,* 633–642.

Mathew, R. J., Wilson, W. H., Blazer, D. G., & George, L. K. (1993). Psychiatry disorders in adult children of alcoholics: Data from the epidemiologic catchment area project. *American Journal of Psychiatry, 150,* 793–800.

McCranie, E. W., Hyer, L. A., Boudewyns, P. A., & Woods, M. G. (1992). Negative parenting behavior, combat exposure, and PTSD symptom severity: Test of a person-event interaction model. *Journal of Nervous and Mental Disease, 180,* 431–438.

McGoldrick, M., Pearce, J. K., & Giordano, J. (Eds.). (1982). *Ethnicity and family therapy.* New York: Guilford.

McLeod, J. D. (1993). Spouse concordance for depressive disorders in a community sample. *Journal of Affective Disorders, 27,* 43–52.

Merikangas, K., Weissman, M., Prusoff, B. A., & Johns, K. (1988). Assortative mating and affective disorders: Psychopathology in offspring. *Psychiatry, 51,* 48–57.

Merikangas, K., Weissman, M., Prusoff, B. A., Pauls, D., & Leckman, J. (1985). Depressives with secondary alcoholism: Psychiatric disorders in offspring. *Journal of Studies on Alcohol, 46,* 199–204.

Miklowitz, D. J., Goldstein, M. J., Doane, J. A., Nuechterlein, K. H., Strachan, A. M., Snyder, K. S., & Magana-Amato, A. (1989). Is expressed emotion an index of a transactional process?: I. Parents' affective style. *Family Process, 28,* 153–167.

Moes, D., Koegel, R. L., Schreibman, L., & Loos, L. M. (1992). Stress profiles for mothers and fathers of children with autism. *Psychological Reports, 71,* 1272–1274.

Murphy, R. T., O'Farrell, T. J., Floyd, F. J., & Connors, G. J. (1991). School adjustment of children of alcoholic fathers: Comparison to normal controls. *Addictive Behaviors, 16,* 275–287.

Mutzell, S. (1994). Coping strategies in children of male alcoholic parents and men from the general population. *Early Child Development and Care, 97,* 73–89.

Nash, J. (1965). The father in contemporary culture and current psychological literature. *Child Development, 36,* 261–297.

Nicol, A. R., Smith, J., Kay, B., Hall, D., Barlow, J., & Williams, B. (1988). A focused casework approach to the treatment of child abuse: A controlled comparison. *Journal of Child Psychology and Psychiatry, 29,* 703–711.

Onstad, S., Skre, I., Torgersen, S., & Kringlen, E. (1993). Parental representation in twins discordant for schizophrenia. *Psychological Medicine, 23,* 335–340.

Orvaschel, H., Walsh-Allis, G., & Ye, W. (1988). Psychopathology in children of parents with recurrent depression. *Journal of Abnormal Child Psychology, 16,* 17–28.

Parsons, J., Kehle, T. J., & Owen, S. V. (1990). Incidence of behavior problems among children of Vietnam war veterans. *School Psychology International, 11,* 253–259.

Patterson, G. R. (Ed.). (1990). *Depression and aggression in family interaction.* Hillsdale, NJ: Erlbaum.

Petersen, A. C., Compas, B. E., Brooks-Gunn, J., Stemmler, M., Ey, S., & Grant, K. E. (1993). Depression in adolescence. *American Psychologist, 48,* 155–168.

Peterson, J. B., Finn, P. R., & Pihl, R. O. (1992). Cognitive dysfunction and the inherited predisposition to alcoholism. *Journal of Studies on Alcohol, 53,* 154–160.

Phares, V. (1992). Where's Poppa? The relative lack of attention to the role of fathers in child and adolescent psychopathology. *American Psychologist, 47,* 656–664.

Phares, V. (1995). Fathers' and mothers' participation in research. *Adolescence, 30,* 593–602.

Phares, V. (1996). *Fathers and developmental psychopathology.* New York: Wiley.

Phares, V., & Compas, B. E. (1992). The role of fathers in child and adolescent psychopathology: Make room for daddy. *Psychological Bulletin, 111,* 387–412.

Pihl, R. O., Peterson, J., & Finn, P. R. (1990). Inherited predisposition to alcoholism: Characteristics of sons of male alcoholics. *Journal of Abnormal Psychology, 99,* 291–301.

Plomin, R., & Daniels, D. (1987). Why are children in the same family so different from one another? *Behavioral and Brain Sciences, 10,* 1–60.

Plomin, R., DeFries, J. C., & McClearn, G. E. (1990). *Behavioral genetics: A primer* (2nd ed.). New York: Freeman.

Plomin, R., Reiss, D., Hetherington, E. M., & Howe, G. W. (1994). Nature and nurture: Genetic contributions to measures of the family environment. *Developmental Psychology, 30,* 32–43.

Pollock, V. E., Schneider, L. S., Gabrielli, W. F., & Goodwin, D. W. (1987). Sex of parent and offspring in the transmission of alcoholism: A meta-analysis. *Journal of Nervous and Mental Disease, 175,* 668–673.

Puig-Antich, J., Kaufman, J., Ryan, N. D., & Williamson, D. E. (1993). The psychosocial functioning and family environment of depressed adolescents. *Journal of the American Academy of Child and Adolescent Psychiatry, 32,* 244–253.

Puig-Antich, J., Lukens, E., Davies, M., Goetz, D., Brennan-Quattrock, J., & Todak, G.

(1985a). Psychosocial functioning in prepubertal Major Depressive Disorders: I. Interpersonal relationships during the depressive episode. *Archives of General Psychiatry, 42,* 500–507.

Puig-Antich, J., Lukens, E., Davies, M., Goetz, D., Brennan-Quattrock, J., & Todak, G. (1985b). Psychosocial functioning in prepubertal Major Depressive Disorders: II. Interpersonal relationships after sustained recovery from an affective episode. *Archives of General Psychiatry, 42,* 511–517.

Radke-Yarrow, M., Cummings, E. M., Kuczynski, L., & Chapman, M. (1985). Patterns of attachment in two- and three-year-olds in normal families and families with parental depression. *Child Development, 56,* 884–893.

Radke-Yarrow, M., Nottelman, E., Martinez, P., Fox, M. B., & Belmont, B. (1992). Young children of affectively ill parents: A longitudinal study of psychosocial development. *Journal of the American Academy of Child and Adolescent Psychiatry, 31,* 68–77.

Reeves, J. C., Werry, J. S., Elkind, G. S., & Zametkin, A. (1987). Attention Deficit, Conduct, Oppositional, and Anxiety Disorders in children: II. Clinical characteristics. *Journal of the American Academy of Child and Adolescent Psychiatry, 26,* 144–155.

Reid, W. J., & Crisafulli, A. (1990). Marital discord and child behavior problems: A meta-analysis. *Journal of Abnormal Child Psychology, 18,* 105–117.

Reisinger, J. J. (1982). Unprogrammed learning of differential attention by fathers of oppositional children. *Journal of Behavior Therapy and Experimental Psychiatry, 13,* 203–208.

Rheingold, J. (1967). *The mother, anxiety, and death: The catastrophic death complex.* Boston: Little, Brown.

Richards, C. A., & Goldenberg, I. (1985). Joint custody: Current issues and implications for treatment. *American Journal of Family Therapy, 13,* 33–40.

Rimmer, J. (1982). The children of alcoholics: An exploratory study. *Children and Youth Services Review, 4,* 365–373.

Rolf, J., Masten, A. S., Cicchetti, D., Neuchterlein, K. H., & Weintraub, S. (Eds.). (1990). *Risk and protective factors in the development of psychopathology.* New York: Cambridge University Press.

Rosenheck, R. (1986). Impact of posttraumatic stress disorder of World War II on the next generation. *Journal of Nervous and Mental Disease, 174,* 319–327.

Rosenthal, R., & Rosnow, R. L. (1975). *The volunteer subject.* New York: Wiley.

Rothbaum, F., & Weisz, J. R. (1994). Parental caregiving and child externalizing behavior in nonclinical samples: A meta-analysis. *Psychological Bulletin, 116,* 55–74.

Russell, J. D., Kopec-Schrader, E., Rey, J. M., & Beumont, P. J. (1992). The Parental Bonding Instrument in adolescent patients with anorexia nervosa. *Acta Psychiatrica Scandinavica, 86,* 236–239.

Sanua, V. D. (1961). Sociocultural factors in families of schizophrenics: A review of the literature. *Psychiatry: Journal for the Study of Interpersonal Processes, 24,* 246–265.

Sanua, V. D. (1963). The sociocultural aspects of schizophrenia: A comparison of Protestant and Jewish schizophrenics. *International Journal of Social Psychiatry, 9,* 27–36.

Sanua, V. D. (1986a). The personality and psychological adjustment of family members with autistic children: I. A critical review of the research in Britain. *International Journal of Family Psychiatry, 7,* 221–260.

Sanua, V. D. (1986b). The personality and psychological adjustment of family members of autistic children: II. A critical review of the literature research in the United States. *International Journal of Family Psychiatry, 7,* 331–358.

Sarason, B. R., Pierce, G. R., Bannerman, A., & Sarason, I. G. (1993). Investigating the antecedents of perceived social support: Parents' views of and behavior toward their children. *Journal of Personality and Social Psychology, 65,* 1071–1085.

Schachar, R., & Wachsmuth, R. (1990). Oppositional disorder in children: A validation study comparing conduct disorder, oppositional disorder and normal control children. *Journal of Child Psychology and Psychiatry, 31,* 1089–1102.

Schuckit, M. A., Tipp, J. E., & Kelner, E. (1994). Are daughters of alcoholics more likely to marry alcoholics? *American Journal of Drug and Alcohol Abuse, 20,* 237–245.

Schwartz-Bickenbach, D., Schulte-Hobein, B., Abt, S., Plum, C., & Nau, H. (1987). Smoking and passive smoking during pregnancy and early infancy: Effects on birth weight, lactation period, and cotinine concentrations in mother's milk and infant's urine. *Toxicology Letters, 35,* 73–81.

Seltzer, J. A. (1991). Relationships between fathers and children who live apart: The father's role after separation. *Journal of Marriage and the Family, 53,* 79–101.

Seltzer, J. A., & Bianchi, S. M. (1988). Children's contact with absent parents. *Journal of Marriage and the Family, 50,* 663–677.

Sher, K. J. (1991). *Children of alcoholics: A critical appraisal of theory and research.* Chicago: University of Chicago Press.

Sher, K. J., Walitzer, K. S., Wood, P. K., & Brent, E. E. (1991). Characteristics of children of alcoholics: Putative risk factors, substance use and abuse, and psychopathology. *Journal of Abnormal Psychology, 100,* 427–448.

Silverstein, L. B., & Phares, V. (1996). Expanding the mother-child paradigm: An examination of dissertation research 1986–1994. *Psychology of Women Quarterly, 20,* 39–53.

Silverton, L., Mednick, S. A., Schulsinger, F., Parnas, J., & Harrington, M. E. (1988). Genetic risk for schizophrenia, birthweight, and cerebral ventricular enlargement. *Journal of Abnormal Psychology, 97,* 496–498.

Singhal, S., & Dutta, A. (1990). Who commits patricide? *Acta Psychiatrica Scandinavica, 82,* 40–43.

Starrels, M. E. (1994). Gender differences in parent-child relations. *Journal of Family Issues, 14,* 148–165.

Steinberg, L. (1987). Recent research on the family at adolescence: The extent and nature of sex differences. *Journal of Youth and Adolescence, 16,* 191–197.

Strachan, A. M., Feingold, D., Goldstein, M. J., Miklowitz, D. J., & Nuechterlein, K. H. (1989). Is expressed emotion an index of a transactional process? II. Patient's coping style. *Family Process, 28,* 169–181.

Szapocznik, J., Perez-Vidal, A., Brickman, A. L., Foote, F. H., Santisteban, D., Hervis, O., & Kurtines, W. M. (1988). Engaging adolescent drug abusers and their families in treatment: A strategic structural systems approach. *Journal of Consulting and Clinical Psychology, 56,* 552–557.

Tannenbaum, L., & Forehand, R. (1994). Maternal depressive mood: The role of the father in preventing adolescent problem behaviors. *Behavioral Research and Therapy, 32,* 321–325.

Tarter, R. E., Blackson, T. C., Martin, C. S., & Loeber, R. (1993). Characteristics and correlates of child discipline practices in substance abuse and normal families. *American Journal on Addictions, 2,* 18–25.

Tarter, R. E., Laird, S., & Bukstein, O. (1991). Multivariate comparison of adolescent offspring of substance abuse parents: Community and treatment samples. *Journal of Substance Abuse, 3,* 301–306.

Telerant, A., Kronenberg, J., Rabinovitch, S., & Elman, I. (1992). Anorectic family dynamics. *Journal of the American Academy of Child and Adolescent Psychiatry, 31,* 990–991.

Thomas, A. M., & Forehand, R. (1991). The relationship between paternal depressive mood and early adolescent functioning. *Journal of Family Psychology, 4,* 260–271.

Tillitski, C. J. (1992). Fathers and child custody: Issues, trends, and implications for counseling. *Journal of Mental Health Counseling, 14,* 351–361.

Truscott, D. (1992). Intergenerational transmission of violent behavior in adolescent males. *Aggressive Behavior, 18,* 327–335.

Ullman, A. D., & Orenstein, A. (1994). Why some children of alcoholics become alcoholics: Emulation of the drinker. *Adolescence, 29,* 1–11.

Vandenberg, S. G., Singer, S. M., & Pauls, D. L. (1986). *The heredity of behavior disorders in adults and children.* New York: Plenum.

Velleman, R. (1992). Intergenerational effects—A review of environmentally oriented studies concerning the relationship between parental alcohol problems and family disharmony in the genesis of alcohol and other problems: I. The intergenerational effects of alcohol problems. *International Journal of the Addictions, 27,* 253–280.

Wachs, T. D., & Weizmann, F. (1992). Prenatal and genetic influences upon behavior and development. In C. E. Walker & M. C. Roberts (Eds.), *Handbook of clinical child psychology* (2nd ed., pp. 183–198). New York: Wiley.

Warren, J. K., Gary, F., & Moorhead, J. (1994). Self-reported experiences of physical and sexual abuse among runaway youths. *Perspectives in Psychiatric Care, 30,* 23–28.

Watt, N. F. (1986). Risk research in schizophrenia and other major psychological disorders. In M. Kessler & S. E. Goldston (Eds.), *A decade of progress in primary prevention* (pp. 115–153). Hanover, NH: University Press of New England.

Watt, N. F., Anthony, E. J., Wynne, L. C., & Rolf, J. E. (Eds.). (1984). *Children at risk for schizophrenia: A longitudinal perspective.* New York: Cambridge University Press.

Webster-Stratton, C. (1985). The effects of father involvement in parent training for conduct problem children. *Journal of Child Psychology and Psychiatry, 26,* 801–810.

Webster-Stratton, C. (1992). Individually administered videotape parent training: "Who benefits?" *Cognitive Therapy and Research, 16,* 31–35.

Webster-Stratton, C., Hollinsworth, T., & Kolpacoff, M. (1989). The long-term effectiveness and clinical significance of three cost-effective training programs for families with conduct-problem children. *Journal of Consulting and Clinical Psychology, 57,* 550–553.

Webster-Stratton, C., Kolpacoff, M., & Hollinsworth, T. (1988). Self-administered videotape therapy for families with conduct-problem children: Comparison with two cost-effective treatments and a control group. *Journal of Consulting and Clinical Psychology, 56,* 558–566.

Weinberg, N. Z., Dielman, T. E., Mandell, W., & Shope, J. T. (1994). Parental drinking and gender factors in the prediction of early adolescent alcohol use. *International Journal of the Addictions, 29,* 89–104.

Weinberger, D. A., Tublin, S. K., Ford, M. E., & Feldman, S. S. (1990). Preadolescents' social-emotional adjustment and selective attrition in family research. *Child Development, 61,* 1374–1386.

Weiss, G., & Hechtman, L. (1986). *Hyperactive children grown up.* New York: Guilford.

Weissman, M. M., Leckman, J. F., Merikangas, K. R., Gammon, G. D., & Prusoff, B. A. (1984). Depression and anxiety disorders in parents and children. *Archives of General Psychiatry, 41,* 845–852.

Weisz, J. R., & Weiss, B. (1993). *Effects of psychotherapy with children and adolescents.* Newbury Park, CA: Sage.

Weller, R. A., Kapadia, P., Weller, E. B., Fristad, M., Lazaroff, L. B., & Preskorn, S. H. (1994). Psychopathology in families of children with major depressive disorders. *Journal of Affective Disorders, 31,* 247–252.

Wellner, Z., & Rice, J. (1988). School-aged children of depressed parents: A blind and controlled study. *Journal of Affective Disorders, 15,* 291–302.

West, M. O., & Prinz, R. J. (1987). Parental alcoholism and childhood psychopathology. *Psychological Bulletin, 102,* 204–218.

Whipple, S. C., & Noble, E. P. (1991). Personality characteristics of alcoholic fathers and their sons. *Journal of Studies on Alcohol, 52,* 331–337.

Wylie, P. (1946). *Generation of vipers.* New York: Rinehart.

Yaccarino, M. E. (1993). Using Minuchin's structural family therapy techniques with Italian-American families. *Contemporary Family Therapy: An International Journal, 15,* 459–466.

Yesavage, J. A., Becker, J. M. T., Werner, P. D., Patton, M. J., Seeman, K., Brunsting, D. W., & Mills, M. J. (1983). Family conflict, psychopathology, and dangerous behavior by schizophrenic inpatients. *Psychiatry Research, 8,* 271–280.

Yoshikawa, H. (1994). Prevention as cumulative protection: Effects of early family support and education on chronic delinquency and its risks. *Psychological Bulletin, 115,* 28–54.

Zahn-Waxler, C., Cummings, E. M., McKnew, D. H., & Radke-Yarrow, M. (1984). Altruism, aggression, and social interactions in young children with a manic-depressive parent. *Child Development, 55,* 112–122.

CHAPTER 16

Achenbach, T. M., & Edelbrock, C. (1983). *Manual for the Child Behavior Checklist and Revised Child Behavior Profile.* Burlington, VT: University of Vermont.

Achenbach, T. M., & Edelbrock, C. S. (1987). *Manual for the Youth Self-Report and Profile.* Burlington, VT: University of Vermont.

American Association for Protecting Children. (1986). *Highlights of official child neglect and abuse reporting, 1984.* Denver, CO: American Humane Association.

Armsden, G. C., & Greenberg, M. T. (1987). The Inventory of Parent and Peer Attachment: Individual differences and their relationship to psychological well-being in adolescence. *Journal of Youth and Adolescence, 16,* 427–454.

Bachman, R., & Salzman, L. E. (1995). *Violence against women: Estimates from the redesigned survey* (Bureau of Justice Statistics Spec. Rep. NCJ-154348). Washington, DC: U.S. Department of Justice.

Belsky, J. (1980). Child maltreatment: An ecological integration. *American Psychologist, 35,* 320–335.

Belsky, J. (1993). Etiology of child maltreatment: A developmental-ecological analysis. *Psychological Bulletin, 114*(3), 413–434.

Bene, E., & Anthony, E. J. (1957). *Manual for the Family Relations Test.* London: National Foundation for Educational Research.

Blankenhorn, D. (1995). *Fatherless America: Confronting our most urgent social problems.* New York: Basic Books.

Bryant, B. K. (1985). The neighborhood walk: Sources of support in middle childhood. *Monographs of the Society for Research in Child Development, 50.*

Burgess, R. L., & Conger, R. D. (1978). Family interactions in abusive, neglectful, and normal families. *Child Development, 49,* 1163–1173.

Caffey, J. (1946). Multiple fractures in the long bones of infants suffering from chronic subdural hematoma. *American Journal of Radiology, 56,* 163–173.

Carlson, V., Cicchetti, D., Barnett, D., & Braunwald, K. G. (1989). Finding order in disorganization: Lessons from research on maltreated infants' attachments to their caregivers. In D. Cicchetti & V. Carlson (Eds.), *Child maltreatment* (pp. 494–528). New York: Cambridge University Press.

Cicchetti, D., & Toth, S. L. (1993). Child maltreatment research and social policy: The neglected nexus. In D. Cicchetti & S. L. Toth (Eds.), *Child abuse, child development and social policy: Advances in applied developmental psychology, Vol. 8.* Norwood, NJ: Ablex.

Crittenden, P. M. (1988). Relationships at risk. In J. Belsky & T. Nezworski (Eds.), *Clinical implications of attachment* (pp. 136–174). Hillsdale, NJ: Erlbaum.

Cummings, E. M., Ballard, M., El-Sheikh, M., & Lake, M. (1991). Resolution and children's responses to interadult anger. *Developmental Psychology, 27,* 462–470.

Cummings, E. M., & Davies, P. (1994). *Children and marital conflict: The impact of family dispute and resolution.* New York: Guilford.

Cummings, E. M., Simpson, K. S., & Wilson, A. (1993). Children's responses to interadult anger as a function of information about resolution. *Developmental Psychology, 29,* 978–985.

Cummings, E. M., Zahn-Waxler, C., & Radke-Yarrow, M. (1981). Young children's responses to expressions of anger and affection by others in the family. *Child Development, 52,* 1274–1282.

Cummings, E. M., Zahn-Waxler, C., & Radke-Yarrow, M. (1984). Developmental changes in children's reactions to anger in the home. *Journal of Child Psychology and Psychiatry, 25,* 63–74.

Curtis, G. C. (1963). Violence breeds violence. Perhaps? *American Journal of Psychiatry, 120,* 386–387.

Daly, M., & Wilson, M. (1984). A sociobiological analysis of human infanticide. In G. Hausfater & S. B. Hrdy (Eds.), *Infanticide: Comparative and evolutionary perspectives* (pp. 487–502). Hawthorne, NY: Archive.

Davies, P. T., & Cummings, E. M. (1994). Marital conflict and child adjustment: An emotional security hypothesis. *Psychological Bulletin, 116,* 387–411.

Dobash, R. E., & Dobash, R. P. (1984). The nature and antecedents of violent events. *British Journal of Criminology, 24,* 269–288.

Doumas, D., Margolin, G., & John, R. S. (1994). The integrational transmission of aggression across three generations. *Journal of Family Violence, 9,* 157–175.

Dubin, R., & Dubin, E. R. (1965). Children's social perceptions: A review of research. *Child Development, 36,* 809–838.

Edelson, J. L. (1995, March). *Mothers and children: Understanding the links between women battering and child abuse.* Paper prepared for Strategic Planning Workshop on Violence against Women, National Institute of Justice, Washington, DC.

Eisikovits, Z. C., Guttmann, E., Sela-Amit, M., & Edelson, J. L. (1993). Woman battering in Israel: The relative contributions of interpersonal factors. *American Journal of Orthopsychiatry, 63* (2), 313–317.

Faeber, R. L., & Long, N. (1991). Children in context: The role of the family in child psychotherapy. *Journal of Consulting and Clinical Psychology, 59,* 813–820.

Fauber, R., Forehand, R., Thomas, A. M., & Wierson, M. (1990). A mediational model of the impact of marital conflict on adolescent adjustment in intact and divorced families: The role of disrupted parenting. *Child Development, 61,* 1112–1123.

Feldman, R. S., Salzinger, S., & Kaplan, S. J. (1995, April). *Perspectives on physically abused children's and adolescent's behavior: Rater effects.* Paper presented to the Society for Research on Child Development, Indianapolis.

Fincham, F. D., Grych, J. H., & Osborne, L. N. (1994). Does marital conflict cause child maladjustment? Directions and challenges for longitudinal research. *Journal of Family Psychology, 8*(2), 128–140.

Finkelhor, D., & Dziuba-Leatherman, J. (1994). Children as victims of violence: A national survey. *Pediatrics, 91*(4), 413–420.

Garbarino, J., Sebes, J., & Schellenbach, C. (1984). Families at risk for destructive parent-child relations in adolescence. *Child Development, 55,* 174–183.

Geffner, R., & Pagelow, M. D. (1990). Victims of spouse abuse. In R. T. Ammerman & M. Hersch (Eds.), *Treatment of family violence* (pp. 113–135). New York: Wiley.

Geffner, R., Rosenbaum, A., Hughes, H., & O'Leary, K. D. (1988). Characteristics and treatment of batterers. *Behavioral Sciences and the Law, 8* (2), 131–140.

Gelles, R. J. (1985). Family violence. *Annual Review of Sociology, 11,* 347–367.

Gelles, R. J. (1989). Child abuse and violence in single parent families: Parent-absent and economic deprivation. *American Journal of Orthopsychiatry, 59,* 492–501.

Gelles, R. J. (1991). Physical violence, child abuse, and child homicide: A continuum of violence, or distinct behaviors? *Human Nature, 2*(1), 59–72.

Gelles, R. J., & Straus, M. A. (1988). *Intimate violence.* New York: Simon and Schuster.

Gil, D. (1973). *Violence against children: Physical child abuse in the United States.* Cambridge, MA: Harvard University Press.

Gil, D. (1975). Unraveling child abuse. *American Journal of Orthopsychiatry, 45,* 346–356.

Gilbert, N. (1993). Examining the facts: Advocacy research overstates the incidence of date and acquaintance rape. In R. J. Gelles & D. R. Loeske (Eds.), *Current controversies on family violence.* Newbury Park, CA: Sage.

Gottmann, J. M., Jacobson, N. S., Rushe, R. H., Short, J. N., Babcock, J., La Taillade, J. J., & Walz, J. (1995). The relationship between heart rate reactivity, emotionally aggressive behavior, and general violence in batterers. *Journal of Family Psychology, 9*(3), 227–248.

Grych, H. J., & Fincham, F. D. (1993). Children's appraisals of marital conflict: Initial investigations of the cognitive-contextual framework. *Child Development, 64,* 215–230.

Hazzard, A., Christensen, A., & Margolin, G. (1983). Children's perceptions of parental behaviors. *Journal of Abnormal Child Psychology, 11,* 49–60.

Helfer, R. E., & Kempe, R. S. (1987). *The battered child* (4th rev. ed.). Chicago: University of Chicago Press.

Hemenway, D., Solnick, S., & Carter, J. (1994). Child-rearing violence. *Child Abuse and Neglect, 18,* 1011–120.

Herrenkohl, E. C., & Herrenkohl, R. C. (1995, August). Paper submitted to the International Society for Behavioral Development, Quebec City, Quebec.

Herrenkohl, E. C., Herrenkohl, R. C., Toedter, L., & Yanushefski, D. (1984). Parent-child interactions in abusive and nonabusive families. *Journal of the American Academy of Child Psychiatry, 23,* 641–648.

Hertzberger, S., Potts, D. A., & Dillon, M. (1981). Abusive and non-abusive parental treatment from the child's perspective. *Journal of Consulting and Clinical Psychology, 49,* 81–91.

Holden, G. W., & Ritchie, K. L. (1991). Linking extreme marital discord, child rearing, and child behavior problems: Evidence from battered women. *Child Development, 62,* 311–327.

Holden, G. W., Willis, D. J., & Foltz, L. (1989). Child abuse potential and parenting stress: Relationships in maltreating parents. *Psychological Assessment: A Journal of Consulting and Clinical Psychology, 1,* 64–67.

Hotaling, G. O., & Sugarman, D. B. (1986). An analysis of risk markers in husband to wife violence: The current state of knowledge. *Violence and Victims, 1*(2), 101–124.

Hughes, H. (1988). Psychological and behavioral correlates of family violence in child witnesses and victims. *American Journal of Orthopsychiatry, 58,* 77–90.

Hughes, H. (in press). Research concerning children of battered women: Clinical implications. In R. Geffner, S. F. Sorenson, & P. K. Windberg-Love (Eds.), *Violence and sexual abuse at home: Current issues, interventions and research in spousal battering and child maltreatment.* Binghamton, NY: Haworth.

Jaffe, E. D. (1983). Fathers and child welfare services: The forgotten clients. In M. E. Lamb & A. Sagi (Eds.), *Fatherhood and family policy* (pp. 113–128). New York: Erlbaum.

Jouriles, E. N., & Norwood, W. D. (1995). Physical aggression toward boys and girls in families characterized by the battering of women. *Journal of Family Psychology, 9*(1), 69–78.

Jouriles, E. N., & O'Leary, K. D. (1985). Interspousal reliability of reports of marital violence. *Journal of Consulting Clinical Psychology, 53,* 419–421.

Kalmuss, D. (1984). The intergenerational transmission of marital aggression. *Journal of Marriage and the Family, 46,* 11–19.

Kaufman, J., Jones, B., Stieglitz, E., Vitulano, L., & Mannanno, A. P. (1994). The use of multiple informants to assess children's maltreatment experiences. *Journal of Family Violence, 9*(3), 227–248.

Kaufman, J., & Zigler, E. (1989). The intergenerational transmission of child abuse. In D. Cicchetti & V. Carlson (Eds.), *Child maltreatment: Theory and research on the causes and consequences of child abuse and neglect* (pp. 129–152). New York: Cambridge University Press.

Kempe, C. H., Silverman, F. N., Steele, B. F., Droegemueller, W., & Silver, H. K. (1962). The battered-child syndrome. *Journal of the American Medical Association, 18,* 105–112.

Kurz, D. (1993). Physical assaults by husbands: A major social problem. In R. J. Gelles & D. R. Loseke (Eds.), *Current controversies on family violence* (pp. 88–103). Newbury Park, CA: Sage.

Lamb, M. E., Gaensbauer, T. S., Malkin, C. M., & Schultz, L. A. (1985). The effects of abuse and neglect on security of infant-adult attachment. *Infant Behavior and Development, 8,* 35–45.

Langhinrichsen-Rohling, J., & Vivian, D. (1994). The correlates of spouses' incongruent reports of marital aggression. *Journal of Family Violence, 9*(3), 265–283.

Lennington, S. (1981). Child abuse: The limits of sociobiology. *Ethology and Sociobiology, 2,* 17–29.

Lenton, R. L. (1990). Techniques of child discipline and abuse by parents. *Canadian Review of Sociology and Anthropology, 27,* 157–184.

Lightcap, J. L., Kurland, J. A., & Burgess, R. L. (1982). Child abuse: A test of some predictions from evolutionary theory. *Ethology and Sociobiology, 3,* 61–67.

Malkin, C. M., & Lamb, M. E. (1994). Child maltreatment: A test of sociobiological theory. *Journal of Comparative Family Studies, 25,* 121–134.

Margolin, G. (1992). Child abuse by mothers' boyfriends: Why the overrepresentation? *Child Abuse and Neglect, 16,* 541–551.

Margolin, G., Sibner, L. O., & Gleberman, L. (1988). Wife battering. In V. B. Van Hasselt, R. L. Morrison, A. S. Bellack, & M. Herson (Eds.), *Handbook of family violence* (pp. 89–117). New York: Plenum.

Martin, S. A. (1983). Neglected fathers: Limitations in diagnostic and treatment resources for violent men. *Child Abuse and Neglect, 8,* 387–392.

Mash, E. J. (1991). Measurement of parent-child interaction in studies of child maltreatment. In R. H. Starr & D. A. Wolfe (Eds.), *The effects of child abuse and neglect* (pp. 203–245). New York: Guilford.

McCloskey, L. A., Figueredo, A. J., & Koss, M. P. (1995). The effects of systematic family violence on children's mental health. *Child Development, 66,* 1239–1261.

McMahon, M., & Pence, E. (1995). Doing more harm than good? Some cautions on visitation centers. In E. Peled, P. Jaffe & J. L. Edelson (Eds.), *Ending the cycle of violence* (pp. 186–206). Beverly Hills, CA: Sage.

Milner, J. S. (1994). Assessing physical child abuse risk: The Child Abuse Potential Inventory. *Clinical Psychology Review, 14* (6), 547–583.

Milner, J. S., & Robertson, K. R. (1989). Inconsistent response patterns and the prediction of child maltreatment. *Child Abuse and Neglect, 13,* 59–64.

National Center on Child Abuse and Neglect. (1988). *Study findings: Study of national incidence and prevalence of child abuse and neglect: 1988.* Washington, DC: U.S. Department of Health and Human Services.

National Research Council, Panel on Child Abuse and Neglect. (1988). *Understanding child abuse and neglect.* Washington, DC: National Academy Press.

Nicholas, K. B., & Bieber, S. L. (1994). Perceptions of mothers and fathers' abusive and supportive behaviors. *Child Abuse & Neglect, 18,* 167–178.

O'Brien, M., John, R. S., Margolin, G., & Erel, O. (1994). Reliability and diagnostic efficacy of parents' reports regarding children's exposure to marital aggression. *Violence and Victims, 9* (1), 45–62.

O'Brien, M., Margolin, G., & John, R. (1995). The relationship between marital conflict, child coping, and child adjustment. *Journal of Clinical Child Psychology, 24,* 346–361.

Office of Human Development Services. (1988). *Study findings: Study of national incidence and prevalence of child abuse and neglect: 1988.* Washington, DC: U.S. Department of Health and Human Services.

O'Keefe, M. (1994). Linking marital violence, mother-child/father-child aggression, and child behavior problems. *Journal of Family Violence, 9* (1), 63–78.

Parke, R. D., & Collmer, C. W. (1975). Child abuse: An interdisciplinary analysis. In E. M. Hetherington (Ed.), *Review of child development research* (Vol. 5, pp. 1–102). Chicago: University of Chicago Press.

Pelton, L. H. (1978). Child abuse and neglect: The myth of classlessness. *American Journal of Orthopsychiatry, 48,* 608–617.

Pfohl, S. J. (1977). The discovery of child abuse. *Social Problems, 24,* 310–323.

Radbill, S. (1968). A history of child abuse and infanticide. In R. E. Helfer & C. H. Kempe (Eds.), *The battered child* (pp. 77–92). Chicago: University of Chicago Press.

Silverstein, L. B. (1996). Fathering is a feminist issue. *Psychology of Women Quarterly, 20,* 3–37.

Starr, R. H., Jr. (1982). A research-based approach to the prediction of child abuse. In R. H. Starr, Jr. (Ed.), *Child abuse prediction: Policy implications* (pp. 105–134). Cambridge, MA: Ballinger.

Starr, R. H., Jr. (1987). Clinical judgement of abuse-proneness based on parent-child interactions. *Child Abuse and Neglect, 11,* 87–92.

Starr, R. H., Jr. (1988). Physical abuse of children. In V. B. van Hasselt, R. L. Morrison. A. S. Bellack, & M. Hersen (Eds.), *Handbook of family violence* (pp. 119–115). New York: Plenum.

Steele, B., & Pollack, C. (1968). A psychiatric study of parents who abuse infants and small children. In R. Helfer & C. H. Kempe (Eds.), *The battered child* (pp. 89–133). Chicago: University of Chicago Press.

Sternberg, K. J., Lamb, M. E., & Dawud-Noursi, S. (in press). Using multiple informants and cross-cultural research to study the effects of domestic violence on developmental psychopathology: Illustrations from research in Israel. In S. S. Luthar, J. A. Burack, D. Cicchetti, & J. Weisz (Eds.), *Developmental psychopathology: Perspectives on risk and disorder.* Cambridge: Cambridge University Press.

Sternberg, K. J., Lamb, M. E., & Dawud-Noursi, S. (1996). *Understanding domestic violence and its effects: Making sense of divergent reports and perspectives.* Manuscript in preparation, National Institute of Child Health and Human Development, Bethesda, MD.

Sternberg, K. J., Lamb, M. E., Greenbaum, C., Cicchetti, D., Dawud, S., Cortes, R. M., Krispin, O., & Lorey, F. (1993). Effects of domestic violence on children's behavior problems and depression. *Developmental Psychology, 29*(1), 44–52.

Sternberg, K. J., Lamb, M. E:, Greenbaum, C., Dawud, S., Cortes, R. M., & Lorey, F. (1994). The effects of domestic violence on children's perceptions of their perpetrating and nonperpetrating parents. *International Society for the Study of Behavioral Development, 17*(4), 779–795.

Straus, M. A. (1993). Physical assaults by wives: A major social problem. In R. J. Gelles & D. R. Loseke (Eds.), *Current controversies on family violence* (pp. 67–87). Newbury Park, CA: Sage.

Straus, M. A., & Gelles, R. J. (1986). Societal change and change in family violence from 1975 to 1985 as revealed by two national surveys. *Journal of Marriage and the Family, 48,* 465–479.

Straus, M. A. & Gelles, R. J. (Eds.) (1990). *Physical violence in American families.* New Brunswick, NJ: Transaction.

Straus, M. A., Gelles, R. J., & Steinmetz, S. (1980). *Behind closed doors: Violence in the American family.* New York: Doubleday/Anchor.

Szinovacz, M. (1983). Using couple data as a methodological tool: The case of marital violence. *Journal of Marriage and the Family, 45,* 633–644.

Trickett, P. K., & Sussman, E. J. (1988). Parental perceptions of child-rearing practices in physically abusive and nonabusive families. *Developmental Psychology, 24,* 270–276.

U.S. Department of Justice. (1984). *Family violence.* Washington, DC: Bureau of Justice Statistics.

Walker, L. E. A. (1979). *The battered woman.* New York: Harper and Row.

Walker, L. E. A. (1995). Current perspectives on men who batter women—Implications for intervention and treatment to stop violence against women: Comment on Gottman et al. (1995). *Journal of Family Psychology, 9* (3), 264–271.

Widom, C. S. (1989a). Child abuse, neglect and adult behavior: Research design and findings of criminality, violence, and child abuse. *American Journal of Orthopsychiatry, 59* (3), 355–367.

Widom, C. S. (1989b). Does violence beget violence? A critical examination of the literature. *Psychological Bulletin, 106* (1), 3–28.

Wolfe, D. A. (1987). *Child Abuse: Implications for child development and psychopathology.* Newbury Park, CA: Sage.

Wolfe, D. A., Jaffe, P., Wilson, S. K., & Zak, L. (1985). Children of battered women: The relations of child behavior to family violence and maternal stress. *Journal of Consulting and Clinical Psychology, 5,* 657–665.

Wolfner, G. D., & Gelles, R. J. (1993). A profile of violence toward children: A national study. *Child Abuse & Neglect, 17,* 197–212.

Wolins, M. (1983). The gender dilemma in social welfare: Who cares for children. In M. E. Lamb & A. Sagi (Eds.), *Fatherhood and family policy* (pp. 129–135). New York: Erlbaum.

Author Index

SUBJECT INDEX